State Building in Putin's Russia

Building a strong Russian state was the central goal of Vladimir Putin's presidency. This book argues that Putin's strategy for rebuilding the state was fundamentally flawed. Brian D. Taylor demonstrates that a disregard for the way state officials behave toward citizens – state quality – had a negative impact on what the state could do – state capacity. Focusing on those organizations that control state coercion, what Russians call the "power ministries," Taylor shows that many of the weaknesses of the Russian state that existed under Boris Yeltsin persisted under Putin. Drawing on extensive field research and interviews, as well as a wide range of comparative data, the book reveals the practices and norms that guide the behavior of Russian power ministry officials (the so-called *siloviki*), especially law enforcement personnel. By examining *siloviki* behavior from the Kremlin down to the street level, *State Building in Putin's Russia* uncovers the who, where, and how of Russian state building after communism.

Brian D. Taylor is Associate Professor of Political Science in the Maxwell School of Citizenship and Public Affairs at Syracuse University. Previously, he served as Assistant Professor at the University of Oklahoma. He earned his Ph.D. from the Massachusetts Institute of Technology in 1998 and holds a master of science from the London School of Economics and a B.A. from the University of Iowa. He is a 2011 Fulbright Scholar to Russia and was a Carnegie Scholar from 2002 to 2003. He was also a Fellow at the Belfer Center for Science and International Affairs and the Olin Institute for Strategic Studies at Harvard University. He is the author of *Politics and the Russian Army: Civil-Military Relations, 1689–2000*, and his work has appeared in *Comparative Politics, Comparative Political Studies, Problems of Post-Communism, Europe-Asia Studies, International Studies Review, Survival, Millennium,* and the *Journal of Cold War Studies*.

"The 'power ministries' of the police, the security services, and the military have been central to state building efforts in post-Soviet Russia, but have been vastly under-studied. Brian Taylor's fascinating book pries open the power ministries to explore how organizational pathologies, weak oversight, and increasingly authoritarian rule undermined efforts to build state capacity in Russia. Taylor demonstrates that in many respects, the state is hardly more effective under Putin than under Yeltsin, despite Russia's return to economic growth and prominence on the international stage. With its keen attention to detail and impressive data collection, *State Building in Putin's Russia* is an important work that should interest Russia watchers and scholars of state building alike."

– Timothy Frye, Columbia University

"Brian Taylor offers a clear-eyed account of Vladimir Putin's efforts to rebuild the power of the state in Russia in the 2000s. Taylor distinguishes between state capacity and state quality, and finds only modest improvements in state capacity under Putin and none in the degree to which the state actually serves the public interest. Focusing in particular on the coercive agencies of the state – the military, police, and security forces – Taylor shows that under Putin, they were largely ineffective in combating crime and terrorism but were often used for the purposes of political repression and intimidation. Taylor concludes that centralizing and consolidating power at the top is a very different enterprise from improving the quality of governance in a state."

– Thomas F. Remington, Emory University

State Building in Putin's Russia

Policing and Coercion after Communism

BRIAN D. TAYLOR

Maxwell School, Syracuse University

 CAMBRIDGE
UNIVERSITY PRESS

CAMBRIDGE UNIVERSITY PRESS
Cambridge, New York, Melbourne, Madrid, Cape Town, Singapore,
São Paulo, Delhi, Dubai, Tokyo, Mexico City

Cambridge University Press
32 Avenue of the Americas, New York, NY 10013-2473, USA

www.cambridge.org
Information on this title: www.cambridge.org/9780521760881

First published 2011

Printed in the United States of America

A catalog record for this publication is available from the British Library.

Library of Congress Cataloging in Publication data
Taylor, Brian D., 1964–
  State building in Putin's Russia : policing and coercion after communism / Brian D. Taylor.
    p. cm.
  Includes bibliographical references and index.
  ISBN 978-0-521-76088-1 (hardback)
  1. Putin, Vladimir Vladimirovich, 1952 – Political and social views. 2. Yeltsin, Boris
Nikolayevich, 1931–2007 – Influence. 3. Russia (Federation) – Politics and government –
1991– 4. Post-communism – Russia (Federation) – History. 5. Power (Social sciences) –
Russia (Federation) – History. 6. Federal government – Russia (Federation) – History.
7. Police power – Russia (Federation) – History. 8. Duress (Law) – Russia (Federation) –
History. 9. State, The – History – 20th century. 10. State, The – History – 21st century.
I. Title.
  DK510.766.P87T39 2010
  947.086'2–dc22   2010037099

ISBN 978-0-521-76088-1 Hardback

Cambridge University Press has no responsibility for the persistence or accuracy of URLs for
external or third-party Internet Web sites referred to in this publication and does not guarantee
that any content on such Web sites is, or will remain, accurate or appropriate.

To
My Parents

Contents

List of Figures, Tables, and Maps   *page* viii
List of Abbreviations   xi
Acknowledgments   xiii
Note on Transliteration and Translation   xvii

Introduction   1
1   Bringing the Gun Back In: Coercion and the State   8
2   The Power Ministries and the *Siloviki*   36
3   Coercion and Capacity: Political Order and the Central State   71
4   Coercion and Capacity: Centralization and Federalism   112
5   Coercion and Quality: Power Ministry Practices and Personnel   156
6   Coercion and Quality: The State and Society   204
7   Coercion in the North Caucasus   250
8   State Capacity and Quality Reconsidered   284

Appendix A   *Publication Abbreviations*   323
Appendix B   *Interview Index*   325
References   331
Index   361

Figures, Tables, and Maps

Figures

1.1	State quality and state capacity	*page* 20
1.2	Political stability and state quality (WGI 2006)	21
2.1	Fragmentation and consolidation of the power ministries, 1986–2006	38
2.2	National defense and security and law enforcement in Russian budget, constant rubles, 1997–2007	53
2.3	Power ministry budget percentage comparison, 1999–2007	54
2.4	Tenure of FSB directors	56
2.5	Militarization of the Russian elite	58
2.6	Putin's *siloviki* network, 2007	60
3.1	Political stability/no violence (WGI)	78
3.2	Deaths from terrorist attacks in Moscow, 1995–2007	85
3.3	Deaths by major terrorist attack, October 2001–June 2007	87
3.4	Government effectiveness (WGI)	90
3.5	Murders per 100,000 population, 1990–2007	92
3.6	Russian state fiscal capacity, 1993–2007	101
4.1	Regional police chief appointments, 1992–2006	136
4.2	Percentage of regional police chief appointments from outside region, 1993–2006	136
5.1	Rule of law (WGI)	159
5.2	Control of corruption (WGI)	160
5.3	Three models of policing	179
5.4	Russian law enforcement types	181
6.1	Trust in the power ministries	206

6.2 How did the work of police and other law enforcement
     agencies change in the last year?   208

6.3 How did the state of citizens' personal safety
     change in the last year?   210

6.4 Can the Russian authorities defend the
     Russian population against new terrorist attacks?   210

6.5 Annual number of pardons, 1995–2007   235

6.6 Voice and accountability (WGI)   245

7.1 Deaths from terrorism/insurgency, major attacks,
     North Caucasus, 2000–2007   259

7.2 Kidnappings, disappearances, and murders in
     Chechnya, 2002–2007   260

7.3 Deaths from terrorist incidents in Dagestan, 2002–2007   261

8.1 State capacity and per capita GNI   291

8.2 State quality and per capita GNI   292

8.3 Russia: State capacity versus state quality (WGI)   303

8.4 Weak state to police state? State building under Putin   304

8.5 Control over coercion: A typology   305

Tables

1.1 Elements of State Building   35

2.1 Main Power Ministries and Their Approximate Size, 2007   39

2.2 Police Personnel per 100,000 Inhabitants   48

3.1 Law Enforcement Capacity under Putin: Routine
     versus Exceptional Decisions   108

4.1 Control over Policing, Federal Political Systems   123

4.2 Legal Authority for Law Enforcement Budgetary Support, 1999   124

4.3 Polpreds by Federal District, May 2000–May 2008   131

4.4 Federal Districts and Power Ministry Personnel, 2002 and 2007 132

4.5 "Outsiders" in Regional Power Ministries, 2000–2007   138

5.1 Police Bribes "Price List," 2002   171

5.2 Main Direction of Activity of Russian Law Enforcement
     Organs, Percent of Responses, 2006   180

5.3 Russian Encounters with Police Violence and Corruption   182

5.4 Turnover, Education, and Experience of MVD
     Investigators, 1993–2002   192

8.1 State Capacity (Dependent Variable) and Structural
     Factors (Wealth, Resource Dependence, Region)   296

8.2   State Quality (Dependent Variable) and Structural Factors
       (Wealth, Resource Dependence, Region)   296
8.3   Predicted Values for State Capacity and State Quality
       Compared to Actual Russian Scores   297

Maps

4.1   Russia's federal districts, 2000–2009   129
7.1   North Caucasus   252

Abbreviations

Cheka	Extraordinary Commission
CJA	Center for Justice Assistance
CPSU	Communist Party of the Soviet Union
EMERCOM	Ministry of Civil Defense and Emergency Situations (see MChS)
FAPSI	Federal Agency for Government Communication and Information
FC	Federation Council
FDSU	Federal Road Construction Administration
FEMA	Federal Emergency Management Agency (U.S.)
FPS	Federal Border Service
FRS	Federal Registration Service
FSB	Federal Security Service
FSIN	Federal Service for the Administration of Sentences
FSKN	Federal Service for Control of the Narcotics Trade
FSNP	Federal Tax Police Service
FSO	Federal Guards Service
FTS	Federal Customs Service
GDP	Gross Domestic Product
GNI	Gross National Income
GONGO	Government-Organized Non-Governmental Organization
GRU	Main Intelligence Directorate
GU MVD	Main Administration of the Ministry of Internal Affairs
GUO	Main Guards Directorate
GUSP	Main Directorate for Special Programs

GUVD	Main Directorate of Internal Affairs
INDEM	Information for Democracy Foundation
KBR	Kabardino-Balkaria Republic
KGB	Committee on State Security
Komsomol	Communist Youth League
MB	Ministry of Security
MChS	Ministry of Civil Defense and Emergency Situations
MO	Ministry of Defense
MOB	Public Order Militia
MVD	Ministry of Internal Affairs
NAC	National Antiterrorism Committee
NGO	Non-Governmental Organization
NKVD	People's Commissariat for Internal Affairs
NPSP	Nizhniy Novgorod Project for Justice Assistance
Politburo	Political Bureau of the Central Committee of the Communist Party
Polpred	Presidential Representative
PPP	Purchasing Power Parity
PRI	Institutional Revolutionary Party (Mexico)
OMON	Special Designation Police Detachment
OMSN	Special Designation Police Detachment
RSFSR	Russian Soviet Federated Socialist Republic
RUBOP	Regional Anti–Organized Crime Directorate
SBP	Presidential Security Service
SSR	Security Sector Reform
SVR	Foreign Intelligence Service
USSR	Union of Soviet Socialist Republics
UVD	Directorate of Internal Affairs
VV	Internal Troops
WDI	World Development Index
WGI	World Bank Worldwide Governance Indicators

Acknowledgments

Many institutions and individuals provided assistance on this project. I apologize in advance for those I forget to mention here and stress that the usual disclaimers most definitely apply – all opinions and errors in the book are my own.

For financial assistance, I would like to thank: The Carnegie Corporation of New York, for a very generous scholarship that got the project started and, among other things, made much of the field research possible; The Smith Richardson Foundation, for a similarly generous grant that supported writing and additional field research, as well as the publication of a policy monograph in which some of the findings from this book were originally presented; The Maxwell School, for several small grants, field research support (through a grant from the Department of State), and support for course buyouts; The University of Oklahoma, for research leave; The Moynihan Institute of Global Affairs and the Department of Political Science at the Maxwell School, for support for a workshop on the first draft of the book.

The most important scholarly community that supported me while working on this project was the Program on New Approaches to Russian Security (PONARS). Specialists will have little trouble spotting the intellectual influences of multiple PONARS members in the book. I thank especially the founder and director (until 2009) Celeste Wallander. Many members offered feedback, data, ideas, and other support, including: Mikhail Alexseev, Pavel Baev, Andrew Barnes, Doug Blum, Georgi Derluguian, Matthew Evangelista, Tim Frye, Vladimir Gel'man, Ted Gerber, Henry Hale, Stephen Hanson, Ted Hopf, Debra Javeline, Mark Kramer, Ivan Kurilla, Pauline Jones Luong, Sarah Mendelson, Robert Orttung, Nikolay Petrov, Vladimir Popov, Regina Smyth, Vadim Volkov, and Cory Welt.

I thank the participants in an April 2008 workshop at Syracuse University for their comments on an earlier draft. I am particularly grateful to Mark Beissinger and Vadim Volkov for their thoughtful criticisms, as well as Elizabeth Cohen, Audie Klotz, Vlad Kravtsov, David Rivera, Mark Rupert, Azamat Sakiev, and Hans Peter Schmitz.

I thank the Russia and Eurasia Program of the Carnegie Endowment for International Peace, especially Marina Barnett, and the Institute for National Security and Counterterrorism of Syracuse University, especially Marlene Diamond and Keli Perrin, for help in organizing a 2007 workshop on the policy monograph *Russia's Power Ministries*. The participants provided valuable feedback that helped shape this book.

A number of research assistants provided important help with this project over the years: Richard Bodnar, Yulia Ivanovskaya, Katya Kalandadze, Ekaterina Mozhaeva, Tamara Polyakova, Honggang Tan, Tatyana Vinichenko, and Naomi Wachs.

I owe a special debt of gratitude to all of those individuals in Russia who helped me in multiple ways with the research on this project, whether in agreeing to be interviewed, helping find contacts, or reminding me that there is much more to Russia than the state and its *siloviki*. I particularly thank: Dmitriy Babich, Boris Bednikov, Andrey and Larissa Berkenblit, Olga Dmitriyeva, Irina Dmitriyevich, Zhanna Gumenyuk, Nikolay Kulikovskikh, Irina Kurenkova, Sarah Lindemann-Komarova, Tatyana Nikitina, Nikolay Petrov, Viktor Rudenko, Mikhail Rykhtik, Maksim Shandarov, Vadim Volkov, and Aleksandr Voronin.

Others who contributed in various ways to this project beyond those listed above include: Pablo Beramendi, Matthew Cleary, Boris Demidov, Mikhail Filippov, Dan Goldberg, Petr Kozma, Cerwyn Moore, Robert Otto, Melanie Peyser, Bill Pridemore, Peter Reddaway, Sharon Werning Rivera, Ekaterina Sokirianskaia, Peter Solomon, Jeffrey Straussman, Daniel Treisman, and Alexei Trochev.

Lewis Bateman of Cambridge University Press was, yet again, a model of efficiency in shepherding this project from manuscript to book, and I thank him for his support. Others who contributed to the production process at Cambridge were Emily Spangler, Anne Lovering Rounds, and Mark Fox. I thank Kavitha Lawrence and Newgen for their management of the copyediting and production process, and Nancy Peterson for compiling the index. David Cox produced the two maps used in this book with great skill and efficiency. I also thank the two anonymous reviewers for their very helpful and detailed comments.

I am grateful to the following publishers for permission to use portions of previously published articles or book chapters in revised form in this book:

Comparative Politics, for: "Force and Federalism: Controlling Coercion in Federal Hybrid Regimes." *Comparative Politics*, 39, 4 (July 2007), pp. 421–440;

M.E. Sharpe, for: "Putin's 'Historic Mission': State-Building and the Power Ministries in the North Caucasus." *Problems of Post-Communism*, 54, 6 (November–December 2007), pp. 3–16;

Rowman & Littlefield, for: "Russia's Regions and Law Enforcement." In Peter Reddaway and Robert W. Orttung, eds., *The Dynamics of Russian Politics: Putin's Reform of Federal-Regional Relations*, Volume II (Lanham, MD: Rowman & Littlefield, 2005), pp. 65–90;

Taylor & Francis, for: "Law Enforcement and Civil Society in Russia." *Europe-Asia Studies*, 58, 2 (March 2006), pp. 193–213.

My final acknowledgments are to my family. I thank my wife Renée de Nevers for her love, encouragement, and sense of humor. Renée is also an academic, which means I am doubly grateful for her willingness to take time away from her own research and writing to tell me how to fix mine. I thank my sons Anatol and Lucian, whose obsession with sports, Star Wars Legos, and general mayhem made it possible for me to finish this book, and whose smiles, hugs, and laughter brightened the times I wasn't working on it. Finally, I thank my parents, Lois and Merlin Taylor, for decades of love and support. I'm sure that they had no idea when they were raising me that I would become keenly interested in Russian *siloviki*, but I'm quite certain that they would have loved me anyway. I dedicate this book to them.

Note on Transliteration and Translation

I use the transliteration system of the U.S. Board on Geographic Names, which I believe is easier for non-Russian speakers to read than the Library of Congress system (Basayev rather than Basaev, Serdyukov rather than Serdiukov, etc.). I have also used the familiar English form for well-known names (e.g., Ingushetia rather than Ingushetiya, Khodorkovsky rather than Khodorkovskiy). Soft signs are omitted from the main text (e.g., Rossel instead of Rossel'), but preserved in the notes. In cases in which Russian authors have published in English under more than one spelling (e.g., Nikolay/Nikolai Petrov) I have tried to preserve the spelling used for that publication. Other exceptions to this system may occur and are accidental; my apologies.

All translations from Russian are mine unless otherwise noted.

NOTE ON INTERVIEWS AND PRIMARY SOURCES

Much of the material in the book comes from interviews and press accounts. Appendix A provides a list of abbreviations used for Russian- and English-language newspapers and magazines. Appendix B provides a key to the interviews, organized by city and then alphabetically. Anonymity was offered to all respondents and provided when requested. Unless otherwise specified, quotes from speeches by Putin and Medvedev are available at one of the following Web sites: http://archive.kremlin.ru/ (Putin) or http://www.president.kremlin.ru (Medvedev).

Introduction

The quality of policing is the quality of ruling.

Otwin Marenin, 1985[1]

Russia needs strong state power and must have it.

Vladimir Putin, December 1999[2]

The Soviet Union has been characterized as "the world's largest-ever police state."[3] But why is "police state" a pejorative, a synonym for brutal dictatorship? After all, if we expect the state to do anything, policing is surely one of those things. Although policing is a function that can and often is carried out by private actors, all modern states create "an organization authorized by a collectivity to regulate social relations within itself by utilizing, if need be, physical force."[4] Try living in a community of any significant size that does not have an authorized organization capable of policing it, and one will quickly see the virtues of such a force. Anarchists aside, most citizens in the modern world would rather live with police than without them. But the term "police state" resonates because state power, as Max Weber recognized, ultimately rests on the ability to coerce. The behavior of its coercive organizations, such as the military, the police, and the secret police, tells us much about the character of a state, as the Marenin epigraph emphasizes.

The collapse of "the world's largest-ever police state" introduced a period of remarkable political and economic change in Russia. Although the Soviet

[1] Otwin Marenin, "Police Performance and State Rule: Control and Autonomy in the Exercise of Coercion" (Review Article), *Comparative Politics*, 18 (1985), p. 101.

[2] Vladimir Putin, "Rossiya na rubezhe tysyacheletiy," *Nez. Gaz.*, December 30, 1999. A key to abbreviations for newspapers and magazines is in Appendix A.

[3] Stephen Kotkin, *Armageddon Averted: The Soviet Collapse 1970–2000* (Oxford: Oxford University Press, 2001), p. 173.

[4] David H. Bayley, "The Police and Political Development in Europe," in Charles Tilly, ed., *The Formation of National States in Western Europe* (Princeton, NJ: Princeton University Press, 1975) p. 328.

collapse is conventionally referred to as peaceful, and by comparative standards perhaps it was, it was not entirely so, with multiple wars and violent
conflicts. Moreover, in the view of many Russians, the collapse ushered in not
just a period of turmoil and uncertainty, but also a period in which the risk of
becoming a victim of crime or violence significantly increased. The need for
competent policing was obvious. Russia did indeed need strong state power.
Vladimir Putin made building this strong state the central goal of his presidency, and he relied heavily on coercive organizations in this endeavor. Unlike
state formation in early-modern Europe, in which states emerged unintention-
ally out of violent struggles for domination and power, *state building* in the
contemporary world, including in Russia, is very much an intentional project.
The modern European state has become a model for the world.[5]

The goal of building a strong state, however, leaves open the question of
what *kind* of state is to be built. The Soviet Union, after all, was a strong state,
but most Russian politicians, including Boris Yeltsin and Putin, rejected the
goal of building a Soviet-type state. In the programmatic statement cited in
the epigraph above, Putin explicitly repudiated a totalitarian state, writing,
"strong state power in Russia is a democratic, law-based, capable, federal
state." To put it in the terminology used in this book, Putin asserted an intention to build not just a high *capacity* state that can adopt and implement policies, but also a high *quality* one that serves the public interest in an impartial
manner.

This book is about Russian state building under Yeltsin and Putin. I am
interested in both the degree of stateness and the kind of state that Russia is.
To explain the trajectory of state building under Yeltsin and Putin, I distinguish between the capacity and the quality of the state, arguing that these are
analytically and empirically separate categories. To make the abstract notion
of the state more concrete, I focus on state coercive agencies, especially law
enforcement ones, based on a Weberian understanding of the centrality of
controlling violence to stateness. I investigate both their role in the state building process and what their behavior tells us about the capacity and quality of
the state. Further, states do not just exist in the capital, but throughout the territory of a country. I therefore examine the central, regional, and street-level
components of these coercive organizations' activities.

In Russia, state coercive agencies are known as "the power ministries," and
officials who come from the power ministries are known as "*siloviki*." The
siloviki and their role in Russian politics have been the subject of considerable
commentary, especially in Russia but also in the West, but they have received

---

[5] On this difference between state formation and state building, see, for example: Charles Tilly,
"Western State-Making and Theories of Political Transformation," in Tilly 1975, pp. 601–
638; Mohammed Ayoob, *The Third World Security Predicament: State Making, Regional
Conflict, and the International System* (Boulder, CO: Lynne Rienner, 1995), pp. 21–45; Vadim
Volkov, *Violent Entrepreneurs: The Use of Force in the Making of Russian Capitalism* (Ithaca,
NY: Cornell University Press, 2002), pp. 155–157.

much less sustained academic study. In Chapter 2, I set out three different lenses for thinking about the influence of the siloviki in Russian politics, which I label the cohort, clan, and corporate (organizational) approaches. These different lenses focus on different issues and yield different conclusions both about how united and how powerful the siloviki were under Putin. Overall, the siloviki were an important cohort of officials under Putin, but they were not a united team, and the Federal Security Service (FSB) and the Procuracy were much more politically powerful than the police or the armed forces.

Despite Putin's claim to have restored the Russian state, I conclude that serious deficiencies remained in both the capacity and especially the quality of the state, and in particular its force-wielding organs, at the time he left the presidency in 2008. The coercive capacity of the state did increase in some respects under Putin, most significantly in the rebuilding of a "regime of repression" that was used to weaken actual and potential opponents of the Kremlin, such as the so-called oligarchs and opposition parties and movements. The fiscal capacity of the state also improved under Putin. On the other hand, the ability to accomplish core law enforcement tasks, such as fighting crime and terrorism, was little different under Putin when compared to the Yeltsin era, although the situation improved in Putin's final years as president. Finally, no progress was made in the key state function of securing property rights. I explain this mixed performance by distinguishing between "routine" and "exceptional" law enforcement tasks. Routine ones are those that are the core functions of an organization as set out in laws and regulations, whereas exceptional ones are set by superiors but are extralegal or even illegal. Examples include allowing some organizations to hold street rallies while prohibiting others based on the political tendencies of the groups, or investigating some cases of tax evasion while ignoring others based on a person's standing with the authorities. Russian law enforcement agencies were much better at implementing exceptional tasks than the routine ones established by law.

A key piece of Putin's state building strategy was to strengthen the central government vis-à-vis Russia's regions. His first major reform as president was a series of changes to Russian federalism, including the creation of seven "federal districts" to impose centralized control over executive bodies in the regions, including law enforcement ones. These changes, although combating a real problem of regional disregard for federal laws, culminated in the abolition of direct elections for governors and serious damage to the development of Russian federalism. The use of the power ministries to decisively alter the federal bargain showed that in hybrid regimes (combining democratic and authoritarian elements), the institutions that structure center-region relations in established democracies, such as courts and political parties, are often too weak to play this role, giving greater weight to the control of coercion. Putin's ability to shift the balance toward the center did not, however, greatly increase state capacity, because centralized law enforcement agencies were no more effective at carrying out their lawful responsibilities than decentralized ones. In the critical case of the North Caucasus, there was some evidence that Putin's repressive approach was successful in reducing terrorist violence in Chechnya, but the situation in neighboring Ingushetia and Dagestan was worse than at the beginning of his presidency, and power ministry officials in the region exhibited similar pathologies to those in the rest of the country.

The modest improvements in state capacity under Putin were directly linked to lack of attention to the equally important issue of state quality. The concept of state quality will be developed further in Chapter 1, but the idea speaks to a key facet often neglected in the literature on states and state strength – not just *what* states do, but *how* they do it. Specifically, state quality asks to what extent state officials are true civil servants, working for the public good in a fair way, rather than pursuing primarily personal or elite interests. In post-Soviet Russia, law enforcement officials too often have engaged in corrupt practices, flouted the law, and preyed on rather than worked for the citizenry. Further, the professional characteristics and behavior of law enforcement personnel remain deficient, despite an infusion of resources due to the economic boom under Putin.

Low state quality in the coercive realm translated into a lack of trust on the part of the citizenry. Efforts by civil society organizations to engage law enforcement structures and promote liberal and professional norms had some success under Yeltsin and in Putin's first term, but ran into increasing obstacles after 2004 because of Kremlin concerns about international influences on domestic politics in the aftermath of the "Orange Revolution" in Ukraine.

What explains the modest improvements in state capacity and absence of change in state quality during Putin's presidency? After all, state building was Putin's top priority, and very high approval ratings and nine years of economic growth provided considerable political and economic resources to push his agenda. I trace these deficiencies in state capacity and quality to three fundamental aspects of organizational practice and public administration: bureaucratic type, monitoring strategy, and organizational mission. Specifically, I highlight:

- the dominance of patrimonialism in bureaucratic practices;
- a faulty monitoring strategy overly reliant on internal state oversight;
- failure to give state agencies and agents a new sense of mission.

Patrimonialism refers to the use of informal and personalistic criteria in personnel decisions (hiring, promotion, etc.) rather than more professional or rational-legal standards. Second, oversight was housed within the executive branch, with the presidential administration and competing power ministries monitoring each other, rather than empowering the legislature, non-governmental organizations (NGOs), or the media to serve as watchdogs; this approach proved ineffective. Third, for most of the Putin presidency, there was too little attention to shaping the values of state officials by giving them something meaningful to work for beyond their own self-interests. Toward the end of Putin's presidency, a more coherent ideological narrative that sought to mobilize power ministry personnel against internal and external enemies took hold, and this project may have helped bolster state capacity, but it was not designed to improve state quality. Moreover, this mission statement regarding "fortress Russia" was not fully embraced by the leadership itself, which made it harder to instill values that would divert officials from short-term self-interested behavior.

In this book, I focus on the practices and norms that guide bureaucratic behavior to explain the disappointing results of Putin's state-building project. Clearly many factors influence the capacity and quality of a state, and in the final chapter, I bring more structural factors, such as wealth, resource dependence, and post-communist legacies, into the story. Primarily, though, I show how the beliefs of those state officials who wear uniforms and carry guns, and the constraints under which they operate, affect their actions, and what these actions mean for Russian political development.

The book investigates state building in the Yeltsin and Putin eras in Russia, with special attention to the 2000–2007 years of Putin's presidency. Of course, it is a bit of a fiction to pretend that the Putin era ended in 2008 when Dmitriy Medvedev became president. Putin carried on as prime minister in the two-headed system that came to be known as "tandemocracy," with every indication that he still called many of the shots and may return as president by 2012, and stay in that role for some time. Still, for our purposes, the end of his second term as president in early 2008 represents a convenient break point. The year 2008 also marked the end of the remarkable economic boom that coincided with Putin's presidency and fueled – quite literally – Russia's growing international ambitions. Thus, for the most part, this book covers the period up to 2007–2008, although in the final chapter, I discuss developments in Medvedev's first two years as president.

RESEARCH APPROACH

Scholars have debated extensively how we should properly assess and measure "stateness." A range of approaches have been in evidence, from quantitative studies of varying sophistication to more detailed, qualitative case studies of one or more states. To place the Russian case in context, in different chapters of the book, I rely on a variety of cross-national data. Most centrally, I use World Bank World Governance Indicators (WGI) to provide a rough indication both of Russia's standing relative to other countries and of changes over time, from 1996 to 2007. Governance scores are based on aggregates of individual indicators produced by a range of organizations, including NGOs, international organizations, and business consulting firms. Although these scores are not flawless, they represent the state of the art in terms of rigorous, comparative data on the performance of governments around the world. The five indicators I use, all of which capture different aspects of state capacity or quality, are: Political Stability and Absence of Violence, Government Effectiveness,

Voice and Accountability, Rule of Law, and Control of Corruption. The first two I treat primarily as indicators of capacity, the latter three of quality.[6] More specific data on Russia are also used to evaluate stateness. Examples include information on budgets, size of forces, murder rates, incidents of terrorism, and survey data on public trust in various institutions.

Much of the research is of a qualitative nature, particularly relying on a wide reading of the Russian press over the last decade and more than 100 interviews conducted over a nine-year period (see Appendix B).[7] This in-depth research serves several important goals in uncovering evidence about the capacity and quality of Russia's coercive agencies. Most importantly, it provides the fullest picture available of the dynamics transforming these agencies, their practices at multiple levels, and their relationships with each other and federal and regional officials. In a certain sense, I hope to provide a "thick description" of the power ministries in post-Soviet Russia, although the level of ethnographic detail present in the work of anthropologists such as Clifford Geertz is obviously absent. Rather, to quote Geertz, I have endeavored to be responsive to both the "need to grasp and the need to analyze."[8] The strength of a single-country study in general, and particularly one of specific government agencies, is to explore in depth the microprocesses that connect state-building strategies with actual outcomes.

The story as it unfolds generally moves in two directions: from the center to the regions to the street level, and from an attention mainly to capacity to a growing focus on quality. I aim to trace the who, where, and how of state building in the coercive realm. In this way, I hope to provide as complete a picture as possible of the Russian power ministries, especially law enforcement structures, and their role in Russian state building from the Soviet collapse in 1991 to the end of the Putin presidency in 2008.

The book is organized as follows. Chapter 1 discusses the key concepts from the statist literature that inform the rest of the book, and develops the core theoretical arguments. Chapter 2 provides an overview of the Russian power ministries and the siloviki. Chapters 3 and 4 examine Russian state capacity in the coercive realm, first at the national level and then at the regional level. Chapters 5 and 6 are about state quality, dealing with bureaucratic practices in the power ministries and how these agencies relate to society. Chapter 7 focuses on the North Caucasus, a particularly difficult area for state building

---

[6] For a positive assessment of the project and its data, see: Carlos Gervasoni, "Data Set Review: The World Bank's Governance Indicators (1996–2004)," *APSA-CP*, 17, 1 (2006), pp. 17–20. A more negative assessment and a response from the directors of the project are in: Marcus J. Kurtz and Andrew Schrank, "Growth and Governance: Models, Measures, and Mechanisms" and "Growth and Governance: A Defense," *Journal of Politics*, 69, 2 (May 2007), pp. 538–554, 563–569; Daniel Kaufmann, Aart Kraay, and Massimo Mastruzzi, "Growth and Governance: A Reply" and "Growth and Governance: A Rejoinder," *Journal of Politics*, 69, 2 (May 2007), pp. 555–562, 570–572.

[7] References to interviews in the footnotes follow the key used in Appendix B.

[8] Clifford Geertz, *The Interpretation of Cultures* (New York: Basic Books, 1973), p. 24.

and one in which state coercion has been especially prominent. In Chapter 8, I summarize the results of Russian state building under Yeltsin and Putin, assess Russian performance in comparative perspective, and consider further the relationship between state capacity and state quality. I also take up the issue of future prospects for the Russian state. Russia still needs strong state power, with a higher quality of policing and ruling.

I

Bringing the Gun Back In

Coercion and the State

A standing army and police are the chief instruments of state power.

Vladimir Lenin[1]

Lenin's blunt emphasis on control over organized coercion as central to what states are and do fits nicely with the dominant social science definition of the state provided by his German contemporary, Max Weber. Weber, we recall, defines the state in the following way: "[A] compulsory political organization will be called 'a state' insofar as its administrative staff successfully upholds the claim to be the *monopoly* of the *legitimate* use of physical force in the enforcement of its order." Alternatively, in a different work, Weber uses a slightly different formulation: "[A] state is a human community that (successfully) claims the *monopoly of the legitimate use of physical force* within a given territory."[2] The minor differences, although potentially interesting, seem less central than the focus on the effort to claim a monopoly on the legitimate use of force.

Although many scholars have criticized Weber's definition and provided alternatives, his approach is still the most widely accepted one and represents the pivot around which most definitional debates turn. For example, Joel Migdal, who pioneered the influential "state-in-society" approach, asserts that Weber's definition of the state "has led scholars down sterile paths." He proposes a "new definition" of the state that will reorient further research. The key to Migdal's definition involves separating "the image of a coherent, controlling organization in a territory" from "the actual practices of its multiple parts."[3]

---

[1] V.I. Lenin, "The State and Revolution," in *Lenin: Selected Works* (Moscow: Progress Publishers, 1968), p. 268.
[2] Max Weber, *Economy and Society*, edited by Guenther Roth and Claus Wittich (Berkeley, CA: University of California Press, 1978), p. 54; Max Weber, "Politics as a Vocation," in H.H. Gerth and C. Wright Mills, eds., *Max Weber: Essays in Sociology* (New York: Oxford University Press, 1946), p. 78. Emphasis in originals.
[3] Joel Migdal, *State in Society: Studying How States and Societies Transform and Constitute One Another* (Cambridge: Cambridge University Press, 2001), pp. 3, 15–16.

Similarly, Margaret Levi objects to Weber's definition on the grounds that both the monopoly on the use of force and its legitimacy are variables.[4] However, there is nothing in Weber's ideal-type definition of the state that impedes the study of actual practices, or from taking account of and attempting to explain variance across countries and across time in the extent to which the monopoly of force is legitimate and successfully claimed. Indeed, Migdal's earlier classic, *Strong Societies and Weak States*, takes the Weberian definition as given and then proceeds to show how and why many real states "vary considerably in how they fit the ideal-type." Weber's definition, far from deflecting attention away from the gap between the ideal and the real, arguably helped inspire the investigation of this gap in the work of Migdal, Levi, and others.[5]

This is not to say that Weber's definition is without difficulties. Theda Skocpol rightly emphasizes the "Janus-faced" (both internally and externally oriented) nature of states, something Weber's approach largely neglects, although his reference to "a given territory" at least nods in that direction.[6] Still, the social science's near-consensus on the dominant status of Weber's definition is a good thing and a step forward from the debate of the 1970s and 1980s that contrasted Weberian approaches with Marxist and pluralist ones.

The more important difficulty in studying the state is not defining it, but operationalizing it. Although it may be possible to see "like a state," it is impossible to see a state.[7] The pitfalls of reification in the study of the state have been noted by many,[8] but at least in principle, there is no obvious reason why this is more true in studies of the state than it is in research that looks at other collectives, such as nations, firms, and societies. And, as Charles Tilly notes, without some form of casual reification when writing about the state, we would sacrifice both succinctness and significance.[9]

---

[4] Margaret Levi, "The State of the Study of the State," in Ira Katznelson and Helen V. Milner, eds., *Political Science: The State of the Discipline*, Centennial Edition (New York: W.W. Norton & Company, 2002), p. 4.

[5] Joel Migdal, *Strong Societies and Weak States: State-Society Relations in the Third World* (Princeton, NJ: Princeton University Press, 1988), p. 19. For more on the state-in-society approach, see: Joel S. Migdal, Atul Kohli, and Vivienne Shue, eds., *State Power and Social Forces: Domination and Transformation in the Thirld World* (Cambridge: Cambridge University Press, 1994); Atul Kohli, "State, Society, and Development," in Katznelson and Milner 2002, pp. 84–117. For Levi's work on the state explaining variation in revenue extraction systems and the success of conscription, see, respectively: Margaret Levi, *Of Rule and Revenue* (Berkeley, CA: University of California Press, 1988); Margaret Levi, *Consent, Dissent, and Patriotism* (Cambridge: Cambridge University Press, 1997).

[6] Theda Skocpol, *States and Social Revolutions: A Comparative Analysis of France, Russia, and China* (Cambridge: Cambridge University Press, 1979), p. 32.

[7] James Scott, *Seeing Like a State: How Certain Schemes to Improve the Human Condition Have Failed* (New Haven, CT: Yale University Press, 1998).

[8] E.g., Robert W. Jackman, *Power Without Force: The Political Capacity of Nation-States* (Ann Arbor, MI: University of Michigan Press, 1993), p. 64; Eric A. Nordlinger, *On the Autonomy of the Democratic State* (Cambridge, MA: Harvard University Press, 1981), p. 9.

[9] Charles Tilly, *Coercion, Capital, and European States, AD 990–1992* (Cambridge: Blackwell, 1992), p. 34.

Still, undoubtedly some of the statist literature is overly abstract. In this vein, Levi correctly argues for a shift from general theories of the state to more detailed studies of "the organizations and individuals who establish and administer public policies and laws."[10] Taking Weber's approach seriously implies a particular focus on the state organizations that wield coercion. As Weber puts it, "organized domination requires the control of those material goods which in any given case are necessary for the use of physical violence. Thus, organized domination requires control of the personal executive staff and the material implements of administration."[11]

The executive staff primarily responsible for what Samuel Huntington calls "the management of violence" are military and police officers.[12] Yet despite the enormous literature on the state produced in recent decades, and the prominence of neo-Weberian perspectives in this work, detailed studies of state coercive organs remain a distinctly niche affair in comparative politics. Gerardo Munck's and Richard Snyder's content analysis of fifteen years' worth of articles in the top three comparative politics journals – *Comparative Politics, Comparative Political Studies*, and *World Politics* – showed that only 2.5 percent of these articles were on the military and police – a total of 8 out of 319 articles. Although articles on political violence and order, such as civil wars and revolutions, were relatively frequent (17.9 percent of all articles), most comparativists eschewed detailed analysis of the actual state organizations that control the means of violence.[13]

There is, of course, a large civil-military relations literature that deals with the state's foremost coercive agency.[14] In *Political Order in Changing Societies*, Huntington directly connects military coups to state weakness in his argument about praetorian governments.[15] However, little of the civil-military relations literature, particularly on coups, self-consciously situated itself in the statist literature, partially because the centrality of the state may have seemed obvious and partially because any connection between state incapacity and coups at least flirted with the danger of tautology.[16] In the 1980s and 1990s, the civil-military relations literature shifted to the study of democratization. Much of

[10] Margaret Levi, "Why We Need a New Theory of Government," *Perspectives on Politics*, 4, 1 (March 2006), p. 6.

[11] Weber 1946, p. 80.

[12] Samuel P. Huntington, *The Soldier and the State: The Theory and Politics of Civil-Military Relations* (Cambridge, MA: Belknap Press/Harvard University Press, 1957), pp. 11–14.

[13] Gerardo L. Munck and Richard Snyder, "Debating the Direction of Comparative Politics: An Analysis of Leading Journals," *Comparative Political Studies*, 40, 1 (January 2007), p. 9.

[14] Overviews include: Martin Edmonds, *Armed Services and Society* (Boulder, CO: Westview Press, 1990); Peter D. Feaver, "Civil-Military Relations," *Annual Review of Political Science*, 2 (1999), pp. 211–241.

[15] Samuel P. Huntington, *Political Order in Changing Societies* (New Haven, CT: Yale University Press, 1968).

[16] My attempt to systematize the large coup literature is in: Brian D. Taylor, *Politics and the Russian Army: Civil-Military Relations, 1689–2000* (Cambridge: Cambridge University Press, 2003), pp. 6–37.

this work was, in some ways, the mirror image of the coup literature, seeking to explain under what conditions the military does *not* intervene against the existing regime. This more recent scholarship also has not explicitly connected to the statist literature.[17]

In terms of coercive state agencies, most notable has been the relative neglect of law enforcement structures in the statist literature in particular and in comparative politics more generally.[18] In Weberian terms, P.A.J Waddington notes, police, more than any other state agency, "are the *custodians* of the state's monopoly of legitimate force." For this reason, as Otwin Marenin argues, "any examination of the nature of the state requires the analysis of the police and policing."[19]

This book, then, combines Weber and Lenin's focus on force-wielding agencies as central to what states are and do with Levi's injunction to study state organizations and personnel in a more detailed, less abstract way. Law enforcement agencies deserve particular attention, both because of their importance and because of their relative neglect in the statist literature.

STATES, STATE FORMATION, AND STATE FAILURE: BRINGING THE GUN BACK IN

The statist revival in social science is a decades-old process that shows little sign of losing steam.[20] Among this enormous and diverse literature, two distinct streams of work are of central importance to us. The first strand, inspired especially by the work of Charles Tilly, examines the relationship between war (or its absence) and state formation.[21] Initially, most of this work was historical and focused largely on Europe.[22] Subsequently, particularly in

---

[17] Andrew Cottey, Timothy Edmunds, and Anthony Forster, "The Second Generation Problematic: Rethinking Democracy and Civil-Military Relations," *Armed Forces & Society*, 29, 1 (Fall 2002), pp. 31–56.

[18] Two review essays on the neglect of policing in comparative politics, which offer similar laments despite a fifteen-year gap in publication dates, are: Otwin Marenin, "Police Performance and State Rule: Control and Autonomy in the Exercise of Coercion" (Review Article), *Comparative Politics*, 18 (1985), pp. 101–122; Murray Scott Tanner, "Will the State Bring You Back In?: Policing and Democratization (Review Article)," *Comparative Politics*, 33 (2000), pp. 101–124.

[19] P.A.J. Waddington, *Policing Citizens: Authority and Rights* (London: UCL Press, 1999), p. 20 (emphasis in original); Marenin 1985, p. 102.

[20] Although the eponymous manifesto of the "bringing the state back in" movement was published in 1985, in hindsight it seems clear that the movement began in 1968, with the publication of J.P. Nettl's "The State as a Conceptual Variable" and Samuel Huntington's *Political Order in Changing Societies*: Peter B. Evans, Dietrich Rueschemeyer, and Theda Skocpol, eds., *Bringing the State Back In* (Cambridge: Cambridge University Press, 1985); Huntington 1968; J.P. Nettl, "The State as a Conceptual Variable," *World Politics*, 20 (1968), pp. 559–592.

[21] Charles Tilly, ed., *The Formation of National States in Western Europe* (Princeton, NJ: Princeton University Press, 1975); Charles Tilly, "War Making and State Making as Organized Crime," in Evans, Rueschemeyer, and Skocpol 1985, pp. 169–191; Tilly 1992.

[22] Important contributions to the so-called "bellicist" account of European state formation include: Otto Hintze, "Military Organization and the Organization of the State" (1906),

the last decade, there has been an explosion of work applying Tilly's arguments to other parts of the world, both in terms of the history of state formation and current concerns about weak states.[23]

The second, and dominant, strand in the statist literature sought to parse, clarify, and illustrate the multiple aspects of "stateness." In particular, the strong/weak state distinction and the differentiation between state autonomy and state capacity provided the basis for productive cumulation in studies of the state.[24] Michael Mann's distinction between the despotic and infrastructural power of states has received somewhat less attention in comparative politics, although a close reading of his definitions shows that these concepts are very close cousins of state autonomy and state capacity.[25] The main difference is more normative, in that state autonomy is generally depicted as a positive trait leading to more rational economic policy making, whereas the label "despotic" obviously carries negative connotations.[26]

in Felix Gilbert, ed., *The Historical Essays of Otto Hintze* (New York: Oxford University Press, 1975), pp. 178–215; Brian M. Downing, *The Military Revolution and Political Change: Origins of Democracy and Autocracy in Early Modern Europe* (Princeton, NJ: Princeton University Press, 1992); Michael Mann, *The Sources of Social Power*, Volumes I and II (Cambridge: Cambridge University Press, 1986/1993); Bruce D. Porter, *War and the Rise of the State: The Military Foundations of Modern Politics* (New York: The Free Press, 1994); Janice Thomson, *Mercenaries, Pirates, and Sovereigns: State-Building and Extraterritorial Violence in Early Modern Europe* (Princeton, NJ: Princeton University Press, 1994); Thomas Ertman, *Birth of the Leviathan: Building States and Regimes in Medieval and Early Modern Europe* (Cambridge: Cambridge University Press, 1997).

[23] Important books in this tradition with a largely historical focus include: Karen Barkey, *Bandits and Bureaucrats: The Ottoman Route to State Centralization* (Ithaca, NY: Cornell University Press, 1994); Miguel Angel Centeno, *Blood and Debt: War and the Nation-State in Latin America* (University Park, PA: The Pennsylvania State University Press, 2002); Jeffrey Herbst, *States and Power in Africa: Comparative Lessons in Authority and Control* (Princeton, NJ: Princeton University Press, 2000); Victoria Tin-Bor Hui, *War and State Formation in Ancient China and Early Modern Europe* (Cambridge: Cambridge University Press, 2005). For my attempt to make sense of how the Tillyian account of state formation applies in the contemporary Third World, with a review of the relevant literature, see: Brian D. Taylor and Roxana Botea, "Tilly Tally: War-Making and State-Making in the Contemporary Third World," *International Studies Review*, 10, 1 (Spring 2008), pp. 27–57.

[24] The essential starting point remains: Evans, Rueschemeyer, and Skocpol 1985. Good overviews include: Kohli 2002; Levi 2002; Joel Migdal, "Studying the State," in Mark Irving Lichbach and Alan S. Zuckerman, eds., *Comparative Politics: Rationality, Culture, and Structure* (Cambridge: Cambridge University Press, 1997), pp. 208–236.

[25] Mann 1986/1993; Michael Mann, "The Autonomous Power of the State: Its Origins, Mechanisms, and Results," in John A. Hall, ed., *States in History* (Oxford: Basil Blackwell, 1986), pp. 109–136.

[26] The despotic label has sometimes lead scholars astray, but Mann's definition – "the range of actions which the elite is empowered to undertake without routine, institutionalized negotiation with civil society groups" – is very close to Skocpol's definition of state autonomy, "states ... may formulate and pursue goals that are not simply reflective of social groups, classes, and society." Mann 1986, p. 113; Theda Skocpol, "Bring the State Back In: Strategies of Analysis in Current Research," in Evans, Rueschemeyer, and Skocpol 1985, p. 9.

Relatively simple concepts such as state strength, autonomy, and capacity (the word simple is meant to imply "easy to understand," not "simplistic") made possible illuminating comparisons within particular states over time and issue area, between states in different regions of the world, and between states within these regions. For example, the neo-statist literature helped explain important differences in national economic policy.[27] Over time, the conceptualization and operationalization of the core concepts grew increasingly more sophisticated. Moreover, this strand of the neo-statist literature produced two important offshoots, the "state-in-society approach" and "new institutionalism."[28]

Despite these important advances in the statist literature, one flaw of this second strand was that the vast majority of it took relatively well-constructed states as a given. Given that this literature really took off in the 1970s and 1980s, this tendency is not that surprising. At this point in post–World War II history, the decolonization in Africa and Asia of the 1950s and 1960s had largely been completed, whereas the collapse of Yugoslavia and the USSR still lay in the future. The possibility of states losing control over coercion, and this loss of control leading to state collapse, was not on most scholars' radar screens. In the 1970s and 1980s, the number of states in the international system was relatively stable compared to preceding and subsequent decades.

In hindsight, though, the tendency to focus on well-established states and treat states as given was a major weakness of this second strand of statist work. State formation and state failure were seen as topics better left for historical sociologists. One consequence of the "taken for granted" nature of states in much of the neo-statist literature of the 1980s and 1990s was that an issue central to the classic Weberian approach – coercion and violence – often faded into the background.[29] Although scholars such as Huntington, Tilly, and Skocpol placed political violence at the center of the major early works that inspired the neo-statist movement, subsequent work focused primarily on economic issues in which the hand of the state is clearly present, but wrapped

---

[27] E.g., Stephen D. Krasner, *Defending the National Interest: Raw Materials Investment and U.S. Foreign Policy* (Princeton, NJ: Princeton University Press, 1978); Kathryn Sikkink, *Ideas and Institutions: Developmentalism in Brazil and Argentina* (Ithaca, NY: Cornell University Press, 1991); David Waldner, *State Building and Late Development* (Ithaca, NY: Cornell University Press, 1999); Atul Kohli, *State-Directed Development: Political Power and Industrialization in the Global Periphery* (Cambridge: Cambridge University Press, 2004).

[28] This claim about the lineage of the "state-in-society" and "new institutiontalist" approaches may be controversial, but it is secondary to our concerns. Discussions include: Kohli 2002; Karen L. Remmer, "Theoretical Decay and Theoretical Development: The Resurgence of Institutional Analysis," *World Politics*, 50 (1997), pp. 34–61; Peter A. Hall and Rosemary C.R. Taylor, "Political Science and the Three New Institutionalisms," *Political Studies*, 44 (1996), pp. 937–938.

[29] For example, there was little explicit attention to coercion in two influential edited volumes in the neo-statist tradition, with the exception of Tilly's 1985 essay: Evans, Rueschemeyer, and Skocpol 1985; Migdal, Kohli, and Shue 1994.

in a velvet glove rather than armor. As Peter Katzenstein noted in his study of the Japanese military and police, this statist literature was "carried forward most actively by students of political economy and the welfare state. Yet the core of the modern state lies, as Max Weber knew, not in economy and society but in the state's monopoly over legitimate means of coercion."[30]

Vadim Volkov usefully distinguishes between "the politics of sovereignty, the effect of which is the formation of a state, and conventional politics, aimed at controlling the state." Once modern states were formed, Volkov notes, "the long and brutal politics of sovereignty ... [gave] way to a different kind of politics that was no longer preoccupied with the foundations of the state – the monopolies of violence, taxation, and justice – but came to rest on them."[31] Roughly speaking, we can think of state building involving a first phase of state formation, when a monopoly over legitimate coercion is more or less successfully claimed, and a second phase that involves building the capacity of an already existing state.[32]

However, although the distinction between "the politics of sovereignty" and "conventional politics" makes sense, the tendency to ignore state coercive organs during periods of "conventional politics," or the second phase of state building, is less justifiable. The monopoly over legitimate coercion is not achieved once and for all, but is rather a continuously claimed and contested state power that can grow, recede, or even collapse. Thus, the references to phases does not mean that states only move in one direction, from phase one to phase two – they can, and do, also move "backward." Further, all successful states ultimately rely on the ability to coerce to maintain their rule. Some scholars even use coercion as a synonym for "government."[33] This, perhaps, goes too far; although politics is always about conflict, in cases of conventional politics, goods and values are allocated through authoritative institutions without the use of force. However, the threat of force to achieve

[30] Peter J. Katzenstein, *Cultural Norms and National Security: Police and Military in Postwar Japan* (Ithaca, NY: Cornell University Press, 1996), p. 6.

[31] Vadim Volkov, *Violent Entrepreneurs: The Use of Force in the Making of Russian Capitalism* (Ithaca, NY: Cornell University Press, 2002), p. 156. David Woodruff similarly distinguishes between the "politics of sovereignty" and the "politics of the cash register" (allocation): David Woodruff, *Money Unmade: Barter and the Fate of Russian Capitalism* (Ithaca, NY: Cornell University Press, 1999). See also Stephen D. Krasner, "Approaches to the State: Alternative Conceptions and Historical Dynamics (Review Article)," *Comparative Politics*, 16 (1984), pp. 223–246.

[32] Thomas Carothers refers to two phases of state building in: Thomas Carothers, "The 'Sequencing' Fallacy," *Journal of Democracy*, 18, 1 (January 2007), p. 19.

[33] Mikhail Filippov, Peter C. Ordeshook, and Olga Shvetsova, *Designing Federalism: A Theory of Self-Sustainable Federal Institutions* (Cambridge: Cambridge University Press, 2004), pp. 1, 22. This usage is also consistent with Weber's understanding, although it creates problems for him in conceptualizing democracy in terms of his typology of authority, which leads him to underestimate the role of deliberation in democracies: Peter Lassman, "The Rule of Man Over Man: Politics, Power, and Legitimation," in Stephen Turner, ed., *The Cambridge Companion to Weber* (Cambridge: Cambridge University Press, 2000), pp. 83–98.

compliance is implicit in much state activity, including in such central realms as redistribution (those who do not pay taxes can go to jail) and regulation (ditto for those who violate, for example, environmental or labor laws). Even minimalist, "night watchman" conceptions of the state require basic coercive organizations such as the police, prisons, and the military.[34]

Real-world events intervened, as they so often do, to call into question this division of the statist literature into a historical stream on state formation (phase one) and a second stream on contemporary polities (phase two). The collapse of communism and the end of the Cold War had profound effects on states throughout the world, and on subsequent scholarship. The collapse of Czechoslovakia, the Soviet Union, and Yugoslavia evidenced a remarkable decline in state strength in a part of the world once seen as epitomizing "developed polities."[35] The end of the Cold War also changed markedly the external opportunities and constraints facing many Third World countries. Moreover, the international security threats posed by failed and failing states have received growing attention, particularly since September 11, 2001. Controlling and managing coercion remains central to state formation in the contemporary world, as evidenced, for example, in Afghanistan, Iraq, and Palestine. Violent state formation is not just a historical topic.[36]

The inability of many states to successfully claim the monopoly of legitimate coercion has featured most prominently in the literature on Africa.[37] But state weakness and controlling coercion is an issue in most other parts of the world, including in countries and regions that historically have had coherent and functioning states. As Anthony Pereira notes, the "near monopoly of legitimate force" can be "temporary and reversible."[38] This is evident in Eurasia in general and Russia in particular, a country with a long history of strong statehood and one that relied considerably on coercion during its formation.[39] With the collapse of the Soviet Union, and the widespread (and accurate) perception that the "transition" to democracy had run aground in

---

[34] Robert Nozick, *Anarchy, State, and Utopia* (New York: Basic Books, 1974).

[35] Huntington 1968.

[36] A good introduction to the rapidly growing literature on state failure is: Robert I. Rotberg, ed., *When States Fail* (Princeton, NJ: Princeton University Press, 2004).

[37] E.g., Robert H. Jackson and Carl G. Rosberg, "Why Africa's Weak States Persist: The Empirical and Juridical in Statehood," *World Politics*, 35 (1982), pp. 1–24; Christopher Clapham, *Africa and the International System: The Politics of State Survival* (Cambridge: Cambridge University Press, 1996); William Reno, *Warlord Politics and African States* (Boulder, CO: Lynne Rienner, 1998); Herbst 2000; Robert H. Bates, *When Things Fell Apart: State Failure in Late-Century Africa* (Cambridge: Cambridge University Press, 2008).

[38] Anthony W. Pereira, "Armed Forces, Coercive Monopolies, and Changing Patterns of State Formation and Violence," in Diane E. Davis and Anthony W. Pereira, eds., *Irregular Armed Forces and Their Role in Politics and State Formation* (Cambridge: Cambridge University Press, 2003), p. 388.

[39] Tilly 1992; Geoffrey Hosking, *Russia: People and Empire 1552–1917* (Cambridge, MA: Harvard University Press, 1997); Marshall Poe, *The Russian Moment in World History* (Princeton, NJ: Princeton University Press, 2003).

much of Eurasia, scholars looked to the state as an important variable and concept in post-communist studies.[40]

Despite this interest in the state in the post-Soviet region, most of this literature has followed the more general tendency in comparative politics noted earlier in the chapter – the state's central coercive agencies are typically ignored.[41] To the extent these institutions are studied, it is not within a statist framework.[42] This book thus attempts to apply standard concepts from the statist literature, as well as a few newer ones, to the study of Russian coercive organs. In the rest of this chapter, I articulate a framework for studying state coercive agencies at multiple levels of government in order to link discussions of the Russian state to the specific organizations implicated in a neo-Weberian approach.

STUDYING COERCIVE ORGANS: STATE CAPACITY AND STATE QUALITY

The neo-statist literature focused particularly on state strength and capacity. I define state capacity, consistent with the standard definitions, as the ability of a state to ensure the reliable implementation of its decisions by its own personnel. Michael Mann's notion of infrastructural power – "the capacity of the state ... to penetrate civil society, and to implement logistically political decisions throughout the realm" – is basically the same.[43] Joshua Forrest and Joel Migdal emphasize that this capacity has an important territorial dimension because states seek to "penetrate" regions and localities.[44]

This notion of capacity or infrastructural power has provided illuminating comparisons across states. One ambiguity in the concept, however, is what it means to "implement decisions." Decisions of state leaders come in two basic forms, *routine* and *exceptional*. The implementation of routine decisions means that state officials in their regular practice attempt to fulfill and comply with standing laws and procedures that govern their activities. In contrast, the implementation of exceptional decisions comes when bureaucrats obey an order from an authorized state superior, such as a president or governor, that comes in response to specific circumstances that may be discretionary, or even potentially unlawful, under existing rules. For example, when the police investigate crimes defined by law, this is consistent with the implementation of routine decisions. When the police implement an order to overlook the crimes of a political ally of the leader, or frame political opponents of the leader for a crime they did not commit, this represents compliance with exceptional decisions. The distinction here is basically the same as Weber's claim

---

[40] This literature is discussed in Chapter 3.
[41] The most important exception in the statist literature on Russia is Volkov 2002.
[42] See the discussion of the literature on the "power ministries" in Chapter 2.
[43] Mann, "The Autonomous Power of the State," 1986, p. 113.
[44] Joshua B. Forrest, "The Quest for State 'Hardness' in Africa," *Comparative Politics*, 20, 4 (July 1988), pp. 423–442; Migdal 1988.

that "the theory of modern public administration" assumes that bureaucratic regulations are "abstract" rather than issued for individual cases.[45] From the normative point of view, official compliance with exceptional decisions may be objectionable (although not all exceptional decisions are of this nature), but the ability to demand compliance of this sort from state officials also represents a form of capacity that may be lacking in other states.

This distinction between routine and exceptional decisions calls attention to a more fundamental difference often elided in the neo-statist literature, that between state capacity and what I call state *quality*.[46] By state quality I mean whether the state and its officials serve the interests of the population in a fair manner that promotes the general welfare. In ideal-typical high-quality states, bureaucrats see themselves as "public servants," bound by the rule of law and resistant to the temptations of corruption. The concept of state quality shifts the perspective from that of the rulers and their goals to the citizens and their needs, and from *what* states do to *how* they do it.

State quality is roughly the same as what used to be called "good government" and is often now referred to as "good governance."[47] There is now a growing literature, especially by economists, on "good governance" or "the quality of government," both as an independent and dependent variable.[48] This literature has connected the quality of government to such desirable and diverse outcomes as economic growth and subjective life satisfaction.[49] However, as Bo Rothstein and Jan Teorell observe, the issue of state quality has received less conceptual attention. They argue that quality of government should be thought of as "*impartiality* in the exercise of public authority." Graham Wilson, in a critique of Rothstein and Teorell, stresses the importance

---

[45] Weber 1978, p. 958.

[46] A similar distinction between the "degree" of the state and the "kind" of state is made by Michael Barnett: Michael N. Barnett, "Building a Republican Peace: Stabilizing States after War," *International Security*, 30, 4 (Spring 2006), pp. 91–92.

[47] Analytically, government, which concerns state activities, and governance, which emphasizes the involvement of nonstate actors in making authoritative decisions, are distinct, but slippery usage has led to the term 'governance' often supplanting the word 'government' even from its proper domain. On government and governance, see: Gerry Stoker, "Governance as Theory: Five Propositions," *International Social Science Journal*, 50, 155 (March 1998), pp. 17–28.

[48] Most influential here has been the work of the World Bank Worldwide Governance Indicators (WGI) Project: World Bank, *A Decade of Measuring the Quality of Governance* (Washington, DC: 2006); Daniel Kaufmann, Aart Kraay, and Massimo Mastruzzi, "The Worldwide Governance Indicators Project: Answering the Critics," World Bank Policy Research Working Paper 4149 (Washington, DC: The World Bank, March 2007). See also: Rafael La Porta et al., "The Quality of Government," *Journal of Law, Economics, & Organization*, 15, 1 (March 1999), pp. 222–279; John F. Helliwell and Jaifang Huang, "How's Your Government? International Evidence Linking Good Government and Well-Being," *NBER Working Papers*, No. 11988 (Cambridge: NBER, January 2006); Alicia Adsera, Carlos Boix, and Mark Payne, "Are You Being Served? Political Accountability and Quality of Government," *Journal of Law, Economics, & Organization*, 19, 2 (2003), pp. 445–490.

[49] La Porta et al. 1999; Helliwell and Huang 2006.

of "a professional bureaucracy with a public service ethos [that] is policed by political institutions that insure adequate accountability." My conception of state quality draws on both of these approaches and includes impartiality (fairness) and a public service ethos. Bureaucratic professionalism and account- ability, as Rothstein and Teorell suggest and as I argue further, can be thought of as institutional arrangements that contribute to state quality.[50]

The concept of state quality has yet to join state autonomy and state capac- ity as a core idea in the statist comparative politics literature. This could be just a matter of time, as the growing literature on good governance and the quality of government by economists and policy specialists begins to influence political science. The first published combination of state capacity and state quality of which I am aware is Verena Fritz's *State-Building*, which looks at the size, capacity, and quality of the state in Belarus, Lithuania, Russia, and especially Ukraine in the fiscal realm. Fritz is more precise about her defini- tions and measures of size and capacity than those of quality, but the basic idea is that a high-quality state is a "source of solutions" for society, whereas a low-quality one is a "source of problems." Corruption is one of her key mea- sures, which I also use (see Chapter 5).[51]

A potential obstacle to wider adoption of the term is the obvious normative element in the term "state quality."[52] Without denying this issue, I would argue that the normative element is not a barrier to a more positive assessment of state quality, any more than the normative element in the concept of democ- racy has been a barrier to productive research on regime types. I bracket as much as possible the normative issues involved, focusing instead on the attempt to precisely measure state quality, to make meaningful comparisons over both time and space in state quality, and to explain the sources of high or low state quality. It is both desirable and possible to rigorously study not only what states do but how they do it. Overall, the risks of normative bias seem less severe than those of real-world irrelevance; by the criterion of whether it influences peoples' lives, state quality warrants greater comparative research.

A concern with the quality of states, and not just their capacity, also fol- lows from the growing confluence between the literature on the state and the democratic transitions literature. Indeed, the notion of state quality is partially inspired by the literature on democratic quality.[53] If some of the

---

[50] Bo Rothstein and Jan Teorell, "What Is Quality of Government? A Theory of Impartial Government Institutions," *Governance*, 21, 2 (April 2008), pp. 165–190 (quote p. 166, emphasis in original); Graham Wilson, "The Quality of Government," *Governance*, 21, 2 (April 2008), pp. 197–200; Bo Rothstein and Jan Teorell, "Impartiality as a *Basic* Norm for the Quality of Government: A Reply to Francisco Longo and Graham Wilson," *Governance*, 21, 2 (April 2008), pp. 201–204.

[51] Verena Fritz, *State-Building: A Comparative Study of Ukraine, Lithuania, Belarus, and Russia* (Budapest: Central European University Press, 2007), esp. pp. 31–33, 74.

[52] Rothstein and Teorell explicitly ground their discussion of the quality of government on nor- mative concerns: Rothstein and Teorell 2008, p. 169.

[53] Larry Diamond and Leonardo Morlino, eds., *Assessing the Quality of Democracy* (Baltimore: The Johns Hopkins University Press, 2005); Guillermo O'Donnell, Jorge Vargas

pioneering "transitology" literature paid little attention to the state,[54] it has become a central feature of more recent scholarship. Indeed, some minimal degree of state capacity, or "stateness," including a recognized population and territory, is perhaps the one "precondition" for democracy that most scholars can agree on. In Juan Linz's pithy formulation, "no state, no *Rechtsstaat*, no democracy."[55] Conversely, the attempt by Huntington in *Political Order in Changing Societies* to separate the question of the "form of government" from the "degree of government" has been called into question, with Francis Fukuyama arguing that "it is not clear whether state capacity (or political development, in Huntington's terminology) can be separated from legitimacy," adding that "in today's world the only serious source of legitimacy is democracy."[56] Cross-national statistical analysis seems to bear out this link between stateness and democracy, including when controlling for wealth.[57]

It is important to emphasize that, despite these recent arguments about the importance of "stateness" for democracy, and the observed tendency of the two factors to co-vary in many countries, they remain conceptually and often empirically distinct. Similarly, and crucial to this book, state capacity and state quality first need to be analytically separated before the linkages between these two concepts can be explored. Figure 1.1 shows the possible relationships between high and low state capacity and state quality.

The upper-right quadrant includes states that are both high capacity and high quality, or what I call "civil states."[58] The most obvious examples of these states are consolidated liberal democracies, representing primarily Guillermo O'Donnell's "originating countries" in Western Europe that generally had strong legal systems and public bureaucracies prior to democratization, although some more recent democratizers also belong in

Cullell, and Osvaldo M. Iazzetta, eds., *The Quality of Democracy: Theory and Applications* (Notre Dame, IN: University of Notre Dame Press, 2004). For an application to the post-communist region, see: Derek S. Hutcheson and Elena A. Korosteleva, eds., *The Quality of Democracy in Post-Communist Europe* (London: Routledge, 2006).

54 E.g., Guillermo A. O'Donnell and Philippe C. Schmitter, *Transitions from Authoritarian Rule: Tentative Conclusions about Uncertain Democracies* (Baltimore: Johns Hopkins University Press, 1986).

55 Linz is quoted in: Larry Diamond, *Developing Democracy: Toward Consolidation* (Baltimore: Johns Hopkins University Press, 1999), p. 12. On stateness and democracy, see, for example: Juan Linz and Alfred Stepan, *Problems of Democratic Transition and Consolidation: Southern Europe, South America and Post Communist Europe* (Baltimore: Johns Hopkins University Press, 1996), pp. 16–37; Valerie Bunce, "Comparative Democratization: Big and Bounded Generalizations," *Comparative Political Studies*, 33 (2000), pp. 711–715. An important precursor is the discussion of "national unity" in: Dankwart Rustow, "Transitions to Democracy: Toward a Dynamic Model," *Comparative Politics*, 2 (1970), pp. 350–352.

56 Francis Fukuyama, *State-Building: Governance and World Order in the 21st Century* (Ithaca, NY: Cornell University Press, 2004), p. 26. See also: Huntington 1968; Francis Fukuyama, *The End of History and the Last Man* (New York: The Free Press, 1992).

57 Adsera, Boix, and Payne 2003; Hanna Back and Axel Hadenius, "Democracy and State Capacity: Exploring a J-Shaped Relationship," *Governance*, 21, 1 (January 2008), pp. 1–24.

58 I thank Steve Hanson for this formulation.

	State quality	
	Low	High
High	Police States	Civil States
Low	Weak States	

State capacity

FIGURE I.I. State quality and state capacity.

this quadrant.[59] Whereas it is important to note that civil states have multiple deficiencies along both dimensions of state quality and state capacity, relative to world practice, these countries perform well. In the upper-left quadrant are police states, which are able to effectively penetrate society and ensure that their most important decisions are implemented, but which serve the goals of the rulers while generally neglecting the needs of citizens. Totalitarian states like the Soviet Union, and most bureaucratic-authoritarian states, would fit here.[60]

In the lower-left quadrant are weak (and sometimes even failing) states that perform poorly both at implementing authoritative decisions and serving the needs of society. Interestingly, the combination of high quality/low capacity seems to be infrequent to nonexistent, which means the lower-right square is largely empty. This implies, as argued earlier, that there is at least some sequencing involved, with the first essential task being the establishment of basic state integrity by creating the rudiments of public order and state control over legitimate violence.[61] In reality, of course, it makes more sense to think of both state capacity and quality as continuums, so actual states would be scattered throughout the grid, although few states probably fall in the lower-right quadrant.

Measures of stateness from the 2006 World Bank Worldwide Governance Indicators (WGI) project provide some preliminary evidence on the relationship between state capacity and state quality globally. Figure 1.2 shows a scatter plot of states in the world on two dimensions – political stability and a

[59] Guillermo A. O'Donnell, "Democracy, Law, and Comparative Politics," *Studies in Comparative International Development*, 36 (2001), esp. pp. 20–21, 27. See also: Richard Rose and Doh Chull Shin, "Democratization Backwards: The Problem of Third-Wave Democracies," *British Journal of Political Science*, 31 (2001), pp. 331–354.

[60] David Collier, ed., *The New Authoritarianism in Latin America* (Princeton, NJ: Princeton University Press, 1979).

[61] On the need for some "minimal functional capacity" and "something resembling a monopoly of force" before democracy and the rule of law are possible, see: Carothers 2007, p. 19. For an argument about the importance of "institutionalization before liberalization" in postconflict settings, see: Roland Paris, *At War's End: Building Peace After Civil Conflict* (Cambridge: Cambridge University Press, 2004), esp. pp. 179–211.

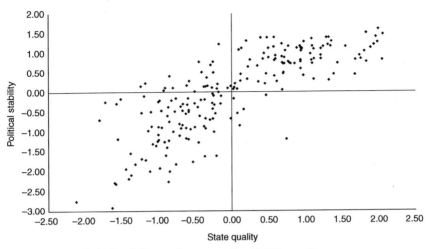

FIGURE 1.2. Political stability and state quality (WGI 2006).

combined measure of state quality. The "Political Stability/No Violence" indicator measures "the perceptions of the likelihood that the government will be destabilized or overthrown by unconstitutional or violent means, including domestic violence and terrorism," which I use here as a proxy for political capacity.[62] The state quality measure is the average of three WGI indicators: rule of law, control of corruption, and voice and accountability.[63]

The scatter plot shows most states in the world in either the civil-state or weak-state category, with a strong correlation between political stability/no violence and state quality.[64] There are also quite a few countries (twenty-one) that have high scores for political stability and low ones for state quality – police states. Examples include Belarus, Cuba, Libya, Mozambique, and Kazakhstan.[65] As expected, the lower-right quadrant is largely empty. The country most clearly in this square is Israel, which has high-quality state institutions but faces a serious terrorist threat. India, another democracy that suffers both from terrorist threats and ethnic violence, is also in the low-stability/high-quality box.

Keith Darden, although using different terminology and different measures, shows a similar tendency of states in the contemporary world to cluster into my three categories of civil states (high quality and capacity), weak states

---

[62] On the use of political violence as an indicator of state capacity, see Jackman 1993.

[63] See also the discussion in Chapter 8.

[64] R = 0.79.

[65] Interestingly, the state quality measure used here does not seem to simply be a proxy for democracy, with several countries with high political stability and low state quality also having relatively high Freedom House scores. For example, Mongolia is in this category and has a 2008 Freedom House combined score of 2 (1 is the highest on a 7-point scale), and Mozambique has a combined score of 3.

(low quality and capacity), and police states (high capacity and low quality), with few states having high quality but low capacity. Using tax collection and government expenditures as a percentage of GDP as measures of state capacity and the Transparency International Corruption Perceptions Index as a measure of corruption, Darden finds that there are "virtually no" states that have low corruption and low tax extraction, which I would classify as high quality but low capacity. Darden is most interested in those states with high corruption and high state capacity, a category in which he finds multiple examples. Darden concludes, "corrupt practices and other violations of the law may signal the absence of a Weberian bureaucracy but do not necessarily imply absence or weakness of administrative hierarchy."[66]

State coercive organs are crucial actors in efforts to build state quality.[67] In the coercive realm, state quality is built, following Norbert Elias, when the state's monopoly of force is wielded not primarily for the interests of the ruler(s), but for society as a whole.[68] Guillermo O'Donnell's work also highlights the importance of state coercive organizations to democratization and state quality. He emphasizes the importance of the rule of law for both democracy and the state, noting that the state is not just a "territorial entity" but also a "legal system." When the legal system does not work for the population, when one "cannot expect proper treatment from the police or the courts," then citizenship is limited, a condition he calls "low intensity citizenship."[69] If Mao was correct that power issues from the barrel of a gun, then authority derives from the gavel of a judge. And strengthening the rule of law, and thus the quality of the state, is intrinsically bound up with state coercive agencies, particularly, of course, law enforcement. Rachel Kleinfeld observes, "the transfer of military and police allegiance from the regime to the citizens is often the first essential step in moving autocratic governments toward becoming governments bound by law."[70]

---

[66] Keith Darden, "The Integrity of Corrupt States: Graft as an Informal State Institution," *Politics & Society*, 36, 1 (March 2008), pp. 35–60. Darden distinguishes between "minimalist" and "maximalist" views of the state, which roughly corresponds to my capacity/quality distinction.

[67] Concern with the quality of state coercive organs is found most directly in the largely policy-focused literature on "security sector reform (SSR)." Work on SSR has largely ignored the social science literature on the state. See: Robert Egnell and Peter Halden, "Laudable, Ahistorical, and Overambitious: Security Sector Reform Meets State Formation Theory," *Conflict, Security & Development*, 9, 1 (April 2009), pp. 27–54.

[68] Norbert Elias, "Violence and Civilization: The State Monopoly of Physical Violence and Its Infringement," in John Keane, ed., *Civil Society and the State: New European Perspectives* (London: Verso, 1988), pp. 179–180.

[69] Guillermo O'Donnell, "On the State, Democratization, and Some Conceptual Problems: A Latin American View with Glances at Some Postcommunist Countries," *World Development*, 21, 8 (1993), pp. 1355–1369 (quote p. 1361); O'Donnell 2001.

[70] Rachel Kleinfeld, "Competing Definitions of the Rule of Law," in Thomas Carothers, ed., *Promoting the Rule of Law Abroad: In Search of Knowledge* (Washington, DC: Carnegie Endowment for International Peace, 2006), p. 38. On the police and democratization, see: David H. Bayley, *Changing the Guard: Developing Democratic Police Abroad* (Oxford: Oxford University Press, 2006), pp. 17–23; Diamond 1991, pp. 90–91, 94–96; Otwin Marenin,

"All State Formation Is Local": Coercion beyond the Capital

One problem with many abstract discussions of "the state" is that they often seem very far away from the actual encounters that citizens have with agents of the state. Arguably Migdal's most important contribution to the study of state capacity was his insistence that understanding states in the developing world requires looking beyond the capital to the local level, where "triangles of accommodation" between state implementers, local political figures, and local strongmen undermine the goals of central leaders and agencies. As Diane Davis puts it, echoing a phrase frequently attributed to former U.S. Speaker of the House Thomas P. O'Neill, "all state formation [is] in essence 'local.'"[71]

State capacity and quality vary not only cross-nationally and temporally, but also geographically within the same state. Jeff Goodwin states, "any claim that a particular state is infrastructurally strong should ideally specify where, for whom, and how."[72] A complete account of state building necessitates moving beyond the capital and looking at the behavior of state agents at the regional, local, and even "street level."[73] The effectiveness of law varies, creating areas where the state is present and functions properly (what O'Donnell terms "blue areas"), where the state may be present but does not function properly ("green areas"), and where it fulfills neither condition ("brown areas").[74]

Studies of state coercive organs need to pay greater attention to this territorial dimension. It is striking, for example, that we have large literatures on the ethno-national and economic aspects of decentralization and federalism, but very little on the coercive aspects of these issues.[75] Mark Ungar notes

"Democracy, Democratization, Democratic Policing," in Dilip K. Das and Otwin Marenin, eds., *Challenges of Policing Democracies: A World Perspective* (Amsterdam: Gordon and Breach, 2000), pp. 311–331; Mark Ungar, *Elusive Reform: Democracy and the Rule of Law in Latin America* (Boulder, CO: Lynne Rienner, 2002).

[71] Migdal 1988; Diane E. Davis, "Contemporary Challenges and Historical Reflections on the Study of Militaries, States, and Politics," in Davis and Pereira 2003, p. 29. See also: Forrest 1988, pp. 427–431.

[72] Jeff Goodwin, *No Other Way Out: States and Revolutionary Movements, 1945–1991* (Cambridge: Cambridge University Press, 2001), p. 250. On within-country variation in, respectively, good government and state capacity, see: Judith Tendler, *Good Government in the Tropics* (Baltimore: The Johns Hopkins University Press, 1997); Catherine Boone, *Political Topographies of the African State: Territorial Authority and Institutional Choice* (Cambridge: Cambridge University Press, 2003).

[73] Michael Lipsky, *Street-Level Bureaucracy: Dilemmas of the Individual in Public Services* (New York: Russell Sage Foundation, 1980).

[74] O'Donnell 1993.

[75] On ethno-national aspects, see, for example: Valerie Bunce, *Subversive Institutions* (Cambridge: Cambridge University Press, 1999); Donald L. Horowitz, *Ethnic Groups in Conflict* (Berkeley, CA: University of California Press, 1985), pp. 601–628; Arend Lijphart, *Democracy in Plural Societies: A Comparative Exploration* (New Haven, CT: Yale University Press, 1977). On economic and fiscal federalism, see, for example: Gabriella Montinola, Yingyi Qian, and Barry R. Weingast, "Federalism, Chinese Style: The Political Basis for Economic Success," *World Politics*, 48 (1995), pp. 50–81; Jonathan Rodden, *Hamilton's Paradox: The Promise and Peril of Fiscal Federalism* (New York: Cambridge University Press, 2006); Erik Wibbels, *Federalism and the Market: Intergovernmental Conflict and Economic Reform in*

the important role provincial law enforcement structures play in rule-of-law issues, sometimes serving as a source for reform initiatives and sometimes providing the worst examples of repression and unresponsiveness.[76] Even more fundamentally, central and regional governments will often fight for control of policing, in both federal states such as Argentina and unitary ones such as France.[77] Migdal contends, "who controls the local police is often one of the most important questions one can ask about the distribution of social control."[78] In some cases, regions exert considerable influence over the military as well.[79]

A key part of the story told in this book is about how the issue of controlling coercion featured heavily in the politics of Russian state building and federalism under Boris Yeltsin and Vladimir Putin. As I elaborate in Chapter 4, the means used for resolving center-region disputes in established democracies were too weak to perform this function in Russia. These struggles for control, however, had no impact on state quality. On the contrary, the focus on control pushed to the background the more important issue for the Russian state: how to transform Russia into a civil state in which coercion serves not just the ruling elite, but society as a whole.

COERCION, STATE CAPACITY, AND STATE QUALITY IN POST-SOVIET RUSSIA

The dramatic events of the 1980s and 1990s in Russia have been characterized variably as a revolution, an imperial collapse, and a transition. In important respects, of course, it was all of these. Stephen Kotkin argues persuasively that it is a mistake to see the political and economic collapse as an event that took place in December 1991, as opposed to a process that began decades before the formal death of the Soviet Union and continued well after this date.[80] And

---

the Developing World (New York: Cambridge University Press, 2005). A unique and important treatment of the territorial aspects of policing is: David H. Bayley, *Patterns of Policing* (New Brunswick, NJ: Rutgers University Press, 1985), pp. 53–73.

[76] Ungar 2002, pp. 19, 86–89, 143, 149, 178, 203.

[77] Laura Kalmanowieci, "Policing the People, Building the State: The Police-Military Nexus in Argentina, 1880–1945," in Davis/Periera 2003, pp. 209–232; Lizabeth Zack, "The *Police Municipale* and the Formation of the French State," in Davis/Periera 2003, pp. 281–302. Zack's account is weakened by her argument that the French state did not monopolize coercion until the second half of the twentieth century because the central state shared this control with cities and provinces. But a Weberian approach makes no specific claim about what *level* of the state asserts a monopoly of control over legitimate coercion; regional or local control is still state control.

[78] Migdal 1988, p. 32.

[79] This was true, for example, in pre–World War II Brazil: Kent Eaton, *Politics Beyond the Capital: The Design of Subnational Institutions in South America* (Stanford, CA: Stanford University Press, 2004), pp. 76–78; Alfred Stepan, *The Military in Politics: Changing Patterns in Brazil* (Princeton, NJ: Princeton University Press, 1971), p. 18.

[80] Stephen Kotkin, *Armageddon Averted: The Soviet Collapse 1970–2000* (Oxford: Oxford University Press, 2001).

the 1990s was not just a period of economic depression in Russia but also one of *political* depression, specifically low stateness.

Such periods of state collapse and weakness are of course not new in Russian history. The cyclical view of Russian history argues that the perennial challenge of Russian statehood has been how to govern such a large and inhospitable territory, particularly in conditions of relative economic backwardness and external threat from more economically advanced and militarily powerful neighbors. The conventional solution has been a revolution from above employing coercive methods, resulting in a strong authoritarian "service state." The pathologies of this model and changing historical conditions lead to liberalizing reforms designed to make the state more effective. These reforms tend to fail, leading to state collapse and the resumption of the cycle anew.[81]

It is tempting to view Putin through this angle, as another authoritarian state builder in the tradition of Peter the Great and Stalin.[82] Putin himself, consciously or unconsciously, promoted these analogies, hanging a portrait of Peter the Great in his office and echoing Stalin's famous line about "those who fall behind get beaten" in his September 2004 speech after the Beslan tragedy.[83] By the end of Vladimir Putin's presidency in 2008, the conventional wisdom, in both Russia and abroad, was that the post-collapse political and economic crisis had ended and that Russia was back on its feet, once again ready to reclaim its rightful place in the world as a major power. Conventional explanations for growing power included both structural factors, such as high world energy prices and the resulting economic growth in Russia, and agency in the person of Putin, who was able to rebuild the state by centralizing power in the Kremlin and weakening alternative centers of power, such as the economic barons known as the "oligarchs" and regional governors who had accumulated considerable power under Yeltsin.[84]

In contrast, I argue that the state-building achievements of Putin, although real, were relatively modest, especially in the coercive realm. Like Peter the Great and Stalin, Putin clearly privileged capacity building over quality building. There was a noticeable increase in the capacity of the Russian state to demand compliance from law enforcement organs to fulfill extraordinary decisions; a new "regime of repression" was built to crack down on political and economic opponents of the Kremlin. The picture with respect to implementing

---

[81] Examples include: Dominic Lieven, *Nicholas II: Twilight of the Empire* (New York: St. Martin's Press, 1993), pp. 252–262; Georgi Derluguian, "Recasting Russia," *New Left Review*, 12 (Nov.–Dec. 2001), pp. 5–31; Poe 2003; Stefan Hedlund, "Vladimir the Great, Grand Prince of Muscovy: Resurrecting the Russian Service State," *Europe-Asia Studies*, 58, 5 (July 2006), pp. 775–801.

[82] See especially Hedlund 2006.

[83] See the discussion in Chapter 3.

[84] See, for example, Thomas Graham, "A Modernizing Czar," *Wall Street Journal Europe*, 22 January 2008. Graham was senior director for Russia on the U.S. National Security Council staff in 2004–2007 and is one of Washington's best and most influential Russia watchers.

routine tasks was more mixed. The fiscal capacity of the state increased, and in Putin's last years as president, law enforcement agencies were apparently doing a better job of fighting crime and terrorism, although by comparative standards, their performance was relatively poor. On the other hand, the state did not establish a stable property rights regime.

The quality of Russian state coercive bodies did not improve; these organizations still neglected societal needs, treated citizens unfairly, and thereby failed to regain the trust of the population. Russia at the end of Putin's reign continued to lag dramatically behind states of comparable wealth around the world in terms of both state capacity and especially state quality; much of this book is devoted to demonstrating this assertion.

Why has state building, particularly in terms of the coercive agencies emphasized by a Weberian approach, been so difficult? I highlight three shortcomings in terms of public administration and political institutions:

1) The continued dominance of patrimonial and informal bureaucratic practices;
2) A faulty strategy for monitoring the behavior of state bureaucracies, especially coercive ones;
3) The failure to institutionalize a new set of values among government employees in the coercive realm that would lead state agents to pursue general rather than particular goods.

These three factors clearly are not the only influences on state capacity and state quality. Stateness is influenced by larger structural factors, such as economic wealth and resource dependence, as well as prior historical legacies, such as inheritances from the Soviet system and the legacies of its collapse.[85] The advantage of the three issues I focus on – bureaucratic type, monitoring strategy, and organizational mission – is that they are directly connected to organizational practice and public administration. They also are manipulable, in the sense that they can be changed by the actions of politicians and state officials.[86] Karl Marx famously observed that "men make their own history, but they do not make it just as they please; they do not make it under circumstances chosen by themselves."[87] Boris Yeltsin and Vladimir Putin both thought of themselves as making history and sought to bend the existing circumstances to further their goal of rebuilding the Russian state. It is thus appropriate that we focus on those factors more subject to short- and medium-term change.

---

[85] Identifying the structural correlates of stateness is best studied using cross-national statistical analysis, although qualitative case studies are necessary for probing in more detail the causal mechanisms at work. In Chapter 8, I return to these issues.

[86] Stephen Van Evera, *Guide to Methods for Students of Political Science* (Ithaca, NY: Cornell University Press, 1997), p. 21.

[87] Karl Marx, "The Eighteenth Brumaire of Louis Bonaparte," in Robert C. Tucker, ed., *The Marx-Engels Reader*, 2nd Edition (New York: W.W. Norton, 1978), p. 595.

Bureaucratic Type: Patrimonial Administration

Central to the Weberian approach to public administration is the distinction between rational-legal and patrimonial bureaucracies. Rational-legal bureaucracies are based on impersonal administration, in which personnel are recruited and promoted based on relatively objective criteria, such as education, examination, length of service, and performance. In contrast, in patrimonial bureaucracies, personnel are recruited and promoted based on connections, family ties, ethnic background, and other characteristics not directly related to their ability to complete their assigned tasks in an effective and efficient manner. In short, in the former, you enter and advance based on "what you know," and in the latter, based on "who you know."[88] Further, in a rational-legal bureaucracy, one's tasks are clearly specified and relatively compartmentalized, whereas in a patrimonial one, both the nature of tasks and the boundary between jobs are fuzzier. Finally, the Weberian approach stresses the importance of attracting high-quality cadres and providing them with competitive salaries, benefits, and stable career prospects.[89]

In Weber's account, patrimonialism is a type of traditional domination similar to the rule of a patriarch over his household. Officials in states and empires cannot literally be members of the ruler's household, but they can be motivated more by personal loyalty than impersonal rules. Further, patrimonial officials historically were maintained by various "benefices" or "prebends," such as land or the right to extract fees for fulfilling administrative functions. Because "official acts ... are discretionary," Weber observes, "the lord and his officials demand a compensation in each case, either arbitrarily or according to established rates."[90] In current parlance, officials in a patrimonial bureaucracy can use their position in the state to extract rents. In Russia, being part of the president's team means access not just to political power, but also to economic wealth.[91] In one sense, this demonstrates the failure to maintain

---

[88] Patrimonialism thus obviously violates the norm of impartiality that Rothstein and Teorell see as fundamental to "quality of government": Rothstein and Teorell 2008, p. 170.

[89] The classic statement on rational-legal bureaucracy and patrimonialism is, of course, Weber 1978, pp. 956–1110. Other very useful discussions include: Robin Theobald, "Patrimonialism," *World Politics*, 34, 4 (1982), pp. 548–559; Ertman 1997; Peter Evans and James E. Rauch, "Bureaucracy and Growth: A Cross-National Analysis of the Effects of 'Weberian' State Structures on Economic Growth," *American Sociological Review*, 64, 5 (October 1999), pp. 748–765; Goodwin 2001.

[90] Weber 1978, p. 1029. For more detailed contemporary discussions of the similarities, differences, and relationships between the concepts of patrimonialism and prebendalism, see: Richard A. Joseph, *Democracy and Prebendal Politics in Nigeria: The Rise and Fall of the Second Republic* (Cambridge: Cambridge University Press, 1987), pp. 55–68; Nicolas van de Walle, "Meet the New Boss, Same as the Old Boss? The Evolution of Political Clientelism in Africa," in Herbert Kitschelt and Steven I. Wilkinson, eds., *Patrons, Clients, and Policies: Patterns of Democratic Accountability and Political Competition* (Cambridge: Cambridge University Press, 2007), pp. 50–67.

[91] On "patronal presidentialism" in Russia and the former Soviet Union, see: Henry E. Hale, "Democracy or Autocracy on the March? The Colored Revolutions as Normal Dynamics

appropriate boundaries between the public and the private, the impersonal and the personal, the state and the market.[92] In Weberian terms, it can be thought of as a departure from rational-legal administration.

The rise of coercive state bureaucracies approximating the rational-legal type can be traced to Western Europe in the nineteenth century. It was at this point that European militaries became "professional" in the sense described by Samuel Huntington in *The Soldier and the State*: entry and promotion for officers based on merit and education rather than class background, the creation of national military academies to train officers, and the rise of modern general staffs devoted to rational planning for war. Similarly, David Bayley dates the rise of professional police forces – uniform recruitment standards, specialized training, and salaries high enough to promote policing as a career option – to the nineteenth century in Western Europe and Japan.[93] In the United States, policing in many important cities remained dominated by patronage-based political machines until well after World War II. It took several generations of good government reformers to succeed in introducing civil service reforms and professional standards to American urban police forces.[94]

The rational-legal and patrimonial categories are obviously ideal types, with neither existing in pure form and many possible variants in between.[95] Moreover, the difficulty of creating rational-legal bureaucracies, especially beyond O'Donnell's "originating countries," has long been acknowledged.[96] Still, scholars have shown that this basic difference is important in explaining such diverse phenomena as state effectiveness, economic growth, and the likelihood of revolution.[97] The more "Weberian" a bureaucracy, the more its behavior is likely to be consistent with both higher state capacity and higher state quality.[98]

of Patronal Presidentialism," *Communist and Post-Communist Studies*, 39, 3 (September 2006), pp. 305–329; Celeste A. Wallander, "The Domestic Sources of a Less-than-Grand Strategy," in Ashley J. Tellis and Michael Wills, eds., *Strategic Asia 2007–2008: Domestic Political Change and Grand Strategy* (Seattle, WA: National Bureau of Asian Research, 2007), esp. pp. 144–148.

[92] Volkov 2002, pp. 164–166; Vadim Volkov, personal communication, April 26, 2008.

[93] Huntington 1957, pp. 19–58; Bayley 1985, pp. 47–52.

[94] Robert M. Fogelson, *Big-City Police* (Cambridge: Harvard University Press, 1977); James F. Richardson, *Urban Police in the United States* (Port Washington, NY: Kennikat Press, 1974). I thank Richard Bodnar for introducing me to this literature.

[95] On the inevitability of some degree of patrimonialism in any bureaucracy, see: Lloyd I. Rudolph and Susanne Hoeber Rudolph, "Authority and Power in Bureaucratic and Patrimonial Administration: A Revisionist Interpretation of Weber on Bureaucracy," *World Politics*, 31, 2 (January 1979), pp. 195–227.

[96] Fred W. Riggs, *Administration in Developing Countries: The Theory of Prismatic Society* (Boston: Houghton Mifflin, 1964); Merilee S. Grindle, ed., *Getting Good Government: Capacity Building in the Public Sectors of Developing Countries* (Cambridge, MA: Harvard Institute for International Development, 1997).

[97] Ertman 1997; Evans and Rauch 1999; Goodwin 2001.

[98] Some have connected the rational-legal/patrimonial divide to the currently popular distinction between formal and informal institutions: see, for example: Vladimir Gel'man, "The

Monitoring Strategy: Internal (Police Patrols) versus External (Fire Alarms)

The economic approach to organizations, grounded in rational choice theory, has endeavored over the last several decades to create a general theory of organizations rooted in what is called principal-agent theory. The basic idea is that all hierarchical relationships involve a principal, or boss, and an agent, or employee. The problem of the principal is to avoid hiring someone poorly suited for the job ("adverse selection") or who will perform poorly once in the position ("moral hazard" and "shirking").[99]

I am generally skeptical of an approach to organizations (or most other aspects of social or political life) based solely on individual self-interest. Agency theory, among other problems, suggests that the position of employees is stronger than that of the ill-informed bosses who cannot control them, that issues of group norms and culture play no role in organizational behavior, and that all agencies would be more efficient if structured around some optimal organizational design that supposedly minimizes adverse selection, moral hazard, and shirking.[100] Perhaps more fundamentally, agency theory to date has been applied primarily and most successfully in situations in which a stable bureaucratic order exists – precisely the thing that needs to be established in many states around the world. In many situations in weak and failing states, it is not clear who the principal and who the agent is, and the principal may be a crime boss or a warlord rather than state or bureaucratic superiors. It is hard to imagine, for example, that the type of agency theory applied to American bureaucracies can tell us much about the behavior of armed bodies, either state, non-state, or quasi-state, in places like Somalia or Afghanistan.

But if an approach to state bureaucracies based entirely on rational choice theory is likely to be both anemic and misleading, an approach without attention to self-interest and problems of monitoring and oversight will be equally misguided. For my purposes, the rationalist model that seems most applicable – and not just because it includes the word "police" – is the congressional oversight model of Matthew McCubbins and Thomas Schwartz. McCubbins and Schwartz suggest there are two basic forms of oversight, "police patrols" and "fire alarms." Police patrols, as the name suggests, involves periodic checking of behavior in a particular sphere. Fire alarms, in contrast, rely on

Unrule of Law in the Making: The Politics of Informal Institution Building in Russia," *Europe–Asia Studies*, 56, 7 (November 2004), p. 1022. Although there are important similarities, the overlap is not 100 percent, and I have chosen to frame the issue more in keeping with the literature on state bureaucracy and public administration. For a useful discussion of what the term "informal institutions" does (and does not) mean, see: Gretchen Helmke and Steven Levitsky, "Informal Institutions and Comparative Politics: A Research Agenda," *Perspectives on Politics*, 2, 4 (December 2004), pp. 725–740.

99 A classic statement is: Terry M. Moe, "The New Economics of Organization," *American Journal of Political Science*, 28, 4 (November 1984), pp. 739–777.

100 For these and other critiques of agency theory, see: Charles Perrow, *Complex Organizations: A Critical Essay*, 3rd Edition (New York: McGraw-Hill, 1986), pp. 219–257; Fukuyama 2004, pp. 43–91.

someone other than the principal informing the principal of a problem in a bureau's behavior.[101] In terms of state agencies, a police patrol approach would involve using some parts of the bureaucracy to check on the behavior of other state officials in different agencies. A fire alarm approach, in contrast, would make use of actors outside the state, such as the media or civil society organizations, to help monitor the behavior of state officials and organizations. McCubbins and Schwartz contend that the fire alarm approach is a more effective oversight mechanism. For my purposes, although an effectively implemented police patrol approach may improve state capacity, a fire alarm approach is more likely to improve not only state capacity, but especially state quality. Of course, both monitoring approaches can be used simultaneously, which may be the best option, but a sole reliance on police patrols is likely to be deficient.[102]

How to best monitor state coercive organs has generated a sizeable literature. For example, in the civil-military relations sphere, the issue of how to control the armed forces and minimize their involvement in politics has been widely discussed.[103] Bayley distinguishes between internal and external forms of control over policing. Internal control involves both bodies explicitly delegated to this task, such as internal affairs departments and special disciplinary procedures, as well as more implicit controls such as peer socialization (which I discuss in the next section). External controls include the courts, legislative bodies, and the media. Similarly, Pablo Policzer has proposed a generalized agency theory of control over state coercion. In Policzer's account, monitoring of coercion can be either internal (police patrol) or external (fire alarm) and varies from low to high, producing a standard two-by-two matrix of different types of monitoring. Both Bayley's and Policzer's frameworks are quite consistent with the agency theory approach used here.[104] In the coercive realm, important external "fire alarms" include not just the media and civil society groups, but also quasi-state institutions such as ombudsmen and civilian review boards.

[101] Matthew D. McCubbins and Thomas Schwartz, "Congressional Oversight Overlooked: Police Patrols versus Fire Alarms," *American Journal of Political Science*, 28, 1 (February 1984), pp. 165–179.

[102] Back and Hadenius distinguish between "steering from above" and "steering from below" in their discussion of the effect of regime type on state capacity. Although authoritarian regimes relying on "steering from above" can build some capacity, those states with the greatest capacity also use "steering from below," in terms of civil society engagement. Back and Hadenius 2008.

[103] An agency theory approach is: Peter D. Feaver, *Armed Servants : Agency, Oversight, and Civil-Military Relations* (Cambridge, MA: Harvard University Press, 2003). Other influential treatments include: Huntington 1957; Eric A. Nordlinger, *Soldiers in Politics: Military Coups and Governments* (Englewood Cliffs, NJ: Prentice-Hall, 1977), pp. 10–19; James T. Quinlivan, "Coup-proofing: Its Practice and Consequences in the Middle East," *International Security*, 24, 2 (1999), pp. 131–165.

[104] Bayley 1985, pp. 159–188; Pablo Policzer, *The Rise and Fall of Repression in Chile* (Notre Dame, IN: University of Notre Dame Press, 2009).

Institutionalizing a New Mission

Douglass North and Robert Putnam both contend that good government is as much a normative issue as a structural or rational one. Under purely rationalist assumptions, North notes, building "third party enforcement" of property rights is impossible, because "if the state has coercive force, then those who run the state will use that force in their own interest at the expense of the rest of society." The problem is how to create self-enforcing moral constraints, and both North and Putnam argue that this depends on the broader culture and are skeptical that this change can take place quickly.[105]

An approach that shares similar premises to those of North and Putnam about the centrality of norms, but locates the problem of changing them at a level of analysis perhaps more tractable to short- and medium-term change, that of bureaucrats and the bureaucracy, is what has become known as the "old institutionalism." Fukuyama, for example, argues for the virtues of an "old institutionalist" approach to building capacity based on norms rather than the rationalist version of "new institutionalism" that relies on principal-agent models. In this older tradition, he notes, "ideas and the attitudes they foster may serve as surrogates for a system of rules and formal discipline."[106]

Philip Selznick's classic formulation of this form of institutionalism states that "'to institutionalize' is to *infuse with value* beyond the technical requirements of the task at hand." James Q. Wilson expresses a similar idea, arguing that "when an organization has a culture that is widely shared and warmly endorsed by operators and managers alike, we say the organization has a sense of *mission*."[107] Creating such an internal consensus that shapes the values and everyday practices of state officials, as organizational theorists have long recognized, can supplement or substitute for the types of external controls that agency theory emphasizes.[108] Organizations that lack such a sense of mission can be said, in Durkheimian terms, to be suffering from "normlessness" (*anomie*). Without such a set of common norms to guide behavior, members of an organization will be more inclined to pursue their own interests.[109]

[105] Douglass C. North, *Institutions, Institutional Change and Economic Performance* (Cambridge: Cambridge University Press, 1990), pp. 59–60; Robert D. Putnam, *Making Democracy Work: Civic Traditions in Modern Italy* (Princeton, NJ: Princeton University Press, 1993). See also Nettl 1968, p. 589.

[106] Fukuyama 2004, p. 79.

[107] Philip Selznick, *Leadership in Administration: A Sociological Interpretation* (Berkeley, CA: University of California Press, 1957), p. 17, emphasis in original; James Q. Wilson, *Bureaucracy: What Government Agencies Do and Why They Do It* (New York: Basic Books, 1989), p. 95, emphasis in original. See also Arthur L. Stinchcombe, "On the Virtues of the Old Institutionalism," *Annual Review of Sociology*, 23 (1997), pp. 1–18.

[108] E.g., Anthony Downs, *Inside Bureaucracy* (Boston: Little, Brown and Company, 1967), pp. 226–228; Jeffrey Pfeffer, *Organizations and Organization Theory* (Boston: Pitman Publishing Inc., 1982), pp. 80–120.

[109] Applications of Durkheim to organizational analysis include: Deborah Vidaver-Cohen, "Ethics and Crime in Business Firms: Organizational Culture and the Impact of Anomie,"

Behavior by state officials that serves neither the state nor society can be thought of as corrupt, or even predatory. Michael Mann writes that "if the state ... loses control of its resources they diffuse into civil society, decentring and de-territorializing it."[110] But this is not necessarily true: State power can become decentered without diffusing into civil society. Rather, lower level officials can simply appropriate the state's power for their own ends. In common language, we call the use of public office for private benefit corruption.[111] Peter Evans distinguishes between "predatory" states that primarily plunder and extract resources from the population and "developmental" ones that create the conditions for economic entrepreneurship and growth. In a somewhat different approach, James Burk labels as predatory those state institutions that have both a high "material presence" in society and low "moral integration," meaning they do not behave in ways consistent with social understandings of what makes a good society, and are thus perceived as illegitimate.[112]

Stephen Hanson has developed this old institutionalist logic to explain the failure of democratic transition in Russia. Hanson argues that democratic consolidation "requires enforcement by a staff that can be counted on with some degree of confidence to uphold the directives of the central authorities." This confidence comes when state officials "genuinely believe in the practices they enforce." Hanson roots his argument in the Weberian distinction between "value rationality" and "instrumental rationality," maintaining that the high degree of uncertainty and the weakness of any overarching set of values or ideological project in post-communist Russia means that the pursuit of short-term material interest has been the dominant mode of individual activity, including by state agents. In such circumstances, corruption and the "unrule of law" are pervasive. Similarly, Kenneth Jowitt traced the rise of corruption in Soviet-bloc countries to the decline of the "combat task," or mission, of the communist party after the revolutionary regimes had consolidated themselves.[113]

in Freda Adler and William S. Laufer, eds., *The Legacy of Anomie Theory* (New Brunswick, NJ: Transaction Publishers, 1995), pp. 183–206; Ken Starkey, "Durkheim and Organizational Analysis: Two Legacies," *Organization Studies*, 13, 4 (1992), pp. 627–642. An important link between Durkheim and Selznick and other "old institutionalists" in organizational theory was Chester Barnard: Chester I. Barnard, *The Functions of the Executive* (Cambridge, MA: Harvard University Press, 1938/1966), pp. 86–89, 118–119, 233, 258–284. See the discussions in Perrow 1986, pp. 62–78; Wilson 1989, pp. 91–92.

[110] Mann 1986, p. 134.

[111] A good introduction is in Susan Rose-Ackerman, *Corruption and Government: Causes, Consequences, and Reform* (Cambridge: Cambridge University Press, 1999).

[112] Peter B. Evans, "Predatory, Developmental, and Other Apparatuses: A Comparative Political Economy Perspective on the Third World State," *Sociological Forum*, 4, 4 (1989), pp. 561–587; James Burk, "The Military's Presence in American Society, 1950–2000," in Peter Feaver and Richard Kohn, eds., *Soldiers and Civilians* (Cambridge, MA: MIT Press, 2001), pp. 247–274.

[113] Stephen E. Hanson, "Defining Democratic Consolidation," in Richard D. Anderson, Jr., M. Steven Fish, Stephen E. Hanson, and Philip G. Roeder, eds., *Postcommunism and the Theory of Democracy* (Princeton, NJ: Princeton University Press, 2001), p. 142; Stephen E. Hanson,

From this more sociological approach to institutions, then, the focus of those seeking to create state quality should be on the infusion of values that make state officials see themselves as "public" or "civil" servants. Judith Tendler maintained that in the Ceara region of Brazil, the regional government was "a remarkably strong moral presence in creating an imagery of calling around public service – in the eyes of the public and of public workers themselves."[114]

The importance of a sense of mission, or internal cultural constraints, has been emphasized by some experts as particularly important for state coercive agencies. Militaries, for example, are "total organizations" that are largely cut off from wider society for extended periods and that adhere to a fairly rigid and enclosed way of life; they also indoctrinate their members from a relatively early age. Thus, they are particularly inclined to develop powerful and more uniform organizational cultures.[115] David Bayley notes that the behavior of police is "powerfully influenced by the vocational sense" of officers, with those who view the job as "a calling, drawing upon motivations of community service" more likely to conduct themselves with rectitude than those who treat policing as "just a job." Otwin Marenin also stresses the importance of "police ideologies which make their work meaningful to themselves."[116]

In Chapter 5, I develop further the argument that law enforcement organs without a sense of mission, either a repressive one in the interests of the state and elites or a protective one based on service to society, will develop toward a "predatory" style of policing that advances the material interests of individual officers.[117] Russian law enforcement organs tend to treat their mission as one of repression or predation, not protection. Predatory policing undermines both state capacity and state quality.[118]

The Difficulty of Building State Capacity and Quality in the Coercive Realm

It should be acknowledged at the outset that there is no "magic bullet" for creating civil states with high capacity and quality. Optimal solutions to

---

"Instrumental Democracy? The End of Ideology and the Decline of Russian Political Parties," in Vicki L. Hesli and William M. Reissinger, eds., *The 1999–2000 Elections in Russia: Their Impact and Legacy* (Cambridge: Cambridge University Press, 2003), pp. 163–185; Ken Jowitt, "Soviet Neotraditionalism: The Political Corruption of a Leninist Regime," *Soviet Studies*, 35, 3 (July 1983), pp. 275–297. I take the phrase "unrule of law" from Gel'man 2004.

[114] Tendler 1997, p. 141.

[115] Elizabeth Kier, *Imagining War: French and British Military Doctrine between the Wars* (Princeton, NJ: Princeton University Press, 1997), p. 29; Taylor 2003, pp. 12, 17. On "total organizations," see: Erving Goffman, *Asylums: Essays on the Social Situations of Mental Patients and Other Inmates* (Garden City, NY: Anchor Books, 1961).

[116] Bayley 1985, p. 169; Marenin 1985, p. 109.

[117] A model of "predatory policing" is applied to Russia in: Theodore P. Gerber and Sarah E. Mendelson, "Public Experiences of Police Violence and Corruption in Contemporary Russia: A Case of Predatory Policing?" *Law and Society Review*, 42, 1 (2008), pp. 1–43.

[118] The military realm also has been marked more by "institutional decay" than the building of state capacity or quality: Zoltan Barany, *Democratic Breakdown and the Decline of the Russian Military* (Princeton, NJ: Princeton University Press, 2006).

organizational dilemmas vary considerably depending on factors such as the type of agency, available technology, and social factors. Fukuyama states, "instead of equilibria or Pareto optimal solutions to organizational problems, there are continuous tradeoffs along a series of organizational dimensions."[119]

If state building is never easy, there are good reasons to believe it is particularly hard to monitor and control the behavior of coercive agencies, especially law enforcement ones. Most noticeable, perhaps, is that state coercive agents by definition possess the physical means for demanding citizen compliance. Analysts of law enforcement have noted the potentially wide gap between "police power," in terms of the formal laws and rules that regulate police functions, and "police action" – the actual behavior of the police.[120]

More generally, both Fukuyama and Wilson have proposed typologies of organizations that suggest law enforcement is one of the most difficult areas to reform. Fukuyama distinguishes between "transaction volume" (the number of regular decisions made by an organization) and "specificity" (the ability to monitor organizational outputs). An area like central bank reform is marked by low "transaction volume" and high "specificity" and is thus most amenable to technocratic solutions that draw on the new organizational economics and principal-agent models. In contrast, a high transaction volume/low specificity area like law enforcement is much more complicated, thus demanding greater attention to "local constraints, opportunities, habits, norms, and conditions." A similar idea is found in Wilson's distinction between four types of agencies (production, procedural, craft, coping) based on whether outputs (bureaucrats' activities) and outcomes (results of those activities) can be observed. Policing, in Wilson's schema, is a difficult area to reform because it is a "coping" organization in which it is difficult for supervisors both to watch what the average cop is doing and assess whether the cop's activities contribute to public order and crime reduction. The considerable autonomy of most police officers led Weber to refer to them as the "representative of God on earth."[121]

While remaining mindful of the difficulties of reforming any state agency, particularly large ones with guns, I argue in this book that a misguided approach to state building has hurt both state capacity and especially state quality in post-Soviet Russia. This is particularly true of Vladimir Putin, who squandered important resources he had available to him (a rapidly growing economy, high personal popularity) and undermined his goal of building a strong and effective Russian state. Under Putin, coercive agencies increased their capacity to carry out extraordinary tasks, such as the repression of economic and political rivals to the state leadership. But they did not improve that much in carrying out their routine tasks of fighting crime and terrorism and

---

[119] Fukuyama 2004, p. 76. On the lack of magic bullets in reforming public administration, see also: Grindle 1997, pp. 5, 32; B. Guy Peters, *The Politics of Bureaucracy*, 5th edition (London: Routledge, 2001), pp. 299–346.

[120] Ungar 2002, pp. 64–70.

[121] Fukuyama 2004, p. 88; Wilson 1989, pp. 158–171; Weber 1978, p. 972.

TABLE 1.1. *Elements of State Building*

	Bureaucratic Type	**Monitoring Strategy**	**Organizational Mission**
Putin	Patrimonial	Police Patrols	Predation & Repression
Civil States	Rational-Legal	Fire Alarms	Protection

protecting private property rights. Further, they remained corrupt and unaccountable to society. If building capacity and quality in the coercive realm is particularly difficult, it is also particularly important, especially for law enforcement agencies, if popular trust in and commitment to the state is to increase. To an important extent, especially from the point of view of average citizens, "the quality of policing is the quality of ruling."[122]

Table 1.1 contrasts the bureaucratic type, monitoring approach, and dominant mission of Russian state coercive agencies under Putin with those that would be required for a high-quality, civil state. These three basic elements of a state-building strategy correspond with the three basic ways in which the police are held accountable, as outlined by Marenin: "by the fact that they are employees, by their own sense of what good policing means, and by the influence of other groups and organizations on them."[123]

The challenge facing President Dmitriy Medvedev since taking office in 2008 has been whether to continue Putin's state-building strategy, which has emphasized building state capacity to repress and has tolerated considerable corruption and predation by coercive agencies, or whether to adopt a radically different approach that stresses state quality and the rule of law.[124]

The prospects for a new strategy under Medvedev are discussed in the last chapter. Overall, if the story I tell about state building in Putin's Russia is convincing, the book will provide one illustration of the benefit of "bringing the gun back in" to the comparative politics literature on the state.

---

[122] Marenin 1985, p. 101.
[123] Marenin 1985, p. 118.
[124] In Chapter 8, I discuss further the difference between what Thomas Ertman calls the "authoritarian" and "constitutionalist" approaches to state building: Ertman 1997, pp. 323–324.

2

The Power Ministries and the *Siloviki*

> The group of FSB personnel assigned to work undercover in the government has successfully carried out the first step of their assignment.
>
> Vladimir Putin, December 1999[1]

> History has arranged it that the burden of upholding Russian statehood has to a considerable extent fallen on our shoulders.
>
> Viktor Cherkesov, KGB veteran and Putin ally, December 2004[2]

Putin presumably was joking when he made the statement quoted in the epigraph at a reception for secret police personnel on December 20, 1999, less than two weeks before he would become acting president when Boris Yeltsin surprisingly resigned on New Year's Eve 1999. But, as Russians like to say, in every joke there is an element of truth. And if Putin was joking, his close friend Cherkesov was deadly serious, arguing that Russia itself would perish if secret police alumni could not unify their forces.

During Putin's tenure as president, he relied heavily on officials who had made their careers in law enforcement and military agencies. State coercive bodies, referred to in Russia as the power ministries (*silovye ministerstva*) or power structures (*silovye struktury*), rose in stature. Russian citizens, for example, believed that Putin represented the interests of the power ministries – more than big business ("the oligarchs"), "ordinary people," the state bureaucracy, or society as a whole.[3] The increased prominence of personnel from these agencies throughout government led the Russian sociologist Olga

---

[1] Vitaliy Yaroshevskiy interview with Ol'ga Kryshtanovskaya, "Operatsiya 'vnedreniye' zavershena!," *Nov. Gaz*, August 30, 2004.

[2] Viktor Cherkesov, "Moda na KGB?," *KP*, December 29, 2004.

[3] Based on national surveys. See: Lev Gudkov, "The Army as an Institutional Model," in Stephen L. Webber and Jennifer G. Mathers, eds., *Military and Society in Post-Soviet Russia* (Manchester: Manchester University Press, 2006), p. 52.

Kryshtanovskaya to dub Putin's regime a "militocracy."[4] The term used to label people with power ministry backgrounds, *siloviki* (singular = *silovik*), swept into general Western usage and became a staple of journalistic accounts.[5]

To set the stage for an investigation of the role of the power ministries in Russian state building, in this chapter, I explain what the power ministries are and who are the siloviki. By the power ministries I mean those state structures, such as ministries and agencies, in which some personnel generally wear uniforms and which possess armed units or formations. I outline their roots in the Soviet period and note the most important organizational changes in these structures. I discuss several important law enforcement structures that are often excluded from the power ministry category, but are important actors in this policy area and thus interact frequently with the power ministries. I also provide some basic information on personnel and budgets, demonstrating the increased stability and resources of these ministries under Putin.

I then move on to examining the "rise of the siloviki" story that became a standard framing device for thinking about Russian politics under Putin. In particular, I stress the importance of distinguishing between the use of the term "siloviki" to refer to a cohort of personnel, a "clan" in Kremlin politics, and a group of state ministries and organizations. These three usages I refer to as the cohort, clan, and corporate understandings of the term "siloviki." These three different lenses suggest that the notion that the power ministries came to dominate Russian politics under Putin had an element of truth, but that there were important differences between the agencies and factions within this group of officials. An examination of the rise of the siloviki also demonstrates the importance of patrimonial bureaucratic practices in Russia.

RUSSIA'S POWER MINISTRIES: AN OVERVIEW

Firm control over the organs of state coercion was a hallmark of Soviet rule. Three large, powerful agencies represented the core Soviet force-wielding institutions: the Committee on State Security (KGB), the Ministry of Defense (MO), and the Ministry of Internal Affairs (MVD). Under the control of the Communist Party, they were the ultimate physical embodiment of Soviet power.

The last years of the Soviet Union and much of the 1990s represented a period of decline and fragmentation for the power ministries. In addition to the territorial disintegration of these structures brought about by the Soviet collapse and the establishment of new state coercive bodies in the Soviet successor states, within Russia, these agencies were splintered into multiple

---

4 Ol'ga Kryshtanovskaya, "Rezhim Putina: liberal'naya militoktratiya?", *Pro et Contra*, 7, 4 (Fall 2002), pp. 158–180; Olga Kryshtanovskaya and Stephen White, "Putin's Militocracy," *Post-Soviet Affairs*, 19, 4 (2003), pp. 289–306.
5 'Silovik' can also be used as an adjectival form.

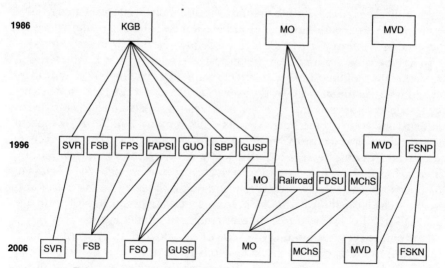

FIGURE 2.1. Fragmentation and consolidation of the power ministries, 1986–2006.

parts. The change was most important for the KGB, the organization that represented the greatest potential threat to the new, more liberal and democratic order, but it affected the Ministry of Defense and MVD as well. The three core organizations were divided into more than a dozen different power ministries. This fragmentation was somewhat reversed under Putin (see Figure 2.1).[6] Overall, probably about 3 million people serve in Russia's various power ministries and law enforcement structures (see Table 2.1).[7]

[6] Key: SVR=Foreign Intelligence Service; FSB=Federal Security Service; FPS=Federal Border Service; GUO=Main Guards Directorate; SBP=Presidential Security Service; GUSP=Main Directorate for Special Programs; FDSU=Federal Road Construction Administration [became independent in 1997, not 1996, but included as illustrative]; MChS=Ministry of Civil Defense and Emergency Situations; FSNP=Federal Tax Police Service; FSO=Federal Guards Service; FSKN=Federal Service for Control of the Narcotics Trade. This figure is not comprehensive, but it does provide a relatively accurate depiction of the general trends. Further issues will be noted in the text. Good overviews of the basic structure and function of the power ministries include: Jonathan Littell, *The Security Organs of the Russian Federation: A Brief History 1991–2004* (Paris: PSAN Publishing House, 2006); A.A. Mukhin, *Kto est' mister Putin i kto s nim prishel?* (Moskva: Gnom i D, 2002), pp. 135–250; Carolina Vendil Pallin, "The Russian Power Ministries: Tool and Insurance of Power," *Journal of Slavic Military Studies*, 20, 1 (2007), pp. 1–25; Bettina Renz, "Russia's 'Force Structures' and the Study of Civil-Military Relations," *Journal of Slavic Military Studies*, 18, 4 (2005), pp. 559–585.

[7] Citations for these figures appear further in the chapter, when each ministry or service is discussed. In addition to those shown in the table, one could include, for example, the several hundred thousand uniformed personnel in the prison system, which is part of the Ministry of Justice: Renz 2005, p. 562. Independent Russian State Duma Deputy Vladimir Ryzhkov in 2006 estimated that the number of employees of the power ministries at four million people, but this figure seems high: Vladimir Ryzhkov, "Kak perepakhat' partiynoye pole," *Nov. Gaz.*, June 22, 2006.

TABLE 2.1. *Main Power Ministries and Their Approximate Size, 2007*

Ministry of Defense (MO)	1,027,000
Ministry of Internal Affairs (MVD)	1,230,000
Internal Troops (VV)	200,000
Special Forces (Spetsnaz – OMON & OMSN)	27,000
Federal Security Service (FSB)	350,000
Federal Border Service (FPS)	160,000
Special Forces units	4,000
Ministry of Civil Defense and Emergency Situations (MChS)	262,831
Civil Defense Troops	20,000
State Fire Service	220,000
Federal Customs Service (FTS)	61,352
Procuracy	53,837
Federal Service for Control of the Narcotics Trade (FSKN)	33,677
Federal Guard Service (FSO)	10,000–30,000

The Ministry of Defense and Its Successors

The Soviet armed forces were the largest in the world, with around 5.3 million personnel in 1985. They received substantial material support from the state, with budgets around 15–25 percent of GDP. Respected at home and feared abroad, the Soviet military was a key pillar of state power. At the same time, its fundamental function was external defense, and for most of the post–World War II period, it played a minor and episodic role in internal politics. As I have argued elsewhere, the Russian and Soviet military for more than 200 years has tried to avoid involvement in sovereign power issues, only playing an important role during periods of state collapse and reconstitution (1917–1920, 1991–1993) or at the impetus of the civilian political leadership (1953, 1957).[8]

The collapse of the Soviet Union brought radical changes in the fortunes and capacities of the military. The military's size and budget were cut drastically, and throughout the 1990s there were frequent predictions of its imminent collapse. Although it lost control briefly over several armed structures and underwent multiple reorganizations, it kept its core components and still remains one of the world's largest militaries.

The Ministry of Defense (MO)

The Ministry of Defense is the main successor to the Soviet military. It was formed in May 1992 and inherited about 2.8 million personnel. Throughout the 1990s, this number was cut, leveling off at slightly more than 1 million

---

[8] Brian D. Taylor, *Politics and the Russian Army: Civil-Military Relations, 1689–2000* (Cambridge: Cambridge University Press, 2003).

troops in the late 1990s, the number it remains at today.[9] A key achievement of the early Yeltsin years was bringing home more than 1 million military personnel and their families from Eastern Europe and the Baltic states. The military also went through multiple internal reorganizations. For example, the main services and branches were reconfigured several times. Currently, there are three main services – army, navy, and air force – and three separate branches – strategic rocket forces, space forces, and airborne forces.[10]

A key issue for the Ministry of Defense in the post-Soviet period has been the issue of "military reform." Despite the considerable downsizing and multiple reorganizations, critics contended that the Russian military under Yeltsin and Putin remained very Soviet in terms of personnel policies (especially conscription and the very weak non-commissioned officers [NCO] system), doctrine, and overall culture. More sympathetic analysts argued that Putin turned the military around after the virtual collapse of the 1990s with an influx of rubles and a series of careful reforms.[11]

In terms of civil-military relations, one notable continuity between Yeltsin and Putin is that, by Western democratic standards, civilian control is weak because of the small number of civilian personnel in the Ministry of Defense and the limited role that the parliament plays in defense oversight, including the budget.[12] Throughout most of Putin's presidency the Minister of Defense was Sergey Ivanov – like Putin, a former KGB foreign intelligence officer from St. Petersburg. A purely civilian Minister of Defense, Anatoliy Serdyukov, was appointed in February 2007, but the Ministry of Defense continued to have a very small number of civilian employees and a huge staff of military officers. The appointment of Serdyukov, the former head of the Federal Tax Service, was certainly a bold move, given his lack of any relevant experience for the job, although he proved to be a more committed reformer than Ivanov was. Serdyukov owed his rapid political ascent to his St. Petersburg background, where he met Putin in the 1990s, when Serdyukov managed a furniture store.[13]

---

[9] *The Military Balance 2008* (London: The International Institute for Strategic Studies, 2008), p. 212.

[10] Branches are independent command structures, but of lesser status than services.

[11] For the pessimistic account, see: Zoltan Barany, *Democratic Breakdown and the Decline of the Russian Military* (Princeton, NJ: Princeton University Press, 2007); Steven E. Miller and Dmitri Tenin, eds., *The Russian Military: Power and Policy* (Cambridge, MA: MIT University Press, 2004). For the optimistic version, see: Dale R. Herspring, *The Kremlin and the High Command: Presidential Impact on the Russian Military from Gorbachev to Putin* (Lawrence, KS: University Press of Kansas, 2006); Dale R. Herspring, "Putin and the Re-emergence of the Russian Military," *Problems of Post-Communism*, 54, 1 (January 2007), pp. 17–27.

[12] Barany 2007, esp. pp. 143–168; David Betz, "No Place for a Civilian?: Russian Defense Management from Yeltsin to Putin," *Armed Forces and Society*, 28, 3 (Spring 2002), pp. 481–504.

[13] On Serdyukov's appointment and reforms, see: V.V. Shlykov, "Tayny blitskriga Serdyukova," *Rossiya v Global'noy Politike*, No. 6, November-December 2009; Dale R. Herspring and Roger N. McDermott, "Serdyukov Promotes Systemic Russian Military Reform," *Orbis*, 54, 2 (Spring 2010), pp. 284–301.

For the most part, the Russian army has maintained its orientation toward external defense. However, the Chechen wars necessitated a larger role in internal fighting than the military had experienced in decades. Thus, after this chapter, the military as an organization is a minor player in this book and largely drops out of the story until we turn to the North Caucasus in Chapter 7. Although the military is a key attribute of state power, because of its organizational culture and the limited role it plays in domestic politics, it is less important than law enforcement and security bodies in the evolution of state capacity and quality in post-Soviet Russia. At the same time, military officers are part of the larger cohort of siloviki placed in key positions throughout the country under Putin, and these individuals are included in calculations about the increase in power ministry personnel in government.

The Railroad Troops and the Construction Troops

The Soviet Ministry of Defense included several components that were ancillary to its core functions. These included railroad and construction troops. In the 1990s, these forces were separated from the regular armed forces. Some of them were made independent entities, such as the Federal Road Construction Administration (later the Federal Service of Special Construction, or *Spetsstroy*), and others were absorbed by other agencies. For example, the Ministry of Atomic Energy, Ministry of Communications, and the State Construction Committee all received their own military construction units. In 2004, the railroad troops and some construction units, notably *Spetsstroy*, were returned to the Ministry of Defense.[14] The likely motive for these steps was economic. Control over construction troops consisting largely of draftees provides a ready source of "slave labor" for agencies that control it, and this labor can easily be converted into money.[15] The commercial value of the power ministries is one of the key drivers of their "reform" and activity. In general, the old Watergate adage "follow the money" serves as an excellent guide to understanding the development of the power ministries.

The Ministry of Civil Defense and Emergency Situations (MChS)

Sometimes known in English as EMERCOM, MChS is a great success story. Formed partially on the basis of Civil Defense troops of the Soviet military, its closest analogue in the US context would be the Federal Emergency Management Agency (FEMA). In reality, it is quite a different animal. Formed

---

[14] Renz 2005, p. 564; Pallin 2007, p. 11; Aleksandr Khramchikhin, "Shestnadtsat' armiy i ni odnoy parallel'noy," *Otechestvennye zapiski*, No. 8, 2002, pp. 183–184; Pavel Gazukin, "Vooruzhennye sily Rossii v postsovetskiy period," *Otechestvennye zapiski*, No. 8, 2002, p. 137.

[15] On the commercial value of construction and railroad troops, see: Khramchikhin 2002, pp. 183–184; Nikolai Petrov, "The Security Dimension of the Federal Reform," in Peter Reddaway and Robert W. Orttung, eds., *The Dynamics of Russian Politics*, Vol. II (Boulder, CO: Rowman & Littlefield, 2005), p. 14.

in the late-Soviet period as a "rescue corps," it became a State Committee for Emergency Situations and then a State Committee for Civil Defense and Emergency Situations after taking over the Civil Defense forces. It was elevated to a ministry, MChS, in 1994. One man, Sergey Shoygu, headed the organization throughout the Yeltsin and Putin presidencies, making him by far the longest serving minister in the Russian government.[16]

The core personnel of MChS was given as 22,831 by the Federal State Statistics Service in 2007. This number obviously does not include the roughly 20,000 personnel in the Civil Defense Forces, as well as the 220,000 employees of the State Fire Service, which MChS succeeded in gaining control over in 2001 after years of efforts by Shoygu. Even so, the Ministry has apparently become considerably smaller in recent years; previous estimates put the size of MChS at 70,000 personnel, including the Civil Defense Forces but not the State Fire Service. Further, the Civil Defense forces are to be removed from MChS by 2011 as part of the long-anticipated "demilitarization" of the agency.[17]

MChS is active both domestically and internationally. Domestically, it is a highly visible presence at the scene of both natural and man-made disasters. This visibility and Shoygu's reputation as a competent official have made MChS one of the most trusted government agencies. Shoygu's popularity made him a logical choice to head the new "Unity" party in 1999, and he remains a prominent member of the successor ruling party, "United Russia."[18] Internationally, it also participates in relief operations after natural disasters. Much of its international activity is done on a commercial basis, some of which has prompted corruption allegations.[19]

MChS also played an important role in the conflict in Chechnya and neighboring regions, dealing with refugees and humanitarian aid. Despite this humanitarian role, MChS personnel, many of whom previously served in the armed forces, wear uniforms, travel in military vehicles, and carry weapons. The Russian journalist Dmitry Babich wryly noted that, given its size and militarized nature, MChS was "capable not only of liquidating emergency situations, but also creating them." Russian expert Ekaterina Stepanova refers to MChS as a "militarized humanitarian agency" but gives it high marks for its competent work in the North Caucasus.[20]

Although Shoygu personally is an important and influential figure, the MChS as an institution is not a prominent political actor, and it is known to

[16] For background, see: http://www.mchs.gov.ru; Renz 2005, pp. 567–569; Pallin 2007, pp. 9–10; Mark Galeotti, "Emergency Presence," *JIR*, January 2002, pp. 50–51.

[17] Federal State Statistics Service, "Chislennost' rabotnikov federal'nykh organov gosudarstvennoy vlasti," 2007 [http://www.gks.ru/free_doc/2007/kadr/tab3.htm]; http://www.mchs.gov. ru; *Lenta.ru*, February 21, 2006; Lev Aleynik, "MChS uydet iz armii," *Gazeta*, February 20, 2006; Khramchikhin 2002, p. 184.

[18] On MChS's popularity, see Renz 2005, p. 568.

[19] Brian D. Taylor, *Russia's Power Ministries: Coercion and Commerce* (Institute for National Security and Counterterrorism, Syracuse University, October 2007), p. 5.

[20] Interview M-4; E.A. Stepanova, *Voyenno-grazhdanskiye otnosheniya v operatsiyakh nevoyennogo tipa* (Moskva: Prava Cheloveka, 2001), pp. 210–218.

most Russians only through their TV screens. Still, its relative competence as a disaster relief organization has arguably contributed to Russian state capacity throughout the post-Soviet period.

The KGB and Its Successors

Although smaller and receiving less money than the armed forces, pride of place among the power ministries as a political actor in the Soviet period goes to the KGB. Its broad mandate of foreign intelligence, border security, communications security, domestic intelligence and repression, and leadership protection made it a central figure in maintaining Soviet rule at home and expanding influence abroad. The KGB played a key role in the overthrow of one General Secretary (Nikita Khrushchev in 1964), the attempted overthrow of another (Mikhail Gorbachev in 1991), and one of its own became the top leader of the country (Yuriy Andropov, KGB head from 1967 to 1982 and General Secretary from 1982 to 1984). Secret police personnel are collectively known as "Chekists," after the name for the KGB predecessor organization, the Cheka, created under Lenin.[21]

Estimates put the size of the KGB at around 500,000–700,000 personnel in the late Soviet period. Given the lead role the KGB played in the August 1991 coup, as well as its traditional major role in domestic politics, not to mention its past role in the bloodiest episodes of Soviet history, Gorbachev and Yeltsin decided to break up the KGB into multiple parts. As Figure 2.1 shows, of the three main Soviet power ministries, the KGB, at least organizationally, was the most affected by the Soviet collapse. Separate agencies were created for foreign intelligence, domestic intelligence and counterintelligence, border protection, government communications, and leadership security.[22]

The Foreign Intelligence Service (SVR)

SVR's functions are relatively standard foreign intelligence work. It is not a particularly influential actor in domestic politics, and except for its first director, Yevgeniy Primakov, the head of the SVR is a generally unknown figure inside Russia. Moreover, it is unclear if it controls any armed units – if it does, it is a relatively small number of special forces. Thus, the SVR, although an important foreign policy actor and typically counted among the power ministries, is not relevant to this book.[23]

---

[21] Amy W. Knight, *The KGB: Police and Politics in the Soviet Union* (Boston: Unwin Hyman, 1990); Amy Knight, "The KGB, Perestroika, and the Collapse of the Soviet Union," *Journal of Cold War Studies*, 5, 1 (Winter 2003), pp. 67–93.

[22] Personnel estimates from: Yevgenia Albats, *The State within a State: The KGB and Its Hold on Russia – Past, Present, and Future* (New York: Farrar, Strauss, and Giroux, 1994), pp. 22–23. See also: Amy Knight, *Spies Without Cloaks: The KGB's Successors* (Princeton, NJ: Princeton University Press, 1996); Littell 2006; J. Michael Waller, *Secret Empire: The KGB in Russia Today* (Boulder, CO: Westview Press, 1994).

[23] Brief introductions can be found in: Renz 2005; Littell 2006; Mukhin 2002; Pallin 2007.

The Federal Security Service (FSB)

The FSB is the most obvious descendent of the KGB and chief inheritor of its domestic functions. It was formed on the basis of the KGB directorates for counterintelligence, military counterintelligence, transportation security, ideology and dissent, economic crime, and surveillance. In its first four years, it was renamed three times (Ministry of Security, Federal Counter-Intelligence Service, Federal Security Service), and was declared "unreformable" by a Yeltsin decree in December 1993, an act likely stimulated by the agency's fence-sitting during the September–October 1993 crisis. Until the Putin era, no individual served as director for more than two years in post-Soviet Russia.[24] In contrast, Nikolay Patrushev became director in the fall of 1999 and occupied the position throughout Putin's presidency. Patrushev was a close Putin ally who shared a KGB and St. Petersburg background with Putin.

Despite the turmoil of the Yeltsin years, the FSB expanded its responsibilities and legal mandate throughout the 1990s and under Putin became one of the most powerful state agencies. Current estimates suggest about 350,000 personnel work for the FSB, including the large border guards service that was autonomous for most of the 1990s but reincorporated into the FSB in 2003.[25] The elite Alpha and Vympel special forces units are part of the FSB. More important than the specific armed units it commands are the FSB's broad functions. It is simultaneously an intelligence, security, and law enforcement body. Its responsibilities include counterintelligence, terrorism and extremism, border security, economic crime and corruption, and information security. In addition to absorbing the Federal Border Service (FPS), it also took over many of the personnel and functions of the Federal Agency for Government Communication and Information (FAPSI) in 2003. The FSB was thus the big winner of the March 2003 reorganization of the power ministries, gaining back key powers and instruments it had lost in the early 1990s.[26] The importance of the FSB as a domestically focused state coercive agency renders it a key actor throughout the book, along with the MVD.

The Federal Guard Service (FSO)

The FSO was formed based on the Ninth Directorate of the KGB, which was responsible for leadership security. Splitting this function from the rest of the KGB became an obvious imperative after Gorbachev's security service participated in his isolation during the August 1991 coup attempt. The FSO protects the president and his family, other top officials, visiting dignitaries, and key government buildings and installations. The FSO is believed to possess two

---

[24] Albats 1994, pp. 26–29, 349–351; Knight 1996, pp. 28–37; Waller 1994, pp. 79–96.
[25] *The Military Balance 2008*, p. 221; Renz 2005, p. 562.
[26] Renz 2005; Littell 2006; Pallin 2007; Andrey Soldatov, "Pod Kolpakom," *Versiya*, March 17–23, 2003; Il'ya Bulavinov, "Vesenneye obostreniye," *K-V*, March 17, 2003; Aleksandr Gol'ts, "Kremlevskiy zvezdopad," *Yezhenedel. Zh.*, March 18, 2003; Natal'ya Kalashnikova, "Silovoi priyem," *Itogi*, March 18, 2003.

military regiments and one brigade, including the famous Presidential (formerly Kremlin) Regiment. Estimates of the FSO's size vary widely.[27]

The FSO also includes the Presidential Security Service (SBP), which from 1993 to 1996 was a powerful independent service not subordinate to the FSO (then GUO – Main Guards Directorate). Yeltsin's chief bodyguard and head of the SBP during his first term, Aleksandr Korzhakov, was one of the dominant figures in Russian politics until his dismissal in 1996. During the Putin years, he served in the Duma.[28]

The FSO, like the FSB, benefited from the consolidation of the power ministries carried out in 2003. The FSO plays a key role in government communications and information security, providing the president with an alternative to the FSB for information on domestic developments. The heads of the FSO and the SBP under Putin, Yevgeniy Murov and Viktor Zolotov, respectively, both worked with him since his days in St. Petersburg in the 1990s. Although not publicly visible, allegedly both Murov and Zolotov were influential figures behind the scenes, and they resumed Korzhakov's inclinations to involve the FSO and the SBP in economic and business matters.[29]

The Main Directorate for Special Programs (GUSP)

GUSP is a small and highly secret state agency formed on the basis of a KGB Directorate. Its chief official function is the security of strategic installations, most specifically the bunkers built to shield the Soviet leadership in the event of nuclear war. It also has a coordination and mobilization function in the event of major war. Some reports also suggest it has "operational-analytical" functions. Given the nature of its tasks and the secrecy that surrounds it, GUSP will not be discussed further.[30]

The Ministry of Internal Affairs (MVD)

The MVD was in some ways the neglected stepchild of the Soviet power ministries. In the early decades of Soviet power, it was sometimes institutionally joined to the KGB's predecessors, such as the NKVD (People's Commissariat of Internal Affairs), but ultimately it developed as an autonomous institution in the post-Stalin era. The MVD suffered in comparison to the KGB and the military in terms of status, power, and resources. But the police (formally the "militia," but I generally use "police" throughout) were the face of Soviet

[27] Renz 2005; Littell 2006; Mukhin 2002; Pallin 2007; *Agentura.ru*, a specialist website on the Russian security services; *The Military Balance 2008*, p. 221.

[28] Korzhakov's memoir, published after his dismissal, remains a highly revealing look at Russian politics during Yeltsin's first term, despite the obviously self-serving nature of the book: Aleksandr Korzhakov, *Boris Yel'tsin: Ot rassveta do zakata* (Moskva, 1997).

[29] See especially Littell 2006, Part IV, and the bios of Murov and Zolotov in the appendix of Littell.

[30] Renz 2005; Littell 2006; Mukhin 2002; Pallin 2007; *Agentura.ru*.

power with which ordinary citizens were most likely to interact, and evidence of pervasive corruption in the MVD in the 1970s and 1980s was an important indicator that Soviet control over coercive force was weakening. Moreover, the MVD, despite its relatively marginal status, did control key bodies from the point of view of domestic security, including the Internal Troops.[31]

Compared to the KGB, the MVD has endured relatively little organizational change since the Soviet collapse. Although internally it has experienced some reorganization, it was not split up into its constituent parts like the KGB. The one significant loss of coercive power and responsibility was the transfer in 1998 of the prison service from the MVD to the Ministry of Justice. The MVD controls not only the ordinary police (militia), but also many other subunits with responsibility for various aspects of internal security and law enforcement. These include, for example, the Road Police, Special Designation Police Detachments (OMON and OMSN), and multiple directorates with specific designations, such as the Department for Countering Extremism, which replaced the Department for Combating Organized Crime and Terrorism. The MVD also controls the 200,000-strong Internal Troops (VV), which has played a major role in the war in Chechnya.[32] After the Yeltsin-era holdover, Vladimir Rushaylo, was removed as minister in 2001, the MVD under Putin was led by someone from his two main sources of officials, either St. Petersburg or the KGB. Boris Gryzlov, who went on to become Speaker of the Duma and head of the pro-Kremlin United Russia party, led the MVD from 2001 to 2004. His successor, Rashid Nurgaliyev, was a KGB veteran who was moved to the MVD as First Deputy in 2002 before being elevated to the top spot.

The MVD employs more than 1.2 million personnel, plus physical plant employees and guards. A 2005 presidential decree listed the size of the MVD financed by the federal budget as 821,268 personnel. Of this number, 661,275 are law enforcement personnel and the remaining 159,993 are civilian employees.[33] However, there are also MVD personnel financed by local and

[31] For background on the Soviet period, see: Louise I. Shelley, *Policing Soviet Society: The Evolution of State Control* (London: Routledge, 1996); V.F. Nekrasov et. al., *Organy i Voyska MVD Rossii: Kratkiy istoricheskiy ocherk* (Moskva: MVD Rossii, 1996); Dennis Desmond, "The Structure and Organization of the Ministry of Internal Affairs under Mikhail Gorbachev," *Low Intensity Conflict & Law Enforcement*, 3, 2 (Autumn 1994), pp. 217–258; William C. Fuller, Jr., *The Internal Troops of the MVD SSSR*, College Station Papers No. 6 (College Station, TX: Center for Strategic Technology, Texas A & M University, 1983).

[32] For basic introductions to the MVD, see: L.K. Savyuk, *Pravokhranitel'nye organy* (Moskva: Yurist, 2001), pp. 283–316; Mark Galeotti, "Policing Russia: Problems and Prospects in Turbulent Times," *JIR*, Special Report No. 15, September 1997; Gordon Bennett, *The Ministry of Internal Affairs of the Russian Federation*, Conflict Studies Research Centre, UK (March 2000).

[33] "Ukaz Prezidenta Rossiyskoy Federatsii ob ustanovlenii predel'noy shtatnoy chislennosti organov vnutrennikh del Rossiyskoy Federatsii," No. 1246, October 31, 2005. See also the figures provided by the official state newspaper *Rossiyskaya Gazeta*, which gives data not only on the total number of personnel, but also those in the Internal Troops and in MVD special forces: Mikhail Falaleyev, "Chist' mundiry," *RG*, November 10, 2006.

regional budgets not included in this decree. According to a report by the MVD Financial-Economic Department, police units supported by local and regional budgets make up about one-third of the total number of MVD personnel.[34] Thus, overall, the MVD employs around 1,230,000 people.[35] For comparison, the Soviet MVD employed roughly 3.5 million personnel in 1988.[36]

Published figures also permit a rough estimate of the total number of police in Russia. Combining the 661,275 federal law enforcement personnel with the more than 400,000 police personnel supported by regional and local governments, minus the 200,000 internal troops, yields a total of 871,909 police in Russia.[37] With a 2006 total population of 142,800,000, this means a ratio of 1 police officer for every 164 citizens, or 611 police for every 100,000 inhabitants.[38] This estimate of the number of police in Russia is imprecise, but if it is at all close, it suggests that the number of Russian police is quite high compared to other post-communist countries or some other developed countries (see Table 2.2). For example, it is almost twice as many on a per capita basis as the United States, Germany, France, or Poland. To put it differently, any weaknesses in Russian state capacity in the law enforcement sphere are not due to a small number of police personnel. Indeed, as we will see when we discuss homicide rates in Chapter 3, Russia does not seem to be getting good value from such a large police force.

This discussion of personnel also points to a key difference between the MVD and other major power ministries, such as the armed forces and the FSB: the important element of regional and local control over the police. According to Article 72 of the Constitution, "the guaranteeing of legality, law and order, and public safety" and "personnel of judicial and law-enforcement bodies" are joint responsibilities of the center and subjects of the Federation.

---

34 FED MVD Rossii, "Voprosy finansovogo obespecheniya MVD Rossii v 2006 godu, material'nogo obespecheniya i predostavleniya garantiy i kompensatsiy sotrudnikam organov vnutrennikh del, voyennosluzhashchim vnutrennikh voysk MVD Rossii i chlenam ikh semey," Ministerstvo Vnutrennikh del Rossiyskoy Federatsii, April 27, 2006 [http://www.mvd.ru/news/8013].

35 This figure is comparable to other estimates. A police colonel from a MVD research institute gave a figure of 1.2 million for total MVD personnel in 2003: Interview M-13. Sergey Stepashin, head of the Accounting Chamber and head of the MVD under Yeltsin, suggested in 2006 that the number is closer to 1.5 million: Natal'ya Melikova, "Sergey Stepahsin: My budem kalenym zhelezom vyzhigat' nechist' v svoikh ryadakh," *Nez. Gaz.*, June 5, 2006. A 2008 report in *Kommersant" Vlast'* put the number of MVD employees as 1.3 million, not counting the Internal Troops: Aleksandr Kukolevskiy, "1 prestupnik na 1 militsionera v god," *K-V*, June 30, 2008. In 2009, Prime Minister Putin put the number at 1.4 million: "Razgovor s Vladimirom Putinym. Prodolzheniye," December 3, 2009, http://premier.gov.ru

36 Shelley 1996, p. 85.

37 Specifically, if local and regional governments support one-third of total MVD personnel in the country, then territorial police units consist of 410,634 officials. 410,634 plus 661,275 federal law enforcement personnel equals 1,071,909, minus 200,000 Internal Troops, for a final total of 871,909 police nationwide.

38 Population estimate from the Russian Federal Service of State Statistics: http://www.gks.ru

TABLE 2.2. *Police Personnel per 100,000 Inhabitants*

Country	Police Per 100,000 Inhabitants
Australia	516
Czech Republic	445
Estonia	265
France	211
Georgia	229
Germany	292
Hungary	289
Italy	559
Japan	182
Kazakhstan	464
Kyrgyzstan	340
Latvia	436
Lithuania	345
Moldova	314
Poland	260
Russia (estimate)	611
Slovakia	374
United States	244

Note: Post-communist countries are italicized.
Source: Seventh United Nations Survey of Crime Trends and Operations of Criminal Justice Systems, 1998–2000; author's estimate.

Although somewhat decentralized in the context of Russia's power ministries, in comparative context, Russian policing has historically been quite centralized for a federation. The federal element of state coercion, especially as it applies to the police, will be explored further in Chapter 4.

The police in general are relatively understudied in the statist literature. The Russian police are also generally understudied in the West. Given this relative neglect both in political science and in Russian studies, and the importance of the police for the post-Soviet Russian state, they receive extensive coverage in this book.

Other Power Ministries and Law Enforcement Agencies

The Military, the FSB, and the MVD, despite the greater fragmentation of the 1990s, remain the fundamental state coercive agencies in Russia. Other organizations, such as the SVR, the MChS, and the FSO, have managed to carve out relatively stable and successful bureaucratic niches for themselves. In addition to these core agencies, there are several other important organizations that play an important law enforcement role and that will feature at various places later in the book.

The Federal Service for the Control of the Narcotics Trade (FSKN)

The FSKN is a relatively new organization, formed in 2003 as part of a larger reorganization of the power ministries undertaken by Putin. The function of combating the drug trade was previously primarily a function of the MVD. Putin's decision to create a separate agency dedicated to this task was motivated both by concern about the escalating drug problem in Russia and the previous inefficiency of the police in dealing with the problem.[39] Like the FSO, it also has sufficient domestic surveillance and intelligence capabilities to serve as a counterweight to the FSB.

The FSKN was formed largely on the basis of the Federal Tax Police Service (FSNP), an organization created after the Soviet collapse to provide some muscle to the state in enforcing tax claims. The FSNP was staffed largely by personnel from the former KGB and became famous for its so-called "mask show" raids on businesses. The FSNP grew to about 53,000 personnel, and it did help the state raise revenue, but it was also widely seen as corrupt.[40] When the FSNP was disbanded, its functions and some of its personnel were transferred to the MVD, while the bulk of the personnel (around 40,000) went to work for the FSKN; the size of the FSKN in 2007 was 33,677.[41] Of course, there are doubts as to whether the same personnel who were accused of corruption in hunting down corporate tax evaders will be any cleaner in cracking down on the drug trade. The FSKN under Putin was headed by Viktor Cherkesov, a close acquaintance of Putin who shared a background in the KGB and who also hails from St. Petersburg. Cherkesov had a reputation as a hardliner, based partially on his persecution of dissidents in Leningrad well into the Gorbachev era.

The Ministry of Justice

The Ministry of Justice is not a traditional power ministry. Most of its functions, such as providing legal expertise on laws and decrees and maintaining official registers of property, political parties, and non-governmental organizations, do not involve state coercion in any direct sense. However, as noted earlier, the ministry does control the prison system, which was transferred from the MVD in 1998 at the request of the Council of Europe to make the Russian prison system more compatible with European standards. The Federal Penitentiary Service – literally the Federal Service for the Administration of Sentences (FSIN) – is responsible for the detention and prison system that holds more than 850,000 prisoners. Its personnel wear uniforms and have ranks,

---

[39] Brief introductions can be found in: Renz 2005; Pallin 2007; Littell 2006.

[40] Gerald M. Easter, "The Russian Tax Police," *Post-Soviet* Affairs, 18, 4 (2002), pp. 332–362; Frank Gregory and Gerald Brooke, "Policing Economic Transition and Increasing Revenue: A Case Study of the Federal Tax Police Service of the Russian Federation, 1992–1998," *Europe-Asia Studies*, 52, 3 (2000), pp. 433–455.

[41] Sergey Topol', "Politseyskikh pozdravili s kontsom," *K-D*, March 19, 2003; Federal State Statistics Service 2007.

and are subject to MVD personnel regulations.[42] The Ministry of Justice also controls the Bailiffs Service, which is responsible for the enforcement of judicial decisions and orders, including civil judgments involving the payment or seizure of money. Peter Kahn argued that Bailiffs' activities are guided more by enriching themselves or the state than the private parties who are seeking compensation.[43]

The Federal Customs Service (FTS)

Other reviews of the power ministries tend not to include the FTS, but it plays an important law enforcement role. It employs more than 60,000 people and allegedly also controls small armed units of up to 10,000 personnel. As a customs agency, it deals with the smuggling of all kinds of illicit goods, including narcotics and weapons.[44] The huge volumes of trade crossing the Russian border obviously provide multiple opportunities for corruption and material enrichment by FTS personnel; in Chapter 5, I examine one of the most notorious post-Soviet corruption cases, the "Three Whales" affair, in which personnel of the FTS were heavily implicated. The head of the FTS from 2005 until the end of Putin's presidency was Andrey Belyaninov, who served with Putin in the KGB in East Germany.[45] This long-standing link to Putin suggests the importance he attached to controlling the customs service.

The Procuracy

The procuracy is one of Russia's most important law enforcement structures, on par with the FSB and the MVD.[46] The procuracy, or prosecutor's office, combines both executive and judicial branch functions but is formally considered part of neither branch. It employees approximately 54,000 people and is headed by the Procurator General (Prosecutor General) of Russia.[47] Although not meeting the formal definition of a power ministry because of its independent status and lack of armed units, the procuracy is closely connected to all

---

[42] Savyuk 2001, pp. 350–378; Renz 2005; Pallin 2007. On the poor state of Russian prisons, see: Anatoly Medetsky, "Prison Life Growing Tougher, Activists Say," *MT*, July 27, 2006; Jonathan Weiler, *Human Rights in Russia: A Darker Side of Reform* (Boulder, CO: Lynne Rienner, 2004), pp. 29–53; Lev Ponomarev, "Revival of the Gulag? Putin's Penitentiary System," *Perspective*, 16, 1 (November–December 2007).

[43] Peter L. Kahn, "The Russian Bailiffs Service and the Enforcement of Civil Judgments," *Post-Soviet Affairs*, 18, 2 (2002), pp. 148–181.

[44] Federal State Statistics Service 2007; Savyuk 2001, pp. 345–349; Federal Customs Service website: http://www.customs.ru/ru/; Petrov 2005, p. 14.

[45] On Belyaninov, see: Rimma Akmirova, "Don Kikhot tamozhennyy," *Sobesednik*, October 8, 2006.

[46] For introductions to the procuracy, see: Gordon B. Smith, *Reforming the Russian Legal System* (Cambridge: Cambridge University Press, 1996), pp. 104–128; Inga Mikhailovskaya, "The Procuracy and Its Problems: Russia," *East European Constitutional Review*, 8, 1/2 (Winter/Spring 1999). For a comparison of the Russian procuracy system to that of other countries, see: V.N. Dodonov and V.E. Krutskikh, *Prokuratura v Rossii i za rubezhom* (Moskva: Norma, 2001).

[47] Federal State Statistics Service 2007.

of the other power ministries, and its personnel are rightly considered part of the siloviki cohort. Peter Maggs, an expert on Russian legal affairs, noted that in reality, the procuracy is closely tied to the executive branch and often fulfills political orders. "The Prosecutor-General isn't called a 'general' for nothing," stated Maggs. "It's a service organized with a military hierarchy and uniforms and so forth."[48]

The law enforcement mandate of the procuracy is extensive. It has two basic functions: criminal prosecution and oversight of all government agencies to ensure that their activities are consistent with the law. Putin once described the Procurator-General as "the one who keeps an eye on whether all citizens comply with the law: the prime minister, the president, everyone."[49] The procuracy, rather than the courts, is often the first venue citizens use to complain against abuses by government officials. It is also supposed to coordinate crime-fighting efforts, although its ability to do this is hampered by bureaucratic competition among the different bodies. The ability of the procuracy to give directions to the FSB, for example, is questionable. Still, given the potential power it wields, it is not surprising that, despite its notional independence, the executive branch in Russia is eager to direct and control this weapon.

In May 2007, a major change in the powers of the procuracy was introduced.[50] The functions of criminal investigation and oversight of the legal process were separated with the creation of an Investigative Committee, located within the procuracy but de facto independent. The head of this new committee is not appointed by the Procurator General, but by the Federation Council, on the recommendation of the president. The first head, Aleksandr Bastrykin, went to law school with Putin and had worked in both the MVD and the procuracy. At the same time, the other law enforcement structures, including the MVD, the FSB, and the FSKN, kept their own investigative units – the idea of unifying all of the investigative services within the law enforcement organs into one powerful, independent investigative department was at least postponed, if not rejected altogether.[51] Whether the change will make the criminal prosecution process more effective and less corrupt is hotly disputed and will only become clear with time.[52]

---

[48] "Legal Reforms Take Giant Leap Forward," *RFE/RL Russian Political Weekly*, 1, 32 (December 18, 2001). The "general" in the title is not actually a military term, but general in the sense of universal, but the joke is still telling.

[49] Natal'ya Gevorkyan, Natal'ya Timakova, and Andrey Kolesnikov, eds., *Ot pervogo litsa: Razgovory s Vladimirom Putinym* (Moskva: Vagrius, 2000), p. 180.

[50] Viktor Paukov, "General'nym stanet sledovatel," *VN*, June 7, 2007; Boris Yamshanov, "Sledstviye popravok," *RG*, June 7, 2007; Yekaterina Zapodinskaya, "Odnokashnik prezidenta vozglavit prokurorskiye sledstviye," *K-D*, June 22, 2007.

[51] For a discussion of this concept by the then deputy head of the Investigative Department within the MVD, see: Boris Gavrilov, "Sledstevennyy apparat organov vnutrennykh del," *Otechestvennye zapiski*, No. 2 (11), 2003.

[52] Two skeptical accounts in English, both of which trace the change to political infighting, are: Ethan S. Burger and Mary Holland, "Law as Politics: The Russian Procuracy and its Investigative Committee," *Columbia Journal of East European Law*, 2, 2 (2008), pp. 143–194;

The procuracy is also, according to the Constitution, "a single centralized system in which lower-level procurators are subordinate to higher-level procurators" (Article 129). This centralization, however, was undermined in the 1990s, with increasing regional control over procurators. The enormous powers of the procuracy, as well as its pivotal role in the law enforcement system, make it a key actor in the coercive realm despite the absence of armed units under its control. It thus features heavily in this book.

POWER MINISTRY BUDGETS AND LEADERSHIP UNDER YELTSIN AND PUTIN

The fragmentation of the power ministries in the 1990s was only one manifestation of the crisis suffered by these organizations during the Yeltsin era. Two other symptoms of their difficulties were the sharp drop in state financing compared to the Soviet past and the frequent turnover in leadership of the key power ministries. Both of these tendencies were reversed under Putin.

Military and Security Spending

The Soviet Union prioritized military and security spending above all other state functions. Two key factors led to a sharp decline in spending on military and security forces in the 1990s. First, the government of Boris Yeltsin self-consciously decided to drastically reduce spending on guns in order to try to rebuild the economy to provide more butter. Second, the economic depression that lasted until 1999 gave the government little choice but to cut back on spending in most areas. More generally, the drop in state spending was part of an overall crisis of the state.

The military, out of all of the power ministries, suffered the most from the economic depression, the weakness of the state, and the shift in government priorities. During Yeltsin's rule, from 1992 to 1999, the military budget was slashed by 62 percent. Moreover, the Finance Ministry frequently failed to pay out all of the military obligations in the budget. For example, in 1998, actual expenditures were only 55 percent of planned allocations.[53] Although the military suffered the most in terms of budget, security spending also declined precipitously in the 1990s. The budget section "state security," which includes the FSB, FSO, SVR, and several other security ministries, dropped from 93 billion rubles in 1994 to 32 billion rubles in 1999 (2003 constant rubles).[54]

William Burnham and Thomas A. Firestone, "Investigation of Criminal Cases under the Russian Criminal Procedure Code," unpublished paper, October 2007.

[53] Taylor, *Politics and the Russian Army*, pp. 307–309.

[54] Andrey Soldatov, interview with Ivan Safranchuk, "Kassa zakrytogo tipa," *Nov. Gaz.*, March 5, 2007. The version of this article at the *Agentura.ru* site contains the budget figures cited here.

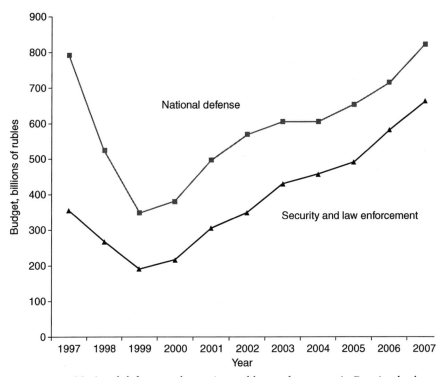

FIGURE 2.2. National defense and security and law enforcement in Russian budget, constant rubles, 1997–2007.

The rapid growth of the Russian economy after the 1998 economic crisis, as well as a shift in state priorities toward the military and security sectors under Putin, allowed a considerable increase in the power ministries' budgets. Between 1998 and 2007, the economy as a whole grew at a rate of more than 6 percent a year, buoyed initially by devaluation and default during the 1998 crisis and subsequently by high global energy prices.[55] Defense and security spending grew accordingly. Figure 2.2 shows spending on "National Defense" and "Security and Law Enforcement" for the Russian state budget for the period 1997–2007. National Defense includes the armed forces and scientific research in the defense sector. Security and Law Enforcement includes most of the other power ministries, including the FSB, the MVD, the procuracy, MChS, and FSKN. Spending on defense more than doubled under Putin, from 382 billion rubles in 2000 to 822 billion rubles in 2007 (all figures in 2007 constant rubles). Although Putin increased defense spending substantially, he

---

[55] Another contributing factor for several years was the use of underutilized capital and labor due to the 1990s depression. On economic growth after 1998 and its causes, see: *OECD Economic Surveys: Russian Federation* (Volume 2006 Issue 17, November 2006), Chapter One.

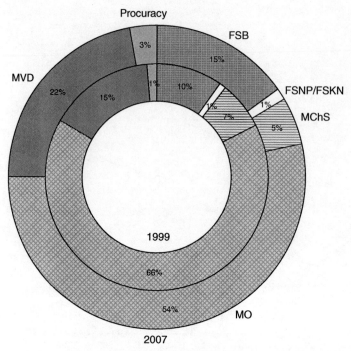

FIGURE 2.3. Power ministry budget percentage comparison, 1999–2007.

only succeeded in restoring the budget to the level prior to the 1998 economic crisis. Moreover, the budget of the armed forces remains between 2 and 3 percent of GDP, well below the target figure of 3.5 percent set by Yeltsin in the 1990s, and a significant cut compared to the Soviet military.[56]

Spending on the security and law enforcement sector increased at an even greater rate in the Putin era. Between 2000 and 2007, spending in the national security and law enforcement sections of the budget more than tripled. Moreover, this increase was not simply a return to the pre-1998 levels, as was the case with defense spending. In general, under both Yeltsin and Putin, the government favored internal security and law enforcement over external security. As a share of the power ministries' budget, military spending dropped from 80 percent in 1992 to 56 percent in 2007. The law enforcement organs – MVD, procuracy, and the FSB – garnered the biggest increase. The procuracy, for example, increased its budget from 3 billion rubles in 2000 to 27 billion rubles in 2006.[57]

Figure 2.3 shows the share of the budget going to the main power ministries in both 1999 (the last year of Yeltsin's presidency) and 2007 (the last full

---

[56] Budget figures for 1997–2007 compiled from: http://budgetrf.ru/ and http://www1.minfin.ru/budjet/budjet.htm. On defense spending as a percentage of GDP, see: Herspring 2007, p. 22.
[57] Soldatov interview with Safranchuk.

year of Putin's presidency). The inner circle shows the percentages in 1999, whereas the outer circle shows the percentages in 2007. Comparing the two circles demonstrates the continuing decline in military spending compared to law enforcement and security bodies (from 66 percent to 54 percent), and the simultaneous big increases received by the FSB (from 10 to 15 percent of power ministry spending), the MVD (from 15 to 22 percent), and the procuracy (from 1 to 3 percent).[58]

Overall, spending on the power ministries increased substantially under Putin, helped by rapid economic growth and much larger state revenues. Internal security was a greater priority than external security. Given the domestic situation – the war in Chechnya, terrorism, and high crime rates – this focus made sense. It is notable, however, that despite Putin's efforts in his second term to reassert Russia's position as a great power, spending priorities still reflected concern about domestic political order.[59]

Power Ministry Leadership

Soviet General Secretary Leonid Brezhnev famously pursued a policy of "stability in cadres," providing greater job security for party officials after the murderous Josef Stalin and the mercurial Nikita Khrushchev. Putin, by temperament, seems somewhat similar to the arch-bureaucrat Brezhnev, whereas Yeltsin shared some of the impulsive characteristics of Khrushchev. Yeltsin's propensity for sudden firings of top officials was most notable with the multiple prime ministers of his second term, but he also frequently changed the heads of the power ministries. For the top four power ministry positions – heads of the FSB, procuracy, MVD, and MO – the average tenure of these officials was noticeably longer under Putin than under Yeltsin.

The difference was most striking in terms of the FSB (see Figure 2.4): The average director of the FSB under Yeltsin served only 14 months, and his longest-serving appointment served only two years, whereas Putin had the same director, Nikolay Patrushev, from the time he became Prime Minister in August 1999 until the end of his presidency.[60] Similarly, Yeltsin had great difficulty finding a General Procurator with whom he felt comfortable, and was deadlocked with the Federation Council for more than a year in 1998–1999 over his attempt to fire Yuriy Skuratov, whereas Putin kept his first General Procurator, Vladimir Ustinov, for more than six years before transferring him to head the Ministry of Justice. In terms of the MVD, Yeltsin appointed four different people to this position in eight years, whereas Putin only appointed two new ministers in the same period of time. Although there was more

---

[58] See note 56.

[59] The 2008 Russian-Georgian war prompted a commitment to further increase defense spending, but the war took place under President Medvedev and thus after the period covered in this book.

[60] Although technically Patrushev was appointed by Yeltsin, Patrushev clearly owed his appointment to Putin.

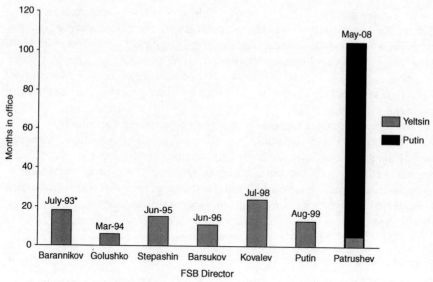

FIGURE 2.4. Tenure of FSB directors.

stability for defense ministers than the other key power ministries under Yeltsin, Putin showed greater constancy in this agency as well, appointing one of his closest allies, Sergey Ivanov, to run the military for the first six years of his presidency, before appointing him to First Deputy Prime Minister.

The reason for this difference is clear. Yeltsin lacked confidence in his appointments, having few close acquaintances from the power ministries. Putin, on the other hand, came from this milieu and was able to appoint people he knew were "his." Putin's appointment policies toward the power ministries were consistent with the patrimonial nature of Russian administration. For most of his presidency, he put the military and the FSB under the control of Ivanov and Patrushev, both Petersburgers from the KGB that he had known since before the Soviet collapse. The police under Putin were headed either by a St. Petersburg politician (Boris Gryzlov), or a KGB veteran (Rashid Nurgaliyev). In the case of the procuracy, Ustinov initially was seen as being backed by the pro-Yeltsin clan known as "the Family," but Ustinov quickly demonstrated his loyalty to Putin and even managed to marry his son to the daughter of one of Putin's top aides, Deputy Head of the Presidential Administration Igor Sechin.[61] In all of these cases, personal loyalty and connections were key.

Putin's reliance on personnel from the security services to fill top positions in the state made an immediate impression. Journalists, analysts, and scholars

[61] Il'ya Bulavinov, "Koloda Rossiyskoy Federatsii," *K-V*, December 1, 2003; Yevgeniy Teplov, "Politika po-semeynomu," *Nashe Vremya*, March 26, 2007.

soon began to talk about a "siloviki" group around Putin dominating Russian politics. The use of the term is somewhat misleading, in that it implies a greater unity among these often warring agencies and officials than exists in practice, but it does capture a prominent feature of Putin's presidency.

THE SILOVIKI: COHORT, CLAN, AND CORPORATE ACTORS

The Yeltsin and Putin eras contrast starkly in terms of the fate of the power ministries. Under Yeltsin, the three dominant Soviet power ministries were replaced with more than a dozen agencies. Spending for military and security needs was cut sharply. The leadership of the most important of these agencies, such as the FSB, the military, and the procuracy, was shuffled frequently as Yeltsin struggled, often in vain, to find personnel he considered trustworthy. Under Putin, the FSB regained control of some of the former elements of the KGB that had been made independent, military and security spending increased dramatically, and Putin loyalists were given long tenures at the head of these agencies.

This reversal of fortune under Putin – and the increased prominence of these agencies and personnel from these agencies – is undeniable. Western journalists noted this shift and began to write about the "rise of the siloviki."[62] A key ambiguity in the "rise of the siloviki" story, however, is that it is often unclear who exactly is rising: Is it the power ministries themselves, personnel from those structures, or is it merely a specific "clan" in Russian politics? It is important to distinguish between the use of the term "siloviki" to refer to a cohort of personnel, a clan in Kremlin politics, and a group of state ministries and organizations. The three usages I refer to as the cohort, clan, and corporate understandings of the term siloviki. The cohort approach is sociological, the clan approach is Kremlinological, and the corporate way of thinking is bureaucratic political.

This distinction leads to several important conclusions. First, the expansion of the siloviki as a cohort in government at all levels is clear – the only debate is about its extent and significance. Second, the clan nature of Russian politics is clearly an important phenomenon, but a closer look shows important divisions between the most prominent top officials from the secret services, who are often lumped together as a coherent siloviki clan. Third, in terms of the power ministries as corporate actors, the FSB is definitely the dominant one, followed by the procuracy, whereas the military and police were relatively weak political forces under Putin.

The Siloviki Cohort

Russian sociologist Olga Kryshtanovskaya pioneered the scholarship that showed the increasing presence of representatives from the power ministries

---

[62] A Lexis-Nexis search in August 2008 uncovered more than 200 references to the siloviki in the U.S. press (newspapers and magazines), with the first instance occurring in 2001.

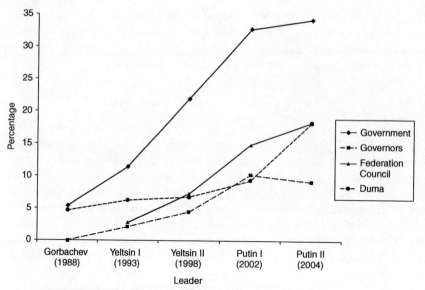

FIGURE 2.5. Militarization of the Russian elite.

throughout the government. She observed that in the Soviet period, it was unusual for power ministry officers to be appointed to civilian posts. Quite the reverse, it was not uncommon for KGB positions around the country to be filled by Communist Party and Komsomol (Communist Youth League) appointments.

The pattern in post-Soviet Russia has been much different. Starting in Yeltsin's second term, and continuing with a much stronger emphasis under Putin, a variety of civilian positions throughout regional and federal government were filled by security and military personnel. Kryshtanovskaya showed that this increasing "militarization" of the elite took place in the federal government, both houses of parliament (the Duma and the Federation Council), and among regional governors (see Figure 2.5). This militarization took place not only at the top level, but also at intermediate and lower levels. For example, many deputy ministers in multiple nonmilitary agencies, such as the Ministry for Economic Development and the Ministry of Communications, also came from the power ministries.[63] It also took place at the regional level.

At times Kryshtanovskaya overstated the extent to which siloviki had taken over the key positions in the state. For example, she argued that the Security Council, 40–50 percent of whose members come from power ministry backgrounds, was the most important decision-making body in the country, equivalent to the Soviet-era Politburo (Political Bureau of the Central Committee of the Communist Party). Although the Security Council does include many

---

[63] Kryshtanovskaya 2002; Kryshtanovskaya and White 2003; Ol'ga Kryshtanovskaya, "I v komnatakh snova sidyat komissary," *Nov. Gaz.*, August 30, 2004.

of the country's top officials, including the heads of the power ministries, it has never been the core locus for decision making. This was true under both Yeltsin and Putin, both of whom tended to concentrate important decision making within the presidential administration. Arguably the peak of the Security Council's influence was in 1999–2001, when first Putin and then Sergey Ivanov headed this body. Since that time, its role has been secondary. Kryshtanovskaya also sometimes counted people likely to have cooperated with the KGB due to their professional past, such as those involved in international affairs, as siloviki. Counting these "affiliated" siloviki, she claimed that up to 77 percent of state officials in 2004 were siloviki, which seems an overstatement.[64] An estimate using a more conservative methodology, a 2007 newspaper survey of the top 100 executive branch positions, showed that about one-third of these slots were filled by those with power ministry backgrounds.[65]

The rise of the siloviki cohort, as Figure 2.5 shows, actually started during Yeltsin's second term. Yeltsin's last three prime ministers – Yevgeniy Primakov, Sergey Stepashin, and Putin – had power ministry ties, and the presidential administration also became populated with higher numbers of the siloviki. For example, the former KGB officer Nikolay Bordyuzha headed both the Security Council and the presidential administration in 1998–1999. Yeltsin himself believed that society was yearning for a leader who was not only a "new-thinking democrat" but also a "strong, military man."[66]

It was Putin's selection, and then election, as president that ensured the rise of the siloviki as a cohort throughout the Russian government. Two factors, one about the nature of Russian politics and one about Putin himself, combined to make such a development not only possible but likely. First, and most important, is the patrimonial nature of Russian state administration.[67] The second issue, specific to Putin, was his meteoric rise to the top. In 1996, he was a briefly unemployed Deputy Mayor of St. Petersburg after his patron, Mayor Anatoliy Sobchak, lost his reelection bid. Brought to Moscow by a group of

---

[64] Yaroshevskiy 2004. For a more detailed critique of Kryshtanovskaya's methodology that shows a noticeable, but smaller, increase in siloviki influence, see: Sharon Werning Rivera and David W. Rivera, "The Russian Elite under Putin: Militocratic or Bourgeois?" *Post-Soviet Affairs*, 22, 2 (2006), pp. 125–144.

[65] Oleg Roldugin, "Kak stat' ministrom," *Sobesednik*, May 7, 2007. See also: Henry Gaffney, Ken Gause, and Dmitry Gorenburg, *Russian Leadership Decision-Making under Vladimir Putin: The Issues of Energy, Technology Transfer, and Non-Proliferation* (Alexandria, VA: CNA Corporation, 2007), pp. 161–169.

[66] Boris Yeltsin, *Prezidentskiy marafon* (Moskva: ACT, 2000), p. 254.

[67] One stark example of the sometimes premodern nature of Russian state administration is the forging of alliances through marriages between families. Yeltsin's daughter, Tatyana, married his chief of staff and ghostwriter, Valentin Yumashev. In addition to the Sechin-Ustinov marriage already mentioned, another siloviki example is that Defense Minister Serdyukov is married to the daughter of Viktor Zubkov, Putin's last prime minister and before that the head of the powerful Federal Financial Monitoring Service. It is perhaps redundant to note that they are both from St. Petersburg. Teplov 2007.

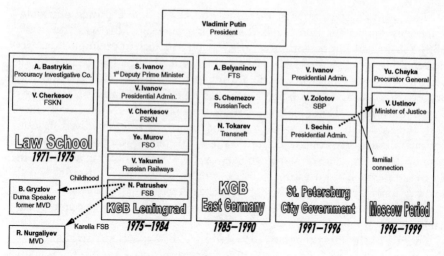

FIGURE 2.6. Putin's *siloviki* network, 2007.

government officials who also came from St. Petersburg, Putin climbed rapidly, so that within two years, by the summer of 1998, he was the director of the FSB. Thirteen months later, he was Prime Minister and on his way to the presidency. Given this ascent and Putin's limited tenure in Moscow, he had a narrow circle of colleagues to draw on in creating his own patronage machine. Perfectly naturally, given the nature of the political system, many of Putin's most important appointments had a KGB background, a St. Petersburg background, or both. Further, Putin's appointees from the secret services brought their own train of former colleagues with them, creating a ripple effect throughout the government.[68]

The extent to which Putin's top appointments in the government, the presidential administration, and even state-controlled corporations were dominated by his former contacts from the KGB and St. Petersburg is evident from Figure 2.6.[69] The diagram shows how Putin used his network of siloviki contacts from law school, the KGB, and the St. Petersburg city government to control key positions in Russian politics. Of course, if we were to

---

[68] For a similar explanation for the expansion of the siloviki cohort, see: Bettina Renz, "Putin's Militocracy? An Alternative Interpretation of *Siloviki* in Contemporary Russian Politics," *Europe-Asia Studies*, 58, 6 (September 2006), pp. 903–924.

[69] Positions listed are for 2007. Details about most of these officials can be found elsewhere in this chapter. The exceptions are the heads of key state companies that Putin also wanted to ensure were in trusted hands, such as Vladimir Yakunin of Russian Railways, Sergey Chemezov of Russian Technology, and Nikolay Tokarev of Transneft. For investigative reports on their KGB pasts, their ties to Putin, and their companies, see, for example: Yevgeniya Al'bats and Il'ya Barabanov, "V. Yakunin: 'Ya – kentavr'," *NV*, September 3, 2007; Vladimir Voronov, "Vsya oboronnaya rat'," *NV*, September 10, 2007; Roman Shleynov, "Na prokachku," *Nov. Gaz.*, October 18, 2007. More generally on leading siloviki and big business, see: Taylor 2007, pp. 48–51; Daniel Treisman, "Putin's *Silovarchs*," *Orbis*, 51, 1 (Winter 2007), pp. 141–153.

include Putin's St. Petersburg allies from outside the siloviki, such as Dmitriy Medvedev, Viktor Zubkov, and Aleksey Kudrin (the Minister of Finance throughout Putin's presidency), the personalistic nature of almost all top appointments would become even more clear.[70] The dominance of people from the KGB, St. Petersburg, or both in Russian politics was captured in the following joke recounted by the journalist Andrew Jack: "Are you from the Kremlin? Are you from the KGB? Are you from St. Petersburg?" asks one man of another in a tramcar. "No? Then get off my foot."[71]

I also include Putin's two Procurator Generals, Vladimir Ustinov and Yuriy Chayka, as part of his network. Putin met both of them in the late 1990s when he worked for Yeltsin in Moscow. Specifically, Putin became acquainted with Ustinov and Chayka during the Skuratov affair, in which Putin, as FSB chief, played a key role. During the episode, Yeltsin sought to fire Procurator General Skuratov, ostensibly for moral failings but more likely for his investigation of people close to Yeltsin. At the time, Ustinov and Chayka were both deputies under Skuratov, but they showed a willingness to cooperate with the Kremlin during the affair, which evidently helped their careers when Putin became president.

Did it matter that so many top officials under Putin had backgrounds in the security service and other power ministries? After all, there were many differences among this large cohort of officials. The clan and corporate differences discussed later in the chapter, for example, clearly show that this was not a unified team. The cohort of siloviki certainly is not politically monolithic. For example, in the 1990s, every political party found army generals to put on their list of candidates, from the democratic-leaning Eduard Vorobev of the Union of Right Forces to the anti-Semitic hardline nationalist Albert Makashov of the Communist Party. Bettina Renz argued that differences in institutional background, rank, and career path of these officials meant that they should not be treated as a homogeneous group.[72]

On the other hand, there are good reasons to think that such a large cohort of power ministry officials in government service would influence the nature of the Russian government. The sociological logic of this approach points to the importance of the organizational culture of these agencies.[73] If this group is just a collection of individuals, and not a true cohort, then their shared background is perhaps not that important. But if their collective backgrounds led to similar socialization, then the expansion of the siloviki cohort had important implications for Russian politics.

---

[70] The two most important exceptions, in terms of key figures lacking personalistic ties to Putin were his first two prime ministers, Mikhail Kasyanov and Mikhail Fradkov. Fradkov, however, is also a silovik; his service in foreign economic relations in the Soviet period suggests KGB ties, he served in the Security Council and as director of the FSNP during Putin's first term, and in 2007 he became head of the SVR.

[71] Andrew Jack, *Inside Putin's Russia* (Oxford: Oxford University Press, 2004), p. 317.

[72] Renz 2006.

[73] For my attempt to develop an organizational culture approach to Russian civil-military relations, see: Taylor, *Politics and the Russian Army.*

Kryshtanovskaya argued that several features of power ministry culture, such as hierarchy, strict discipline, and patriotism, pushed out more democratic ideas and procedures with the rise of the siloviki cohort. The desire for control predominates among former Chekists (secret police personnel), the most important group within the siloviki cohort and the Putin team. Kryshtanovskaya described siloviki culture in the following way:

What is "disorder" in the eyes of a man in uniform? It's the absence of control. If there is not control, there is the possibility of independent influence. And siloviki perceive the presence of alternative centers of power in the country as a threat to the country's integrity. The Duma is not subordinate to the presidential administration? Disorder. Gazprom is led by Vyakhirev [Rem Vyakhirev, former director of Gazprom from 1992–2001 – B.T.] and not the Kremlin? Disorder. Political parties wanted something, the mass media talked about something? All of this is disorder that must be liquidated. And they liquidated it. In seven years the chekists have completely changed the political system in the country, not changing one letter of the Constitution.[74]

Kryshtanovskaya's account of siloviki culture is primarily impressionistic, based on her study of this cohort. Although there are some polls on the political views of Russian military officers, primarily from the 1990s, I know of no such polls on the beliefs of siloviki as a whole, or the FSB in particular.[75] Still, Russian and foreign scholars who study the FSB tend to agree that the dominant culture of the organization emphasizes order, control, and the primacy of the state over more liberal values. They also stress that, despite the multiple reorganizations of the 1990s, the basic ethos of the organization is a direct descendant of that of the Soviet KGB. At the very beginning of Putin's tenure, the leading Western expert on the KGB, Amy Knight, noted "legitimate concerns about a 'KGB mindset' penetrating Kremlin politics." Yevgenia Albats, one of Russia's top analysts of the FSB, argued in 2004 that "by training, Putin is a man of control …. The KGB taught its soldiers well; its institutional culture has not been easily thrown off and its imperatives have proved stronger than Putin's leanings toward democracy."[76]

Memoir accounts by former KGB and FSB personnel also suggest an organizational culture that values statism and order and is skeptical of, if not hostile to, liberalism and democracy. Yusif Legan, who worked for the KGB and FSB for more than thirty-five years, maintained in his 2001 memoirs that attempts to introduce Western reforms and values into Russia are "pernicious," and that Russians value collectivism over individualism. Legan contended that the

---

[74] Viktor Khamrayev, interview with Ol'ga Kryshtanovskaya, "'Polozheniye chekistov segodnya fantastitecheski ustoychivo'," *K-V*, March 19, 2007. See also her longer articles cited above.

[75] My discussion of these military polls is in *Politics and the Russian Army*, pp. 271–272, 311–313. Polls of the police are discussed in Chapter 5, but these polls focus on law enforcement practices, not political views.

[76] Amy Knight, "The Enduring Legacy of the KGB in Russian Politics," *Problems of Post-Communism*, 47, 4 (July/August 2000), p. 13; Yevgenia Albats, "In Putin's Kremlin, It's All About Control," *Washington Post*, December 12, 2004. See also: Knight 1996; Albats 1994.

"main state ideology" for Russians is the view that the state is "sacred and indivisible ... its greatness and interests are higher than any individual citizen." Nikolay Leonov, former deputy head of foreign intelligence in the KGB, suggested that the increased prominence of the Chekists under Putin was a natural phenomenon:

> They are patriots and proponents of a strong state grounded in centuries-old tradition.... *History recruited them* to carry out a special operation for the resurrection of our Great Power [*Derzhava*].... What is a KGB officer? He is, above all, a servant of the state.... The only people that can bring order to the state are state people [*gosudarstvennye lyudi*].[77]

One of Putin's closest colleagues from the KGB, Viktor Cherkesov, who occupied several top jobs under Putin, set out what amounted to a "Chekist manifesto" in two extraordinary newspaper articles, the first in December 2004 and the second in October 2007. Both came at a time of internecine warfare between siloviki clans (see further discussion), and in both articles Cherkesov appealed for Chekist unity for the good of the country. According to Cherkesov, attempts to sow discord among the Chekists were designed to undermine the "territorial integrity and national sovereignty" of Russia. The Chekists, as he stated in the epigraph to this chapter, had to assume responsibility for preserving the Russian state. Indeed, Cherkesov asserted that the Chekists were a "hook" that society was clinging to in order to avoid plunging into an abyss. Putin and the Chekists, he continued, were preventing Russia from falling to its death. But enemies of Russia very much wanted the Chekists to fail and therefore tried to divide them against each other. If the "comradely solidarity" of the Chekist corporation was broken, it could not carry out its historic mission. In that case, Cherkesov concluded, Russia itself was at risk, "awaiting the fate of many African nations – practically complete annihilation, plunging into chaos and multiracial genocide."[78]

The available evidence, then, including expert assessments and the writings of former Chekists, tends to support Kryshtanovskaya's argument that siloviki in general, and the Chekists in particular, are more likely than elites from other backgrounds to be both adherents of a strong state internally (in Russian, *gosudarstvenniki*) and of a strong Russia internationally (*derzhavniki*). Liberal democracy is at best a lower priority, and more likely perceived as a threat to political order and stability. Importantly, these views were apparently shared by Putin himself. Thus, the expansion of the silovik cohort could have important implications for Russian state building, democracy, and federalism. The behavior of the siloviki detailed in subsequent chapters tends to support this

[77] Yusif Legan, *KGB-FSB. Vzglyad iznutri* (Moskva: "Tsentrkniga," 2001), Vol. 2, pp. 223–226, 297; Leonov quoted in: Laurent Murawiec and Clifford C. Gaddy, "The Higher Police: Vladimir Putin and His Predecessors," *The National Interest*, 67 (Spring 2002), p. 35, emphasis in original.

[78] Cherkesov 2004; Viktor Cherkesov, "Nel'zya dopustit', chtoby voiny prevratilis' v torgovtsev," *K-D*, October 9, 2007.

conclusion, although, as we will see in Chapter 5, material self-interest often trumps state goals and priorities.

Siloviki Clans

A second way of understanding the influence of the siloviki in Russian politics is based not on the group as a cohort of officials, but as a more narrow "clan" connecting top Kremlin officials with key power ministry leaders. Understanding the key groupings and alliances at the top of Soviet politics was a key feature of Kremlinology and remained equally vital after the so-called "transition to democracy." This point was made forcefully by the U.S. diplomat Thomas Graham in 1995, who, highlighting the patrimonial character of Russian politics, argued that under Yeltsin, several political and economic groupings struggled for power. Graham highlighted four different clans, headed by powerful patrons such as Prime Minister Viktor Chernomyrdin, Moscow Mayor Yuri Luzhkov, State Property Committee Head Anatoliy Chubais, and Aleksandr Korzhakov, the head of the Presidential Security Service.[79]

Although the players changed, the game under Putin remained the same. In his first term, analysts highlighted three or four key groupings. There were the leftover elements of the so-called Yeltsin "Family," such as Prime Minister Kasyanov and Chief of the Presidential Administration Aleksandr Voloshin, the siloviki, and the "Saint Petersburg liberals," a group sometimes further subdivided into the "economists" (German Gref and Aleksey Kudrin, who headed the two most important economic ministries) and the "lawyers" (Dmitriy Medvedev and Dmitriy Kozak, who in the first term both worked for the presidential administration).[80]

The siloviki clearly became the most powerful grouping. Traditionally, the center of the clan was said to be in the presidential administration, headed by the Deputy Head of the presidential administration Igor Sechin and Viktor Ivanov, a key assistant to Putin. Both Ivanov and Sechin are from St. Petersburg, with Ivanov having a definite KGB past and Sechin presumed to have at least some contacts with the KGB, given his work as a military translator in Mozambique and Angola in the 1980s.[81]

---

[79] Thomas Graham, "Noviy rossiyskiy rezhim," *Nez. Gaz.*, November 23, 1995.
[80] See, for example: Jack 2004, p. 320.
[81] Good introductions to the siloviki as a clan include: Pavel Baev, "The Evolution of Putin's Regime: Inner Circles and Outer Walls," *Problems of Post-Communism*, 51, 6 (2004), pp. 3–13; Ian Bremmer and Samuel Charap, "The *Siloviki* in Putin's Russia: Who They Are and What They Want," *The Washington Quarterly*, 30, 1 (2006–2007), pp. 83–92. In a thoughtful discussion of the siloviki, Thomas Gomart suggested that "the group is probably less an active clan than a media construct:" Thomas Gomart, *Russian Civil-Military Relations: Putin's Legacy* (Washington, DC: Carnegie Endowment for International Peace, 2008), p. 42. As should become clear, I think the siloviki are more than a media construct, although I agree that they are not a homogeneous clan.

The key to the power of the siloviki group in the Kremlin, other than their obvious closeness to Putin, was their alliance with Patrushev at the FSB. One symbol of this alliance was that Patrushev's son Andrey was an advisor to Sechin in Sechin's capacity as Chair of the Board of the state oil company Rosneft. Further, Procurator General Vladimir Ustinov, previously part of the Yeltsin "Family" grouping, joined the siloviki clan. The two heads of the MVD under Putin after 2001, Boris Gryzlov and Rashid Nurgaliyev, were also believed to be close to Patrushev. Gryzlov and Patrushev not only went to school together in St. Petersburg, but allegedly sat next to each other in class, and Nurgaliyev served in the Karelia FSB under Patrushev. Thus, throughout most of the Putin presidency, this clan controlled the three key law enforcement structures: the FSB, the procuracy, and the MVD. The power of this clan was evident in the taking down of Russia's richest man, Mikhail Khodorkovsky, in the Yukos affair.[82]

One advantage of the siloviki-as-clan approach is that it allows for greater analysis of the divisions *within* the siloviki. Former Defense Minister and First Deputy Prime Minister Sergey Ivanov was often grouped with the siloviki because of his KGB and St. Petersburg background, but Ivanov and Sechin were believed to be bitter enemies. For example, the scandal in the press over the mutilation of army private Andrey Sychev by other soldiers on New Year's Eve 2006 was said to be promoted by Sechin and Ustinov as an attack on Ivanov and his management of the army. Similarly, Cherkesov and Patrushev were opponents, and Cherkesov's 2004 and 2007 manifestoes were apparently motivated by what he viewed as attacks inspired by Patrushev. Cherkesov was believed to be allied with the head of the Presidential Security Service, Viktor Zolotov, also a long-time associate of Putin from St. Petersburg (Zolotov was Sobchak's bodyguard), and perhaps also Procurator General Chayka.[83]

These intra-siloviki clan squabbles were most evident in autumn 2007, as the search for Putin's successor reached its final phase. The new Investigative Committee under the procuracy arrested one of Cherkesov's top deputies at the FSKN, Lieutenant General Aleksandr Bulbov, and accused him of abuse of office and several other crimes. Cherkesov fought back publicly with one of his "Chekist manifestoes" in *Kommersant*, a leading newspaper. Most commentators linked the Bulbov affair to a dispute between Sechin, Patrushev, and

[82] Baev 2004; Bremmer and Charap 2006–2007; Roman Shleynov, "Donoschiki snaryadov," *Nov. Gaz.*, April 26, 2007; Rimma Akhmirova, "Ochen' nezametnyy Patrushev," *Sobesednik*, June 25, 2007.

[83] On intra-siloviki disagreements, see: Il'ya Zhegulev, "Pochti kak Putin," *Smart Money*, July 9, 2007; Vladimir Voronov, "Sychevym po Sechinu," *Sobesednik*, October 9, 2006; Shleynov 2007; Mikhail Fishman, "Shchit i kit," *RN*, November 13, 2006; V. Pribylovksiy, "Pyat' Bashen. Politicheskaya Topografiya Kremlya," 2006, at http://www.anticompromat.ru/putin/5bashen.html; Aleksandr Khinshteyn, "FSB zanimayetsya dur'yu," *MK*, October 3, 2007; Roman Shleynov, "Skandal v prezidentskom gareme," *Nov. Gaz.*, October 11, 2007; Yuliya Latynina, "Bol'shoy brat slyshit tebya," *Nov. Gaz.*, October 11, 2007; Olesya Yakhno, "Noch' chekista," *Glavred* (Ukraine), November 9, 2007.

Bastrykin on the one hand and Cherkesov, Zolotov, and Chayka on the other. Indeed, the entire development of the Procuracy in 2006–2007, including the removal of Ustinov in 2006 and the creation of the Investigative Committee in 2007, were linked to battles between these clans and the need for Putin to firmly control law enforcement on the eve of the 2007–2008 electoral cycle.[84]

Divisions within the siloviki became more apparent in Putin's second term for three reasons, all of them interrelated. First, the successful assault on "the Family" eliminated a key common enemy of the siloviki and allowed submerged divisions within this group to come to the forefront. Second, Putin himself had obvious incentives to not let one clan become predominant, because it would weaken his position as chief arbiter. Thus, he made sure to maintain a balance among the different siloviki factions. Third, the approach of the 2008 succession motivated all major elite factions to seek to increase their power. For example, Dmitriy Medvedev, who lacked a power ministry background, worked to place his people within these structures even before being tapped by Putin as successor. Some analysts argued that the Sechin–Viktor Ivanov relationship, the foundation of the siloviki clan, broke down, with the siloviki clan split into multiple factions.[85]

The clan approach to the siloviki, although serving to highlight important factional differences within the broader cohort, implies that the divisions between siloviki were more about power and resources than ideas. Indeed, top officials such as Sechin, Patrushev, Sergey Ivanov, and Cherkesov were believed to have broadly similar policy views stressing statism and nationalism.[86] Siloviki disputes with other clans, such as with the liberals, could be based on policy. But inter-siloviki disagreements did not seem to have a significant policy difference, and thus were assumed to be about patron-client ties and advancing the material interests of the clan.[87] Although this approach is open to the possibility of a heterogeneous siloviki cohort, the source of this heterogeneity is rooted in patrimonial rent seeking.

Siloviki Corporate Actors

The third way of thinking about the influence of the siloviki is not as a cohort or a clan (or group of clans), but as the corporate bodies that make up the power ministries. In contrast to the sociological approach of the cohort view,

[84] In addition to the cites in the previous note, see: Burger and Holland 2008; Burnham and Firestone 2007; Francesca Mereu, "Sechin's Clan the Loser in a Week of Surprises," *MT*, December 17, 2007; Natal'ya Royeva, "Putin – zalozhnik sobstvennoy svity, kotoraya poidet na vse, tol'ko by on ostalsya u vlasti," *Forum.msk.ru*, November 19, 2007; Interview M-30; Interview M-45.

[85] Shleynov 2007; Anton Zlobin, "Gruppy Krovnykh," *RN*, June 11, 2007; Pribylovksiy 2006.

[86] Bremmer and Charap 2006–2007.

[87] A classic statement on the difference between Kremlinologists who emphasize disputes over power and those who emphasize disagreements over policy is: Carl A. Linden, *Khrushchev and the Soviet Leadership 1957–1964* (Baltimore: The Johns Hopkins Press, 1966).

or the Kremlinological methods of the clan perspective, seeing the siloviki primarily as a group of corporate actors is consistent with a traditional bureaucratic politics approach. Policy is seen as the outcome of "pulling and hauling" between competing agencies.[88]

Like the clan approach, one virtue of the corporate perspective is that it highlights potential divisions between the power ministries and within the broad cohort of siloviki. The power ministries do not just represent a bloc of agencies united around their control of coercive force – they often have overlapping jurisdictions and are competitors for power and resources. These rivalries are long-standing. The MVD and the KGB/FSB have historically been mutually antagonistic; President Putin once remarked, "those of us in the Cheka never liked the police."[89] Similarly, the Red Army resented KGB monitoring and oversight of its activities and loyalties. These institutional conflicts continued into the post-Soviet period. For example, the military greatly resented the influence and resources directed at other power ministries in the 1990s and the presence of multiple "parallel armies," such as the Internal Troops of the MVD, the MChS, and the Federal Border Service (FPS).[90]

These institutional conflicts also exist at the microlevel of everyday interactions between officials from different agencies. The military is largely aloof from these conflicts because it does not play an internal role, although the war in Chechnya created many clashes between the army, the MVD, and the FSB in the North Caucasus.[91] All of them have troops in the area, and operational control has shifted between them several times. In the domestic law enforcement sphere, there are both everyday tensions and important cultural differences between police, secret police, and prosecutors. KGB/FSB agents always have considered themselves the elite "blue bloods" among the law enforcement agencies (and among state officials in general), viewing the average cop as someone who is overburdened with unimportant grunt work and frequently corrupt. Police, in return, see themselves as the real fighters against crime, soldiers who shed blood while FSB agents and procurators just sit at their desks. Procuracy officials, for their part, see themselves as the linchpin of the system, with everything dependent on them. Although legally this is somewhat true, given their key role in the criminal prosecution system and as the coordinators of law enforcement, in reality they often are dependent on information provided by other agencies, the police in ordinary crimes and the FSB in high-profile cases. Moreover, given the elite status of the FSB, the ability of the procuracy to exercise genuine oversight of the Chekists is limited.

---

[88] Graham T. Allison, *Essence of Decision: Explaining the Cuban Missile Crisis* (Boston: Little, Brown, and Company, 1971).

[89] Gevorkyan et. al., 2000, pp. 25, 128–129. On MVD/FSB competition, see also: "Siloviki snova stali sil'nymi," *VN*, March 11, 2004.

[90] Interview with Minister of Defense Igor' Rodionov, "Sdelat' moguchey ekonomiku za schet nizkoy oboronosposobnosti strany – avantyura," *NVO*, July 17, 1998.

[91] See, for example: Aleksey Malashenko and Dmitriy Trenin, *Vremya Yuga* (Moskva: Carnegie Moscow Center, 2002), pp. 114–115, 123–124.

These cultural differences are long-standing and remain with officials as they climb the ladder. Good personal relationships – that is, do they drink vodka together? – can overcome these differences in some localities, and obviously some cooperation does takes place, but overall, the law enforcement structures are hardly a unified team.[92]

At the macrolevel, the 1990s was a time of flux. Yeltsin clearly distrusted the secret police, which explains the decision to break the KGB into multiple parts and the frequent leadership changes at the top of the FSB. Beyond the "big three" of the MO, MVD, and FSB, other agencies were able to assert themselves, particularly if their director enjoyed close ties to Yeltsin. The most obvious example here is the enormous power accumulated as head of the Presidential Security Service by Aleksandr Korzhakov in Yeltsin's first term. After Korzhakov played a crucial rule in defeating Yeltsin's opponents in the violent October 1993 conflict, Yeltsin instructed Korzhakov to make his service into a "mini-KGB."[93] In 1995, Korzhakov made the top five of *Nezavisimaya Gazeta*'s well-known "100 Leading Politicians" index, which charted the shifting influence of Russia's political and economic elite. MChS's Shoygu and FPS head Andrey Nikolayev also were both closer to Yeltsin and arguably more powerful than some directors of the FSB, such as Nikolay Kovalev (1996–1998).[94]

The FSB's power, although already wide-ranging on paper, really began to grow when Putin became its head and demonstrated his loyalty to Yeltsin. Once he became the head of state, the FSB's rise to dominance over the other power ministries was assured. In 2003, as noted earlier, the FSB regained control over border protection and some important government communication functions. More importantly, FSB personnel spread throughout the other power ministries, a form of bureaucratic colonization. The most obvious manifestation of this was the appointment of Ivanov to head the Ministry of Defense in March 2001 and Nurgaliyev to run the MVD in March 2004. Nurgaliyev, in fact, already had been sent to the MVD from the FSB in 2002, when he became the First Deputy Minister of Internal Affairs. This example can be multiplied many times over. For example, in 2004, five of the second-tier positions in the MVD, such as Deputy Minister or the heads of MVD directorates or services, were occupied by former KGB/FSB personnel. Similarly, in

---

[92] Interview M-5; Interview M-6; Interview M-7; Interview M-10; Interview M-13; Interview M-32; Interview M-43; Interview M-47; Interview P-2; Interview P-9; Interview P-12; Interview N-13.

[93] Korzhakov 1997, p. 404; Yuriy Baturin et. al., *Epokha Yel'tsina: Ocherki politicheskoy istorii* (Moskva: Vagrius, 2000), pp. 213–214.

[94] For the ratings of these officials' influence, see: "100 Naibolee vliyatel'nykh politikov Rossii v 1996 godu," *Nez. Gaz.*, January 17, 1997; *NG-Stsenarii*, January 28, 1998; *Nez. Gaz.* January 12, 2000; *Nez. Gaz.* January 15, 2002. Shoygu headed the pro-Putin "Unity" Party in the 1999 Duma elections, and Nikolayev was considered a serious contender for the presidency: Sergey Chugayev, "Sleduyushchim prezidentom strany mozhet stat' general Nikolayev," *Izvestiya*, December 23, 1997.

the MO, the Deputy Minister in charge of cadres came from the secret police, as did the Director of the military-technical cooperation service. The head of the Federal Customs Service (FTS) in Putin's second term, Andrey Belyaninov, was a Chekist, as were several officials in second-tier positions in that agency. This was also true of the FSKN, Cherkesov's agency.[95]

Second in stature behind the FSB has been the procuracy, primarily because of its wide-ranging powers and responsibilities. Although in principle the procuracy is independent from the executive branch, it still largely takes its direction from the president, just as it did from the Party during the Soviet period. In the early 1990s, legal reformers sought to limit the procuracy's extensive mandate and strengthen the power and independence of the courts, but these efforts failed.[96]

The 2007 creation of the semiautonomous Investigative Committee represented a major weakening of the procuracy, because the prosecutorial weapon is of great political and economic importance in Russia. This reform also somewhat strengthened the FSB and the MVD, but it was far from the last word in the battle for influence between the main law enforcement structures. The first head of the committee, Aleksandr Bastrykin, was a long-time Putin associate and was viewed as an ally of Sechin and Patrushev. Indeed, the creation of the committee, as discussed earlier, showed the influence of clan battles on corporate power.

The advantage of thinking of siloviki as corporate actors, rather than as a cohort, is that it calls attention to the sources not just of unity, but also disagreement and difference, between the power ministries. Putin seemingly encouraged conflict between agencies, such as between the FSB and the FSKN and between the procuracy and its investigative committee, as a way to maintain the desired balance between agencies and ensure his own control. The advantage of this approach compared to the clan perspective is that it points to the type of bureaucratic battles that are considered the norm in states with more rational-legal modes of bureaucracy. Indeed, Russian state administration is a combination of patrimonial and rational-legal modes of bureaucratic action, and has been at least since Peter the Great.[97] At the same time, treating the power ministries solely as self-contained organizations warring for power and resources with each other, without noting that they share some cultural

[95] "Siloviki snova stali sil'nymi" 2004; "Agenty vliyaniya," *Nov. Gaz.*, August 30, 2004; Shleynov 2007.
[96] Smith 1996; Gordon B. Smith, "The Struggle Over the Procuracy," in Peter H. Solomon, Jr., ed., *Reforming Justice in Russia, 1864–1996: Power, Culture, and the Limits of Legal Order* (Armonk, NY: M.E. Sharpe, 1997), pp. 348–373.
[97] Vadim Volkov, "Patrimonialism versus Rational Bureaucracy: On the Historical Relativity of Corruption," in Stephen Lovell, Alena Ledeneva, and Andrei Rogachevskii, eds., *Bribery and Blat in Russia: Negotiating Reciprocity from the Middle Ages to the 1990s* (New York: St. Martin's Press, 2000), pp. 35–47; Peter H. Solomon, Jr., "Administrative Styles in Soviet History: The Development of Patrimonial Rationality," in Thomas Lahusen and Peter J. Solomon, Jr., eds., *What Is Soviet Now?: Identities, Legacies, Memories* (Berlin: Lit Verlag, 2008), pp. 78–89.

similarities and that patronage ties cut across these bureaucratic boundaries, would also provide a limited picture of their activity.

CONCLUSION

The 1990s was a time of great upheaval for the power ministries in almost all respects: organizationally, financially, and in terms of leadership. The Soviet "police state" gave way to a new order in which the military, security, and law enforcement structures were on the ropes. For the power ministries, Vladimir Putin arrived as a savior, promising to restore the power and status of Russia's force structures. Putin delivered, consolidating the fragmented agencies, increasing their budgets, and entrusting their management to loyal allies who were granted long tenures.

His presidency also led to a significant increase in the number of current and former power ministry officials occupying key state positions. The patrimonial nature of Russian politics was no more evident than in the rise of the siloviki as a cohort under Putin. But the image of a monolithic "militocracy" dominating Russian politics fades away once we look inside the clan politics that determined the major directions of Russian policy under both Yeltsin and Putin, or the bureaucratic battles between the various power ministries. Former KGB officials benefited the most from Putin's rule, and the FSB established itself as the preeminent power agency in post-Soviet Russia. Whether these patterns will continue under President Medvedev remains unclear. He himself is not from this milieu, but his independence from Putin is yet to be demonstrated.

The power ministries and the siloviki, both as a cohort and a clan, benefited from Putin's rule. Putin viewed this bolstering of the power ministries as a central component of his major policy priority of strengthening the Russian state. Did he succeed? The next two chapters address this question.

3

Coercion and Capacity

Political Order and the Central State

> A strong state for a Russian is not an anomaly, not something to fight against, but on the contrary is the source and guarantor of order, the initiator and driving force of any change.
>
> Vladimir Putin, December 1999[1]

From his first days in office as Russia's second president, Vladimir Putin made strengthening the state the primary goal of his rule. Putin's objective responded not only to the wishes of Russian citizens, but arguably to a real and serious problem. By the end of Boris Yeltsin's presidency in 1999, the weakness of the Russian state was being compared to African failed states.[2] A host of pathologies in the 1990s – economic depression culminating in default, the spread of alternative monetary instruments in place of the ruble, demographic crisis evidenced by a rising death rate and declining birth rate, high crime and murder rates, the power of the so-called oligarchs and regional barons – were blamed on state incapacity. Throughout the decade, observers asked, as Matthew Evangelista put it, "will Russia go the way of the Soviet Union?"[3]

---

[1] Vladimir Putin, "Rossiya na rubezhe tysyacheletiy," *Nez. Gaz.*, December 30, 1999.

[2] Donald N. Jensen, "Is Russia Another Somalia?" *RFE/RL Newsline*, 3, 18, January 27, 1999; David Hoffman, "Yeltsin's Absentee Rule Raises Specter of a 'Failed State'," *WP*, February 26, 1999, p. 1. For a stimulating comparative study of stateness in Africa and the former Soviet Union, see: Mark R. Beissinger and Crawford Young, eds., *Beyond State Crisis? Postcolonial Africa and Post-Soviet Eurasia in Comparative Perspective* (Washington, DC: Woodrow Wilson Center Press, 2002). Also using the African failed state literature is: John P. Willerton, Mikhail Beznosov, and Martin Carrier, "Addressing the Challenges of Russia's 'Failing State': The Legacy of Gorbachev and the Promise of Putin," *Demokratizatsiya*, 13, 2 (Spring 2005), pp. 219–239.

[3] Peter Reddaway, "Russia Comes Apart," *NYT*, January 10, 1993, p. E23; Jessica Eve Stern, "Moscow Meltdown: Can Russia Survive?" *International Security*, 18, 4 (Spring 1994), pp. 40–65; Douglas W. Blum, ed., *Russia's Future: Consolidation or Disintegration?* (Boulder, CO: Westview Press, 1994). Assessments of the same question several years into Putin's rule include: Matthew Evangelista, *The Chechen Wars: Will Russia Go the Way of the Soviet Union?* (Washington, DC: Brookings Institution Press, 2002); Henry E. Hale and Rein Taagepera, "Russia: Consolidation or Collapse?" *Europe-Asia Studies*, 54, 7 (2002),

By the end of his second term, Putin was proclaiming the rebuilding of the state as one of his most important achievements.[4] This chapter begins the assessment of the capacity and quality of the Russian state, particularly the coercive organs, pursued throughout this book by examining the role of the power ministries at the national level. How should we evaluate Putin's claim to success, one echoed by many Russian and Western observers?

The evidence from this chapter shows a noticeable increase in state capacity in several realms, but the overall picture is mixed. Evidence for an increase in capacity in the coercive realm was most obvious in the absence of violent clashes for power in the state capital, such as happened in 1991 and 1993. It also seems clear that the fiscal capacity of the state was higher under Putin than in the 1990s, an increase that is at least in part related to the power ministries. This higher fiscal capacity represented an improvement in the ability to fulfill routine tasks. Other signs of improvement came in the fulfillment of exceptional decisions: A "regime of repression" was reconstituted and directed against political enemies, such as opposition parties and candidates and out-of-favor economic oligarchs.

On the other hand, the power ministries performed comparatively poorly in fulfilling key core tasks, such as fighting terrorism and crime. They did better in these respects in the last years of Putin's rule, but overall their performance was little better under Putin than it was under Yeltsin. More importantly, in comparative terms, Russia lagged behind countries of similar wealth in terms of state capacity, and was one of the most violent countries in the world in terms of both homicide and terrorist attacks. Moreover, Russia still lacked a stable private property rights regime, with arbitrary application of the law to businesses of all sizes. State coercive agencies continued to exhibit multiple dysfunctions that suggested the increase in capacity was only partial and perhaps temporary.

Putin succeeded more in increasing the capacity of law enforcement organs to implement exceptional state directives designed to increase the power of the Kremlin than in coping with their routine, core tasks. To the extent that there was some improvement in state capacity, especially in terms of the fulfillment of exceptional tasks, this was primarily due to three factors: Putin's overall popularity while president, a much stronger economy, and an ideological project of statism for its own sake that grew particularly prominent in Putin's second term. This last factor is consistent with historical episodes of Russian and Soviet state building, a circling of the wagons against internal and external enemies. Overall, the relatively moderate increase in state capacity under Putin should be seen as a disappointment, given the available political and economic resources he commanded compared to Yeltsin.

---

pp. 1101–1125; Vladimir Popov, "The State in the New Russia (1992–2004): From Collapse to Gradual Revival?" *PONARS Policy Memo*, 342 (November 2004).

[4] Vladimir Putin, "Stenograficheskiy otchet o vstreche s uchastnikami tret'ego zasedaniya Mezhdunarodnogo diskussionnogo kluba 'Valday'," September 9, 2006; Vladimir Putin, "Intervyu zhurnalistam pechatnykh sredstv massovoy informatsii iz stran – chlenov 'Gruppy vos'mi'," June 4, 2007.

The remainder of the chapter provides an account of the role of the power ministries in building state capacity at the national level. This assessment of the capacity of Russia's power ministries, especially law enforcement organs, is based on two comparisons: diachronic (from Yeltsin to Putin) and cross-national (Russia and the rest of the world). I examine three different areas: political violence, law enforcement capacity, and coercion in the economic realm. I begin with a brief overview of the academic literature on the post-Soviet Russian state.

BRINGING THE RUSSIAN STATE BACK IN[5]

In the first half of the 1990s, most academic writing on Russia focused on "transitions" – to democracy and free markets.[6] Claus Offe astutely noted early on that there was a third transition in post-communist Europe involving what he called "the territorial" issue of nation and state building, but even his conception was more about borders and nationalism than government institutions and administration. Taras Kuzio later argued that nation and state building should be considered separate tasks, suggesting that a "quadruple transition" was taking place in many post-communist states.[7]

By the second half of the 1990s, a growing number of analysts were attributing problems with the democratic and market transitions to the weakness and dysfunctionality of post-communist states. Prominent symptoms of the problem in Russia included the inability of the state to fulfill some of its core functions, including control over monetary emissions and currency (evidenced by the rise of barter and alternative payment instruments at the local and regional level), securing private property rights (evidenced by the rise of the mafia and other protection rackets), and tax collection. Challenges to central authority from multiple regions, most dramatically in the case of Chechnya, were further evidence of Russian state crisis.[8]

---

[5] Cynthia Roberts and Thomas Sherlock, "Bringing the Russian State Back In: Explanations of the Derailed Transition to Market Democracy," *Comparative Politics*, 31 (1999), pp. 477–498; Peter B. Evans, Dietrich Rueschemeyer, and Theda Skocpol, eds., *Bringing the State Back In* (Cambridge: Cambridge University Press, 1985).

[6] Jordan Gans-Morse shows that most scholars of post-communism did not unquestioningly accept the implicit teleology of the transition paradigm, but the large number of articles identified by Gans-Morse on regime change (more than 130 in 12 years) does show the scholarly preoccupation with this topic: Jordan Gans-Morse, "Searching for Transitologists: Contemporary Theories of Post-Communist Transitions and the Myth of a Dominant Paradigm," *Post-Soviet Affairs*, 20, 4 (2004), pp. 320–349. The classic critique of the assumptions of the transitions literature is: Thomas Carothers, "The End of the Transition Paradigm," *Journal of Democracy*, 13, 1 (January 2002), pp. 5–21.

[7] Claus Offe, "Capitalism by Democratic Design? Democratic Theory Facing the Triple Transition in East Central Europe," *Social Research*, 58, 4 (1991), pp. 865–892; Taras Kuzio, "Transition in Post-Communist States: Triple or Quadruple?", *Politics*, 21, 3 (2001), pp. 168–177.

[8] For good discussions of barter, the mafia, and the first Chechen war as manifestations of state crisis, see, respectively: David Woodruff, *Money Unmade: Barter and the Fate of*

To the extent that scholars were a bit late in recognizing the problem of state capacity, there were two primary, related reasons.[9] First, for understandable historical reasons, the dominance of the state over society was believed to be the key problem in the region, not state weakness. Second, the dominant models of communist politics, from totalitarianism to bureaucratic politics approaches, had shared an emphasis on the state as the central topic of analysis. In the Russian context, this emphasis on the dominance of the state over society was also prevalent in much scholarship on the prerevolutionary period.[10] After 1991, there was a rush to incorporate more "bottom up" perspectives and connect to broader literatures in comparative politics on regime change, elections, public opinion, and civil society.

When scholars did return to the state, the key concepts developed in the comparative statist revival discussed in Chapter 1 were employed and put to good use. In an early contribution, for example, Arista Maria Cirtautus invoked Michael Mann's distinction between infrastructural and despotic power to show how the weakness of post-communist states could be traced, following Ken Jowitt, to the decline of ideological commitment among party officials and the rise of corruption and patronage in the late communist period.[11] Other scholars, such as Valerie Sperling and Michael McFaul, tended to emphasize the well-known concepts of state capacity and autonomy to analyze Russian state weakness.[12]

Russian Capitalism (Ithaca, NY: Cornell University Press, 1999); Vadim Volkov, *Violent Entrepreneurs: The Use of Force in the Making of Russian Capitalism* (Ithaca, NY: Cornell University Press, 2002); Anatol Lieven, *Chechnya: Tombstone of Russian Power* (New Haven, CT: Yale University Press, 1998), esp. pp. 150–185.

[9] Arista Maria Cirtautus, "The Post-Leninist State: A Conceptual and Empirical Examination," *Communist and Post-Communist Studies*, 28 (1995), pp. 379–392; Anna Gryzmala-Busse and Pauline Jones Luong, "Reconceptualizing the State: Lessons from Post-Communism," *Politics & Society*, 30, 4 (December 2002), pp. 529–531; Timothy J. Colton, "Introduction: Governance and Postcommunist Politics," in Timothy J. Colton and Stephen Holmes, eds., *The State after Communism: Governance in the New Russia* (Lanham, MD: Rowman & Littlefield, 2006), pp. 1–3.

[10] Geoffrey Hosking, *Russia: People and Empire 1552–1917* (Cambridge, MA: Harvard University Press, 1997); Marshall Poe, *The Russian Moment in World History* (Princeton, NJ: Princeton University Press, 2003). In Nettl's terminology, Russia has a cultural tradition of a "high degree of stateness": J.P. Nettl, "The State as a Conceptual Variable," *World Politics*, 20 (1968), pp. 559–592.

[11] Cirtautus 1995; Ken Jowitt, "Soviet Neotraditionalism: The Political Corruption of a Leninist Regime," *Soviet Studies*, 35, 3 (July 1983), pp. 275–297. Others who at least partially employ Mann include: Colton and Holmes 2006; Kathryn Stoner-Weiss, *Resisting the State: Reform and Retrenchment in Post-Soviet Russia* (Cambridge: Cambridge University Press, 2006). Tilly is put to good use in: Venelin I. Ganev, "Post-Communism as an Episode of State Building: A Reversed Tillyan Perspective," *Communist and Post-Communist Studies*, 38, 4 (2005), pp. 425–445.

[12] Valerie Sperling, "Introduction: The Domestic and International Obstacles to State-Building in Russia," in Valerie Sperling, ed., *Building the Russian State: Institutional Crisis and the Quest for Democratic Governance* (Boulder, CO: Westview Press, 2000), pp. 1–23; Michael McFaul, "State Power, Institutional Change, and the Politics of Privatization in Russia,"

These statist explanations for Russian political and economic difficulties were an important correction to both overly optimistic early accounts of the "transition" and later, more pessimistic verdicts that blamed Russian political culture or misguided foreign advice for Russia's political and economic difficulties.[13] To the extent the statist literature was lacking, besides its relative paucity compared to other topics, it tended to exhibit two problems, the exact problems found with the broader social science literature on the state discussed in Chapter 1. First, much of this literature provided general accounts of the crisis of the Russian state rather than more detailed studies of "the organizations and individuals who establish and administer public policies and laws."[14] Second, despite the usual invocation of the Weberian definition of the state, state coercive organs were generally absent from this work.

There were, of course, exceptions. Edited volumes by Valerie Sperling, Gordon Smith, and Timothy Colton and Stephen Holmes provided detailed studies of specific aspects of Russian state performance.[15] Kathryn Stoner-Weiss focused on the center-regional component of state weakness.[16] Eugene Huskey and Alexander Obolonsky explored public administration reform.[17] These more detailed studies put flesh on the bones of more general accounts of Russian state development.[18]

World Politics, 47 (1995), pp. 210–243; Michael McFaul, "Russia's 'Privatized' State as an Impediment to Democratic Consolidation," *Security Dialogue*, 29 (1998), pp. 191–199, 315–332.

[13] For prominent examples see, respectively: Anders Aslund, "Russia's Success Story," *Foreign Affairs*, 73, 5 (September/October 1994), pp. 58–71; Richard Pipes, "Flight From Freedom: What Russians Think and Want," *Foreign Affairs*, 83, 3 (May/June 2004), pp. 9–15; Stephen F. Cohen, *Failed Crusade: America and the Tragedy of Post-Communist Russia* (New York: W.W. Norton, 2000).

[14] Margaret Levi, "Why We Need a New Theory of Government," *Perspectives on Politics*, 4, 1 (March 2006), p. 6.

[15] Sperling 2000; Colton and Holmes 2006; Gordon B. Smith, ed., *State-Building in Russia: The Yeltsin Legacy and the Challenge of the Future* (Armonk, NY: M.E. Sharpe, 1999).

[16] Stoner-Weiss 2006.

[17] Eugene Huskey and Alexander Obolonsky, "The Struggle to Reform Russia's Bureaucracy," *Problems of Post-Communism*, 50, 4 (July/August 2003), pp. 22–33; Eugene Huskey, "Nomenklatura Lite? The Cadres Reserve in Russian Public Administration," *Problems of Post-Communism*, 51, 2 (March/April 2004), pp. 30–39. Placing current Russian bureaucracy in historical perspective is: Karl W. Ryavec, *Russian Bureaucracy: Power and Pathology* (Lanham, MD: Rowman & Littlefield, 2003).

[18] Important general contributions include: Stephen Holmes, "What Russia Teaches Us Now: How Weak States Threaten Freedom," *The American Prospect* (July/August 1997), pp. 30–39; Roberts and Sherlock 1999; Thomas E. Graham, Jr., "The Fate of the Russian State," *Demokratizatsiya*, 8, 3 (Summer 2000), pp. 354–375; Stephen Kotkin, *Armageddon Averted: The Soviet Collapse 1970–2000* (Oxford: Oxford University Press, 2001), esp. pp. 142–170; Allen C. Lynch, *How Russia Is Not Ruled: Reflections on Russian Political Development* (Cambridge: Cambridge University Press, 2005); Ottorino Cappelli, "Pre-Modern State-Building in Post-Soviet Russia," *Journal of Communist Studies and Transition Politics*, 24, 4 (2008), pp. 531–572; Gerald M. Easter, "The Russian State in the Time of Putin," *Post-Soviet Affairs*, 24, 3 (2008), pp. 199–230.

The neglect of coercion was in some ways more widespread and more serious. Stoner-Weiss sidestepped the issue, despite an approach to the state drawing on Weber, Mann, and Tilly, by maintaining that in modern states, enforcing compliance does not involve the use of force.[19] This is undoubtedly true in many policy areas, including the economic and social domains on which she focuses. But Russian citizens, from Mikhail Khodorkovsky, Russia's former richest man and most famous prisoner, to your average urban pedestrian shaken down by a corrupt cop, know that state coercive organs often do use or threaten to use force to achieve compliance. Other studies, such as the Colton and Holmes project, also tended to follow the comparative statist literature by focusing more on political economy issues such as banking, pensions, taxation, and energy policy.[20] Sperling's *Building the Russian State* was an important exception to this general neglect, with separate chapters on the military, the courts, and crime.

The most important work on state capacity and coercion was Vadim Volkov's *Violent Entrepreneurs*, which provided a highly original account of the crisis of the Russian state in the 1990s. Volkov contended that Russia in the early 1990s "was close to the state of nature, where anarchy rather than hierarchy prevails."[21] In these conditions appeared "violent entrepreneurs," often athletes or former power ministry officials, who converted their superiority in the use of force into money. Extortion and protection rackets evolved over time into what Volkov, citing the leader of a criminal group, calls "enforcement partnership." Enforcement partnership includes such activities as security, contract enforcement, information gathering, dispute resolution, and many other activities that the Russian state in the 1990s provided to private economic actors either sparsely or inefficiently. By the late 1990s, however, the mafia was being pushed aside by state actors and legal private actors (private security companies). The most successful violent entrepreneurs became businessmen and politicians, whereas weaker competitors were pushed out (or jailed or killed). Protection rackets still existed, but by and large, they were run by the police rather than criminals. The state appeared to be successfully claiming a monopoly on legitimate force. In a concurrent paper, Volkov summarized the state of the state in Russia in Putin's first term in the following way: "The first step in reconstructing the state has been made: the bandit has gone; the state employee has taken his place. The second

---

[19] Stoner-Weiss does note in passing that "the reemerging coercive aspect of the security forces" could play a key role in Putin's state-building project, but does not explore the issue further. Stoner-Weiss 2006, pp. 7–9, 25.

[20] Gerald Easter's excellent chapter on fiscal capacity does emphasize the importance of state coercion in this sphere: Gerald Easter, "Building Fiscal Capacity," in Colton and Holmes 2006, pp. 21–52. See also: Verena Fritz, *State-Building: A Comparative Study of Ukraine, Lithuania, Belarus, and Russia* (Budapest: Central European University Press, 2007), esp. pp. 285–314. I return to this issue further in this chapter.

[21] Volkov 2002, p. 26.

step – making him act as a state employee rather than a bandit – is still a problem."[22]

This volume is in some ways an extension of Volkov's story, with some key differences. First, Volkov focused on the "street level" and viewed the process of state formation from the bottom up, whereas my approach is more top-down. Second, Volkov concentrated on the bandits, whereas I give primary attention to the power ministries. Third, Volkov's story is primarily about the Yeltsin years, whereas I cover both the Yeltsin and Putin periods, focusing most closely on the Putin era. Volkov believed that a rebuilding of state capacity in the coercive realm was well underway by 2000. Were these hopes realized?

POLITICAL VIOLENCE FROM YELTSIN TO PUTIN

Max Weber observed that states try to claim a monopoly of *legitimate* violence. This implies that some violence is *illegitimate*, meaning that those who employ it do not have the "right" to do so. The most common example of such illegitimate violence is crime. The most extreme examples are a coup d'état, a literal "blow to the state," or acts of terrorism that kill large numbers of innocents. Both everyday forms of illegitimate violence such as crime, and more political violence like terrorism and coups, have been used as indicators of state capacity.[23] In this section, I concentrate on political violence, turning later in the chapter to crime.

Political Violence and Stability: A Comparative Assessment

One key component of state capacity is the ability of the state to deter or prevent illegitimate political violence like coups and terrorism. Samuel Huntington famously argued that coups are a consequence of state weakness, the natural mode of political behavior for the military in weakly institutionalized, praetorian states.[24] The World Bank Worldwide Governance Indicators (WGI) project ranks countries on "the perceptions of the likelihood that the government will be destabilized or overthrown by unconstitutional or violent means, including domestic violence and terrorism," which they label the "political stability/no violence" indicator.[25]

---

[22] Vadim Volkov, "The Selective Use of State Capacity in Russia's Economy: Property Disputes and Enterprise Takeovers After 2000," *PONARS Policy Memo*, 273 (October 2002).

[23] Robert W. Jackman, *Power Without Force: The Political Capacity of Nation-States* (Ann Arbor, MI: University of Michigan Press, 1993); Ekkart Zimmerman, *Political Violence, Crises, and Revolutions: Theories and Research* (Cambridge, MA: Schenkman Publishing, 1983).

[24] Samuel P. Huntington, *Political Order in Changing Societies* (New Haven, CT: Yale University Press, 1968), pp. 192–263.

[25] The "Political Stability/No Violence" indicator is a composite based on 10 different sources. For project data, see: http://info.worldbank.org/governance/wgi2007/. The World Bank

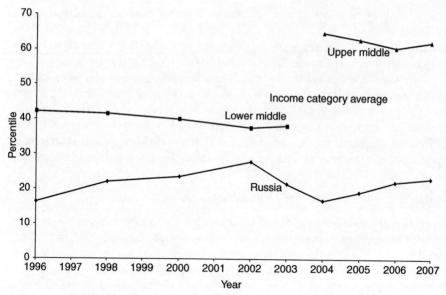

FIGURE 3.1. Political stability/no violence (WGI).

Russia's scores on this indicator show a slight improvement from 1996 to 2007, but no overall change during Putin's tenure from 2000 to 2007 (see Figure 3.1). There was a steady increase from 1996 to 2002, followed by a several-year drop, and then a rebound in 2005–2007. The dip in the middle

Governance project does not provide income group average percentiles for the entire series from 1996–2007, but only for the most recent evaluation. The income group averages shown in this and subsequent figures using WGI data were calculated using World Bank income categories. I thank Massimo Mastruzzi for clarification on this issue, and Richard Bodnar for calculating and graphing these averages. The year 2007 income classifications, and an explanation, are at: http://go.worldbank.org/K2CKM78CC0. In 2007, the lower middle income group was $936–$3,705 GNI per capita (Atlas Method), upper middle income group was $3,706–$11,455. Russian GNI per capita (Atlas Method) for 2006 was $5,770. A couple of caveats are also in order. First, the WGI data show Russia moving to the upper middle income only in its 2006 issue, but according to general Bank income averages, Russia moved to this income category in 2004. I thus use 2004 as the year this change took place. The discrepancy may be caused by differences in timing in when the data were released, or may simply be an error. Second, I have not provided margins of error in the graphs, although the WGI reports these margins. In most cases in this book, the differences between Russia and its income category peers are so large that they are well outside these margins, and recalculating all of these margins for the entire series would have been quite laborious. Third, because of differences in underlying data and changes in the sources from year to year, as well as technical issues about how the raw scores and percentages are calculated, some scholars have raised questions about comparing both across countries and across years. I am confident that, for my rather general and descriptive purposes, the WGI data provide one of the best cross-national set of data on state capacity and state quality, and interested readers are encouraged to consult the WGI website for further information. For discussion of critiques of WGI, and responses by the project coordinators, see: Daniel Kaufmann, Aart Kraay, and Massimo Mastruzzi, *The Worldwide Governance*

of Putin's presidency is likely explained by major terrorist attacks during this period, such as the *Nord-Ost* theater hostage incident in 2002 and the 2004 Beslan school siege. The two most striking conclusions from the figure are the absence of change during Putin's presidency and the extent to which Russia lags behind other states at the same level of income, particularly after it shifts to a higher income category in 2004.

Looking at the issue of political violence more generally over the entire post-Soviet period, two key trends stand out. First, the possibility of a violent confrontation for state power in Moscow, such as the ones that occurred in 1991 and 1993, has diminished greatly. This shows an increase in state capacity that began under Yeltsin and continued under Putin. Questions of who rules the state are no longer decided on the streets. Second, the other main type of political violence experienced by post-Soviet Russia has been terrorism. In the terrorism realm, there are legitimate concerns about the capacity of Russia's force structures to cope with this threat.

Sovereign Power Issues

Sovereign power issues concern who rules the state and who decides who rules.[26] In a stable constitutional democracy, the power ministries play no role in such issues. The intervention of coercive agencies into sovereign power issues, most commonly the military in the form of coups, is often taken as an indicator of state weakness. Under Yeltsin, the power ministries were directly involved in a sovereign power crisis in October 1993, and narrowly avoided a similar crisis in March 1996. In contrast, under Putin, there were no crises in the sovereign power realm.

For the most part, the Soviet power ministries did not play a role in sovereign power issues because deciding who ruled the state was the responsibility of the Communist Party. The key exception was during the Khrushchev era (1953–1964), when the military and the secret police were brought into these decisions on several occasions by various party factions contending for power.[27] The August 1991 coup attempt was thus a break with tradition, brought about by the potential collapse of the state. The heads of the KGB, MVD, and military were three of the coup plotters who tried to overthrow Mikhail Gorbachev in August 1991, and the foot-dragging and resistance of some of their subordinates played a key role in the failure of the putsch.

Indicators Project: Answering the Critics, World Bank Policy Research Working Paper 4149 (Washington, DC: The World Bank, March 2007), as well as the discussion in Chapter 1.

[26] Timothy J. Colton, "Perspectives on Civil-Military Relations in the Soviet Union," in Timothy J. Colton and Thane Gustafson, eds., *Soldiers and the Soviet State* (Princeton, NJ: Princeton University Press, 1990), 7–11.

[27] Brian D. Taylor, *Politics and the Russian Army: Civil-Military Relations, 1689–2000* (Cambridge: Cambridge University Press, 2003), pp. 175–192.

Similarly, the inactivity of these ministries in December 1991 permitted the collapse of a powerful military empire without a shot being fired.[28]

The new Russian state that came into being in January 1992 was weak in almost every respect, including in terms of its core political institutions. The constitution in place was still the heavily amended 1978 Soviet-era constitution, onto which had been grafted both the presidency and the key legislative body, the Congress of People's Deputies (CPD). The years 1992 and 1993 were marked by frequent and tense confrontations between President Yeltsin and the CPD, especially its speaker, Ruslan Khasbulatov. Khasbulatov was joined in his opposition to Yeltsin by Yeltsin's own vice-president, Aleksandr Rutskoy.

These confrontations culminated in Yeltsin's decision on September 21, 1993 to disband the legislature and call for new elections and a new constitution. Khasbulatov, Rutskoy, and a majority of the legislature resisted this move and swore in Rutskoy as an alternative president. Rutskoy promptly named his own directors of the three main power ministries – the Ministry of Defense (MO), the Ministry of Internal Affairs (MVD), and the Ministry of Security (MB), the main successor to the KGB, now called the Federal Security Service (FSB). Russia's power ministries were thus faced with two chief executives who both claimed authority over state coercive organs. The crisis escalated into violent confrontation on October 3, when pro-parliament forces attacked the Moscow mayor's office and the main television tower. Yeltsin called on the power ministries to repress this uprising, and the affair ended on October 4 when army tanks shelled the parliament building, the so-called White House, and pro-president special forces detained Rutskoy, Khasbulatov, and their allies.[29]

The violent October 1993 events were significant in terms of assessing state capacity in the coercive realm in two key respects. First, they demonstrated the fundamental importance of the power ministries in deciding who ruled the state. Other key actors – the Constitutional Court, regional leaders, even the Orthodox Church – that intervened in the standoff ultimately were unable to broker a compromise, and the side with the stronger claim over state coercion won the day.

Second, the weakness of the state's claim over a monopoly of legitimate violence, even in the ultimate question of who rules the state, was made clear. On the night of October 3–4, it was touch-and-go whether Yeltsin could mobilize government forces to his side. He was forced to go personally to the Ministry of Defense and meet with the military brass to secure the participation of army

---

[28] John B. Dunlop, "The August 1991 Coup and Its Impact on Soviet Politics," *Journal of Cold War Studies*, 5, 1 (Winter 2003), pp. 94–127; Amy Knight, "The KGB, Perestroika, and the Collapse of the Soviet Union," *Journal of Cold War Studies*, 5, 1 (Winter 2003), pp. 67–93; Brian D. Taylor, "The Soviet Military and the Disintegration of the USSR," *Journal of Cold War Studies*, 5, 1 (Winter 2003), pp. 17–66.

[29] I have covered these events in detail in: Taylor, *Politics and the Russian Army*, pp. 283–301. Cites to the relevant primary and secondary literature can be found there.

units, and the Minister of Defense, Pavel Grachev, only agreed after Yeltsin signed a public decree stating his responsibility for the use of the army. The situation was even worse with elite commando units, "Alpha" and "Vympel," that were, at the time, part of the Main Guard Directorate (GUO) responsible for leadership security; most of its members initially refused to participate in the operation. First Deputy Prime Minister Yegor Gaidar felt compelled to call on the public to rally in support of the government, and he made arrangements with Sergey Shoygu, the head of the Committee (later Ministry) on Emergency Situations, to arm private citizens, if necessary, to defend the government. The Ministry of Security proved ineffectual throughout the crisis, prompting Yeltsin to reorganize it once again after the events and to give greater power to the Presidential Security Service (SBP) and its head, Aleksandr Korzhakov.[30]

A second sovereign power crisis that narrowly avoided a possible repetition of the October 1993 events took place in March 1996. Yeltsin was up for reelection in June, and some of his closest confidants believed he was likely to be defeated by the Communist Party candidate, Gennadiy Zyuganov. Korzhakov and several others urged Yeltsin to cancel the elections, and Yeltsin actually ordered his staff to prepare a decree on disbanding the Duma, banning the Communist Party, and postponing the presidential elections. Yeltsin, however, eventually decided not to go ahead with the plan due to opposition from several key officials. Not only did his main political advisers object to the plan, but his Interior Minister, Anatoliy Kulikov, did as well. Kulikov claims he was motivated both by the knowledge that Yeltsin's decision was unconstitutional and by his belief that the government lacked reliable military and security forces to enforce the proposed measures. Tellingly, Minister of Defense Grachev was not brought into the planning for internal security; the MVD and the FSB were to take the lead role.[31]

Both the October 1993 and March 1996 events demonstrated the tenuous hold of the Russian president over the coercive organs of the executive branch. The capacity of the Russian state in the sovereign power realm was weak under Yeltsin.

Putin became president on the eve of the millennium, when Yeltsin unexpectedly resigned, and Putin, as Prime Minister, was elevated to acting president. Three months later, he was elected president. Whether his meteoric rise to the presidency involved the use of state coercive resources is a highly controversial issue. Specifically, multiple observers have argued that the series of apartment bombings in Moscow and elsewhere in September 1999 were not the work of pro-Chechen terrorists but the government itself, particularly the

---

[30] Yegor Gaidar, *Dni porazheniy i pobed* (Moskva, 1997), pp. 288–289; Aleksandr Korzhakov, *Boris Yel'tsin: Ot rassveta do zakata* (Moskva, 1997), p. 404; Yuriy Baturin et al., *Epokha Yel'tsina: Ocherki politicheskoy istorii* (Moskva: Vagrius, 2000), pp. 213–214.

[31] Anatoliy Kulikov, *Tyazhelye zvezdy* (Moskva: Voyna i Mir, 2002), 390–403; Baturin et al., 2000, 558–563; Boris Yel'tsin, *Prezidentskiy marafon: Razmyshleniya, vospominaniya, vpetchatleniya ...* (Moskva: AST, 2000), pp. 31–33; Interview M-30.

FSB, as part of an elaborate campaign to propel Putin to the presidency. The evidence for these claims is incomplete and ambiguous, however, so I discuss this episode further with other terrorist incidents.

This episode aside, there were no sovereign power crises under Putin like those under Yeltsin. However, the power ministries did have to cope with a different form of political violence – terrorism – during both the Yeltsin and Putin presidencies. How did they perform in coping not with exceptional tasks due to a sovereign power crisis, but the routine task established by law of preventing and responding to acts of terrorism?

Terrorism

Russia has faced a serious terrorist threat for most of the post-Soviet period. More than a thousand Russians have been killed in terrorist attacks since 1991. Most of these attacks are associated with the protracted war in Chechnya and political instability and violence elsewhere in the North Caucasus. For example, the first terrorist attack with substantial casualties took place in June 1995, when Chechen terrorists attacked a hospital in the city of Budennovsk in southern Russia (Stavropol region), taking more than 1,000 people hostage. More than 150 people were killed when Russian forces attempted to storm the building.[32] Other major terrorist attacks, such as the September 2004 Beslan school incident, also took place in and around Chechnya and the North Caucasus. Given the importance of this region for assessing the contribution of Russian power ministries to state capacity and quality, I devote a separate chapter to the North Caucasus. In this chapter, I discuss attacks in Moscow, including those associated with terrorists from Chechnya and neighboring republics.

Terrorism hit the Russian capital in spectacular fashion in September 1999, when two apartment buildings were destroyed in late-night bombings, killing over 200 people. The bombings came immediately after two major events in August 1999, the resumption of the Chechen war and the appointment of Putin as Prime Minister. In early August 1999, a group of Chechen rebels attacked the neighboring republic of Dagestan, hoping to expand the area in the North Caucasus under Islamic rule and de facto independent from Russia.[33] Putin made restoring order and Russian control in the region his top priority. In September, the conflict escalated dramatically when apartment buildings were blown up not only in Moscow but also in Dagestan and Volgodonsk in southern Russia. The government blamed these attacks on Chechens and used the reaction to the bombings to bolster support for a second war in Chechnya.

[32] A useful reference on major incidents is: Radio Free Europe/Radio Liberty, "Russia: A Timeline of Terrorism since 1995." Available at: http://www.rferl.org/

[33] Another part of the alleged conspiracy discussed here suggests that the Kremlin itself engineered the attack on Dagestan as a justification for a new war. For a discussion, see: Evangelista 2002, pp. 77–80.

Subsequently, the government tried and convicted several alleged Islamic radicals from the North Caucasus, and blamed a group of rebel field commanders, some now dead and some still at large, for organizing the attacks.[34]

Almost immediately after the bombings, it was suggested that the government, or elements within the government, were behind the attacks. The supposed rationale was to whip up public support for a new war in Chechnya and for the new prime minister and potential president Putin. The primary evidence for this conspiracy is actually a bombing that did not take place, in the city of Ryazan in central Russia on September 22. A vigilant citizen noticed a suspicious car and its occupants unloading sacks into the basement of an apartment building, and called the police. At first the authorities claimed they had averted a terrorist attack, but two days later FSB head Nikolay Patrushev said it had been a training exercise. Other fishy details, such as whether the sacks involved contained explosives or sugar, further raised suspicions. And the peculiarities of the Ryazan incident led to the conclusion that if the FSB was conducting an attack in Ryazan, it was behind the other bombings as well.[35] Eight years after the attacks, according to a 2007 poll, the Russian public had no clear sense of who stood behind the attacks. Only 5 percent of poll respondents declared themselves fully satisfied with the work of investigators and law enforcement, whereas 54 percent were either completely or partially dissatisfied with law enforcement work, with the reason for the attack remaining unclear.[36]

If there really was a conspiracy to propel Putin to the presidency by blowing up multiple apartment buildings, with the active involvement of the FSB and perhaps the Main Intelligence Directorate (GRU) of the armed forces, the role of the power ministries in sovereign power issues and the post-Yeltsin succession would have to be evaluated as not only crucial, but also criminal. The currently available evidence on these bombings, however, is so ambiguous, fragmented, and contradictory that firm conclusions seem unwarranted.

There are several good reasons to doubt the conspiracy version, however. First, the cause-and-effect relationship posited by the theory – provoke another war in Chechnya (three years after the end of a very unpopular war) and blow up some apartment buildings in order to elect our preferred candidate

---

[34] For the government version, see the General Procuracy account in a letter to State Duma Deputy A. Kulikov: http://terror99.ru/documents/doc24.htm. This website contains many materials about the 1999 events and subsequent investigations, particularly those that emphasize the likelihood of FSB involvement.

[35] The conspiracy version of the 1999 apartment bombings is summarized in: David Satter, *Darkness at Dawn: The Rise of the Russian Criminal State* (New Haven, CT: Yale University Press, 2003), pp. 24–33, 64–69, 250–252. For the view that North Caucasian Islamic radicals were behind the bombings, see Robert Bruce Ware, "Revisiting Russia's Apartment Block Blasts," *Journal of Slavic Military Studies*, 18 (2005), pp. 599–606. Presenting both sides are: Evangelista 2002, pp. 80–84; Andrew Jack, *Inside Putin's Russia* (Oxford: Oxford University Press, 2004), pp. 102–110.

[36] Levada Tsentr, "Osen' 1999," September 28, 2007 [http://www.levada.ru/press/2007092806.html]; Yevgeniya Zubchenko, "'Polnoy kartiny net do sikh por," *NI*, October 1, 2007.

as president – is dubious. Although it is true that these events did help propel Putin to the presidency, this in and of itself is not evidence that this was the goal of the attacks. In hindsight, we can see the results, but the conspiracy version posits that Putin, Yeltsin, or people close to them decided in the summer of 1999 that this was the best possible strategy to make Putin president. If it was a conspiracy, it was a very desperate one. Second, the invasion of Dagestan, on top of the multiple kidnappings in the region in previous years, presented sufficient cause for war, even without the bombings. Third, a key problem with the conspiracy version is the number of actual bombings. Why blow up five different apartment buildings in four different cities? One or two in Moscow would have been more than adequate to justify a new war and the election of a "strong man" as president to restore order. Each subsequent bombing arguably was not only unnecessary but potentially dangerous because it increased the risk of the conspiracy coming to light. Fourth, it suggests considerable confidence in those behind the conspiracy that a plot involving multiple players in and out of government, and presumably a considerable number of FSB operatives, could be kept secret – a proposition that also seems dubious.

The most obvious explanation could well be the correct one – that Islamic radicals from the North Caucasus, who both before and after 1999 showed a willingness to carry out deadly terrorist attacks, also were responsible for the apartment bombings. The major problem with this version is the Ryazan incident, but recognizing the peculiarities of this episode does not lead inevitably to the conspiracy theory. For example, it is plausible that the FSB really did simulate an attack in Ryazan in order to subsequently "uncover" it and claim credit for doing so, but the vigilance of local citizens and law enforcement personnel in responding foiled these plans. The "training exercise" justification was improvised once the plan fell apart.[37]

Which version of the 1999 bombings is correct has important implications for our understanding of Russian state capacity vis-à-vis the power ministries. If there really was a conspiracy, then one would have to evaluate the state's capacity to implement exceptional decisions involving the use of the power ministries against innocent citizens as very high. Although the conspiracy did not go off without a hitch, given the controversy about it, the goals were accomplished with no definitive proof coming out. On the other hand, if the bombings really were the result of North Caucasian terrorists, then how to evaluate state capacity is less clear. Failure to prevent one or two attacks is not in itself an indictment, unless we are going to assess the capacity of states such as the United States, the United Kingdom, and Spain

---

[37] This version has been suggested by two of Russia's most astute political observers, Vladimir Pribylovskiy and Yuliya Latynina: Gregory Feifer, "Three Years Later, Moscow Apartment Bombings Remain Unsolved," *RFE/RL*, September 6, 2002; Yuliya Latynina, "Poymayut li terroristov, obvarivshikh rebenka kipyatkom?" *Yezhednev. Zh.*, June 14, 2005.

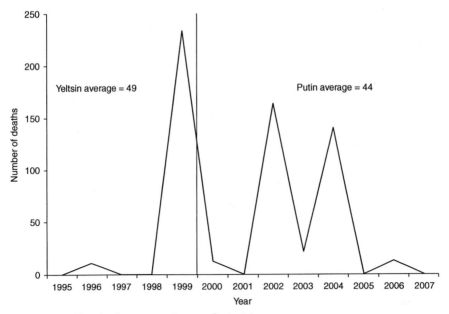

FIGURE 3.2. Deaths from terrorist attacks in Moscow, 1995–2007.

as weak. But four major attacks in less than two weeks in September 1999 suggest that Russian security services were ill-prepared for terrorist attacks. On the other hand, the Russian government claims to have either arrested and sentenced or killed in conflict most of the alleged organizers and implementers of the attacks. In my view, we do not have enough evidence to decide which version of the 1999 bombings is correct and thus to draw any firm conclusions about what these attacks demonstrate about the capacity of Russian power ministries.

Additional attacks in Moscow in subsequent years, especially from 2002 to 2004, further suggest the difficulty Russia's security and law enforcement services had in coping with the terrorist challenge. Terrorists attacked the subway, restaurants and hotels, a theater, an outdoor rock concert, and airplanes. Almost all of these attacks were carried out by groups or individuals affiliated with or sympathetic to Chechen rebels. From the time the Chechen war began in late 1994 through 2007, nearly 600 people were killed in terrorism-related violence in Moscow (see Figure 3.2). In general, there is a very small improvement from Yeltsin to Putin in terms of deaths from terrorism in the capital when comparing the two presidencies, with slightly lower average yearly death figures under Putin (forty-four per year) compared to Yeltsin (forty-nine per year), although if the period before the Chechen war was included, the Yeltsin average would drop to thirty-one per year. Moreover, all of the major attacks under Yeltsin took place in autumn 1999, when Putin was already Prime Minister and thus also responsible for Russia's "war on terror." The figure also shows that, rather than presenting a consistent threat, major attacks were concentrated in three different years (1999, 2002, and 2004).[38]

More important than the number of deaths in assessing state capacity is how the power ministries coped with this major challenge. In this respect, particularly in the deadliest attacks, there is clear evidence of these agencies' failings and their weak capacity to cope with one of their core tasks. The largest single attack in Moscow was the October 2002 *Nord-Ost* theater attack, in which nearly 1,000 theater-goers were held hostage by 40 terrorists who sought an end to the Chechen war. The siege ended after two and a half days when special forces pumped a special gas into the theater, intended to knock out the terrorists (and, by necessity, the hostages). Special forces subsequently shot all of the terrorists, and 140 hostages died, primarily as a result of the gas. Observers later pointed to multiple security and law enforcement lapses during the crisis, including evidence that some of the terrorists acquired residency registration illegally from the police, and the failure of the secret services to inform medical personnel about the nature of the gas attack, which caused many unnecessary deaths. The ability of dozens of terrorists to arrive in Moscow, with weapons and explosives, and move around the city undetected also raised questions, including whether they had illegally acquired special transportation passes or bribed traffic police.[39] In another key attack, the August 2004 airplane bombings of two flights originating in Moscow, similar lapses were evident. The two terrorists purchased their plane tickets from a scalper shortly before boarding, paid a bribe to an airline employee to get around the document check, and an antiterrorism officer at the airport let them board without searching their baggage (although no formal accusations of a bribe were issued in the case of this officer).[40]

The number and lethality of terrorist attacks in Russia under Putin demonstrate a state failing to cope with a serious security threat. Indeed, Russia experienced more major terrorist attacks (defined as more than ten people

---

[38] Data from: Pavel K. Baev, "The Targets of Terrorism and the Aims of Counter-Terrorism in Moscow, Chechnya, and the North Caucasus," Paper for the annual meeting of the International Studies Association, Chicago, March 2007; Pavel K. Baev, "Putin's 'Crushing Blow' on Terrorism: Is Chechnya Really Pacified and Is Stability Restored in the North Caucasus?" unpublished paper, June 2008. I thank Pavel Baev for sharing his updated data with me.

[39] Dmitry Babich, "Terrorists' Not-So-Little Helpers," *RP*, October 25, 2004; Nabi Abdullaev, "Picture Emerges of How They Did It," *MT*, November 6, 2002; Peter Baker and Susan Glasser, *Kremlin Rising*, updated edition (Dulles, Virginia: Potomac Books, 2007), pp. 156–178; John B. Dunlop, *The 2002 Dubrovka and 2004 Beslan Hostage Crises: A Critique of Russian Counter-Terrorism* (Stuttgart: ibidem-Verlag, 2006). Dunlop provides the most detailed account in English of the *Nord-Ost* event. He argues that the incident was a "joint venture" between Chechen extremists and the Russian special services to scuttle the prospects for a settlement of the conflict, because both sides had an interest in the war continuing. His evidence on this point, however, is far from conclusive.

[40] Babich 2004; Kim Murphy, "Russia May Pay for Bribes in Lives," *Los Angeles Times*, November 8, 2004.

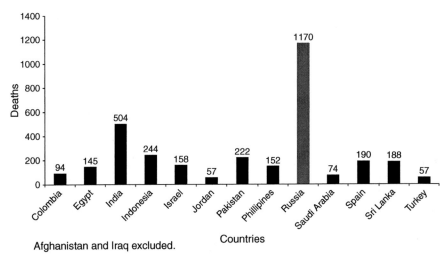

FIGURE 3.3. Deaths by major terrorist attack, October 2001–June 2007.

killed) from October 2001 to June 2007 than any country other than Iraq and Afghanistan. Russia had fourteen such incidents, followed by Pakistan with ten and Israel and India with nine. The number of people killed in major terrorist attacks in Russia during this period was 1,170, the highest total in the world, again excluding Afghanistan and Iraq. Countries with serious terrorist problems, including Israel, India, Pakistan, Colombia, Indonesia, and Sri Lanka, had both fewer attacks and significantly fewer deaths during this period, although Pakistan experienced a major wave of terrorist attacks after these data were published (see Figure 3.3).[41]

Perhaps Russia really faced a more serious and determined threat than all of these countries, and this explains the higher number of attacks and casualties. Also, terrorism is typically thought of as a "weapon of the weak," so these attacks can at least in part be explained by the inability of extremist Islamic groups from the North Caucasus to defeat Russia's military and security forces on the battlefield. There is good reason, however, to think that weak capacity in the law enforcement and security realm contributed to these results. The Russian terrorism expert Anatoliy Tsyganok noted that throughout the post-Soviet period, there has been a "game of leapfrog in terms of responsibility for fighting terrorism." Between 1998 and 2006, there were five different laws or presidential decrees that rearranged organizational responsibility for terrorism between the FSB, the MVD, the military, and other state bodies. Despite these multiple reorganizations, or perhaps because of them,

---

[41] William C. Banks, Mitchel B. Wallerstein, and Renée de Nevers, *Combating Terrorism: Strategies and Approaches* (Washington, DC: CQ Press, 2008), pp. 234–236. Supplemental data collected from: List of Terrorist Incidents, *Wikipedia* [http://en.wikipedia.org/wiki/List_of_terrorist_incidents].

long-standing barriers between agencies were not broken down. For example, the FSB traditionally has not shared information received from other countries' law enforcement and intelligence services, such as the FBI, with the MVD or the armed forces.[42]

The 2006 antiterrorism law placed responsibility for fighting terrorism on the FSB at both the national and regional level, and created a National Antiterrorism Committee (NAC) chaired by the FSB director. Similar structures were created at the regional level. The NAC routinely issued press statements claiming responsibility for preventing hundreds of attacks, but the precise meaning of those numbers is very unclear. The decline in major terrorist incidents after 2004 may be explained by FSB work, including the death of Russian "Terrorist Number 1" Shamil Basayev, but it also reflected a change in strategy by Islamic rebels after the counterproductive Beslan incident. There was little concrete evidence that the capabilities of the power ministries had significantly improved. For example, Tor Bukkvoll showed very limited organizational learning in the power ministries about how to cope with hostage crises, despite facing multiple such incidents since 1995. Bukkvoll attributed this poor learning to a range of factors, including: the tendency to ignore formal regulations during crises, relying instead on specific persons in an ad hoc fashion; fear of responsibility on the part of officials; and distrust between different institutions. Bukkvoll also noted a very high tolerance for civilian casualties and an inexplicable "self-congratulatory attitude" after crises. Even after major events such as the *Nord-Ost* and Beslan attacks, the federal authorities were disinclined to critically evaluate their own performance.[43] It is hard to imagine that the political leadership of any of the major industrial democracies, or indeed of most other countries, would be so complacent about power ministry performance if an average of more than forty people per year were killed by terrorists in the country's capital for a period of more than a decade. The March 2010 Moscow subway terrorist bombing, which killed forty people, demonstrated that the threat to the capital remained serious under Medvedev. The capacity of the state to cope with political violence was still shaky.

STATE CAPACITY AND LAW ENFORCEMENT

Coping with extraordinary political violence, like terrorism and sovereign power crises, is only part of what state coercive agencies are expected to do. Maintaining public order and fighting crime are also key spheres of

---

[42] Anatoliy Tsyganok, "Anti-terroristicheskaya bezotvetstvennost'," *Polit.Ru*, March 21, 2006 [http://www.polit.ru/analytics/2006/03/21/zakon.html]. The unwillingness of the KGB/FSB to share information with the MVD was also true in the Soviet period: Interview M-5.

[43] Andrei Smirnov, "No Terrorist Acts in Russia Since Beslan: Whom to Thank?" *CW*, May 24, 2007; Tor Bukkvoll, "Waiting for the next Beslan – Russia's handling of major hostage-takings," Norwegian Defence Research Establishment (FFI) Report No. 2007/01888, August 8, 2007. See also: Baev 2007.

responsibility. I first assess the effectiveness of the Russian government in general in comparative context, and then turn to an evaluation of the capacity of Russian law enforcement in both routine and exceptional activities. A key routine task for law enforcement is fighting crime, and the murder rate is one key indicator of state effectiveness. Although maintaining public order is also a routine task, what happened in Russia under Putin was the rebuilding of a "regime of repression" that was directed against political and economic opponents of the Kremlin, which involved the implementation of exceptional decisions.

Government Effectiveness: A Comparative Assessment

The most common understandings of state capacity, and the one used here, is the ability of a state to ensure the reliable implementation of its decisions by its own personnel – what Michael Mann calls infrastructural power. The World Bank Governance project includes six different measures of good governance, one of which is "government effectiveness," defined as "the quality of public services, the quality of the civil service and the degree of its independence from political pressures, the quality of policy formulation and implementation, and the credibility of the government's commitment to such policies."[44] Although this definition combines several issues I would keep analytically separate, including distinctions between autonomy and capacity and capacity and quality, it does give us some purchase on evaluating Russian state capacity in comparative terms.

Russia's scores on this indicator moved it up from the bottom thirtieth percentile in 1996 to around the fortieth percentile in 2005–2007. Russia's percentile ranking was noticeably higher in Putin's last year in office than during his first year in office (42 percent compared to 33 percent). However, after reaching the fiftieth percentile in 2003, Russia's ranking declined markedly from 2003 to 2006 before registering a slight increase in 2007 (see Figure 3.4). Russia's rating on this indicator was actually slightly above average for its income category for a couple of years, the only such result among the five WGI that we evaluate in this book. However, once Russia moved to a higher income category in 2004, it again became a comparative underperformer. To put it differently, Russia's growing wealth has not been matched by a corresponding increase in government effectiveness.

Still, the increase from 2000 to 2003 was substantial and impressive. What does this increase, and the subsequent decrease, reflect? WGI are based on perceptions – what did outside experts observe? Given the sources for this measure, the big increase in Putin's first term is most likely attributable to the passage of a large number of liberal economic reform measures that had

[44] Sources used to measure Government Effectiveness include several business competitiveness and risk surveys, the Economist Intelligence Unit, and the Bertelsmann Transformation Index.

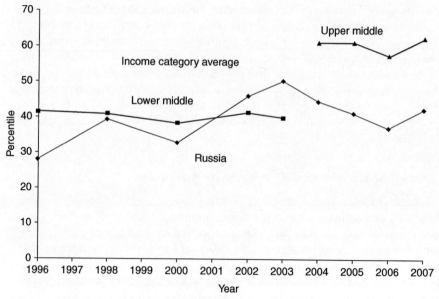

FIGURE 3.4. Government effectiveness (WGI).

been stymied by the more communist-leaning Duma under Yeltsin. Prominent examples include tax reform, new land and labor codes, judicial reform, a law on bankruptcy, and a series of changes designed to reduce government regulation in the economic sphere. In contrast, by 2003, the pace of economic reform measures slowed noticeably, and Putin concentrated on political measures that restricted opposition to Kremlin power.[45]

William Tompson argued persuasively in 2005 that "the progress of Putin's drive to rebuild the state has been decidedly uneven." Tompson noted a rise in the state's coercive and extractive capacities, but continuing weaknesses in service provision, administrative and regulative abilities, and "rule-enforcement powers." He observed that "the mere fact that the state's coercive capacities are far greater than its other capabilities creates incentives to rely heavily on coercion or the threat of coercion." Similarly, Gerald Easter highlighted a "renewed readiness to use coercion" under Putin.[46]

How did the state use these coercive abilities? In terms of routine tasks, Russia has very high homicide rates comparatively, and they were no lower overall under Putin than under Yeltsin, but they did drop steadily after 2003. One exceptional task that law enforcement did cope with effectively was

---

[45] A good overview of legislation passed and the shift in priorities is: Thomas F. Remington, "Putin, the Parliament, and the Party System," in Dale R. Herspring, ed., *Putin's Russia: Past Imperfect, Future Uncertain*, 3rd edition (Lanham, MD: Rowman & Littlefield, 2007), pp. 53–73.

[46] William Tompson, "Putting Yukos in Perspective," *Post-Soviet Affairs*, 21, 2 (2005), pp. 165, 175–176; Easter 2008, p. 206.

undermining opposition parties and candidates during elections. This task reflected a more fundamental change in Russian law enforcement under Putin, evidenced most clearly in the aggressive policing of opposition demonstrations in 2007: Russia was returning to a more repressive type of policing compared to that under Yeltsin, consistent with the overall shift toward authoritarianism under Putin.

Fighting Crime: Russia's Homicide Problem

The Soviet government claimed that crime was less of a problem in socialist countries than capitalist ones. We now know that these claims were dubious and, not surprisingly, that Soviet crime data were unreliable. Data made available since the Soviet collapse show, for example, that the homicide rate in the Soviet Union was comparable to that in the U.S. since at least the mid-1960s. Criminologists often use murder rates as a proxy for overall crime in cross-national studies, because other crime statistics, particularly those compiled by police and law enforcement agencies, are notoriously unreliable. In Russia, there have been multiple reasons over the decades for suppression of crime statistics, including police evaluation criteria based on crime rates and crime clearance rates.[47] Moreover, criminologists find the Russian Ministry of Health mortality data more reliable than murder statistics provided by the MVD. In the 1990s, the MVD regularly reported less than 75 percent of the homicides recorded by the health ministry.[48] Thus, we use Ministry of Health homicide data as a proxy for analyzing patterns of violent crime in Russia.

Post-Soviet Russia has one of the highest homicides rates in the world. It shot up dramatically in the early 1990s, declined in the second half of the decade, and then rose again after the 1998 economic crisis. It kept rising until 2002 and declined steadily after that, with the 2007 level (18 per 100,000 people) the lowest since the 1991 collapse (see Figure 3.5).[49] Despite this sharp decline in Putin's second term, the average for the Yeltsin (1992–1999) and Putin (2000–2007) years is virtually identical, between 26 and 27 homicides per 100,000 people annually.

[47] On this problem, see: Demos, *Reforma pravookhranitel'nikh organov: preodoleniye proizvola* (Moskva: Demos, 2005), pp. 13–17; K.K. Goryainov, V.S. Ovchinskiy, L.V. Kondratyuk, *Uluchsheniye vzaimootnosheniy grazhdan i militsii: Dostup k pravosudiyu i sistema vyyavleniya, registratsii i ucheta prestupleniy* (Moskva: INFRA-M, 2001); Adrian Beck and Annette Robertson, *Public Attitudes to Crime and Policing in Russia* (Scarman Centre, University of Leicester, United Kingdom, 2002).

[48] William Alex Pridemore, "Demographic, Temporal, and Spatial Patterns of Homicide Rates in Russia," *European Sociological Review*, 19, 1 (2003), pp. 42–43; Natalia S. Gavrilova et al., "Patterns of Violent Crime in Russia," in William Alex Pridemore, ed., *Ruling Russia: Law, Crime, and Justice in a Changing Society* (Lanham, MD: Rowman & Littlefield, 2005), pp. 117–121.

[49] Russian Ministry of Health data, available from the Federal State Statistics Service website [www.gks.ru.]. I thank Bill Pridemore, Vladimir Popov, and Mark Kramer for help with homicide statistics.

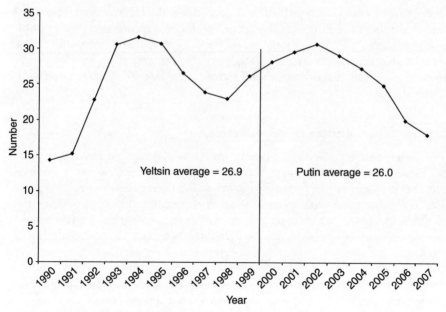

FIGURE 3.5. Murders per 100,000 population, 1990–2007.

Moreover, Russia's murder rate is extremely high on a comparative basis; only some countries of Southern Africa and Central and South America have higher rates. In Western Europe, the average is 1–2 per 100,000 population, in the U.S. the rate is 5–7 per 100,000, the world average is about 8 per 100,000, and in very high-crime countries like Mexico and Brazil, the rate is approximately 15–20 per 100,000. Of seventy-four countries in a 2002 World Health Organization study, based on data from the 1990s, Russia had the fourth-highest murder rate in the world. It is true that homicide rates are relatively high in almost all post-Soviet countries, including the Baltic states, but even among this subset of countries, Russia has the highest rate. Throughout the post-Soviet era, Russia has had one of the highest murder rates in the world and the highest in Europe.[50]

The reasons for Russia's high homicide rate are multiple and in dispute, but several factors stand out, including historically high patterns of murder,

[50] Etienne G. Krug et al., eds., *World Report on Violence and Health* (Geneva: World Health Organization, 2002), pp. 308–313; United Nations, *The Seventh United Nations Survey on Crime Trends and the Operations of Criminal Justice Systems (1998–2000)*; United Nations, *The Eighth United Nations Survey on Crime Trends and the Operations of Criminal Justice Systems (2001–2002)* [both available at: http://www.unodc.org/]; Jan Van Dijk, *The World of Crime: Breaking the Silence on Problems of Security, Justice, and Development Across the World* (Los Angeles: Sage Publications, 2008), pp. 77–78; Gavrilova et al., 2005, p. 121.

alcohol abuse, and social and economic dislocation.[51] The last factor obviously increased substantially in the last two decades, and researchers have linked high Russian homicide rates to the economic depression, increased poverty, and social changes (such as family situation) of the transition.[52] Although cross-national studies are contradictory, poverty generally seems to be related to homicide, whereas economic growth is inversely related.[53] Yuriy Andriyenko predicted in 2001 that stable economic growth would lead to a drop in violent crime, and this seems the most likely explanation for the post-2002 decline in Russia's homicide rate.[54] Further, the economic and social dislocation brought about by the revolutionary changes of the early 1990s is gradually disappearing as people find their place in the new order. In other words, Russia's lower murder rate over the last few years is not due to an increase in the capacity of state law enforcement organs, but rather to broader socio-economic changes.[55] At the same time, poor law enforcement obviously is not to blame for many homicides that involve, as one U.S. government official put it to me, "drunks killing drunks."[56]

Some researchers suggest that poor law enforcement work contributes to Russia's relatively high murder rate.[57] As shown in Chapter 2, Russia has a more than adequate number of police officers; indeed, its police force is comparatively quite large. Russia's continued extremely high murder rate on a comparative basis is a disappointment given the increased power and resources of Russia's law enforcement and security organs under Putin. On the other hand, the sharp decline since 2002, if the data are to be believed, may show that law enforcement capacity has started to increase.[58]

---

[51] For an overview of the scientific literature connecting high alcohol consumption to Russia's high homicide rate, see: William Alex Pridemore, "The Role of Alcohol in Russia's Violent Mortality," *RAD*, No. 35 (February 19, 2008).

[52] Gavrilova et al., 2005, pp. 137, 141–144; Yu. V. Andriyenko, "V poiskakh ob"yasneniya rosta prestupnosti v Rossii v perekhodnyy period: kriminometricheskiy podkhod," *Ekonomicheskiy zhurnal VShE*, 5, 2 (2001), p. 213; Pridemore 2003, p. 50.

[53] Travis C. Pratt and Christopher T. Lowenkamp, "Conflict Theory, Economic Conditions, and Homicide: A Time-Series Analysis," *Homicide Studies*, 6, 1 (February 2002), pp. 61–83; Gary LaFree, "A Summary and Review of Cross-National Comparative Studies of Homicide," in M. Dwayne Smith and Margaret A. Zahn, eds., *Homicide: A Sourcebook of Social Research* (Thousand Oaks, CA: Sage Publications, 1999), pp. 140–141; personal communication from William Pridemore, October 5, 2007.

[54] Andriyenko 2001, p. 215.

[55] It is also possible that coroners are again manipulating cause of death decisions to reduce the homicide rate, as they did in the Soviet period; there is some anecdotal evidence of this. See: Pridemore 2003, p. 43; Gavrilova et al., 2005, p. 120; personal communication from William Pridemore, October 7, 2006.

[56] Dan Goldberg, Department of Defense, personal communication, November 2007.

[57] Gavrilova et al., 2005, pp. 141–142; Andriyenko 2001.

[58] It is worth noting that WB Governance measures of government effectiveness for Russia do not covary in logical ways with murder rates. Assessments of government effectiveness increased while the murder rate was going up, and generally decreased while the murder rate

Looking at law enforcement effectiveness more broadly, attempts to measure police capacity in cross-national studies are in their infancy, but available measures suggest Russian performance in this respect is weak. For example, Jan Van Dijk and his collaborators have constructed a cross-national index of "police performance" based on five variables, such as surveys from the International Crime Victims Survey about the propensity to report crimes to the police, and satisfaction with police performance. On this index, Russia scored 33.6 out of 100 (100 being the best) with data from the early 2000s, which ranked it 85th out of 114 countries. The average "police performance" scores for the ten other post-Soviet countries included in the index was 45.53, although several countries, including Lithuania and Ukraine, scored lower than Russia. On Van Dijk's Composite Organized Crime Index, Russia ranked 7th out of 156 countries, with a score of 88.2 out of 100 (100 indicating the most organized crime), with only Haiti, Paraguay, Albania, Nigeria, Guatemala, and Venezuela ranking higher.[59] Although only suggestive, these comparative data, like the homicide figures, suggested that the law enforcement capacity of the Russian state in dealing with its core routine competency – crime – was relatively low.

Policing the Opposition: Rebuilding a Regime of Repression

An important task of the power ministries in the Soviet period was enforcing what Mark Beissinger calls a "regime of repression." According to Beissinger, a regime of repression includes both "a set of regularized practices of repression" and "internalized expectations" among citizens about how the state will respond to challenges. By the late-Soviet period, from the mid-1960s to the mid-1980s, the Soviet state had created a highly effective regime of repression based on "the predictable, consistent, and efficient application of low level and moderate coercion." This regime, however, unraveled under Gorbachev, when the authorities tried to make room for legal demonstrations but were unable to establish consistent practices for maintaining order at the local level, especially in some of the national republics. In effect, the Soviet regime of repression collapsed in the face of nationalist mobilization.[60]

The task of maintaining public order and policing protest changed under Boris Yeltsin. A Soviet-style regime of repression was no longer appropriate once democratic rights were at least formally established. But the Russian state still needed procedures for sanctioning and policing legal protests, and repressing violent challenges to the state. Street violence and bloodshed that

---

was going down (see Figures 3.4 and 3.5). The most likely explanation for this pattern is that effectiveness assessments are based more on economic policy making than law enforcement work.

[59] Van Dijk 2008, pp. 165–166, 224, 360–362, 375–377.

[60] Mark R. Beissinger, *Nationalist Mobilization and the Collapse of the Soviet State* (Cambridge: Cambridge University Press, 2002), pp. 320–384 (quotes pp. 326, 334).

accompanied the sovereign power crisis of September–October 1993 was further evidence that the power ministries, using the techniques developed in the Soviet period for dealing with protests, were not up to the task. The regime of repression that collapsed under Gorbachev had not yet been reconstituted as a mechanism for public order maintenance in a democracy. This was further confirmed in March 1996, when Interior Minister Kulikov told Yeltsin that he doubted the ability of the power ministries to implement an order closing down the Duma and canceling elections.

Under Putin, especially in his second term, a more concerted effort was made to rebuild a regime of repression, adapted to the new circumstances of "competitive authoritarianism."[61] We see this regime of repression both in the aggressive policing of opposition demonstrations in 2007 and in the systematic harassment of opposition politicians and parties, especially during elections. The latter task – harassing opposition parties and candidates during elections – clearly counts as the implementation of exceptional decisions. How to categorize the policing of demonstrations is more complicated. Although the maintenance of public order during protests surely counts as a routine task, the techniques used against opposition groups compared to those used against pro-Putin organizations also suggest that law enforcement organs were implementing exceptional decisions in these cases.

The use of what Steven Levitsky and Lucan Way call "low intensity coercion" against opposition parties and politicians occasionally took place in the 1990s under Yeltsin, but most of this activity was locally instigated and directed, particularly by regional governors.[62] After 2000, the Kremlin steadily increased its power to manipulate the electoral process, including through the use of law enforcement organs. Although less dramatic than the violent street confrontations of October 1993, this state use of the police and procuracy against opposition parties and politicians was important. In particular, it showed how under Putin, the exceptional decisions of state leaders (as opposed to routine tasks) were implemented by law enforcement organs, a phenomenon that suggests an increase in state capacity but is problematic for assessing state quality.

Russians euphemistically call the manipulation of elections by the executive branch the use of "administrative resources." Vladimir Pribylovskiy distinguishes between "honest" and "dishonest" administrative resources. Honest ones are basically advantages of incumbency. Dishonest ones, or "low intensity coercion," include preventing opposition candidates from registering to run or mounting an effective campaign, as well as outright falsification of the vote. The primary administrative resources used by the executive branch at both

---

[61] Steven Levitsky and Lucan A. Way, "The Rise of Competitive Authoritarianism," *Journal of Democracy*, 13, 2 (2002), pp. 51–65.

[62] Lucan A. Way and Steven Levitsky, "The Dynamics of Autocratic Coercion after the Cold War," *Communist and Post-Communist Studies*, 39 (2006), pp. 387–410.

the federal and regional level are electoral commissions and courts. On occasion, however, law enforcement organs, specifically the procuracy, the FSB,
and the MVD, are also used against opposition candidates. Pribylovskiy gives
a stylized example, the opening of a criminal case, "including a completely
fabricated one," against an undesirable candidate.[63]

One prominent case of the use of law enforcement organs to shape an election was the fall 2003 election of Putin ally Valentina Matviyenko as mayor
of Putin's hometown, St. Petersburg. Matviyenko, at the time Putin's envoy
to the Northwest Federal District, was endorsed by Putin and became the
clear favorite to become mayor, particularly after several potentially viable
candidates were persuaded not to run. Putin and his team, however, were leaving nothing to chance. The local procurator, appointed by Moscow, set up a
working group to monitor the elections, which included representatives from
the MVD and FSB. The police engaged in multiple dubious acts during the
campaign, including seizing campaign materials of Matviyenko opponents,
detaining opposition campaign workers, and issuing questionable opinions
about the number of falsified signatures in the filing papers of Matviyenko's
main opponent, Deputy Mayor Anna Markova. A criminal case was even
opened against the director of a printing company for "slander"; his company
had printed opposition materials that criticized Matviyenko. Matviyenko
won the election in the second round, but the low turnout (28 percent) and
high percentage of those voting "against all" (11 percent) suggested that many
Petersburg voters were turned off by the aggressive use of administrative
resources on Matviyenko's behalf.[64]

Another example of the use of law enforcement assets as administrative
resources in Russian elections was the 2002 presidential election in the republic of Ingushetia (the heads of Russia's twenty-one ethnic republics usually
carry the title of president, although they are equivalent to a governor). The
candidate with the highest public opinion rating, Ingush Interior Minister
Khamzat Gutseriyev, was forced from the ballot on the eve of the election.
The Kremlin could not rely on local militia personnel, given Gutseriyev's position, or trust the local courts, so Putin's envoy to the North Caucasus, Viktor
Kazantsev, accompanied by armed men, interrupted and stopped the Ingush
Supreme Court hearing on Gutseriyev's candidacy. Kazantsev argued that the
Russian Supreme Court should hear the case, and Gutseriyev was disqualified
by the national court two days before the election. Putin's favored candidate,
Murat Zyazikov, a FSB general and Kazantsev's deputy, still finished thirteen
percentage points behind another candidate in the first round, so in the second

[63] Vladimir Pribylovskiy, "Upravlyaemye vybory: Degradatsiya vyborov pri Putine," in
Vladimir Pribylovskiy, ed., *Rossiya Putina: Istoriya bolezni* (Moskva: Tsentr Panorama,
2004). Available at: http://www.scilla.ru/works/uprdem/putiros2.html
[64] Pribylovskiy 2004; Gordon M. Hahn, "Managed Democracy? Building Stealth
Authoritarianism in St. Petersburg," *Demokratizatsiya*, 12, 2 (Spring 2004), pp. 195–231;
Nick Paton Walsh, "Dirty tricks alleged in St Petersburg poll," *The Guardian* (UK), September
20, 2003; Nikolai Petrov, "A Mismanaged Election," *MT*, September 23, 2003.

round, no observers were allowed and the FSB monitored the voting. Zyazikov won.[65]

In both the 2003 Duma elections and the 2004 presidential elections, there were credible reports of opposition candidates being harassed by law enforcement officials. The detention of campaign workers and impoundment of campaign materials by the police during the 2003 Duma elections were reported in such diverse locales as the Moscow oblast, Volgograd, Bashkortostan, and Vladivostok. One of Putin's more competitive opponents during his reelection campaign in 2004, Sergey Glazev, faced repeated obstacles in trying to arrange campaign appearances, including unannounced fire inspections and police investigations of bomb threats. Glazev and other opposition candidates faced multiple procuracy investigations into their signature drives to get on the ballot. In contrast, United Russia and candidates supported by Putin, as well as Putin himself, routinely receive favorable court and electoral commission decisions even when there was credible evidence of violations of the electoral law. Gordon Hahn calls this the "negative" use of administrative resources, "that is, they refuse to deploy against officially backed candidates." European election observers also raised concerns about the behavior of police at some polling stations and the lack of clear guidelines for militia conduct.[66] In other cases, law enforcement organs were used after the elections to suppress popular protests, including blocking roads, tear-gassing protesters, and seizing radio stations by force.[67]

Not all of these and similar instances of the use of administrative resources, including law enforcement, can be attributed to the Kremlin. Certainly in some cases, local officials acted on their own, either to advance their own interests or to conform to perceived Kremlin expectations. Most observers agree, however, that if in the 1990s, law enforcement tended to be used by regional and local officials in some areas to interfere with elections, after 2000, the process became much more controlled by the national executive branch.[68] In 2003, a directive from the central MVD to its regional branches included monitoring the violation of election laws as one of the militia's key tasks for the year. The head of the Novosibirsk police, Aleksandr Soinov, expressed puzzlement concerning Putin's call for the police to insure good elections, noting that the

[65] M. Steven Fish, *Democracy Derailed in Russia: The Failure of Open Politics* (Cambridge: Cambridge University Press, 2005), pp. 63–64; Matthew Evangelista, "Ingushetia as a Microcosm of Putin's Reforms," *PONARS Policy Memo*, 346 (November 2004).

[66] *OSCE/ODIHR Election Observation Mission Report: Russian Federation: Elections to the State Duma 7 December 2003* (Warsaw: OSCE/ODIHR, January 27, 2004), pp. 13, 18, 21, 27; *OSCE/ODIHR Election Observation Mission Report: Russian Federation: Presidential Election 14 March 2004* (Warsaw: OSCE/ODIHR, June 2, 2004), pp. 12, 19, 23, 27; Hahn 2004, p. 215.

[67] Pribylovskiy 2004.

[68] Pribylovskiy 2004; Cameron Ross, "Federalism and Electoral Authoritarianism under Putin," *Demokratizatsiya*, 13, 3 (Summer 2005), pp. 363–365; Nikolai Petrov, "Regional Elections under Putin and Prospects for Russian Electoral Democracy," *PONARS Policy Memo*, 287 (February 2003).

"Law on the Militia" does not permit police interference in politics.[69] The tendency for law enforcement involvement in elections grew even more wide-spread during the 2007 Duma campaign and the 2008 presidential election, when there were multiple incidents of police and procuracy harassment of opposition parties.[70]

Moreover, the use of law enforcement against the opposition became more frequent not only during elections, but in general. This was most noticeable in 2006 and 2007 during rallies, known as the "March of the Dissidents," orga-nized by the opposition group "Other Russia." Small protests of several thou-sand demonstrators in Moscow and St. Petersburg were met by much larger groups of regular police and OMON troops, many of them brought in from other regions. Journalists reported on unprovoked violence, including against journalists and random passersby, and unnecessary arrests on the part of the police. In Nizhniy Novgorod, for example, the local administration and police made every effort to prevent a march, including the arrest of several organizers before the march and the confiscation of opposition newspapers. Those pro-testers who were able to assemble were arrested or dispersed immediately.[71]

Russian and western commentators alike were struck by the disproportion-ate response by the authorities to this series of relatively small protests, which seemed to reflect an irrational fear that Russia could fall victim to a "colored revolution" like in Georgia in 2003 or Ukraine in 2004. A Russian NGO noted that almost all opposition demonstrations were banned or dispersed by the police in 2007. At the same time, pro-Kremlin groups, like the youth movement *Nashi* ("Ours"), had no difficulty conducting marches and rallies. This is clear evidence that the new regime of repression was deployed in an exceptional fashion against antigovernment forces and was not simply part of a stronger capacity to uphold public order during legal demonstrations. Mikhail Rostovskiy, writing for the popular newspaper *Moskovskiy Komsomolets* after particularly aggressive police tactics were used to shut down an April 2007 march in Moscow, stated that "the siloviki have been given a clear sig-nal: now everything is permissible." Rostovskiy clearly is using siloviki in the corporate sense here, particularly the law enforcement structures.[72]

[69] Interview Ye-13; Interview N-7.
[70] Natal'ya Kostenko, "Demokratizatory – 2007," *Nez. Gaz.*, November 15, 2007; Clifford Levy, "Putin's Iron Grip on Russia Suffocates Opponents," *NYT*, February 24, 2008; Robert Coalson, "Russia: How the Kremlin Manages to Get the Right Results," *RFE/RL*, March 7, 2008. The extensive role of the MVD in election monitoring is detailed and explained by First Deputy Minister of Internal Affairs A.A. Chekalin in: Mikhail Falaleyev and Svetlana Alikina, "Militsiya kompromat ne sobirayet," *RG*, November 22, 2007.
[71] Julian Evans, "Two Russias," *Eurasianhome.org*, December 18, 2006; Lynn Berry, "Making Threats," *MT*, December 19, 2006; Yevgeniya Zubchenko, "Kto pozval OMON v Piter," *NI*, March 8, 2007; Michael Schwirtz, "Meager Efforts to Protest Meet Subterfuge and Nightsticks," *NYT*, March 26, 2007; Yekaterina Savina and Andrey Kozenko, "Farsh neso-glasnykh," *K-D*, April 16, 2007.
[72] Robert Coalson, "Russia: Demonstrations, But No Protests," *RFE/RL*, October 12, 2007; Mikhail Rosotvskiy, "Vsya vlast' – OMONu," *MK*, April 16, 2007.

The MVD and other power ministries expanded their capacity to monitor the opposition in Putin's second term. The number of special designation police units (OMON and OMSN) increased, with higher budgets and increasing coordination. A new spetsnaz unit was also created in 2006 in the MVD Internal Troops, specifically designed for dealing with mass disorder in Moscow or St. Petersburg. Not only did coercive capacity to deal with internal threats increase, but the monitoring of the opposition became more systematic. Civil society activists could find their name on police "black lists," prompting multiple stops and document checks if they traveled to demonstrations or meetings in other cities. It appeared as if this rebuilt regime of repression was moving from an extraordinary task to a routine one for the police.[73]

Overall, under Vladimir Putin, the Russian state showed a much greater capacity and willingness to deploy state coercive organs against opposition political parties, candidates, and groups. Russia's power ministries were able to respond to exceptional tasks set by the state leadership in terms of fixing elections and cracking down on opposition demonstrations. A new-style regime of repression was built for competitive authoritarianism circumstances, in which elections are held but are so unfree and unfair that the opposition has no prospect of challenging the ruling party. The widespread and successful use of these techniques of "low-intensity coercion" showed an increase in Russian state coercive capacity under Putin. In Way and Levitsky's framework, this new regime of repression demonstrated both an increase in coercive *scope* – the ability to penetrate society – and *cohesion* – the compliance with instructions from superiors.[74] It must be stressed, however, that this greater capacity was used to implement exceptional decisions of the Kremlin. In the area of crime and law enforcement, state agencies have problems dealing with routine tasks, but they are more adept at fulfilling exceptional tasks and, under Putin, have rebuilt their capacity to repress challenges from political opponents.

THE COERCION OF ECONOMICS

In Chapter 2, I reviewed the economics of coercion in post-Soviet Russia, demonstrating the significant drop in power ministry funding under Yeltsin

[73] This institutionalization of the regime of repression can be seen in the 2008 creation of a MVD Department for Countering Extremism on the basis of the Department for Combating Organized Crime and Terrorism. Irina Borogan of Agentura.ru wrote a series of articles critical of the use of police resources against the political opposition for *Yezhednevnyy zhurnal* in 2009 and 2010 under the rubric "The Kremlin's anti-crisis package." On the points in the above paragraph, see the following articles: "Kogda OMON speshit na pomoshch'," December 15, 2009; "Krapovye berety v pomoshch' OMONu," February 11, 2010; "Kak i dlya chego sostavlyayut 'chernye' spiski," June 2, 2009.

[74] Way and Levitsky 2006. They argue that low intensity coercion, like harassing the opposition, requires an increase in state coercive scope, whereas "high intensity coercion," such as violently repressing large protests, requires an increase in state coercive cohesion. At least in the Russian case, however, it seems clear that this new regime of repression, while used mainly for low intensity coercion, relies on both greater scope and greater cohesion.

and the equally momentous increase in spending under Putin, especially for internal security and law enforcement. In this section, I examine what might be called the coercion of economics, specifically how state capacity can be assessed by looking at two key economic realms: fiscal capacity, and the establishment of a stable property rights regime. Both of these issues are well-established as indicators of "stateness" in the comparative literature on state capacity. In post-Soviet Russia, fiscal capacity increased somewhat under Putin compared to Yeltsin, but private property rights have been insecure throughout the post-Soviet period, and subject to state predation under Putin in particular.

Fiscal Capacity

The ability of the state to extract revenue from society has long been viewed as one of the best indicators of state capacity.[75] A state can only pursue its goals, whatever they may be, if it has access to money. For our purposes, it is also important that revenue extraction is at some level backed by state coercive power. In Russia between 1993 and 2003, a Federal Tax Police Service (FSNP) of 40–50 thousand people was an important power ministry; in 2003, it was disbanded, with most of its personnel going to the Federal Service for the Control of the Narcotics Trade (FSKN), and its main functions and some personnel transferred to the MVD.[76]

Experts on the Russian tax system agree that the fiscal capacity of the state increased under Vladimir Putin. Specialists maintain that weak fiscal capacity under Yeltsin played a role in the economic crisis of 1998, including the devaluation of the ruble and default on foreign loans, and that an increase in fiscal capacity contributed to the subsequent economic growth that began in 1999 and continued through Putin's presidency. Of course, multiple factors not related to revenue extraction, such as low world oil prices in 1998 and high world oil prices subsequently, contributed to both the collapse and the subsequent growth. But an inefficient tax system, combined with tax resistance on the part of powerful regions and corporations, definitely contributed to the state's fiscal woes during Yeltsin's presidency. After becoming president, Putin moved both to reform the tax system and to enforce better compliance by elite actors and average citizens alike. A key role was played by tax

---

[75] On revenue extraction as a measure of state strength see, for example: Jacek Kugler and William Domke, "Comparing the Strength of Nations," *Comparative Political Studies*, 19 (1986), pp. 39–69; Cameron G. Thies, "State Building, Interstate and Intrastate Rivalry: A Study of Post-Colonial Developing Country Extractive Efforts, 1975–2000," *International Studies Quarterly*, 48 (2004), pp. 53–72. See also: Mick Moore, "Revenues, State Formation, and the Quality of Governance in Developing Countries," *International Political Science Review*, 25, 3 (2004), pp. 297–319.

[76] See Chapter 2.

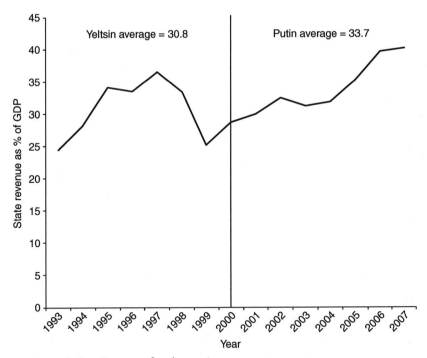

FIGURE 3.6. Russian state fiscal capacity, 1993–2007.

reform, which began in 1998 and continued under Putin, with a particularly important package of reforms pushed through parliament in 2000.[77]

One standard measure of fiscal capacity is state revenue as a percentage of GDP. Of course, big government may not always be better government, but the ability to extract resources from society for the pursuit of state goals is one obvious component of state strength. Figure 3.6 shows Russian state revenue as a percentage of GDP from 1993 to 2007. The figure comes from the Russian "consolidated budget," which includes federal, regional, and local budget revenue. Overall, the figure shows higher fiscal capacity under Putin on average, and especially a consistent growth throughout his presidency, reaching 40 percent of GDP in 2007. It should also be noted that if we used absolute numbers (rubles), the capacity of the Putin years would be considerably higher compared to the 1990s, because the size of the economy shrank throughout most of Yeltsin's presidency and grew during Putin's tenure; adjusting for size of GDP, therefore, does not show this overall growth in revenue. Another shift

---

[77] Easter 2006; Fritz 2007, pp. 285–314; Pauline Jones Luong and Erika Weinthal, "Contra Coercion: Russian Tax Reform, Exogenous Shocks and Negotiated Institutional Change," *American Political Science Review*, 98, 1 (2004), pp. 139–152.

these data do not show is greater central control over revenue compared to the regions under Putin.[78]

Overall, Russia had higher fiscal capacity under Putin, especially by the end of his presidency. Extracting revenue is clearly a routine task of any state, although it falls less directly under the power ministries than fighting crime or terrorism. On the other hand, the state's coercive power played a lead role in the assault on the oil giant Yukos, allegedly for tax noncompliance, among other crimes. As Gerald Easter put it, "the tax collection system was mobilized as a coercive instrument by which the central state reasserted its dominance over the corporate elite."[79] The Yukos affair also speaks to the issue of state protection of property rights.

Guns Over Money: Property Rights, Law Enforcement, and the Oligarchs

Another core task of law enforcement in the economic realm in capitalist states is the protection of private property rights. Indeed, Margaret Levi includes the establishment of property rights as a core component of her definition of what a state is, and Douglass North famously made reliable third party (i.e., state) enforcement of private property rights the centerpiece of his explanation for successful economic performance in the modern world.[80] In the Soviet Union, of course, most major factors of production were not private but "socialist property," and the virtual absence of reliable third-party enforcement of private property rights in the late Soviet Union/early post-Soviet Russia played a significant role in the rise of the mafia. Vladimir Putin noted that the protection of property rights is a key task of Russian law enforcement.[81]

The privatization of state property under Yeltsin led not only to the rise of the Russian mafia but also to the emergence of a small number of extremely powerful and wealthy businessmen, known conventionally as the oligarchs.

---

[78] Data for 1993–2006 in Figure 3.6 from multiple years of: Economist Intelligence Unit, *Russia Country Profile*. Data for 2007 from the Russian Federal State Statistics Service [http://www. gks.ru/]. Economist Intelligence Unit data also were obtained from this source; I checked multiple years of the data to ensure that I am comparing apples and apples. I thank David Rivera for suggesting that I include this measure, and Timothy Frye, Pauline Jones Luong, Katya Kalandadze, Mark Kramer, and Vladimir Popov for advice and help with data.

[79] Easter 2006, p. 47. Although state coercive power definitely played a role in increased revenue extraction, it also should be noted that the tax reform of 1998–2002 was a product of bargaining between the state and private companies, especially in the oil sector: Jones Luong and Weinthal 2004. Easter emphasizes "coercion" more than "contracts" (negotiation) in his account, although noting the role of major corporations in bargaining over tax reform.

[80] Margaret Levi, "The State of the Study of the State," in Ira Katznelson and Helen V. Milner, *Political Science: The State of the Discipline*, Centennial Edition (New York: W.W. Norton & Company, 2002), p. 40; Douglass C. North and Robert P. Thomas, *The Rise of the Western World: A New Economic History* (Cambridge: Cambridge University Press, 1973); Douglass C. North, *Structure and Change in Economic History* (New York: Norton, 1981).

[81] Volkov 2002; Vladimir Putin, "Vystupleniye Vladimira Putina pered doverennymi litsami," Feburary 12, 2004 [http://www.putin2004.ru/putin/press/402C2C3E].

These oligarchs gained control over major companies, most notably in such key sectors as oil and metals. The political and economic weight of the oligarchs under Yeltsin is debated, but there is no doubt that wealth in Russia was highly concentrated, and that leading oligarchs sought – sometimes successfully – to influence state policy.[82]

The relationship between state guns and private money was a complicated one.[83] All of the oligarchs created powerful security firms headed by and staffed by former power ministry personnel. For example, the head of security for Vladimir Gusinsky's MOST organization was Filipp Bobkov, former first deputy chief of the KGB. These security services maintained close links to their former colleagues still working for the state and used these contacts to collect information on business rivals and to smooth any problems that might arise with the authorities.

At the same time, the power ministries sometimes clashed with leading oligarchs under Yeltsin. Two famous incidents illustrate the phenomenon. In 1994, an armed battle nearly broke out in central Moscow between the Presidential Security Service (SBP) headed by Aleksandr Korzhakov and MOST's security service. The SBP, according to Korzhakov, had been ordered by Yeltsin to put some pressure on Gusinsky, perhaps at the instigation of rival oligarch Boris Berezovsky or due to the manner in which Gusinsky's NTV television channel was covering Yeltsin. After the incident, Gusinsky temporarily left the country, and the head of the Moscow FSB, who had sided with Gusinsky, was fired.[84] Ultimately, though, Gusinsky was able to return and his businesses flourished under Yeltsin, whereas Korzhakov lost his position as head of the SBP as a result of intrigues surrounding the June 1996 presidential elections.

Another epic clash between elements of the power ministries and a top oligarch occurred during the 1999 Skuratov affair. Yuriy Skuratov, who became Procurator General in 1995, was investigating several cases that implicated people close to Yeltsin in corruption, including both his actual family (his two daughters) and the "Family" clan, which included Berezovsky. Whether the investigations were genuine or political is contested by the different parties, but there is no doubt that Skuratov and Berezovsky went to war against each other.

---

[82] A 1996 study estimated that twelve financial industrial groups accounted for almost one-third of Russian GDP: Michael McFaul, *Russia's Unfinished Revolution: Political Change from Gorbachev to Putin* (Ithaca, NY: Cornell University Press, 2001), p. 318.

[83] The guns-versus-money formulation has been used by others, with somewhat different conceptions of what the labels refer to: Robert Cottrell, "The Emperor Vladimir," *The New York Review of Books*, 53, 2 (February 9, 2006); Michael McFaul, "Vladimir Putin's Grand Strategy … for anti-democratic regime change in Russia," *The Weekly Standard*, November 17, 2003.

[84] Korzhakov 1997, pp. 282–290; Volkov 2002, pp. 171–173; David Remnick, *Resurrection: The Struggle for a New Russia* (New York: Vintage Books, 1998), pp. 191–195; David E. Hoffman, *The Oligarchs: Wealth and Power in the New Russia* (New York: Public Affairs, 2002), pp. 284–295; Paul Klebnikov, *Godfather of the Kremlin: Boris Berezovsky and the Looting of Russia* (New York: Harcourt, 2000), pp. 153–158.

In February 1999, special forces conducted raids on two companies linked to Berezovsky, including his private security firm Atoll. Berezovsky suspected that Prime Minister Yevgeniy Primakov was behind the attack. Berezovsky and the Family hit back at Skuratov by arranging for the showing on national TV of a pornographic video of "someone who looks like Skuratov" in bed with two prostitutes. Intervening on the side of the Family was Putin, then chair of the FSB, who asserted that technical analysis confirmed that the man in the video was Skuratov. However, Yeltsin's effort to sack Skuratov ran aground in the Federation Council (FC), which had to approve the move. Primakov's ally, Moscow Mayor Yuriy Luzhkov, led the effort in the FC to keep Skuratov. For more than a year, Skuratov was suspended from his duties, with several acting procurators filling the void until Putin was elected. The investigations into Berezovsky stopped temporarily when Primakov was removed as Prime Minister in May 1999, and Putin's loyal service during the Skuratov affair played a key role in his rise to the presidency.[85]

Episodes like the SPB-MOST showdown and the Skuratov affair, as well as countless similar episodes of smaller import, revealed several things about power ministry–big business relations under Yeltsin. First, business and state coercion were closely intertwined with each other. Second, the power ministries were not a unified team, but were divided both within and between themselves, and could end up directly confronting each other in major clan battles. Third, although sometimes under pressure from the state, leading oligarchs usually found some accommodation or were able to fight back successfully. Volkov observed that the December 1994 MOST episode "attested not to the strength of the state but rather to its weakness."[86] Law enforcement capacity was low both in terms of carrying out routine tasks, fighting economic crime and corruption, and protecting property rights, as well as in implementing exceptional tasks directed against specific oligarchs (although stronger in the latter than the former).

The relationship between guns and money changed radically under Putin. He showed this in his first year of office by successfully pushing both Gusinsky and Berezovsky out of the country and depriving them of control over major companies, especially key television stations. For our purposes, the central feature of these legal and political processes is the aggressive use of law enforcement structures by the Kremlin. In the case of Berezovsky, the procuracy and the tax police (FSNP) went after two Berezovsky-controlled

[85] Skuratov, Yeltsin, and Primakov provide widely-varying memoir accounts: Yel'tsin 2000, pp. 262–279; Yuriy Skuratov, *Variant Drakona* (Moskva: Detektiv-Press, 2000); Yevgeniy Primakov, *Vosem' mesyatsev plyus...* (Moskva: Mysl', 2001), pp. 184–211. Putin's reflections are in: Natal'ya Gevorkyan, Natal'ya Timakova, and Andrey Kolesnikov, eds., *Ot pervogo litsa: Razgovory s Vladimirom Putinym* (Moskva: Vagrius, 2000), pp. 178–180. Secondary accounts include: Hoffman 2002, pp. 459–462; Peter Reddaway and Dmitri Glinski, *The Tragedy of Russia's Reforms: Market Bolshevism Against Democracy* (Washington, DC: United States Institute of Peace Press, 2001), pp. 603–608.
[86] Volkov 2002, p. 173.

companies, the carmaker Avtovaz and the state airline Aeroflot. Gusinsky's Media-MOST came under heavy pressure immediately after Putin became president, with a FSNP raid on its headquarters four days after his inauguration in May 2000.[87] In June, Gusinsky was summoned to the General Procuracy, where he was questioned and then arrested. He was released after a few days and left the country, this time for good, shortly thereafter. Dozens of raids by the FSNP and the procuracy would follow in the coming year before the final takeover of his media holdings by the state gas company, Gazprom. In the same period, other large companies also found themselves receiving high-profile visits from the tax inspectors.[88]

The 2003 attack on Mikhail Khodorkovsky and his oil company Yukos was equally momentous and used similar methods. In July 2003, the General Procuracy opened a major investigation into the oil giant Yukos, which led to the October arrest of Khodorkovsky by FSB agents. There were several political and economic reasons for the clash, including a power struggle between "the Family" and the siloviki, retribution for Khodorkovsky's political activities and potential political ambitions, and the enormous and growing power of Yukos as an energy player on the domestic and international stage, including planned independent pipelines and a possible merger with a major international oil company. A more general cause of the affair, Philip Hanson noted, was the Putin leadership's fear of any independent, potentially uncontrollable social forces.[89]

Putin maintained throughout, as he had in the 2000 attacks on Berezovsky and Gusinsky, that these were simply legal matters being pursued by independent law enforcement agencies. *The Economist* rightly called this claim a "pretense"; it is clear that Berezovsky, Gusinsky, and Khodorkovsky had been selectively targeted, even if some of the criminal accusations against them were true.[90] An anonymous FSB official was quoted in the press claiming that the Yukos affair was directed from "the very-very top."[91] Most Russian observers believed it was "no accident" that the ultimate beneficiary of the breaking up of Yukos, the state oil company Rosneft, was chaired by key Kremlin aide and

[87] The journalist Dmitriy Babich characterized the affair as an assault of the "Big-KGB" (the FSB, FSNP, etc.) on the "Little-KGB" (MOST's security service, headed by a former KGB general): Interview M-4.

[88] Jack 2004, pp. 131–178; Baker and Glasser 2007, pp. 78–98; Hoffman 2002, pp. 475–489; Andrew Barnes, *Owning Russia* (Ithaca, NY: Cornell University Press, 2006), pp. 172–175.

[89] See: Baker and Glasser 2007, pp. 272–292; Tompson 2005; Barnes 2006, pp. 209–226; Stephen Fortescue, *Russia's Oil Barons and Metal Magnates: Oligarchs and the State in Transition* (New York: Palgrave Macmillan, 2006), pp. 108–111, 121–172; Philip Hanson, "The Russian Economic Puzzle: Going Forwards, Backwards, or Sideways?" *International Affairs*, 83, 5 (2005), p. 880. For an illuminating comparison to U.S. robber barons, see: Vadim Volkov, "'Delo Standard Oil' i 'delo Yukosa'," *Pro et Contra*, 9, 2 (September–October 2005), pp. 66–91.

[90] "After Yukos," *The Economist*, May 12, 2007. See also: Hanson 2007, p. 880.

[91] "A ne nado v sviterke khodit' k prezidentu," *Nov. Gaz.*, November 13, 2003. This same FSB official suggests that the Jewish backgrounds of Gusinsky, Berezovsky, and Khodorkovsky

the purported head of the siloviki clan, Igor Sechin, or that the key instrument of the destruction of Yukos, the General Procuracy, was headed by Vladimir Ustinov, who was closely allied with Sechin and, indeed, his son was married to Sechin's daughter. Putin's philosophy toward the use of the law seemed similar to that of former Brazilian President Getulio Vargas, who allegedly said, "for my friends, everything; for my enemies, the law."[92]

Another noteworthy outcome of the redistribution of property under Putin was the rise of a new generation of oligarchs with backgrounds in the power ministries. Indeed, Daniel Treisman argued that Putin's oligarchs should be called *silovarchs*, a combination of siloviki and oligarchs. In terms of the relationship between big business and the state, Putin reasserted the primacy of the state. But this reassertion of state power, as William Tompson emphasized, is based on the state's power to arbitrarily coerce, and not on a stronger rule of law or greater regulative capacity.[93] Although business and the power ministries continued to be intertwined under Putin, the Kremlin was able to deploy the key law enforcement structures against leading oligarchs in a much more concerted way than was the case under Yeltsin. Certainly clan and corporate divisions between the siloviki persisted, but Putin was able to overcome those when it really mattered to him. Oligarchs could no longer resist when faced with the coercive power of the state. As Robert Cottrell put it, "under Yeltsin, the people with guns could get money, and the people with money could get guns. By sending Khodorkovsky to Siberia, Putin showed that the people with money could no longer get guns."[94]

The Yukos affair was far from the last dispute between the Kremlin and big business in Russia that showed the weakness of private property rights. In Putin's second term, it was not only domestic companies, but major international oil companies like Royal Dutch Shell and British Petroleum that ran into trouble with the authorities, both of which were forced to sell majority stakes in lucrative gas fields to Gazprom. The expatriate investment banker William Browder had to flee Russia and watch helplessly as his fund, Hermitage Capital, was raided with the participation of law enforcement officials. Commenting on his own situation and the troubles of British Petroleum's joint venture

played an important role in their fall from power. This official evidently made this claim to multiple observers, because Olga Krysthanovskaya and Stephen White also quote an anonymous FSB official asserting the importance of big business being controlled by loyal Russians, not Jewish "traitors": Ol'ga Kryshtanovskaya and Stephen White, "Inside the Putin Court: A Research Note," *Europe-Asia Studies*, 57, 7 (November 2005), p. 1072. Quantitative evidence that members of the business elite were more likely to be "ostracized" (i.e., subject to punitive actions such as investigations and detention by law enforcement organs) under Putin if they were Jewish is in: Serguey Braguinsky, "Post-Communist Oligarchs in Russia: Quantitative Analysis," *Journal of Law and Economics*, 52 (May 2009), pp. 307–349.

[92] Quoted in Guillermo O'Donnell, "Why the Rule of Law Matters," *Journal of Democracy*, 15, 4 (October 2004), p. 40. Stephen Fortescue provides a detailed analysis of the role of the siloviki clan in the Yukos affair: Fortescue 2006.

[93] Daniel Treisman, "Putin's *Silovarchs*," *Orbis*, 51, 1 (2007), pp. 141–153; Tompson 2005.

[94] Cottrell 2006.

BP-TNK in 2008, Browder stated, "property rights and the rule of law don't exist in Russia."[95] In Chapter 5, we will see how not only oligarchs but small-businesspeople and average citizens often had their property rights violated by law enforcement structures.

CONCLUSION: STATE CAPACITY AND THE POWER MINISTRIES

The conventional wisdom in Russia is that there was a weak state under Yeltsin and a strong state under Putin. The evidence presented in this chapter on the capacity of Russia's power ministries shows that the picture is more complicated. The capacity of the power ministries from the point of view of Russia's leaders is higher when it comes to carrying out exceptional decisions rather than routine implementation of their core tasks. For example, although the performance of the police in fighting violent crime is quite poor, they are fully capable of mobilizing enormous shows of force against opposition protests when required by the authorities. The FSB has been more adept at taking down major oligarchs than preventing or managing major terrorist attacks. The most important increase in state coercive capacity under Putin was the rebuilding of a regime of repression that could be deployed against the Kremlin's political and economic enemies. In fairness, a drop in homicide rates and major terrorist attacks in Moscow was evident in Putin's last years, and the fiscal capacity of the state also improved under Putin. On the other hand, the Russian state under Putin was not a neutral third-party enforcer of private property rights (see Table 3.1).

This ability to carry out exceptional tasks in some ways represented an increase in capacity compared to the Yeltsin era. Sovereign power crises like those in October 1993 and March 1996, and siloviki-oligarch clashes like the MOST affair of 1994 or the Skuratov affair of 1999, showed that the power ministries were so divided among themselves and so penetrated by societal actors that their reliability even during exceptional events was suspect. Under Putin, in contrast, they became an important weapon in the hands of the Kremlin. *Novaya Gazeta* reporter Roman Shleynov even classified the power ministries as different types of weapons: The MVD is used for "artillery preparation, preliminary fire on the opposing camp before the decisive attack"; the FSB is a "guidance system" used to target an objective; and the General Procuracy is an "assault cannon, capable of destroying any walls."[96]

Why were the power ministries so much more capable of carrying out exceptional tasks than routine ones, and why did this specific capacity increase under Putin? Their ineffectiveness at dealing with routine responsibilities is

[95] Peter Rutland, "Putin's Economic Record: Is the Oil Boom Sustainable?", *Europe-Asia Studies*, 60, 6 (August 2008), p. 1059; Clifford J. Levy, "An Investment Gets Trapped in Kremlin's Vise," *NYT*, July 24, 2008; Brian Whitmore, "Beware the Russian Bear Market," *RFE/RL Russia Report*, August 1, 2008.
[96] Roman Shleynov, "Donoschiki snaryadov," *Nov. Gaz.*, April 26, 2007.

TABLE 3.1. *Law Enforcement Capacity under Putin: Routine versus Exceptional Decisions*

		Law Enforcement Capacity	
		Low	*High*
Type of Activity	*Routine*	Terrorism → Crime → Protection of Property Rights	Fiscal Capacity
	Exceptional		Regime of Repression – Elections – Opposition Marches – "Bad" Oligarchs

Note: The arrows show improvement in Putin's last years, but over the course of his entire presidency, the capacity of the power ministries to fight terrorism and crime was no better than under Yeltsin, and was weak comparatively.

investigated in more detail in Chapter 5, in which I look at corruption and patrimonialism in the power ministries. Their greater capacity in exceptional matters under Putin can be explained by several factors. First, as Yeltsin's former chief legal advisor Mikhail Krasnov stressed, the simple fact that Putin maintained high approval ratings throughout his presidency, in stark contrast to Yeltsin, allowed him to undertake actions that were unthinkable in the 1990s.[97]

Second, the economic boom under Putin both fueled his popularity and allowed him to increase spending on the power ministries, including personnel salaries. A very important piece of this economic turnaround was extremely high world energy prices. Political scientists have argued convincingly in recent decades that resource wealth is bad for democracy, and this argument has been extended to Russia. One reason this is said to be true is what Michael Ross called the "repression effect": high energy prices allow the state to invest heavily in coercive resources. Steven Fish argued that resource wealth has indeed undermined Russian democracy, but reserved judgment on this specific issue because "we do not have data that allow for a firm conclusion on a repression effect in Russia."[98] Yet the data provided in Chapter 2 on the size and budgets of the power ministries, as well as the specific cases investigated in this chapter, suggest that this "repression effect" mattered in Putin's Russia. Nicolas van de Walle maintained that in Africa, resource wealth has helped build state capacity in some states, "even when there is considerable

[97] Interview M-19. A similar point was made in Interview N-5. See also: Fritz 2007, p. 287.
[98] Michael Ross, "Does Oil Hinder Democracy?," *World Politics*, 53, 3 (April 2001), pp. 325–61; Fish 2005, pp. 122–123.

leakage through corruption and rent-seeking."[99] A similar account seems to fit Russia, where at least some types of coercive capacity have been strengthened due to oil and gas money.

A third reason for greater state coercive capacity, especially regarding exceptional decisions, was an ideological project that became increasingly prominent and coherent in Putin's second term. His statism was evident from the beginning of his presidency, but this was tempered by a simultaneous rhetorical commitment to Russia's European identity and the importance of freedom and democracy. Starting around 2004, his rhetoric became noticeably more anti-Western. Putin blamed both the Beslan terrorism incident of September 2004 and the Ukrainian Orange Revolution of December 2004 on outside powers interested in encircling and undermining Russia. For example, after Beslan, Putin appeared to blame the attack on foreign countries, stating: "We appeared weak. And the weak are beaten. They want to cut from us a tasty piece of pie, others are helping them.... Terrorism is only an instrument for achieving these goals." The statement that "the weak are beaten" consciously or unconsciously referenced a famous 1931 speech by Stalin, in which he justified his industrialization campaign by arguing that the Soviet Union must not fall behind the leading industrial powers, because "those who fall behind get beaten."[100]

Putin's deputy chief of staff Vladislav Surkov, widely considered the chief Kremlin ideologist, propagated the notion of "sovereign democracy," arguing that Russia must pursue its own conception of democracy without outside interference. It would be "stupid," Surkov stated, to think that the "unprecedented pressure on Russia" was due to deficiencies in its democracy. Rather, the true motive of external critics was "control over Russia's natural resources by means of weakening its state institutions, defense capability, and independence."[101]

The essence of Putin's ideology in his second term became the need for a strong state to protect Russia against internal and external enemies. Putin and his supporters made clear that these enemies were in league with each other. For example, on the eve of the December 2007 Duma elections, Putin told a rally of supporters that "those who oppose us ... need a weak, sick state" and

[99] Nicolas van de Walle, "The Economic Correlates of State Failure," in Robert I. Rotberg, ed., *When States Fail: Causes and Consequences* (Princeton, NJ: Princeton University Press, 2004), pp. 101–102.

[100] Vladimir Putin, "Obrashcheniye Prezidenta Rossii Vladimira Putina," September 4, 2004; "Stalin on the Ends and Means of Industrialization," in Robert V. Daniels, ed., *A Documentary History of Communism in Russia: From Lenin to Gorbachev* (Hanover, NH: University Press of New England, 1993), pp. 180–183. For an insightful analysis of Putin's post-Beslan speeches, see: Sergei Medvedev, "'Juicy Morsels': Putin's Beslan Address and the Construction of the New Russian Identity," *PONARS Policy Memo*, 334 (November 2004).

[101] Vladislav Surkov, "Russkaya politicheskaya kul'tura. Vzglyad iz utopii," in Konstantin Remchukov, ed., *Russkaya politicheskaya kul'tura. Vzglyad iz utopii. Lektsiya Vladislava Surkova* (Moskva: Nezavisimaya Gazeta, 2007), p. 15.

that there are forces inside Russia who are "jackals," seeking the support of "foreign foundations and governments." Multiple Russian and foreign specialists noted that this ideological approach to state building had deep roots in Russian history. Lilia Shevtsova, for example, referred to the "image of the besieged fortress" as a return to an old "mobilization model of Russian development" based on "the search for an enemy." Echoing Shevtsova, Stefan Hedlund pointed to "the imagery of enemies that has served over the centuries, time and again, to trigger programmes for forced mobilisation of resources, with the aim of enhancing the country's war-fighting capabilities."[102]

Putin's ideology resonated with the power ministry officials called upon to rebuild a regime of repression to protect Russian statehood. Statist views are particularly strong among Russian siloviki, as well as a heightened concern for control and order. Putin's background in this milieu explains both his embrace of these views and how they resonated so much with the broader cohort of siloviki. Another feature of power ministry culture is a tradition of subordination and hierarchical authority.[103] Although this cultural disposition came under considerable stress under Gorbachev and Yeltsin, it did not disappear. The somewhat notorious Russian journalist Sergey Dorenko put it starkly and dramatically in 2000 after Gusinsky's arrest: "Today the security structures throughout the whole country are taking a message from Putin's rise to power.... They hear music that we do not hear, and they get up like zombies and walk."[104]

Although Dorenko's prose was somewhat purple, there was a definite feeling among power ministry personnel as early as 2000 that something serious had changed under Putin. I was in Moscow at the time of Gusinsky's arrest, shortly after Putin's inauguration, and several interviewees expressed their firm conviction that Putin was going to change Russian politics radically. Major-General (retired) V.I. Slipchenko stated that Putin was trying to create "Soviet-style power (*vlast'*)." Military journalist and retired Lieutenant-Colonel Aleksandr Zhilin maintained that "a very firm dictatorship is coming; people will feel it and fall into line."[105] Slipchenko and Zhilin heard the music,

[102] Vladimir Putin, "Vystupleniye na forume storonnikov Prezidenta Rossii," November 21, 2007; "Vlast'," *EM*, September 12, 2008; Stefan Hedlund, "Vladimir the Great, Grand Prince of Muscovy: Resurrecting the Russian Service State," *Europe-Asia Studies*, 58, 5 (July 2006), p. 796. For similar arguments, see: Medvedev 2004; Igor' Klyamkin and Tat'yana Kutkovets, *Kremlevskaya shkola politologii: Kak nas uchat lyubit' Rodinu* (Moskva: "Liberal'naya missiya," 2006), p. 25; Alfred B. Evans, "Putin's Legacy and Russian Identity," *Europe-Asia Studies*, 60, 6 (2008), pp. 899–912; Celeste A. Wallander, "Russia: The Domestic Sources of a Less-than-Grand Strategy," in Ashley J. Tellis and Michael Wills, eds., *Strategic Asia 2007–2008: Grand Strategy and Domestic Politics* (Seattle, WA: National Bureau of Asian Research, 2007), pp. 158–160. See also the discussion in Chapter 1 on cycles in Russian history.
[103] On the military, see: Taylor, *Politics and the Russian Army*. On the KGB, see: Knight 2003; On the procuracy, see: Gordon B. Smith, *Reforming the Russian Legal System* (Cambridge: Cambridge University Press, 1996), pp. 104–128.
[104] Quoted in Hoffman 2002, pp. 480–481.
[105] Interview M-32; Interview M-44.

which became loud enough in Putin's second term that it was impossible to miss.

It would be a mistake, however, to uncritically conclude that this harmony between Putin's statism and power ministry organizational culture led to an across-the-board increase in state capacity. Instead, the achievements of the state-building project were modest and partial, with the greatest gains in capacity taking place in rebuilding a regime of repression to implement extraordinary decisions of the Kremlin. Much less progress was made in coping with the core, routine tasks of the power ministries. Repressing opposition figures and "bad" oligarchs certainly came much more naturally to Russian law enforcement officials than establishing a stable private property rights regime. Moreover, as we see in Chapter 5, there was money to be made when property rights were insecure.

Still, when Putin came to power in 2000, the ability of the Kremlin to direct and control the power ministries was not secure even in terms of extraordinary tasks. One reason for this was that under Yeltsin, regional governors had gained considerable influence over state coercive organs. This alternative center of power had to be undermined, and Putin launched this effort in his first week as president. The next chapter explains how.

4

Coercion and Capacity

Centralization and Federalism

Everyone was saying that the administrative vertical had been destroyed and that it had to be restored.

Vladimir Putin, 2000[1]

Vladimir Putin first became familiar with the details of Russian federalism and regional politics in 1997–1998, when he worked in the presidential administration of Boris Yeltsin in two different positions concerning regional politics and relations with the heads of Russia's eighty-nine subunits (conventionally referred to as "governors"). It was at this time that "everyone was saying" that decentralization had gone too far and federal relations were in crisis, including (or perhaps especially) in the Kremlin.[2] Putin became convinced that Russia did not have a "full-fledged federal state" but a "decentralized state," and that "regional independence often is treated as permission for state disintegration."[3] This diagnosis was widely shared, not only in Russia but by many foreign experts.[4]

"Strengthening vertical power" became a key slogan of Putin's presidency, especially in his first term. He was guided by his statist ideology and his belief, as his close ally Viktor Cherkesov put it, that in Russia, it has

[1] Natal'ya Gevorkyan, Natal'ya Timakova, and Andrey Kolesnikov, eds., *Ot pervogo litsa: Razgovory s Vladimirom Putinym* (Moskva: Vagrius, 2000), p. 123.

[2] Interview M-33; Interview M-19.

[3] Vladimir Putin, "Vystupleniye pri predstavlenii yezhegodnogo Poslaniya Prezidenta Rossiyskoy Federatsii Federal'nomu Sobraniyu Rossiyskoy Federatsii," July 8, 2000.

[4] Although they differed on how serious the problems were, all of the following works from the late-Yeltsin years pointed to major deficiencies in Russian federalism: Mikhail A. Alexseev, ed., *Center-Periphery Conflict in Post-Soviet Russia: A Federation Imperiled* (New York: St. Martin's, 1999); Graeme P. Herd, "Russia: Systemic Transformation or Federal Collapse?", *Journal of Peace Research*, 36 (May 1999), pp. 259–269; Gail W. Lapidus, "Asymmetrical Federalism and State Breakdown in Russia," *Post-Soviet Affairs*, 15, 1 (1999), pp. 74–82; Alfred Stepan, "Russian Federalism in Comparative Perspective," *Post-Soviet Affairs*, 16 (April–June 2000), pp. 133–176; "Federalism in Russia: How Is It Working," National Intelligence Council, 1999 [http://www.dni.gov/nic/confreports_federalrussia.html].

always been important "to have supreme state control over the activity of local bureaucrats."[5] It was particularly important to Putin that the central state reassert its control over the power ministries. This control had weakened considerably under Yeltsin, particularly in the law enforcement realm, but there were significant concerns about regionalization of the military as well. Powerful regional governors were seen as amassing substantial political, economic, and even coercive resources, which was of great concern to central authorities. Max Weber pointed to the potential danger when he noted that in ancient patrimonial states, "the fusion of the military and economic power of an administrative district in the hands of one person soon tended to encourage the administrator's disengagement from the central authority."[6]

Putin set his goal as reversing this "disengagement from the central authority." He launched a successful effort to recentralize the Russian state that relied heavily on the power ministries. His centralization drive went so far that, particularly after the end of direct gubernatorial elections in 2004, Putin arguably had saved Russian federalism by killing it, returning to a form of "sham federalism" similar to that of the Soviet Union.[7] How such a radical turnaround was possible, and what this tells us about both theories of federalism and the state of the Russian state, is the theme of this chapter. I begin with a discussion of federalism theory and the absence of the issue of coercion from this literature. I then describe the vertical distribution of coercive power in the late-Soviet and Yeltsin periods. The core of the chapter examines Putin's federal reforms and the role of the power ministries in these changes. I conclude by asking whether this recentralization of state coercion has increased the capacity of the Russian state, and what reforms might help build this capacity.

FORCE AND FEDERALISM

A federation is a polity in which decision-making power is divided between central and regional governments.[8] Federalism, much recent literature argues, is a delicate institutional balance. If the subunits are too powerful, the federation may face the threat of secession or dissolution. If the central government is too strong, it may impose itself on the subunits, rendering federalism a fiction.[9] This literature points to three major institutions – political parties,

[5] Peter Baker and Susan Glasser, *Kremlin Rising*, updated edition (Dulles, VA: Potomac Books, 2007), p. 252.
[6] Max Weber, *Economy and Society* (Berkeley, CA: University of California Press, 1978), p. 1044.
[7] On Russia in Putin's second term as a "sham federation," see: Cameron Ross, "Federalism and Electoral Authoritarianism under Putin," *Demokratizatsiya*, 13 (Summer 2005), 347–271.
[8] Arend Lijphart, *Patterns of Democracy* (New Haven, CT: Yale University Press, 1999), p. 186.
[9] Jenna Bednar, William N. Eskridge Jr., and John Ferejohn, "A Political Theory of Federalism," in John Ferejohn, Jack N. Rakove, and Jonathan Riley, eds., *Constitutional Culture and Democratic Rule* (Cambridge: Cambridge University Press, 2001), pp. 223–267; Rui J.P. de

constitutions, and courts – as central to designing federal political systems that are "self-enforcing" and stable.

William Riker famously argued that "the structure of parties parallels the structure of federalism." Thus, federations like the Soviet Union under the Communist Party of the Soviet Union (CPSU) and Mexico under the Institutional Revolutionary Party (PRI) were highly centralized, whereas countries like the United States and Canada have more decentralized political parties and thus more decentralized federations.[10] Another line of work has stressed the importance of constitutions and courts to managing federal relations. For example, Rui de Figueiredo and Barry Weingast claim that constitutions serve as "focal points" that help make federal institutions "self-enforcing."[11] Others highlight the importance of the judicial system in adjudicating boundary disputes between different levels in a federal system.[12]

Combining these two strands of argument, Jenna Bednar, William Eskridge, and John Ferejohn have proposed a "political theory of federalism" that seeks to explain the durability of federal arrangements. They argue that subunit cheating on the federal bargain is best checked by an independent national judiciary, whereas encroachment by the national government is best limited by "fragmenting power at the national level." National power can be fragmented, following Riker, through procedures that hinder the development of strong centralized parties or through checks and balances that prevent a unified central government.[13]

Much of this work (although not Riker's) assumes that federalism is a viable form of government only in a liberal democracy because the division of powers that is central to federalism is only meaningful with constitutional guarantees.[14] Post-Soviet Russia thus fits uneasily into this discussion, because even in the best of times, most analysts classified Russia as an electoral democracy, lacking such features of liberal democracy as a robust civil society and the rule of law.[15] Many analysts classified Russia as a "hybrid

Figueiredo, Jr. and Barry R. Weingast, "Self-Enforcing Federalism," *Journal of Law, Economics, & Organization*, 21 (April 2005), pp. 103–135; Mikhail Filippov, Peter C. Ordeshook, and Olga Shvetsova, *Designing Federalism* (Cambridge: Cambridge University Press, 2004).

[10] William H. Riker, "Federalism," in Fred I. Greenstein and Nelson W. Polsby, eds., *Handbook of Political Science*, Vol. 5 (Reading, MA: Addison-Wesley, 1975), p. 137. See also: William H. Riker, *Federalism* (Boston: Little, Brown and Company, 1964); Filippov, Ordeshook, and Shvetsova 2004.

[11] de Figueiredo and Weingast 2005. See also Ronald L. Watts, *Comparing Federal Systems in the 1990s* (Kingston, Canada: Institute of Intergovernmental Relations, Queens University, 1996), ch. 10.

[12] Stepan 2000, p. 147; Maxwell A. Cameron and Tulia G. Faletti, "Federalism and the Subnational Separation of Powers," *Publius*, 35 (Spring 2005), pp. 245–271.

[13] Bednar, Eskridge, and Ferejohn 2001.

[14] See, for example: Alfred Stepan, "Toward a New Comparative Politics of Federalism, (Multi)Nationalism, and Democracy," in Alfred Stepan, *Arguing Comparative Politics* (Oxford: Oxford University Press, 2001), pp. 318–319.

[15] On the distinction between liberal and electoral democracy, see: Larry Diamond, *Developing Democracy* (Baltimore: Johns Hopkins University Press, 1999), pp. 7–17. For a detailed

regime," meaning a political regime that combines democratic and authoritarian features, such as electoral democracies and competitive authoritarian regimes.[16]

In most hybrid regimes the institutions that are said to regulate federal relations – parties, constitutions, the judiciary – tend to be weak and poorly developed. There are federations that lie between the extremes of consolidated liberal democracy and politically closed authoritarian systems in Europe (Russia), Latin America (Argentina, Brazil, Mexico, Venezuela), Asia (India, Malaysia, Pakistan), and Africa (Comoros, Ethiopia, Nigeria). In all of these countries, obviously in varying degrees, there are notable problems with party development, the rule of law, or both.

What substitutes for party development and the rule of law in Russia and other federal hybrid regimes? I have argued elsewhere that coercion is central to the operation of federalism in countries with hybrid regimes.[17] Thomas Hobbes famously asserted that "in matter of Government, when nothing else is turn'd up, Clubs are Trump."[18] Clubs are often trump in resolving political disputes in semidemocratic or semiauthoritarian federations because other institutions, such as courts and political parties, are not up to this task. Coercion can thus alter the federal bargain in hybrid regimes, the way high court decisions and changes in party system centralization are said to in liberal democratic federations.

Both national and subnational politicians view control over coercion as a key resource in negotiating this bargain. To put it differently, the allocation of the power to coerce is endogenous. Center-region disputes about military and law enforcement powers and organization are not simply about efficiency, but about the fundamental political questions of whether the state will hold together, and whether it will maintain meaningful (as opposed to sham) federalism. Moreover, politicians in hybrid regimes are hesitant to rely solely on written constitutions, the judiciary, or other political arrangements, such as the party system, to resolve these questions. This ability of disputes over force to change fundamentally the federal bargain makes the issue of controlling coercion markedly different than, say, center-region disputes about who controls education or health policy.

accounting of the reasons for classifying Russia as an electoral but not liberal democracy in its first decade, see: Michael McFaul, *Russia's Unfinished Revolution: Political Change from Gorbachev to Putin* (Ithaca, NY: Cornell University Press, 2001), pp. 301–339.

[16] Larry Diamond offers the sixfold classification – liberal democracies, electoral democracies, ambiguous regimes, competitive authoritarian, hegemonic electoral authoritarian, and politically closed authoritarian – with apparently the third through fifth categories counting as hybrid. I would also include electoral democracies in the category of hybrid regimes, particularly in discussing theories of federalism. See Larry Diamond, "Thinking About Hybrid Regimes," *Journal of Democracy*, 13 (April 2002), 21–35.

[17] Brian D. Taylor, "Force and Federalism: Controlling Coercion in Federal Hybrid Regimes," *Comparative Politics*, 39, 4 (July 2007), pp. 421–440.

[18] Thomas Hobbes, *A Dialogue Between a Philosopher and a Student of The Common Laws of England* (Chicago: University of Chicago Press, 1971), p. 140.

Thus, coercion needs to play a larger role in the study of the operation of federations. Federations can be studied at three distinct points in their existence: birth, life, and death. By birth, I mean the decision to create a federal political system. Federation death can occur in two ways: the state can cease to exist, breaking into multiple parts, or the state can become unitary. Some of the most influential works on federalism stress the importance of force and coercion to the birth and death of federal political systems.[19] However, coercion is largely neglected in studies of the life of federations.

Experts on Russian federalism and regional politics have generally followed the broader comparative literature by focusing on constitutions and the courts,[20] party system development,[21] or fiscal federalism.[22] Although not denying the importance of these issues, the account that follows suggests that any understanding of how federalism is managed in Russia needs to take account of the role of coercion. Vladimir Putin used the club more than any other weapon to rebuild the "power vertical" in Russia.

FEDERALISM AND COERCION IN THE SOVIET UNION

The Soviet Union was federal in form but unitary in content. The vertically integrated Communist Party was the linchpin of this system. Centralized power ministries reinforced Moscow's control. Most importantly, the KGB and the procuracy were reliable instruments by which the Party could monitor and enforce compliance by lower-level officials. The armed forces were also available in a pinch, but for the most part were only used internally during crises or major challenges to Soviet power, such as the one posed by armed nationalist groups after World War II in western Ukraine and Belorussia and the Baltic states, or large strikes and demonstrations such as the one in Novocherkassk

---

[19] Riker 1964; Valerie Bunce, *Subversive Institutions* (Cambridge: Cambridge University Press, 1999); Stepan 2001.

[20] Jeffrey Kahn, *Federalism, Democratization, and the Rule of Law in Russia* (Oxford: Oxford University Press, 2002).

[21] Kathryn Stoner-Weiss, "Central Governing Incapacity and the Weakness of Political Parties," *Publius*, 32 (Spring 2002), pp. 125–146; Kathryn Stoner-Weiss, *Resisting the State: Reform and Retrenchment in Post-Soviet Russia* (Cambridge: Cambridge University Press, 2006), pp. 111–146; Henry Hale, *Why Not Parties in Russia? Democracy, Federalism, and the State* (Cambridge: Cambridge University Press, 2006); Andrew Konitzer and Stephen K. Wegren, "Federalism and Political Recentralization in the Russian Federation," *Publius*, 36 (Fall 2006), pp. 503–522.

[22] Steven L. Solnick, "The Political Economy of Russian Federalism," *Problems of Post-Communism*, 43 (November/December 1996), pp. 13–25; Daniel S. Treisman, *After the Deluge* (Ann Arbor, MI: University of Michigan Press, 1999); Elizabeth Pascal, *Defining Russian Federalism* (Westport, CT: Praeger, 2003); Donna Bahry, "The New Federalism and the Paradoxes of Regional Sovereignty in Russia," *Comparative Politics* 37 (January 2005), pp. 127–146.

in 1962.[23] The Soviet MVD was also generally a centralized body, but there were periods in which it was decentralized. Under Nikita Khrushchev, not only were the political police (KGB) and the regular police (MVD) separated from each other once and for all in 1954, but the regular police were decentralized in several stages. In 1956, local government organs were given greater control over the police, and in 1960, the central MVD was abolished entirely, with control over the police devolving to the fifteen constituent republics (Russia, Ukraine, Kazakhstan, etc.). Under Leonid Brezhnev, the police were recentralized under an all-union ministry in 1966 and remained so until the late-Gorbachev period.[24]

Of course, in a country as large as the Soviet Union, there were both formal and informal linkages at the local level. For example, in the military sphere, both the regular armed forces and the MVD Internal Troops had Military Soviets, or Councils, in their regional districts (*okrugs*). The local party leader was a member of these councils.[25] Regional military commanders worked closely with local party leaders, particularly to resolve material questions related to food, construction, and similar matters. The Communist Party Secretary in an area, such as a republic or oblast, could create career problems for power ministry officials through his ties to the national party leadership, which generally ensured compliance with his wishes on at least nonpolitical questions.[26] One former military General maintained that local party leaders were "very powerful – god and tsar," so that requests for assistance with transport, the harvest, and the like were definitely met. At the same time, party leaders would help military units on their territory if necessary; one example noted by a retired Colonel was help with food supplies and electricity in case of an accident.[27]

There were also formal and especially informal horizontal links in the law enforcement realm. Vadim Bakatin served as the Communist Party Secretary for Kirov Oblast and then Kemerovo Oblast from 1985–1988 before being appointed by Gorbachev to head the Soviet MVD in 1988. Bakatin stated

[23] Alfred J. Rieber, "Civil Wars in the Soviet Union," *Kritika*, 4, 1 (Winter 2003), pp. 157–160; Samuel H. Baron, *Bloody Saturday in the Soviet Union: Novocherkassk, 1962* (Stanford, CA: Stanford University Press, 2001).

[24] V.F. Nekrasov et al., *Organy i Voyska MVD Rossii: Kratkiy istoricheskiy ocherk* (Moskva: MVD Rossii, 1996), pp. 208–211; Louise I. Shelley, *Policing Soviet Society: The Evolution of State Control* (London: Routledge, 1996), pp. 41–47.

[25] For brief descriptions, see: *Voyennyy entsiklopedicheskiy slovar'* (Moskva: Voyennoye Izdatel'stvo, 1984), p. 147; *MVD Rossii: Entsiklopediya* (Moskva: MVD Rossii, 2002), p. 87; Harriet Fast Scott and William F. Scott, *The Armed Forces of the USSR*, 3rd Edition (Boulder, CO: Westview Press, 1984), pp. 289–290.

[26] In this chapter, I use male pronouns to refer to regional party, government, and power ministry officials because virtually no females have held these positions, either in the Soviet or post-Soviet period.

[27] Interview M-5; Interview M-26; Interview M-28; Interview M-32; Interview M-35; Interview M-40; Interview M-42.

that in his capacity as regional Party chief, he could give orders to the head of the oblast police or procuracy on any matter that he thought he would have support from the Party Central Committee. It was "complete lawlessness (*proizvol*)," he said. Although the MVD was "super-centralized" – the head of regional MVD commands were decided not just by the Soviet MVD, but by the Politburo – it was still subject to local interference. Leonid Smirnyagin, Yeltsin's adviser on regional affairs, provided a similar picture, noting that despite the centralized nature of the MVD in the Soviet period, the police played by the local rules of the game. He said there was a list of local "untouchables" close to the party secretary that the police would leave alone. Smirnyagin noted that this was a traditional situation in Russia, where there was strong central control in principle but local interests were in practice very powerful, even if they were not considered legitimate. Smirnyagin stated, "Moscow was awesome, but far away."[28]

Bakatin maintained, in contrast, that he could not interfere with the oblast KGB when he was Kirov and Kemerovo Party Secretary. The most he could do was provide general direction in speeches at oblast KGB party meetings, based on the party's general line. The KGB was the "vertical of verticals," completely controlled from the center.[29]

In sum, although there were horizontal linkages between local and regional political leaders and their counterparts in the power ministries, there were definite limits that could not be crossed, and there was little danger of the power to coerce slipping away from Moscow's grasp. Although there was some slippage of control over the MVD, the armed forces and the KGB remained extremely centralized. And of course the Communist Party itself was a highly centralized "vertical power" that held everything together.

Under Gorbachev, to paraphrase William Butler Yeats, things fell apart, and the center could not hold. The role of both force and federalism in the Soviet collapse has been examined at length elsewhere and will not be repeated here.[30]

---

[28] Interview M-5; Interview M-33.

[29] Interview M-5.

[30] On force, see, for example: Yevgenia Albats, *The State within a State: The KGB and Its Hold on Russia – Past, Present, and Future* (New York: Farrar, Strauss, and Giroux, 1994); Robert V. Barylski, *The Soldier in Russian Politics: Duty, Dictatorship, and Democracy Under Gorbachev and Yeltsin* (New Brunswick, NJ: Transaction Publishers, 1998), pp. 35–170; Amy Knight, "The KGB, Perestroika, and the Collapse of the Soviet Union," *Journal of Cold War Studies*, 5, 1 (Winter 2003), pp. 67–93; William E. Odom, *The Collapse of the Soviet Military* (New Haven, CT: Yale University Press, 1998); Brian D. Taylor, *Politics and the Russian Army* (Cambridge: Cambridge University Press, 2003), pp. 206–258; Brian D. Taylor, "The Soviet Military and the Disintegration of the USSR," *Journal of Cold War Studies*, 5, 1 (Winter 2003), pp. 17–66. On federalism, prominent contributions include: Mark R. Beissinger, *Nationalist Mobilization and the Collapse of the Soviet State* (Cambridge: Cambridge University Press, 2002); Bunce 1999; Henry Hale, "The Makeup and Breakup of Ethnofederal States: Why Russia Survives Where the USSR Fell," *Perspectives on Politics*, 3, 1 (March 2005), pp. 55–70; Kahn 2002, pp. 83–141; Philip G. Roeder, "Soviet Federalism and Ethnic Mobilization," *World Politics*, 43, 2 (1991), pp. 196–232; Edward W. Walker, *Dissolution: Sovereignty and the Breakup of the Soviet Union* (Lanham, MD: Rowman and Littlefield, 2003); Viktor

It is worth stressing, however, that the central Soviet government retained strong control over coercive bodies until almost the very end. Bakatin took steps to decentralize the MVD when he led the ministry from 1988 to 1990, transferring more power and resources to the republics, and there was widespread resistance to the military draft from multiple republics, but it was only after the failure of the August 1991 coup that uncontrolled decentralization of the power ministries took place.[31]

FEDERALISM AND COERCION UNDER YELTSIN

The newly independent state of Russia was born federal. In the Soviet system of "matryoshka federalism," Russia was a federation – the Russian Soviet Federated Socialist Republic (RSFSR) – within the larger Soviet federation. When the Russian Federation became independent after the Soviet collapse, a new federal treaty was quickly signed in March 1992 and grafted on to the 1978 RSFSR Constitution, which continued to hold force until a new Constitution was adopted by referendum in December 1993.[32]

Existing theories of the birth of federations do not capture this process of federal formation in Russia. William Riker argued that all federations are formed through a political bargain between two or more units, a process Alfred Stepan later labeled "coming together" federalism. Stepan maintained, contra Riker, that there are two other modes of federal creation, "holding together" and "putting together." "Holding together" federalism is when an existing unitary state decides to become a federation to deal with the distinct challenges of governing a diverse society; India and Spain are Stepan's major examples. "Putting together" federalism is Stepan's label for what happened when the Soviet Union was created, what he calls an instance of "nonvoluntary, nondemocratic federation formation."[33]

None of these approaches apply to what happened in Russia in 1992. The subjects of the Russian Federation did not "come together" or "hold together," and they were not "put together." Rather, they "stayed together" in a path-dependent fashion. A "staying together" federation is a political unit that either was part of an existing federation that lost some constituent elements or had a federal structure within a larger unit, either a state or empire, and gained independence after the collapse of the state or empire.[34]

Zaslavsky, "Nationalism and Democratic Transition in Postcommunist Societies," *Daedalus*, 121, 2 (1992), pp. 97–122.

[31] Interview M-5; Vadim Bakatin, *Doroga v proshedshem vremeni* (Moskva: Dom, 1999), pp. 191–193, 215–216, 224–227; Vladimir Nekrasov, *MVD v litsakh: Ministry ot V.V. Fedorchuka do A.S. Kulikova 1982–1998* (Moskva: Molodaya Gvardiya, 2000), pp. 67–71, 75–76; Odom 1998, pp. 292–297.

[32] On this process, see: Kahn 2002, pp. 102–141.

[33] Riker 1964; Riker 1975; Stepan 2001; Alfred Stepan, "Federalism and Democracy: Beyond the U.S. Model," *Journal of Democracy*, 10, 4 (October 1999), pp. 19–34.

[34] Several cases that Riker treats as "coming together" federations seem to be "staying together" cases, in particular the post-British colonial federations of Nigeria and Malaysia. Also worth

Although post-Soviet Russia's status as a federation was largely an inheritance, the *terms* of the federal bargain were still in dispute.[35] In addition to Chechnya, which sought outright independence, several other republics, such as Tatarstan and Bashkortostan, sought wide-ranging "sovereignty." Yeltsin had famously declared in 1990 during a visit to the Tatar capital of Kazan that the republics should "take as much sovereignty as you can swallow," and at least some of the leaders of Russia's eighty-nine subunits, or regions, tried to take him at his word.[36] This was true not only in political and economic spheres but also in the coercive one.

Multiple regions, especially some of the ethnic republics, sought considerable independence from the center in both the law enforcement and even the military sphere. Pro-independence groups in Tatarstan and Bashkortostan began forming their own militias or "national guards," and the Tatarstan parliament adopted a resolution stating that Tatar citizens should not serve outside the local Volga-Urals Military District, a resolution that apparently many youth from the republic at least initially followed. Conscription became a major sticking point of the bilateral treaty negotiations between Moscow and Tatarstan in 1992–1993. Similar moves were taken in the North Caucasus, and not just in Chechnya. In the Far East, The Tuva Constitution claimed the right to veto military commander appointments in the republic.[37]

Similar powers were sought in the law enforcement realm. The Federation Treaty signed in March 1992 made control over law enforcement a shared power between the center and the regions, leaving room for further bargaining. The following year, Yeltsin made an important concession to the regions by issuing a decree on policing in February 1993 that gave regional executives

noting is the high failure rate of many federations that were imposed by a departing colonial power, a category that Nancy Bermeo calls "forced-together federalism." Examples include the Central African Federation set up by the British or the Mali Federation established by the French. See: Nancy Bermeo, "The Import of Institutions," *Journal of Democracy*, 13, 2 (April 2002), pp. 106–108.

[35] Scholars conceptualizing Russian federalism as a bargaining game in the 1990s include: Filippov, Ordeshook, and Shvetsova 2004, pp. 131–141; Pascal 2003; Solnick 1996.

[36] Russia's subjects of the federation are divided into multiple categories. Ethnically based units are called republics or autonomous okrugs (and one autonomous oblast). Other units are called oblasts, krais, or federal cities (Moscow and St. Petersburg). By 2008, there were eighty-three regions, after several mergers were implemented. For descriptions of Russia's complex federal system, see: "Understanding Russian Regionalism," *Problems of Post-Communism*, 54, 2 (March/April 2007), pp. 72–74; Kahn, pp. 5–12. On the merger process, see: Julia Kusznir, "Russia's Territorial Reform: A Centralist Project that Could End Up Fostering Decentralization?" *RAD*, No. 43, June 17, 2008, pp. 8–12.

[37] Jessica Eve Stern, "Moscow Meltdown: Can Russia Survive?" *International Security*, 18, 4 (Spring 1994), pp. 57, 60–61; Matthew Evangelista, *The Chechen Wars: Will Russia Go the Way of the Soviet Union?* (Washington, DC: Brookings Institution Press, 2002), p. 101; Mary McAuley, *Russia's Politics of Uncertainty* (Cambridge: Cambridge University Press, 1997), p. 72; Steven L. Solnick, "Federal Bargaining in Russia," *East European Constitutional Review*, 4 (Fall 1995), pp. 52–53; Gordon M. Hahn, "The Impact of Putin's Federative Reforms on Democratization in Russia," *Post-Soviet Affairs*, 19, 2 (2003), p. 115.

a larger say in controlling police forces. It granted regions the right to fund additional units and personnel out of their budgets, a power that increased regional control over the police, particularly in wealthy regions.[38]

The critical role of force in the Russian federal bargain was made starkly apparent in the very manner in which the 1993 Constitution was adopted. The 1993 constitutional negotiations that were supposed to resolve not only issues of federal design but also legislative and executive power were abruptly terminated in September–October 1993 as a consequence of the violent confrontation between Yeltsin and his parliamentary opponents. Control over the army, police, and secret police was fundamental to Yeltsin's victory in this showdown.[39] After the confrontation, the constitutional framework for Russian federalism was largely imposed by Yeltsin. Although the new Constitution was formally adopted by referendum in December 1993, the October events ended the negotiations on a new document and allowed Yeltsin to put forward his preferred version for public ratification.

The new Constitution retained federalism as a key feature, stating the commitment to federalism in Article 1 and elaborating the specific components in chapter 3 (Articles 65–79). Experts on both comparative and Russian federalism treated Russia as a federation under Yeltsin, or, at a minimum, a nascent federation, contingent on future developments, such as the consolidation of constitutional democracy. For example, a 1999 U.S. government conference on Russian federalism reported substantial agreement among twenty-two outside experts that "Russia today meets the classical definition of a federation."[40] Russia includes such typical features of a federation as a written constitution (including articles enumerating which powers are federal, which are shared, and which are subunit [the latter being merely a residual category of those not specified in the previous two articles]), a constitutional court empowered to resolve jurisdictional disputes between the center and the subunits, and an upper house of the legislature formed on the territorial principle.

At the same time, the Constitution clearly privileges the center in important respects, such as the absence of autonomous subunit courts and the stipulation that there is a "unified system of executive power" in the country (Article 77).[41] However, it would be going too far to say that, at least in terms of original institutional design, Russian federalism is simply a fiction.[42] Rather, like

---

[38] Kahn 2002, p. 128; *Pravovye osnovy deyatel'nosti sistemy MVD Rossii*, Vol. I (Moskva: INFRA-M, 1996), pp. 262–271.

[39] Taylor, *Politics and the Russian Army*, pp. 282–301.

[40] Watts, *Comparing Federal Systems*; Filippov, Ordeshook, and Shvetsova; Stepan, "Russian Federalism"; Kahn; Pascal; National Intelligence Council 1999.

[41] On subnational courts, see: Cameron and Faletti 2005; Aleksandr Deryugin, "Osobennosti rossiyskogo federalizma," *Neprikosnovennyy Zapas*, No. 38 (June 2004).

[42] Nikolai Petrov, "Federalizm po-rossiyski," *Pro et Contra*, 5 (Winter 2000), pp. 7–33. Petrov's argument about Russia's nonexistent federalism had almost nothing to say about the original constitutional design – he pointed to other problems, such as huge political and economic asymmetries between the units, and the general weakness of Russian democracy.

many other federations, the Constitution provides a framework in which real federalism can develop, but further bargaining and agreement is necessary for this to take place. Moreover, the move to direct elections of regional leaders under Yeltsin gave them more independence from the center, particularly compared to local first party secretaries in the USSR, who could be removed easily by a decision of the Politburo.[43]

The 1993 Constitution opened the door to further bargaining over the control of coercion. Defense and security are naturally specified as federal powers, but in the law enforcement sphere, there is a combination of shared powers and those reserved for the center. Specifically, "the guaranteeing of legality, law and order and public safety" and "personnel of judicial and law-enforcement bodies" are powers to be shared by federal and regional authorities (Article 72). Furthermore, local self-government is charged with "the protection of public order" (Article 132). On the other hand, one key law enforcement body, the procuracy, is placed largely under federal control. Article 129 of the Constitution describes the procuracy as "a single centralized system," but it does provide one concession to shared control in the provision that the appointment of regional procurators is to be agreed with the subunits.

Making law enforcement a shared power, with certain biases toward the center, is not atypical for federations, as Table 4.1 makes clear. Policing can be a federal, shared, or subunit power, and all of these variants are practiced by current federations. At least constitutionally, then, Russia is neither particularly centralized nor decentralized compared to other federations in this respect. Historically, though, Russia has tended more toward centralized policing.

In practice, in post-Soviet Russia, law enforcement was a topic for center-subunit bargaining, one that both Moscow and the regions believed to be significant for managing federal relations. Beyond the Constitution, the major political and legal mechanism regulating Russian federalism under Yeltsin was a series of bilateral treaties between Moscow and forty-six of the regions. Jurisdictional agreements on controlling coercion were sometimes explicitly part of these treaties. For example, law enforcement, domestic security, or military affairs were explicitly incorporated into the bilateral treaties with Tatarstan, Bashkortostan, and Udmurtia.[44] De facto, law enforcement in particular was almost always a key part of the federal bargaining process.

A first cut at understanding the varying degree of central versus regional control over Russian law enforcement can be gained by looking at the legal

[43] This point was stressed by multiple Russian experts, for example: Interview M-25; Interview M-29; Interview P-1. On regional governor elections in the 1990s, see: Hale 2006; Andrew Konitzer, *Voting for Russia's Governors: Regional Elections and Accountability under Yeltsin and Putin* (Baltimore: Johns Hopkins University Press, 2005).

[44] Kahn, pp. 142–188 (esp. p. 167); Evangelista 2002, p. 111; McAuley 1997, p. 78; Solnick 1995, p. 55.

TABLE 4.1. *Control over Policing, Federal Political Systems*

	Federal Power	Concurrent or Shared Power	Subunit Power
Argentina		X[a]	
Australia			X
Austria		X	
Belgium	X		
Brazil		X	
Canada	X[b]		
Germany			X
India			X[a]
Malaysia	X		
Mexico		X	
Nigeria	X		
Pakistan		X	
Russia		X	
South Africa		X	
Spain	X[b]		
Switzerland			X
United States			X
Venezuela			X

Source: Daniel J. Elazar, ed., *Federal Systems of the World*, 2nd ed. (Harlow, Essex: Longman Group, 1994).

Key: a = general government retains right of intervention or extensive emergency powers

b = exceptions for certain subunits

basis for budget support for the major law enforcement agencies. As Alexander Hamilton noted, "a power over a man's support is a power over his will,"[45] or, as many Russians have told me when discussing federal relations, "he who pays the piper also calls the tune." Table 4.2 shows the legal basis for federal, regional, and local budget support for law enforcement as of 1999, the last year of Yeltsin's presidency.[46] As is clear from the table, the FSB was the most centralized law enforcement agency in terms of its budget, followed by the Tax Police (FSNP), the Procuracy, and the MVD. Within the MVD there was a distinction between the centralized Internal Troops (VV), the shared OMON (police special forces), and general police units supported more from regional and local budgets.

The police, then, were the law enforcement agency most likely to fall under regional control. This was partially by design. The MVD is divided into the

---

[45] *The Federalist Papers*, No. 73 (Alexander Hamilton).

[46] "Rezul'taty inventarizatsii normativno-pravovykh aktov...." (2000). *Byudzhetnaya sistema Rossiyskoy Federatsii*. http://www.budgetrf.ru/Publications/2000/Budgeting/Federal/Regnpd/ fedminfino1071999regnpdinv/fedminfino1071999regnpdinvooo.htm

TABLE 4.2. *Legal Authority for Law Enforcement Budgetary Support, 1999*

Federal	Regional	Local
FSB Financing		
FSNP Financing and Salaries	FSNP Supplemental Support	FSNP Supplemental Support
Procuracy Financing	Procuracy Financing	Procuracy Supplemental Financing
MVD VV Financing, Maintenance of Armaments, Construction and Housing	MVD VV Construction and Housing	
MVD Units & OMON Financing	MVD Units, MOB, Patrol Police, & OMON Financing	MVD Units Financing, OMON Housing, Local Police Leadership, Support of Additional Police

Key:
FSB   = Federal Security Service
FSNP = Federal Tax Police
MVD   = Ministry of Internal Affairs
VV   = Internal Troops
OMON = Special Designation Police Detachments
MOB   = Public Order Police

"public order militia" (*militsiya obshchestvennoy bezopasnosti*, or MOB) and the criminal police, such as criminal investigation and police responsible for organized crime, terrorism, and economic security. The public-order militia are also referred to as the "local militia" and include beat cops and traffic police, as well as Special Designation Police Detachments (the OMON). Seventy percent of Russian police are in the MOB. A significant share of MOB funding comes from local and regional governments, as well as "nonbudget" sources, such as the collection of fines. Under Yeltsin, for example, 80 percent of the funding for the Moscow MOB came from the city. Even under Putin, regional and local governments played a large role in funding the MOB; for example, in Novosibirsk, 60 percent of the MOB budget in 2003 came from the oblast. Additionally, the regional governor has to agree with the central MVD who will head the MOB in that region.[47]

In the Yeltsin era, the degree of governor influence over not only the MOB but also the criminal police was often significant. The central government had to gain the approval of regional leaders to appoint or fire chiefs of the

[47] Interview M-13; Interview N-7; Interview N-11. For discussions of the different functions and subordination of the public order and criminal police, see: A.Yu. Shumilov, *Novyy zakon o militsii: Uchebnoye posobiye*, 4th edition (Moskva: Shumilova I.I., 2002), pp. 7–10; L.K. Savyuk, *Pravookhranitel'nye organy* (Moskva: Yurist, 2001), pp. 283–316.

regional Directorate of Internal Affairs (UVD).[48] Even when Moscow insisted on "its" candidate, this person tended to develop a close relationship with the regional governor. In other words, such appointments from "outside" (i.e., from a different region) were often insufficient to prevent their capture by the local executive. Because of continual budget problems throughout the 1990s, regional and city governments often played an important role in delivering salaries, equipment, housing, and other benefits to the police. Thus, they came to command much of the police's loyalty.[49]

Some regions went further. For example, in Sverdlovsk Oblast, the regional charter adopted in 1994 stated that the creation of oblast and municipal police forces was a possibility, and in 1996–1997, the oblast considered creating its own police force. However, scholars from the Institute of Philosophy and Law who looked into the question for the governor concluded that from a legal point of view, the oblast could not create its own police force, although it could increase the number of public-order police and finance them from its budget.[50]

Concerned about the increased control of governors over the police, the central MVD sought to strengthen the power of regional anti-organized crime directorates (RUBOPs) as a check on governors' influence over the police. Twelve RUBOPs divided up the country and were directly subordinate to a Deputy Minister of the central MVD, and, in the words of one former top MVD official, were used to "control" the regional police chief. Regional police chiefs apparently did resent the role of the anti-organized crime directorates; the head of the Novosibirsk police referred to the RUBOP as a "criminal organization."[51]

The procuracy, although remaining a more centralized control weapon than the MVD, also was the subject of serious power struggles. Stephen Holmes noted that "the unsteered devolution of power to the regions ... has inflicted great strains on an office that is traditionally hierarchical and unified

---

[48] Formally republics have ministries of internal affairs (MVDs), and major regions have main directorates of internal affairs (GUVDs). When referring generally to the regional internal affairs bureaucracy, I use the abbreviation UVD.

[49] Interview M-13; Interview M-33; Interview NN-7; Interview P-9; Interview P-12; Interview Ye-10; Interview Ye-11.

[50] Interview Ye-9. For discussions of local and regional powers over the police, including in the budget realm, see: V.N. Kolemasov et al., *Kommentariy k Zakonu Rossiyskoy Federatsii "O militsii": Postateynyy* (Moskva: Os'-89, 2007), pp. 361–369; E.V. Pershin and M.V. Gligich-Zolotareva, "Aktual'nye voprosy razgranicheniya kompetentsii mezhdu Rossiyskoy Federatsiey i sub"ektami Rossiyskoy Federatsii," *Analiticheskiy Vestnik: Sovet Federatsii Federal'nogo Sobraniya Rossiyskoy Federatsii (Analiticheskoye Upravleniye Otdel Gosudarstvennogo Stroitel'stva)*, No. 27 (344), December 2007, p. 26.

[51] Interview M-23; Interview M-47; Interview N-7; Vitaliy Ivanov, *Putin i regiony: Tsentralizatsiya Rossii* (Moskva: "Evropa," 2006), p. 90. On the Northwest RUBOP in Petersburg, see: Vadim Volkov, *Violent Entrepreneurs: The Use of Force in the Making of Russian Capitalism* (Ithaca, NY: Cornell University Press, 2002).

at the center."[52] Governors sought to control as much as possible the procurator in their region, and provided financing for housing and other benefits in an attempt to gain his support.[53] The procurator could be a crucial ally or a dangerous enemy because of his far-reaching powers to investigate the unlawful behavior of government officials. In practice, a lot depended on local conditions, in particular on the power of the governor and his relationship with the procurator. Although some procurators remained loyal to the center, many others developed close and friendly relationships with regional governors.[54]

With the police, procuracy, and often the courts partially reliant on governors, it was difficult for the center to use law enforcement as a weapon against recalcitrant or oppositional governors. Given this weakening of influence, Yeltsin made sure to keep the Federal Security Service (FSB) under firm central control, both in terms of financing and appointments. Indeed, regional FSB directors would keep dossiers of compromising information on governors. Even in the case of the FSB, however, close relations often developed between governors and FSB regional chiefs. For example, in Sverdlovsk Oblast, G.I. Voronov headed the regional FSB from 1992 through 2000, and was close enough to Governor Eduard Rossel that he went to work for him as secretary of the oblast Security Council when he was removed as FSB chief.[55]

The mere fact that Rossel created an oblast security council modeled on the federal one indicated his interest in coordinating the work of the regional power ministries, who – in theory at least – worked for the central government and not for him. The oblast Security Council included the governor and the local representatives from all of the power ministries, including the FSB, the MVD, the procuracy, and the Ministry of Defense and MVD Internal Troops district commanders for the Urals. Similarly, in St. Petersburg in the early 1990s, Mayor Anatoliy Sobchak made the local MVD and FSB chiefs members of his cabinet.[56]

Russian and international observers became seriously concerned about the degree of decentralization of control over coercion by the late 1990s, and discussion of the prospect of state collapse became increasingly prominent in both journalistic and academic accounts.[57] The most alarmist voices pointed not

---

[52] Stephen Holmes, "The Procuracy and its Problems: Introduction," *East European Constitutional Review*, 8, 1–2 (Winter/Spring 1999).

[53] Interview Ye-9; Kahn 2002, p. 182.

[54] Interview M-33; The Procurator-General from 1995 to 1999 noted several cases in which regional procurators opened criminal cases against governors or their deputies: Yuriy Skuratov, *Variant Drakona* (Moskva: Detektiv-Press, 2000), p. 111.

[55] Interview M-13; Interview M-33; Interview Ye-1; Interview Ye-11; "Ukaz ob obrazovanii Soveta Obshchestvennoy Bezopasnosti Sverdlovskoy Oblasti," Gubernator Sverdlovskoy Oblasti, November 27, 1995; "Ukaz o sostave Soveta Obshchestvennoy Bezopasnosti Sverdlovskoy Oblasti," Gubernator Sverdlovskoy Oblasti, May 13, 2002.

[56] Interview Ye-9; "Ukaz ob Obrazovanii Soveta Obshchestvennoy Bezopasnosti Sverdlovskoy Oblasti"; "Zakon o Sovete Obshchestvennoy Bezopasnosti Sverdlovskoy Oblasti," May 20, 1997; Interview P-1.

[57] Representative cites from 1999 are: Donald N. Jensen, "Is Russia Another Somalia?" *RFE/RL Newsline*, 3, 18, Part I (January 27, 1999); David Hoffman, "Yeltsin's Absentee

only to the substantial weakening of Moscow's control over law enforcement, but also of the armed forces. Knowledgeable experts spoke of "Kalashnikov confederalism," "military regionalization," and "the collapse of the military machine ... along regional fault lines."[58] These observers pointed in particular to the increasing provision of material resources, such as food and housing, by governors to military units based on their territory. This practice was encouraged and supported by the armed forces themselves as a way of compensating for shortfalls in federal financing.[59]

The problem with these scenarios is that in Russia, the army is a much less useful "weapon" in federal-regional bargaining than law enforcement. Neither the center nor the regions can call on military units to use force as part of this process, absent an armed secessionist movement. The Russian military traditionally has seen its primary focus as external defense and generally has not intervened in domestic politics.[60] In this respect, Russia is much more like India, where the military is also apolitical in terms of high politics and loyal to the center, than like Nigeria or Brazil in the past, where the military historically played a key domestic political role and local military officials sometimes sided with governors.[61] Moreover, for purely geographic and organizational reasons, the military is not situated to be used by governors. The Russian armed forces are organized in large military districts (currently six) that encompass multiple regions, and the commanders of these districts thus have no quasi-dependent relationship with any particular governor. Russian military experts, including multiple retired officers, were virtually unanimous when queried in 1999 and 2000 that the military could not be used to further separatist impulses and that they would not back governors in a conflict with the center, and that this had been true under Yeltsin, even when military financing was very low. Former Colonel and Duma Deputy Sergey Yushenkov (he was assassinated in 2003) argued that governors supported army units on their territory financially in order to promote stability, not to try to control them. Retired General Aleksandr Vladimirov stated in 1999, "economic assistance does not and will not influence the behavior of the army."[62]

That scenarios for military regionalization were seriously discussed in the late-Yeltsin period, even if implausible, suggests the degree to which control over coercion had become "decentered." Thomas Graham stated in 1999,

Rule Raises Specter of a 'Failed State'," *WP*, February 26, 1999, p. 1; Lapidus 1999; Herd 1999.

[58] Mark Galeotti, "Kalashnikov Confederalism," *JIR*, 11 (September 1999), 8–9; Herd, p. 265; Pavel K. Baev, "The Russian Armed Forces," *The Journal of Communist Studies and Transition Politics*, 17 (March 2001), p. 39.

[59] Indeed, the official military newspaper, *Krasnaya zvezda (Red Star)*, ran a series of interviews with governors and local military commanders on the topic in 1999 and 2000. Examples include: Igor' Budykin and Oleg Bedula, "Bez takogo edinstva ne vyzhit'," *KZ*, May 25, 1999; Yuriy Karacharov, "Nuzhdam voyennykh," *KZ*, February 29, 2000.

[60] Taylor, *Politics and the Russian Army*.

[61] On coercion and federalism in India, Brazil, and Nigeria, see Taylor 2007.

[62] Interviews: M-7; M-8; M-12; M-25; M-26; M-28; M-35; M-36; M-37; M-40; M-42. The one exception was Aleksandr Zhilin, who argued that military regionalization had been a real

"the Center does not enjoy the monopoly over the legitimate institutions of coercion it once did, nor does it necessarily reliably control those nominally subordinate to the Center." Alfred Stepan asserted in 2000 that the "territorial dispersion" of coercive power in Russia "has greatly complicated the tasks of a centralizing dictatorship."[63] This prediction was quickly put to the test, because Vladimir Putin made the restoration of the "power vertical" the primary objective of his first term, insisting, as later observed in *Izvestiya*, that the regions "return everything they had swallowed."[64] Central to Putin's efforts was regaining central control over state coercion.

PUTIN'S FEDERAL REFORMS AND THE POWER MINISTRIES

One week after taking his presidential oath in May 2000, Putin announced a major reform of Russian federalism. He decreed the creation of seven "federal districts (*okrugy*)" headed by an envoy or "presidential representative" (*polpred* is the Russian abbreviation).[65] The seven federal okrugs were the Northwest, Central, Southern, Volga, Urals, Siberian, and Far Eastern (see Map 4.1).[66] These polpreds (*polpredy* is the Russian plural form) were given the functions of coordinating the activity of federal executive branch organs in the regions, resolving disputes between federal and regional bodies, and monitoring the compliance of regional laws with federal laws and decrees. Another major function was the analysis of "the effectiveness of law enforcement organs' activity in the federal district," including the appointment of officials.[67] According to Galina Kovalskaya of *Itogi* magazine, the presidential representatives were created by Putin because "executive power in the regions had become practically uncontrollable: law enforcement organs, which according to the Constitution are supposed to fight lawlessness in the regions, had become completely dependent on the governors."[68]

The federal districts were the most important piece of a series of federal reforms launched by Putin in his first year.[69] These reforms responded to clear deficiencies in Russian federalism under Yeltsin, and it was obvious that some

---

threat in the late-Yeltsin period because of the dependence of commanders on governors for material support, but that Putin had quickly eliminated that threat: Interview M-44.

[63] National Intelligence Council 1999; Stepan, "Russian Federalism," p. 170.

[64] Yekaterina Grigor'eva, "Kak zakalyalas' vertikal'," *Izvestiya*, July 20, 2005.

[65] I use the terms "federal district" and "okrug," as well as the titles "envoy" and "polpred," interchangeably in the rest of the chapter.

[66] In 2009, the Southern Federal District was split in two with the creation of the North Caucasus Federal District.

[67] "O polnomochnom predstavitele Prezidenta Rossiyskoy Federatsii v federal'nom okruge," May 13, 2000. Available at: http://document.kremlin.ru/doc.asp?ID=001937

[68] Galina Koval'skaya, "Bessmennye besprizornye," *Itogi*, Feburary 6, 2001.

[69] The most thorough treatment of Putin's federal reforms in his first term is: Peter Reddaway and Robert W. Orttung, eds., *The Dynamics of Russian Politics*, Two Volumes (Lanham, MD: Rowman & Littlefield, 2004/2005). Updating the story to the second term is: Nikolai Petrov and Darrell Slider, "Putin and the Regions," in Dale R. Herspring, ed., *Putin's*

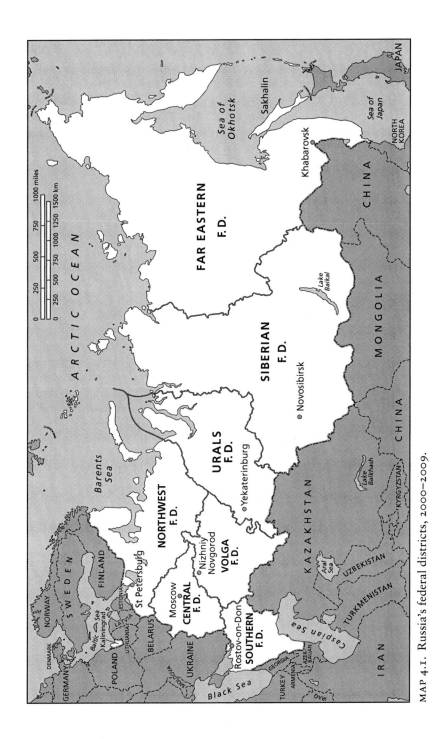

MAP 4.1. Russia's federal districts, 2000–2009.

recentralization was necessary. The ultimate result of Putin's federal reforms, however, was the return to a de facto unitary state, killing Russian federalism in order to save it. The power ministries were both an important subject and object of these reforms. The centrality of coercion to the federal reforms was made clear by the very boundaries of the federal districts, which corresponded exactly with the boundaries of the districts for the Internal Troops of the MVD.[70] In the following sections, I first show how the center wrested control over law enforcement personnel from the regional governors, and then examine how the polpreds used the recentralized power ministries to reimpose central dominance. I pay particular attention to the law enforcement agencies – MVD, FSB, and Procuracy – which were much more important than the armed forces, although some military personnel did occupy key positions. Finally, I demonstrate the importance of the power ministries and the siloviki to Putin's imposed "renegotiation" of the federal bargain, trumping the role of parties, the courts, and the Constitution itself.

"Cadres Decide Everything": Siloviki in the Regions[71]

Not only the boundaries of the new federal districts showed the centrality of the power ministries to the process, but the personnel chosen for the first and second tiers of these new structures came with pronounced siloviki backgrounds. Putin's initial choice of two army generals, two former KGB colleagues, and one MVD general to head five of the seven federal districts set the tone for the activities of the *polpredy*. Indeed, it seems clear that the whole reform plan was worked out in two key power structures that Putin had headed in 1999 before becoming Prime Minister and then President: the FSB and the Security Council. In 1999 and 2000, these bodies were headed by two of his closest allies, Nikolay Patrushev and Sergey Ivanov, both of whom, like Putin, came from St. Petersburg and began their careers in the KGB.[72]

Over the course of Putin's eight years as president, the polpreds in most of the districts were changed one or more times. Two envoys, however, kept their positions throughout Putin's tenure: KGB veteran Georgiy Poltavchenko in the Central Federal District and MVD General Petr Latyshev in the Urals Federal District. The reliance on power ministry personnel as polpreds was consistent from May 2000 to May 2008, with ten of the fifteen people serving in that capacity under Putin coming from power ministry backgrounds (see Table 4.3).[73]

Russia: Past Imperfect, Future Uncertain, 3rd Edition (Lanham, MD: Rowman & Littlefield, 2007), pp. 75–97.

[70] Nikolai Petrov, "The Security Dimension of the Federal Reform," in Reddaway and Orttung, Vol. II, p. 7.

[71] "Cadres decide everything" is one of Stalin's most famous quotes, still used frequently by Russians, including law enforcement officials. Examples from my interviews include: Interview N-7; Interview P-13; Interview P-14.

[72] Petrov, "Security Dimension," pp. 9–10.

[73] The polpreds are shown from May 2000, when the Federal Districts were created, to May 2008, when Dmitriy Medvedev succeeded Vladimir Putin as president. Although Dmitriy

TABLE 4.3. *Polpreds by Federal District, May 2000–May 2008*

Federal District	Polpreds
Central	*Georgiy Poltavchenko (2000–2008) (KGB/FSNP)*
Northwest	*Viktor Cherkesov (2000–2003) (KGB/FSB)* Valentina Matviyenko (2003) Ilya Klebanov (2003–2008)*
Volga	Sergei Kiriyenko (2000–2005) *Aleksandr Konovalov (2005–2008) (Procuracy)*
Southern	*Viktor Kazantsev (2000–2004) (Armed Forces)* *Dmitriy Kozak (2004–2007) (Procuracy)* *Grigoriy Rapota (2007–2008) (KGB/SVR)*
Urals	*Petr Latyshev (2000–2008) (MVD)*
Siberian	Leonid Drachevskiy (2000–2004) *Anatoliy Kvashnin (2004–2008) (Armed Forces)*
Far Eastern	*Konstantin Pulikovskiy (2000–2005) (Armed Forces)* Kamil' Iskhakov (2005–2007) *Oleg Safonov (2007–2008) (KGB/MVD)*

Italics = silovik.
* Klebanov was considered "affiliated" with the siloviki because of his background in the military-industrial complex.

A similar preponderance of siloviki was evident at the second tier in the federal districts. Second-tier positions include deputies and assistants to the polpred and the Main Federal Inspectors appointed to oversee the work of federal agencies in each region. I collected data on these officials at two different periods, in mid-2002 and mid-2007. At both periods, roughly 40 percent of these second-tier officials had power ministry backgrounds (see Table 4.4).[74] At the same time, there were noticeable differences between districts and over time. The Northwest Federal District under both Viktor Cherkesov and Ilya Klebanov was the most "militarized," with more than two-thirds of second-tier officials coming from the power ministries, whereas in 2002, the most civilian federal district was the Siberian one, headed by former diplomat Leonid Drachevskiy. When he was replaced by Army General Anatoliy

Kozak is not traditionally thought of as a silovik, he served in the Leningrad procuracy for five years in the 1980s.

[74] The 2002 data were collected mid-2002 from the website Rambler.Ru: Rossiyskaya Vlast' [http://Vlast.rambler.ru/], which is no longer active. I first reported this data in: Brian D. Taylor, "Strong Men, Weak State: Power Ministry Officials and the Federal Districts," *PONARS Policy Memo*, No. 284 (Washington, DC: Center for Strategic and International Studies, 2002). The 2007 data were collected mid-2007 from the official websites of the Federal Districts. Other analysts have put the silvoki presence in the federal districts even higher, with some estimates as high as 70–75 percent of second-tier officials: Petrov, "Security Dimension," pp. 22–23; Nikolai Petrov, "*Siloviki* in Russian Regions: New Dogs, Old Tricks," *Journal of Power Institutions in Post-Soviet Societies*, 2 (2005); Ol'ga Kryshtanovskaya, "Rezhim Putina: liberal'naya militoktratiya?" *Pro et Contra*, 7, 4 (Fall 2002), p. 163.

TABLE 4.4. *Federal Districts and Power Ministry Personnel, 2002 and 2007*

Federal District	Deputies & Assistants with Power Ministry Background		Main Federal Inspectors with Power Ministry Background		Totals	
	2002	2007	2002	2007	2002	2007
Central	3 of 8	No Data	10 of 18	No Data	13 of 26 (50%)	No Data
Northwest	4 of 6	5 of 10	7 of 10	9 of 11	11 of 16 (69%)	14 of 21 (67%)
Volga	1 of 6	2 of 7	6 of 13	8 of 14	7 of 19 (37%)	10 of 21 (48%)
Southern	2 of 7	1 of 4	5 of 9	No Data	7 of 16 (44%)	1 of 4 (25%)
Urals	1 of 5	1 of 4	3 of 6	2 of 6	4 of 11 (36%)	3 of 10 (30%)
Siberian	2 of 6	4 of 9	2 of 11	3 of 12	4 of 17 (24%)	7 of 21 (33%)
Far Eastern	3 of 6	2 of 6	1 of 8	0 of 8	4 of 14 (29%)	2 of 14 (14%)
Totals	16 of 44 (36%)	15 of 40 (38%)	34 of 75 (45%)	22 of 51 (43%)	50 of 119 (42%)	37 of 91(41%)

Kvashnin, the percentage of siloviki increased, whereas in the neighboring Far Eastern District, the proportion of siloviki dropped in half after Army General Konstantin Pulikovskiy was replaced by Kamil Iskhakov, the former mayor of the Tatar capital of Kazan.

The tendency to rely on siloviki for key first- and second-tier positions in the federal districts under Putin was consistent with his general reliance on a cohort of siloviki for key appointments, as shown in Chapter 2. Both Putin and the envoys filled positions with familiar faces from similar backgrounds, consistent with the general tendency toward patrimonial appointment patterns in the Russian state.

Putin used the federal district structures, dominated by siloviki, as the spearhead of an effort to impose greater centralization on the regions. Nikolay Fadeyev, the Main Federal Inspector for the Perm region, maintained that the federal district structures were designed as "administrative *spetsnaz* (special forces)," noting that they were directly subordinate to the presidential administration in the Kremlin.[75] Control over coercion was fundamental to this process of recentralization. Three of the main law enforcement structures – the MVD, the procuracy, and the FSNP – established federal district

---

[75] "Appendix A: Interview with the Chief Federal Inspector (CFI) for the Perm Region, Nikolai Anatolevich Fadeyev," in Reddaway and Orttung 2005, Vol. II, p. 488.

structures, creating an intermediate zone between the central ministry and the regional directorates, as did several smaller but still important organs, such as the Federal Customs Service and the Federal Financial Monitoring Service. Of the major law enforcement bodies, only the FSB did not follow suit – presumably it was felt that special efforts were not required to recentralize this agency, which had remained under Moscow's control throughout.[76]

The creation of a federal district MVD structure took place despite the fact that originally sources in the MVD said that such a change was not necessary and would simply duplicate the work of regional UVDs.[77] However, in June 2001, Putin signed a decree creating a Main Administration of the Ministry of Internal Affairs (GU MVD) in each of the okrugs. These GU MVD were created on the basis of existing RUBOP (organized crime) structures. Although the national directorate for fighting organized crime continued to exist, RUBOP personnel at the district level were incorporated into the GU MVD, and in most cases, the GU MVD was housed in the old RUBOP building.[78] Each of these administrations has a considerable staff, ranging from 150 to more than 300.[79]

The GU MVD had several explicit functions. The original decree in June 2001 listed three functions: "coordination, control, and analysis" of regional UVD; fighting organized crime, particularly of an "inter-regional" nature; and cooperation with the polpred's office in their district. Officials in the Northwest, Urals, and Siberian federal district MVD offices echoed these tasks, describing their functions, respectively, as "coordination, control, and analysis," "coordination and analysis," and "management and control." In practice, there were two key lines of work. First, the Operational-Investigative Bureau of each GU MVD worked on combating large organized crime groups whose activities crossed the borders of more than one region. These Operational-Investigative Bureaus were supposed to deal with the "biggest cases" of "inter-regional significance." One official also noted that they were able to deal with corruption associated with regional governors, something that regional UVD often did not do because of their dependence on the region for financing. The second line of work was as an intermediate body that

---

[76] Ivanov 2006, pp. 90–91. Yekaterina Zapodinskaya, the law enforcement correspondent for *Kommersant"-Daily*, stated that the FSB did not need a federal district level because of its strong centralization: Interview M-43.

[77] "V kazhdyi okrug – general-prokurora," *KD*, May 25, 2000.

[78] In the Urals Federal District in Yekaterinburg, the GU MVD had to be built more from scratch, because the Urals RUBOP had been headquartered in Tyumen. Information on the organization of the GU MVD from: Interview N-11; Interview NN-7; Interview P-13; Interview P-14; Interview Ye-14.

[79] In Siberia, the GU MVD in 2003 had 150 personnel; in the Volga, the number was put at 300–400: Interview N-11; "Appendix: Interview with the Chief Federal Inspector (CFI) for the Perm Region, Nikolai Anatolevich Fadeyev," in Reddaway and Orttung 2004, Vol. I, p. 305. Other analysts suggested 150 was the target figure for GU MVD staffs: Pavel Isayev, "B. Gryzlov vystraivayet novuyu vertikal' MVD," *RRB*, 3, 2 (June 18, 2001); Nikolai Petrov, "Seven Face's of Putin's Russia," *Security Dialogue*, 33, 1 (March 2002), p. 81.

provided information to the central MVD and the polpred in their district. In essence, they acted as a filter for statistics, reports, and major personnel decisions. Receiving information from seven federal district structures greatly simplified the work of the central MVD compared to the old system of information from eighty-nine regions, and also allowed the polpred and thus the presidential administration to keep tabs on regional police forces. The Main Federal Inspector in the Northwest Federal District during Putin's first term, Nikolay Vinnichenko, stated in 2002 that the main advantage of the okrug-level power ministry structures is that they are "closer to local conditions, but look out for Moscow's interests." Furthermore, he maintained, regional law enforcement organs feel the support of the federal district agencies and thus "are not allowed to weaken."[80]

At the same time, federal district police officials were at pains to stress that they did not "interfere" with the work of local and regional police, who still answered for crime in their cities and regions. Regional and local police officials were often openly skeptical of the GU MVD. The head of the Novosibirsk regional police, A. Soinov, said the goals and tasks of the federal district police structures were "unclear" and "not necessary." A police colonel in Yekaterinburg similarly believed that the GU MVD had unclear functions, referring to their personnel as "do nothings" (*bezdel'niki*) who engage in "endless meetings." A police colonel in Moscow also described the district MVD structures as "falsely created" and "unnecessary." Even some GU MVD officials were inclined to admit that the lines of authority remained unclear, and that their structure might be "temporary." One went so far as to refer to his own organ as "superfluous" and "an experiment."[81]

One key function of the federal district police structures, as well as the polpred and other power ministry agencies at the district level, was to replace regional and local police personnel who were seen as "captives" of the governors. What Joel Migdal has labeled "the big shuffle" – the power of leaders to remove and appoint local officials – was crucial to undermining "threatening conglomerates of power."[82] Indeed, arguably depriving governors of influence over regional power ministry agencies and personnel was the key function of these new bureaucracies. Personnel replacement became a key task of the GU MVD. In 2001, the Putin government successfully pushed through the parliament an important change in the law on the police. Previously, the central government had to gain the approval of regional leaders to appoint or fire chiefs of regional UVDs. The "Law on Militia" was amended to give the president the power to appoint and remove regional police chiefs, on the

[80] Ukaz Prezidenta Rossiyskoy Federatsii No. 644, "O nekotorykh voprosakh Ministerstva Vnutrennikh Del Rossiyskoy Federatsii," June 4, 2001; Interview N-11; Interview NN-7; Interview P-13; Interview P-14; Interview Ye-14; Interview P-11.

[81] Interview N-11; Interview N-7; Interview Ye-13; Interview M-46; Interview Ye-14; Interview P-13. Similar assessments were given by: Interview NN-8; Interview P-2; Interview P-9; Interview Ye-11.

[82] Joel S. Migdal, *Strong Societies and Weak States: State-Society Relations in the Third World* (Princeton, NJ: Princeton University Press, 1988), pp. 214–217.

recommendation of the head of the MVD. Under the amended law, the head of the MVD only has to solicit the opinion of the regional leader; now the governor merely has an important say in who controls the public-order police (MOB).[83]

In many federal districts, the MVD and the presidential envoy wrested control over the regional UVDs from the local leader. Important regions in which the head of the UVD was replaced in Putin's first three years included Moscow, St. Petersburg, Yekaterinburg, Nizhniy Novgorod, and Primorskiy Krai (Vladivostok).[84] Similarly, regional procurators were changed in many cases. For example, two-thirds of the procurators in the Volga Federal Okrug were changed in the first year after the district was created.[85]

It is important not to overstate the change from Yeltsin to Putin in this respect. Under Yeltsin, about seventeen regional police chiefs changed every year, whereas in Putin's first six years this number increased to more than nineteen, on average. Furthermore, there was no obvious yearly pattern in the replacements, with the number of replacements fluctuating between fifteen and twenty-five a year (see Figure 4.1).[86]

More important than the number of appointments per year were the geographic origins of the new police chiefs. In the Soviet period, there was a tradition of "rotation of cadres" outside of their home region for many state officials. For some law enforcement agencies, especially the FSB and the Procuracy, this rotation continued under Yeltsin. In the MVD, however, the principle, according to one police specialist, became much less formal in the 1990s. A more concerted effort was made under Putin to rotate police cadres from region to region, and both Putin and his close ally and former Interior Minister (2001–2003) Boris Gryzlov publicly advocated such a policy, with the goal of bringing in outsiders to break up existing local ties.[87] As shown in Figure 4.2, the percentage of "outsiders" appointed to regional police jobs increased from 42 percent under Yeltsin to 67 percent under Putin.[88]

---

[83] Shumilov 2002; Petr Koz'ma, "Gosduma reshayet, kto budet uvol'nyat' nachalnikov UVD v regionakh," *RRB*, 2, 9 (May 5, 2000); *RRB*, 3, 14–15 (July 23, 2001).

[84] The following several paragraphs are based largely on a database of regional police chief appointments for the years 1992–2006 compiled by the author and his research assistants. Appointments to regional UVD were monitored from multiple sources, including: *Rambler: Rossiyskaya vlast'* [http://vlast.rambler.ru]; *Shchit i Mech*, the MVD newspaper; *MVD Rossii: Entsiklopediya* (Moskva: MVD Rossii, 2002); the Presidential website [http://www.kremlin.ru]. In addition to my research assistants Yulia Ivanovskaya and Katya Kalandadze, I thank Nikolai Petrov for invaluable assistance.

[85] Peter Baker and Susan Glasser, "Regions Resist Kremlin Control," *WP*, May 31, 2001.

[86] On this issue I somewhat disagree with Nikolai Petrov, who argued that there was an "abrupt renewal" of the regional MVD leadership in Putin's first years; in fact, the number of changes in 2001–2002 was not radically different than 1998–1999: Petrov, "*Siloviki* in Russian Regions."

[87] Interview M-33; Interview NN-7; Elena Shishkunova, "Putin otdal militsiyu polpredam," *Gazeta.ru*, May 31, 2002; Interfaks, "Novye naznacheniya v UIN i UVD," *Gazeta*, March 18, 2003; Anastasiya Kornya, "Rotatsiya vmesto 'chistki'," *Vremya-MN*, June 1, 2002.

[88] These data are for the officials on which we were able to collect information on their previous appointment. Although the data are not complete, we believe they are not biased and thus are representative of general trends.

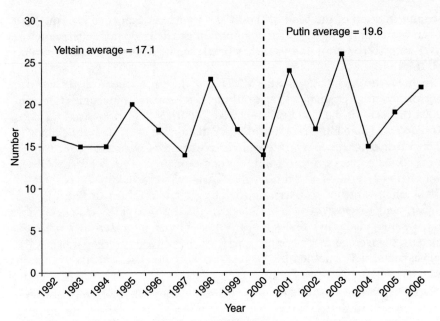

FIGURE 4.1. Regional police chief appointments, 1992–2006.

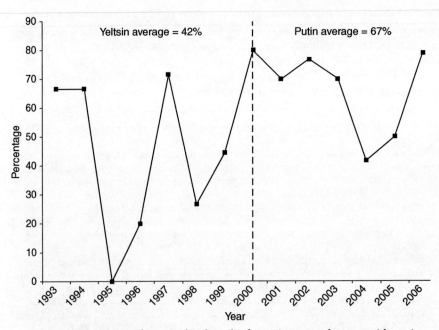

FIGURE 4.2. Percentage of regional police chief appointments from outside region, 1993–2006.

A few examples will demonstrate the pattern. A.M. Belozerov was born in Krasnodar Krai in the Southern Federal District and rose to head the city police in two cities in the Krai, Sochi and Novorossiysk. In 2001, he was appointed to head the UVD in Orenburg Oblast in the Volga Federal District, then in 2003 returned to the Southern Federal District, this time in Rostov Oblast. A.A. Antonov was born in Tula Oblast in the Central Federal District, served in the Moscow police for many years, and then rose to work in the central MVD, before being named to head the Irkutsk Oblast GUVD in the Siberian Federal District in 2004. V.P. Ponomarev was born in Mordovia in the Volga Federal District, was deputy head of the Saratov UVD (also in the Volga region), was tapped in 2001 to be the deputy head of the GU MVD in the Southern Federal District, became head of the Republic of Kalmykia MVD in 2003, and then in 2006 transferred to head the MVD of the Republic of Khakasia in Siberia.[89] Nikolai Petrov documented similar rotation patterns in not only the MVD but also the FSB in Putin's first term, while noting that the principle of rotation in the FSB had been retained under Yeltsin as well.[90]

It is important to note that the replacement and renewal of regional power ministry officials did not always go smoothly. Some of the most powerful regional governors and presidents resisted the Kremlin's efforts to recapture control. From 1999 to 2001, a major battle, with multiple court cases, raged between powerful Moscow Mayor Yuri Luzhkov and the federal government over the power to appoint the head of the Moscow police. A compromise candidate was eventually found, but the central government won the fight over the power to appoint regional police chiefs.[91]

Two of the most independent and powerful republican presidents under Yeltsin and Putin were Tatarstan President Mintimer Shaymiyev and Bashkortostan President Murtaza Rakhimov. After 2000, the control of both Rakhimov and Shaymiyev over the power ministries in their republics declined somewhat, but they remained stronger in this realm than most governors. Both of them managed to keep the same republican MVD head throughout Putin's presidency. In Bashkortostan, Rafail Divayev, who had been appointed police chief in 1996, even weathered a major national scandal about violent police abuse against innocent citizens in the town of Blagoveshchensk in December 2004.[92] On the other hand, several investigations launched by the center in 2001 led to new Bashkir procuracy and FSB

---

[89] All data from author's database. On the struggle to appoint Ponomarev to the Kalmykia MVD in 2003, see: Petrov "*Siloviki* in Russian Regions."

[90] Petrov "*Siloviki* in Russian Regions."

[91] Brian D. Taylor, "Law Enforcement and Russia's Federal Districts," in Reddaway and Orttung 2005, p. 71.

[92] On the events in Blagoveshchensk, see: Peter Finn, "For Russians, Police Rampage Fuels Fear," *WP*, March 27, 2005. Divayev was replaced in October 2008: Tat'yana Romenskaya, "Ministr MVD respubliki Bashkortostan osvobozhden ot dolzhnosti," *RG*, October 20, 2008.

TABLE 4.5. *"Outsiders" in Regional Power Ministries, 2000–2007*

Agency	2000	2007
FSB	58	72
Procuracy	32	55
MVD	15	50
Main Federal Inspector	15	31

heads being appointed in 2002.[93] In Tatarstan, an "outsider" was eventually brought in to head the FSB, but both the MVD and Procuracy remained under the control of locals.[94]

Nikolay Petrov demonstrated a pronounced tendency toward greater reliance on outsiders in regional power ministries from the beginning to the end of the Putin presidency (see Table 4.5). Of the eighty-nine regions in 2000, only in the case of the FSB were the majority of agency heads outsiders. By 2007, when the number of regions had been reduced to eighty-five, in the three main law enforcement structures – the FSB, the MVD, and the procuracy – there were a majority of outsiders heading the regional branches in Russia. The position of Main Federal Inspector, which is not a power ministry job but is often filled by siloviki, also saw a pronounced increase in the percentage of outsiders in these positions.[95]

To summarize, under Putin, control over law enforcement and security personnel shifted drastically back toward the center in comparison to the Yeltsin years. By all accounts, the degree of central financing for the power ministries also increased under Putin, although this is harder to verify on a region-by-region basis.[96] How did the central government use this reacquired ability to control the behavior of the power ministries in the regions?

The Federal Districts: Coercion and the "Power Vertical"

Why did Moscow care about controlling the power ministries in the regions? After all, some dispersion of coercive control is a common feature of many federations. Boris Yeltsin apparently decided, for example, that it was okay

[93] Igor Rabinovich, "Center Cracks Down on Bashkortostan Police, Procurator," *RRR*, 6, 17 (May 9, 2001); Igor Rabinovich, "Bashkortostan's Tax Police Limit Rakhimov's Power," *RRR*, 6, 30 (August 29, 2001).

[94] Interview M-23; Nikolay Petrov, "Naslediye imperiy i regionalizm," in Aleksey Miller, ed., *Naslediye imperiy i budushcheye Rossii* (Moskva: Fond "Liberal'naya missiya," 2008), pp. 381–454.

[95] Petrov 2008. Note that the number of positions does not always equal the number of regions: for example, the head of the St. Petersburg city police is also responsible for neighboring Leningrad Oblast, and several Main Federal Inspectors cover multiple territories. For specifics, see: Petrov and Slider 2007, p. 87.

[96] Interview M-47; Interview NN-8; Interview Ye-1.

to allow the governors to have considerable power over the police.[97] Vladimir Putin thought differently, viewing the decentralization of coercion as a potential threat to state integrity. Russian social scientist Andrey Kortunov put it in Hobbesian terms at the beginning of the Putin presidency, noting that by trying to put the power ministries under them, the governors were trying to "take away the trump card of the center."[98] With the creation of the federal districts and the recentralization of the power ministries, Putin got his trump card back. He proceeded to use it to fulfill both routine and extraordinary tasks. Here I highlight two issues, the "harmonization of laws" campaign and the use of the federal districts and the power ministries to pursue political tasks for the center.

The Harmonization of Laws

A major initiative of Putin and the presidential envoys in his first term was the effort to bring local laws and ordinances into compliance with federal law. The procuracy in particular played a key role in this process.[99]

The process of trying to harmonize federal and regional laws did not begin with Putin's federal reforms. For example, in January 1998, Procurator-General Yuri Skuratov claimed that in the previous two-year period, procurators throughout Russia had annulled more than 2,000 laws and resolutions that violated the Constitution. The Kremlin under Yeltsin was well aware of the problem, and Putin even organized a conference on the issue when he worked for the presidential administration in Yeltsin's second term. Thus, Putin's claim that procurators in the year 2000 were "starting from scratch" in this process was a clear overstatement. Still, although efforts were occasionally made to focus on these legal discrepancies, the central government was too weak at the time to make significant progress; a legal expert in Yekaterinburg noted that under Yeltsin, there was "a lack of political will from the center" on this issue. It was also true that some Yeltsin advisers were not overly alarmed by the situation, arguing that national laws took precedence over regional and local laws, so if they were in conflict, the lower one was invalid anyway.[100]

Putin gave new impetus to the process of legal harmonization, and the personnel and organizational changes discussed earlier in many cases severed or weakened governors' control over the local procuracy. In 2002, both the Main Federal Inspector for St. Petersburg, Nikolay Vinnichenko, and the Vice-Governor Anna Markova credited this campaign with bearing fruit. Markova's office expended considerable effort on the process, which it undertook by going back to the late Soviet period and systematically working through decrees and

---

97 Interview M-33.
98 Interview M-18.
99 For other treatments of this issue, see: Alexei Trochev and Peter H. Solomon Jr., "Courts and Federalism in Putin's Russia," in Reddaway and Orttung, 2005, pp. 91–122; Kahn 2002, pp. 234–278; Hahn 2003.
100 Lapidus 1999, p. 78; Interview M-19; V.V. Putin, "Vystupleniye Prezidenta Rossiyskoi Federatsii V.V. Putina na kollegii General'noi prokuratury RF," February 21, 2002; Interview Ye-4; Interview M-30.

laws year by year. Further, Markova contended that the judicial system and
the procuracy could not have accomplished this work on their own, given their
other responsibilities. Law enforcement officials in Nizhny Novgorod similarly
lauded the process of bringing laws into compliance. The head of the Volga
Okrug procuracy, Deputy Procurator-General Aleksandr Zvyagintsev, headed
a commission to bring laws into compliance throughout the okrug. Specialists
and experts were enlisted in the process, and the commission sent representatives to the okrug's republics. The commission also reviewed new and draft
legislation. Previously, according to these officials, no one had paid attention
to this issue except specialists. In this respect they viewed the creation of the
okrugs and envoys as a success. Similar procedures were established in the
Urals Federal District, with an expert commission working with the procurator, the Ministry of Justice, and the polpred to review old laws and bring them
into correspondence with federal law.[101] Envoys themselves reported major successes in this campaign during its first few years, claiming to have brought
hundreds of laws into compliance with federal ones.[102]

There was considerable regional variation in both the nature of the law
standardization process and the extent of the problem. In some okrugs, the
envoys worked most closely with the procuracy, in others with the Ministry
of Justice, and in yet others, joint commissions from the two agencies were
created.[103] In addition, some regions had many violations whereas others had
few, and some regional leaders resisted changes whereas others adopted them
willingly. Not surprisingly, in Tatarstan and Bashkortostan, the process was
much more contentious than in most other regions. Moreover, regional leaders could seek special exemptions from the presidential envoy; in Moscow, for
example, Mayor Luzhkov was allowed to continue his anticonstitutional policy of restricting internal immigration of Russian citizens to the capital.[104]

President Putin hailed the work of the procuracy on the standardization
of laws, claiming that it "played the most important role in implementing
the important task of creating a unified legal space in the country." At the
same time, his Urals envoy Latyshev noted some flaws in the process. In particular, he observed that many so-called violations of federal law contained
in regional law occur because of the absence of corresponding federal law.
Similarly, then Samara Governor Konstantin Titov complained to Kiriyenko
that in some cases it was the federal, not the regional, laws that contradicted

---

[101] Interview P-5; Interview P-11; Interview NN-7; Interview NN-8; Interview Ye-4; Interview
Ye-5; Interview Ye-9.

[102] Taylor 2005, pp. 73–74.

[103] Interviews cited in note 101. The different procedures by Federal District also are discussed
in the different chapters of Reddaway and Orttung 2004.

[104] "Bringing Regional Laws into Line," *RRR*, 6, 18 (May 16, 2001); Interview NN-1; Artem
Vernidub, "Korruptsiya dolzhna byt' upravlyayemoy," *gazeta.ru*, May 15, 2002; Taylor
2005, p. 74; Elena A. Chebankova, "The Limitations of Central Authority in the Regions
and the Implications for the Evolution of Russia's Federal System," *Europe-Asia Studies*, 57,
7 (November 2005), pp. 935–936; Baker and Glasser 2001.

the Constitution. He also complained about overzealous behavior on the part of procurators. Further, Yekaterinburg legal specialists Konstantin Kiselev and Viktor Rudenko noted that most of the violations in regional law were technicalities, and that other violations arose because federal laws were amended after regional laws were passed, thereby rendering noncompliant laws that were previously congruent with federal law. Rudenko also noted, in tune with Titov's complaint, that okrug and regional level procurators were "overfulfilling the plan" to demonstrate their loyalty to Moscow. Similarly, experts in Novosibirsk thought that the Siberian polpred Drachevskiy had overstated the importance of the campaign, given that most of the legal discrepancies did not result from political disagreements but rather technicalities similar to those pointed to by Kiselev and Rudenko. Although the process may have been useful in Novosibirsk, it was neither controversial nor symptomatic of fundamental disagreements between the region and the center.[105]

The process of harmonizing federal, regional, and local laws in Russia will be an ongoing one. Putin's federal reforms, if nothing else, did focus attention on the importance of these legal questions, although, as noted earlier, some experts thought the issue was overblown. In the long run, what is needed are institutionalized administrative and legal processes for dealing with these issues, not public campaigns, and such processes did indeed emerge. Far Eastern envoy Pulikovskiy created a mechanism by which the Ministry of Justice reviewed both draft and new legislation in his okrug's regions. Similar processes were created in the Siberian, Urals, and Volga Federal Districts. In Saratov, a committee including members from the procuracy, the Ministry of Justice, the legislature, the governor's administration, and the envoy's office was established to harmonize laws.[106] In short, the envoys, in conjunction with procuracy officials, played a useful role in coordinating the work of executive and legislative branch officials at multiple levels to make Russian law more coherent. By the end of the Putin presidency, legal experts concluded, Russian law had become substantially unified and centralized; indeed, perhaps too centralized for a notionally federal state.[107] What is most important, of course, is a different and much harder task than centralization alone: regular and predictable implementation of the law.

The Federal Districts and the Manipulation of Law Enforcement
In Chapter 3, I argued that at the level of the central government, the Putin government increased its ability to use the power ministries for exceptional

---

[105] Pushkarev 2001; Anisim Tarasov, "Privolzhskiy forum: Stremleniye uyti ot praktiki partkhozaktivov," *RRB*, 3, 21 (November 5, 2001); Interview Ye-5; Interview Ye-9; Interview N-1; Interview N-8; Interview N-10.

[106] Chebankova 2005, pp. 934–935; *RRR*, 6, 39 (November 7, 2001); *RRR*, 6, 18 (May 16, 2001); Interview NN-7; Interview NN-8; Interview N-6; Interview Ye-4; Interview Ye-5; Interview Ye-9; Interview Ye-10.

[107] Jeffrey Kahn, Alexei Trochev, and Nikolay Balayan, "The Unification of Law in the Russian Federation," *Post-Soviet Affairs*, 25, 4 (2009), pp. 310–346.

tasks, such as repressing economic and political rivals, but made less progress in increasing state capacity to fight crime and terrorism and protect private property rights. The story at the regional level is similar, in that greater central control was used at the regional level to further particular political interests rather than establish the rule of law after the so-called "legal anarchy" of the Yeltsin years.[108] Although polpreds and federal district law enforcement agencies did in some cases make efforts to sever the link between business, politics, and the law at the regional level, more often it appeared that federal district structures themselves manipulated law enforcement organs for political ends.

The need for truly independent procurators and police was clear after a sometimes brutal and often legally questionable decade of redistributing power and property in Russia. Vladimir Ovchinskiy, a former assistant to ex-Interior Minister Anatoliy Kulikov, applauded the changes in the police law that weakened the governors' role in MVD appointments, calling them a necessary condition "for the liberation of regional police from the yoke of local corrupt clans and the criminal fraternity." Even procurators themselves admitted that, in the words of Pskov's regional procurator Nikolay Lepikhin, "procuracy offices fulfill political orders all the time."[109] Some observers, such as Igor Rabinovich, hoped that Putin's federal reforms would "strengthen the level of legality and the observation of human rights," at least in more authoritarian regions such as Bashkortostan.[110]

What happened turned out rather differently. The federal districts became a further source for the manipulation of law enforcement, not an instrument for combating such practices.

In Chapter 3, I described how law enforcement organs were used to shape elections, and some of the examples involved the Federal District structures, including in the Northwest and Southern federal districts. Similar practices were seen in other federal districts. In the Urals Federal District, a deputy of envoy Latyshev (himself an MVD general) ran for governor in the Tyumen region, with the support of MVD offices around the okrug. In the Volga okrug, law enforcement structures established a commission to investigate the President of the Mariy-El Republic, Vyacheslav Kislitsyn, before an election: A candidate backed by the Kremlin and polpred Kiriyenko then defeated him.[111] The procuracy and the courts also were heavily involved in elections for mayor of Nizhniy Novgorod and for the regional legislature in 2002. The

[108] References to "legal anarchy" under Yeltsin include: Masha Lipman, "Constrained or Irrelevant: The Media in Putin's Russia," *Current History*, October 2005, p. 321; Peter Rutland, "Russia 2001: Putin in Charge," *Transitions Online*, January 9, 2002.

[109] Vladimir Ovchinskiy, "Yur'ev den' dlya militsii," *MN*, June 12, 2001; *RFE/RL Newsline*, 6, 39 (February 28, 2002).

[110] Rabinovich, "Center Cracks Down...," 2001.

[111] *RFE/RL Crime, Corruption, and Terrorism Watch*, 1, 6 (December 6, 2001); Jeffrey Kahn, "Canaries in the Coal Mine: Early Warning Signals for Putin's Federal Reforms," *RFE/RL Russian Federation Report*, 4, 5 (February 13, 2002); Sergei Kondrat'ev, "Urals Federal Okrug," in Reddaway and Orttung 2004, p. 201; Gul'naz Sharafutdinova and Arbakhan Magomedov, "Volga Federal Okrug," in Reddaway and Orttung 2004, p. 167.

favored mayoral candidate of Kiriyenko was eventually declared the winner after a scandal-plagued election that commentator Yulia Latynina described as an "orgy of filth." One mayoral candidate was removed from the ballot by court order, and criminal cases were opened against the incumbent mayor and his associates; local observers attributed these acts to pressure from Kiriyenko. The head of the Nizhny Novgorod police was removed a year later, allegedly at least in part because of his refusal to carry out instructions from Kiriyenko during the mayoral election.[112]

Other law enforcement investigations apparently were related to similar political disputes. For example, in the Southern Okrug, Stavropol Governor Aleksandr Chernogorov was investigated by the procuracy and other federal organs. Local observers suggested that the investigations stemmed from a struggle for control over the pro-Putin "United Russia" party.[113] Former St. Petersburg Governor Vladimir Yakovlev was another prominent regional leader whose position came under heavy attack from okrug officials. Indeed, it appeared that the primary task of the first Northwest Okrug polpred, Viktor Cherkesov, was to unseat Yakovlev, who successfully ran for mayor against Putin's former boss and patron, St. Petersburg Mayor Anatoliy Sobchak, in 1996. The Northwest Federal District Procurator-General opened corruption investigations against four of Yakovlev's deputy governors, something the city procurator was less likely to do. Several other top officials were also investigated, and Vladimir Zubrin, head of the okrug procuracy, stated: "The corruption investigation of the city's administration is a serious warning to St. Petersburg Governor Vladimir Yakovlev, and our demand to him is to instill order among his associates." Federal pressure was widely believed to be behind Yakovlev's June 2003 decision to resign as governor.[114]

Thus, the successful wresting of control over law enforcement structures from regional leaders did not put an end to the manipulation of their work in order to implement extraordinary decisions. The use of the FSB, procuracy, and police for political purposes continued, but it took place more at the okrug and federal levels and at the direction of the Kremlin. Of course, in all of these cases, it is quite possible that the targets were indeed guilty of various forms of malfeasance. But the timing and nature of the law enforcement

---

[112] Yulia Latynina, "Nizhny Vote Descends Into Orgy of Filth," *MT*, September 18, 2002; Oleg Rodin, "Democratic Procedures or Electoral Games?", *RFE/RL Russian Political Weekly*, 2, 37 (November 6, 2002); Andrei Makarychev, "Nizhny Journalists, Politicians Examine State of Media, Elections," *RRR*, 8, 5 (April 8, 2003); Interview NN-1; Interview NN-3; Interview NN-6; Interview NN-7; Interview NN-8; Sergei Anisimov, "Politika i militsiya – veshchi nesovmestnye," *Nez. Gaz.*, May 20, 2003. Putting these elections in a larger context is: Gulnaz Sharafutdinova, "Why was democracy lost in Russia's regions? Lessons from Nizhnii Novgorod," *Communist and Post-Communist Studies*, 40 (2007), pp. 363–382.

[113] Natalia Zubarevich, "Southern Federal Okrug," in Reddaway and Orttung 2004, p. 123.

[114] Interview P-1; Interview P-6; Interview P-8; *RFE/RL Newsline*, 6, 88 (May 13, 2002); *RFE/RL Newsline*, 6, 19 (January 30, 2002); *Ot pervogo litsa*, pp. 104–108; "Severo-Zapadnyy FO. V okruge luchshe boryutsya s korruptsiey, chem v drugikh regionakh Rossii, schitaet zamestitel' genprokurora RF," *Regions.ru*, February 20, 2003.

investigations and actions suggested that political motives were at work. The return to federal dominance of law enforcement did not change the basic rules of the game – the power ministries were manipulated for political advantage by whoever could control them, which undermined their capacity to carry out their lawful tasks.

The Power Vertical Restored

Putin's federal reforms in his first term were designed to alter the terms of the federal bargain that existed under Yeltsin sharply in the direction of the center. The power ministries in general, and law enforcement structures (the MVD, the FSB, and the procuracy) in particular, were key objects in this struggle. In particular, the new federal districts and the district-level power ministry structures presided over a series of efforts to diminish the power of the regions, including the appointment of new regional law enforcement officials. The polpreds launched efforts to coordinate the work of the siloviki in their federal districts, creating security councils bringing together the power ministries in their regions. Although these collegiums were only empowered to give recommendations and not directives, one GU MVD colonel in the Siberian Federal District noted that in reality, these "recommendations" were fulfilled – tersely adding, "try not to." Similarly, the main federal inspectors, who were, in the words of one of them, a "mini-polpred," met regularly with power ministry officials in their region. One Russian expert concluded as early as 2001 that these reforms "undoubtedly seriously undermine the opportunities for regional leaders to use 'their' power structures in conflict with the federal center."[115]

In many regions, governors offered little or no resistance to this diminution of their power. For example, of the forty-six bilateral treaties in force when Putin took power, twenty-eight were annulled by April 2002, often at the initiative of the regional governor himself as a sign of loyalty to the center. In 2003, the rest of the bilateral treaties lost their power due to national legislation, although a handful of regions still insisted their agreements were in force.[116] In most cases, governors saw little to gain and much to lose, both economically and politically, in challenging the popular Putin, particularly now that he had taken his club back.

Other regional leaders offered more resistance. For example, Sverdlovsk Governor Eduard Rossel was one of Russia's most powerful and independent governors. He quickly clashed with the Urals Federal District polpred, MVD General Latyshev, and their early relations were extremely poor. Latyshev held the ultimate trump card, however, and moved quickly to undermine

[115] Interview P-13; Interview P-14; Interview N-11; Interview P-11; Pavel Isayev, "B. Gryzlov vystraivayet novuyu vertikal' MVD," *RRB*, 3, 2 (June 18, 2001).
[116] Julia Kusznir, "The New Russian-Tatar Treaty and Its Implications for Russian Federalism," *RAD*, No. 16 (March 6, 2007), p. 3; Ross 2005, p. 359; Chebankova 2005, pp. 936–937.

Rossel by getting a new procurator, GUVD head, Tax Police chief, and head of the regional State Customs Committee (later the Federal Customs Service) appointed within his first year. Yekaterinburg political scientist Ilya Gorfinkel remarked in May 2001, "on the field in which [Rossel] could put up pressure – control over federal structures, law enforcement, police, the procurator – he either has lost already or is losing now."[117]

Symptomatic of the change in the coercive realm was the altered composition of the Sverdlovsk Oblast Security Council. As noted above, Rossel created the council in 1995 to coordinate the work of the power ministries in his region, and all of the key officials participated. In contrast, after Latyshev arrived on the scene, the head of the Urals Military District (Volga-Urals Military District after September 2001) stopped attending these meetings, as did the oblast procurator. The regional heads of the other power ministries lowered their level of participation, sending their deputies instead of attending themselves, a move described by a member of Rossel's staff as a "show of loyalty to the center." The okrug procurator insisted that the Sverdlovsk charter be amended to strike the provision on creating its own police force – a provision, as noted earlier, that was inconsistent with the federal "Law on the Militia." Sergey Belyayev, the head of a Yekaterinburg human rights organization, observed, "the polpred has taken control of all power ministries – this is his main function, and his main accomplishment."[118]

Other powerful regions, such as Tatarstan and Bashkortostan, as noted earlier, were able to maintain greater autonomy in the coercive realm. Volga Federal District envoy Kiriyenko remained quite deferential to Tatarstan President Shaymiyev in particular.[119] In his home base of Nizhniy Novgorod, however, Kiriyenko used the power ministries to impose okrug dominance on the region. As Kiriyenko's political rival and controversial businessman/convicted criminal Andrey Klimentev asserted, "Kiriyenko as presidential envoy has taken control of the local power structures – the police, the tax police, and the special services."[120]

These changes in the distribution of coercive power between federal and regional leaders were not the only aspects of Putin's federal reforms, but they were, in my view, the most fundamental.[121] Further, it was necessary to start with the power bodies because they were both more reliable mechanisms for changing the terms of the federal bargain than other possibilities, and because they could help determine outcomes in other aspects of federal reforms. A brief overview of these other possible mechanisms, and other key Putin reforms,

---

[117] Kondrat'ev 2004, pp. 196–199; Baker and Glasser 2001; *RRB*, 3, 11 (June 4, 2001).
[118] Interview Ye-1; Interview Ye-9; "Ukaz o sostave Soveta Obshchestvennoy Bezopasnosti Sverdlovskoy Oblasti," 2002; Interview Ye-3.
[119] Sharafutdinova and Magomedov 2004; Interview NN-3; Interview NN-5; Interview NN-8.
[120] Oleg Rodin, "Strange Bedfellows in Nizhnii Novgorod," *RFE/RL Russian Federation Report*, 4, 12 (April 3, 2002).
[121] See also Petrov, "The Security Dimension of the Federal Reform."

demonstrates that force was not the only mechanism available for shifting the federal balance, but it was pivotal.

The Constitutional Court, although obviously not an irrelevant player in the process, did not have the authority to enforce decisions regulating jurisdictional disputes between the center and the subunits. Indeed, the Constitutional Court had ruled against the regions in several cases under Yeltsin, but these decisions had little effect because the regions involved either disputed the standing of the Court or simply ignored the rulings. Jeffrey Kahn noted that the Court had "consistently (but futilely) opposed" the regions, and that it had been "an ineffective and infrequent arbiter in federal disputes." One member of the Court noted that it took a signal from the top to rule against key regions, stating that the Court acted "only after President Putin announced his crackdown on recalcitrant regions; we would not have been brave enough to do this under Yeltsin." Although under Putin, the center exerted greater control over courts at all levels, this was a far cry from the role of the judiciary envisioned by comparative theories of federalism, which expect the courts to be independent and authoritative bodies whose judgments are respected and enforced.[122]

Political parties and the party system also were unable to regulate the federal balance both under Yeltsin and in Putin's first term. National parties in this period had very weak roots in the regions, and in political life generally (neither Yeltsin nor Putin joined a political party). Even by 2003, most regional leaders "remained staunchly independent of parties." Although subsequent steps by the Kremlin strengthened the United Russia party and changed the rules of the game to make regional penetration easier, these changes came well *after* the changes in state coercion that shifted the balance toward the center.[123]

Other federal reforms enacted by Putin also were enabled at least in part by his initial steps in the coercive realm. For example, another key move in 2000 was to remove governors from the upper house, the Federation Council, where their presence not only gave them considerable influence on national policy but also immunity from prosecution. The Kremlin, in the person of its representative to the Duma, Aleksandr Kotenkov (a former Soviet army officer who held the rank of Major-General), openly threatened at least sixteen unnamed governors with criminal prosecution if such immunity was lifted, relying on information from a top MVD official. Although such a threat seemed counterproductive in terms of encouraging governors to back Putin's proposal, Kotenkov was primarily seeking to detach Duma members from regional governors who had been pressuring deputies from their regions to oppose the reforms. Moreover, sending the signal that the Kremlin was willing to use

---

[122] Kahn, pp. 178, 249, n45; Kathryn Hendley, "Putin and the Law," in Herspring 2007, p. 110; Trochev and Solomon, p. 115.

[123] Stoner-Weiss 2006, pp. 111–146; Henry E. Hale, "Party Development in a Federal System," in Reddaway and Orttung, Vol. II, p. 184; Konitzer and Wegren 2006.

federal law enforcement organs against outspoken opponents was part of a broader effort to fracture a potential anti-Putin coalition and to "cow the governors into submission." After Putin tossed in a few sweeteners, such as delaying the implementation of the change, the governors relented and gave up their seats.[124]

Even in terms of the important issue of fiscal federalism, the changes in controlling coercion preceded and helped enable a renegotiation of the provisions of the fiscal bargain. Legally, the regions were supposed to receive half of Russia's total tax income. Putin slowly eroded that split, so the federal government received 51 percent in 2001 and 62 percent in 2002. By 2008, the central government took 70 percent of tax receipts.[125] Not only did this change temporally follow the changes in state coercion by more than a year, but it also was enabled by them. As one Russian commentator noted at the time, governors' control over law enforcement was a key tool in their ability to pressure local economic interests and to resist the center. Writing in May 2000, the commentator observed that "after governors lose their control over force bodies it will be just a matter of time [before] they lose their financial independence."[126]

Because of the weakness of other mechanisms for regulating Russian federalism, Putin and the governors understood that much would depend on controlling the power ministries. Putin cleverly used the weapons at his disposal, including his high popularity rating, divisions between regional leaders, and, not least, his dominance of the procuracy at the federal level and the FSB at all levels of government, to undermine the cozy relations between law enforcement and governors that had developed under Yeltsin. After these changes, incompliant governors, as Russian politician Sergey Glazev stated in 2004, "can expect trouble from the law enforcement organs." The flip side of this, as the Russian journalist Aleksandr Zhilin accurately predicted in 2000, was that the new rule for governors became "be loyal, and you won't be touched."[127]

In summary, the changes in the federal bargain in Russia in the Yeltsin and Putin periods show the centrality of force to center-subunit relations in hybrid regimes. The mechanisms that regulate and stabilize federalism in liberal democracies, such as courts and parties, were too weak to play this role. The dynamics in the center-region balance also cannot be explained by the

---

[124] "Governors Begin to Untuck Tails While Putin Switches to 'Carrot and Stick'," *Jamestown Foundation Monitor*, 6, 106 (May 31, 2000); Matthew Hyde, "Putin's Federal Reforms and their Implications for Presidential Power in Russia," *Europe-Asia Studies*, 53 (July 2001), pp. 727–731.

[125] Robert Orttung, "Key Issues in the Evolution of the Federal Okrugs and Center-Region Relations under Putin," in Reddaway and Orttung 2004, p. 32; Interview M-16.

[126] "Governor-Generals Will Deprive Governors of Their Generals," *smi.ru*, May 23, 2000, in JRL #4321, May 24, 2000.

[127] Sergey Glaz'ev, "Parad suverenitetov nachalsya s naznacheniya gubernatorov," *Nov. Gaz.*, December 16, 2004; Interview M-44.

original institutional design embedded in the Constitution, which of course did not vary. Further, it is not a simple story of central neglect under Yeltsin and renewed vigor under Putin. Rather, a complicated process of both de jure and de facto decentralization and recentralization unfolded in stages and varied across power structures. Finally, the importance of force is further emphasized by the fact that Putin's federal reforms began in this realm and helped make possible other important reforms in different arenas.

THE DEATH OF FEDERALISM?

In September 2004, in the aftermath of the Beslan terrorist incident, Putin made two major speeches in which he decried the continuing weakness of the Russian state in general and the power ministries in particular, and proposed a series of political reforms to mobilize the state and society to confront the terrorist threat.[128] Most relevant for the purposes of this work, he fundamentally altered the nature of Russian federalism by suggesting that the heads of the subjects of the federation (presidents, governors, and the mayors of St. Petersburg and Moscow) be appointed by the president rather than popularly elected. Although technically the heads of the regions are confirmed by the regional legislatures after a recommendation from the president, the proviso in the final law that the president can disband the legislature if they reject his nominee twice gave the regions little leverage against the president. In the first three years of the new system (2005–2007), not only did every presidential candidate get confirmed, but they did so by overwhelming margins, with around 85–90 percent of the vote from the regional assembly. The president also gained the ability to remove governors who had lost his trust; although Putin only employed this weapon three times in this period, in each case, the procuracy brought a criminal case against the governor before he was dismissed.[129]

It is also important to note that these changes allowed some republic presidents and oblast governors to continue in power indefinitely. By 2007, a total of fifteen regional leaders were in their fourth term in office.[130] The longevity of some of the most prominent regional bosses, such as Luzhkov in Moscow, Shaymiyev in Tatarstan, Rakhimov in Bashkortostan, and Rossel in Sverdlovsk, not only served their interests, but also that of Putin, who was willing to tolerate these bosses if they joined the United Russia party, delivered votes to United Russia in national elections, and maintained regional stability,

---

[128] See the discussion in Chapter 3.

[129] Ross 2005, p. 360; Aleksey Titkov, "Krizis naznacheniy," *Pro et Contra*, 11, 4–5 (July–October 2007), pp. 94–96. See also: Paul Goode, "The Puzzle of Putin's Gubernatorial Appointments," *Europe-Asia Studies*, 59, 3 (May 2007), pp. 365–399; Nikolay Petrov, "Naznacheniya gubernatorov: Itogi pervogo goda," *Brifing Moskovskogo Tsentra Karnegi*, 3, 8 (April 2006).

[130] Titkov 2007, p. 94.

especially during the managed succession from Putin to Medvedev that took place in 2007–2008.[131]

Overall, the move to appointed governors, coupled with the absence of independent regional courts and other centralizing features of federal design in Russia, as well as the more general undermining of democracy under Putin, have gravely weakened Russian federalism. This outcome is consistent with the view that federalism is a very precarious institutional form in the absence of a robust constitutional democracy. Russian federalism is now more akin to the "sham federalism" of the Soviet Union, another federation that also sought to dominate the regions, not only through the mechanism of a highly centralized party à la Riker, but also via a complete dominance over state coercive organs.

The power ministries were crucial actors not only in carrying out the assault on federalism in Putin's first term, but also managing regional politics in Putin's second term. One indication of the importance of the power ministries came from an expert survey on regional influence conducted by the Institute of Situational Analysis and New Technology (ISANT) in Russia. ISANT published survey results in 2003 and 2007 on the most politically influential figures in the regions by position. The heads of the three main law enforcement bodies – the FSB, the procuracy, and the MVD – each moved up in ranking between 2003 and 2007. The FSB chief moved up from sixteenth to fifth, the procurator moved up from thirteenth to seventh, and the head of the UVD moved up from tenth to eighth. In the top ten positions, only one – the mayor of the regional capital – was now directly elected by voters. "Simply speaking," Nikolay Petrov concluded in 2007, "politics in the regions is now conducted not by [legislative] deputies and mayors, but FSB employees and procurators."[132]

If Putin's recentralization sticks, which is by no means guaranteed, the 1990s may have turned out to be simply a short-term anomaly in terms of the dispersion of state control over coercion in Russia. David Bayley argues that the degree of centralization/decentralization in the control over law enforcement is very path-dependent, even in the face of major political, social, and economic changes. In the case of Russia, Bayley notes that "tension between local initiative and central control in Russia has always been resolved in favor of the latter."[133] Given Stepan's finding that for a large, multinational state to be a democracy it must be federal, this historical centralizing tendency creates another potential obstacle to successful Russian democratization.[134]

---

[131] In sixty-five of eighty-five regions in the 2007 parliamentary elections, the governor appeared first or second on the United Russia party list: Nikolai Petrov, "The Faces of United Russia," *MT*, October 23, 2007. See also: Konitzer and Wegren 2006. Most of these long-serving regional leaders were replaced in Medvedev's first term.

[132] Nikolai Petrov, "Korporativizm vs regionalizm," *Pro et Contra*, 4–5, 38 (July–October 2007), pp. 81–83; "Reyting politicheskoy vliyatel'nosti," *Ekspert*, March 26, 2007.

[133] David H. Bayley, *Patterns of Policing* (New Brunswick, NJ: Rutgers University Press, 1985), pp. 60–61.

[134] Stepan, "Toward a New Comparative Politics."

Decentralizing the Russian Police as a Path to Renewed Federalism

I have argued that in conditions faced by Russia and other hybrid regimes – particularly the weakness of parties, constitutional norms, and judiciaries – force may serve as a substitute in "policing" jurisdictional boundaries and the division of powers between levels of government. The key issue for federations is giving the central government enough power to prevent subunit cheating on the federal bargain, but reserving some power for the subunits to resist encroachment by the national government. Relying on a "balance of power" in controlling coercion to regulate federal relations is unlikely to produce a stable, long-term equilibrium. It may be difficult, if not impossible, to find the right mix of central and subunit coercive resources that simultaneously will prevent subunit cheating and central encroachment, as well as adequately balance the values of state integrity, local autonomy, and democracy. Scholars who point to the importance of a well-institutionalized party system, strong constitutional norms, and an independent judiciary for stable federalism are clearly, at one level, correct. Unfortunately, many countries with imperfect federalism and imperfect democracy may lack these attributes and have no easy or short-term methods for acquiring them. In these situations, clubs may indeed be trump.

Given the importance of coercion in managing federal relations in hybrid regimes, an important issue is if there are particular organizational patterns that have proven their utility at simultaneously maintaining the state and federalism. This shifts the question to a more normative one: What are the "best practices" for organizing coercion in federal hybrid regimes? Since control over coercive institutions in itself is unlikely to create long-term federal stability, the goal should be institutional arrangements that can, in the short and medium term, help preserve federal stability and contribute to the development of more reliable democratic institutions. Institutional arrangements can either help or hinder the promotion of a "culture of federalism" identified by some as necessary for federal stability.[135]

The most obvious principle for federations in organizing coercion is centralized control over the armed forces. Indeed, if subunits control the military then the situation more closely resembles, in the best case, confederation, and in the worst case, warlordism. Even in the United States, which has an externally oriented military with severe restrictions on domestic usage, it has on occasion been necessary to use the army to ensure public order and preserve fundamental rights when local courts and law enforcement were either unwilling or unable to perform this function.

Finding the proper balance of central and subunit control is more difficult when it comes to law enforcement. Although many of the oldest and most consolidated democratic federations give considerable law enforcement

---

[135] de Figueiredo and Weingast 2005, p. 128; Daniel Elazar, *Exploring Federalism* (Tuscaloosa, AL: University of Alabama Press, 1987).

power to state and local government, such as the United States, Germany, and Switzerland, there is no universal pattern, as shown in Table 4.1. Moreover, in Europe recently, there has been a convergence on policing systems that combine local, national, and international (particularly EU) bodies, whether the country is federal or unitary.[136]

Thinking of government responsibility in a federation as shared across many levels, rather than as divided into distinct spheres, is consistent with models of American federalism that stress federalism's interdependent nature. As opposed to alternative models that stress either the autonomy of different levels or a hierarchy of relations with the center clearly dominant, the interdependent model sees overlapping spheres of responsibility, with bargaining the dominant pattern of relations. Further, these interdependent models note that power in a federation is not necessarily zero-sum, and that both the central government and the subunits can gain capacity in a properly functioning system.[137]

Constructing appropriate federal relations thereby involves bargaining and shared powers rather than exclusive powers or hierarchical relations. The difficulty in hybrid regimes is that many key actors see power in zero-sum terms and will seek to increase their power relative to other actors rather than to pursue power sharing. For every argument decentralizers can advance in favor of their position (local responsiveness, better innovation, competition between units, proximity to citizens), centralizers can provide reasonable counterarguments (coordination problems, localistic biases, capture by wealthy interests, redundancy, inequality).[138] The recent political economy literature on federalism has produced no clear verdict on the relative merits of centralization versus decentralization, with much of the devil remaining in the details.[139]

The best possible outcome in controlling law enforcement in semidemocratic/semiauthoritarian federal states is for relatively equal power balances that necessitate shared powers and bargaining between different levels. This outcome is desirable primarily because of the congruence between institutional power sharing and bargaining and norms of democratic decision making – norms that may ultimately lead to strengthening the judicial and party-based mechanisms used for resolving jurisdictional disputes in consolidated democratic federations. Indian federalism has appeared to work, for example,

---

[136] M.G.W. den Boer, "Internationalization," in R.I. Mawby, ed., *Policing Across the World* (London: Routledge, 1999), pp. 59–74.

[137] Deil Wright, *Understanding Intergovernmental Relations*, 2nd edition (Monterey, CA: Brooks/Cole, 1982); David C. Nice and Patricia Fredericksen, *The Politics of Intergovernmental Relations*, 2nd edition (Chicago: Nelson-Hall Publishers, 1995).

[138] Nice and Fredericksen, pp. 15–21; Larry Diamond, *Developing Democracy* (Baltimore: Johns Hopkins University Press, 1999), pp. 121–138.

[139] Pablo Beramendi, "Federalism," in Carlos Boix and Susan Stokes, eds., *Oxford Handbook of Comparative Politics* (Oxford: Oxford University Press, 2007), pp. 752–781; Erik Wibbels, "Madison in Baghdad?" *Annual Review of Political Science*, 9 (2006), pp. 165–188; Daniel Treisman, *The Architecture of Government: Rethinking Political Decentralization* (Cambridge: Cambridge University Press, 2007).

because of the development of "formal and informal political institutions" – including parties – that "make the politics of bargaining work."[140] But Indian federalism has also worked because the center has always maintained enough coercive power, and mechanisms for using it, to deter or defeat secessionists. One model for law enforcement organization in hybrid federal regimes, particularly in multinational federations, may be one that decentralizes some structures (public-order police, for example), while also maintaining a small reserve force if central intervention becomes necessary in emergency situations, akin to the Indian Central Reserve Police Force.[141]

The possibility of at least partially decentralizing the Russian police is a persistent debate among Russian law enforcement experts.[142] As noted earlier, under Khrushchev, the entire central MVD was dismantled and policing was transferred to the republics – a move reversed under Brezhnev. Debates about decentralizing the police reemerged under Gorbachev. His Minister of Internal Affairs, Vadim Bakatin, argued for greater regional and local control over the local militia (public-order militia, or MOB), but Gorbachev resisted this idea. Similarly, under Yeltsin, reformers such as his legal adviser, Mikhail Krasnov, pushed a similar proposal, which would have transferred the MOB to governors or mayors while leaving the criminal police, such as criminal investigation and police responsible for organized crime, terrorism, and economic security, under the federal MVD. The federal police would be responsible for serious crimes, whereas the municipal militia would have responsibility for public order and minor street crime. One of Putin's top officials, Dmitriy Kozak, indicated in 2002 that legislation to turn control over public-order policing to municipalities was soon to be introduced, but nothing came of this proposal.[143]

One reason that decentralized public-order policing has been stymied is that serious opposition to this reform exists within the MVD. Although some of the opposition can be linked to bureaucratic conservatism, there are also serious principled objections. The two basic objections are that it will contribute to separatism in Russia, and that it will de facto put many militia forces under local political and economic "clan" interests. For example, a former

---

[140] James Manor, "Making Federalism Work," *Journal of Democracy*, 9 (July 1998), p. 23.

[141] On the Indian police and federalism, see: R.K. Raghavan, "The Indian Police: Problems and Prospects," *Publius*, 33, 4 (Fall 2003), pp. 119–133. On policing in federal hybrid regimes, see: Taylor 2007.

[142] A compilation of press and expert commentary on the debate can be found in: Demos, *Reforma pravookhranitel'nikh organov: preodoeniye proizvola* (Moskva: Demos, 2005), pp. 105–108, 131–140.

[143] Interview M-5; Interview M-19; Svetlana Babayeva, "Dmitriy Kozak: 'Eto – vlast', a ne samodeyatel'nost'," *Izvestiya*, November 19, 2002. See also: Ivan Sas, "Silovikov stanet men'she," *Nez. Gaz.*, November 4, 2002; Valeriy Novikov, "Kak reformirovat' MVD," *Parlamentskaya gazeta*, April 10, 2003; Vitaliy Tseplyayev, Svetlana Evdokimova, Aleksandr Kolesnichenko, "Menyaem militsiyu na politsiyu, nedorogo," *AiF*, No. 20, May 14, 2003; Peter H. Solomon, Jr., "The Reform of Policing in the Russian Federation," *The Australian and New Zealand Journal of Criminology*, 38, 2 (2005), pp. 230–240.

high-ranking MVD official argued that such a change would create "89 armies of Dudayev," a reference to the former Chechen separatist leader. Further, he argued that, except in a handful of well-off regions, the only source of funds to support the police will inevitably be the powerful "oligarchs and financial industrial groups," and that "he who pays will also call the tune."[144] Others in law enforcement were not definitively opposed but suggested the need for caution, given the difficulty some local governments might have in coping with this new task.[145] Opposition is not confined to the police, with some legal scholars and even human rights activists and officials highly skeptical of the idea. For example, the Sverdlovsk human rights ombudsman Tatyana Merzlyakova stated that local governments were not prepared to cope with financing issues, especially pensions, and that "nothing good will come of it" if the police are divided between federal and local services.[146]

Proponents of the police reform, including within the police, counter that the risk of separatism is overstated, given that a considerable portion of the police will remain under central control, as will control over the other power ministries. Further, they contend that what needs to be transferred to local jurisdiction is not just power over the municipal militias, but also government funds to support them. Sergei Tushin of the Yekaterinburg city administration argued that as long as appropriate financing was available, municipalities could manage the local police, and that this would bring them closer to the people. Russia is simply too big, proponents argue, for the entire police force to be controlled from Moscow. Some advocates of police decentralization even argue, along the model of American sheriffs, for electing the local head of police to make him more responsible to the public.[147]

The decentralizing of Russian policing probably would be successful only in the context of further reform to strengthen local self-government and of greater democratization at the local level. Otherwise the danger of significant control over law enforcement by local political and economic clans certainly would be a real one, although Georgiy Satarov rightly asked, "which is worse – the control of local or federal clans?"[148] Local control is not an end in itself and will not automatically lead to better policing from the perspective of average citizens – witness the role of local law enforcement in the American South prior to the civil rights movement, or the dominance of police "machines" in northern American cities well into the post–World War II period, or even the close links between the local police and drug cartels in Mexico today.[149] In

---

[144] Interview M-47. Other interviewees made similar points: Interview M-13; Interview NN-7; Interview NN-8.

[145] Interview P-11; Interview P-13; Interview P-14.

[146] Interview Ye-7; Interview Ye-9; Interview NN-4; Interview M-6.

[147] Interview M-5; Interview M-19; Interview M-29; Interview M-30; Interview M-46; Interview Ye-10; Interview N-6.

[148] Interview M-30.

[149] James C. McKinley Jr., "Mexico Hits Drug Gangs With Full Fury of War," *NYT*, January 22, 2008; Marc Lacey, "In Mexico, Sorting Out Good Guys From Bad," *NYT*, November 2, 2008.

theory, however, in a democratic and federal system, local government officials should be able to exercise some degree of civilian oversight and control of the state's coercive agencies, particularly law-enforcement bodies. Under Putin, in contrast, the general tendency was to weaken the powers not only of the regions, but also of local government.[150]

FORCE, FEDERALISM, AND RUSSIAN STATE CAPACITY

Leonid Smirnyagin, Yeltsin's regional affairs adviser, observed in 2001 that Putin "does not need or understand federalism." Indeed, he noted, the very idea of building "vertical power" is inconsistent with the logic of federalism.[151] Federalism was an obstacle to Putin's conception of strengthening the state, and he progressively undermined it without formally changing the constitution. The power ministries, law enforcement in particular, were central to this effort.

Putin undoubtedly strengthened the center vis-à-vis the regions. But did this strengthen the state? His supporters, such as former Main Federal Inspector in St. Petersburg, Nikolay Vinnichenko, maintained that the federal district reforms made the state more effective because polpreds were the "eye of the state" who could "intervene and discipline" federal officials at the regional level if necessary. Opponents, such as Vladislav Yegorov, a top communist party official in Nizhniy Novgorod, referred to the federal districts as "gendarme okrugs" with "repressive functions" that were creating a "police state."[152] Of course, both Vinnichenko and Yegorov could be correct – the ability to "intervene and discipline" might have both increased state capacity while making it more repressive. No less an expert on the state than Charles Tilly contended in 2007 that "Putin's regime was aggressively expanding state capacity as it squeezed out democracy."[153]

Experts on Russian federalism, however, were not as confident as Tilly that Putin had indeed strengthened the state. For example, Kathryn Stoner-Weiss concluded that Putin had built "authoritarianism without authority" and, by and large, had not increased the capacity of the state.[154] Indeed, the evidence discussed in Chapter 3 showed that under Putin, the power ministries had become more subject to direction from the Kremlin for extraordinary tasks, but their ability to carry out their core functions of fighting crime and

---

[150] Cameron Ross, "Municipal Reform in the Russian Federation and Putin's 'Electoral Vertical'," *Demokratizatsiya*, 15, 2 (Spring 2007), pp. 191–208. For a more benign interpretation of local government reform under Putin, see: John F. Young and Gary N. Wilson, "The View from Below: Local Government and Putin's Reforms," *Europe-Asia Studies*, 59, 7 (November 2007), pp. 1071–1088.

[151] Interview M-33; Leonid Smirnyagin, "Federalizm po Putinu ili Putin po federalizmu (zheleznoy pyatoy)?" *Brifing Moskovskogo Tsentra Karnegi*, 3, 3 (March 2001).

[152] Interview P-11; Interview NN-6.

[153] Charles Tilly, *Democracy* (Cambridge: Cambridge University Press, 2007), p. 137.

[154] Stoner-Weiss 2006, esp. pp. 147–155.

terrorism, although improving in Putin's last years, remained low in comparative terms. The results in this chapter were also mixed. Some reforms to the practice of Russian federalism were definitely needed, and the "harmonization of laws" campaign was necessary and important. But the broader assault on the regions went too far, including in the coercive realm. Indeed, much of the activity of the polpreds and federal district law enforcement structures seemed directed more at political and economic rivals than toward fighting crime and strengthening law enforcement capacity – once again, extraordinary decisions took priority over routine tasks. There were also the opportunity costs of Putin's approach; the resources and efforts devoted to bringing the governors to heel could have been directed toward raising the professionalism and administrative capacity of law enforcement bodies.

Putin's state-building efforts were devoted most of all to making the regions accountable to the *center*; however, in a federal democracy, regions should be accountable most of all to the *voters*. As a monitoring strategy, the creation of the federal districts was akin to the police patrol approach, in which state agents are enlisted to periodically check up on other state agents. The capacity of the central government to monitor the regions, including power ministry structures at this level, undoubtedly increased. But the federal reforms also undermined the fire alarm strategy of trusting citizens and civil society actors to monitor state behavior – an issue I take up directly in Chapter 6.

In short, the methods used to fix the problems with center-region relations that arose under Yeltsin were not long-term solutions to achieving Putin's stated goal of creating a "strong state." Greater central government control over the power ministries reduced the influence of regional governors over law enforcement, but it did not transform these officials into disinterested or public-spirited administrators. Rather, law enforcement officials became subject to manipulation by federal and okrug-level politicians. In other words, the same problems that previously afflicted Russian power ministry behavior continued to exist under Putin, just at a different level. Rather than eighty-nine regional patrimonial machines, an effort was made to create one national patrimony centered in the Kremlin. The rebuilding of the "power vertical" in the coercive realm directed attention away from the more important task of increasing not just state capacity, but state quality. The consequences of this neglect of quality are explored in the next two chapters.

5

Coercion and Quality

Power Ministry Practices and Personnel

> The state, including its law enforcement and security services, is there to work for the people, to defend their rights, interests and property, not to mention their security and their lives.
>
> Vladimir Putin, 2004[1]

Do Russian law enforcement and security services work for the people and defend their rights? On the eve of his second term, Putin put his finger on what is central to thinking about not just the capacity, but the quality, of state coercive organs. In a civil state with high state quality, the state's monopoly of force is wielded not primarily for the interests of the ruler(s), but for society as a whole.[2]

In the previous two chapters, we focused on the capacity of the Russian power ministries. At the national level, there is some evidence that the capacity of the power ministries increased during Putin's presidency. Violent clashes for sovereign power in the capital were off the table, the fiscal capacity of the state increased, and toward the end of Putin's tenure, there seemed to be some improvement in fighting violent crime and terrorism, although Russia continued to lag comparatively in these areas. The greatest increase in coercive capacity, however, came in the rebuilding of a "regime of repression" that the Kremlin used to help fix elections and repress economic and political rivals. Moreover, private property rights remained insecure, both for oligarchs and for ordinary businesspeople and citizens, as we will see in this chapter.

The power ministries also were a crucial actor in building the "power vertical" and undermining federalism under Putin. Although the decentering of force under Boris Yeltsin had probably gone too far, the recentralization of

---

[1] Vladimir Putin, "Speech to campaign supporters," February 12, 2004 [http://www.putin2004. ru/english/authorized/402D773F]. The original speech in Russian referred to the "power structures" rather than specifying "law enforcement and security services."

[2] Norbert Elias, "Violence and Civilization: The State Monopoly of Physical Violence and its Infringement," in John Keane, ed., *Civil Society and the State: New European Perspectives* (London: Verso, 1988), pp. 179–180.

coercion as part of the federal reforms, and the use of this reacquired club against the regions, increased the power of the center without necessarily building state capacity overall. In a federal state, coercive capacity should be assessed not in terms of which level of government controls it, but whether the lawful decisions of different levels of government are implemented by state personnel. In this respect, law enforcement structures still were subject to manipulation in the pursuit of particular rather than state interests, to the neglect of both law and order.

The surprisingly modest improvements in state capacity under Putin are tightly linked to the neglect of state quality. I conceptualize state quality as the extent to which the state and its officials serve the interests of the population in a fair manner that promotes the general welfare. Russia's rulers have been more concerned that the power ministries serve their interests than those of society. The upshot of this orientation has been that, when not fulfilling extraordinary tasks, law enforcement and security personnel often serve not societal but individual interests. Specifically, they engage in corrupt and predatory activities. The rule of law and state quality thereby suffer.

In this chapter, I show that the quality of state coercive bodies in post-Soviet Russia has been relatively low and, equally important, that their quality did not increase as a consequence of Putin's state-building strategy. This discouraging performance can be traced in part to patrimonial bureaucratic forms and the failure to inculcate a culture of public service among power ministry personnel. I begin with a discussion of how Russia compares to other states in terms of the rule of law and controlling corruption. I then turn toward a more detailed discussion of the evidence for corrupt and predatory law enforcement practices, drawing on surveys, interviews, and press and academic accounts. The third section develops a theory of predatory power ministry behavior that encompasses the multiple empirical examples of corruption within a broader framework about Russian law enforcement culture and practice. Fourth, I examine personnel policy and the problem of recruiting and retaining high-quality personnel in these bodies, demonstrating the weakness of Weberian rational-legal mechanisms. The concluding section argues that Russian state quality in the coercive realm has remained low due both to the continuation of patrimonial bureaucratic forms and the failure to instill a new mission in the power ministries that orients officials' behavior toward serving society rather than either state or personal interests.

CORRUPTION AND THE RULE OF LAW: RUSSIA
IN COMPARATIVE CONTEXT

Putin promised at the beginning of his first term that the only dictatorship that would be established in Russia would be a "dictatorship of the law." Critics such as Mikhail Krasnov, Yeltsin's former legal advisor, branded the very formulation "illiterate." The generous interpretation of this statement

was that Putin was interested in the creation of a "rule of law" state.[3] Both
defining and measuring the "rule of law" are subjects of vigorous dispute,
and Judith Shklar has called the very notion a "self-congratulatory rhetorical
device" of "Anglo-American politicians." At a minimum, the concept implies
that the law applies equally to everyone, and that the government and state
personnel are also bound by the law. These two definitional components alone
make clear that the rule of law is an ideal that has nowhere been fully realized.
Rachel Kleinfeld adds three other elements to her definition: respect for human
rights, predictable and efficient justice, and law and order.[4] Many experts distinguish between "rule *by* law," which, as Thomas Carothers notes, implies
"the regular, efficient application of law," and the "rule *of* law," which highlights the importance of limits on the power of the state through government
subordination to the law.[5]

The World Bank Governance project defines the rule of law as "the extent
to which agents have confidence in and abide by the rules of society, and
in particular the quality of contract enforcement, the police, and the courts,
as well as the likelihood of crime and violence."[6] Although this definition
includes features that I would consider more about capacity than quality, such
as the likelihood of crime, in general it provides a rough measure of state quality, including that of the law enforcement system. Russia's percentile ranking
for "Rule of Law" has been consistently around the 20 percent range since the
project began in 1996 (see Figure 5.1). Although there was a small improvement at the beginning of Putin's first term, the Rule of Law measure for Russia
declined in Putin's second term, leaving Russia in 2007 roughly where it had
been in 2000, and below the level it was when first measured in 1996 under
Yeltsin. Overall, it seems fair to conclude that, by these measures, the rule of
law has changed little in Russia throughout the post-Soviet period. Indeed,
Dmitriy Medvedev maintained in January 2008 that Russia is a country of
"legal nihilism," with a respect for law lower than in any other European
state.[7] Most importantly, perhaps, Russia's score in this category remains

[3] Interview M-19. On Putin's early use of the "dictatorship of law" notion, see: Jeffrey Kahn,
    Federalism, Democratization, and the Rule of Law in Russia (Oxford: Oxford University
    Press, 2002), pp. 238–239.
[4] Rachel Kleinfeld, "Competing Definitions of the Rule of Law," in Thomas Carothers, ed.,
    Promoting the Rule of Law Abroad: In Search of Knowledge (Washington, DC: Carnegie
    Endowment for International Peace, 2006), pp. 31–73. The Shklar quote is on p. 31 of
    Kleinfeld.
[5] Thomas Carothers, "The Rule-of-Law Revival," in Carothers 2006, p. 5. See also: Kahn
    2002, p. 54; Stephen Holmes, "Lineages of the Rule of Law," in Jose Maria Maravall and
    Adam Przeworski, eds., *Democracy and the Rule of Law* (Cambridge: Cambridge University
    Press, 2003), pp. 19–61.
[6] Like their other indicators, the Rule of Law score is a composite measure that draws on polls,
    government and international organization reports, think tank evaluations, and business and
    political risk analysis services.
[7] "Kandidat v prezidenty Dmitriy Medvedev oglasil svoi predvybornye tezisy," *Newsru.com*,
    January 22, 2008. Medvedev added that this "legal nihilism" was responsible for state corrup-
    tion, "which exists today on an enormous scale."

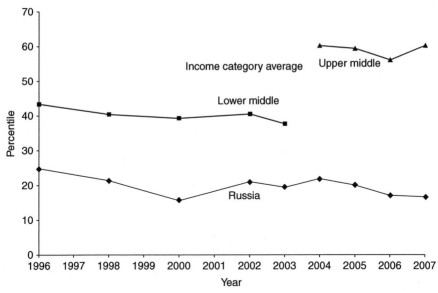

FIGURE 5.1. Rule of law (WGI).

considerably below the average for states in its income category, particularly after it moved into the World Bank Higher Middle Income group in 2004.

Another key component of state quality is the amount of corruption. Corruption, defined as the use of public office for private benefit, weakens state quality. If state officials are using their office for personal gain, then they are by definition not serving the population and the general welfare in a fair way. Of course, the danger of external actors using corruption allegations as another "self-congratulatory rhetorical device," and of holding states to unrealistic and unattainable standards, is as present in the study of corruption as it is in rule of law promotion.[8] Indeed, several decades ago, "revisionists" argued that corruption provides certain economic and political benefits, such as overcoming administrative inefficiencies and integrating new groups into politics during modernization. More recently, scholars have rehabilitated these revisionist arguments to suggest that corruption can help bind together elites in divided societies and even increase state capacity by providing leaders a means to blackmail subordinates to enforce compliance.[9] Although these

[8] Excessive moralizing by outsiders is one of the major targets of Stephen Kotkin and Andras Sajo, eds., *Political Corruption in Transition: A Sceptic's Handbook* (Budapest: Central European University Press, 2002).

[9] Samuel P. Huntington, *Political Order in Changing Societies* (New Haven, CT: Yale University Press, 1968), pp. 59–71; Robert Hislope, "Corrupt Exchange in Divided Societies: The Invisible Politics of Stability in Macedonia," in Mitchell A. Orenstein, Stephen Bloom, and Nicole Lindstrom, eds., *Transnational Actors in Central and East European Transitions* (Pittsburgh, PA: University of Pittsburgh Press, 2008), pp. 142–161; Keith Darden, "The Integrity of Corrupt States: Graft as an Informal State Institution," *Politics & Society*, 36, 1 (March 2008), pp. 35–60.

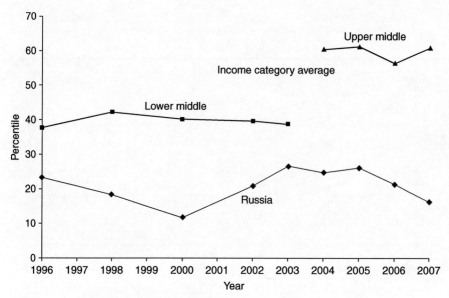

FIGURE 5.2. Control of corruption (WGI).

arguments may be partially true, most recent studies have argued persuasively that, in general, corruption has negative political and economic consequences, undermining growth, state strength, and democracy.[10]

The World Bank Governance project defines corruption as "the extent to which public power is exercised for private gain, including both petty and grand forms of corruption, as well as 'capture' of the state by elite and private interests." Russia's percentile ranking for "Control of Corruption" is slightly higher for 2007 than it was in 2000 when Putin took office (see Figure 5.2).[11] On the other hand, Russia's percentile ranking was lower in 2007 than it was in 1996 (16 percent versus 23 percent), and it had declined markedly from the 2003 high of 27 percent. The two most striking features of these scores are the downward trend in Putin's second term, and how Russia's scores were considerably below the average for states in its income category. To use a different set of ratings, in the 2007 Transparency International Corruption Perceptions Index, Russia was tied for 143rd place out of 179, along with Gambia, Indonesia, and Togo. Its raw score was 2.3 (out of 10), down from a high of 2.8 in 2004 and comparable to the scores of Yeltsin's last years, 1998 and 1999, when it scored a 2.4.[12]

[10] Overviews include: Susan Rose-Ackerman, *Corruption and Government: Causes, Consequences, and Reform* (Cambridge: Cambridge University Press, 1999); Rasma Karklins, *The System Made Me Do It: Corruption in Post-Communist Societies* (Armonk, NY: M.E. Sharpe, 2005), pp. 6–9.

[11] Detailed studies of corruption conducted by the INDEM Foundation found that corruption in Russia got worse between 2001 and 2005: INDEM, "Diagnostika rossiyskoy korruptsii 2005," available at: http://www.anti-corr.ru/

[12] See: http://www.transparency.org

Overall, these comparative data are fairly blunt instruments for assessing state quality. Still, they represent the best available cross-national comparative data on the issue, and they do suggest a couple of important tentative conclusions. First, Russian performance in improving the rule of law and controlling corruption changed little under Putin, and indeed throughout the post-Soviet period. Second, Russia remains a relative underperformer on these measures compared to other states at similar levels of income. In the next section, I use more detailed information on corruption in the power ministries to show that the quality of the Russian state was relatively low and improved little, if at all, under Yeltsin and Putin.

CORRUPTION IN RUSSIAN LAW ENFORCEMENT

Corruption and weak adherence to the rule of law are a particular problem in the power ministries. For example, surveys of Russian citizens show that they believe corruption is particularly widespread among the police, the traffic police, customs officials, the procuracy, and the courts.[13] In other words, Russians believe that the very structures that are supposed to uphold the law are the most consistent violators of it.[14] This belief is well founded.

Law enforcement in general, and policing in particular, is an activity that, perhaps paradoxically, is prone to corruption everywhere. This is true for several reasons, including:

1) Police officers, unlike most state officials, can use or threaten to use violence to achieve compliance;
2) Police have regular contact with lawbreakers who obviously do not want the police to do their jobs, and these criminals may have both the means to buy off the police and strong incentives and few disincentives to seek to influence the police in such a way;
3) Police officers, as "street-level bureaucrats," have substantial autonomy and discretion in how they carry out their duties;
4) Police managers have difficulty in monitoring the activity and effectiveness of individual police officers.[15]

---

[13] Lev Gudkov, Boris Dubin, and Anastasiya Leonova, "Militseyskoye nasiliye i problema 'politseyskogo gosudarsta'," *Vestnik obshchestvennogo mneniya*, 4, 72, (July–August 2004), pp. 33–34; Interfax, "Russians Worried Over Widespread Corruption – Public Opinion Poll," January 12, 2006 [JRL, 2006-#13, January 13, 2006].

[14] This view is also the dominant one in Russian pulp detective novels. In his survey of the genre, Anthony Olcott notes, "the fact that a person was a law enforcement official seemed now almost to guarantee that he was a villain, rather than a pillar of virtue." Anthony Olcott, *Russian Pulp: The* Detektiv *and the Way of Russian Crime* (Lanham, MD: Rowman & Littlefield, 2001), p. 141.

[15] David H. Bayley, *Patterns of Policing* (New Brunswick, NJ: Rutgers University Press, 1985), pp. 7–8; John Kleinig, "Gratuities and Corruption," in Tim Newburn, ed., *Policing: Key Readings* (Cullompton, Devon, UK: Willan Publishing, 2005), pp. 596–597; Michael Lipsky, *Street-Level Bureaucracy: Dilemmas of the Individual in Public Services* (New York: Russell

Indeed, it is not just in Russia, but around the globe, that the police are perceived to be one of the most corrupt institutions; in Transparency International's 2007 Global Corruption Barometer the police tied with legislatures for second place (political parties were first) among fourteen different sectors in terms of the degree of corruption. Still, there is a great deal of cross-national variance, between 1.8 (Finland) and 4.6 (Cameroon and Ghana) on a five-point scale ranging from "not at all corrupt" to "extremely corrupt." In Russia, the police were in first place among all institutions, with a rating of 4.1.[16] In polls conducted between 2004 and 2006, consistently about 80 percent of Russians said that "lawlessness and arbitrary despotism (*bezzakoniye i proizvol*)" was either "a rather serious problem" or "a very serious problem" among the police; only around 10–15 percent said it was not a problem or not a very serious problem.[17] The forms of corruption described in this section show that there are ample reasons for such results.

Forms of Corruption

It is important to stress that corrupt behavior by Russian power ministry officials, particularly in the law enforcement realm, is not the episodic work of a few bad apples, nor is it new, although by all accounts the problem has worsened considerably in the last twenty years.[18] Rather, law enforcement structures now operate within a system of commercialization in which illegal activity is viewed as normal by all parties. What follows are some examples of common forms of converting guns into money, or what Vadim Volkov memorably dubbed "violent entrepreneurship."[19]

Shakedowns

This is the kind of police corruption most common for average Russians and visitors to Russia.[20] The method is simple: A police officer stops someone on

Sage Foundation, 1980), p. 3; James Q. Wilson, *Bureaucracy: What Government Agencies Do and Why They Do It* (New York: Basic Books, 1989), pp. 168, 327–329.

[16] Transparency International, *Report on the Transparency International Global Corruption Barometer 2007*, December 6, 2007, p. 22.

[17] Levada Tsentr, *Obshchestvennoye mneniye 2006: Sbornik*, Table 7.5.12. [available at: www.levada.ru/files/1172574635.doc].

[18] On corruption in the Soviet police, see: Louise I. Shelley, *Policing Soviet Society* (New York: Routledge, 1996), pp. 101–102; Vladimir Nekrasov, *Trinadtsat' 'zheleznykh' narkomov* (Moskva: Versty, 1995), p. 301; Zhil' Favarel'-Garrig [Gilles Favarel-Garrigues], "Sovetskaya militsiya i eye bor'ba s rostom ekonomicheskikh prestupleniy v epokhu 'zastoya'," *Neprikosnovennyy Zapas*, No. 42, July 2005.

[19] Vadim Volkov, *Violent Entrepreneurs: The Use of Force in the Making of Russian Capitalism* (Ithaca, NY: Cornell University Press, 2002). Volkov, in turn, took the term from writings on the Italian mafia.

[20] Good discussion of shakedown practices, with examples, are in: David Satter, *Darkness at Dawn: The Rise of the Russian Criminal State* (New Haven, CT: Yale University Press, 2003), pp. 114–118; Maksim Glikin, *Militsiya i bespredel: Kto oni – oborotni v pogonakh ili nashi zashchitniki?* (Moskva: Tstenrpoligraf, 1998), pp. 62–71.

the street and asks to see her documents. If the person does not have appropriate documents, she pays a "fine" on the spot. If she does have the right documents, some "administrative violation" is found and she also can pay a "fine." Racial profiling often lies behind these stops: If in the United States, African Americans talk both bitterly and ironically about the crime of "driving while black," in Russia, the equivalent is "walking while Caucasian" (meaning, in this case, originating ethnically from the Caucasus region of Russia), and Caucasians in major Russian cities experience document checks by the police quite frequently. For example, a study conducted in the Moscow subway system in 2005 found that more than half of those people stopped by the subway police appeared to be from the Caucasus or Central Asia, even though they represented less than five percent of the passengers.[21] Allegedly, people from the Caucasus or Central Asia who live in Moscow sew their pockets shut so police officers have a harder time planting drugs on them. Another common variant of the individual shakedown is that inflicted on drivers by the ubiquitous and notoriously corrupt traffic police, who extract "fines" for real or alleged traffic violations. It should be noted that until recently, the procedure for paying a fine was so clumsy and time-consuming that most drivers far preferred to pay the "fine" (i.e., bribe) directly to the traffic cop; in recent years, the payment procedure has been simplified in many Russian cities.

A more time-consuming but potentially more lucrative version of the shakedown is to actually detain someone because of a violation discovered during a stop. The police might hold someone in a cell for several hours, or threaten to charge him with a more serious crime. Usually at that point, most people are prepared to part with all the money they have with them to get out of the situation. Another variant is to take all of the property on the "suspect" – cash, cell phones, and so on – before putting him in a holding cell. Once he is released, the property is not returned. If the person refuses to sign the property declaration, he is beaten until he agrees to sign.[22]

In February 2003, aware of the image problem of the police, the head of the Moscow police decreed that police should stop "baseless document checks." He further insisted on the importance of "polite and cultured relations with people," stating that police are "obligated to defend and respect people regardless of their citizenship, place of residence, social, material, and occupational status, racial or national background, sex, age, education, language, and religious, political, or other beliefs." The popular tabloid *Komsomolskaya pravda* cheekily printed a copy of the decree inside a dotted line with the suggestion that readers cut it out and carry it with them. Another paper sent out reporters a month later to investigate how police were reacting to the new decree. Some officers were unaware of it. Those who knew of it were openly skeptical, with some declaring it "silly" or "stupid." Street cops claimed that

[21] Jurix, *Etnicheski izbiratel'nyy podkhod v deystviyakh militsii v Moskovskom metro* (Moskva: Novaya Yustitsiya, 2006), p. 7.
[22] Interview M-24.

document checks were necessary to fight crime, and that taking bribes was justified because of their low pay.[23] Regardless, the reporters found plenty of shakedowns taking place on the street that day. The paper concluded that the decree and publicity around it was simply a "PR-action."[24]

"Roofing" (Kryshevaniye)

One of the most common forms of enrichment for power ministry personnel is the provision of protection (a "roof," or *krysha* in Russian parlance) to businesses of all sizes.[25] In the immediate post-Soviet period, state law enforcement agencies proved unable or unwilling to protect the property rights of newly legal stores and companies, so mafia groups created demand for "roofs" by running protection rackets. Over time, however, much of this activity was taken over by state agencies – not as part of their legal responsibilities, but on a for-hire basis. For example, the notorious Moscow bar "The Hungry Duck" started with a Chechen mafia roof, then switched to a private security service run by a former KGB general, and finally settled with the extremely reliable services provided by RUBOP, the MVD's regional organized crime directorate.[26] One Russian crime journalist estimated that if in the early 1990s, 70 percent of roofs were criminal, ten years later, 70 percent were provided by the police and another 10 percent by the FSB. Large enterprises were more likely to have an FSB roof.[27] Medium and large enterprises usually hire a former officer from the FSB or the MVD to serve as the "vice president" for security, who manages the firm's relations with law enforcement authorities.

The other major players in the "roofing" business are private security firms, which generally employ former military and law enforcement personnel. Indeed, many of the mafia-type groups originally formed to provide "protection" to private firms went legit in the 1990s and became private security firms. In 2008, the value of this industry was estimated to be about $3 billion annually, employing more than 740,000 people in more than 27,000 firms. The police interact with private security firms and extract rents from them; for example, the head of the municipal militia in St. Petersburg in the early 2000s reportedly oversaw roofing operations in the city, partially by controlling licenses for private security companies.[28]

[23] The tendency to justify bribe taking because of low police pay was ubiquitous among interviewees who either worked in or closely with the police: Interview M-5; Interview M-47; Interview P-2; Interview P-9; Interview P-13.

[24] "- Pred"yavite pasport! – A s kakoy stati?" *KP*, April 1, 2003; Anastasiya Kornya, Armen Urikhanyan, Dmitriy Chernov, "Proveryay, no doveryay," *Vremya MN*, April 4, 2003.

[25] Volkov 2002; Evgeniy Anisimov, "Pod 'kryshey'," *KP*, October 31, 2002; Sergey Kanev, "Kak ustroyeny 'kryshi' v Rossii," *Nov. Gaz.*, October 22, 2007.

[26] Satter 2002, pp. 147–155.

[27] Interview M-43; Dmitriy Rudnev et al., "Proshchay, 'krysha'!" *Profil'*, April 2006.

[28] Yekaterina Barova, "CHOP: Chego Oni Pritsepilis'? MVD protiv chastnykyh okhrannikov," *Sobesednik*, April 8, 2008; Inteview P-6. On the development of the private security industry, see: Volkov 2002.

In 2008, the MVD promoted legislation that would seriously weaken private security firms by tightening licensing procedures and even depriving them of the right to own firearms. Most observers believed the legislation was designed to allow the police to expand their roofing activities. Gennadiy Gudkov, a Russian State Duma deputy, stated, "for the Interior Ministry, commercial interests are the priority, not those specified in the Constitution, i.e. fighting crime. Unfortunately, this law cannot be called anything else but a commercial law lobbied by [the Interior Ministry.]"[29]

Under Putin, it appeared that the FSB also was expanding its roofing operations. The Russian scholar and journalist Yevgeniya Albats, an expert on the FSB, claimed that the FSB was trying to push the MVD out of many of its roofing "contracts," as well as increase the fees for businesses.[30]

Forced Takeovers

Law enforcement personnel are frequently involved in so-called "commissioned cases" (*zakaznye dela*), in which a company secures law enforcement support for an attack on a business rival.[31] The phenomenon of commissioned cases is one among multiple tactics used by "corporate raiders" in Russia.[32] These criminal takeovers can involve firms ranging in size from a corner store to Russia's biggest companies, such as Oleg Deripaska's Basic Element, which engineered several such high-profile takeovers in 2000–2002. Carrying out such commissioned cases involves not only the use of the courts to initiate lawsuits or bankruptcy cases, but also armed state units, such as MVD OMON troops to physically seize the assets, and police or procuracy support to bring criminal cases against one's rivals. FSB officers have also actively participated in the redistribution of property. Putin called attention to the problem at a February 2003 meeting of the MVD Collegium, declaring: "the involvement of MVD employees in corporate wars and economic disputes is, I would like to stress, very dangerous. I ask you to stay far away from that."[33]

---

[29] Barova 2008; Ivan Petrov, "Okhrannik s rogatkoy," *RBK daily*, March 17, 2008; "Russian Ministry Lobbies for New Law to Seize Private Security Business," *REN-TV*, October 30, 2007 [*BBC Monitoring International Reports*, October 30, 2007].

[30] Interview M-2. A good account of FSB business interests, and how these took them away from their core tasks, is: Sergey Mikhalych and Konstantin Poleskov, "Kto i kak prevratil FSB v khozyaystvuyushchego sub"ekta," *Nov. Gaz.*, September 22, 2003.

[31] Russian legal affairs journalist Leonid Nikitinskiy wrote a novel based on one such commissioned case, and the experiences of the jurors who heard the case: Leonid Nikitinskiy, *Tayna soveshchatel'noy komnaty* (Moskva: AST, 2008). See the discussion of the real case in the afterword.

[32] Thomas Firestone, "Criminal Corporate Raiding in Russia," *International Lawyer*, 42 (2008), pp. 1207–1229.

[33] Vadim Volkov, "Hostile Enterprise Takeovers: Russia's Economy in 1998–2002," *Review of Central and East European Law*, 29, 4 (2004), pp. 527–548; Sergey Mikhalych and Konstantin Poleskov, "Khronika peredelov," *Nov. Gaz.*, September 22, 2003; "Vystupleniye Prezidenta Rossiyskoi Federatsii Vladimira Putina na rasshirennom zasedanii Kollegii MVD RF," *Shchit i Mech*, February 13, 2003.

For example, the Nizhniy Novgorod region was the scene for two such commissioned cases in 2003, both involving food production companies. In both cases, courts and law enforcement organs were enlisted by both sides, the "attacker" and the "defender." In an attack on the Lysovsky Beer Factory, a colonel from the MVD administration of the Volga Federal District organized a meeting between the factory director and an agent of the hostile party and then brought in fifteen MVD agents to pressure the factory leadership with the threat of a criminal investigation. The regional prosecutor, however, sided with the factory, and the colonel faced potential dismissal.[34]

Vadim Volkov noted that in one sense, the increasing prominence of such cases in the early 2000s showed the strengthening of the state relative to the early 1990s, when mafia groups were much more active in such disputes. Now, he stated, "the major instruments of aggressive enterprise takeovers are corrupt state organizations that have judicial and coercive power." The problem, Volkov continued, is that state employees behave like bandits. Similarly, the *Moscow Times* noted that the use of law enforcement organs to settle commercial disputes represents "an assault on the state by the state."[35]

The importance of commissioned cases to Russia's commercialized law enforcement structures was apparent in the protracted struggle over which agencies have the legal right to initiate criminal proceedings. In the 2002 Criminal Procedure Code, the law was changed so only procurators could formally initiate criminal proceedings against someone. Police complained that the new requirement represented an unnecessary burden, but other observers thought the real objection was that the police had lost the ability to formally instigate commissioned cases, although police and other law enforcement agencies could still open investigations, which often could be enough to pressure a business. The 2002 change was reversed in 2007, although procurators retained the power to reverse a decision by an investigator (police or otherwise) initiating a criminal case. Police investigators lobbied heavily for this change. One observer characterized this protracted fight as a "battle over who gets bribes."[36]

[34] Sergei Ovsyannikov, "Prokuratura trebuyet uvolit' polkovnika MVD," *K-D-Nizhniy Novgorod*, April 29, 2003; Tat'yana Krasil'nikova, "Rossiyskoye zakonodatel'stvo bessil'no," *K-D-Nizhniy Novgorod*, April 29, 2003; Sergei Ovsyannikov, "Lysovskiy pivzavod pytayutsya zakhvatit'," *K-D-Nizhniy Novgorod*, April 29, 2003; "Pryamaya rech'," *K-D-Nizhniy Novgorod*, April 29, 2003.

[35] Vadim Volkov, "The Selective Use of State Capacity in Russia's Economy: Property Disputes and Enterprise Takeovers after 2000," *PONARS Policy Memo No. 273* (Washington, DC: Center for Strategic and International Studies, October 2002); "An Assault On the State By the State (Editorial)," *MT*, August 2, 2002.

[36] Peter H. Solomon, Jr., "The Criminal Procedure Code of 2001," in William Alex Pridemore, ed., *Ruling Russia: Law, Crime, and Justice in a Changing Society* (Lanham, MD: Rowman & Littlefield, 2005), p. 88; Victor V. Filippov, "The New Russian Code of Criminal Procedure: The Next Step on the Path of Russia's Democratization," *Demokratizatsiya*, 11, 3 (Summer 2003), pp. 397–398; William Burnham and Thomas A. Firestone, "Investigation of Criminal Cases Under the Russian Criminal Procedure Code," unpublished manuscript, October 2007; B.Ya. Gavrilov, *Sovremennaya ugolovnaya politika Rossii: tsifry i fakty* (Moskva: Prospekt, 2008), pp. 196–205; Interview M-45; Interview M-46.

The Yukos affair that began in 2003 and continued for several years was in some sense post-Soviet Russia's largest "commissioned case," with the firm Rosneft using its access to the power ministries (top Kremlin aide and silovik Igor Sechin was chair of the Rosneft board of directors at the time) to carry out a forceful redistribution of property. Further evidence for the importance of the practice of forced takeovers came in late 2007, when Russian business-man Oleg Shvartsman caused a miniscandal with his public assertions that his company had strong backing from prominent siloviki such as Sechin, and that they relied on their ties to current and former power ministry officials to conduct their business, including the use of "voluntary-coercive instruments" to reduce the price of enterprises. Although questions were raised about some particulars of Shvartsman's account, and it was speculated that he was being used as part of clan battles around the Kremlin, few doubted that his general account of business methods accurately reflected reality.[37]

Selling Assets

This category of commercialized siloviki behavior should be thought of broadly: Assets to be exchanged for money include information, documents, positions, and even people. The type of assets sold depend on those possessed by the specific agency or officer, but the principle is the same – valuable resources that theoretically belong to the state can be sold (or rented) to willing buyers. Roofing and commissioned cases are in this sense just a subset of this more general category. A few examples from 2007 will illustrate the phenomenon:

- The subdivision of the Moscow police responsible for phone tapping alleg-edly carried out illegal phone taps on business competitors for a variety of companies.
- A group of current and former siloviki, including personnel from the MVD and the FSO (Federal Guards Service, responsible for leadership secu-rity), reportedly sold access passes to government buildings, including the Kremlin, and special permission documents for automobiles, including government license plates complete with flashing blue lights (migalki).
- MVD officers sold positions and ranks within the militia. For example, the head of the criminal police in Tyumen Oblast allegedly paid a $200,000 bribe to be promoted to general.[38] The amount of the bribe is an indication of how lucrative corruption can be at the top of the MVD.

[37] Maksim Kvasha, "'Partiyu dlya nas olitsetvoryayet silovoy blok, kotoryy vozglasvlyayet Igor' Ivanovich Sechin'," *K-D*, November 30, 2007. See also: Jonas Bernstein, "Finansgroup: How Russia's Siloviki Do Business," *EDM*, 4, 222 (November 30, 2007); Jonas Bernstein, "Shvartsman's Description of Siloviki Business Practices – Truth or Fiction?" *EDM*, 4, 227 (December 7, 2007); Andrew Kramer, "Former Russian Spies Are Now Prominent in Business," *NYT*, December 18, 2007.

[38] Aleksandr Zheglov, "Novyy korruptsionnyy skandal v Moskovskom GUVD," *K-D*, June 22, 2007; Kirill Mel'nikov, "Signal'nyy srok," *VN*, March 20, 2007; Andrey Sharov and Vladimir Fedosenko, "Torgovtsy dolzhnostyami," *RG*, May 31, 2007.

Corrupt police officers attract the most press attention, but there are examples from all of the power ministries. In some ways, the armed forces should be an exception to the commercialization of the power ministries, because army officers do not have law enforcement responsibilities and therefore cannot open and close criminal cases, carry out court orders to seize property, and so on. But officers have also figured out how to sell or rent military assets for money. For example, conscripts and even contract soldiers are "rented" by their commanding officers to businessmen to perform menial labor, such as construction, and military firing ranges admit paying customers to shoot weapons. In Chechnya, military personnel have engaged in oil smuggling and sold weapons on the black market or to rebel forces.[39]

Connections to Organized Crime

Russian mafia groups link to and overlap with the power ministries in multiple ways. The explosive growth of the mafia upon the introduction of capitalism drew many former siloviki into organized crime because they possessed the necessary skills and training to wield violence effectively (sportsmen represented another major segment of these new mafia groups). These criminal groups either maintained contacts with former colleagues in the security and law enforcement structures or built new relationships with the underpaid people who stayed in these agencies. In 2001, Putin noted that grounds exist "for thinking that a fusion has taken place between criminal entities and law enforcement agencies."[40]

Mafia cooperation with state coercive structures is rife in traditional organized crime sectors, such as prostitution, gambling, and drugs. For example, the customs service (FTS) has close links to smugglers in many regions. Other forms of interaction include law enforcement officials sharing information about planned operations or arrests, favoring one gang over another in a dispute, selling weapons, and releasing gang members from prison or custody. In a 2002 poll, 39 percent of respondents expressed "firm confidence" that there are ties between the police and organized crime.[41]

Moreover, units within the MVD responsible for fighting organized crime sometimes cooperate with organized crime and sometimes are its

---

[39] "Russian TV says contract servicemen desert over extortion," *Ren TV* via *BBC Monitoring*, May 22, 2007 [JRL 2007-#116, May 22, 2007]; Kevin O'Flynn, "2 Arrested for Running Firing Range Business," *St. Petersburg Times*, April 17, 2007; Anna Politkovskaya, *Vtoraya Chechenskaya* (Moskva: Zakharov, 2002), pp. 195–227. For a good overview of Russian military corruption, see: Tor Bukkvoll, "Their Hands in the Till: Scale and Causes of Russian Military Corruption," *Armed Forces & Society*, 34, 2 (January 2008), pp. 259–275.

[40] Volkov 2002; *RFE/RL Security Watch*, 2, 6 (February 12, 2001).

[41] Interview M-50; Mark Galeotti, "Organised Crime and Russian Security Forces: Mafiya, Militia, and Military," *Conflict, Security & Development*, 1, 2 (2001), pp. 103–111; Alexander Salagaev, Alexander Shashkin, and Alexey Konnov, "One Hand Washes Another: Informal Ties Between Organized Criminal Groups and Law-Enforcement Agencies in Russia," *The Journal of Power Institutions in Post-Soviet Societies*, Issue 4/5 (2006); Gudkov, Dubin, and Leonova 2004, p. 37.

competitor in selling protection services. One gang member from Kazan, Tatarstan, stated, "The Department for Struggle against Organized Crime is very active.... They usually work like gang members; it means invasion and then 'rescue' from it.... For example, the Department examines a business, exerts pressure, and then offers the [sic] services." General Aleksandr Soinov, the head of police in Novosibirsk Oblast, in a 2003 interview characterized the regional Organized Crime Directorate (RUBOP) as a "criminal organization."[42]

One of the most spectacular cases of power ministry involvement with criminal groups involved the murder of the well-known Russian journalist Anna Politkovskaya in October 2006. In June 2008, the procuracy charged Sergey Khadzhikurbanov, a former employee of the Central (Moscow) Regional Organized Crime Directorate, with being the organizer of the plot to kill Politkovskaya, although the actual shooter and the "client" for the contract killing remained at large. Khadzhikurbanov was also charged in a second, unrelated case for extortion; his alleged accomplice in the attempt to extort a businessman was FSB Lt.-Col. Pavel Ryaguzov, who had initially been named as a suspect in the Politkovskaya murder but was not charged. Khadzhikurbanov and his co-defendants were acquitted in 2009, but the Supreme Court ordered a retrial. Politkovskaya's paper, *Novaya Gazeta*, conducted its own investigation into her murder and suspected that, at a minimum, Ryaguzov, Khadzhikurbanov, and others, including two brothers also charged in Politkovskaya's murder, were members of a criminal gang that included multiple members from the power ministries, although the lead procuracy investigator denied this version. In 2007, the Chief Editor of *Novaya Gazeta*, Dmitriy Muratov, maintained, "Politkovskaya's murderers are people in uniform who in their free time carry out different orders. This is a widespread practice, and practically all high-resonance crimes in recent times have been conducted precisely by these professionals."[43]

Corruption as a System

The previously described examples represent the tip of the iceberg in terms of the illegal economic activities of power ministry officials. Perhaps the most damaging aspect of the widespread corruption in the power ministries is that the phenomenon is so systemic that there is no one in these structures who has an interest in combating it. One MVD official remarked that those in a position to push for "the systematic extermination of corruption" are

---

[42] Salagaev et al. 2006; Interview N-7.

[43] Sergey Sokolov, "My vplotnuyu zanimayemsya zakazchikami," *Nov. Gaz.*, October 6, 2008; Andrey Soldatov and Irina Borogan, "Chto znayet podpolkovnik," *Nov. Gaz.*, October 6, 2008; Dmitriy Bykov, "Dmitriy Muratov: Delo Politkovskoy razvalivayut," *Sobesednik*, September 3, 2007. For an example of Politkovskaya's own reporting on corruption in Russian law enforcement, see: Anna Politkovskaya, *Putin's Russia: Life in a Failing Democracy* (New York: Metropolitan Books, 2004), pp. 114–158.

unwilling to because it would "hurt their commercial interests."[44] As the quote implies, corruption goes up and down the administrative hierarchy. If a beat cop makes extra money from people with improper registration papers and small street traders, then higher-ranking officers can oversee more organized schemes involving payoffs from various businesses, such as markets, restaurants, and construction firms.[45] More than two-thirds of law enforcement officials polled in 2005 claimed that they knew of or "constantly heard about" law enforcement officers "using their position for corrupt or other personal goals," while less than one-third said they did not know of such cases.[46] By most accounts, this understated the extent of the problem. Further, in a 2002 survey, 58 percent of Russians thought police corruption, such as bribes and roofing, had become a "stable system," and such phenomena were not simply isolated events. Fully 83 percent of those surveyed thought that bribe taking and corruption were either spread "quite widely" or that the police were "completely corrupt."[47]

The systemic nature of the problem was illustrated starkly by a December 2002 article in *Komsomolskaya pravda* that produced a "price list" for various services provided by the police, based on interviews with officers (See Table 5.1). These services included the closing of a criminal case, the release of a criminal, the sharing of documents with private individuals and companies, and providing a *krysha* or "roof" for a business. The "cost" of such services varied depending on the level within the police to which one needed to appeal. For example, according to *Komsomolskaya pravda* the cost of closing a criminal case in 2002 could vary from $10 to $500,000, depending on the level within the MVD, the individual involved, and the nature of the crime.[48] Russian academic experts came to similar conclusions about the variability of costs, pegging them to such factors as "the complexity of the problem (sometimes to solve it, the officer should break the law)" and "the position of a person offering the service." Not much had changed by 2008, when *Business Week* listed the price of getting the police to open a criminal investigation as $20–50,000, buying a favorable court ruling as $10–200,000, and a police raid on a business could run up to $30,000.[49]

More scientifically, a group of researchers from the Academy of Sciences' Institute for the Socio-Economic Problems of Society conducted a multi-year study on the economic activity of police officers. In a survey of more than 2,000 officers in eight regions of Russia between 2000 and 2002, these researchers arrived at a series of startling conclusions, including:

[44] Oleg Khrabryy, "Krizis vneshnego upravleniya," *Ekspert*, October 18, 2004.

[45] Evgeniya Borodina, "Zemlekopy: Komu v militsii zhit' khorosho," *MK*, December 16, 2002.

[46] Lev Gudkov and Boris Dubin, "Privatizatsiya politsii," *Vestnik obshchestvennogo mneniya*, 1, 81 (January–February 2006), p. 62.

[47] Gudkov, Dubin, and Leonova, p. 37.

[48] "Menty bez grima: glava 3. Korruptsiya," *KP*, December 12, 2002. UVD stands for Internal Affairs Department, which refers to the regional units of the MVD.

[49] Salagaev et al., 2006; Jason Bush, "Russia's Raiders," *Business Week*, June 5, 2008.

TABLE 5.1. *Police Bribes "Price List,"* 2002

The Price List of Police Services	Rural Police Department	City Police Department	Oblast' UVD	Krai UVD (Autonomous Oblast')	Republican UVD	St-Petersburg UVD	Moscow UVD	Central Command MVD
Close a criminal case	300 to 2,000 rubles	5 to 20,000 rubles	$2,000 to $100,000	$5,000 to $150,000	$10,000 to $200,000	$5,000 to $250,000	$10,000 to $300,000	$10,000 to $500,000
Free a criminal	1,000–2,000 rubles	2,000–3,000 rubles	$3,000 to $100,000	$5,000 to $100,000	$3,000 to $150,000	$10,000 to $200,000	From $200,000	From $500,000
Forge documents	50 to 300 rubles	100 to 2,000 rubles	$50 to $100	$100 to $1000	$1,000 to $2500	$10 to $4,000	$10 to $7,000	$5,000 to $10,000
Sell information to the criminals	From 800 rubles	From 2,500 rubles	From $200	From $200	From $200	$3,000 to $10,000	$5,000 to $10,000	$100 to $200 per day
Provide a "krysha" (protection) to business	From $50	From $1,000	From $1,000	From $2,000	From $2,000	$2,000 to $5,000	$3,000 entering a business	$5,000
Give permission for petty trade	From 100 rubles	100 to 500 rubles	From 500 rubles	500 to 1,000 rubles	500 to 1,000 rubles	From 1,000 rubles	From 1,000 rubles	
Sell an office	From $50	From $1,000	$1,000 to $100,000	$5,000 to $200,000	From $20,000	From $50,000	$250,000	From $250,000
Free a hooligan	50 rubles	100 to 300 rubles	100 to 300 rubles	100 to 300 rubles	From 200 rubles	200 to 500 rubles	$1,000 to $3,000	
"Forgive" the absence of a registration	20 rubles	From 50 rubles	From 50 rubles	From 50 rubles	From 50 rubles	50 to 100 rubles	100 rubles	
Forcibly extracting debts	40–50 % of the debt sum							

- The Russian police received more from non-state actors than they did from the state budget.
- Forty-one percent of police officers thought that illegal types of second jobs were more common among their fellow officers than legal ones (another survey showed that more than 80 percent of police officers had outside employment of some kind).[50]
- The ratio of legal to illegal second jobs was 3–1 during free time, but 2–3 during work time. It seemed that "police employees engage in illegal activity to a greater extent during work time, that is, when they should be fighting crime."

The authors of the report concluded that law enforcement had been "spontaneously privatized," and that the government was not "the only and often not the main sponsor" of law enforcement organs.[51]

Power Ministry Corruption and Clan Politics: The "Three Whales" Case

Many of the previously described examples come from lower- to medium-level law enforcement officials, but it must be stressed that high-ranking officers have been implicated in serious corruption also. For example, the so-called "werewolves in uniform" campaign that began in June 2003 was launched with the arrest of six colonels and lieutenant-colonels from the Moscow Criminal Investigations division and of Lt.-Gen. Valentin Ganeyev, head of the security department at the MChS (Emergency Situations Ministry).[52]

Perhaps the power ministry corruption case with the greatest resonance in Russia under Putin, however, was the "Three Whales" case, named after a Moscow furniture store accused of customs violations. Trivial and commonplace on the face of it, the case was anything but – Putin at one point said he was personally controlling the case, and the case was at the center of some of the biggest siloviki clan battles under Putin. Almost all of the main Russian law enforcement agencies, including the FSB, MVD, procuracy, FSKN (narcotics control), and FTS (customs), were involved in one way or another with the case. A member of the Duma and well-known investigative journalist, Yuri Shchekochikhin, may well have been killed for digging into the affair. The case shows not only the potential involvement of top power ministry officials

---

[50] Gudkov and Dubin 2006, p. 68.

[51] O. Kolesnikova, L. Kosals, R. Ryvkina, and Yu. Simagin, *Ekonomicheskaya aktivnost' rabotnikov pravookhranitel'nykh organov postsovetskoi Rossii: Vidy, masshtaby i vliyaniye na obshchestvo* (Moskva: 2002), pp. 31–32, 38–39; Interview N-3.

[52] Leonid Berres and Vladimir Demchenko, "Oborotni," *Izvestiya*, June 24, 2003; Sergey Topol' and Andrey Sal'nikov, "Vnutrenniye dela vyshli naruzhu," *K-D*, June 24, 2003. The "werewolves" campaign was widely viewed, both within law enforcement and society at large, as a "PR show" in advance of the December 2003 Duma elections. At the time, Boris Gryzlov was both Minister of Internal Affairs and the leader of the United Russia party. Gudkov, Dubin, and Leonova 2004, p. 32; Gudkov and Dubin 2006, pp. 67–68; Interview P-2.

in covering up crime and corruption, but the clientelistic nature of the system of corruption in Russia.[53]

The Three Whales case began in the summer of 2000, when officials of the State Customs Committee (now the Federal Customs Service) launched an investigation against the "Three Whales" furniture store and its owner, Sergey Zuyev, for importing contraband furniture and not paying customs duties equal to $5 million. The case was turned over to the MVD for investigation. The police investigator in charge, Pavel Zaytsev, allegedly turned up evidence of additional crimes, including money laundering and illegal trade in weapons and oil. Zaytsev's investigation was abruptly curtailed in November 2000, when the General Procuracy demanded the case be transferred to it. In December 2000, the procuracy opened a case against Zaytsev for illegal conduct during his investigation, and in May 2001 closed the Three Whales case.[54]

Why was the case closed, and why was Zaytsev arrested? Investigative journalists working for the independent paper *Novaya Gazeta*, and other media outlets, contended that Zaytsev ran into trouble because Three Whales had a very powerful "roof" – the FSB. Specifically, the head of security for Three Whales was retired KGB General Yevgeniy Zaostrovtsev. Zaostrovtsev's son Yuriy was the deputy head of the FSB responsible for economic security when the case broke in 2000. The FSB director throughout Putin's presidency was Nikolay Patrushev, who had been subordinate to the senior Zaostrovtsev in the KGB of the Republic of Karelia and who had served as the junior Zaostrovtsev's patron. As noted in Chapter 2, Vladimir Ustinov, the General Procurator from 2000 to 2006, is by most accounts part of the same siloviki clan as Patrushev. Additionally, it was alleged that those under investigation paid $2 million to close the case.

In 2003, Zaytsev received a two-year probationary sentence for abuse of office. A Moscow city judge who, by her account, had resisted pressure to convict Zaytsev was removed from the case and eventually forced out of the judiciary.[55] Two investigators for the State Customs Committee were also charged with abuse of office and lost their jobs. The case might well have died, but Shchekochikhin used his position in the Duma Security Committee and at *Novaya Gazeta* to investigate the affair and to call witnesses from the General

---

[53] On the connection between corruption and clientelism in post-communist countries, see: Kotkin and Sajo 2002.

[54] The summary of the case in this and subsequent paragraphs comes from: Yuriy Shchekochikhin, "Delo o 'Trekh kitakh'," *Nov. Gaz.*, June 2, 2003; "Khronologiya dela "Trekh kitov," *Nov. Gaz.*, June 19, 2006; Roman Shleynov, "Gnutye spinki," *Nov. Gaz.*, June 19, 2006; Victor Yasmann, "Russia: Corruption Scandal Could Shake Kremlin," *RFE/RL*, September 26, 2006; Yekaterina Zapodinskaya, "Delo 'Trekh kitov' vyshlo na yavku," *K-D*, June 22, 2007; Semen Stolyarov, "Delo 'Trekh kitov'," *Gazeta.ru*, October 3, 2007; "Titry k delu," *Nov. Gaz.*, July 7, 2008.

[55] On former judge Ol'ga Kudeshkina, see: Jeremy Page, "Judges take stand against Putin," *The Times* (UK), March 19, 2005. Kudeshkina's 2005 open letter to Putin, with details on the Zaytsev case and the pressure she received from her superiors to decide the case the "right way," is available at: http://archive.khodorkovsky.ru/society/docs/1935.html

Procuracy, MVD, and State Customs Committee to testify before the Duma. Pressure from the Duma to keep the investigation going led Putin to appoint a special prosecutor from Leningrad Oblast, allegedly a law school classmate of his. In 2002, Putin claimed the case was under his "personal control." Shchekochikhin died under mysterious circumstances in 2003 – his friends, family, and colleagues believe he was poisoned, but the official cause of death was an allergic reaction. Another key witness was killed, and several other figures in the case were physically attacked or threatened.

The Three Whales case remained largely dormant until June 2006, when Ustinov was replaced as Procurator General by Yuriy Chayka. Two weeks later, the procuracy announced the arrest of five people, including the head of Three Whales, Zuyev. However, none of these five individuals were state officials. Still, there was little doubt, according to observers, that the case was revived by Putin.

Over the next few months and into 2007, it became increasingly clear that the case had become a weapon in the siloviki clan battles that grew more intense as the "2008 problem" (the end of Putin's second term) became more pressing.[56] In the fall of 2006, a major house cleaning was ordered in the FSB, with more than a dozen officials, including several top generals, losing their jobs. The roughly simultaneous attack on Ustinov at the General Procuracy and Patrushev at the FSB was believed to have come partially at the instigation of Viktor Cherkesov, head of the FSKN and another key Petersburg silovik with close and long-standing ties to Putin. Cherkesov's FSKN had been given operational authority in the "Three Whales" investigation, which apparently led to wiretaps of several highly placed FSB generals. Another case involving the FSB and contraband furniture, this time from China, was also bundled together with the Three Whales affair and placed under FSKN investigation.[57]

The "Three Whales" case thus became another very useful weapon in siloviki clan struggles. Moreover, the ultimate target was not just Ustinov or Patrushev, but the deputy head of the presidential administration Sechin, the purported head of the dominant Kremlin siloviki clan. Sechin and Patrushev managed to strike back at Cherkesov, with the help of the new independent Investigative Committee within the procuracy, by arresting FSKN Lieutenant-General Aleksandr Bulbov for abuse of office in October 2007. Bulbov was in charge of investigating the "Three Whales" case within the FSKN and was

---

[56] On the connection of clan battles to the Three Whales case, discussed in the next several paragraphs, see: Yasmann 2006; Mikhail Fishman, "Shchit i kit," *RN*, November 13, 2006; Aleksandr Khinshteyn, "FSB zanimayetsya dur'yu," *MK*, October 3, 2007; Roman Shleynov, "Skandal v prezidentskom gareme," *Nov. Gaz.*, October 11, 2007; Yuliya Latynina, "Bol'shoy brat slyshit tebya," *Nov. Gaz.*, October 11, 2007; Semen Stolyarov and Mayk Gabriyelyan, "Gosnarkokontrol' kroyut za 'Trekh kitov'," *Gazeta.ru*, October 3, 2007. See also the discussion of siloviki clans in Chapter 2.

[57] On the Chinese contraband furniture case, see: Valeriy Ushakov, Anastasiya Mel'nikova, and Andrey Kuleshov, "Generaly shirokogo potrebleniya," *Nov. Gaz.*, October 2, 2006.

considered Cherkesov's right-hand man. This step was also connected to the coming succession at the top of Russian politics.

The affair appeared to wind down in early 2010, when Three Whales head Zuyev and eight of his business associates were convicted of smuggling and received sentences ranging up to eight years. Most notable about this dénouement was that none of the state officials connected to the case were charged with any crimes. The investigative journalist and Duma deputy Aleksandr Khinshteyn observed, "the principle heroes of the main political scandal of the Putin era – those who protected the smugglers and impeded the investigation – were left to the side. Only some of them lost their positions, not losing, however, their former influence."[58] Although the only convictions were of private individuals for smuggling, the Three Whales affair was ultimately not about smuggling. Rather, the episode was instructive because of how power ministry officials, in the words of journalist Roman Shleynov, "turned state service into business," with little regard for the law and complete impunity. It also showed how different clans tried to exploit the case for their own commercial and political gain.[59] At its most basic, Three Whales represented just one instance of such common practices as roofing and the selling of assets. More importantly, patrimonial linkages within and between law enforcement agencies, and with former colleagues who had gone into the private sector, facilitated corruption in the state bodies charged with upholding and enforcing the rule of law.

Summary

Corruption is a serious problem in the Russian power ministries in general, and law enforcement in particular, and has undermined state quality. Russia, of course, is not unique in this respect. In Mexico, Diane Davis observed, there is "a culture of corruption and impunity among the police"; in Ukraine before the Orange Revolution, Bohdan Harasymiw maintained, a "corrupt" and "politicized" law enforcement system was a key piece of "an incompetent, corrupt, police state."[60] Multiple examples exist around the world of weak states with corrupt – indeed predatory (see the following section) – law enforcement organs. In countries with high state quality, corruption in law enforcement structures is abnormal and episodic, as opposed to the routine and systemic form it takes in countries with low state quality.

Russian law enforcement clearly fits in the low state quality category, with pervasive and systemic pathologies, as the comparative data on corruption

---

[58] Aleksandr Khinsteyn, "Poslesloviye k prigovoru," *MK*, May 5, 2010.

[59] Roman Shlyenov, "Kak kitov prevratili v myshey," *Nov. Gaz.*, July 7, 2008; Shleynov, October 11, 2007; "Titry k delu" 2008.

[60] Diane E. Davis, "Undermining the Rule of Law: Democratization and the Dark Side of Police Reform in Mexico," *Latin American Politics and Society*, 48, 1 (2006), p. 62; Bohdan Harasymiw, "Policing, Democratization, and Political Leadership in Postcommunist Ukraine," *Canadian Journal of Political Science*, 36, 2 (June 2003), p. 320.

and the rule of law discussed earlier suggested. Several key points about the commercialization of the Russian power ministries bear emphasizing. First, it is not confined to one agency – there are multiple examples of such behavior from the MVD, the FSB, the Procuracy, the armed forces, as well as from less prominent bodies such as the FTS (customs) and MChS (emergency situations). Second, it is not just lower-level operatives but officials at all levels who engage in such practices. Third, there is little evidence that the problem got better under Putin, despite his anticorruption and state-building rhetoric. Writing a month after Putin left the presidency in 2008, well-known Russian commentator Yulia Latynina stated:

> The most striking thing about everyday life in the Russia of Vladimir Putin … is the incredible corruption of the courts, the police, the special forces – all the institutions that are supposed to uphold law and order in a democracy and that in Russia today have been transformed into a cancer that is devouring the state.[61]

The enormous problem of power ministry corruption is also recognized by top state officials. For example, Sergey Stepashin, the head of the Audit Chamber and a close Putin ally (as well as a silovik from Petersburg), publicly railed against corruption and economic activity in the power ministries in a 2007 speech to a procuracy conference:

> Former employees of the FSB, MVD, Procuracy, GRU [military intelligence], militia, moving into commerce and working against us for big money, with other technical capabilities – this is an enormous problem for our state.... Observing the inactivity and helplessness of the Procuracy, even law enforcement employees themselves are going down the criminal path and committing such serious crimes as kidnapping, drug trafficking, and "roofing" commercial structures. What do you expect, when corrupt officials have been uncovered in the Procuracy itself.[62]

Stepashin did not add, although he might have, that given the low risk of being caught or prosecuted, as well as the obvious personal enrichment going on at higher levels within the state machinery, the temptations facing your average officer must be enormous.[63] Further, given prevailing practices and organizational culture within Russian law enforcement structures, such behavior is the norm.

PREDATORY POLICING

State employees in general, and law enforcement officials in particular, can orient their work toward one of three basic goals: serving the state and its

---

[61] Julia Latynina, "Life in Putin's Russia," *WP*, June 22, 2008.

[62] Yevgeniy Mal'kov, "Prokuror za vsye v otvete," *Novgorodskiye vedomesti*, February 27, 2007.

[63] One brief example of the low risk of being punished for corruption will suffice – in 2005, in all of Russia, a total of 109 officers in the notoriously corrupt traffic police were sentenced for taking bribes, a rate of about 1.25 per region. "Sotrudniki GIBDD pochti ne berut vzyatok," *Novoye Vremya*, March 5, 2007. The Russian sketch comedy show "Nasha Russia (Our Russia)" spoofed the idea of an "honest traffic cop" with the fictional character Nikolay Laptev, whose family lived in abject poverty due to his unwillingness to take bribes.

rulers, society as a whole, or their own personal interests. These three options are ideal types, and most employees will serve some combination of these goals. For state bureaucracies to be high quality, however, most employees should view their job as serving society as a whole and allocate their efforts accordingly. This is not to say that even the most public-spirited officials are not interested in a good salary and benefits, or that they are not supposed to comply with directives from their bosses or other higher-placed state officials. The question, rather, is whether they steal on top of their salary and benefits, and whether they implement extraordinary tasks assigned by their superiors that violate the law, unjustly privilege one group over another, or have obviously harmful consequences for society as a whole.

This issue of whose interests bureaucrats ultimately serve can be conceptualized in either rationalist or culturalist terms. Agency theory, based on rational-choice assumptions, would think of the problem in terms of who is the principal (society or "voters" versus the state or "elites") and whether employees "work" or "shirk." Organizational culture perspectives would characterize the issue in terms of prevailing norms that guide employee behavior. In reality some combination of a "logic of consequences" (rational self-interest) and a "logic of appropriateness" (culture and norms) is likely to shape the conduct of state officials, including in law enforcement.[64]

The comparative literature on policing has long recognized the basic tension faced by the police in terms of whether they serve primarily the state and the maintenance of order or whether they serve the community and society and work to uphold the law and protect citizens from crime. Some studies, for example, differentiate between "Anglo-Saxon," "continental," and "colonial" models of policing, with the Anglo-Saxon model more decentralized, focused on crime control, and more accountable to the law and the citizenry, whereas the continental and the colonial models are more centralized and devoted first of all to maintaining political order and serving the state (or the colonial authority). Others distinguish between "democratic" and "authoritarian" forms of policing, with democratic policing oriented toward public accountability and committed to respect for civil and human rights. Otwin Marenin suggests a key difference is whether police power is used predominantly for repression or protection, whereas Ronald Weitzer contrasts a "functionalist" model of policing in which the police serve society as a whole to a "conflict" or "divided-society" model in which the police uphold the interests of the powerful and repress subordinate groups.[65]

---

[64] James G. March and Johan P. Olsen, *Rediscovering Institutions* (New York: Free Press, 1989).

[65] R.I. Mawby, ed., *Policing Across the World* (London: Routledge, 1999); P.A.J. Waddington, *Policing Citizens: Authority and Rights* (London: UCL Press, 1999), pp. 20–28; Shelley 1996, pp. 3–16; Dilip K. Das, "Challenges of Policing Democracies: A World Perspective," in Dilip K. Das and Otwin Marenin, eds., *Challenges of Policing Democracies: A World Perspective* (Amsterdam: Gordon and Breach, 2000), pp. 4–5; David H. Bayley, *Changing the Guard: Developing Democratic Police Abroad* (Oxford: Oxford University Press, 2006),

This binary opposition leaves out, as Ted Gerber and Sarah Mendelson pointed out in an excellent article on Russian policing, the possibility that police officers will use their position mainly in pursuit of corrupt or other self-interested goals. Gerber and Mendelson call this form of policing "predatory policing."[66] As noted in Chapter 1, the notion of predatory policing fits nicely with Peter Evans's description of "predatory" states that primarily plunder and extract resources from the population. A somewhat different approach to predatory state institutions is that of James Burk; in Burk's use, institutions are predatory when they both command significant societal resources while also behaving in morally illegitimate ways.[67] Arguably, given the data in Chapter 2 on the size and budgets of the power ministries, and the evidence in this chapter for significant corruption in these structures, Russian law enforcement structures are also predatory in the way Burk describes.

I call these three ideal-type models of policing, following Marenin and Gerber/Mendelson, the protection, repression, and predation models. In the protection model, police see their core task as serving society by fighting crime and upholding the law. This is what we might call the ideal ideal type, found in a high-quality, civil state. In the repression model, law enforcement agents primarily uphold the interests of the powers that be, maintaining political order and securing the regime and other elites from internal challenges. This type of policing might be found, for example, in high-capacity but low-quality authoritarian states – what are traditionally called "police states." In the predation model, as noted, police officers mainly serve their own interests by extracting rents from the population. In this type of state, both state capacity and state quality are low (see Figure 5.3).

No law enforcement organ or system will correspond exactly to one of the ideal types – in Iceland, some cops take bribes, and in Burma, some police solve actual crimes. Even at the level of the individual officer, both their role beliefs and actual practices are likely to combine various elements. The trick is to determinate the dominant tendency and, even more specifically, the mix

---

p. 8; Otwin Marenin, ed., *Policing Change, Changing Police: International Perspectives* (New York: Garland Publishing, 1996), p. 317; Ronald Weitzer, *Policing Under Fire: Ethnic Conflict and Police-Community Relations in Northern Ireland* (Albany, NY: State University of New York Press, 1995).

[66] Theodore P. Gerber and Sarah E. Mendelson, "Public Experiences of Police Violence and Corruption in Contemporary Russia: A Case of Predatory Policing?" *Law and Society Review*, 42, 1 (2008), pp. 1–43.

[67] Peter B. Evans, "Predatory, Developmental, and Other Apparatuses: A Comparative Political Economy Perspective on the Third World State," *Sociological Forum*, 4, 4 (1989), pp. 561–587; James Burk, "The Military's Presence in American Society, 1950–2000," in Peter Feaver and Richard Kohn, eds., *Soldiers and Civilians* (Cambridge, MA: MIT Press, 2001), pp. 247–274. See also: Richard A. Joseph, *Democracy and Prebendal Politics in Nigeria: The Rise and Fall of the Second Republic* (Cambridge: Cambridge University Press, 1987). I first used the notion of predation to describe Russian power ministry behavior in: Brian D. Taylor, "Putin's 'Historic Mission': State-Building and the Power Ministries in the North Caucasus," *Problems of Post-Communism*, 54, 6 (November–December 2007), pp. 3–16.

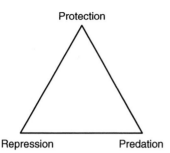

FIGURE 5.3. Three models of policing.

of types. Rather than relying on my own judgment, I use survey data from Russian citizens to situate the special services (e.g., the FSB), the militia, and the General Procuracy within this space.[68] An October 2006 survey by the Levada Center polling agency asked Russians what the main direction of activity for the three principal law enforcement organs was: the security of the population, the interests of the powers that be (*vlast*), or their own personal interests. Those responses are shown in Table 5.2.[69]

These survey data can then be used to plot the extent to which the law enforcement activity of the Russian special services, procuracy, and police correspond to one of the three ideal types of policing. Leaving aside the "hard to say" responses, Figure 5.4 shows Russian perceptions of the dominant orientation of the special services, procuracy, and militia, represented by points in the triangle.[70] The militia are believed to be dominated by predatory behavior (serve their own personal interests), with some protective tendencies (the security of the population) as well, and no repressive (the interests of the powers that be) ones. The special services and procuracy are perceived as quite similar to each other, with their activities directed first of all toward upholding the interests of the powers that be (repression), with some efforts at both predation and protection. The special services are seen as slightly more protection-oriented than the procuracy.

[68] William Pelfrey investigated the dominant style of Russian policing by interviewing eighteen officers, who were in the United States for a training course, using James Q. Wilson's distinction between watchman, legalistic, and service styles of policing. He found that the watchman style dominated, which Pelfrey described as the one "most prone to corruption and malfeasance due to the significant levels of discretion allocated to the officer." William V. Pelfrey, Jr., "Perceptions of Police Style by Russian Police Administrators," *The Journal of Slavic Military Studies*, 18, 4 (2005), pp. 587–598 (quote p. 590).

[69] Levada Tsentr, *Obshchestvennoye mneniye 2006: Sbornik*, Table 7.5.2. [available at: www.levada.ru/files/1172574635.doc]. The 2007 figures were within two to three percentage points, showing considerable stability: Levada Tsentr, *Obshchestvennoye mneniye 2007: Yezhegonik* (Moskva: Levada Tsentr, 2007), p. 86.

[70] The recalculated percentages once the "hard to say" responses are dropped out, in the order protection/repression/predation, are: special services – 31/48/23; procuracy – 24/52/26; militia – 29/0/71. Not all figures sum to 100 percent due to rounding.

TABLE 5.2. *Main Direction of Activity of Russian Law Enforcement Organs,*
Percent of Responses, 2006

	Special Services	General Procuracy	Militia
The security of the population	27	20	24
The interests of the powers that be	42	44	0
Their own personal interests	20	22	60
Hard to say	12	15	16

Although one might quibble with the exact placement of the different law
enforcement agencies – for example, it is hard to sustain the notion that the
Russian police do not at least in part serve the powers that be, particularly
after their aggressive policing of opposition marches and political parties in
2007, not to mention the 200,000-strong Internal Troops of the MVD – the
overall placement seems to fit with other evidence.[71] Given the crucial role
that the procuracy and the FSB played in Putin's assault on potential alternative centers of power, such as the oligarchs and regional governors, it is not
surprising that Russians believe that these agencies primarily serve the powers that be. Historically, the procuracy was known as the "eye of the tsar" or
the "eye of the state," whereas the KGB was the "shield of the state."

Gerber and Mendelson asked a question very similar to the one asked by
the Levada Center about the predominant activity of the police in a 2004 survey. In the Gerber and Mendelson survey, 37 percent of respondents think that
"most of all" the militia "serve their own material interests," 28 percent think
the police most "serve the interests of elites," and 25 percent think they most
"preserve public order and protect citizens." In other words, in this survey, just
like in the Levada poll, only about 25 percent of respondents think Russian
police are primarily protectors. Moreover, nearly half (47 percent) said that
preserving order and protecting citizens was either the police's third priority,
or something they did not do at all. The big difference between the two surveys
is that in the Gerber/Mendelson poll, the respondents are much more likely
to view the police as repressors, and therefore less likely to see them as preda-
tors, although the plurality still sees this as the dominant activity of Russian
police.[72] A similar finding about the low priority of protection for the Russian
police was reported by a Russian sociologist based on expert interviews; he

---

[71] The poll used for this figure was taken in October 2006, before the late 2006 and early
2007 "Other Russia" marches. It is also possible that the option "the powers that be" was
not given for the militia; it did not appear that it was in the 2007 survey: Levada Tsentr,
Obshchestvennoye mneniye 2007, p. 86.

[72] Gerber and Mendelson 2008, pp. 28–29. They also note that they know of no cross-national
surveys that ask this specific question.

FIGURE 5.4. Russian law enforcement types.

noted that not a single expert listed serving the public as a top priority of the police, concluding that such an orientation was "basically absent."[73]

Gerber and Mendelson also provide additional evidence, including further survey data, about the predatory behavior of the Russian police. Respondents were asked how often they or members of their family had experienced police violence or corruption in the last two-to-three years. The average totals for 2002–2004 (the survey was given annually during those three years) are shown in Table 5.3. Overall, between one in seven and one in eight Russians or members of their immediate family had experienced either physical or nonphysical abuse by the police within the previous two-to-three years. Levada Center polls conducted in 2002 that asked virtually identical questions came to very similar results, with 6 percent of respondents saying they had experienced police violence (10 percent when family members were included) and 5 percent stating they had been victims of police corruption (12 percent when family members were included). Fifteen percent said they had personally been inappropriately searched, stopped, or detained by the police in the last two-to-three years.[74]

---

[73] V.L. Rimskiy, "Predstavleniya intervyuiruyemykh o vozmozhnosti pridaniya rossiyskim pravookhranitel'nym organam sotsial'no oriyentirovannykh kachestv," in Demos, *Reforma pravookhranitel'nikh organov: preodoleniye proizvola* (Moskva: Demos, 2005), pp. 402–403.

[74] Gerber and Mendelson 2008, pp. 16–17; Gudkov, Dubin, and Leoneva 2004, p. 36. Because the Gerber/Mendelson poll was conducted by the Levada Center, it is possible that some of the same data are being used, but slight differences in the results and description of the survey sample suggest they were conducted separately. Either way, the results are highly consistent with each other.

TABLE 5.3. *Russian Encounters with Police Violence and Corruption*

	Total
Experienced Violence by the Police	
Respondent	5.2%
Family Member	4.9%
Either or Both	8.6%
Experienced Corruption by the Police	
Respondent	6.3%
Family Member	5.1%
Either or Both	9.4%
Experienced Any Form of Police Abuse (Violence or Corruption)	
Respondent	9.0%
Family Member	7.9%
Either or Both	13.8%

Note: Question was regarding experiences in last two-to-three years.
Source: Gerber and Mendelson 2008.

Gerber and Mendelson, comparing their data to data on the United States, conclude that, roughly speaking, "Russians experience about twice as much police violence and corruption in the course of 2–3 years as Americans experiences in the course of their lifetimes." They find some statistically significant differences based on ethnicity and status, with non-Europeans more likely to experience police violence and lower-status (education/employment) individuals more likely to encounter corruption, but overall these differences are relatively small.[75]

The routine use of violence by the police, rising to the level of torture, is consistent with either the predation or repression models of policing and completely incompatible with the protection model. The data from Gerber and Mendelson's survey about police violence are consistent with other surveys on the topic, as well as NGO reports and expert evaluations. For example, in 2005, Russian NGOs documented more than 100 cases of police torture in Russia, not including the North Caucasus.[76] In the same year, Russia's human

---

[75] Gerber and Mendelson 2008, pp. 18–23 (quote p. 18). By relatively small, they mean in comparison, for example, to the differences between whites and minorities in the United States, where the differences are much larger.

[76] Amnesty International, *Russian Federation: Torture and Forced "Confessions" in Detention* (London: Amnesty International Publications, November 2006), p. 2. Earlier reports documenting multiple cases of police use of torture are: Amnesty International, *Rough Justice: The Law and Human rights in the Russian Federation* (London: Amnesty International Publications, 2003); Amnesty International, *The Russian Federation: Denial of Justice* (London: Amnesty International Publications, 2002). For further examples from journalists, see: Glikin 1998, pp. 173–221; Michael Mainville, "Russia's 'Werewolves in Uniform'," *Toronto Star*, August 15, 2004.

rights ombudsman, Vladimir Lukin, highlighted the problem in his annual report. Lukin stated:

The number of crimes committed by employees of the internal affairs organs continues to grow. Particularly alarming are activities of members of the militia that can be characterized as torture, inhuman and degrading treatment. Data of non-governmental human rights organizations shows that the scale of police violence has grown significantly over the last 10 years.[77]

The use of torture and beatings against those in detention by Russian police has at least two prominent causes. First, violence is often used by the police to extract confessions to crimes. These "confessions" are often the easiest way to "solve" a crime, which improves the statistics used in performance review for officers.[78] As noted earlier, beatings can also be administered during shakedowns. Second, regular police officers have been rotated through Chechnya for short tours of duty (three months or so), both because of the need for personnel to augment the armed forces and the Internal Troops, and because of the desire to depict the operation as a law enforcement task rather than a counterinsurgency war. Power ministry personnel have regularly used beatings and torture against suspected militants in the North Caucasus (see Chapter 7). One human rights activist noted that the practice of sending regular police to Chechnya tended to make them "trigger happy" when they came back to regular service, whereas another claims that torture has become a "norm" for the police due to their experience in Chechnya.[79]

Overall, the predatory and repressive behavior of Russian law enforcement structures hurts state quality by diverting them from the protection of ordinary citizens, the role formally assigned to them in legislation. To put it differently, there is a large gap between "police power" as established by law and "police action" – what the police actually do.[80] For the police in particular, predation

---

[77] Vladimir Lukin, *Doklad o deyatel'nosti upolnomochennogo po pravam cheloveka v Rossiyskoy Federatsii v 2005 godu* [available at: http://www.ombudsmanrf.ru/doc/ezdoc/05. shtml#e].

[78] Demos 2005, pp. 13–17; Ol'ga Shepeleva, "Proizvol v rabote militsii: Tipichnye praktiki," in Demos 2005, pp. 40–43. The Demos report discusses in detail the procedures for recording crimes and assessing police performance, and notes how attempted reforms have not had the desired effects. A good earlier discussion of the problem is: K.K. Goryainov, V.S. Ovchinskiy, and L.V. Kondratyuk, *Uluchsheniye vzaimootnosheniy grazhdan i militsii: Dostup k pravosudiyu i sistema vyyavleniya, registratsii i ucheta prestupleniy* (Moskva: INFRA-M, 2001). An assessment of the problems with crime statistics in Russia is in: Gavrilov 2008, pp. 24–44.

[79] Interview P-8; Ye-3. The most detailed discussion is: Demos, *Militsiya mezhdu Rossiey i Chechney: Veterany konflikta v rossiyskom obshchestve* (Moskva: Demos, 2007). See also: Mainville 2004; Andrei Smirnov, "Chechnya Deployment 'Deprofessionalizes' Russian Policemen," *CW*, 8, 27 (July 5, 2007); Susan B. Glasser, "Chechnya Duty Hardens Russian Police," *WP*, November 28, 2003; Valentinas Mite, "Russia: Police Who Serve in Chechnya Bring Trauma of War Back Home," *RFE/RL*, June 27, 2002.

[80] The responsibility to uphold the law, protect citizens, and uphold human rights is set out in the first section, if not the very first article, of the laws on the procuracy, the FSB, and the militia. See: *Organy okhrany pravoporyadka: Sbornik normativnykh aktov 2004* (Moskva: Kodeks,

has come to dominate over either repression or protection. The police them-selves, according to surveys, are inclined to feel that in the post-Soviet period, they have lost their position as defenders of the state and order, with their "boss" (the state) having lost its legitimacy. They thus tend to pursue mainly their own interests rather than those of the state or society.[81] As David Satter stated, "the police in postcommunist Russia do not want to defend ordinary citizens because they regard it as an unproductive use of their time .... Their obsession with making money left them with neither the time nor the energy to enforce the law."[82]

Because of these predatory practices, Russian citizens fear the police almost as much as they fear terrorists and criminals. In a 2005 survey, 33 percent of respondents feared attacks by criminals and street hooligans, 29 percent feared terrorist attacks, and 26 percent feared arbitrary and despotic behavior (*proizvol*) by the police. One of Russia's best known authors of detective novels, Boris Akunin (Grigoriy Chkhartishvili), unfavorably com-pared this distrust of the state and police in Russia to that in democratic countries. Although the common police motto in the West – to serve and pro-tect – "sounds like something a dog does," Akunin thinks it is a good slogan. In contrast, he states, "The motto of our state, and especially of the police (which is perceived of as the state in the mass consciousness): 'To squeeze and rob.'" Similarly, Canadian journalist Michael Mainville wrote in 2004, "with extortion, harassment and, increasingly, murders, beatings, and rapes being carried out at the hands of police, Muscovites feel terrorized by those meant to serve and protect." Although Mainville's claim is perhaps hyper-bolic, the survey data suggests a significant problem.[83]

Indeed, this fear of the police has been noted by leading Russian state offi-cials. In 2001, Dmitriy Kozak, one of Putin's closest allies and, at the time, the deputy head of the presidential administration responsible for legal reform, referred to citizens' "panic-like fear" of law enforcement bodies. Putin him-self called attention to the problem in his 2005 State of the Union address to parliament:

We need law enforcement organs that honest citizens will be proud of, rather than crossing to the other side of the street when they see a man in uniform. Those who make personal profit their main task, and not defense of the law, have no place in law

---

2004). On police power versus police action, see: Mark Ungar, *Elusive Reform: Democracy and the Rule of Law in Latin America* (Boulder: Lynne Rienner, 2002), pp. 64–70. As Otwin Marenin notes, the difficulty is how to make formal principles of democratic polic-ing enshrined in law an important part of police culture: Otwin Marenin, "Democracy, Democratization, Democratic Policing," in Das and Marenin 2000, p. 313.

[81] Gudkov and Dubin 2006, p. 61.

[82] Satter 2002, p. 113.

[83] Gudkov and Dubin 2006, pp. 58–59; Mainville 2004; "One of the World's Richest Men Went to Solitary Because of This Interview," www.esquire.com, October 10, 2008 [English translation of correspondence between Grigoriy Chkhartishvili and Mikhail Khodorkovsky, originally published in the Russian version of *Esquire*].

enforcement structures. Employees of these structures should be motivated above all by the defense of citizens' rights and freedoms.[84]

It must be stressed again that it would be a gross error to view all Russian law enforcement officials as corrupt and predatory, or to pretend that such problems do not afflict law enforcement bodies in civil states. I personally have encountered multiple honest and decent Russian law enforcement officials, including average street cops who were helpful and friendly. Some observers believe that the Moscow metro police, for example, became considerably more professional in Putin's second term due to persistent reform efforts in the wake of several scandalous cases of predatory behavior.[85] However, the bulk of evidence shows, unfortunately, that the behavior of power ministry personnel is frequently oriented toward serving their own interests, or those of the powers that be, rather than upholding the law and protecting society as a whole. As one former police investigator put it, "among some people there is a sense of responsibility, that they are there to serve the public. But they are definitely in the minority."[86] These predatory and repressive behaviors, which are arguably based in both rational motives and cultural practices, weaken Russian state quality in the coercive realm. To understand the prevalence of these practices, we need to look more closely at personnel policies, including recruitment, compensation, and training in these bodies.

THE CADRES PROBLEM AND LOW PROFESSIONALISM

Russian bureaucratic practices have for centuries deviated greatly from the rational-legal type of administration outlined by Weber. Anyone who has read the novels or short stories of Gogol will not find this surprising. In Tsarist Russia, state officials originally operated through the use of prebendalist methods, meaning they received payment from citizens for performing their functions rather than receiving a salary from the state. This practice was known in Russia as "feeding" (*kormleniye*).[87] Although this practice was eventually replaced, at least on paper, in Weberian terms, Russian imperial bureaucracy

---

[84] *RFE/RL Newsline*, 5, 122 (June 27, 2001); Vladimir Putin, "Poslaniye Federal'nomu Sobraniyu Rossiyskoy Federatsii," April 25, 2005.

[85] Interview M-50.

[86] Mainville 2004.

[87] Vadim Volkov, "Patrimonialism versus Rational Bureaucracy: On the Historical Relativity of Corruption," in Stephen Lovell and Alena Ledeneva, eds., *Bribery and Blat in Russia: Negotiating Reciprocity from the Middle Ages to the 1990s* (New York: St. Martin's, 2000), pp. 42–43; Karl W. Ryavec, *Russian Bureaucracy: Power and Pathology* (Lanham, MD: Rowman & Littlefield, 2003), p. 177. On prebendalism, see: Max Weber, *Economy and Society* (Berkeley, CA: University of California Press, 1978), pp. 235–236, 966–967; Fred W. Riggs, *Administration in Developing Countries: The Theory of Prismatic Society* (Boston: Houghton Mifflin, 1964), p. 44; Joseph 1987.

tended toward the patrimonial type or at best toward a hybrid of patrimonial and rational forms.[88]

Soviet state administration might have been expected to move away from patrimonial forms, given the "high modernist" views of Lenin and other founders of the Soviet state. Yet the quest for "scientific management" resulted not in rational-legal bureaucracy, but simply overbureaucratization.[89] Soviet bureaucratic practices diverged from the Weberian ideal type in multiple ways, including the weakness of legal norms, arbitrariness, the personalization of office, overlapping lines of authority and responsibilities, and entry and promotion criteria and standards that mixed professional standards with political and personal, including clientelistic, ones. As Jan Pakulski concluded, "political-administrative systems in Soviet-type societies seriously deviate from almost all the important features of Weber's type of modern rational bureaucracy."[90]

It is not surprising, given this history, that the post-Soviet bureaucracy continues to be dominated more by patrimonial than rational-legal norms. Robert Brym and Vladimir Gimpelson carefully sifted the available data on civil service employment to show that, although contrary to conventional wisdom, the Russian bureaucracy is not particularly large in comparative terms, it exhibits a number of features – rapid turnover, poor-quality personnel, failure to adhere to employment qualifications, and so forth – that make it far from "the Weberian ideal of bureaucratic efficiency."[91]

---

[88] Suzanne Shattenberg, "Kul'tura korruptsii, ili k istorii rossiyskikh chinovnikov," *Neprikosnovennyy Zapas*, No. 42, July 2005; Alexander V. Obolonsky, "The Modern Russian Administration in the Time of Transition: New Challenges Versus Old Nomenclature Legacy," *International Review of Administrative Sciences*, 65 (1999), pp. 569–577; Peter H. Solomon, Jr., "Administrative Styles in Soviet History: The Development of Patrimonial Rationality," in Thomas Lahusen and Peter J. Solomon, Jr., eds., *What Is Soviet Now?: Identities, Legacies, Memories* (Berlin: Lit Verlag, 2008), pp. 78–89; Volkov 2000. Volkov contrasts the patrimonialism of Muscovy with the more rationalist orientation of imperial St. Petersburg, resulting in a mixed form of "patrimonial rationality" in which traditional practices persist but in a more covert form. The classic statement on the influence of Muscovite culture on both Imperial and Soviet political culture is: Edward L. Keenan, "Muscovite Political Folkways," *Russian Review*, 45, 2 (April 1986), pp. 115–181.

[89] James C. Scott, *Seeing Like a State: How Certain Schemes to Improve the Human Condition Have Failed* (New Haven, CT: Yale University Press, 1998), esp. pp. 147–179; Mark R. Beissinger, *Scientific Management, Socialist Discipline, and Soviet Power* (Cambridge, MA: Harvard University Press, 1988).

[90] Jan Pakulski, "Bureaucracy and the Soviet System," *Studies in Comparative Communism*, 19, 1 (Spring 1986), pp. 3–24 (quote p. 10); Jerry F. Hough, *The Soviet Union and Social Science Theory* (Cambridge, MA: Harvard University Press, 1977), p. 65. On the role of patrimonialism in the building of the Soviet state, see: Gerald M. Easter, *Reconstructing the State: Personal Networks and Elite Identity in Soviet Russia* (Cambridge: Cambridge University Press, 2000).

[91] Robert J. Brym and Vladimir Gimpelson, "The Size, Composition, and Dynamics of the Russian State Bureaucracy in the 1990s," *Slavic Review*, 63, 1 (Spring 2004), pp. 90–112 (quote p. 111).

Further, as Eugene Huskey has argued and as I demonstrated for Putin and the power ministries in Chapter 2, personal loyalty has dominated over professionalism or technical expertise in bureaucratic appointments.[92] Patrimonialism in the specific sense of family ties also continues to play a role. At the top of government under Putin, examples included the marriage of Defense Minister Anatoliy Serdyukov to the daughter of Prime Minister Viktor Zubkov, the marriage of the son of Procurator General Vladimir Ustinov to the daughter of top Kremlin official and siloviki clan head Igor Sechin, and the appointment of the son of FSB head Nikolay Patrushev as an advisor to Sechin at the state oil company Rosneft.

Similar favoritism toward family members is also common at lower levels of government. For example, a particularly lucrative legal profession in Moscow is notary public – estimates suggest that a monthly income of $50,000–$60,000 is not atypical, with the best-paid making up to $100,000 a month. To work as a notary public, one must be chosen by a commission. In 2005–2006, those receiving the position included the son of the Moscow police chief, the daughter of the speaker of the Moscow city Duma, the son-in-law of MChS head Sergey Shoygu, the wife of a member of the Supreme Court, relatives of multiple notary officials, and the wife of the chair of the very commission choosing notary publics. The commission head during that period, Aleksandr Buksman, later rose to the post of First Deputy General Procurator of Russia, where he was responsible for fighting corruption. Inna Ermoshkina, a lawyer who filed multiple suits about the influence of connections (*blat*) on commission decisions, stated, "experienced lawyers who do not have a big family name have practically no chance of becoming a notary public." For her troubles, Ermoshkina and her husband were charged with fraud in a property dispute and spent months in prison before being released. In 2008, a court declared many of the commission decisions illegal and removed dozens of Moscow notary publics from office.[93]

Efforts to build a more Weberian civil service in post-Soviet Russia also have been hampered by a huge loss of cadres to the private sector, particularly the most qualified members at the middle of the administrative hierarchy. As Georgiy Satarov, one of Yeltsin's top political advisers, put it in 1999, "the old

[92] Eugene Huskey, "Putin as Patron: Cadres Policy in the Russian Transition," in Alex Pravda, ed., *Leading Russia: Putin in Perspective* (Oxford: Oxford University Press, 2005), p. 168; Eugene Huskey, "Nomenklatura Lite? The Cadres Reserve in Russian Public Administration," *Problems of Post-Communism*, 51, 2 (March/April 2004), p. 35; Eugene Huskey and Alexander Obolonsky, "The Struggle to Reform Russia's Bureaucracy," *Problems of Post-Communism*, 50, 4 (July/August 2003), p. 23.

[93] Elizaveta Mayetnaya, "Novoye pravilo povedeniya samykh krupnykh rossiyskikh chinovnikov: khochesh' khorosho ustroit' rodstvennika – sdelay ego notariusom," *RN*, December 11, 2006; Yekaterina Zapodinskaya, "Basmannyy sud zastupilsya za zhenu pervogo zamestitelya genprokurora," *K-D*, June 27, 2008; Yekaterina Butorina, "Nuzhnoye mesto," *VN*, October 20, 2008; Elizaveta Mayetnaya, "Uvolit' po-rodstvennomu," *RN*, October 20, 2008.

system of state cadres collapsed, and a new one is still being created." Satarov added that Russia still lacked a clear distinction between civil service and political appointments, a point echoed by others.[94]

Administrative reform was an important concern of both the first and second Putin terms, with several major initiatives launched to try to create a more modern civil service based on Western models. Although there is now considerable consensus among Russian experts about the type of public administration that the country needs – specifically "a merit-based professional civil service based on the promotion of the public interest" – and some important legislation has been adopted, the implementation of these projects has lagged considerably. One public administration expert estimated that the 2004 Law on Civilian State Service was only about 10–20 percent implemented, and that overall it was merely an "imitation of change" that did not change either state personnel or the way they related to society.[95] Surveys of Russian civil servants suggest that they themselves are highly aware of the disjuncture between what they believe to be appropriate bureaucratic behavior and how the system actually works.[96] Thus, many of the pathologies that have plagued Russian bureaucracy for centuries persist, with the administrative type being, at best, a hybrid of patrimonial and rational forms. Public administration reform seems to have followed the general pattern of post-Soviet politics outlined in the memorable quote of former Prime Minister Viktor Chernomyrdin: "we wanted things to be better, but they turned out the way they always do" (*khotelos kak luchshe, a poluchilos kak vsegda*).

In the rest of this section, I argue that in the law enforcement sphere, and in particular in the police, many of the general problems of Russian state administration are also apparent. Although firm quantitative data on many issues are not available, qualitative evidence – including from interviews, press accounts, and expert reports – all indicate that Russian law enforcement tends toward patrimonial rather than rational-legal forms of administration, and that these tendencies weaken state quality.

Cadres: Recruitment and Retention

In the Soviet period, there was a sharp difference in the quality of cadres recruited by the KGB and by the MVD for the police. The KGB in the

---

[94] Alexei Barabashev and Jeffrey D. Straussman, "Public Service Reform in Russia, 1991–2006," *Public Administration Review*, 67, 3 (May/June 2007), pp. 373–382; Interview M-30; Interview Ye-12.

[95] Interview M-22. The 2004 law replaced an earlier civil service reform law from 1995. On the history of civil service reform, see especially Barabashev and Straussman 2007.

[96] Debra W. Stewart, Norman A. Sprinthall, and Jackie D. Kem, "Moral Reasoning in the Context of Reform: A Study of Russian Officials," *Public Administration Review*, 62, 3 (May/June 2002), p. 289; Ryavec 2003, pp. 4–5, 14; Larry Luton, "The Relevance of U.S. Public Administration Theory for Russian Public Administration," *Administrative Theory and Praxis*, 26, 2 (2004), p. 219.

post-Stalin era was able to attract well-educated, high-quality recruits to stable careers that were both high status and, relatively speaking, financially well compensated. In contrast, the MVD in general, and the militia in particular, was unable to pay and reward its employees as well and consequently attracted recruits who were undereducated relative to the Soviet norm. The prestige of serving in the police, in sharp contrast to the KGB, was low, and the conditions of employment were more difficult. Training for average cops was considered rudimentary and overly ideological. The primary incentives to take a job in the police were urban residence permits and housing, and the police attracted many recruits from rural areas who had recently completed their obligatory military service. Vladimir Putin made clear in his 2000 campaign memoir the elite mindset of the KGB and the disdain with which secret policemen viewed the regular police.[97]

The collapse of the Soviet state led to a huge exodus of cadres from all of the major law enforcement structures. Louise Shelley notes that under Mikhail Gorbachev, job conditions worsened, the prestige of the militia fell even further, and the state was not able to offer either competitive salaries or job security, which might have compensated for lower wages. The Soviet collapse, followed by the attempt to introduce capitalism in Russia, accelerated the loss of power ministry officials to the private sector. Volkov reported one estimate suggesting that between 1991 and 1996, the MVD lost 200,000 employees *per year* – an enormous percentage of ministry employees – with one quarter of these dismissed for disciplinary reasons. Another report claimed that by 1993, more than half of MVD personnel had worked in the police for less than three years.[98]

Losses from the KGB and its successor bodies were not as dramatic but were still considerable. Investigative journalist Aleksandr Khinshteyn, known for his close ties to the secret services, argued after the Beslan incident of September 2004 that the state was unable to confront terrorism because the KGB had been mindlessly dismantled after 1991. Before 1990, Khinshteyn wrote, the KGB was "the most prestigious organization in the country," which attracted "the best of the best, the elite." After 1991, this elite "lived through an oppressive feeling of their own irrelevance, dispensability, uselessness." According to Khinshteyn, tens of thousands of people left the secret police, and it was the best cadres who left, including the organization's "skeleton" – mid-level officials. The most capable officials went to work in private security companies, banks, or oil companies. As I noted in Chapter 2, there were good

---

[97] Amy W. Knight, *The KGB: Police and Politics in the Soviet Union* (Boston: Unwin Hyman, 1990), pp. 159, 176–177; Shelley 1996, pp. 83–84, 86–88, 90–96; Natal'ya Gevorkyan, Natal'ya Timakova, and Andrey Kolesnikov, eds., *Ot pervogo litsa: Razgovory s Vladimirom Putinym* (Moskva: Vagrius, 2000), pp. 25, 128–129.

[98] Shelley 1996, pp. 103–104; Volkov 2002, pp. 130–132; Yakov Gilinskiy, "Challenges of Policing Democracies: The Russian Experience," in Das and Marenin 2000, pp. 188–189; Ol'ga Shepeleva and Asmik Novikova, "Osnovnye problemy sovremennoy militsii," in Demos 2005, p. 57.

reasons for the leaders of an aspiring democracy to dismantle the KGB, but Khinshteyn was probably correct about the consequences of this decision for the quality of cadres in the secret police.[99]

Other observers agreed that the power ministries were particularly hard hit at the middle ranks. Crime journalist Andrey Konstantinov maintained that the middle level of law enforcement "suffered mightily" in the 1990s, with the best leaving service. This view was echoed by law enforcement officials themselves. Two police colonels in Yekaterinburg independently stressed that the best cadres left in the 1990s. A police colonel in Nizhniy Novgorod made the same point, noting in particular that middle-aged men took better positions elsewhere, so the proportion of women in the MVD increased because it was harder for them to get work in the private sector. A city official in Nizhniy also noted the loss of middle-aged law enforcement personnel.[100] The loss of many experienced officials at middle levels meant that remaining employees were either "old-timers" who were less able to jump to the private sector or very young and inexperienced officers. According to MVD Head Rashid Nurgaliyev, in 2005, more than half of MVD employees at the local level (cities and districts [*rayon*]) were younger than thirty and thus lacking in the requisite experience. Nurgaliyev contended that the personnel situation at the local level was "catastrophic." Another report maintained that at the lowest levels of service, personnel changed every two years.[101]

Not only did law enforcement bodies lose some of their best, most experienced personnel, but they had a hard time recruiting and retaining replacements in sufficient quantity and quality. The head of the police in Novosibirsk noted a perennial shortage of personnel throughout his service. In Nizhniy Novgorod in 2003, a colonel noted a 50 percent shortage of criminal investigators in the police. Konstantinov similarly claimed a 40 percent shortage in the St. Petersburg procuracy, particularly in terms of investigators. In one district of St. Petersburg, he joked ruefully, murder investigators are so overworked that they "simply go from corpse to corpse." Experts in St. Petersburg and Nizhniy Novgorod noted a tendency of people to rotate through both the police and procuracy very quickly.[102] Given these shortages and the tendency of employees not to stay in one position very long, the quality of employees was universally declared to be low – a point made both by academic experts and law enforcement officials themselves.[103]

[99] Aleksandr Khinshteyn, "Izbavleniye ot KGB," *MK*, September 8, 2004.

[100] Interview P-2; Interview Ye-13; Interview Ye-14; Interview NN-7; Interview NN-8. See also: Shepeleva and Novikova 2005, pp. 55–56.

[101] Yuriy Spirin, "Reforma MVD budet kosmeticheskoy," *Izvestiya*, July 29, 2004; "Ministr vnutrennikh del Rossii Rashid Nurgaliyev dovol'no zhestko otzyvayetsya o rabote svoikh podchinennykh na mestakh," *EM*, October 26, 2005; Demos 2005, p. 12. For descriptions of the organization of city and district MVD structures, see: Shelley 1996, pp. 66–68; A.P. Korenev, ed., *Administrativnaya deyatel'nost' organov vnutrennikh del*, 3rd Edition (Moskva: Moskovkaya akademiya MVD, 2001), pp. 90–97.

[102] Interview N-7; Interview NN-7; Interview P-2; Interview P-7; Interview P-12; Interview NN-4.

[103] Interview M-20; Interview M-39; Interview M-47; Interview N-7; Interview NN-7.

Specific data are available on the difficulty of retaining quality personnel in the investigative apparatus of the MVD. All three of the main law enforcement organs – Procuracy, MVD, and FSB – have investigators (*sledovateli*), with cases assigned based on the nature of the crime. For example, procuracy investigators are responsible for cases of rape, murder, and certain types of economic and administrative crimes. MVD investigators are responsible for the large majority of general criminal cases; in 1999, the MVD investigated 89.2 percent of all cases handled by law enforcement structures (up from 61 percent in 1964 and 76 percent in 1978). In 2003, the Deputy Head of the MVD Investigative Committee, Boris Gavrilov, published data on turnover, education, and experience of MVD investigators (see Table 5.4). Although Gavrilov did not provide a baseline figure for the number of MVD investigators in Russia, a rough estimate of 49,000 for the year 1999 can be calculated from the data.[104]

The table shows that turnover of MVD investigators was roughly between 10 percent and 20 percent per year in the decade from 1993 to 2002. In total over that decade, nearly 65,000 MVD investigators left service. Gavrilov asserted than many of them left for more lucrative positions, either in the private sector or in other law enforcement organs with higher salaries, such as the procuracy. These people were generally replaced by less qualified individuals, since the MVD academies could not replace such a large outflow of cadres. The share of those with higher legal education in this position dropped considerably compared to the late Soviet period. In 1989, the percent of MVD investigators with such an education was 87 percent, but this number dropped precipitously in the coming years, down to 60 percent in 1993 and 44 percent in 1996. In other words, the percent of MVD investigators with a higher legal education was cut in half in a period of seven years. By 2002, this percentage had climbed back to the 60 percent mark of 1993, still far below the late-Soviet standard. Similarly in 1989, the percent of investigators with more than three years of service was 69 percent. By 1993, this figure had dropped to 55 percent and by 2000, less than 40 percent of MVD investigators had been in that position for more than three years.[105]

Entry into both law enforcement educational establishments and entry-level positions has become much less competitive since the Soviet collapse. Several police officials reported that there is no longer competition for positions in the police in large cities like Yekaterinburg and Nizhniy Novgorod, so they end up taking everyone.[106] Similarly, in the Republic of Komi, an official noted that

---

[104] Specifically, data in the article on the number of registered crimes, the percent of these investigated by the MVD, and the average case burden per MVD investigator yields a number of 48,950 investigators in 1999. Data from 2002 on the number of investigators leaving service and the annual percentage of "employment fluctuation" provides a rough check; using these figures, the number of investigators in 2002 was slightly more than 45,000. See: Boris Gavrilov, "Sledstvennyy apparat organov vnutrennikh del," *Otechestvennye zapiski*, No. 2 (11), 2003.

[105] Gavrilov 2003.

[106] The risks of loose recruiting standards were experienced in Washington D.C. in the early 1990s, when a rapid expansion of the force in 1989–1990 led to an influx of unqualified

TABLE 5.4. *Turnover, Education, and Experience of MVD Investigators, 1993–2002*

	1993	1994	1995	1996	1997	1998	1999	2000	2001	2002
Employees Dismissed or Resigned	2,978	4,134	4,478	4,595	4,333	4,027	3,916	4,658	5,981	6,614
Transferred to Other Service	1,407	1,441	1,590	1,786	1,836	1,958	2,111	2,065	2,368	2,475
Total Leaving Investigative Organs	4,385	5,575	6,068	6,381	6,169	5,985	6,027	6,723	8,349	9,089
Percent with Higher Legal Education	59.8	49.1	46.0	43.6	44.5	46.7	50.9	55.6	58.2	60.0
Percent Employed as Investigator for <3 Years	55.2	62.5	60.6	55.4	47.7	44.1	41.5	39.4	42.2	43.2

anyone who was not sick would immediately be hired. In some cases, according to an official in Nizhniy Novgorod, both legal and illegal businesses (i.e., organized crime) send "their" people, who can help them from the inside, to work in law enforcement. One police colonel at a Moscow MVD academy described the current crop of investigators as "accidental" (*sluchaino*) people, in the sense of they got the job "by accident," without qualifications and without any particular sense of responsibility about their work.[107] Further, many of those who do go through MVD higher education establishments do not go into state service but take their legal and economic education to work in the private sector. In the procuracy, according to Procurator General Yuriy Chayka, as of 2007, a large number of investigators still did not have either a higher professional education or sufficient work experience.[108]

Of course, in reality, the situation is more complicated than this one-sided picture. In some localities, service in the police is still a relatively attractive and respectable career. Small and medium-sized towns, for example, reportedly have more success attracting qualified applicants than big cities. And toward the end of the Putin era, the head of the MVD cadres department was reporting that the personnel situation had "stabilized," although it is hard to imagine that the "catastrophic" situation described by Nurgaliyev in 2005 could be corrected in two years. The dominant tendency in police personnel policy, according to one scholar, is for informal connections to play the most important role for high- and medium-level appointments, and for entry-level positions to be filled by whoever is willing to serve, with little quality control.[109]

Indeed, the sense that the police will hire anyone was humorously conveyed in the opening scene of one of the iconic Russian films of the 1990s, *Brother (Brat)*. The hero, Danila, a young man recently demobilized from the army after serving in Chechnya, inadvertently wanders onto a film set and ends up in a fight with the security guard. He is arrested by the police, and the police commander proceeds to offer him a job as a cop. Danila declines, but in the sequel, *Brother 2*, Danila's older brother, a former mafia hit man in St. Petersburg, has returned to their village and taken a job with the police. In another fictional genre, the detective story, Petersburg writer Nikita

---

police officers, including some with criminal and gang backgrounds. Many of these new officers were involved in criminal behavior as police officers. In D.C. at the time they took one in four applicants, compared to the previous norm of one in twelve, and the national average of one in ten. Compared to contemporary Russia, a one in four acceptance rate looks extremely selective. See: Keith A. Harriston and Mary Pat Flaherty, "D.C. Police Paying for Hiring Binge," *WP*, August 28, 1994.

[107] Interview Ye-13; Interview NN-8; Demos 2005, pp. 11–12; Interview M-46.

[108] Alik Khabibulin and Dmitriy Shumkov, "Novye militsionery," *RG*, December 27, 2006; Aleksey Levchenko, "Chaike vykrutili ruki," *gazeta.ru*, April 13, 2007.

[109] Interview M-21; "Interv'yu nachal'nika Departmenta kadrovogo obespecheniya MVD Rossii general-leytenanta militsii Vladimira Kikotya gazeta 'Shchit i mech'," *Shchit i mech*, September 23, 2007; Interview M-11.

Filatov begins a collection of short stories with the epigraph "You'd have to be a complete idiot to work in the militia right now!" Konstantinov similarly said that "only alcoholics and dimwits remain" in the police.[110] Although Filatov and Konstantinov were exaggerating, their comments captured general attitudes about the low status of the policing profession in contemporary Russia.

Conditions of Employment

Russian experts universally agree that the employment conditions of law enforcement personnel have declined considerably since the Soviet collapse. Even for the police, whose jobs had lower prestige, pay, and benefits than those in the KGB or the procuracy, the Soviet system did offer housing, a living wage, and an adequate pension. The economic collapse that followed the Soviet break-up put great stress on the financial and social rewards of service, representing to a certain extent a return to the practice of *kormleniye* ("feeding") prevalent in Tsarist Russia. As professor Vyacheslav Zhitenev of the Urals Academy of State Service in Yekaterinburg put it, "in the 1990s the MVD was simply sent out to the market [*rynok*, a literal street market, not simply the abstract market of economic theory – B.T.] to make their own money."[111] Although corruption in the police had become widespread even before the collapse, in the 1990s, it became institutionalized in the sense of becoming part of standard practices and norms.

Kormleniye by the police is justified, both by themselves and by others, as a necessary response to their inadequate salaries.[112] As the St. Petersburg crime journalist Konstantinov put it, "can you live on $250 a month? I can't. The police feel morally justified in taking bribes. The very best try to make it somewhat legal, or not so bad." For example, a traffic cop might only give on-the-spot "fines" for actual legal violations, as opposed to for imaginary ones. Those who do not take bribes in the police or procuracy, perhaps because a spouse or relative makes enough money in her job to provide for a comfortable standard of living, are looked at by their colleagues as if they are "a white crow." Echoing Konstantinov, an MVD employee told the paper *Izvestiya* that "a normal person can't live on that amount of money." He added that any structural changes in the MVD are irrelevant to raising police quality given current conditions of employment.[113]

Konstantinov's figure of $250 a month, or $3,000 per year, provided in late 2004, was not hyperbolic, but a legitimate reflection of actual salaries in the MVD during Putin's first term. A police colonel in Petersburg in 2002, the head of a department with more than twenty-five years of service, made

---

[110] Olcott 2001, p. 93; Interview P-2.
[111] Interview Ye-12; on the revival of *kormleniye* more generally, see also: Ryavec 2003, pp. 183–189 (esp. p. 186).
[112] See note 23 to this chapter.
[113] Interview P-2; Spirin 2004.

around $250–300 a month. A police colonel in Moscow with a Ph.D. was paid $220 a month in 2003. A former high-ranking MVD official cited a figure of $300 per month for MVD generals in 2003. A 2005 Moscow newspaper story cited a figure of $200–250 per month for police in Moscow. According to a different paper, the average salary for beat cops in Moscow in 2004 was $172 per month (5,000 rubles), with plans to double it in the following year.[114] To put these numbers in perspective, per capita GDP in Russia in 2004 using the exchange rate method was about $4,000. Thus, police officers in Russia's largest and most expensive cities were paid well below the national average for annual income. In comparison, in New York City, police officers with six years experience were paid $58,000 in 2004, well above the per capita income for the city of $27,000 according to the 2006 census.[115] Overall, more than 90 percent of militia employees surveyed in 2005 considered the level of pay of an average cop as either insufficient or low.[116]

Rising world oil prices and strong economic growth after 1999 made it possible to increase spending on the power ministries under Putin. During his second term, a concerted effort was made to increase police salaries, which doubled between 2005 and 2008. For example, a captain with ten years experience saw his monthly salary increase from 7,500 rubles to 15,500, and an entry-level private had her salary increased from 4,800 rubles to 10,300 (not controlling for inflation). For comparison, the average salary in Russia in 2008 was around 15–16 thousand rubles, although it was double that (30–31 thousand) in Moscow. In dollar terms, the increase was even starker because of the appreciation of the ruble in Putin's second term, with the average monthly salary for a captain going up from $262 to $660. According to then-First Deputy Prime Minister Dmitriy Medvedev, police salaries tripled between 2002 and 2008. This impressive increase in wages was consistent with overall trends in wages in the country.[117] The increase in salaries certainly helped improve the conditions of employment for law enforcement personnel.

Compensation for state employees compared to the private sector remained low, however, especially when benefits were included. For example, a 2003 study conducted by the Russian Higher School of Economics for the World Bank found that total compensation (salary and benefits) in average private sector jobs was four-to-six times greater than in the civil service at lower

---

[114] Interview P-13; Interview M-46; Interview M-47; Rustem Falyakhov and Andrey Kovalevskiy, "MVD budet kryshevat' aeroporty," *Gazeta*, February 16, 2005; Anatoliy Gusev, "Ty chto, davno v obez'yannike ne byl?" *Izvestiya*, October 21, 2004. Ruble/dollar conversions calculated using the exchange rate at the time of the article, twenty-nine rubles to the dollar.

[115] The 2004 per capita GDP for Russia from the UN Statistics Division [http://unstats.un.org/]; New York City police salaries from: William K. Rashbaum, "Police Union Wants Billboard To Send Message About Salary," *NYT*, January 6, 2004; 2006 census data from the U.S. Census Bureau [http://factfinder.census.gov].

[116] Gudkov and Dubin 2006, p. 68.

[117] "Rossiyskim militsioneram podnimut zarplatu," *Gazeta.ru*, August 22, 2005; "Srednyaya zarplata rossiyskogo militsionera – 10 tys. rubley," *RIA Novosti*, March 13, 2008; Nikolaus von Twickel, "Rich Get Richer as Poor Get Poorer," *MT*, August 8, 2008.

and medium levels, and more than three times greater at top levels (deputy minister or head of department in the state sector). Several power ministries, including the MVD and the MChS, were included in this study. The report concluded that this large gap made it difficult to attract and retain capable staff in state service. Moreover, the study noted dryly that "the size of the pay gap must create pressure for people in the Civil Service to find ways, legal or illegal, of supplementing their income." Reportedly, the study prompted greater state efforts to close the gap, although one expert said that by 2008, state compensation was still three-to-five times lower than in the private sector. Moreover, efforts to increase state pay did not, at least in the short run, lead to an increase in professionalism or a decrease in corruption.[118]

Law enforcement personnel and specialists noted that the poor benefits provided to MVD employees, as well as their lack of confidence in the long-term stability of these benefits, were an important reason why it was difficult to attract and retain high-quality personnel. A police general and head of a MVD academic institute maintained that officers who retire or go on disability have no real safety net in terms of benefits. He contrasted this situation both with that in other countries and in the Soviet past, where officers have access to good medical care and other benefits, and can look forward to a comfortable retirement. A sociologist similarly noted that there were not adequate benefits for disabled police officers or their families in the event of death on the job. Forty-six percent of surveyed officers declared themselves dissatisfied with both their current social benefits and future retirement security for them and their families. Forty-nine percent declared themselves dissatisfied with overall work conditions, and dissatisfaction was even higher among better-educated and longer-serving MVD employees. Overall, sociologists studying the militia concluded that police officers in Russia feel underpaid and undervalued, and have a consciousness of someone who has been "tossed away."[119]

There is less reliable data on employment conditions and benefits, as well as work satisfaction, among procuracy and FSB employees. Anecdotally, both organizations provide better salaries and benefits, but firm data is hard to come by. Relative to the regular police, secret police and prosecutors are probably well compensated, but less than they could command in the private sector. Of course, for those who engage in *kormleniye*, the financial returns from service are higher, sometimes far higher, as the previous example of a $200,000 bribe to become an MVD general shows. Indeed, government critics argued that the increasing attractiveness of state service under Putin noted in some studies can be explained by the opportunity to illegally supplement one's income.[120]

---

[118] Andrey Klimenko and Hugh Grant, "Russia Civil Service Modernisation: Pay Reform. Comparative Pay and Benefits Survey, Public and Private Sectors," unpublished report, 2003; Interview M-16; Ol'ga Gorelik, "Zarplaty podnyali – ocheredi ostalis'," *Izvestiya*, September 17, 2007. I thank Professor Nikolay Klishch for sharing this report with me.

[119] Khabibulin and Shumkov 2006; Rimskiy 2005, p. 401; Gudkov and Dubin 2006, pp. 62–64.

[120] Francesca Mereu, "Bureaucrat Numbers Booming Under Putin," *MT*, April 13, 2006; Nikolaus von Twickel, "Red Tape Reaching Its Soviet Heights," *MT*, August 7, 2007. See

Professionalism

David Bayley suggested the following criteria for professionalism in law enforcement: "recruitment according to specified standards, remuneration sufficiently high to create a career service, formal training, and systematic supervision by superior officers." Louise Shelley applied these criteria to the Soviet militia and found that it fell short due to inadequate education and training, politicization (in the sense of ultimate subordination to Communist Party diktat, not impartial legal standards), and low technical standards.[121]

The problems outlined here in terms of recruiting and retaining quality law enforcement personnel, and poor conditions of employment, especially in the police, indicate that the gap between modern professional law enforcement standards and actual Russian practice has gotten worse since the Soviet collapse, not better. At the most basic level, as the head of the Novosibirsk police noted in 2003, the quality of cadres in the police force is low.[122] More specifically, law enforcement, especially the police, has been unable to recruit according to specific standards or offer adequate pay and benefits for a stable career. Further, Russian law enforcement officials are poorly trained and unmotivated to work in a professional manner. Professional civil service standards for promotion and for protecting workers from unwarranted dismissal are absent.

In terms of training, the difficulty of attracting and retaining high-quality personnel has lowered entry standards, as noted above. Those who are accepted into the police ranks often receive only a brief training period, described by experts as "out-dated and formalistic." Stated one former police instructor: "Between the man on the street and a police officer, that is, a person invested with power, called to stand in defense of our rights and interests, stands only three months of training, half of which is spent on fighting and weapons drills. It's absurd." Half of surveyed police officers evaluated the legal culture of the police, defined as knowledge of laws, rights, and responsibilities, as low or very low. Police reformers have argued for a basic training course in law and civil rights, with an exam that applicants would have to pass before joining the force. One police colonel noted that conservative inertia has meant that police training continues Soviet practices in which the police were thought of as a repressive organization, and that a new training approach should inculcate a "correct culture" in which service to the public is the dominant value. Journalist Leonid Nikitinskiy noted that police forces everywhere attract some people inclined to self-interested or aggressive behavior, but the measure of the "civilization level of the state" (state quality) is how effective the mechanisms are for filtering

also: Institute of Sociology (Russian Academy of Sciences), *Byurokratiya i vlast' v novoy Rossii: pozitsii naseleniya i otsenki ekspertov* (Moskva: 2005).

[121] Bayley 1985, p. 47; Shelley 1996, pp. 83–84.

[122] Interview N-7.

out these people. In Russia, he concluded, these mechanisms are completely absent.[123]

Another piece of professional development and training that has suffered in the last two decades has been the relationship between more experienced and rookie officers. Several respondents noted that the loss of the core "middle zone" in law enforcement structures meant that young recruits were not receiving the type of professional socialization from their superiors that officials did in the late-Soviet period, when more stable career paths predominated. A U.S. government official noted that in Russian law enforcement structures, there is little serious oversight of the professional development of investigators after their appointment, such as a trial period with greater oversight or periodic checks on performance; he also noted the weakness of middle management in these agencies. Instead of on-the-job training in professional standards and techniques, new officers are now introduced into the aprofessional practices of predation, such as corruption, violence, and arbitrary despotism (*proizvol*). Former Soviet Minister of Internal Affairs Vadim Bakatin lamented that all ethical norms had disappeared from the police.[124]

Awareness of the poor state of police ethics led to a joint MVD-NGO effort to develop a new "Code of Professional Ethics" (see Chapter 6). As part of this effort, a series of experiments with cadets was conducted at the MVD Academy in Moscow. What the researchers found was that the students were not open to the system of ethics that the experiments sought to impart, which was that police should see themselves as service providers and helpers to the population. Rather, cadets already came to the academy with a conception of the "good cop" as someone who is firm to the point of being brusque, even rude. Cops are expected to "behave like bandits" and are seen by the population as such. Nonetheless, the new Code was adopted in December 2008.[125]

The tendency to engage in predation is closely connected to low pay and uncertainty about stable career options and benefits. The forms of corruption outlined earlier in the chapter – shakedowns, commissioned cases, bribe taking, roofing, and so on – are justified by officers as a necessary means of survival. Similarly, the tendency of officers to take second jobs, sometimes in illegal realms, is explained by poor compensation. The head of a human rights NGO in Yekaterinburg noted that its cleaning woman was a police captain who needed a second job; presumably any cop who takes such a position is one of the more honest ones. Overall, more than 80 percent of police

[123] Demos 2005, p. 12; Shepeleva and Novikova 2005, pp. 58–60; Gudkov and Dubin 2006, p. 62; Pavel Chikov, "Yazva vnutrennikh organov," *gazeta.ru*, May 9, 2007; Interview M-13; Leonid Nikitinskiy, "Grazhdanin ordy," *Nov. gaz.*, May 23, 2005. Shelley noted the poor legal training of Soviet police officers: Shelley 1996, p. 93.

[124] Interview NN-8; Interview P-2; Shepeleva and Novikova 2005, pp. 60–61; Interview M-50; Interview M-5.

[125] Interview M-11; Interview M-30; "Prikaz MVD Rossii No. 1138," December 24, 2008; "Kodeks professional'noy etiki sotrudnika organov vnutrennikh del Rossiyskoy Federatsii," 2008.

personnel reported some form of external employment or source of income.[126] The increases in salaries under Putin were an important step in the right direction, although it is too early to tell whether they will change the sense of professional uncertainty that contributes to corruption and predation.

Patrimonial hiring and promotion practices are also par for the course in Russian law enforcement organs. Putin's patrimonial appointment decisions led to all of the major power ministries being headed by close colleagues from his own personal networks in the KGB and in St. Petersburg. A similar tendency was noted at the second tier in these bodies. For example, the independent Investigative Committee under the General Procuracy was established in 2007; Putin's law school classmate Aleksandr Bastrykin was named as its director. Two of his top deputies were brought in from the FSB. Critics charged that cadres selection in the Investigative Committee "is taking place not based on professional qualities, but exclusively by the principle 'ours – not ours' (*svoy – chuzhoy*)." Well before his March 2008 election, Dmitriy Medvedev was putting "his" people in second-tier positions in the power ministries.[127]

The same tendency is evident at lower levels, where officers are admitted to service and promoted based on personal ties or corrupt payoffs or relationships. One journalist claimed the practice of buying ranks and positions was widespread in the power ministries; some examples were given earlier in this chapter, and more will be detailed in Chapter 7 on the North Caucasus. There were also reports of students paying bribes to enter MVD academies, not because it was that competitive but because students in police higher education institutions can avoid the draft and thus the possibility of service in Chechnya.[128]

Law enforcement officials also lack legal protections against unlawful firing and other punishments for refusing to follow illegal orders.[129] Police respondents reported that internal control mechanisms, such as internal affairs

---

[126] Demos 2005, pp. 11–12; Kolesnikova et al., 2002; Interview Ye-3; Gudkov and Dubin 2006, p. 68.

[127] See Chapter 2 for further discussions of patrimonialism at the top of the power ministries. On the specific points here, see: Aleksandr Khinshteyn, "Prokuratura netraditsionnoy orientatsii," *MK*, February 8, 2008; Roman Shleynov, "Donoschiki snaryadov," *Nov. Gaz.*, April 26, 2007. In fairness to Bastrykin, it should be noted that Khinshteyn, a Duma deputy and investigative journalist with close ties to the power ministries, was quite likely a mouthpiece for a rival clan to Bastrykin's; this article was one of a series by Khinshteyn critical of Bastrykin.

[128] Adrian Beck and Annette Robertson, "Policing in Post-Soviet Russia," in Pridemore 2005, p. 252; Rimskiy 2005, p. 398; Interview M-44; Interview P-9.

[129] Professional civil service standards on promotion and dismissal are included in the draft "Federal Law on Law Enforcement Service of the Russian Federation." This law was part of a series of laws on civil, military, and law enforcement service envisioned in the administrative reform of Putin's first term, as set out in the 2003 "Federal Law on the System of State Service in the Russian Federation." As of early 2010 the draft law was still being worked on in the presidential administration. As of 2008, experts reported little chance for law enforcement personnel to defend their interests in the event of unlawful dismissal: Interview M-11.

bureaus, are used most often to fire subordinates who are "disagreeable" for their superiors. Your average officer was highly dependent on her or his superior and dared not question or resist unlawful instructions. Rank-and-file officers believed they needed more information about their legal rights.[130] Russian bureaucrats in general do not feel that they are protected and that they have a stable career; this sense of stability and protection is central to creating a Weberian system of public administration.[131]

These deficiencies in professional training and standards have real implications for citizens. Olga Shepeleva catalogued many such consequences, including violations of procedural norms, unlawful detention, denial of rights, and arbitrary violence.[132] These abuses were both further evidence of low state quality in Russian state coercive agencies and a real cause of societal distrust toward the state and the previously noted "panic-like fear" of law enforcement bodies.

CONCLUSION

This chapter has shifted the focus from state capacity to state quality. Cross-national data showed that Russia performed poorly in terms of the rule of law and controlling corruption and, equally important, that this performance did not improve over time, despite additional resources and Putin's state-building project. Russian citizens concurred that the rule of law did not become stronger under Putin. A September 2007 poll found that 20 percent of respondents thought that during Putin's tenure, the authorities began to observe the law "more strictly and rigorously" than before, 22 percent thought they did so less strictly and rigorously than before, and 46 percent said "everything is like it was before."[133]

A wide range of evidence showed that corruption and the "unrule of law" were common, even systemic, in Russian law enforcement bodies. Predation and repression dominated over protection. Russian law enforcement personnel, especially in the police, tended to be poorly qualified, poorly compensated, and poorly trained. Russia remained far from the creation of professional law enforcement agencies that provide adequate compensation, good benefits, and stable career paths based on rational-legal principles of public administration.

This result is in some sense surprising. Putin made state building the top priority of his presidency, and fighting corruption and strengthening the rule of law figured prominently in his rhetoric as president. Further, budgetary

[130] Rimskiy 2005, p. 404; Shepeleva and Novikova 2005, pp. 56–57; Interview P-8; Interview P-9.

[131] Interview M-22.

[132] Shepeleva 2005.

[133] "Soblyudeniye zakonov i korruptsiya," *Levada Tsentr*, October 9, 2007 [http://www.levada.ru/press/2007100902.html].

support for the power ministries, especially the key law enforcement bodies of the FSB, MVD, and procuracy, increased substantially during his rule, and during his second term, there were substantial pay increases for power ministry officials. Indeed, in a speech to FSB employees in January 2008, Putin noted that military and security personnel saw pay increases of 45 percent in 2006–2007. However, as Vadim Volkov persuasively argued, "if the state has been turned into a business, then an increase in its resources and powers only enhances the entrepreneurial opportunities of state employees." Russian state weakness, he noted, is not due to insufficient personnel or resources, but due to the tendency of state coercive organs to serve particular rather than general or societal interests. In these conditions, efforts to strengthen the state increased the opportunities for arbitrary despotism of its components, rather than building the legal and administrative capacity of the state as a whole.[134] More cynically, as a former high-ranking MVD official put it, why should a local police boss obey the law when the president does not? The Russian journalist Masha Lipman noted, well before the Yukos case, that the political use of law enforcement "encourages corruption and hampers development of the rule of law."[135]

Of course, any effort to change state quality is likely to take some time. It took a generation or two to professionalize the police in major American cities in the face of well-entrenched corrupt and patrimonial practices. So far, however, Russian civil service reform efforts that started in the early 1990s, including in the law enforcement sphere, have repeatedly failed to be implemented in a manner that would change the behavior of state officials. In the police sphere, Adrian Beck and Annette Robertson noted, the "democratic ideals" set out in national legislation have not been incorporated into "operational policies and regulations." The gap between "police power" and "police action" remains large.[136]

The failure to improve state quality in the law enforcement realm was linked, in particular, to the absence of an effective strategy to combat both patrimonialism and predation. Peter Evans has argued that two key mechanisms for countering the type of state privatization Volkov pointed to are a dependable system of "long-term career benefits" and "powerful internal norms."[137] The failure to create professional long-term career incentives has already been described in detail and is tightly connected to the weakness of Weberian state administration. Perhaps even more damaging has been the

---

[134] Vladimir Putin, "Vystupleniye na rasshirennom zasedanii kollegii Federal'noy sluzhby bezopasnosti," January 30, 2008; Vadim Volkov, "Po tu storonu sudebnoy sistemy, ili pochemu zakony rabotayut ne tak, kak dolzhni," *Neprikosnovennyy Zapas*, 42 (July 2005).

[135] Interview M-46; Masha Lipman, "Putin's Halting Progress," *WP*, April 24, 2002.

[136] Beck and Robertson 2005, p. 257.

[137] Peter Evans, "Government Action, Social Capital, and Development: Reviewing the Evidence on Synergy," in Peter Evans, ed., *State-Society Synergy: Government and Social Capital in Development* (Berkeley, CA: International and Area Studies, University of California, Berkeley, 1997), pp. 194–195.

inability to create internal norms against predatory and repressive power ministry behavior.

"Old institutionalism" in sociology stressed the need to build institutions by, in Philip Selznick's formulation, infusing them with value. In this respect, both Yeltsin and Putin's state-building efforts were inadequate. Alexei Barabashev and Jeffrey Straussman noted that a key problem with civil service reform in Russia has been that the "ideologically driven" ethical norms of state service in the communist period have not been replaced with new ethical norms that would lead bureaucrats to pursue public interests rather than personal ones. Rather, according to Aleksandr Obolonskiy, Russian state officials entered a "period of Durkheimian anomie." Vadim Bakatin, the head of the MVD under Gorbachev, maintained that even in the late-Soviet period, when corruption was a growing problem, there were ethical norms that guided the behavior of officials who felt the need to uphold "Leninist principles." After the collapse, Bakatin continued, there were "no limits" restraining bureaucrats. Two police colonels in Petersburg also stated that police officers in the Soviet period "knew what they were working for" and held some commitment to communist ideals, including a respect for the state and "socialist property." A local official in Nizhniy Novgorod lamented that in law enforcement now, "those who work for an idea are fewer and fewer."[138]

Barabashev and Straussman argued that for civil service reform to succeed in Russia, new "ethical safeguards" are needed so state officials serve not selfish personal interests but the public interest. This can be done, they contended, "either through a return to an ideologically driven state – which is, of course, unacceptable – or through the promotion of civil society values." But commitment to "civil society values" – by which they presumably mean liberal democracy – is also a form of ideological commitment. Liberal democracy, though, has failed as an alternative form of ideological legitimation in post-Soviet Russia, as Stephen Hanson has repeatedly stressed.[139] Although the rhetorical commitment to democracy, civil society, and the rule of law begun under Gorbachev and Yeltsin continued after 2000, the reality under Putin was a fairly consistent effort to build a centralized, authoritarian state. The apotheosis of this project came in Putin's second term, with a new ideology rooted in a more traditional Russian idea about the need to build a strong state to modernize the country and resist foreign powers. But this ideological project was obviously at odds with the liberal effort envisioned by reformers

[138] Barabashev and Straussman 2007, pp. 380–381; Interview M-22; Interview M-5; Interview P-13; Interview P-14; Interview NN-8.
[139] Barabashev and Straussman 2007, pp. 380–381; Stephen E. Hanson, "Instrumental Democracy? The End of Ideology and the Decline of Russian Political Parties," in Vicki L. Hesli and William M. Reissinger, eds., *The 1999–2000 Elections in Russia: Their Impact and Legacy* (Cambridge: Cambridge University Press, 2003), pp. 163–185; Stephen Hanson, "The Uncertain Future of Russia's Weak State Authoritarianism," *East European Politics and Societies*, 21, 1 (February 2007), pp. 67–81.

to transform state officials into public servants.[140] Putin's program may have led to some increases in state capacity, but it did nothing to improve state quality, and arguably made matters worse.

Statism as a goal in itself resonated with many power ministry personnel. But the neglect of service to society in the new ideology meant that state officials did not develop a sense of professional ideals and ethics that would steer their behavior away from corruption and predation. The quality of the Russian state consequently remained low. Further, as discussed in the next chapter, the building of authoritarianism under Putin helped weaken societal monitors of law enforcement, which further contributed to the persistence of low state quality in the coercive realm.

[140] Interview M-22.

6

Coercion and Quality

The State and Society

> There is no more effective mechanism for fighting corruption than the development of civil society and freedom of the press.
>
> Vladimir Putin, February 2007[1]

The quality of Russian state coercive organs is generally low. Power ministries employees tend to work for their own interests or serve the powers that be rather than working for the interests of the population. Corruption and predation are widespread among law enforcement officers, and the rule of law is weak. Putin admitted toward the end of his second term that the fight against corruption had gone "badly" and lamented that there was no "reaction from civil society" to corruption. With this lament, Putin echoed his silovik ally Viktor Cherkesov, head of the drug control agency (FSKN), who wrote in 2007 that the best option for Russia would be the transformation into a "normal civil society," but doubting the likelihood of that possibility and fearing another state collapse, argued that it was necessary for the "Chekist corporation" to unify and take the lead role in rebuilding Russia.[2]

Putin is correct, as he stated in 2007 in the epigraph to this chapter, that civil society and the press are important weapons for combating corruption. However, Putin's actions as president seemed to be guided by Cherkesov's conviction that, since civil society was weak, the Chekists (secret police personnel and veterans) had to step in to save Russia. Indeed, especially in his second term, Putin's efforts seemed more designed to cripple a nascent civil society rather than to help it to mature and grow. The power ministries were enlisted to crack down on independent groups that were tied either materially or ideationally to supporters in the West. Although many of these groups were able to continue functioning, their ability to work effectively was noticeably

---

[1] Vladimir Putin, "Stenograficheskiy otchet o press-konferentsii dlya rossiyskikh i inostrannykh zhurnalistov," February 1, 2007.

[2] Vladimir Putin, "Interv'yu zhurnalu 'Taym'," December 19, 2007; Viktor Cherkesov, "Nel'zya dopustit', chtoby voiny prevratilis' v torgovtsev," *K-D*, October 9, 2007.

limited compared to the Yeltsin era. The deliberate weakening of Russian civil society has made improving the quality of the Russian state through greater accountability more difficult.

Civil society can play an important role in bolstering not only the quality of law enforcement but also its capacity. For example, when citizens trust rather than fear the police, they are more likely to report crime. In Russia, trust in all state institutions is low, and this is particularly true of law enforcement. At the end of Putin's presidency, the public remained just as disillusioned with the work of the power ministries as they were under Yeltsin. This disillusionment reflected the low quality work of these agencies.

Despite the obstacles in their way, some Russian civil society groups remain committed to working with reformers inside the state to try to change the way in which Russian law enforcement structures work. These efforts are premised on the notion that civil society should serve not just as a check on the state, but as a partner of the state that can increase state quality and state capacity by pushing for liberal norms and rational-legal bureaucratic practices inside government agencies. Such state-society partnerships became increasingly difficult in the law enforcement realm during Putin's presidency. Instead, the state actively worked to disable mechanisms of popular account-ability, favoring internal "police patrols" over external "fire alarms" as a way to monitor state law enforcement. The reforms pushed by non-governmental organizations (NGOs) threatened the patrimonial nature of public adminis-tration, and the NGOs themselves were a convenient target in an ideological project that stressed the need to rally around the state in the face of the threat from the West. The potential for reform from below thus remained largely unrealized.

In this chapter, I first discuss some survey data on societal views of the power ministries and the situation with crime and personal security in Russia. Second, I set out the ways that civil society can contribute to state building in general and in the law enforcement realm in particular. In the third sec-tion, I describe efforts by Russian NGOs to engage the police in order to change police practices and norms. Fourth, I show how public accountability declined under Putin, and how restrictions on NGOs and the media under-mined the work of the most effective mechanisms for fighting corruption in state agencies.

RUSSIAN SOCIETY AND THE POWER MINISTRIES: LACK OF TRUST

Throughout his presidency, Vladimir Putin maintained consistently high approval ratings from the Russian public.[3] But this popular support for Putin did not carry over to a broader belief in the quality of government. Russians

---

[3] Timothy J. Colton, "Putin and the Attenuation of Russian Democracy," in Dale R. Herspring, ed., *Putin's Russia: Past Imperfect, Future Uncertain*, 3rd Edition (Lanham, MD: Rowman & Littlefield, 2007), pp. 37–52.

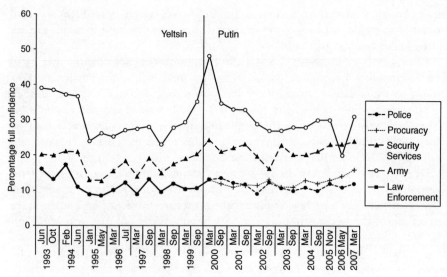

FIGURE 6.1. Trust in the power ministries.

remained cynical and disengaged from government, and the level of trust in state institutions remained virtually unchanged from the 1990s.

There is, of course, substantial variation in the degree to which Russians trust government bodies. The most trusted agencies under Putin were the presidency (this was presumably an indication of trust in Putin, not the institution in general, since under Yeltsin the presidency rated very low) and the armed forces. The most trusted non-state bodies were the Orthodox Church and religious organizations. The police and procuracy were the least trusted state institutions in the country, with only two non-state institutions, political parties and trade unions, rated lower. Within the power ministries, there was a clear hierarchy, with the army commanding the most trust, followed by the security services, and the law enforcement organs (police and procuracy) at the bottom. Figure 6.1 shows the percentage of respondents who stated that a particular power structure earned their complete trust over a fifteen-year period, from 1993 to 2007. Prior to September 2000, the question referred to law enforcement organs (police, procuracy, courts). From September 2000, separate questions were asked about these institutions.[4]

Figure 6.1 shows two important tendencies besides the relative ranking. The first is that the public's evaluation of the different power ministries was

[4] The polls were conducted by firms directed by Yuriy Levada or his successors: VTsIOM, VTsIOM-A, and the Levada Center. Data compiled from multiple issues of: VTsIOM, *Monitoring obshchestvennogo mneniya: ekonomicheskiye i sotsial'nye peremeny*; Levada Center, *Vestnik obshchestvennogo mneniya*; Levada Center website (http://www.levada.ru). I particularly thank Mikhail Alexseev, Katya Kalandadze, and Tatyana Vinichenko for help with these data.

quite consistent throughout the Yeltsin and Putin eras. The level of trust in the army showed the most volatility, with a big drop during the first Chechen war, a big jump at the beginning of the second Chechen war, and a sharp fall in spring 2006, presumably related to bad publicity in early 2006 surrounding the brutal hazing of Private Andrey Sychev. But the army was usually somewhere between 25 percent and 30 percent from 1995 to 2007, quite a narrow range. The second important tendency was the lack of noticeable improvement in public trust in the power ministries under Putin. For example, the percentage of respondents expressing complete trust in the security services was identical in March 2000 and March 2007 – 24 percent. Only the procuracy exhibited an increase in trust after 2000, and that increase was a very modest four percentage points (the margin of error was three percent). There also was virtually no change over time in the percentage of respondents claiming a complete lack of trust, with the police again at the bottom with around 40 percent and the army and the secret services around 20 percent.

This lack of trust in almost all institutions, including state ones, is striking, particularly given both the popularity of the country's leader and the considerable improvement in the economic situation from 1999 to 2008. The absence of trust revealed under Yeltsin did not change under Putin. Further, on a comparative basis, Russia lags well behind the developed world and also many developing countries; Vladimir Shlapentokh argued that the level of trust in state bodies in Russia is "the lowest in the world." Russian trust in the police is also low by comparative standards. Around 80 percent of West European respondents trust the police, according to the World Values Survey, and U.S. surveys show trust in the police at around 70 percent. Other surveys show somewhat lower results in some Western countries, but the U.S., Great Britain, Germany, France, Italy, and Spain are all around 55–75 percent for the level of trust in the police. Available data suggest that Russia lags behind other post-communist countries in this respect also.[5]

It is also noteworthy that, among the power ministries, Russians trust the least the institutions with which they are most likely to interact. The Levada Center, based on two decades of polling about popular trust in state institutions, stated that "the Russian population does not trust *all* law enforcement organs; however, the activity of the police is evaluated as particularly low." Most Russians have either had an encounter with a corrupt or abusive police officer or know someone who has. In contrast, they are much less likely to interact with a FSB or military officer in their everyday life. Georgiy Satarov

[5] Vladimir Shlapentokh, "Trust in Public Institutions in Russia: The Lowest in the World," *Communist and Post-Communist Studies*, 39 (2006), pp. 153–174; Theodore P. Gerber and Sarah E. Mendelson, "Public Experiences of Police Violence and Corruption in Contemporary Russia: A Case of Predatory Policing?" *Law and Society Review*, 42, 1 (2008), p. 25; Levada Tsentr, *Otnosheniye naseleniya k reforme militsii: Otchet po rezul'tatam oprosa rossiyskogo naseleniya* (Moskva: 2008), p. 4.

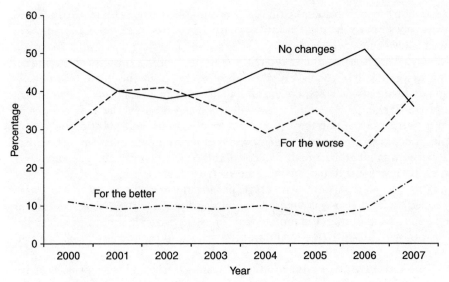

FIGURE 6.2. How did the work of police and other law enforcement agencies change in the last year?

of the Information for Democracy (INDEM) Foundation, one of the leading Russian NGOs in the study of corruption, maintained that trust in the FSB is higher than for the militia because of this lack of contact on the part of average citizens. In contrast, he stated, businesspeople are very dissatisfied with the FSB, because they are more likely to experience FSB intervention in economic matters. Police corruption is also much more publicized in the mainstream press than corruption in the FSB. Finally, Boris Dubin of the Levada Center argued that the "legend" of the honest KGB propagated under Brezhnev is still believed by some citizens.[6] And even though the army is generally trusted relative to other institutions, other surveys show that it commands little respect, and almost 40 percent of respondents state their willingness to go to any lengths to keep family members from serving in the military. Less than 30 percent of men and only 15 percent of women would like to see a close relative serve in the armed forces.[7]

Surveys of Russian citizens also showed that they did not believe that the work of law enforcement agencies improved under Putin (see Figure 6.2). Consistently throughout Putin's presidency (2000–2007), between 75 percent and 80 percent of respondents said that police work had either gotten worse or not changed. A positive trend was noticeable in 2007, when those stating the work of the police had improved in the previous year jumped from 9

[6] Levada Tsentr 2008; Interview M-30; Interview M-2; Interview M-9.
[7] Shlapentokh 2006, p. 162; Lev Gudkov, "The Army as an Institutional Model," in Stephen L. Webber and Jennifer G. Mathers, eds., *Military and Society in Post-Soviet Russia* (Manchester: Manchester University Press, 2006), p. 54.

percent to 17 percent. Unfortunately, in the same year, the percentage saying the work of the police had gotten worse also increased, from 25 percent to 39 percent. Overall, although the results showed some change over time in the various categories, the percentage of Russians who thought that police work had improved under Putin from year to year was swamped by the overwhelming majority who thought it had gotten worse or not changed.[8]

The lack of trust in Russian law enforcement organs, and the related concerns about the low quality of police work, led average Russians to relate to the police and other law enforcement organs with fear and anxiety rather than trust and confidence. For example, further polls by the Levada Center from 2004 to 2006 yielded the following results:

- More than two-thirds of Russians stated that they feel more anxiety toward the police than trust.
- More than 70 percent said that they or someone close to them could suffer abuse at the hands of the police.
- More than 80 percent said they did not feel defended against law enforcement abuse.
- Less than one-third said that if they suffered from police abuse, they could seek redress from the procuracy or the courts.[9]

A similar picture emerges when we look at surveys of citizens' personal safety (see Figure 6.3). Throughout Putin's presidency, only 5–10 percent of Russians thought that personal safety had improved in the previous year. Consistently between 85–90 percent of respondents thought that it had not changed or gotten worse. The only improvement was that the percentage thinking citizens' personal safety had changed for the worse declined between 2004 and 2006 from half of the population to one-third.[10]

During Putin's presidency, Russian residents also generally felt unprotected against terrorist attacks, although there was a marked improvement in the last two years of his rule (see Figure 6.4).[11] The impact of events such as the 1999 apartment bombings, the 2002 *Nord-Ost* Theater attack in Moscow, and the 2004 Beslan school crisis was reflected in the large majority of respondents who felt that the state could not defend them against terrorist attacks. The decline in major terrorist attacks in 2006 and 2007 discussed in Chapters 3 and 7 led to a more positive assessment of state performance in this respect. It is worth noting, as discussed elsewhere, that a change in tactics by Chechen rebels was an important reason for the drop in incidents. Still, unlike surveys

---

[8] Levada Tsentr, *Obshchestvennoye mneniye 2007: Yezhegodnik* (Moskva: Levada Tsentr, 2007), p. 85.

[9] Levada Tsentr, *Obshchestvennoye mneniye 2006: Sbornik*, Tables 7.5.11, 7.5.14, 7.5.15, 7.5.16. See also: Lev Gudkov and Boris Dubin, "Privatizatsiya politsii," *Vestnik obshchestvennogo mneniya*, 1, 81 (January–February 2006), pp. 58–71.

[10] Levada Tsentr, *Obshchestvennoye mneniye 2006: Sbornik*, Table 7.5.17; Demos, *Reforma pravookhranitel'nikh organov: preodoleniye proizvola* (Moskva: Demos, 2005), p. 9.

[11] Levada Tsentr 2007, p. 157.

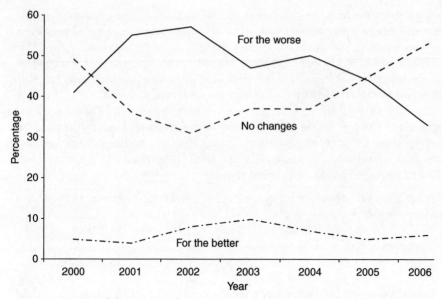

FIGURE 6.3. How did the state of citizens' personal safety change in the last year?

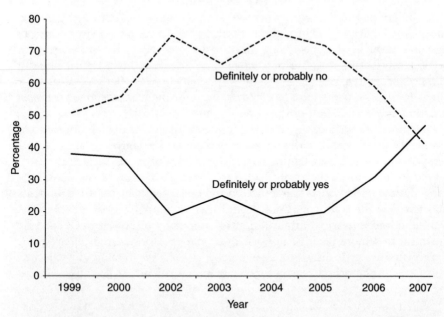

FIGURE 6.4. Can the Russian authorities defend the Russian population against new terrorist attacks?

on law enforcement performance, citizens' personal safety, and especially trust in the power ministries, a clear positive trend was noticeable here.

In general, available survey data show a striking lack of confidence in the work of law enforcement organs on the part of Russians, although in some surveys, positive trends became evident toward the end of Putin's presidency. Why do Russian citizens distrust law enforcement organs, in many cases even fear them, and generally have little confidence in their work? The most obvious explanation is probably the correct one: Because Russian law enforcement works badly. The evidence for this conclusion is myriad and scattered throughout this book. Post-Soviet Russia has comparatively high rates of homicide and domestic terrorism; a decline in the homicide rate and especially major terrorist attacks in 2006 and 2007 did lead to somewhat better assessments by the population. At the same time, the rebuilt regime of repression meant that Russian law enforcement and security organs were often directed against opponents of the Kremlin – oligarchs, regional governors, opposition political parties and movements – and therefore less focused on defending the population. When not engaged in repression, they often are engaged in predation – shaking down ordinary citizens, "roofing" small and medium-sized businesses, selling their services on the open market, and even cooperating with organized criminal groups. Protection of the public is a secondary or even tertiary concern. Both the capacity and quality of the state in the coercive realm are low.

The conclusion that the Russian people do not trust law enforcement because these agencies work badly is one that Russian police and law enforcement personnel and experts often draw themselves. The head of the Novosibirsk police for more than a decade, General Aleksandr Soinov, said that popular trust in the police will increase when the quality of police work increases. Viktor Luneyev, a leading criminologist at the Institute of State and Law in Moscow, echoed Soinov, stating that trust in law enforcement is low because these organs work poorly and do not show the population that it is protecting them. Nikolay Vinnichenko, in 2002 the Chief Federal Inspector in St. Petersburg and a law school classmate of Dmitriy Medvedev, argued that the way to increase trust in the police is to stop police corruption. Robert Simonyan, a former procuracy official and deputy of the national ombudsman, generalized the problem of trust to the arbitrary behavior of the bureaucracy as a whole. "Of course the entire system is corrupt from top to bottom," he stated, maintaining that the people had a basis for their mistrust.[12]

Multiple police officials and experts compared the poor quality of law enforcement work to that of police in the West. Police Colonel K.K. Goryainov maintained that the level of trust in Russian police is low because they are not open to the population. In Europe, in contrast, the police are trained to help citizens, and if the problem is outside police responsibility, to refer them to the correct agency. A police colonel from Yekaterinburg lamented that there was a "big wall" between the population and the police, and that police "work for themselves" and not society, often treating people rudely. Specifically, this officer noted that the police often ignore petty crime; citizens see that the police do not help them, leading them to not share information with the

---

[12] Interview N-7; Interview M-20; Interview P-11; Interview M-31.

police. In the West, in contrast, the police have a different "philosophy of work" that prioritizes service to society. A St. Petersburg human rights activist who worked closely with the police for many years noted that his "most striking impression" from a trip to London in 1990 was how happy an old woman of Indian descent was to see a bobby when she was having trouble crossing the street. The implication of this anecdote was that an old woman of, say, Chechen descent in a major Russian city would probably have a different reaction to seeing a cop.[13] Although these observers may have an idealized view of Western policing, comparative survey data suggests a much higher degree of trust in police in the West than in Russia.

Several current or former Russian cops argued that the lack of trust in police is in part due to a shortage of police resources at the "street level" – beat cops, police patrols, low-level criminal investigators, and the like. In contrast, they argued, the tendency has been to strengthen specialized directorates and higher-level sections of the MVD. An obvious example of this was the creation of the GU MVD at the Federal District level in 2001; it is not surprising that local police officials resented the resources going to a new structure while they had trouble buying gas for patrol cars.[14] One Novosibirsk political official, however, expressed skepticism that more resources would solve anything, arguing that the police already had enough money and asking rhetorically, "if citizens don't feel that the police help them, why give them money? If you want to create a police state, no amount of money is enough." In a similar vein, a U.S. embassy official argued that trying to adopt a community policing model in Russia, in which emphasis is placed on the visibility of "street-level" police to the citizens, would not work because the police are so despised.[15]

Further evidence for the impact of poor police work on popular distrust comes from Vladimir Lukin, Russia's human rights ombudsman. When issuing his report on the state of human rights in Russia in 2007, Lukin asserted that "overall the main subject causing citizens' anxiety is arbitrary despotism (*proizvol*) of law enforcement organs." Survey data indicate, not surprisingly, that those who have experienced police abuse are more inclined to distrust the police, further evidence that the low level of trust in Russian law enforcement organs is directly tied to the actual performance of these bodies.[16]

In short, the power ministries, especially law enforcement organs, do not behave in a way that earns citizens' trust. What are the implications of this low level of public trust for the capacity and quality of Russian state coercive organs?

---

[13] Interview M-13; Interview Ye-13; Interview P-8.
[14] Interview P-12; Interview P-13; Interview M-13; Interview N-7; Interview NN-8; Interview M-30.
[15] Interview N-6; Interview M-45.
[16] Elena Novoselova, "Upolnomochen dolozhit'," *RG*, March 14, 2008; Gerber and Mendelson 2008, pp. 30–31.

CIVIL SOCIETY AND BUILDING STATE QUALITY

The study of trust connects to a broader literature on social capital, civil society, and political culture. Most prominent in this literature is a debate about the effects of trust on democracy, both in terms of the relationship between trust and democratization and the effects of trust on democratic quality. Less discussed is the relationship between trust and stateness, either state capacity or state quality. Before returning to that issue as it applies to law enforcement, I briefly review the broader literature.

First, it is important to note that the type of trust discussed here is what can be called "institutional trust" rather than "interpersonal trust," which concerns whether, as the standard survey question asks, "people can be trusted." The relationship between interpersonal trust and both democratization and the quality of democracy is contentious, but is a different issue than the trust in political institutions discussed here.[17] At any rate, low levels of interpersonal trust do not seem to be a good explanation for the low level of democracy in Russia.[18]

In terms of institutional trust, what do the low levels of popular trust in Russian state institutions mean? Although, as I discuss further, there are important *consequences* for the state because of this lack of trust, the most likely *cause* of low trust was discussed earlier: poor performance. Matthew Cleary and Susan Stokes, in a review of the literature on democracy and trust, contend that low levels of institutional trust are best understood as a rational response of citizens to poor quality government. For example, they show that higher corruption is correlated with lower levels of trust in Latin America. Ronald Inglehart and Christian Welzel also find no association between trust in state institutions and democracy, arguing that a willingness to criticize authority can be conducive to democracy. In the Russian case, Shlapentokh comes to the same conclusion as Cleary and Stokes, stating that popular distrust toward Russian institutions is "mostly rational" and reflects a reasoned assessment that the "efficiency of these institutions [is] very low."[19]

---

[17] The most influential account of interpersonal trust and democratic quality is: Robert D. Putnam, *Making Democracy Work: Civic Traditions in Modern Italy* (Princeton, NJ: Princeton University Press, 1993). Recent large-N work by scholars associated with the literature on trust finds a relationship between interpersonal trust and democracy, but not between institutional trust and democracy: Ronald Inglehart and Christian Welzel, *Modernization, Cultural Change, and Democracy: The Human Development Sequence* (Cambridge: Cambridge University Press, 2005), pp. 245–271. For an overview and critique of the trust and democracy literature, see: Matthew R. Cleary and Susan C. Stokes, "Trust and Democracy in Comparative Perspective," in Karen Cook, Russell Hardin, and Margaret Levi, eds., *Whom Can We Trust? How Groups, Networks, and Institutions Make Trust Possible* (New York: Russell Sage Foundation, 2009), pp. 308–338.

[18] M. Steven Fish, *Democracy Derailed in Russia: The Failure of Open Politics* (Cambridge: Cambridge University Press, 2005), pp. 108–110.

[19] Cleary and Stokes 2008; Inglehart and Welzel 2005, pp. 250–254; Shlapentokh 2006, pp. 154, 168.

Beyond the issue of institutional and interpersonal trust are broader debates about the effect of social capital, political culture, and civil society on Russian political development. Many scholars have highlighted low social capital and weak civil society as important obstacles to democratization in Russia.[20] Much of the general literature on democracy and democratization contends that an active civil society is a key component of a strong liberal democracy.[21] Civil society, following Juan Linz and Alfred Stepan, is "that arena of the polity where self-organizing groups, movements, and individuals, relatively autonomous from the state, attempt to articulate values, create associations and solidarities, and advance their interests." Civil society is thus situated in a space between the state and the household, a space also occupied by "political society" and "economic society."[22] Marc Howard notes that although there is some overlap between the three arenas of society, civil society is distinct in that actors in civil society seek neither power, as in political society, nor profit, as in economic society. Although NGOs are the most common type of civil society organization to be studied, a variety of religious, social, and community organizations also fit in this arena.[23]

Howard, consistent with other literature on civil society, stresses two main ways in which a strong civil society can help promote and strengthen democracy.[24] The first argument is that participation in civil society teaches citizens the norms and values associated with liberal democracy, such as tolerance and compromise. This perspective, associated in particular with the work of Robert Putnam, is labeled "Civil Society I" by Michael Foley and Bob Edwards.[25] The Civil Society I approach is closely linked to the arguments about trust discussed earlier. Recent literature has probed the posited connection between democracy and trust or social capital (the distinction between these two is not always clear), particularly whether high social capital should be thought of as a cause or consequence of liberal democracy. This debate is beyond our immediate concerns, but it is easy to imagine that the causal arrow might go both directions, and that it is at least as likely that living in a

---

[20] Putnam predicted bad outcomes for Russia immediately after the Soviet collapse, based on his assessment of the low levels of social capital after communism: Putnam 1993, p. 183. See also: Marc Morjé Howard, *The Weakness of Civil Society in Post-Communist Europe* (Cambridge: Cambridge University Press, 2003).

[21] Larry Diamond, *Developing Democracy: Toward Consolidation* (Baltimore: Johns Hopkins University Press, 1999), pp. 218–260. For an important dissent, see: Sheri Berman, "Civil Society and the Collapse of the Weimar Republic," *World Politics*, 49, 3 (1997), pp. 401–429.

[22] Juan J. Linz and Alfred Stepan, *Problems of Democratic Transition and Consolidation: Southern Europe, South America, and Post-Communist Europe* (Baltimore: Johns Hopkins University Press, 1996), pp. 7–15.

[23] Howard 2003, pp. 32–38.

[24] Howard 2003, pp. 45–47, 151–152.

[25] Putnam 1993; Robert D. Putnam, *Bowling Alone: The Collapse and Revival of American Community* (New York: Simon & Schuster, 2000); Michael W. Foley and Bob Edwards, "The Paradox of Civil Society," *Journal of Democracy*, 7, 3 (1996), pp. 38–52.

country with strong liberal democratic institutions would promote high social capital, rather than the other way around.[26]

A second argument about the importance of civil society concentrates not on civic norms, but on the relationship between civil society and the state. The "Civil Society II" approach stresses the role of autonomous social organizations as a potential counterweight to an overreaching state. Daniel Posner calls this the "watchdog" model of civil society.[27] Similarly, the literature on transnational activists stresses networks that work to oppose antiliberal and antidemocratic behavior on the part of governments.[28] The Civil Society II perspective is more explicitly political than Civil Society I and would also seem to connect to arguments that skepticism about the state may do more to produce good government than trust because it leads to demands for greater accountability.[29]

A third approach, what might be called the "Civil Society III" argument, stresses the possibility of a more positive relationship of mutual assistance and partnership between the state and civil society. This approach thus contrasts most sharply with Civil Society II, at least in theory.[30] Thomas Carothers notes that this approach is gaining ground in democracy assistance programs: "civil society programs at both the national and local level in transitional countries now typically seek a productive dialogue with state institutions and view state and civil society as partners more than opponents." Similarly, the comparative policing expert David Bayley maintains that reformers outside the state need to make "common cause" with those inside the police who want to raise

[26] For discussions, see: Cleary and Stokes 2008; Omar G. Encarnacion, "Civil Society Reconsidered (Review Article)," *Comparative Politics*, 38, 3 (April 2006), pp. 372–373; Natalia Letki and Geoffrey Evans, "Endogenizing Social Trust: Democratization in East-Central Europe," *British Journal of Political Science*, 35 (2005), pp. 515–529. On Civil Society I/social capital in Russia, see: Howard 2003; James L. Gibson, "Social Networks, Civil Society, and the Prospects for Consolidating Russia's Democratic Transition," *American Journal of Political Science*, 45, 1 (2001), pp. 51–68; Richard Rose, "When Government Fails: Social Capital in an Antimodern Russia," in Bob Edwards, Michael W. Foley, and Mario Diani, eds., *Beyond Tocqueville: Civil Society and the Social Capital Debate in Comparative Perspective* (Hanover, NH: University Press of New England, 2001), pp. 56–69.

[27] Foley and Edwards, "The Paradox of Civil Society"; Daniel N. Posner, "Civil Society and the Reconstruction of Failed States," in Robert I. Rotberg, ed., *When States Fail: Causes and Consequences* (Princeton, NJ: Princeton University Press, 2004), pp. 237–255.

[28] Margaret E. Keck and Kathryn Sikkink, *Activists beyond Borders: Advocacy Networks in International Politics* (Ithaca, NY: Cornell University Press, 1998).

[29] Matthew R. Cleary and Susan C. Stokes, *Democracy and the Culture of Skepticism: Political Trust in Argentina and Mexico* (New York: Russell Sage Foundation, 2006).

[30] Jonah Levy, *Tocqueville's Revenge: State, Society, and Economy in Contemporary France* (Cambridge, MA: Harvard University Press, 1999); Suzanne Mettler, *Soldiers To Citizens: The G.I. Bill and the Making of the Greatest Generation* (Oxford: Oxford University Press, 2005); Theda Skocpol, Marshall Ganz, and Ziad Munson, "A Nation of Organizers: The Institutional Origins of Civic Voluntarism in the United States," *American Political Science Review*, 94, 3 (2000), pp. 527–546.

police effectiveness, rather than treating the police as adversaries. The literature on "security sector reform" notes the importance of civil society serving not only as a "watchdog" of the government, but also as a "resource" for the government. In some cases, civil society can actually "substitute" for the state, providing public goods that the state provides poorly or not at all.[31]

Marcia Weigle developed this Civil Society III argument most fully in the Russian context, writing in 2002:

> Russian civil-society activists do not see themselves as a permanent opposition to an authoritarian-oriented state. They adhere to a 'strong state – strong society' model: The institutionalization of state power is a prerequisite for civil society development, and a strong civil society is vital to ensuring the state's democratic orientation. The 'weak state – weak society' model of the Yeltsin era only exacerbated problems of civil society development.[32]

Some observers quite explicitly contrast a "statist" approach to state-society relations with a "liberal" approach, which is seen by some as inconsistent with Russian traditions and political culture.[33] In the following two sections, I investigate the work of several Russian NGOs that are premised on a Civil Society III approach, and then discuss how the Putin strategy of deliberately weakening civil society oversight of the state (Civil Society II), including that by NGOs and the media, undermined the external fire alarms that are an important component of building both state capacity and state quality.

Before turning to these issues, it is worth considering the ways in which societal engagement can enhance state capacity in the law enforcement realm, and therefore the importance of higher-quality policing (more fair, less corrupt) for fighting crime and establishing law and order. David Bayley listed a series of reasons for this proposition, based on cross-national crime research, including:

- Police find out about crime from the public. Citizens who distrust or fear the police will not report crime.

[31] Thomas Carothers, *Aiding Democracy Abroad: The Learning Curve* (Washington, DC: Carnegie Endowment for International Peace, 1999), p. 250; David H. Bayley, *Changing the Guard: Developing Democratic Police Abroad* (Oxford: Oxford University Press, 2006), p. 85; Nicole Ball, "Good Practices in Security Sector Reform," in *Security Sector Reform: Brief 15* (Bonn International Center for Conversion, 2000), pp. 16–17; Posner 2004.

[32] Marcia A. Weigle, "On the Road to the Civic Forum: State and Civil Society from Yeltsin to Putin," *Demokratizatsiya*, 10, 2 (2002), p. 127. The "strong state-strong society" argument is made by Putnam: Putnam 1993, p. 176.

[33] See, for example: Alexander N. Domrin, "Ten Years Later: Society, 'Civil Society,' and the Russian State," *The Russian Review*, 62 (2003), pp. 193–211; Henry E. Hale, "Civil Society from Above? Statist and Liberal Models of State-Building in Russia," *Demokratizatsiya*, 10, 3 (2002), pp. 306–321; Janet Elise Johnson, "Public-Private Permutations: Domestic Violence Crisis Centers in Barnaul," in Alfred B. Evans, Jr., Laura A. Henry, and Lisa McIntosh Sundstrom, eds., *Russian Civil Society: A Critical Assessment* (Armonk, NY: M.E. Sharpe, 2006), pp. 266–283.

- The most serious crimes – murder, rape, assault, robbery – are rarely solved without public information, specifically the identity of the most likely suspects.
- Crime control depends on public activity – the police cannot be everywhere.
- People are more law-abiding if they have been treated fairly by law enforcement personnel in the past.
- Abusive policing redirects public resources from fighting crime to monitoring the police and leads to mutual distrust.[34]

In short, as Peter Katzenstein noted in his study of the Japanese police, "trust between police and citizens [is] an essential precondition for police effectiveness."[35] Institutional trust in the police can enhance state capacity in the law enforcement realm.

The relationship between institutional trust and state performance, then, is reciprocal. Better policing can increase citizens' trust in the state, but citizen engagement is also necessary for better policing.[36] This suggests that law enforcement–societal relationships may be prone to vicious and virtuous circles, in which high-quality policing and institutional trust reinforce one another, and low-quality policing and institutional distrust are also mutually reinforcing.[37]

Russian Interior Minister Rashid Nurgaliyev acknowledged the importance of social support in a 2005 interview. Nurgaliyev stated that the main task facing the MVD was to become "maximally open and accessible for society and law-abiding citizens." This included more politeness and a higher "cultural level" in interactions with citizens and greater attention to their problems. He promised a series of measures to "improve work with the population and raise the level of citizens' trust toward the militia." He also committed the MVD to working more closely with civil society and human rights groups.[38]

LAW ENFORCEMENT AND CIVIL SOCIETY IN RUSSIA

Greater pluralism in the post-Soviet era has made it possible for civil society groups, including NGOs, to operate in Russia. In this section, I examine the

[34] Bayley 2006, pp. 75–78.
[35] Peter J. Katzenstein, *Cultural Norms and National Security: Police and Military in Postwar Japan* (Ithaca, NY: Cornell University Press, 1996), p. 63.
[36] Evidence from sub-Saharan Africa indicates that better police work and positive trends in crime rates also leads to higher interpersonal trust: Jennifer A. Widner, "Building Effective Trust in the Aftermath of Severe Conflict," in Rotberg 2004, p. 225.
[37] On virtuous and vicious cycles and social capital, see: Putnam 1993, pp. 163–185.
[38] Yevgeniy Katyshev, "Novoye vremya – novaya militsiya," *PG*, September 30, 2005. He renewed this commitment to work with civil society groups under Medvedev, although, as noted further, there seemed to be some divergence between rhetoric and reality on this point: Petr Tverdov, "Militsiya otkryta dlya pravozashchitnikov," *Nez. Gaz.*, October 28, 2008.

work of NGOs across Russia who have tried to take Nurgaliyev and other law enforcement officials at their word that they seek greater engagement with civil society. I particularly focus on the efforts of those groups who pursue a Civil Society III approach that involves working with the state to try to change its dominant norms and practices in a more liberal direction. They seek to break out of the vicious circle of poor police performance and societal distrust that currently plagues Russian law enforcement. Surveys suggest that the Russian public would like to have greater confidence in state law enforcement organs, and that if the police changed its behavior, confidence might be restored.[39]

Most literature in the Civil Society III vein, including on Russia, focuses on two different mechanisms of state-civil society interaction: the provision of social services that state bodies have difficulty providing, and shaping legislation at the local or national level. The type of interaction I examine in the law enforcement realm uses a different mechanism, in which civil society organizations and actors partner with state bodies in an attempt to transform the norms and practices of officials in a more liberal and democratic direction. NGOs work directly with state officials, particularly "street-level bureaucrats," to persuade them that they can perform their functions better if they adopt certain practices that are consistent with liberal, democratic, or rational-legal norms. Rather than employing standard activist strategies involving "shaming" by disseminating information about illegal or undemocratic practices by the state, NGOs try to work with state officials by "framing" their efforts as assistance that will promote the successful fulfillment of core organizational tasks.[40] It is important to stress that such joint projects are not premised on the notion that the bureaucrats involved hold strong ideological commitments to liberal democracy, although the presence of a few such individuals can certainly help a great deal. Rather, it is assumed that the motivations of both those who embrace such projects and those who reject them may range from selfishly rational to strongly principled.[41]

The NGO strategy outlined here can be labeled a "street-level Civil Society III" approach. It targets lower levels of state agencies and tries to work inside state bureaucracies or alongside state officials performing their normal functions. It is neither "grass roots" work that endeavors to build a large movement

---

[39] Gerber and Mendelson 2008, p. 35.

[40] On framing, see: Rodger A. Payne, "Persuasion, Frames, and Norm Construction," *European Journal of International Relations*, 7, 1 (2001), pp. 37–61. Keck and Sikkink discuss both framing and shaming: Keck and Sikkink 1998.

[41] On mixed motives for individual behavior, see: Max Weber, *Economy and Society: An Outline of Interpretive Sociology* (Berkeley, CA: University of California Press, 1978), pp. 24–26; Jon Elster, *The Cement of Society: A Study of Social Order* (Cambridge: Cambridge University Press, 1989); Stephen E. Hanson, "Instrumental Democracy: The End of Ideology and the Decline of Russian Political Parties," in Vicki L. Hesli and William M. Reisinger, eds., *The 1999–2000 Elections in Russia: Their Impact and Legacy* (Cambridge: Cambridge University Press, 2003), pp. 163–185.

of individual citizens, nor is it public advocacy that seeks to target top state officials and other elites who will then push a reform through national legislation. The street-level Civil Society III approach is thus about teaching the state, as opposed to teaching citizens (Civil Society I) or balancing the state (Civil Society II). Ultimately, the goal is for civil society engagement to transform an illiberal state into a "civil state."

Of course, such a strategy will touch only a small number of individuals in one specific area. The local goal is thus the creation of virtuous pockets of trust and higher-quality law enforcement. For any changes in practice or norms to have a larger impact in a country, it needs to diffuse to other actors and areas. There are two possible paths of diffusion, horizontal and vertical, through which they can spread. First, and most simply, the officials exposed to these new norms and practices will interact with others in their agency and other bureaucracies and hopefully spread these ideas. Second, and more ambitiously, is the potential that a successful project will catch the eye of a sympathetic official at a higher level in the state, or in another part of the state, and the practices will be adopted in a greater area than the initial project. Indeed, the most successful projects will plan for the further spread of new norms and practices beyond an isolated experiment from the very beginning. Further, a successful experience with an NGO may make it more likely that previously skeptical state agencies and officials will agree to work with civil society groups in the future. As Wade Jacoby notes, institutions and practices will more successfully transfer to other locales when there are local actors working to "pull in" proposed innovations.[42]

Finally, it is important to stress that not only are different NGO strategies not mutually exclusive, they are often complementary. This is particularly the case with Civil Society II and Civil Society III approaches. For example, arguably elements of the Russian police have been open to cooperation with NGOs precisely because of a perceived need to change their public image brought about by the shaming effects of reports by NGOs and the media about civil rights abuses by the police.[43] Restrictions on media reporting on this issue potentially could undermine Civil Society III efforts to engage the police on liberalizing reforms. To date, despite the significant drop in press freedom in Russia since 2000, print media in particular are able to report on police corruption and abuse (this is significantly less true in terms of reporting on corruption in the procuracy or the FSB).

In general, civil society cooperation with Russian law enforcement has been difficult. The FSB retains much of the ethos of the old KGB and often remains aloof from cooperation even with the MVD, let alone NGOs. The procuracy is also a difficult target for cooperation, although it is more open

---

[42] Wade Jacoby, *Imitation and Politics: Redesigning Modern Germany* (Ithaca, NY: Cornell University Press, 2000).

[43] Many Russian human rights NGOs do valuable work of this nature; one example is "Public Verdict": http://www.publicverdict.org/

than the FSB. Of the three main law enforcement organs, the police interacts most closely with the wider society and is the likeliest partner for civil society organizations.[44]

Despite the difficulty of developing close relations with Russian law enforcement organs, multiple NGOs worked hard to develop such ties and improve state quality in this realm by making these organizations more responsive to society. Several cases of tangible success were evident, especially in the late-Yeltsin and early-Putin years, as NGOs became more experienced, the Soviet-era insularity of the police began to break down, and cooperative relationships developed across the state-society divide. However, the dominance of the ideology of "sovereign democracy" in Putin's second term, with its emphasis on the rejection of Western influence on Russian internal development, made it increasingly difficult for NGOs espousing liberal values and receiving foreign support to work with the power ministries. Instead, the Kremlin pursued a project of turning civil society into yet another "power vertical" that served state interests.

In this section, I discuss three cases of the type of state-civil society interaction sketched out earlier in this chapter. These cases are the activities of the St. Petersburg human rights organization "Citizens' Watch"; several projects of the Center for Justice Assistance, a rule-of-law reform NGO based in Moscow that conducted several projects in Nizhniy Novgorod; and some aspects of the work of the Yekaterina Crisis Center, a domestic violence organization in Yekaterinburg. Taken together, they demonstrate both the potential promise of a "street-level Civil Society III" approach to building state quality in the law enforcement realm and the limits to state-society cooperation in this area with the return to authoritarianism under Putin.[45]

Citizens' Watch: St. Petersburg

Citizens' Watch (*Grazhdanskiy Kontrol'*) is a small, St. Petersburg-based human rights NGO. It was created in 1992 and receives most of its funding from foreign foundations and international organizations. Citizens' Watch describes itself as a human rights organization with the goal of assisting in the establishment of "parliamentary and civic control" over state law enforcement organs "in order to help prevent violations of constitutional rights by these governmental agencies."[46] At first glance, Citizens' Watch seems to be a "typical" human rights organization, using standard shaming tactics to try to call the government to account for violations against individuals and NGOs. This is certainly one aspect of their work. At the same time, however, they worked

---

[44] Interview M-17; Interview M-30; Interview P-8.
[45] More detailed cases studies for the period through 2004 can be found in: Brian D. Taylor, "Law Enforcement and Civil Society in Russia," *Europe-Asia Studies*, 58, 2 (March 2006), pp. 193–213.
[46] http://www.citwatch.org/

hard to build bridges to law enforcement personnel for many years, although most of their projects with the police were terminated in 2007.

Boris Pustyntsev, the director of Citizens' Watch and a member of the Presidential Council for Facilitating the Development of Civil Society Institutions and Human Rights, chaired by Ella Pamfilova, contends that a key task of NGOs is to "civilize the bureaucracy." Openly strategic, Pustyntsev says that NGOs should try to "corrupt, in the good sense" bureaucrats through the use of personal ties, material incentives, and enhanced prestige. He is just as happy to work with "cynics" and "careerists" as committed reformers. The prospect of foreign travel, for example, may lead an official to get involved with NGOs with international contacts.[47]

Citizens' Watch had several projects in the late 1990s–early 2000s that involved law enforcement, and the police and procuracy in particular. One area of work was joint scientific research (particularly polling) on relations between police and citizens in St. Petersburg. They received cooperation and support from the Main Administration of Internal Affairs (GUVD) for St. Petersburg and the Leningrad Oblast, which stated its intention to use this material in training police officers.[48] Significantly, the motivations for this project were clearly inspired by Civil Society III notions about a state-society partnership. Mary McAuley, who was the Ford Foundation Representative in Moscow at the time of the research, noted that the goal of the project was not to generate press articles about the "bad work of the militia." Rather, the goal was to "find practical methods by which the work of the militia and relations between the militia and citizens can be improved."[49] Thus, the foundation that funded the project clearly preferred a framing strategy to a shaming one, one that would facilitate cooperation between civil society and law enforcement in Russia.

Citizens' Watch also developed good ties with the St. Petersburg MVD University. A key goal of their work was to make European norms and human rights a larger part of the education of new police officers. To this end, they translated into Russian several important brochures on policing in Western Europe, such as *The European Code of Police Ethics* (Council of Europe). Thousands of these different brochures were requested for training by the University, the local militia, and the central MVD.

Another key aspect of Citizens' Watch's work on changing police norms and behaviors involved preparing training films to be used in St. Petersburg and throughout the country. They prepared films for police officers on the rights of citizens in "hot spots" such as Chechnya, the rules for checking documents on the street, and the rights of detainees. The films were shown to officers and

---

[47] Interview P-8. All further comments attributed to Pustyntsev are from these interviews.
[48] *"Naseleniye i militsiya v bol'shom gorode": Kruglyy stol (prezentatsiya issledovaniya), stenograficheskiy otchet* (Sankt-Peterburg: Grazhdanskiy Kontrol', 2000), pp. 12–13.
[49] *"Naseleniye i militsiya v bol'shom gorode* 2000, p. 19.

cadets, sometimes with an accompanying lecture on the legal issues discussed in the film.

Citizens' Watch also took a somewhat unusual step for a human rights NGO by hiring a police colonel, a professor at the St. Petersburg MVD University, to work for them. Colonel Mikhail Rodionov became their coordinator on police reform and conducted seminars around the country for police on political extremism. Pustyntsev stated that Citizens' Watch needed someone who "understands police ways." Rodionov believed that his informal and personal contacts helped create good working relationships with the police.[50]

Starting in 2006, however, it became increasingly difficult for Citizens' Watch to work with the police and other law enforcement structures. In 2004 and 2005, clear signals were sent by top state officials, including Putin and FSB head Nikolay Patrushev, that NGOs, especially those with foreign support, were potentially dangerous, and in January 2006, new NGO legislation was signed that was widely interpreted as a crackdown on civil society (see further in this chapter). Moreover, in March 2007, the Law on State Civil Service was amended to prohibit state officials from receiving money from foreign-financed programs.[51] Although there were ways to continue such programs even after this law was adopted, it was generally interpreted in the police as a ban on participating in any NGO project that received foreign funding. Indeed, a Council of Europe official working on police and human rights issues told Pustyntsev in 2008 that the situation with cooperation with the Russian MVD was "disastrous" and that all joint programs had to be canceled, even though similar programs were successfully underway with judges and procurators. Pustyntsev attributed this new MVD attitude against cooperation with NGOs receiving foreign funding to a broader policy of the Chekist clan, with which Nurgaliyev is traditionally associated as a protégé of Patrushev.

In light of this changed atmosphere, Citizens' Watch was forced to cancel several law enforcement projects. One project that they had been pursuing for years was on ethnic minorities in the police. Pustyntsev believes that more diverse police forces in countries like the United States and the United Kingdom, as compared to countries like France and Germany (and Russia), help the police manage relations with minority communities better.

[50] Interview P-9.

[51] "O gosudarstvennoy grazhdanskoy sluzhbe Rossiyskoy Federatsii," Article 17. Loopholes in the article allow such projects if there is written permission from the employer, or if it is covered by an international agreement. Although the U.S. Embassy was able to continue its projects under this provision, both Pustyntsev and Georgiy Satarov of INDEM stated this amendment had a crippling effect on foreign-financed NGO projects: Interviews M-30; M-45; P-8. Technically this law does not even apply to law enforcement organs, which will be covered in a separate law on law enforcement service that as of 2010 was still being drafted in the presidential administration. However, the draft law contains the same prohibition: "O pravookhranitel'noy sluzhbe Rossiyskoy Federatsii," Draft, Article 16; copy in possession of the author.

He hoped to persuade the St. Petersburg police to make greater efforts to recruit ethnic minorities to serve in the police, especially in visible positions like traffic and patrol units. He received Council of Europe support for a project involving the German and Dutch police in comparative research on the issue, to be followed with recommendations to the police on recruitment and training. In June 2006, representatives of the Dutch police visited St. Petersburg and met with officials from the GUVD, and everything seemed okay; several months later, however, the police ceased cooperation. Citizens' Watch then tried to reformulate the project as a purely scientific one in cooperation with the local MVD University, but the university refused. Indeed, according to Pustyntsev, the national MVD sent word that Citizens' Watch is a "bad organization" and it would be better if the university did not cooperate with them.

A second project involving the MVD University that Pustyntsev had worked on for years, the establishment of a department of human rights at the university, was also canceled.[52] Starting around 2001, he pursued the idea with the director of the university, who was generally supportive but skeptical that the national MVD would allow such a step. Pustyntsev received agreement in principle in 2002 from several deputy ministers of the national MVD, but no final order mandating the new department was issued, and eventually the effort was killed. Indeed, the head of the MVD University who had supported international projects was replaced by someone less interested in such work. After an inspection of the university by the national MVD, the new head decided to cancel all cooperation with NGOs that receive foreign money.

As of 2008, both the St. Petersburg GUVD and the MVD University had ended all cooperation with Citizens' Watch on international projects. Indeed, one police colonel told Pustyntsev that joint projects had to cease because "America is now enemy number one!" Citizens' Watch also ran into trouble with the Federal Registration Service under the 2006 NGO Law (see further in this chapter), and clearly remained a target in 2008. For example, a local paper linked to Mayor Valentina Matviyenko ran a story, entitled "Dutch cheese only exists in a mousetrap," which insinuated that Dutch foreign aid projects with Citizens' Watch were designed to collect information on the methods and personnel of the St. Petersburg police. In essence, the article implied that the Netherlands was using its foreign aid department to spy on the Russian government, with the connivance of local NGOs. Pustyntsev threatened to sue the paper if they did not retract the portions of the story about his organization, which they did ten days later.[53]

---

[52] *"Problemy zashchity prav cheloveka v uchebnykh programmakh Sankt-Peterburgskogo universiteta MVD Rossii: Kruglyy stol (Sbornik materialov)* (Sankt-Peterburg: Sankt-Peterburgskiy universitet MVD Rossii i Grazhdanskiy Kontrol', 2004).

[53] Vasiliy Lenskiy, "Gollandskiy syr byvayet tol'ko v myshelovke," *Nevskoye vremya*, April 8, 2008; "'Grazhdanskiy kontrol' deystvoval po zakonu," *Nevskoye vremya*, April 18, 2008.

In light of this virtual prohibition on work with the police, Citizens' Watch devoted greater efforts to working with other pieces of the justice system, such as the courts and the prisons. Pustyntsev still remained hopeful that Citizens' Watch would at some point be able to resume joint projects with the police, remarking in July 2008 that "this plague won't last long," by which he meant the anti-Western tendencies of the central government. Before their joint projects were terminated, Pustyntsev believed that minor changes in police conduct were starting to be felt even at the "street-level" in St. Petersburg due to their training efforts, even if many officers still "get corrupted by the system." Even in the best of times, state-civil society cooperation in the law enforcement sphere is likely to be slow and difficult; the obstacles put in the way of such collaboration in Putin's second term put a halt to positive steps previously underway.

Center for Justice Assistance, INDEM: Moscow and Nizhniy Novgorod

The Center for Justice Assistance (*Tsentr Sodeystviya Pravosudiyu*, hereafter CJA), even more than Citizens' Watch, positioned itself as an NGO working cooperatively with the state to improve the rule of law. CJA works "in partnership with government agencies and nongovernmental organizations to design and implement projects that test innovations in the justice system." CJA was created in 2000 and is part of the INDEM Foundation, a think tank headed by former Boris Yeltsin advisor, Georgiy Satarov. CJA initially came about due to the initiative of the Vera Institute of Justice, an international rule of law NGO based in New York, which proposed joint work with INDEM in a center under the INDEM umbrella. In reality, after 2004, most of their work was absorbed into INDEM's operations, with INDEM continuing to work in the law enforcement and judicial reform area. CJA's small staff from 2000 to 2004 was headquartered in Moscow, although they had an office with several staffers in Nizhniy Novgorod while they were conducting experimental programs there. Most of CJA's funding came from foreign foundations and states, but it also received support from Russian sources, including foundations and government contracts.[54]

CJA had multiple projects in the rule-of-law area and conducted several with Russian law enforcement. Their work was marked by close collaboration with reformist elements within the law enforcement and legal community at both the national and regional level. Indeed, CJA official Ivan Komaritskiy explicitly noted that they are not "watchdogs," and that they chose projects that would benefit not only citizens but state law enforcement agencies as well. They conducted several experiments in Nizhniy Novgorod that were intended to demonstrate that progressive legal reforms can serve the interests of both state agencies and society.

---

[54] Interview M-30. CJA's website is at: http://www.cja.ru/. INDEM's website is at: http://www.indem.ru/

One of their major efforts was the Nizhniy Novgorod Project for Justice Assistance (NPSP). The main goal of the project, which ran from 2000 to 2003, was to reduce the amount of time suspects spent in pretrial detention.[55] Law students hired by NPSP worked with investigators in the police and procuracy to speed up the investigation of cases, while other legal assistants helped judges prepare for cases. NPSP also created an interdepartmental computer system that facilitated data sharing between the police, procurators, courts, and the prison system.[56]

Overall, the project worked for three years on thousands of cases, and succeeded in reducing the time in pretrial detention compared to those cases in the control group by around twenty days. Although the reduction in detention time was impressive, the project was not picked up for wider usage. The basic problem, according to Komaritskiy, was that the project dealt with two separate agencies, the police and the prison system. The money saved by reducing pretrial detention saves money for the prison system but costs money to the police because of the extra personnel required during the investigative phase. Thus, a project that may be rational from the point of view of the state law enforcement system in general is not necessarily rational for the specific ministries involved.

A second major project, and one that arguably helped change police practice at the national level, was called "First Contact." The basic goal of the project was to "build public confidence in law enforcement by improving the very first contact between police and a crime victim or citizen seeking help."[57] The pilot project, which ran in Nizhniy Novgorod in 2002–2003, set up "Citizen Assistance Centers" in three of the eight regional police stations in the city. Volunteer students from the local police academy or law schools worked in police stations taking citizens' statements and complaints. The "First Contact" staff also provided more general assistance to people approaching the police, such as referrals to social service organizations or information on how to get new copies of stolen documents; the police generally did not provide that kind of assistance.

The pilot project had several important successes. First, in areas where "First Contact" worked, there were better crime data than in other parts of

---

[55] On problems with pretrial detention in Russia, such as overcrowding and infectious diseases, see: Peter H. Solomon, Jr. and Todd S. Fogelsong, *Courts and Transition in Russia: The Challenge of Judicial Reform* (Boulder, CO: Westview Press, 2000), pp. 151–157.

[56] The description of the project that follows is based on: TsSP (CJA), *NSNP: Itogi i perspektivy. Metodicheskiy material po sokrashcheniyu srokov soderzhaniya v SIZO*, n.d. [http://www.cja.ru/pages/publications/npsp-itogi.htm]; *Nizhegorodskiy proyekt sodeystviya pravosudiyu*, Nizhniy Novgorod, 2002, brochure; Interview NN-4; Interview M-24.

[57] Jennifer Trone, "For the Police, a Good First Impression Could be Crucial," *Just Cause* (Newsletter of the Vera Institute of Justice), 10, 4 (2003), p. 3. Other materials used in the description of the project include: K.K. Goryainov, ed., *Uluchsheniye vzaimootnosheniy grazhdan i militsii: rezul'taty eksperimenta "Pervyy Kontakt"* (Moskva: Fond INDEM, 2004); Interview M-24; Interview NN-2.

the city. Second, and perhaps more significantly, a series of surveys of citizens appealing to the police in those areas of the city before and after the experiment showed a marked increase in popular approval. Konstantin Golovshchinskiy, a research fellow at the Higher School of Economics in Moscow, described "First Contact" as "uniquely successful" because of the way it changed the way these police stations worked and helped real people in a very practical way.[58] Members of the police also were surveyed after the experiment, and they were generally pleased with the results of the project. The project was also favorably evaluated by the then-deputy head of the MVD Investigative Committee, Boris Gavrilov, who also claimed the experiment reflected well on the MVD:

One additional very important thing the project demonstrated is that in the internal affairs organs there are officials prepared to take on themselves the risk and responsibility to try new mechanisms raising the quality of their work, and concerned with improving relations with citizens. At the same time the project overturned the myth about the militia as an organ which resists all innovation and is not willing to cooperate with societal organizations.[59]

In 2004, there was a conference at the central MVD to discuss the results of the "First Contact" project. CJA proposed further experiments, but no further projects were pursued. In what INDEM director Satarov described as a "strange story," he was told by someone at the MVD that CJA was "too late" for further work because MVD head Nurgaliyev had already signed an internal order requiring the use of citizen surveys in police evaluation criteria. When asked why the MVD had not done more to publicize this apparently important change, Satarov was told that it was not consistent with MVD traditions to do so. Regardless, Satarov ultimately judged the program a success because it helped influence the desire to change police assessment criteria, getting away from a singular focus on crime clearance rates. Indeed, in 2001, CJA had published a report on the problem that had reached then MVD head Boris Gryzlov, a close Putin ally, and Satarov believed that Nurgaliyev's interest in changing police evaluation methods was a continuation of a policy begun under Gryzlov.[60]

Indeed, in 2002, an MVD decree widened the evaluation criteria beyond the level of crime and the crime clearance rate to add additional administrative criteria. However, all of these new measures were also quantitative measures that just further encouraged police officials to "cook the books" to get positive assessments, which led officers to spend more time filing reports and statistics than fighting crime and serving citizens. In December 2007, Nurgaliyev issued an internal order on the use of citizen surveys, conducted by independent sociologists (not police ones), in evaluating MVD performance and also

---

[58] Interview M-11.
[59] Goryainov 2004, p. 119.
[60] Interview M-30. See the discussion of this issue in Chapter 5.

in getting a more complete picture of crime in the country. The surveys were to focus on the degree to which people feel secure and protected against crime and other rights' violations. However, by 2010, it became clear that basically no progress had been made on including citizen surveys in police evaluation criteria, with the old "quota system" remaining in place. Still, the efforts of NGOs like CJA, as well as journalists and police and academic researchers, did manage to keep pressure on the government and the MVD to reform its evaluation system.[61]

After these two major projects, INDEM/CJA did two other programs with the MVD before they lost support for further joint work. In 2004, they were awarded an MVD contract, together with scholars from the Higher School of Economics, to prepare a code of ethical conduct for law enforcement officials. In this case, it was not CJA that had approached the state, but the state that approached them on this issue.[62] A new code of professional ethics was issued by the MVD in December 2008.

Second, in 2006–2007, INDEM partnered with Altus Global Alliance to participate in an international action, "Police Station Visitors Week," conducted in twenty-three countries. The goal of the project was to assess the quality of police work and to make the police more accountable to society. A key ally for INDEM in the project was Russian Human Rights Ombudsman Vladimir Lukin, who wrote to Minister Nurgaliyev, as well as to regional police officials, to encourage the MVD to support the project. Although Nurgaliyev did not endorse the project in 2006, several regional police departments agreed to participate, and overall, thirty-nine police stations in eight regions were visited either by observers from NGOs or by law students. All police stations were scored in five categories of service, such as conditions of detention and transparency and accountability. The overall assessment was meant to evaluate "professionalism, effectiveness, and the observation of human rights." A police station in the Chuvash Republic received particularly high ratings and was recognized as one of the best in Europe by Altus. This success must have led Nurgaliyev to reconsider, because the program was repeated in 2007 and he heralded the project as an important example of the openness of the MVD to working with civil society.[63]

---

[61] Demos 2005, pp. 13–17; Rustam Taktashev, "Rossiyane otsenyat rabotu militsii," *Gazeta*, February 13, 2008; Andrey Sitkovskiy, "Sostoyaniye kriminal'nogo viktimizatsii v Rossiyskoy Federatsii," *Professional*, 2 (2008); O.V. Yakovlev, "Sostoyaniye i perspektivy vnevedomstvennogo izucheniya obshchestvennogo mneniya ob urovne bezopasnosti lichnosti i deyatel'nosti organov vnutrennikh del Rossiyskoy Federatsii," *VNII MVD*, February 2008 [available at: www.vnii-mvd.ru/files/Текст%20выступления%20-%20февраль.doc]; Interview M-11; Interview M-21; Interview M-30; Afanasiy Sborov, "Instruktsiya dlya 'oborotney'," *K-V*, February 1, 2010.

[62] Interview M-11; Interview M-30.

[63] TsSP (CJA), *Nedelya poseshcheniy otdeleniy militsii/politseyskikh uchastkov 29 oktyabrya – 4 noyabrya 2006 g.: Otcheta o rezul'tatakh proyekta v Rossiyskoy Federatsii*, n.d. [http://www.indem.ru/en/cja/reprfru.htm]; Tverdov 2008.

Despite this history of close cooperation with the MVD, INDEM Director Satarov stated in 2008 that in the last few years, it had become harder to work with the police. He pointed to a series of changes and events during Putin's second term, including the British "spy-rock" case (see further in this chapter), the 2006 NGO law, and the 2007 change in the state civil service law, as contributing to difficult NGO-police relations. The main change, however, was a "change of atmosphere" that led to a different attitude by law enforcement personnel about cooperating with civil society organizations. Like Citizens' Watch, judicial reform was now a key direction of their work because it was easier to work with the judiciary than with the police or other law enforcement bodies.[64]

Yekaterina Crisis Center, Yekaterinburg

One area in which one would not expect significant cooperation between law enforcement and civil society organizations is in the area of domestic violence. Russian police are widely believed to be at best indifferent to the problem; one activist states that the police "will rarely investigate a complaint unless the woman has been murdered."[65] N.A. Latygina, of the Novosibirsk Women's Crisis Center, maintained that police often do not help with cases of domestic violence. It is hard for her organization to work with the militia, she said, which is a "very closed structure."[66]

Given these obstacles, it is somewhat remarkable that in Yekaterinburg, the Yekaterina Crisis Center, a domestic violence NGO, has had moderate success in working with the local police. The center was established in 1998 and relies on a small staff and volunteers to conduct their activities, including a telephone "help line" for victims of domestic violence. A cooperation agreement between the police and the center was signed in 2001 and, according to one activist, was the first such agreement between the police and a NGO in Yekaterinburg.[67]

One aspect of the joint work between the police and the center was a training program for "beat cops" (*uchastkovyy*) in the city on the issue of domestic violence. The training was provided by psychologists from the regional MVD academy. The Yekaterina Crisis Center also prepared training manuals for police officers on the issue and conducted training for police supervisors from Yekaterinburg and other surrounding cities. Finally, they opened a joint center at one police station in the city where a lawyer and a psychologist

---

[64] Interview M-30.

[65] Jonathan Weiler, *Human Rights in Russia: A Darker Side of Reform* (Boulder, CO: Lynne Rienner, 2004), p. 73.

[66] Interview N-4.

[67] *Krizisnyy tsentr "Yekaterina"*, 1998–2003, brochure, n.d., in possession of author. Other sources for this section are: *Zhizn' bez strakha: Prakticheskoye posobiye* (Yekaterinburg: Krizisnyy tsentr dlya zhenshchin "Yekaterina," 2002); Interview Ye-6; Interview Ye-13.

were available several times a month for consultations on domestic violence issues.

Another part of their collaboration was the preparation of stands and posters to place in police stations with information about domestic violence, including attached brochures with additional information. The "Life Without Fear" campaign featured a brochure partially authored by a local police colonel who was head of the police juvenile service and a consultant to a national project on violence against women. The brochure has a substantial section on the legal and criminal aspects of domestic violence and instructions to beat cops about how to handle domestic disputes and domestic violence. Although these steps may seem small, compared to the standard police response to domestic violence in Russia, it represented a definite step forward.

The relative success of domestic violence NGOs in Yekaterinburg in working with the police was largely dependent on the personal commitment of a small group of people and the ability to find someone inside the police sympathetic to change.[68] In this case, one key officer seemingly played an important role, based on her own personal commitment to the issue. The officer had the opportunity to travel to both the United States and the United Kingdom on police exchange programs and to observe how the police work on domestic violence issues in these countries. Yekaterinburg, however, is not alone – similar training efforts have been conducted by domestic violence NGOs in other regions.[69]

Other Projects

The three organizations highlighted here do not, of course, represent the only examples of law enforcement–civil society engagement in Russia. There are many other examples of similar work. Other NGO projects that have included Civil Society III work with law enforcement organs include international police exchanges and training and seminars on issues such as human rights, extremism, and human trafficking. Such efforts have been undertaken all across Russia.[70]

Many groups also work with the Federal Service for the Administration of Sentences (FSIN), the penitentiary service, on a range of issues, including conditions for prisoners and rehabilitating former prisoners; juvenile justice has

---

[68] Joint NGO-police work on domestic violence continued in Yekaterinburg after 2003. For example, the Yekaterina Crisis Center's webpage provides details on a 2007 conference on domestic violence in which the local police played an important role: http://www.kc-ekaterina.ru

[69] Claire Bigg, "Russia: Domestic Violence Continues to Take Heavy Toll," *RFE/RL*, December 15, 2005. See also: Johnson 2006.

[70] Community Policing Training Initiative: http://cpti.projectharmony.ru/; Interview P-10; Thomas Firestone, "The Russian Connection: Sex Trafficking into the United States and What the United States and Russia Are Doing About It," *International Organized Crime*, 51, 5 (2003), pp. 39–42; Interview M-45; Interview N-2.

also been a frequent area for NGO activity. In 2008, a new law was adopted on social control over prisons and detention facilities controlled by other agencies (such as the MVD and the FSB). Human rights groups, who had pushed for such a law for a decade, were generally critical of the law in the form it was adopted, with some arguing that it would actually reduce the amount of outside control over prisons. Lyudmila Alpern, the deputy director of the Moscow Center for Prison Reform, agreed that the version passed was "weak" and that an earlier version was better, but hoped that the law would provide a legal basis for developing social control over the prisons further. At the same time, human rights activists in 2008 described the situation in Russian prisons as "catastrophic."[71]

It is also worth mentioning the ombudsman institution in Russia, which exists both at the national level as well as in more than half of Russia's regions (forty-seven as of July 2008). Although this institution is a state one mandated by the Constitution, it also has a strong civil society element and works closely with human rights organizations. Both the previous national ombudsman (formally the Commissioner for Human Rights), Oleg Mironov (1998–2004), and the current one, Vladimir Lukin (2004–), have made one of their priorities highlighting human rights deficiencies in law enforcement structures, shaming the police and other law enforcement agencies for gross violations of human rights and pressing these agencies to punish violators in their midst. At the same time, there are also efforts to engage the MVD in more positive cooperative efforts to change the behavior of its personnel. For example, the MVD and the ombudsman's office cosponsored a conference in November 2004 on "Human Rights and Civil Society," and they also concluded a memorandum of cooperation that included provisions for joint inspections of regional police departments, as well as civil society cooperation with the MVD. Lukin stressed the need for ombudsman monitoring of the police, and joint efforts to change the culture of the police. Nurgaliyev maintained in 2008 that these ties with both the national ombudsman and regional ombudsmen were productive and ongoing.[72]

[71] Interview N-2; Moscow Center for Prison Reform website: http://www.prison.org/; Interview M-1; Interview M-3; Fond zashchitu prav zaklyuchennykh, *Vestnik*, pp. 3–4, 12–13 (March–April–May 2008), pp. 1–6. For an assessment of the prison system under Putin, see: Mary McAuley, "Prisons in Russia and the Rule of Law," in Mary McAuley, Alena Ledeneva and Hugh Barnes, *Dictatorship or Reform? The Rule of Law in Russia* (London: Foreign Policy Centre, 2006), pp. 8–23.

[72] Armen Urikhanjan, "Mironov: People do not Tolerate Humiliation," *Vremya MN*, April 22, 2003 [in JRL #7151, April 22, 2003]; Kira Latukhina, "Lukin ne khochet nachinat' s 'uzhastikov'," *Nez Gaz.*, April 9, 2004; Aleksandr Kolesnichenko, "Glavnyy narushitel' u nas–MVD," *NI*, June 17, 2004; Viktor Gavryushenko, "Stanet li MVD Ministerstvom prav cheloveka?" *Nov. Gaz.*, December 16, 2004; *Prav cheloveka i grazhdanskoye obshchestvo: Programma mezhdunarodnoy nauchno-prakticheskoy konferentsii* (Moskva: November 23, 2004); Interview M-31; "Most human rights complaints caused by welfare issues, ombudsman tells Putin," *RTR Russia TV*, BBC Monitoring, March 1, 2005 [JRL #9074, March 2, 2005]; Tverdov 2008.

Teaching the State: An Impossible Task?

The three NGOs highlighted in this section all set for themselves the goal of partnering with Russian law enforcement structures to transform their norms and practices in a more liberal and rational-legal direction. Each of them achieved some success in implementing programs that, at least at the micro level, seemed to change in small but important ways the behavior of the police. In one case, the work of CJA/INDEM on the system of registering crimes and assessing police performance, an NGO arguably helped contribute to an important change in police practice at the national level, although it is too early to tell if the addition of citizens' evaluations will be implemented in a way that improves either the capacity or the quality of the Russian militia. On the other hand, starting around 2005, it became increasingly difficult for NGOs to partner with law enforcement, and several programs were terminated. This was due to a Kremlin crackdown on foreign-sponsored activities in the wake of the 2003–2004 "colored revolutions" in Georgia and Ukraine.

Even if the government had not decided to tighten the screws, there were legitimate reasons for skepticism about how much change one could expect from such bottom-up initiatives. First of all, it is a truism in the police studies literature that the police resist outside influence over internal practices. Although this insularity has started to break down in some Western democracies, it remains common in most countries, including post-authoritarian and post-communist transitional countries.[73] The pathologies of Russian law enforcement structures, including frequent lack of respect for human rights, low public trust, and pervasive corruption, are long-standing and deeply ingrained. They will not be remedied in a few years by a handful of NGOs.

Second, the work of the NGOs profiled here, although admirable, is marked by some of the deficiencies noted in the literature on democracy assistance and Russian civil society.[74] To varying degrees, the projects relied heavily or

---

[73] Bayley 2006, p. 53; A. Goldsmith and C. Lewis, eds., *Civilian Oversight of Policing: Governance, Democracy and Human Rights* (Oxford: Hart Publishers, 2000); Mark A. Gissiner, "The Role of NGOs in Civilian Oversight of the Police," in András Kadar, ed., *Police in Transition: Essays on the Police Forces in Transition Countries* (Budapest: Central European University Press, 2001), pp. 187–195; Renate Weber, "Police Organization and Accountability: A Comparative Study," in Kadar 2001, p. 52; Mark Ungar, *Elusive Reform: Democracy and the Rule of Law in Latin America* (Boulder, CO: Lynne Rienner, 2002), pp. 67, 77. On a successful effort to open up the Chicago police to the influence of community organizations, see: Archon Fung, *Empowered Participation: Reinventing Urban Democracy* (Princeton, NJ: Princeton University Press, 2004).

[74] Valerie Sperling, *Organizing Women in Contemporary Russia: Engendering Transition* (Cambridge: Cambridge University Press, 1999); Sarah E. Mendelson and John K. Glenn, eds., *The Power and Limits of NGOs: A Critical Look at Building Democracy in Eastern Europe and Eurasia* (New York: Columbia University Press, 2002); Sarah L. Henderson, *Building Democracy in Contemporary Russia: Western Support for Grassroots Organizations* (Ithaca, NY: Cornell University Press, 2003); Julie Hemment, "The Riddle of the Third Sector: Civil Society, International Aid, and NGOs in Russia," *Anthropological Quarterly*, 77, 2 (2004), pp. 215–241; James Richter, "Integration from Below? The Disappointing Effort to Promote

exclusively on foreign funding, their fortunes were dependent on a small number of committed and well-placed individuals, and the long-term sustainability
of the work was in doubt. None of these groups are "grassroots" organizations with large membership rolls or significant financial contributions from
individual Russians. In the cases of Citizens' Watch and the Center for Justice
Assistance in particular, the criticism that they are more attuned to the wishes
of foreign funders than Russian citizens has some validity.

It surely would be a mistake, however, to insist on one model of NGO
activity, based only on grassroots, indigenous sources. It is not obvious that
a large domestic membership is needed for the kind of work pursued by CJA
and Citizens' Watch, but successful projects do benefit broader society. One
role foreign foundations and organizations like the Council of Europe can
play is bankrolling domestic reformers, who can then press the state to pursue liberal and democratic reforms.[75] Further, many of the particular projects pursued by the organizations profiled here were directly or indirectly
inspired by a variety of transnational actors, including international NGOs
such as the Vera Institute of Justice and foreign police officials encountered
in exchanges and conferences. Wade Jacoby argues persuasively that external
actors can most successfully promote change when they go beyond inspiration
to working in coalition with domestic reformers. Jacoby calls these domestic
factions "minority traditions," groups who have fought unsuccessfully for
a particular solution to a given issue. He asserts, "outsiders may be able to
provide material or intellectual resources that allow such minorities to finally
get their way." Bayley similarly emphasizes the importance of "buy-in" by
"crucial stakeholders" if foreign actors are going to have any influence on law
enforcement reform. Of course, these outsiders may also act so ham-handedly
that they undermine the very goals they seek to promote.[76] But, at least in the
cases discussed above, that is not the reason for failure to achieve broader success. Indeed, many Russian activists see this outside support, both material
and ideational, as essential. Alpern, of the Moscow Center for Prison Reform,
said that her ability to travel to Europe and North America and exchange
ideas with activists there has been critical, both in terms of learning about
how good prisons are run and especially learning the "techniques of civil
society."[77]

Civil Society in Russia," in Douglas W. Blum, ed., *Russia and Globalization: Identity, Security, and Society in an Era of Change* (Baltimore: The Johns Hopkins University Press, 2008), pp. 181–203.

[75] On the Council of Europe, which has made rule of law and security sector reform key aspects of its relationship with Russia, see: Pamela A. Jordan, "Russia's Accession to the Council of Europe and Compliance with European Human Rights Norms," *Demokratizatsiya*, 11, 2 (2003), pp. 281–296.

[76] Jacoby discusses some works that argue this position: Wade Jacoby, "Inspiration, Coalition, and Substitution: External Influences on Postcommunist Transformations (Review Article)," *World Politics*, 58, 2 (July 2006), pp. 623–651 (quote p. 629); Bayley 2006, p. 96.

[77] Interview M-3.

The main problems of NGOs seeking to transform Russian law enforcement are not ham-handed outsiders, but the sheer enormity of the task and the relative political weakness of these actors compared to more conservative forces. Although NGO reformers have been able to find allies inside the police at both the national and local levels, these gains were threatened by powerful actors who are at best suspicious and at worst openly hostile to reforms that would make Russian law enforcement more accountable and less patrimonial. Most importantly, Putin himself and close allies like Patrushev sent the signal that foreign NGOs, foundations, and governments were hostile forces that threatened Russian sovereignty. Under these conditions, it is not surprising that local police colonels would blurt out that "America is now enemy number one!" when asked to explain why a police-NGO project had to be terminated. Indeed, I know of at least four cases of police officials who were receptive to greater international and civil society cooperation losing their jobs during Putin's second term. This includes the head of the MVD international cooperation department, who allegedly was perceived as too close to foreigners.[78] Although it is impossible to know if this openness to cooperation was the major reason for their dismissal, in several of the cases it seemed to play an important role.

The goal of any minority tradition has to be to move beyond small projects to institutionalizing their solutions. In the law enforcement realm, innovations such as civilian review boards, rigorous codes of ethics, and empowered ombudsmen are institutional embodiments of liberal values.[79] To achieve greater success at the national level in breaking out of the vicious circle of low-quality law enforcement and institutional distrust, civil society groups need stronger allies inside the state, especially in the executive branch.[80] Indeed, a common feature of insider accounts about how joint NGO-state projects were implemented is the need for a "roof" (*krysha*) inside the state that can protect the NGO and push their projects through a hostile bureaucracy. Just as businesses in Russia are forced to buy "roofs" to protect them from predation by other parts of the state, NGOs sought "roofs" – in the Duma, in the Public Council, in the Ombudsman's office, and especially in the executive branch – to protect them from government attacks.

Without some strong reformers inside the state, whatever institutional innovations that are adopted, such as ombudsmen, are likely to be more exercises in mimicry than institutions in the true sociological sense, infused with

---

[78] Interview M-50.

[79] On NATO's efforts in Central and Eastern Europe to inculcate norms of democratic civil-military relations in officials in prospective member countries, so these officials would "create institutions that ... embody these norms and principles," see: Rachel A. Epstein, "When Legacies Meet Policies: NATO and the Refashioning of Polish Military Tradition," *East European Politics and Societies*, 20, 2 (2006), pp. 254–285 (quote p. 272).

[80] On the importance of alliances across the civil society/government divide, see: Judith Tendler, *Good Government in the Tropics* (Baltimore: The Johns Hopkins University Press, 1997), p. 157.

value and a sense of mission.[81] In Russia under Putin, there was a sharp break between the authorities' rhetoric about the importance of democracy, civil society, and the rule of law and the actual policies pursued, which seemed designed to gut real state accountability to society.

MONITORING THE STATE: THE DECLINE OF ACCOUNTABILITY

Civil society can use multiple strategies to influence the state and thus can play different roles in affecting state performance. Some Russian NGOs have sought to partner with the state to transform its practices and values (Civil Society III). Other parts of civil society, including NGOs and the media, try to play a watchdog role and hold the state accountable for violations of the law and citizens' rights (Civil Society II). These watchdogs can be thought of as forms of external monitors, or fire alarms, to assist or substitute for internal monitors, or police patrols, within state agencies.

During his presidency, despite his frequent rhetorical support for the positive role civil society can play in Russian development, Putin systematically weakened forms of state accountability to the public and civil society. Some of these efforts were apparent from the beginning of his presidency, such as the attacks on the two oligarchs with the largest media empires, Vladimir Gusinsky and Boris Berezovsky.[82] Signs of a more skeptical attitude toward NGOs, especially those in the human rights and environmental spheres, also were evident in the first term. Journalists and scholars working on military and security issues also came under attack. For example, in 2004, think tank researcher Igor Sutyagin was sentenced to fifteen years in prison for espionage for allegedly passing on classified information, although he never had a security clearance or access to classified material.[83]

One example from the criminal justice sphere from Putin's first term demonstrated how an apparent openness to more civil society involvement in state decision making in reality masked greater centralized control. In 1992, Yeltsin created a Presidential Pardons Commission that considered pardon petitions from individual prisoners. The Commission was headed by the well-known writer Anatoliy Pristavkin and consisted primarily of members of the intelligentsia – writers, academics, journalists, and the like. From 1992 to 2001, the Commission pardoned nearly 70,000 prisoners; in the vast majority of cases,

---

[81] On mimicry and civil-military relations reform in the post-communist region, see: Piotr Dutkiewicz and Sergei Plekhanov, "The Politics of 'Mimicry': The Case of Eastern Europe," in Albert Legault and Joel Sokolsky, eds., *The Soldier and the State in the Post Cold War Era* (Special Issue of the *Queen's Quarterly*, 2002), pp. 113–142.

[82] Overviews include: Andrew Jack, *Inside Putin's Russia* (Oxford: Oxford University Press, 2004), pp. 131–178; Peter Baker and Susan Glasser, *Kremlin Rising*, updated edition (Dulles, VA: Potomac Books, 2007), pp. 78–98.

[83] Sarah Mendelson, "Russian Rights' Imperiled: Has Anybody Noticed?", *International Security*, 26, 4 (Spring 2002), pp. 47–49; Zoltan Barany, *Democratic Breakdown and the Decline of the Russian Military* (Princeton, NJ: Princeton University Press, 2007), p. 121.

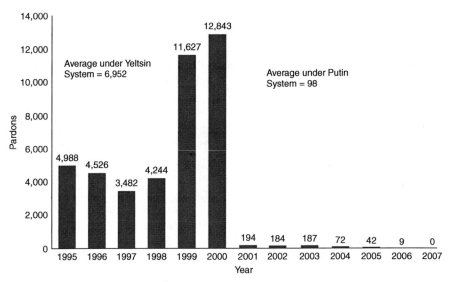

FIGURE 6.5. Annual number of pardons, 1995–2007.

the pardon involved a reduction in sentence rather than immediate freedom. However, power ministry personnel never trusted the Commission. During Yeltsin's second term, they successfully lobbied to include siloviki representatives from the MVD and the Federal Penitentiary Service. In 2001, Putin abolished the Commission and replaced it with a commission in every region. These regional commissions often included civil society representatives, such as NGO activists and journalists. For example, in St. Petersburg, the well-known crime journalist Andrey Konstantinov was a member for several years. Some members of regional commissions saw the new process as more democratic than under Yeltsin because of its decentralized nature. However, it quickly became apparent that these regional commissions were what one human rights activist called a "Potemkin village." This was because the regional commissions did not have final say; their recommendations were passed first to the governor and then to the presidential administration. Almost all pardon appeals were rejected at the national level. After two years, Konstantinov resigned because it became obvious that the regional commissions had no influence. The drastic change from Yeltsin to Putin can be seen in Figure 6.5, which shows the number of pardons from 1995 to 2007.[84]

As the figure shows, the average number of pardons per year from 1995 to 2001 under the Pristavkin Commission was nearly 7,000. Under the regional system created by Putin, the national average for pardons approved was less

[84] Interview P-2; Interview N-12; Interview M-3. A complete account of the change from Yeltsin to Putin is in: Irina Gordiyenko, "Ne ver', ne boysya, ne prosi," *Nov. Gaz.*, June 30, 2008. Data from: "Iz zhizn' otbyvayushchikh," *K-V*, June 30, 2008.

than 100. In Putin's last full year as president, 2007, not a single pardon was approved by the presidential administration. Given that the acquittal rate for judge-only trials in Russia is around 1 percent (the acquittal rate in jury trials is around 15–20 percent), pardons under Yeltsin were an important mechanism for correcting judicial mistakes. Not surprisingly, the change in practice has drastically decreased prisoner appeals, since the prospects of a positive decision at the national level are so low.[85] The changing practice of pardon commissions under Putin is one example of how civil society oversight of the law enforcement system, although theoretically welcomed, in practice was severely limited.

In Putin's second term, he and his allies began to stress, as he stated in 2004, that although civil society was a good thing, some NGOs were not working for the "real interests of people" but were more interested in getting support from "influential foreign foundations" or "serving doubtful group or commercial interests." FSB head Patrushev stated in 2005 that some NGOs were "conducting intelligence operations under the guise of charity." In 2007, Putin denounced forces inside Russia who are "jackals," seeking the support of "foreign foundations and governments."[86]

Observers traced the harsher attitude toward NGOs, particularly those whose activities were more political, to a Russian government overreaction to the so-called "colored revolutions" that took place in Georgia, Ukraine, and Kyrgyzstan in 2003–2005. These events were interpreted by some Kremlin officials and advisers as being orchestrated by foreign governments, foundations, and NGOs.[87] A prominent act symbolizing the new, harsh line was the January 2006 accusation by the FSB that four British embassy employees were spies who had used a fake high-tech "rock" to exchange information with their Russian informants. One of the accused was responsible for overseeing grants to a variety of Russian NGOs; human rights activists believed the scandal was an attempt by the FSB to smear NGOs who received

[85] Gordiyenko 2008. Acquittal date from: Peter H. Solomon, Jr., "Assessing the Courts in Russia: Parameters of Progress under Putin," *Demokratizatsiya*, 16, 1 (Winter 2008), p. 68.

[86] Vladimir Putin, "Poslaniye Federal'nomu Sobraniyu Rossiyskoy Federatsii," May 26, 2004; Fred Weir, "Russian government sets sights on 'subversion'," *Christian Science Monitor*, June 1, 2005; Vladimir Putin, "Vystupleniye na forume storonnikov Prezidenta Rossii," November 21, 2007.

[87] Human Rights Watch, *Choking on Bureaucracy: State Curbs on Independent Civil Society Activism*, February 2008, pp. 13–14; Thomas Carothers, "The Backlash Against Democracy Promotion," *Foreign Affairs*, 85, 2 (March/April 2006), pp. 55–68. For a careful analysis of the relative contribution of foreign ideational and material support to the Orange Revolution, see: Michael McFaul, "Ukraine Imports Democracy: External Influences on the Orange Revolution," *International Security*, 32, 2 (Fall 2007), pp. 45–83. On colored revolutions more generally, see, for example: Mark R. Beissinger, "Structure and Example in Modular Political Phenomena: The Diffusion of Bulldozer/Rose/Orange/Tulip Revolutions," *Perspectives on Politics*, 5, 2 (June 2007), pp. 259–276; Henry E. Hale, "Democracy or Autocracy on the March? The Colored Revolutions as Normal Dynamics of Patronal Presidentialism," *Communist and Post-Communist Studies*, 39, 3 (September 2006), pp. 305–329.

foreign funding. The accusations received prominent coverage in the Russian press.[88]

Legislation passed in 2006 substantially increased the reporting and registration burdens for NGOs and gave the state considerable authority and discretion to investigate and shut down NGOs for violations of this law. A Communist Party Deputy who opposed the legislation, Oleg Smolin, contended, "instead of reinforcing civil society's control over the bureaucracy, this reinforces the bureaucracy's control over civil society." A detailed analysis by Human Rights Watch on the effect of the legislation two years later showed that NGOs that received foreign funding or that worked in the human rights sector were particularly likely to be investigated for violations of the law. Law enforcement organs, including the police, the procuracy, and the FSB, were often involved in these efforts.[89]

This apparent state pressure on NGOs in the human rights realm appeared to be particularly pronounced toward the end of Putin's second term, 2006–2008. For example, one of the groups profiled in this chapter, Citizen's Watch, was subjected to a detailed two-month inspection in 2007 by the Federal Registration Service (FRS, part of the Ministry of Justice) and was accused of violating several laws. The FRS claimed, for example, that by listing its supporters on its publications, Citizens' Watch was providing commercial advertising for these organizations and needed to pay taxes on these grants, since this was not charitable activity. As part of the inspection, the FRS ordered Citizens' Watch to produce all written correspondence outside the organization, including e-mail, for a three-year period from July 2004 to July 2007. Citizen's Watch went to court against the FRS in 2008, but later that year, the FSR backed off. Pustyntsev attributed the change at least in part to his membership on the Presidential Council for Facilitating the Development of Civil Society Institutions and Human Rights, where he was able to confront the deputy head of the FRS about the matter.[90]

The Citizens' Watch case was not an isolated incident, and sometimes law enforcement harassment of NGOs reached absurd levels. For example, in Novorossiysk in 2007, several human rights activists from a local NGO were fined for holding an "unsanctioned meeting," which involved a small-group conversation over tea in an elementary school with several visitors from Germany.[91]

---

[88] Julie A. Corwin, "'Spy-Rock' Scandal Has NGOs Worried," *RFE/RL*, January 24, 2006.

[89] AFP, "Russian Parliament Passes Controversial Bill Restricting NGOs," December 23, 2005 [JRL #9326, December 23, 2005]; Human Rights Watch 2008; Nikolaus von Twickel, "NGOs Buried by Mountain of Paper," *MT*, August 24, 2007; Robert W. Orttung, "Russia," in Freedom House, *Nations in Transit* 2007 (Washington, DC: Freedom House, 2007), pp. 341–343.

[90] Interview P-8; Human Rights Watch 2008; von Twickel 2007; "Petersburgskiy pravozashchitnik Boris Pustyntsev v programme Viktora Rezunkova: nuzhno li vesti dialog s vlast'yu," March 4, 2009, at: http://www.sovetpamfilova.ru/mvd/publ_mvd/1569

[91] Sergey Perov, "Kriminal'noye chayepitiye," *NI*, February 26, 2007; Sergey Perov, "Vsemirnoye chayepitiye protesta," *NI*, April 2, 2007.

Although the reaction to the colored revolutions certainly played an important role in the NGO crackdown in Putin's second term, perhaps more fundamental was Putin's basic conception of the proper relationship between civil
society and the state. This concept was variously described as "managed civil
society," "quasi-civil society," or "pseudo-civil society," in which NGOs and
other social groups were expected to assist the state in pursuing goals set
by the country's leadership.[92] One of Russia's most prominent human rights
activists and a former dissident from the Soviet period, Lyudmila Alekseyeva,
denounced this approach in 2005:

There has been this idea to organize civil society, which has already developed in our
country, according to this vertical of power. But this is a crazy idea. As soon as you
organize civil society into this vertical of power, it stops being civil society. It becomes
a pathetic appendage of the government. And it is destroyed.[93]

This approach to state-civil society relations was evident in the creation
of the Public Chamber in 2005. The Public Chamber is a consultative organ
of 126 members; 42 members are appointed by the president, these 42 members choose another 42, and then these 84 choose the last 42 members. The
Chamber was billed as another oversight mechanism to monitor state bodies
and to serve as an intermediary between the state and society. One of its functions has been to distribute state money to NGOs, and in 2007, it distributed
more than $50 million worth of grants to a wide variety of NGOs. Indeed, in
2005, Putin suggested that NGOs would be better off taking money from the
state than dubious foreign organizations, and the state is now the main source
of funding for Russian NGOs.[94]

In principle, greater internal support for NGOs, both public and private,
would be in the long-run interest of civil society and would reduce the pathologies associated with heavy foreign funding, such as weak grassroots and
a greater orientation to external rather than internal priorities.[95] However,
groups that are critical of the state face serious obstacles to finding substitute
domestic sources of funding, because wealthy corporations and individuals
prefer to limit their charitable giving to noncontroversial causes.[96]

In the law enforcement sphere, the Public Chamber, like the Ombudsman,
received reports and complaints about law enforcement activity and pres-
sured these agencies to investigate these complaints. The Public Chamber also

---

[92] Human Rights Watch 2008, p. 10; Alfred B. Evans, Jr., "Vladimir Putin's Design for Civil
Society," in Evans, Henry, and Sundstrom 2006, pp. 147–158.

[93] Jeremy Bransten, "Public Chamber Criticized as 'Smokescreen'," *RFE/RL Russian Political
Weekly*, 5, 13 (April 1, 2005).

[94] Human Rights Watch 2008, pp. 21–22; Interfax, "Rights NGO Says It Receives No State
Funding," November 19, 2007 [JRL #239 2007, November 19]; "NGOs Feel Squeeze as
Western Grants Dry Up," *RFE/RL Newsline*, 12, 11 (January 16, 2008); "Stenografichsekiy
otchet o zasedanii Soveta po sodeystviyu razvitiyu institutov grazhdanskogo obshchestva i
pravam cheloveka," *kremlin.ru*, July 20, 2005.

[95] See note 74 in this chapter.

[96] Human Rights Watch 2008, pp. 19–20.

worked, at the direction of Putin, to create "public councils" attached to the main power ministries, including the Ministry of Defense, the MVD, the FSB, and MChS. Putin had argued for greater public oversight of the power ministries after the September 2004 Beslan terrorist incident.[97]

At the time of Putin's 2006 decree on creating public councils in the power ministries, representatives of some of Russia's most prominent human rights NGOs expressed skepticism that these bodies would have sufficient independence and authority. For example, Lev Levinson of the Institute of Human Rights said that the decree "depreciates the role of civil society in the country," predicting that only "good NGOs" would be represented, and that their representatives would "nod obediently and give the appearance of human rights activity." Although not opposed to public councils in principle, the top-down nature of their creation made some activists wary. Others adopted a wait-and-see attitude, arguing that much depended on how the minister of any particular agency worked with the body.[98]

The MVD created a Public Council in late 2006, which began its activities in 2007. The MVD Public Council is an advisory body that can make recommendations to the Ministry. Its major priorities include defending citizens' rights, supporting state internal affairs policy, and "raising the authority and prestige of internal affairs organs." Forty-three members were appointed to the MVD Public Council in 2007, for two-year terms. The largest contingents were religious figures (nine), cultural notables (nine), and journalists (seven).[99]

The 2007–2008 MVD Public Council had three members from NGOs, and the identity of these three individuals suggested that the fears of human rights critics were at least partially correct. The oldest and best-known human rights NGOs were not represented on the council, and two of the three NGO members, Olga Kostina and Vladimir Khimanych, headed NGOs created in 2004 or 2005. Kostina's NGO in particular has raised eyebrows among the traditional NGO community. Kostina was a key witness in the Yukos affair against the head of Yukos security Aleksey Pichugin and top Yukos executive Leonid Nezvlin, accusing them of trying to kill her in the late 1990s. In 2005, Kostina cofounded the NGO "Soprotivleniye" (Resistance) as a victims'

[97] Interfax, "Press Conference with Public Chamber Secretary Yevgeny Velikhov," January 22, 2007 [JRL 2007-#18, January 25]; "Ukaz Prezidenta Rossiyskoy Federatsii ot 4 Avgusta 2006 goda N 842 'O poryadke obrazovaniya obshchestvennykh sovetov pri federal'nykh ministerstvakh ...'," August 4, 2006; Vladimir Putin, "Vystupleniye na rasshirennom zasedanii Pravitel'stva s uchastiyem glav sub"ektov Rossiyskoy Federatsii," September 13, 2004.

[98] Irina Nagornykh and Andrey Kozenko, "Silovikov otpravili v palatu," *K-D*, August 7, 2006; Natal'ya Kostenko, "Palatki dlya ministrov," *Nez. Gaz.*, August 7, 2006; Oksana Yablokova, "Citizens to Gauge Power Ministries," *MT*, August 8, 2006.

[99] "Polozhenie ob Obshchestvennom sovete pri Ministerstve vnutrennikh del Rossiyskoy Federatsii," December 14, 2006; "Reglament Obshchestvennogo soveta pri Ministerstve vnutrennikh del Rossiyskoy Federatsii," n.d.; "Sostav Obshchestvennogo soveta pri Ministerstve vnutrennikh del Rossiyskoy Federatsii," n.d. All documents on the MVD Public Council are from the MVD website: http://www.mvd.ru/about/sovet/

rights organization. Soprotivleniye quickly received state grants, as well as support from big business. Press accounts also noted that she served on an advisory council at the FSB and that her husband was a top official in the pro-Putin United Russia party. Top human rights activists labeled Soprotivleniye a GONGO – a government-organized NGO.[100]

Khimanych's organization, although relatively new, also quickly received grants from the state in recent competitions. On the Public Council, Khimanych often sought to justify poor police practices. For example, in 2007, Khimanych argued that the media focused too much on illegal activity by the traffic police without mentioning the many bad drivers on the roads, and stated that many accusations against the traffic police are without basis because citizens do not understand the law. It was left to Minister Nurgaliyev to note that many of the objections to the work of the traffic police are both serious and objectively based, and that the quality of cadres is low, with little experience or legal education. In another case, Khimanych dismissed the results of an NGO monitoring of document checks in the Moscow metro, which found that more than half of those stopped by the police were ethnic minorities; Khimanych said this was understandable, because the police stop people suspected of crimes, and Slavs are much less likely than people from the Caucasus or Asia to be criminal suspects.[101]

Given that the MVD Public Council only started to function in 2007, it is too early to say whether its effect will be positive, negative, or irrelevant to the work of the police. The Public Council only met twice during its first year of existence and can only make recommendations, so it is unlikely to have a major impact, but it could help focus a spotlight on issues of police quality. Its 2007 sessions, however, suggested that public relations was a higher priority. For example, at its first meeting, Minister Nurgaliyev singled out the "tendentious" approach of some media outlets toward the police and called for greater efforts to encourage a more "objective approach." Similarly, the secretary of the Public Council stated that a top priority was support of films, books, and shows that would help "create a positive image" of the police.[102] It is doubtful, however, that a more positive portrayal of the police on television will raise the image of the police if people still continue to experience regular predation and

---

[100] http://www.soprotivlenie.org/; Liliya Mukhamed'yarova, "N'yu-pravozashchitniki sygrayut v gongo," *Nez. Gaz.*, July 20, 2005; "Vse v Rossii zavisit ot interpretatsii ...," *Marketing i konsalting*, July 25, 2005; Interview P-8. On Kostina's testimony in the Yukos affair, see: Igor' Kovalevskiy, "Neustanovlennye litsa Genprokuratury," *Nov. Gaz.*, October 4, 2004.

[101] "Protokol zasedaniya Obshchestvennogo soveta pri Ministerstve vnutrennikh del Rossiyskoy Federatsii ot 3 sentyabrya 2007 g. No 2"; Valeriy Gorbachev, "Militsiyu opyat' obvinili v predvzyatosti," *MN*, June 16, 2006. See also the comments of Khimanych and Andrey Babushkin at: "Prestupleniye i nakazaniye: kto i ot kogo zashchishchayet rossi-yan," *EM*, November 20, 2007. The study of ethnic profiling in the metro was discussed in Chapter 5.

[102] "Protokol zasedaniya Obshchestvennogo soveta pri Ministerstve vnutrennikh del Rossiyskoy Federatsii ot 11 maya 2007 g. No 1"; "Protokol zasedaniya Obshchestvennogo soveta pri Ministerstve vnutrennikh del Rossiyskoy Federatsii ot 3 sentyabrya 2007 g. No 2."

corruption. As the survey data discussed in this and the last chapter suggest, people's attitudes toward the police have been quite consistent throughout the post-Soviet period. Two NGO experts on the police saw the Public Council as not particularly effective, with Andrey Babushkin as the sole legitimate NGO representative on the council and thus a "decorative figure."[103]

Developments at the regional and local level will probably be more important for societal monitoring of law enforcement than public councils at the national level. One potentially positive impact of the creation of national public councils was that it seemed to accelerate the creation of public councils at the regional level. This institution had long been pushed by activists such as Pustyntsev, and some regions had created them before Putin's 2006 decree on public councils, but this push from the top encouraged other regions to follow suit. By March 2008, at least seventeen of Russia's eighty-four regions had UVD Public Councils.

Much will depend on how these public councils are created and organized at the regional level, and what responsibilities they have. In the last years of Putin's presidency, there was considerable variance in how much they were open to real civil society input, with some serving as a real forum for state-society interaction and others at best acting as window dressing. In some regions, these public councils were created before the national one and already have a history of serious work. In the Republic of Mariy El, a public council was established in 2005 in which the deputy head of the council was the head of a local human rights organization, Man and Law, that just six months before had released a report on police torture. Nonetheless, Man and Law developed good relations with the Republic MVD and carried out multiple Civil Society III projects. For example, NGO representatives and police officials conducted joint inspections of pretrial detention centers, which have long been infamous in Russia for their brutal conditions. A brochure prepared by Man and Law on detainee rights was made available at pretrial detention centers in the republic. Man and Law also conducted legal and human rights training for police officers. MVD Head Nurgaliyev pointed to Mariy El as a good example of positive police-civil society interaction.[104]

[103] Interview M-21. Babushkin, sometimes in cooperation with Khimanych, was involved in several Civil Society III projects that engaged the police about issues such as police ethics. He wrote a brochure for ordinary cops on human rights that addressed such questions as the circumstances under which document checks are legal, and whether Russian citizens or foreigners are required by law to carry passports with them (no in both cases). See: Il'ya Vasyunin, "Militsiya ob"edinilas' s pravozashchitnikami," *Nov. Gaz.*, December 1, 2005; Rustam Taktashev, "Militsionerov prizvali soblyudat' prava cheloveka," *Gazeta*, October 10, 2007; A. Babushkin, "Sotrudniku militsii – o pravakh cheloveka," January 2008 [http://www.zagr.org/133.html].

[104] Inna Biletskaya, "Marii El Group Exposes Police Abuse," *RRR*, 10, 1 (January 14, 2005); "Marii El Police Establish Social Council," *RRR*, 10, 9 (May 23, 2005); "Pravozashchitniki Marii El posetili izolyator vremennogo soderzhaniya Gornomariyskogo rayona," http://mvd.gov12.ru/, March 30, 2007; "25 marta sostoyalsya seminar Regional'noy obshchestvennoy organizatsii 'chelovek i zakon' s sotrudnikami OGIBDD OVD po munitsial'nym obrazovaniyam," http://mvd.gov12.ru/, March 28, 2008; Tverdov 2008.

In other regions, the public councils, created after a push from Moscow, seemed to be more pro forma organizations. This included the Public Council for the St. Petersburg and Leningrad Oblast GUVD. Pustyntsev was asked to serve on the council, something he had championed for many years, but he refused once he saw the list of members. Of the forty-one proposed members, there were only two from NGOs, and he saw himself as the only well-known human rights figure. Many of the members were from medium and large businesses, the media, or were well-known cultural figures. Examples from the latter category included Valeriy Gergiyev, the internationally renowned director of the Mariinsky Theater, Mikhail Piotrovskiy, the director of the Hermitage Museum, and the captain of the Russian national soccer team, Andrey Arshavin, one of the stars of the 2008 European Cup. "What would I do there?" asked Pustyntsev. He saw the appointment of business figures to the council as a cynical attempt by the police to "solve their problems," that is, garner private financing for the police.[105]

Pustyntsev's refusal to participate in what he saw as a charade may, however, have been a mistake and seemed inconsistent with his years of efforts to work with law enforcement structures, no matter what the obstacles. In other regions, figures from human rights NGOs reportedly were influential in these councils. For example, in Nizhniy Novgorod, the head of the "Committee Against Torture" served on the public council with multiple high-ranking police officials, where reportedly he would "orate" at them and they would feel compelled to react to his complaints. Olga Shepeleva and Asmik Novikova of the "Demos" NGO maintained that in some regions, human rights activists had been able to use the UVD public councils to push their agenda, and that results varied much by region, and Pustyntsev agreed with this view.[106]

On the other hand, Pustyntsev was right that in some cases, the councils appeared to be window dressing, with little NGO participation and a mission and agenda that mimicked that of the Public Council of the central MVD. Deputy Minister of Internal Affairs N.A. Ovchinnikov, at the first meeting of the national MVD Public Council, stated that one of the goals of forming the council was to "raise the role of the Ministry in forming civil society." Similarly, one of the stated goals of the 2008 Nizhniy Novgorod MVD Public Council was to "strengthen the participation of internal affairs organs in the formation of a democratic state and civil society."[107] These statements seemed to have the goal of public councils exactly backward, in that civil society should participate in monitoring the police rather than the police building civil society.

---

[105] Interview P-8.

[106] "V Obshchestvennyy sovet pri GUVD Nizhegorodskoy oblasti voydut v osnovnom 'siloviki'," *Komitet protiv pytok*, June 17, 2005 [http://www.pytkam.net/web/]; Interview M-21; Interview P-8.

[107] "V GUVD po Sverdlovskoy oblasti sostoyalos' pervoye zasedaniye Obshchestvennogo Soveta," http://www.mvd.ru, March 4, 2008; "Protokol zasedaniya Obshchestvennogo soveta pri Ministerstve vnutrennikh del Rossiyskoy Federatsii ot 11 maya 2007 g. No 1"; "V GUVD po Nizhegorodskoy oblasti sostoyalos' zasedaniye Obshchestvennogo Soveta," http://www.mvd.ru, March 28, 2008.

In the worst-case scenario, then, public councils in the power structures will act more as Leninist "transmission belts" for conveying state policy to the masses than as an independent form of public oversight and accountability.[108] They would be one element of a pseudo-civil society that existed as a "pathetic appendage" of the state while simultaneously choking off truly independent organizations; "good NGOs" could work on state money for state priorities, and "bad NGOs" would be harassed and marginalized. More neutrally, they could just be a form of window dressing that will have no impact either way. In the most optimistic scenario, over time, they could become effective mechanisms for state-society interaction and a means for encouraging more liberal norms and more rational-legal bureaucratic practices. At this point, it is simply too early to tell, and there will probably be considerable variation around the country.[109] What should be clear is that these public councils are in no way comparable to civilian review boards in countries like the United States, United Kingdom, and Canada. Civilian review boards are quite intrusive forms of monitoring in which individual cases of police misbehavior can, in some instances, be investigated and punished by civilians independent from, and external to, the police. They also fall far short of the "specialized, independent oversight of the police" that, David Bayley argues, is essential to making the police more democratic and accountable.[110]

Ultimately, the problem with pseudo-civil society organizations like the Public Chamber and power ministry public councils was not so much any harm they created directly, but that they seemed to be what Nikolay Petrov labeled "substitute institutions," designed to take the place of more independent civil society organizations and more publicly accountable state institutions. For example, the creation of the Public Chamber coincided with the growing irrelevance of the State Duma, dominated by United Russia and rapidly becoming, as Speaker Boris Gryzlov put it in 2005, "not a place for discussion." Duma member Gennadiy Gudkov noted in August 2006, when Putin decreed the creation of power ministry public councils, that the first priority should be the establishment of meaningful parliamentary control, and that these new forms of citizens' control, although "better than nothing," were not an adequate substitute. In other comments, however, Gudkov stated his opposition to any

---

[108] On public organizations in the Soviet period as "transmission belts" (Lenin's description of the role of trade unions), see: Alfred B. Evans Jr., "Civil Society in the Soviet Union?" in Evans, Henry, and Sundstrom 2006, pp. 28–54.

[109] There is also variation over time and across organization. For example, the Public Council of the Federal Penitentiary Service when it was under the Ministry of Justice had multiple well-known human rights figures on it, but the new public council after it was reformed as an independent agency had no such prominent people: Interview M-3; Interview M-21. In 2008, a top prison official wrote an article denouncing human rights activists in Russia working on prison issues for living the "good life" on money from "generous foreigners": Yuriy Aleksandrov, "Besovstvo," *Otechestvennye zapiski*, 2, 41 (2008).

[110] David H. Bayley and Clifford D. Shearing, "The Future of Policing," in Tim Newburn, ed., *Policing: Key Readings* (Cullopton, Devon, UK: Willan Publishing, 2005), p. 720; Bayley 2006, pp. 52–54.

public oversight of law enforcement, maintaining that "everything related to the methods of fighting crime should remain closed to the public."[111]

The weakening of the Duma was another piece of the general effort under Putin to undermine checks on the presidency and the executive branch. Overall there was a significant decline in state accountability during Putin's presidency. In a seminal article, Guillermo O'Donnell noted that accountability in a democracy comes in two basic forms – vertical and horizontal. Vertical accountability is that of the state to society – most directly that of state officials to voters, but also to non-state actors from civil society. NGOs and the media, for example, are also components of vertical accountability. Horizontal accountability refers to the accountability of state agents to other state agents. Note that horizontal accountability is different than either the separation of powers or checks and balances, because horizontal accountability involves, according to O'Donnell, the ability to formally sanction. Charles Kenney points out that although the separation of powers, checks and balances, and horizontal accountability are all forms of limiting state power and checking tyranny, they are analytically distinct.[112]

The World Bank in its Worldwide Governance Indicators (WGI) project measures what O'Donnell calls vertical accountability in its "Voice and Accountability" measure. Voice and Accountability is defined as "the extent to which a country's citizens are able to participate in selecting their government, as well as freedom of expression, freedom of association, and a free media." Given this definition and the nature of the separate components that make up the WGI scores for Voice and Accountability, this measure has been used by some as a measure of the extent of democracy in a country.[113] Figure 6.6 shows Russia's performance in this WGI category from 1996 to 2007.

Russia's performance on Voice and Accountability under Putin shows the most marked deterioration of any of the WGI categories. After a noticeable increase in 2002 to the fortieth percentile of all countries in the world, starting in 2003, this score declined every year and was down to the twentieth percentile by 2007. Under Yeltsin, Russia consistently scored around 32–33 percent.

---

[111] Nikolay Petrov, "Substituty institutov," *Otechestvennye zapiski*, 6, 40 (2007); Nabi Abdullaev, "Elections to Deliver Duller Deputies," *MT*, November 26, 2007; Kostenko 2006; Nabi Abdullaev, "Journalist Enjoying a Security Monopoly," *MT*, June 18, 2008. See also: Thomas F. Remington, "Putin, the Parliament, and the Party System," in Herspring 2007, pp. 67–71. For an early assessment of the Public Chamber and how it fit into Putin's hierarchical conception of state-society relations, see: James Richter, "Putin and the Public Chamber," *Post-Soviet Affairs*, 25, 1 (2009), pp. 39–65.

[112] Guillermo O'Donnell, "Horizontal Accountability in New Democracies," *Journal of Democracy*, 9 (1998), pp. 112–128; Andreas Schedler, Larry Diamond, and Marc F. Plattner, *The Self-restraining State: Power and Accountability in New Democracies* (Boulder, CO: Lynne Rienner, 1999); Charles D. Kenney, "Horizontal Accountability: Concepts and Conflicts," in Scott Mainwaring and Chris Welna, eds., *Democratic Accountability in Latin America* (Oxford: Oxford University Press, 2003), pp. 55–76.

[113] Using WGI Voice and Accountability scores as a democracy measure is, for example: Fish 2005, pp. 21–22.

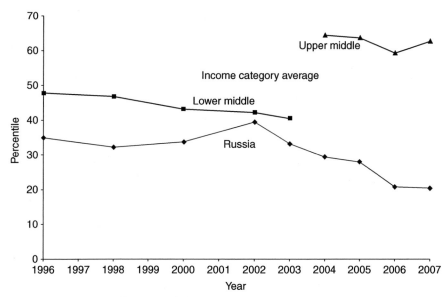

FIGURE 6.6. Voice and accountability (WGI).

The significant drop under Putin is particularly noticeable when Russia is compared to its income category peers; as Russia got wealthier and moved into the upper-middle income category, the degree of vertical accountability, judging by WGI scores, was deteriorating markedly. By the end of Putin's presidency, Russia lagged well behind its peers with similar levels of wealth.

This decline in vertical accountability was reflected in multiple ways, including the decline in freedom and fairness in Russian elections, the weakening of independent media, especially television, and the civil society crackdown described earlier.[114] What O'Donnell calls vertical accountability is what I have described as "fire alarms," when non-state actors in the media or civil society raise the alarm about problems in state quality. By weakening these fire alarms, Putin deprived himself of an effective mechanism for policing the behavior of state agents. Further, he also undermined the types of horizontal accountability described by O'Donnell, such as legislatures, courts, and independent prosecutors or ombudsmen with the power to bring executive branch figures to account and sanction them for illegal behavior.

Instead, Putin tried to use internal police patrols, such as the FSB and the General Procuracy, to monitor and punish corruption and other forms of low-quality behavior by state officials. After the 2004 Beslan terrorist incident, a government commission was set up to reexamine forms of control over the

---

[114] On widespread and increasing electoral fraud under Putin, see: Mikhail Myagkov, Peter C. Ordeshook, and Dimitri Shakin, *The Forensics of Election Fraud: Russia and Ukraine* (Cambridge: Cambridge University Press, 2009), pp. 1–11, 71–137.

power ministries. The commission emphasized the strengthening of internal "police patrols," by which the FSB would check up on the MVD, and the MVD would monitor the FSB. Raising the autonomy of the procuracy investigative committee was also proposed by this commission as a way of separating the oversight and investigative functions within the procuracy; this reform was implemented in 2007. Police experts noted that the main form of control over police behavior was from within the MVD itself, with the procuracy also having secondary control functions. These forms of internal control were regarded as ineffective. The system of control over the police is not oriented toward citizens or, to put it differently, toward external "fire alarms."[115]

Given the problems within law enforcement agencies in terms of adherence to the law, corruption, and their connections to various economic and political clans, they generally have not been effective monitors over poor quality work. Of course, there are occasional press accounts about FSB "stings" ensnaring corrupt police officials for taking bribes or "roofing," but there has been no systematic evidence of less corruption in the law enforcement sphere.[116] It is not that police patrols are never effective; it is that they are less effective than fire alarms. This is especially true because a reliance on police patrols raises Juvenal's classic dilemma – who is to guard the guardians? Moreover, the power ministries are subject to direction from the Kremlin in their monitoring activities. Instead of serving as objective and aggressive monitors of law breaking and corruption, the FSB and procuracy were more likely to be used as a club to hit regime opponents; to extend the metaphor, the "police" patrolled in some neighborhoods but not in others.

Russia's poor performance in voice and accountability, then, is directly connected to similarly weak efforts in promoting the rule of law and control of corruption. Despite Putin's consistent rhetoric about respect for the law and the need to target corruption, he undermined many of the most effective tools for fighting it. Susan Rose-Ackerman contends that autocratic anticorruption campaigns are inherently fragile. Particularly in situations in which corruption is pervasive, she notes, civil service reform alone is not enough – public accountability must be increased. Governments that resist restraints on their power and cripple independent monitoring by the media and civil society undermine accountability. She concludes, "governments that make it very difficult for independent voices to be raised in criticism … will have an especially difficult time establishing a credible commitment to honest and transparent government." More specifically, a cross-national study of efforts to fight police

---

[115] Marina Saydukova, "Pravitel'stvennykh silovikov ozhidayet novaya reforma," *Nez. Gaz.*, July 20, 2005; Ol'ga Shepeleva and Asmik Novikova, "Osnovnye problemy sovremennoy militsii," in Demos, *Reforma pravookhranitel'nikh organov: preodoleniye proizvola* (Moskva: Demos, 2005), pp. 63–64; V.L. Rimskiy, "Predstavleniya intervyuiruyemykh o vozmozhnosti pridaniya rossiyskim pravookhranitel'nym organam sotsial'no oriyentirovannykh kachestv," in Demos 2005, p. 404.

[116] See, for example: Aleksandr Zheglov, "Militsionera vzyali za gastarbayterov," *K-D*, June 28, 2008.

corruption in twenty-five countries found that these endeavors cannot succeed without support and cooperation from the public.[117]

Scholars of post-communist transition have argued that there is a clear connection between political competition, especially between strong parties, and successful state building. State building here refers to both attempts to replace patrimonial bureaucratic practices with rational-legal ones, and efforts to fight corruption.[118] By any reasonable measure, Russia would have to be rated low both in terms of robust party competition and the building of a state with low patrimonialism and corruption – central parts of what I call state quality. More generally, the key mechanisms of horizontal accountability – a strong legislature with meaningful powers of oversight and sanction and independent courts and prosecutors – are absent in Russia.

CONCLUSION

Russian society does not trust the Russian state. This is particularly true in terms of law enforcement. This lack of trust did not change during the Putin presidency, despite his own personal popularity and the improved economic situation. This lack of trust, even fear, toward law enforcement in general and the police in particular is a direct reflection of the poor work of these agencies. This poor performance also affects the capacity of the power ministries. Comparative evidence suggests that police performance is enhanced when the public trusts them and is willing to engage with them. But this trust has to be earned. Russia is currently trapped in a vicious circle in which poor state quality leads to popular distrust, and popular distrust makes good policing even harder. Ted Gerber and Sarah Mendelson believe that poor police performance has wide-ranging negative consequences: "because they [the police] directly hurt rather than protect the individual security of Russian citizens, they do more to undermine democracy and civil society than any other institution."[119]

Arguably Gerber and Mendelson go too far – in Russia's hyperpresidential system, the presidency has the greatest effect on the development of democracy and civil society. And Vladimir Putin's presidency was bad for both democracy and civil society, as WGI Voice and Accountability scores indicate. Rhetoric about the importance of democracy, the rule of law, civil society, and a free

---

[117] Susan Rose-Ackerman, *Corruption and Government: Causes, Consequences, and Reform* (Cambridge: Cambridge University Press, 1999), pp. 209, 84, 162–174, 229 (quote p. 229); Pavol Fric and Czeslaw Walek, *Crossing the thin blue line: An international annual review of anti-corruption strategies in the police* (Prague: Transparency International CR, 2001), p. 29.

[118] Anna Grzymala-Busse, *Rebuilding Leviathan: Party Competition and State Exploitation in Post-Communist* Democracies (Cambridge: Cambridge University Press, 2007); Conor O'Dwyer, *Runaway State-Building: Patronage Politics and Democratic Development* (Baltimore: The Johns Hopkins University Press, 2006).

[119] Gerber and Mendelson 2008, p. 37.

press was matched by practical steps that undermined all of these things. The ultimate result, in the words of Andrey Soldatov, one of Russia's leading independent experts on the power ministries, is that since Putin became president, "the special services have grown increasingly secretive and powerful, making any idea of outside control impossible."[120]

In the civil society realm, Putin's efforts at their most generous can be characterized as an attempt to create civil society from above. One NGO activist from Novosibirsk, generally positively disposed toward Putin, labeled this "Putin's biggest mistake," stating that only activity from below can create a real civil society.[121] In the law enforcement realm, there are multiple NGOs all over Russia working both to serve as watchdogs that monitor the state (Civil Society II) and partners of the state that seek to spread more liberal norms among state personnel (Civil Society III). NGO legislation adopted in Putin's second term seemed designed to harass and cripple the monitors and constrain even those willing to partner with the state unless they worked for state-designated goals on government money. If the "weak state – weak society" model of the Yeltsin years was problematic, under Putin, there was no movement toward a "strong state – strong society" model that would yield better results. Instead, the ideology of "sovereign democracy" led to greater suspicion of NGO activity designed to either balance the state or teach it a new set of values.[122]

In Putin's state-building project, external "police patrol" monitors, such as the media and NGOs, were weakened, apparently viewed more as a threat to state power than the asset they can be. Instead, in Putin's vision, internal "police patrols" by other law enforcement agencies, like the FSB and the procuracy, were supposed to fight corruption and uphold the law. Putin's plan seemed based on a nostalgic vision of incorruptible Chekists, ignoring the overwhelming evidence that many personnel in the Russian power ministries work for their own interests and not those of the state or society.[123] The more difficult environment for reform-minded NGOs helped those state officials who benefited from the patrimonial and corrupt nature of the Russian bureaucracy. Putin's reliance on internal monitoring to build state quality failed, and

---

[120] Abdullaev 2008.

[121] Interview N-12.

[122] Some experts viewed developments under Putin in the civil society realm more positively than I do here. At least in the law enforcement realm, the available evidence suggests a considerably more difficult environment in Putin's second term than previously was the case, although many NGOs continued to work hard to make use of available channels to seek influence and public oversight. For the more positive interpretation, see, for example: Debra Javeline and Sarah Lindemann-Komarova, "How We Assess Civil Society Developments: The Russia Example," *PONARS Eurasia Policy Memo*, 34 (August 2008). My views are closer to those in: James Richter, "Civil Society in the New Authoritarianism," *PONARS Eurasia Policy Memo*, 35 (August 2008).

[123] This vision of incorruptible Chekists is best reflected in two well-known articles by Viktor Cherkesov; see Chapter 2.

the performance of Russia's power ministries did not improve much during his tenure.

Russian state law enforcement bodies are not subject to adequate external monitoring. The weakness of these "fire alarms" hurts efforts to build state quality. As Russian policing experts Adrian Beck and Annette Robertson argued in 2005, "without some form of external oversight, it is difficult to see how the Russian militia can break out of the cycle of corruption in which it appears to be caught."[124]

Vicious cycles are, by definition, hard to break out of. One Russian police colonel contended that it would take 10–30 years to improve popular trust in the police. Most important, according to this officer, is recruiting a new generation of cadres with a new system of education and a new set of values.[125] Time is an indispensible element of state building, but the right strategy is also essential. To get new cadres with new values that citizens trust, the Russian state needs to change its dominant bureaucratic practices from patrimonial to rational-legal, open itself up to effective external monitors, and develop a new sense of mission.

[124] Adrian Beck and Annette Robertson, "Policing in Post-Soviet Russia," in William Alex Pridemore, ed., *Ruling Russia: Law, Crime, and Justice in a Changing Society* (Lanham, MD: Rowman & Littlefield, 2005), p. 256.
[125] Interview M-46.

7

Coercion in the North Caucasus

> My mission, my historic mission – it sounds pompous, but it is true – is to resolve the situation in the North Caucasus.
>
> Vladimir Putin[1]

The power ministries have been central to state building throughout Russia, but nowhere have their activities been more important than in the North Caucasus. The major reason for this is the war in Chechnya that began in 1994. Further, particularly since 1999, the conflict and political violence has spread to other parts of southern Russia. The North Caucasus, more than any other region in Russia, has been closest to what Guillermo O'Donnell calls a "brown area," where the state not only does not function properly but is largely absent.[2] Beyond the issues of state capacity and state quality, in the North Caucasus, post-Soviet Russia has faced a threat to *state integrity*, in which the soundness of its external borders was potentially at risk.

Vladimir Putin's meteoric rise to power was closely tied to the conflict in the North Caucasus. In some ways, a Putin presidency is unthinkable if not for the resumption of war between Russia and Chechnya in 1999. When he declared in early 2000 that resolving the situation in the region was his "historic mission," he also stated that when he was named prime minister in August 1999, he figured that he only had a few months to "bang away at these bandits," but that he was willing to sacrifice his political career to "stop the collapse of the country."[3] As we now know, banging away at the bandits made his career.

---

[1] N. Gevorkyan, A. Kolesnikov, and N. Timakova, *Ot pervogo litsa* (Moskva: Vagrius, 2000), p. 133.

[2] "Blue areas" are where the state is present and functions properly, and "green areas" are where the state is present but does not function properly: Guillermo O'Donnell, "On the State, Democratization, and Some Conceptual Problems: A Latin American View with Glances at Some Postcommunist Countries," *World Development*, 21, 8 (1993), pp. 1355–1369.

[3] Gevorkyan, Kolesnikov, and Timakova 2000, p. 133.

This chapter returns to some of the themes of Chapter 4 by highlighting the territoriality of state building. Unlike the rest of Russia, where the "politics of sovereignty" had been settled before Putin's rise to power, with the state already having created the rudiments of public order and control over legitimate violence, in Chechnya, this first stage had yet to occur.[4] Moreover, between 2003 and 2005, violence, terrorism, and instability appeared to be spreading uncontrollably from Chechnya to the other republics of the North Caucasus. After 2005, however, the state seemed to have stanched the violent disorder. By the end of Putin's tenure as president, Chechnya in particular was much more stable than in the past, although it would be an overstatement to say that the rebels had been defeated, and neighboring Ingushetia and Dagestan still experienced considerable political violence.

This pacification campaign relied heavily on violent repression exercised by armed state bodies and their allies, such as the security forces of Chechen president Ramzan Kadyrov. An effort to claim a monopoly on legitimate violence was a necessary first step before further state capacity could be built. During Putin's presidency, arguably some headway was made on this first stage of state formation, albeit at a significant human cost. Moreover, the violent methods used, although not atypical for European state building historically, have greatly hindered any effort to create state quality, at least in the short run. If in O'Donnell's scheme, the North Caucasus had fewer brown areas by 2007 than it did earlier in Putin's presidency, it was at best largely a green area, where the state was present but did not function properly.

This chapter provides an assessment of state capacity and state quality in the North Caucasus under Putin, especially in the coercive realm. I pay particular attention to the dynamic element of state building. One notable change from previous chapters is the central role played by the armed forces, not just as a source of personnel as part of the silovik cohort, but as an important corporate actor, especially in Chechnya. I begin with a brief overview of the crisis of the state in the region.

STATE CRISIS IN THE CAUCASUS: A BRIEF INTRODUCTION

The break-up of the Soviet Union along national-federal lines raised the obvious question of whether Russia – also a multinational federation – would face a similar fate.[5] Of the eighty-nine units of the federation in 1992, twenty-one were granted the status of "republic," a status that reflected the ethnic distinctiveness of what was called the titular nationality – Bashkirs in Bashkortostan, Tatars in Tatarstan, and so on. These republics had pushed for greater rights in the late-Soviet period, and the prospect of greater autonomy

---

[4] See the discussion in Chapter 1.

[5] A good introduction to these debates is: Henry E. Hale, "The Makeup and Breakup of Ethnofederal States: Why Russia Survives Where the USSR Fell," *Perspectives on Politics*, 3, 1 (March 2005), pp. 55–70.

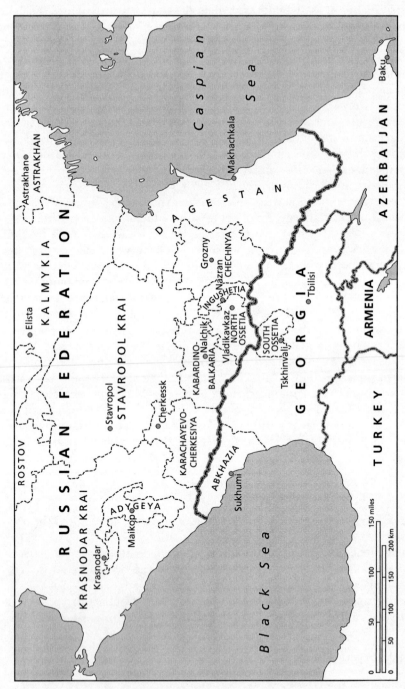

MAP 7.1. North Caucasus

or even independence remained on the agenda in a newly independent Russian Federation. The North Caucasus is the home of seven of the twenty-one ethnic republics. Moreover, of the seven republics in which the titular nationality or nationalities constituted a majority of the population in 1992, five of them – Chechnya, Dagestan, Ingushetia, Kabardino-Balkaria, and North Ossetia – were in the North Caucasus.[6] All five of these had an external border.

Chechnya was the most independence-minded of the North Caucasus republics.[7] An opening of sorts for those Chechen elites pushing for independence came in the aftermath of the failed August 1991 coup in Moscow, when the unraveling of the Soviet Union reached its final, pell-mell phase. In September–November 1991, the National Congress of the Chechen People, headed by Dzhokar Dudayev, a Soviet Air Force General who reinvented himself as a Chechen nationalist, seized power from the communist leadership of the region, engineered new elections of questionable legitimacy, and declared independence. Russian President Boris Yeltsin initially sought to send troops to resist this gambit, but faced opposition both from Mikhail Gorbachev, who was still President of the Soviet Union for another month, and the legislature of the Russian Federation, the Supreme Soviet. From December 1991 to December 1994, Chechnya under Dudayev's rule was de facto independent from Russian control while remaining de jure a part of the Russian Federation.[8]

The other major violent conflict in the early 1990s in the North Caucasus was the Ingush-Ossetian hostilities of 1992. Through most of the Soviet period, Ingushetia and Chechnya had been joined together in a Chechen-Ingush Republic, but in 1991–1992, these two components split apart, creating the Chechen Republic and the Republic of Ingushetia. The primary territorial struggle facing the Ingush at the time was not for independence, but a bid to regain territory that had been lost to neighboring North Ossetia under Stalin. Tense relations between Ingush and Ossetians and sporadic violence in the 1988–1992 period erupted into several days of intense warfare in November 1992, which resulted in hundreds of deaths and tens of thousands of ethnic Ingush expelled from their homes in a contested region of North Ossetia. Russian military and MVD troops intervened to quell the violence, although

---

[6] The other two republics in which the titular nationality was a majority in 1992 were Chuvashia and Tuva. Technically there is no "Dagestani" nationality, but multiple indigenous nationalities. The key point is that ethnic Russians were less than 10 percent of the population in Dagestan as of 1989. Ann Sheehy, "Russia's Republics: A Threat to Its Territorial Integrity?" *RFE/RL Research Report*, 2, 20 (May 14, 1993), p. 38.

[7] A controversial discussion of the historical and cultural reasons for this is: Anatol Lieven, *Chechnya* (New Haven, CT: Yale University Press, 1998), pp. 96–101, 301–368. An account that argues these factors were of little importance is: James Hughes, *Chechnya: From Nationalism to Jihad* (Philadelphia: University of Pennsylvania Press, 2007), pp. 1–29.

[8] Overviews of this period include: Lieven 1998, pp. 56–101; Hughes 2007, pp. 1–29, 56–81; Matthew Evangelista, *The Chechen Wars* (Washington, DC: Brookings Institution Press, 2002), pp. 12–33; Georgi Derluguian, *Bourdieu's Secret Admirer in the Caucasus* (Chicago: University of Chicago Press, 2005), pp. 243–257.

the impartiality of their actions was questioned. This Ingush-Ossetian conflict remains unresolved.[9]

The event that really destabilized the North Caucasus, and made it such a state-building challenge, was the First Chechen War of 1994–1996. Although the southern part of Russia was likely to be a difficult one to govern in the best of circumstances, given the combination of challenging geography, ethnic heterogeneity, and economic poverty, it was Boris Yeltsin's decision to opt for a violent solution to Chechnya's bid for independence that played the largest role in undermining Russian stateness throughout the North Caucasus.[10] From a human perspective, the costs of the war were enormous, with up to 10,000 combatant (Russian and Chechen) deaths and tens of thousands more civilian deaths.[11] The war represented a humiliating defeat for the Russian military and security services. Many officers opposed the 1996 truce negotiated by General Aleksandr Lebed with the Chechens, which gave rise to a "stab in the back" thesis that festered in the unstable interregnum before the war resumed in 1999.[12]

Perhaps the most important consequence of the First Chechen War was the radicalization of many of the Chechen fighters themselves and the increasing prominence of a radical form of Islam, usually referred to as "Wahhabism," within Chechnya. Most important and prominent in this respect was Shamil Basayev, a leading field commander in the first war. James Hughes states, "the apparent conversion of Basayev, from a secular nationalist in the early 1990s to the concept of jihad in the mid-1990s, was a profound turning point for the conflict in Chechnya." Over the course of a decade, Basayev masterminded some of the most notorious terrorist attacks in Russian history, including a 1995 attack on a hospital in Budennovsk in the neighboring Stavropol region and the Beslan school attack in 2004 in North Ossetia. The inability of Chechen President Aslan Maskhadov to control Basayev and other field commanders in the years after the 1996 settlement played a key role in the resumption of the Chechen war in 1999. Finally, Basayev's stated goal of creating a North Caucasian Islamic caliphate led directly to his strategy of organizing pan-Caucasian armed rebel groups, known as military jamaats, in the other predominantly Muslim republics of the region. The war in Chechnya,

[9] Lieven 1998, pp. 70–73; Olga Osipova, "North Ossetia and Ingushetia: The First Clash," and David Mendeloff, "Commentary on North Ossetia and Ingushetia," in Alexei Arbatov et al., eds., *Managing Conflict in the Former Soviet Union: Russian and American Perspectives* (Cambridge, MA: MIT Press, 1997), pp. 27–82.

[10] A persuasive argument for Yeltsin's ultimate responsibility for the war is: Evangelista 2002.

[11] Hughes 2007, pp. 81–82.

[12] On military performance, see: Lieven 1998, pp. 269–299; Aleksey Malashenko and Dmitriy Trenin, *Vremya Yuga* (Moskva: Carnegie Moscow Center, 2002), pp. 113–179; Mark Kramer, "The Perils of Counterinsurgency: Russia's War in Chechnya," *International Security*, 29, 3 (2004), pp. 5–62. On officers' opposition to the 1996 truce, see, for example, the following memoir accounts from high-ranking generals: Anatoliy Kulikov, *Tyazhelye zvezdy* (Moskva: Voyna i Mir, 2002), pp. 455–469; Gennadiy Troshev, *Moya Voyna: Chechenskiy dnevnik okopnogo generala* (Moskva: Vagrius, 2002), pp. 128–135.

which from 1994–1996 was relatively contained to that republic, threatened to spread to the whole North Caucasus.[13]

It was this fundamental transformation of the Chechen conflict that Putin faced when he declared his "historic mission" in 2000. Without entering into the debate about the morality or political wisdom of Putin and Yeltsin's decision to opt for all-out war in 1999, or the counterfactual discussions of whether an alternative political or military strategy would have been both more successful and more humane, it seems clear that Putin and those around him perceived an existential threat to the Russian state after the attack by Basayev and his troops on the neighboring republic of Dagestan in August 1999, which marked the start of the Second Chechen War. Putin stated in early 2000, "I was certain that if we did not stop the extremists now we were threatened with a second Yugoslavia throughout the Russian Federation, the Yugoslavization of Russia."[14]

Did Putin accomplish his "historic mission?" The assessment of Putin and his supporters is that he has indeed fulfilled this task. For example, First Deputy Prime Minister Sergey Ivanov, one of Putin's closest allies, confidently proclaimed victory in Chechnya, stating in February 2007, "we have scored a success ... the problem has been solved."[15] Other observers were more skeptical about Putin's accomplishments in the North Caucasus. For example, the Russian journalist Andrei Smirnov remarked in February 2007, "the real war on the Caucasian insurgency looks less confident than the Russian president's speeches." Similarly, the Chechen academic Mairbek Vachagaev stated in September 2006, "the events in the region are unfolding in accordance to the guerillas' plans. The Russian military and security services are unable to staunch [sic.] the spreading conflagration in the Caucasus."[16]

In the rest of the chapter, I investigate in greater detail the development of Russian state capacity and state quality in the North Caucasus under Putin. I concentrate in particular on the ethnic republics that have seen the worst violence, particularly Chechnya, Dagestan, Ingushetia, North Ossetia,

---

[13] James Hughes describes how the nature of the Chechen conflict was changed from "nationalism" to "jihad" by its own dynamics: Hughes 2007 (quote p. 100). See also: Julie Wilhelmsen, "Between a Rock and a Hard Place: The Islamisation of the Chechen Separatist Movement," *Europe-Asia Studies*, 57, 1 (January 2005), pp. 35–59; Gordon M. Hahn, "The *Jihadi* Insurgency and the Russian Counterinsurgency in the North Caucasus," *Post-Soviet Affairs*, 24, 1 (2008), pp. 1–39.

[14] Gevorkyan, Kolesnikov, and Timakova 2000, p. 135. Some analysts have argued that Basayev's attack on Dagestan, as well as the apartment bombings in Moscow in September 1999, were part of a conspiracy by a group in the Russian elite promoting Putin's presidential candidacy. See the discussion in Chapter 3.

[15] C.J. Chivers, "Russian Official Says Insurgency in Chechnya Has Been Tamed," *NYT*, February 12, 2007. See also: Sergey Markov, "Zadachi Kadyrova," *Izvestiya*, March 19, 2007.

[16] Andrei Smirnov, "Putin Overlooks Assassination Campaign Sweeping the North Caucasus," *CW*, February 8, 2007; Mairbek Vachagaev, "The Chechen Resistance: Yesterday, Today and Tomorrow," Paper presented at the North Caucasus Conference, Jamestown Foundation, September 14, 2006, p. 21.

Kabardino-Balkaria, and Karachayevo-Cherkesiya.[17] In contrast to the 2003–2005 period, when violence, terrorism, and instability appeared to be spreading uncontrollably from Chechnya to the other republics of the North Caucasus, by the end of Putin's presidency, some degree of order and stability seemed to have been imposed. Arguably, Russia was on the path to success in the first stage of state building. At the same time, the imposition of order involved the widespread use of corrupt and predatory practices by state coercive organs. Further, the relative stability in Chechnya was achieved by a feudalistic deal with the most powerful local warlord, Ramzan Kadyrov, which raised questions about the long-term sustainability of Putin's state-building efforts in the North Caucasus. Overall, although the last years of Putin's presidency saw an increase in state capacity in the coercive realm in most (but not all) of the North Caucasus, state quality remained extremely low.

STATE CAPACITY IN THE CAUCASUS

"Banging away at the bandits" in the North Caucasus was central to Putin's rise to power, but the conflict in the region was perhaps the weakest link in his state-building project. Although he was able to dominate the oligarchs, the governors, the media, the legislature, and other major obstacles to the power of the Kremlin by the end of his first term, the continuing weakness of the Russian state in the North Caucasus was evident. Indeed, by the end of 2004, the first year of Putin's second term, the almost universal consensus was that Putin had failed.[18] The horrific Beslan school incident in North Ossetia, in which more than 300 people died, many of them children, was the most notorious event, but 2004 witnessed a whole host of violent episodes that showed not only that Russia did not have control in Chechnya, but that violence and instability was spreading throughout the North Caucasus. For example, the pro-Russian Chechen President, Akhmad Kadyrov, was killed by a terrorist bombing at Dinamo stadium in Grozny on May 9, 2004 during Victory Day celebrations, and a group of insurgents launched a major assault on Nazran and Karabulak in Ingushetia in June 2004 during which scores of law enforcement and security personnel were killed. In 2002–2004, there were multiple terrorist attacks in Moscow related to Chechnya, including the 2002 *Nord-Ost* theater hostage incident and bombings of the subway and two airliners in August 2004. The October 2005 armed attacks on law enforcement

[17] Introductions to the region as a whole include: "The North Caucasus," *RAD*, No. 22 (June 5, 2007); John B. Dunlop and Rajan Menon, "Chaos in the North Caucasus and Russia's Future," *Survival*, 48, 2 (Summer 2006), pp. 97–114; Domitilla Sagramoso, "Violence and Conflict in the Russian North Caucasus," *International Affairs*, 83, 4 (July 2007), pp. 681–705; Natalia Zubarevich, "Southern Federal Okrug," in Peter Reddaway and Robert W. Orttung, eds., *The Dynamics of Russian Politics*, Vol. I (Lanham, MD: Rowman & Littlefield, 2004), pp. 111–152.

[18] See, for example: Mikhail A. Alexseev, "Security Sell-Out in the North Caucasus, 2004: How Government Centralization Backfires," *PONARS Policy Memo*, 344 (November 2004).

structures in Nalchik, the capital of the Kabardino-Balkaria Republic (KBR), which left more than 100 people dead, was another indication of the further spread of unrest in the North Caucasus.[19]

The Beslan attack had the widest resonance both in Russia and around the world. The bloody storming of the school by Russian military and security forces on September 3, 2004, the key details of which are still disputed, led to hundreds of deaths and seemed to show that, despite Putin's popularity and unchallenged supremacy, the Russian state was still gravely ill. The large number of civilian casualties during the storming of the school, even taking into account the barbarity of the terrorists, showed at best gross incompetence on the part of the power ministries and at worst a criminal disregard for the lives of innocents.[20] Putin's two major speeches after Beslan emphasized what he called the "weakness of state administration," with a particular focus on security and law enforcement structures. He argued that insufficient attention had been paid to security questions, which allowed corruption to undermine the work of the courts and law enforcement organs. He vowed in the future to "perfect the system of internal security" in the country as a whole, and specifically in the North Caucasus.[21]

Russian and Western commentators offered similar verdicts, with more scathing language and an abundance of details on the failings of the state in general and the power ministries in particular. The British journalist John Kampfner asserted that "four years into Putin's rule, there may be less stability than there has ever been.... The state is flailing." Analysts from across the political spectrum in Russia laid into the police and secret police. For example, the liberal commentator Yulia Latynina asserted that "the security services are failing miserably" in their key mission of protecting society against terrorist attacks and other threats to national security. In the nationalist weekly *Zavtra*, Vladislav Shurygin wrote, "Does Putin really still not understand that his 'siloviki' are not a pillar of the state, but third-class bureaucrats, mired in intrigues and corruption, who long ago forgot about their duty and their oath?" Yuliya Kalinina, in the popular, generally pro-government tabloid *Moskovskiy Komsomolets*, stated:

---

[19] An overview is: Dunlop and Menon 2006. A useful reference on major incidents is: Radio Free Europe/Radio Liberty, "Russia: A Timeline Of Terrorism Since 1995." Available at: http://www.rferl.org/. Terrorism in Russia as a whole, and in Moscow, was discussed in Chapter 3.

[20] The literature on Beslan is enormous. For a gripping account from the point of view of the hostages, see: C.J. Chivers, "The School," *Esquire*, June 2006; for a more detailed, critical account in English, see: John B. Dunlop, *The 2002 Dubrovka and 2004 Beslan Hostage Crises* (Stuttgart: ibidem-Verlag, 2006). A good summary of the major contending accounts of what happened is: Vladimir Voronov, "Glavnaya tayna Beslana," *NV*, September 10, 2006. For the full texts of the different official and unofficial reports, see: http://www.pravdabeslana.ru

[21] Vladimir Putin, "Obrashcheniye Prezidenta Rossii Vladimira Putina," September 4, 2004; Vladimir Putin, "Vystupleniye na rasshirennom zasedanii Pravitel'stva s uchastiyem glav sub'ektov Rossiyskoy Federatsii," September 13, 2004.

The fatal mistake of President Putin is that he refuses to understand that he doesn't have any instruments.... There is no FSB, no police, no army ... The only real, firm thing [in those structures] is associated with money – kickbacks, bribes, and services carried out on private orders. Real is their own pocket, everything else – a mirage.[22]

Multiple analysts specifically linked the inability of the Russian state to deal with terrorist incidents such as Beslan to inefficiency, incompetence, and corruption in the power ministries. The ease with which heavily armed militants could travel around the North Caucasus was generally attributed to the well-known practice of police and military personnel accepting bribes. Although the charges of government failure usually were of a general nature, there were also specific accusations of malfeasance concerning particular attacks, such as with the August 2004 airplane bombings.[23]

The Russian political scientist Dmitriy Oreshkin summed up the conventional wisdom in June 2005 in the following manner:

The fact that the North Caucasus is on the verge of an explosion, with the subsequent collapse of the Russian Federation, is not a secret for any expert for at least the last three years.... The North Caucasus is an enormous, corrupt source of enrichment and a zone of uncontrolled abuse of power, from which the siloviki are getting rich.[24]

By 2007–2008, however, the situation appeared much different. In 2005–2006, the three most important figures in the Chechen insurgency –Basayev, former Chechen President and head of the Chechen rebel government Maskhadov, and Maskhadov's successor as head of the rebel government, Abdul-Khalim Sadullayev – were killed. Although violence continued throughout the region, not only in Chechnya but also in particular in Ingushetia and Dagestan, in general, the North Caucasus seemed more stable by the end of Putin's presidency. The number of major attacks in the region had decreased, with the last major incident with dozens of casualties taking place in Nalchik in October 2005. As journalist C.J. Chivers put it in 2008, "Anyone suggesting four years ago, after the school siege in Beslan, that the war would be reduced to skirmishes in Ingushetia and Dagestan, and that Grozny (think: Mogadishu) would be largely rebuilt in a thousand days, would have been dismissed as a fool."[25] Chivers was right: Particularly compared to the *annus horribilis* of 2004, the situation in the region looked much better by 2008.

[22] John Kampfner, "Special report – A president craves understanding," *New Statesman*, September 13, 2004; Yulia Latynina, "Heroism and Monstrous Incompetence," *MT*, September 8, 2004; Vladislav Shurygin, "Postskriptum k 'chernoy pyatnitse," *Zavtra*, September 15, 2004; Yuliya Kalinina, "Impotency," *MK*, September 10, 2004.

[23] See Chapter 3.

[24] Ivan Rodin et al., "Kavkazizatsiya politicheskogo byta strany," *Nez. Gaz.*, June 20, 2005.

[25] C.J. Chivers, "Power: The Vladimir Putin Story," *Esquire*, October 2008.

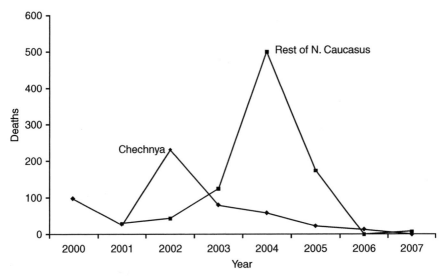

FIGURE 7.1. Deaths from terrorism/insurgency, major attacks, North Caucasus, 2000–2007.

Terrorism and Political Violence in the North Caucasus

Political violence is a key indicator of state capacity, especially in the security and law enforcement sphere. As shown in Chapter 3, Russia had one of the highest rates of deadly terrorist attacks in the world between 2001 and 2007, and Russia's WGI score for "political stability/no violence" was consistently below that of other middle-income countries from 1996 to 2007. Most of the terrorist attacks suffered by Russia, including those in Moscow, were directly connected to the Chechen wars and the wider conflict in the region.

The general trend in political violence in the region is indicated by the following three figures. Figure 7.1 shows the contrasting patterns in major violent episodes over the period 2000–2007 in both Chechnya and the rest of the North Caucasus.[26] The data include deaths from major terrorist incidents and insurgent attacks. They do not include attacks by Russian federal forces on rebel fighters or civilian populations, or rebel ambushes of Russian military units in Chechnya. In Chechnya, after a series of bombings of government buildings and missile attacks on Russian military helicopters in 2002, the ability of the rebels to carry out attacks with large numbers of deaths steadily declined. In the rest of the region, in contrast, the picture of spreading violence

[26] Data from: Pavel K. Baev, "The Targets of Terrorism and the Aims of Counter-Terrorism in Moscow, Chechnya, and the North Caucasus," Paper for the annual meeting of the International Studies Association, Chicago, March 2007; Pavel K. Baev, "Putin's 'Crushing Blow' on Terrorism: Is Chechnya Really Pacified and Is Stability Restored in the North Caucasus?" draft report for the *Russie.Nei.Visions* collection at IFRI, June 2008.

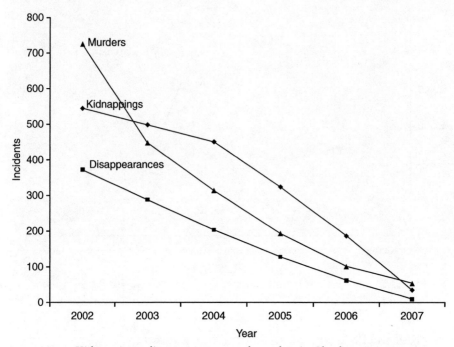

FIGURE 7.2. Kidnappings, disappearances, and murders in Chechnya, 2002–2007.

in the 2003–2005 period was clearly evident, as Basayev in particular sought to widen the Chechen conflict to the entire region. By 2006, however, major attacks had virtually ceased, and the trend continued in 2007. The contrast between 2006–2007 and earlier in Putin's presidency was stark.

Figure 7.2 focuses specifically on Chechnya. The human rights organization Memorial noted a steady decline in reported kidnappings, disappearances, and murders from 2002–2007.[27] It is important to note that these data understate all of these phenomena; Memorial was only able to monitor 25–30 percent of Chechen territory, and there was understandable fear about reporting incidents. What the data do show, however, is the general trend. In all categories, the number of incidents dropped by more than an order of magnitude in six years.

One important trend of the Second Chechen War was the widening of violence beyond that republic. Figure 7.1 showed a big upsurge in major terrorist events outside Chechnya in 2003–2005, when major attacks in Beslan (North Ossetia), Nazran (Ingushetia), and Nalchik (KBR) took place. Dagestan is the largest, most populous, and most ethnically diverse Muslim republic in the North Caucasus, and has witnessed significant political violence since the

---

[27] Data from http://www.memo.ru. See also: Liz Fuller, "Rights Situation May Be Improving in Chechnya," *RFE/RL Newsline*, June 27, 2007.

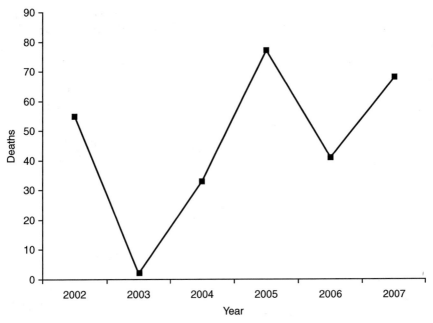

FIGURE 7.3. Deaths from terrorist incidents in Dagestan, 2002–2007.

Soviet collapse, both as a spillover from Chechnya and from internal sources. Figure 7.3 shows the trend in deaths for all terrorist attacks in Dagestan from 2002 to 2007.[28] The data show that, unlike Chechnya, there was no consistent trend in political violence. Indeed, the number of deaths in terrorist attacks in 2005–2007 was more than double (186 versus 90) that of 2002–2004. Attacks on law enforcement and security personnel were a common occurrence. Despite some tactical successes, such as the killing of rebel leader Rappani Khalikov in September 2007, in general, there was little evidence of an improving security situation in Dagestan by the end of Putin's presidency.[29]

Overall, data on terrorism and political violence in the North Caucasus seemed to indicate improving state capacity in 2006–2007, particularly in Chechnya.[30] The death of Shamil Basayev, sometimes referred to as Russia's

---

[28] Data from "Dagestan: chronika terrora (1996–2007 gg.)," *Kavkazskiy uzel* website. Current data at: http://www.kavkaz-uzel.ru/articles/73122/. Deaths of civilians and state officials were counted, but not of rebels.

[29] Negative assessments of trends in Dagestan in 2007–2008 include: Mairbek Vatchagaev, "Dagestan's Jamaats Widen Their Theater of Operations," *CW*, May 8, 2008; International Crisis Group, *Russia's Dagestan: Conflict Causes*, June 3, 2008. A more mixed assessment is: Michael Coffey, "Progress in Dagestan: Taking a Backseat to Other Republics," *Central Asia-Caucasus Institute Analyst*, October 3, 2007.

[30] It must be stressed that, as elsewhere in the book, my assessments of state capacity and state quality apply specifically to the coercive realm. The ability of authorities in Chechnya and elsewhere to deliver public goods beyond security, such as a variety of economic and social

Osama Bin Laden, was especially important, although a change in rebel strategy away from high-profile and arguably counterproductive terrorist attacks may also have been important.[31] On the other hand, state coercive capacity in Dagestan and Ingushetia did not improve in Putin's second term, and arguably the situation in those republics was both worse than in previous years and worse than in Chechnya itself.[32] Although the spectacular attacks of 2004–2005 in the North Caucasus dropped off in 2006–2007, the level of political violence in at least some republics remained significant. Declarations of Russian victory over Islamic insurgents were premature, but by the end of Putin's presidency, the Russian authorities could, if not breathe easier, at least believe that trends were moving in the right direction.[33]

Explaining the Improvement in State Capacity

The evident progress in Russian stateness in the North Caucasus after 2005, with a diminishment of "brown areas" and an increase in "green areas," gives some credence to the claim that Putin presided over successful state building as president. Even with the necessary and important caveats about the dynamic nature of the situation in the region and the continuing widespread problems, the improvement in Putin's second term still requires explanation. Several factors were significant, including the efforts of Putin's 2004–2007 envoy to the region, Dmitriy Kozak, greater economic resources, and the war-weariness of the population. Most important, and controversial, was a classic state-building strategy: cutting a deal with the most powerful local warlord, Ramzan Kadyrov of Chechnya. The last step, however, may ultimately backfire if Kadyrov turns on Moscow.

Dmitriy Kozak was appointed as Putin's representative to the Southern Federal District (*okrug*) in 2004, after the Beslan tragedy. His appointment led observers to expect a more rational, vigorous, and far-sighted Russian

     services, was still quite limited. I thank Ekaterina Sokirianskaia for emphasizing this point, especially with regard to Chechnya.

[31] Andrei Smirnov, "No Terrorist Acts in Russia Since Beslan: Whom to Thank?" *CW*, May 24, 2007.

[32] On Ingushetia, see: Memorial, "Ingushetia: 2007 god: Kuda Dal'she?" January 2008, at: http://www.memo.ru/; Marina Vladimirova and Vladislav Trifonov, "Dmitriy Kozak razzhaloval ingushskikh militsionerov," *K-D*, September 14, 2007; Fred Weir, "Rising Violence in Russia's Ingushetia," *Christian Science Monitor*, September 14, 2007; International Institute for Strategic Studies, "Insurgency in Ingushetia: Russia's Failing North Caucasus Strategy," *Strategic Comments*, 14, 6 (August 2008).

[33] For similar assessments, see: Pavel Baev, "The Russian Military Campaign in the North Caucasus: Is a Victory in Sight?," Paper presented at the North Caucasus Conference, Jamestown Foundation, September 14, 2006; Pavel Baev, "Has Russia Achieved a Victory in Its War Against Terror?" *PONARS Policy Memo*, 415 (December 2006); Mark Kramer, "The Changing Context of Russian Federal Policy in the North Caucasus," *PONARS Policy Memo*, 416 (December 2006); Anna Matveeva, "Chechnya: Dynamics of War and Peace," *Problems of Post-Communism*, 54, 3 (May/June 2007), pp. 3–17; Hahn 2008.

policy in the region.[34] Kozak, one of Putin's closest allies during his presidency, developed a reputation as one of Russia's most competent and intelligent officials, although the results of the policies he is most closely associated with – legal reform, local government reform, administrative reform – were decidedly mixed. Regardless, the mere fact of his appointment demonstrated Putin's seriousness about the region.

Kozak was a tireless troubleshooter in his three years as envoy, moving from flashpoint to flashpoint in the North Caucasus. He carried both a carrot and a stick or, as Russians say, a cake and a whip. His most important stick was his ability to engineer the removal of unpopular leaders and officials by virtue of his closeness to Putin. In 2005–2006, Kozak succeeded in removing the old and corrupt presidents of Dagestan and Kabardino-Balkaria, the discredited KBR MVD head Khachim Shogenov (whose policies prior to Nalchik are discussed below), and the procurator general in Dagestan. In KBR, both the new president, Arsen Kanakov, and the new head of the MVD, Yuriy Tomchak, emphasized that they were taking a more tolerant approach to Islam in the republic than their predecessors, and that the policies of Shogenov had made the situation worse.[35] Kozak also quarreled with the president of the Republic of Adygeya, Khazret Sovmen, who was not reappointed by Putin when his term ran out in January 2007.[36]

Putin's ultimate appointment authority meant that some leaders who were likely candidates for dismissal, at least based on their performance, nonetheless kept their posts. Most prominently, Kozak was not able to persuade Putin to replace the failed president of Ingushetia, Murat Zyazikov (a former FSB official), who presided over a steady deterioration of the political and security situation after he was virtually imposed on the republic in 2002 in place of the competent but insufficiently loyal (from Putin's perspective) Ruslan Aushev. Zyazikov was eventually replaced in October 2008.[37] It also was clear that Kozak had no real authority over the Chechen President Ramzan Kadyrov, who had a direct tie to Putin.

Kozak's most important carrot was the windfall of oil and gas profits sloshing through Russian state coffers. The North Caucasus is the poorest area of

[34] On Russian policy in the region prior to Kozak's appointment, see: Zubarevich 2004.

[35] Kramer 2006; Baev, "The Russian Military Campaign …"; Baev, "Has Russia Achieved a Victory …"; Gennadiy Petrov, "'Podlinnaya prichina tekh sobytiy – korrumpirovannaya i zakrytaya vlast'," *Gazeta*, October 12, 2006; Yuriy Tomchak, "Vakhkhabizm – ne prestupleniye, eto religioznoye techeniye," *Gazeta Yuga*, February 1, 2007.

[36] Ivan Sukhov, "Ekzamen dlya rektora," *VN*, October 16, 2006; Dmitriy Vinogradov, "Prezident dva protsenta," *Gazeta.ru*, October 25, 2006; Ivan Sukhov, "Smena Sovmena," *VN*, December 7, 2006.

[37] Zyazikov's fraudulent election was discussed in Chapter 3. On Aushev and Zyazikov, in addition to the sources in note 32, see: Matthew Evangelista, "Ingushetia as a Microcosm of Putin's Reforms," *PONARS Policy Memo*, 346 (November 2004); Liz Fuller, "Militant Attacks Increase as Cracks Emerge within Ingushetia's Leadership," *RFE/RL Newsline*, August 2, 2007. On Zyazikov's removal, see: Liz Fuller, "Moscow Finally Replaces Discredited Ingushetian President," *RFE/RL Russia Report*, October 31, 2008.

Russia. The Southern Federal District, which under Putin included the ethnic republics of the North Caucasus as well as predominately Russian regions such as Krasnodar, Stavropol, Volgograd, and Rostov, had a per capita GDP less than half of that of the rest of the country.[38] The area also had the highest unemployment rate in the country and suffered the greatest economic depression in the 1990s compared to other parts of Russia. Economic issues, such as unemployment and poverty, were the primary concerns of young men in the region.[39] All of the North Caucasus republics are heavily subsidized, with between 50 and 90 percent of their budgets financed from Moscow. Kozak won additional funding for the south during his tenure from 2004 to 2007, and also succeeded in attracting private investment to the region.[40] The improved financial situation was most notable in Chechnya, where, for the first time since 1994, major reconstruction began in 2005–2007. The bulk of the financing for reconstruction came from Moscow, which distributed more than 70 billion rubles to the republic between 2001 and 2005, and which contributed more than 85 percent of Chechnya's annual budget.[41] The economic situation in the North Caucasus remained extremely difficult, particularly in the poorest republics like Dagestan. But, as in the country as a whole, the marked improvement in the economy had a stabilizing effect.

After three years as envoy, Kozak was recalled to Moscow to head the Ministry of Regional Development in September 2007. At the time, one journalist contended that "he was able to essentially reconstruct the administrative system in the most problematic okrug in Russia."[42] His replacement by another silovik, former intelligence official Grigoriy Rapota, suggested that Putin believed Kozak had succeeded in stabilizing the North Caucasus. Rapota lacked both Kozak's stature and closeness to Putin and was less dynamic than Kozak had been during his tenure as presidential representative. President Dmitriy Medvedev removed Rapota in May 2008 and replaced him with Vladimir Ustinov, the former Procurator General and Justice Minister.

---

[38] In 2009, Medvedev split the Southern Federal District in half, creating a North Caucasus Federal District.

[39] On the economic situation, see: Sagramoso 2007, pp. 690–693; Zubarevich 2004, pp. 113–114. Polling data on the concerns of young men in three North Caucasian republics are in: Theodore P. Gerber and Sarah E. Mendelson, "Security through Sociology: The North Caucasus and the Global Counterinsurgency Paradigm," *Studies in Conflict & Terrorism*, 32 (2009), pp. 831–851.

[40] Liz Fuller, "Russian President Demonstrates Support for Embattled Envoy," *RFE/RL Newsline*, October 3, 2005; Kramer 2006; Baev, "Has Russia Achieved a Victory ..."; Alena Sedlak, "Faktor Kozaka," *Ekspert Yug*, October 15, 2007; Aleksandr Popov, "Sozdatel' druzheskoy atmosfery," *Ekspert*, October 8, 2007.

[41] "Lokshina: Grozny is a City of Construction and Fear," *CW*, August 2, 2007; C.J. Chivers, "Signs of Renewal Emerge from Chechnya's Ruins," *NYT*, May 4, 2006; *Byulleten' Schetnoy palaty Rossiyskoy Federatsii*, 9, 105 (2006).

[42] Popov 2007. A more detailed assessment of Kozak's efforts as envoy is in: Darrell Slider, "Putin's 'Southern Strategy': Dmitriy Kozak and the Dilemmas of Recentralization," *Post-Soviet Affairs*, 24, 2 (April–June 2008), pp. 177–197.

Kozak came to the okrug at a time when the societal desire for order and stability was high after years of war in Chechnya and terrorist attacks in other republics in the North Caucasus. The majority of the Chechen population desired an end to the fighting, regardless of whether the territorial issue was resolved or whether Chechnya achieved independence. Although referendum and election results favorable to Moscow in 2003 and 2004 were clearly manipulated and falsified, they did seem at least partially to reflect the war-weariness of many Chechens. Support for separatism declined due to a desire for peace, and because of the radicalization of the guerrilla's aims and tactics during the second war. Long-time observer Thomas de Waal noted the growth over time of the "silent pragmatic constituency" in Chechnya.[43]

A desire for political stability, as well as the avoidance of violent conflict, also was strong in the other ethnic republics of the North Caucasus. A 2006 survey of young men in Dagestan, Kabardino-Balkaria, and North Ossetia showed very low levels of support for Islamic radicalism and generally low levels of ethnic animosity toward Russians or other groups, with the exception of that toward the Ingush professed by North Ossetians. The Harvard scholar Mark Kramer, after a trip to the North Caucasus in 2006, reported both a widespread desire to avoid the fate of Chechnya, as well as revulsion about the events in Beslan, which also reinforced support for stability and the avoidance of violence.[44]

The Role of Repression

The issues highlighted so far in explaining greater state capacity in the North Caucasus toward the end of Putin's presidency – Kozak's efforts and abilities, greater economic resources, and popular conflict fatigue – are either tactical or subject to change in the short-to-medium term. A final factor that may explain the apparent increase in state coercive capacity, and one that at least potentially held out the prospect of greater long-term stabilization, is violent repression by the state. This explanation is the least palatable and goes against the conclusion of many analysts that state violence further destabilized the region, but deserves a sober assessment. After all, massive violence directed against the North Caucasus by both the Imperial Russian and Soviet regimes did succeed in pacifying the region for multiple decades. To put it bluntly, did Russia bomb the North Caucasus into submission?

I argued in Chapter 1 that it is useful to think of state building as something that happens in stages, with the first stage being about the "politics of sovereignty" – claiming a monopoly on legitimate violence in a given territory.

---

[43] Kramer, 2004, p. 11; Matveeva 2007; Dzabrail Gakaev, "Chechnya in Russia and Russia in Chechnya" and Tom de Waal, "Chechnya: The Breaking Point", both in Richard Sakwa, ed., *Chechnya* (London: Anthem Press, 2005), pp. 41, 195. The war-weariness of the Chechen population was stressed by three activists from the local branch of the human rights organizational Memorial during a speaking tour in the United States, including Syracuse, in April 2007.

[44] Gerber and Mendelson 2009; Kramer 2006.

Until this condition is met, it is hard to move to building more capacity, because the state as such does not even exist. By this criterion, Chechnya was for the most part "stateless," or a "brown area," after the Soviet collapse. After the First Chechen War and into the Second Chechen War, this brown area began to spread into neighboring regions, such as Ingushetia and Dagestan.

Historical accounts of state formation in Europe stress the importance of coercion to the first stage of state building. The utility of violent repression in state building was emphasized most famously by Charles Tilly, who argued, "the central, tragic fact is simple: coercion *works*; those who apply substantial force to their fellows get compliance, and from the compliance draw the multiple advantages of money, goods, deference, access to pleasures denied to less powerful people."[45]

This description seems to apply to Ramzan Kadyrov, who in March 2007, at the age of 30, became Chechnya's president and who has been the de facto master of the republic since his father's assassination in 2004. His power, consistent with Mao's famous dictum about power growing out of the barrel of a gun, originated with his control over pro-Russian Chechen security forces, the so-called *Kadyrovtsy*. He was given Russia's highest honor, Hero of Russia, and even made a member of the Russian Academy of Natural Sciences. He clearly does not lack for wealth. And he achieved his power, status, and wealth due to his willingness to use extremely harsh means. Journalists Owen Matthews and Anna Nemtsova, after an assessment of Kadyrov's "simple, violent, and effective" methods, concluded, "chalk up a victory for the politics of brutal repression."[46]

Chechnya, of course, has experienced more than a decade of "the politics of brutal repression." The human toll of the war was discussed earlier. Tens of thousands of people have been killed, thousands more "disappeared," and torture and kidnapping has been practiced on a widespread scale by Russian, Chechen government, and Chechen rebel combatants.[47] The major turning point was the decision to give Kadyrov (and his father Akhmad before his 2004 assassination) a relatively free hand to impose order by any means necessary after the mixed results of the efforts of Russian military and security bodies. As James Hughes noted in 2007, "the brutality of the Kadyrovtsy approach is now the central plank not only of the security strategy, but also

---

[45] Charles Tilly, *Coercion, Capital, and European States, AD 990–1992* (Cambridge: Blackwell, 1992), p. 70. The literature on European state building is discussed in Chapter 1.

[46] Owen Matthews and Anna Nemtsova, "Ramzan's World," *Newsweek International*, September 25, 2006.

[47] On human rights abuses, see, for example: Sarah E. Mendelson, "Anatomy of Ambivalence: The International Community and Human Rights Abuse in the North Caucasus," *Problems of Post-Communism*, 53, 6 (November/December 2006), pp. 3–15; Memorial and Demos, "Praktika provedeniya 'kontrterroristicheskoy operatsii' Rossiyskoy Federatsiyey na Severnom Kavkaze v 1999–2006 gg.," January 26, 2007, at: http://www.memo.ru/; Anna Politkovskaya, *Vtoraya Chechenskaya* (Moskva: Zakharov, 2002), pp. 195–227; John Russell, *Chechnya – Russia's "War on Terror"* (New York: Routledge, 2007), pp. 12–16.

of Putin's political strategy for Chechnya."[48] This strategy of outsourcing state building to the most powerful local bandit is familiar from the historical and comparative literature.[49]

This policy of "Chechenization" elevated the role of the Kadyrovtsy in the fighting, and in law and order more generally. In 2007, the number of federal forces in Chechnya was cut in half, from 50,000 to 25,000, while Kadyrov built up a force of comparable size loyal to him. Kadyrov's people took over most of the key posts in the Chechen power ministries. Evidence of abuses by these forces was abundant, including kidnapping, torture, "disappearances," and murders. Harsh methods were sometimes used to encourage rebel fighters to surrender and join the Kadyrovtsy, including kidnapping and torturing family members. The Russian journalist Anna Politkovskaya argued before her murder in October 2006 that the Chechenization policy deliberately exploited the cultural practice of "blood feuds," pitting Chechens against Chechens and thus reducing the participation of Russian units in the violence.[50]

It must be stressed that Kadyrov's success is due not only to his embrace of violence, but steady material and financial support from Moscow. Further, some argued that Kadyrov is a Frankenstein's monster, who could turn on his Kremlin master if driven to it. Under Kadyrov, almost all of the top positions in Chechnya are occupied by those, like himself, who fought against Russia either in the first war or even in the second war. With his control over the republic's coercive structures, Kadyrov has de facto independence from federal control, and, according to this view, Moscow would not dare to cut off financial resources and risk a confrontation. Turning over the keys to the republic means, as Vyacheslav Izmaylov put it, "the rebels won," and thus demonstrates the weakness and not the strength of the Russian state in the North Caucasus.[51]

Kadyrov repeatedly sought to demonstrate his independence from Russian forces in Chechnya and to limit and weaken their role. For example, in April 2008, a major conflict broke out between Kadyrov and the Kadyrovtsy and a Ministry of Defense unit, the Vostok (East) battalion, which was controlled

---

[48] Hughes 2007, p. 125.

[49] Diane E. Davis and Anthony W. Pereira, eds., *Irregular Armed Forces and Their Role in Politics and State Formation* (Cambridge: Cambridge University Press, 2003).

[50] Irina Borogan and Andrey Soldatov, "Kavkazskiy front: novaya taktika chuzhikh oshibok," *Nov. Gaz.*, August 9, 2007; Memorial, "Chechenskaya Respublika: posledstviya 'chechenizatsii' konflikta," March 2, 2006; Human Rights Watch, "Widespread Torture in the Chechen Republic," November 13, 2006, at: http://hrw.org/; Aleksandr Cherkasov, "'Rasprostranennaya ili sistematicheskaya praktika'," *Yezhednev. Zh.*, October 27, 2006; Cerwyn Moore, "Counter-Insurgency and Counter Hostage-Taking in the North Caucasus," *Central Asia-Caucasus Analyst*, August 23, 2006; Anna Politkovskaya, "Karatel'nyy sgovor," *Nov. Gaz.*, September 28, 2006.

[51] Vyacheslav Izmaylov, "Rossiya proigrala voynu Ichkerii," *Nov. Gaz.*, February 19, 2007; Sergey Markedonov, "Vernut'sya na Kavkaz," *Apologiya*, 9 (December 2006); Sergei Markedonov, "New Means, Same End," *RP*, July 2006, pp. 7–8. The Frankenstein analogy is from Baev, "Has Russia Achieved a Victory...."

by a rival Chechen clan, the Yamadayev brothers. Kadyrov wanted the battalion removed from Yamadayev control. The army had backed the battalion and the Yamadayev brothers as a counterweight to Kadyrov, who had an obvious interest in eliminating an armed group not loyal to him. The Yamadayev brothers lost this power struggle, and two of the brothers, Ruslan and Sulim, were subsequently assassinated, in Moscow and Dubai respectively. Many observers believe Kadyrov was behind these murders.[52] Russian officers do not trust Kadyrov, who had fought against Russia in the first war. One officer stated in November 2007, "the people in charge in the republic now understand that it is more advantageous to milk Russia than to fight with it. But if the financing is cut off ... they could once again make a deal with Arabs prepared to pay for armed confrontation."[53]

Still, Kadyrov's methods do seem to have "worked" in the sense that Tilly describes.[54] The brutal violence inflicted in Chechnya by Russian forces and their Chechen allies demobilized many potential oppositionists in the republic and killed some of the most prominent rebel leaders, particularly Basayev and Maskhadov. At the same time, the repression in Chechnya has been a constant reminder to those elsewhere in the region about the danger of supporting violent insurgency in their republics. Further, if Kadyrov does succeed in establishing order through brutal repression, Chechnya's role as a source of spillover violence to the rest of the North Caucasus probably will decline. Indeed, the Kadyrovtsy sometimes ventured into Dagestan and Ingushetia, and Kadyrov offered to provide "help and support" to Zyazikov in Ingushetia, adding that Ingushetia is a small republic and that he could impose order "without a problem."[55]

This assessment of the potentially stabilizing role of repression in Chechnya, setting aside the troublesome moral implications, is not definitive. The situation remains unstable, and much could change in the republic in a short period of time.[56] Further, repressive behavior by the power ministries in the

[52] Vladimir Mukhin, "Ramzan vstupil v bitvu za mezhu," *Nez. Gaz.*, January 22, 2008; Simon Saradzhyan, "Tensions in Chechnya Boil Over," *MT*, April 17, 2008; Vyacheslav Izmaylov, "Prichin ubit' mnogo, prichin zashchishchat' ne ostalos'," *Nov. Gaz.*, September 29, 2008; Liz Fuller, "Who Wanted To Kill Sulim Yamadayev, And Why?", *RFE/RL*, April 1, 2009.

[53] Georgiy Aleksandrov, "Chechnya mezhdu shariatom i byudzhetom," *AiF*, November 1, 2007.

[54] Jason Lyall has conducted careful academic assessments of the effectiveness of both indiscriminate violence and the use of pro-Moscow Chechen fighters in the Second Chechen War. In both cases, Lyall found that these tactics were effective: Jason Lyall, "Does Indiscriminate Violence Incite Insurgent Attacks?: Evidence from Chechnya," *Journal of Conflict Resolution*, 53, 3 (June 2009), pp. 331–362; Jason Lyall, "Are Coethnics More Effective Counterinsurgents? Evidence from the Second Chechen War," *American Political Science Review*, 104, 1 (February 2010), pp. 1–20.

[55] Borogan and Soldatov 2007; Aleksandr Gamov, "Ramzan Kadyrov: Russkim devushkam v shortakh mozhno. No zakrytaya zhenshchina interestnee," *KP*, September 10, 2007.

[56] On the persistence of the Chechen resistance, written shortly after Putin stepped down as president, see, for example: Vadim Rechkalov, "Pomoch' Ramzanu," *MK*, June 18, 2008.

neighboring republics of Ingushetia and Dagestan seems to have been generally counterproductive. Most observers believe that the situation in the North Caucasus began to worsen again starting in 2008.[57] The use of harsh measures also may make it harder to build capacity further in the future. As we will see in the next section, the poor quality of the work of state coercive organs shows the limitations of Putin's state-building strategy in the North Caucasus.

STATE QUALITY IN THE CAUCASUS

It should already be clear from the previous discussion that the quality of state coercive organs in the North Caucasus is low. In this section, I discuss in more detail the prevalence of corruption and predation in the power ministries in the region. Corruption among military and security bodies has undermined the effectiveness of these agencies and arguably played a key role in prolonging the Chechen wars. Predation has involved not only the widespread use of official positions for private benefit, but also the other type of predation, morally illegitimate behavior, such as kidnapping and torture.[58]

Corruption

Power ministry corruption in the North Caucasus manifests itself in multiple ways. One common example already mentioned is the payment of bribes to bypass military and police checkpoints. Irina Kuksenkova, a young journalist who interviewed some Chechen rebels after Beslan, reported that "the fighters kept saying their main weapon was corruption in the Russian police and army. They can cross any borders." Police, military, and border guard personnel, who are part of the FSB, routinely take a cut of the profits in exchange for permitting contraband, such as smuggled oil and gas, to pass through checkpoints in and around Chechnya.[59]

The Russian police have general responsibility for the issuing of passports, visas, and other identity documents. Control over this function provides a ready source of enrichment for personnel. After the Beslan tragedy, an investigation into the North Ossetian MVD uncovered 7,000 cases per year of the sale of passports, at a cost of $1,500–$2,000, including to insurgents. In Chechnya,

---

[57] For reports documenting the increase in violence, see: Center for Strategic and International Studies: Human Rights & Security Initiative, *Violence in the North Caucasus: Interim Report: January 2008–July 2009* (Washington, DC: CSIS, 2009); Center for Strategic and International Studies: Human Rights & Security Initiative, *Violence in the North Caucasus: Spring 2010: On the Rise, Again?* (Washington, DC: CSIS, 2010); Parliamentary Assembly of the Council of Europe, *Situation in the North Caucasus Region: Security and Human Rights: Second Information Report*, AS/JUR (2009) 43, September 29, 2009.

[58] On predation, see Chapter 5.

[59] Babich 2004; Bakhtiyar Akhmedkhanov and Dmitriy Starostin, "'Gorets' brosayet vyzov Kadyrovu," *MN*, October 20, 2006; Vadim Rechkalov, "Den'gi Basayeva," *Izvestiya*, December 8, 2004.

many fighters have passports and identity papers acquired illegally through the MVD or middlemen. Chechen terrorists conducting attacks beyond the region, including the 2002 *Nord-Ost* theater attack in Moscow, are also often shown to have acquired residency registration illegally from the police.[60]

A form of corruption that very directly undermines both state capacity and state quality, and leads to the death of state officials and innocent citizens, is the sale of weapons by power ministry personnel to rebels. In Chechnya, the insurgents rarely lack for weaponry. Most of their arms apparently come from Russian government sources, either from individual soldiers or networks that connect military and security personnel to the rebels. One counterintelligence officer remarked that it is very easy to sell part of uncovered arms caches back to the rebels simply by not recording them in the inventory.[61]

Finally, positions in law enforcement are up for sale in the region, as they are elsewhere in Russia. Reportedly, the standard fee for becoming a police officer in the North Caucasus was $1,000 in 2004. By 2007, allegedly the price of becoming a cop in Dagestan was $3,000, with a job in the traffic police going for $7,000. More generally, 37 percent of those surveyed in the North Caucasus reported that they had to pay a bribe to receive employment, compared to 9 percent for the entire country. In Dagestan, allegedly entry into any state position requires a bribe, although disentangling corrupt and patrimonial (see further in this chapter) mechanisms for job placement in highly diverse Dagestan is difficult.[62]

Power ministry corruption in the North Caucasus, like in the rest of Russia, penetrates all levels of the state and has become routine and systemic. For example, the former Ingush Internal Affairs Minister, Beslan Khamkhoyev, alleged that President Zyazikov personally received tens of thousands of dollars every month in kickbacks from misappropriated police pay. The corruption is so extensive, Pavel Baev stated, that "local law enforcement structures became undistinguishable from criminal groupings." More generally, many argue that the material interests of siloviki in the region, and in Chechnya in particular, favor a persistent conflict in order to continue their enrichment through the trafficking of various forms of contraband, including oil and weapons. However, Chechenization may have reduced the access of federal military and law enforcement personnel to these sources of income, which are now more controlled by Kadyrov.[63]

---

[60] Oleg Khrabryy, "Krizis vneshnego upravleniya," *Ekspert*, October 18, 2004; Vadim Rechkalov, "Armiya Basayeva," *Izvestiya*, December 6, 2004; Vladimir Mukhin, "Minoborony neset boyevye poteri," *Nez. Gaz.*, August 22, 2006; Babich 2004.

[61] Lieven 1998, pp. 285–286; Andrei Smirnov, "Police Officers Meet in Nalchik to Discuss Insurgency Options," *EDM*, May 23, 2007; Rechkalov, "Armiya Basayeva."

[62] Khrabryy 2004; International Crisis Group 2008, p. 13; "Kavkaz ostanetsya zazhitochno-nestabil'nym," *K-D*, February 20, 2006; Aleksandr Khinshteyn, "Chikago s kavkazskim aktsentom," *MK*, April 26–27, 2006.

[63] Khrabryy 2004; Fuller, "Militant Attacks Increase ..."; Baev, "The Russian Military Campaign in the North Caucasus." On the "commercial character" of the war, see, for example: Malashenko and Trenin 2002, p. 154; Politkovskaya 2002, pp. 195–227.

In short, the same types of corrupt behavior described in Chapter 5 for Russian law enforcement officers – shakedowns, roofing, selling assets, and so forth – are also prevalent among police, security, and military personnel in the North Caucasus. The only question is whether the south of Russia is worse than the rest of the country. Anecdotal evidence suggests it is. Unfortunately, good cross-regional measures of corruption are hard to come by for Russia. The best-known study of regional corruption in Russia was released in 2002 by the Russian branch of Transparency International and the INDEM Foundation. These data are of limited utility for us because they only examined forty of Russia's then eighty-nine regions, and left all of the ethnic republics of the North Caucasus out of the survey for safety reasons, as well as concerns about the validity of any polls. Three regions in the Southern Federal District were included, and they all were toward the bottom of the combined corruption index: Krasnodar (twenty-nine out of forty), Rostov (thirty-two), and Volgograd (thirty-four). Phyllis Dininio and Robert Orttung argued that those regions with the highest number of state officials and the lowest level of economic development are the most corrupt, and therefore suggested that the North Caucasus would likely have high levels of corruption.[64]

The best available comparative data on power ministry corruption in the North Caucasus comes from a survey conducted by Sarah Mendelson and Theodore Gerber in 2006. Their survey of young adult males (ages sixteen to thirty-nine) in three ethnic republics – Dagestan, Kabardino-Balkaria, and North Ossetia – produced some surprising, even stunning, results that seem to contradict much of the conventional wisdom about the power ministries in the region. The survey, administered by the Levada Center, found, among other results:

- Fears of violent abuse by the police were somewhat *lower* than the national average.
- Fears of arbitrary arrest were somewhat *lower* than the national average.
- Actual experiences of violent abuse by the police were somewhat *lower* than the national average.
- Experiences of police corruption were high (36 percent), but still a minority of respondents, and comparable to national levels.
- Trust in the police, although low, was no lower than the national average.[65]

These findings, if valid, do not by themselves negate the many individual reports discussed earlier, but they do present them in a new light.[66] Specifically,

---

[64] http://www.anti-corr.ru/rating_regions/index.htm; Phyllis Dininio and Robert Orttung, "Explaining Patterns of Corruption in the Russian Regions," *World Politics*, 57, 4 (July 2005), pp. 500–529.

[65] Theodore P. Gerber and Sarah E. Mendelson, "Cauldron of Terrorism or Bowl of Kasha? What Survey Data Say About the North Caucasus," Center for Strategic and International Studies, Unpublished manuscript, July 2006.

[66] There are obvious reasons why young men in these regions might not answer questions about police corruption and violence truthfully. The relevant question is whether this tendency is

they suggest that the power ministries in most of the North Caucasus may behave in broadly similar ways to their counterparts elsewhere in Russia. To put it differently, they are no more corrupt or predatory than is typical for Russia as a whole.

Some experts on the region, such as Yulia Latynina, contend that even though the patterns of violent law enforcement behavior in the North Caucasus are similar to the rest of the country, the effects are different because of cultural specificities of the region. She contends that the tradition of vendettas or "blood feuds" lead victims of torture and abuse, or their relatives, to seek vengeance against their tormentors, either by joining violent extremist groups or taking up arms against the state. Thus, even though the percentage of victims of police abuse is small, the total number of militants can be enough to unleash major attacks.[67] This argument, however, is also challenged by some of Gerber and Mendelson's other findings. They find little support among their respondents for radical Islam, as well as generally low levels of ethnic hostility. The predominant concern of young men in the region was economic.

Overall, the survey data combined with the secondary accounts in the press still give us a firm basis to conclude that power ministry personnel in the North Caucasus engage in corruption relatively frequently, which indicates low state quality. This conclusion is strengthened when we turn to the issue of predation.

Predation

I define predatory behavior as either plunder or morally illegitimate activities. Both types of actions by power ministry personnel in the region have already been noted. Accepting bribes and selling weapons, documents, and even jobs are all forms of plunder in a conflict zone. Murder and torture by state officials are clearly morally illegitimate. And activities such as kidnapping, which is by definition a business by which armed groups can raise money, fits into both categories of predation.

The other factor, besides moral illegitimacy, that James Burk considers relevant to evaluating predation is material presence. The material presence of the power ministries in the North Caucasus is undoubtedly high. Putin noted

---

more pronounced in the North Caucasus than elsewhere. That is a judgment call; Gerber and Mendelson do not believe that this issue makes the results invalid. Another factor that may explain somewhat lower rates of police corruption and police violence in the region toward young males is that, as discussed below, a much larger percentage of this cohort actually works in the power ministries than is typical for Russia as a whole. Young men who work for the police are obviously less likely to be harrassed by the police.

[67] Yuliya Latynina, "Militseyskoye gosudarstvo v otdel'no vzyatoy respublike," *Nov. Gaz.*, October 31 and November 3, 2005; John Dunlop, "Putin, Kozak, and Russian Policy Toward the North Caucasus," Paper presented at the North Caucasus Conference, Jamestown Foundation, September 14, 2006. See also: Yevgeniy Natarov, "Terrorizm fundamentalistskiy i antimilitseyskiy," *Gazeta.ru*, August 31, 2006.

in 2005 that in the Southern Federal District, which encompasses the North Caucasus, there was the "highest density" of law enforcement personnel not only in Russia, but in all of Europe: almost 12 law enforcement personnel per 1,000 population (by comparison, the United States has 2.3 police officers per 1,000 residents). Eighteen percent of employed males age eighteen to thirty-nine in three republics in the region work for the power ministries, compared to 8 percent for the country as a whole.[68]

There is also considerable evidence of morally illegitimate behavior by military, security, and law enforcement personnel in the region. Although the use of torture, kidnappings, and "disappearances" is most widespread and best-documented in Chechnya, similar activities take place in multiple republics in the region.[69] In neighboring Ingushetia, for example, according to the human rights group Memorial, the use of torture against suspects "developed a systematic character" after the June 2004 Nazran attack. In Kabardino-Balkaria (KBR), the police conducted a series of repressive operations in which many practicing Muslims were accused of being "Wahhabists," the term used by Russian state officials for fundamentalist Islamic terrorists. The republic MVD drew up a list of suspected "militants," who were rounded up at mosques and frequently beaten while under detention. Some believers had their beards shaved and crosses shaved into their hair. The head of the KBR MVD from 1992 until 2006, Khachim Shogenov, was instrumental in the use of these tactics. At the same time, he was widely believed to be responsible for running protection rackets (*kryshevaniye*) in the republic. Allegedly it was possible to pay a bribe and have one's name removed from the list of suspected militants. Further, police officers also removed the names of friends and family members from the list of militants.[70]

The widespread use of violence by power ministry personnel across the region, particularly in Dagestan, Chechnya, Ingushetia, North Ossetia, and Kabardino-Balkaria, attained such levels that some observers compared the region to Central America in the 1980s. Sergey Arutyunov, the Director of the Caucasus Department, Institute of Ethnology, Russian Academy of Sciences,

---

[68] Vladimir Putin, "Vstupitel'noye slovo na soveshchanii s rukovoditelyama sub" ektov Federatsii Yuzhnogo federal'nogo okruga," September 23, 2005. Another source claims the 11.8 per 1,000 ratio is for all power ministry personnel, not just law enforcement: Aleksandr Khinshteyn, "Prodayem Kavkaz. Torg umesten," *MK*, June 16, 2005. For U.S. police numbers, see: James T. Quinlivan, "Burden of Victory: The Painful Arithmetic of Stability Operations," *RAND Review*, 27, 2 (Summer 2003), pp. 28–29. On male employment, see: Gerber and Mendelson 2009.

[69] On military and police participation in kidnapping in Chechnya, see, for example: Vyacheslav Izmaylov, "Tovarishchi khvatki," *Nov. Gaz.*, May 28, 2007.

[70] Memorial, "Eskalatsiya konflikta za predelami Chechni v 2004–2005 godakh (Ingushetiya i Kabardino-Balkariya)," March 2, 2006; Latynina 2005; Ivan Sukhov, "Ruslan Nakhushev: 'Moskva dayet den'gi, shtoby vzryva ne bylo'," *VN*, September 29, 2005; Ivan Sukhov, "Gorod posle boya," *VN*, October 17, 2005; "Spetssluzhby na doverii," *Gazeta.ru*, October 19, 2005; Julius Strauss, "Russia's 'war on terror' tainted by brutality and corruption," *The Electronic Telegraph*, May 21, 2005.

remarked in 2006 that antiterrorist operations in the region take place "without any rules. Precisely as it was done, for example, in El Salvador." Indeed, in 2006 and 2007, reports appeared in the opposition press in Russia claiming the existence of officially sanctioned death squads, both in the North Caucasus and throughout the country. Although these claims were impossible to verify, the grounds for suspicion certainly existed, especially in Chechnya.[71]

In much of the North Caucasus, then, we find considerable evidence of both types of predation – plunder and morally illegitimate behavior – among power ministry personnel. Officials serve their own interests and those of the powers that be rather than those of society. One Russian military general acknowledged, "law enforcement organs occupy themselves protecting the interest of clan elites, getting kickbacks, and roofing businesses, and therefore residents look down on them."[72] The response to terrorist incidents such as Beslan also indicated greater attention to regime interests than protecting the population.[73] In the next section, I argue that, even more than in the rest of Russia, patrimonialism and very weak monitoring help account for low state quality in the region.

Explaining Low State Quality in the Caucasus

The most obvious explanation for low state quality in the North Caucasus is straightforward and largely correct: The civil war in Chechnya has been fought with considerable brutality by all sides – the rebels, the federal forces, and the Kadyrovtsy. War is always hell, and this war has been particularly hellish.[74] Moreover, partially due to the efforts of Basayev and partially due to the failings of federal and local officials, the conflict spilled over into neighboring regions. But acknowledging that war is hell is not enough – the parties to the conflict made choices about how to fight the war, and not all of the corrupt and predatory behavior of military, security, and police personnel can be attributed to the war, especially outside Chechnya. Putin's strategy in the North Caucasus was a more extreme version of his overall approach to state building, privileging the use of state coercive power in defense of the regime

---

[71] Natarov 2006; Igor' Korol'kov, "Zapasnye organy," *Nov. Gaz.*, January 11, 2007; Aleksandr Cherkasov, "Sistema 'eskadronov smerti' deystvuyets 2000 goda," *Yezhednev. Zh.*, January 13, 2007; Politkovskaya 2006.

[72] Vladimir Mukhin, "Postoyannaya boyegotovnost' pri vysokoy nestabil'nosti," *Nez. Gaz.*, November 19, 2007. Incidentally, the general in question, Vladimir Shamanov, was accused of, and appeared to condone, war crimes at the beginning of the Second Chechen War: Evangelista 2002, pp. 159–160; Peter Baker and Susan Glasser, *Kremlin Rising*, updated edition (Dulles, VA: Potomac Books, 2007), p. 107.

[73] See, for example: Dunlop 2004, pp. 79–100.

[74] The English translation of Politkovskaya's *Vtoraya Chechenskaya* [The Second Chechen War] was published as: Anna Politkovskaya, *A Small Corner of Hell: Dispatches from Chechnya* (Chicago: University of Chicago Press, 2003). For contrasting discussions of international humanitarian law and war crimes in Chechnya, see: Evangelista 2002, pp. 139–177; Anatol Lieven, "Chechnya i zakony voyny," in Malashenko and Trenin 2002, pp. 230–248.

as opposed to constructing a high-quality state that serves society as a whole. Without attempting a complete account of the multiple reasons for problems of low state capacity in the North Caucasus, I connect the discussion here back to larger themes of the book by briefly noting the role of patrimonialism and the absence of, indeed complete lack of interest in, effective monitoring of the power ministries in the region.

Patrimonialism

The extensive reliance on patrimonial forms of government and administration in post-communist Russia is well documented, and these informal authority networks are arguably the strongest in the North Caucasus. General accounts of patrimonialism tend to emphasize either economic (poverty) or cultural (ethnic or clan) reasons for the dominance of this type of administration, but there is no reason to see them as mutually exclusive. Given both the relative poverty of the North Caucasus and the complex and heterogeneous nature of cultural identity in the region, this tendency toward patrimonialism is not surprising. As North Caucasus expert Georgi Derluguian stresses, many parts of the world have "modern formal institutions that are often superficial or simply superfluous. In such locales people know from daily experience how much their life chances depend on access to various patrons and informal networks."[75]

Kozak, Putin's top aide in the region, called attention to the phenomenon and warned of potentially negative consequences in a report to Putin that was leaked to the press in June 2005. Kozak wrote:

Corporative associations have formed in the power structures that monopolize political and economic resources. In all of the North Caucasus republics the leading positions in the organs of power, and in the most powerful economic entities, are occupied by people with kin ties to each other. As a result the system of checks and balances has collapsed, leading to the spread of corruption. The dominant clan-corporative associations, due to their closed nature, are not interested in feedback mechanisms that enable open dialogue with citizens.

The report was leaked to Aleksandr Khinshteyn, an investigative journalist and State Duma deputy with close ties to the power ministries, who backed up Kozak's central point with more colorful language: "All Caucasian republics long ago were turned into family enterprises, where numerous relatives of the president 'privatized' the tastiest pieces of the pie." Khinshteyn further noted that in Dagestan, the principle of "family succession" operates for many government positions, with one family member replacing another.[76]

---

[75] Derluguian 2005, p. 75. Derluguian provides the best account of patrimonialism in the North Caucasus.

[76] Khinshteyn 2005; Khinshteyn 2006. As Irina Voytsekh remarked at the time, Kozak seemed not to have noticed how much his observations about the North Caucasus applied to the whole country: Irina Voytsekh, "Kreml' vspotel ot kavkazskikh koshmarov," *Utro. ru*, June 17, 2005.

A prominent example of the pernicious effects of patrimonialism in the region took place in Karachayevo-Cherkesiya. In October 2004, seven men were murdered at the home of President Mustafa Batdyev's son-in-law, Ali Kaitov, in a dispute concerning control over major factories in the region. The local police and prosecutors initially protected Kaitov, which led relatives of the victims to storm the president's office and demand the resignation of Batdyev and law enforcement officials. Kozak managed to defuse the situation by removing the chief procurator and regional MVD head, and having the General Procurator investigate the crime and bring charges against Kaitov. The whole episode showed the extent to which law enforcement personnel in the republic are tied into local political and economic clan networks.[77]

The importance of family ties and informal networks is clearly evident in the power ministries in the North Caucasus. For example, local procurators in North Ossetia allegedly refused to bring cases against traffic police accused of assisting rebel fighters because the officers had family ties to high members of the government. Even more damaging, there are multiple reports of family members serving on opposite sides of the conflict, with one brother working for the police and the other fighting for the rebels. In those circumstances, the population is unlikely to report rebel activity to the police for fear that they will be targeted for retribution because their identity will be passed on to the rebels.[78]

Indeed, given the weakness of rational-legal mechanisms for filling spots in the police and other law enforcement and security organs, it is not surprising that it is relatively easy for the rebels to insinuate sympathizers into these bodies. When Shamil Basayev and a group of fighters attacked government buildings and arms depots in Ingushetia in June 2004, they received assistance from multiple members of the Ingush police. Insiders fed him information on the location, identity, work patterns, addresses, and cell phone numbers of members of the police and security structures. They also provided weapons and even escorted Basayev around Ingushetia, using their police IDs to bypass police and military checkpoints.[79]

In Chechnya, Ramzan Kadyrov has made recruiting former rebels into the police and security services a routine practice. There is a certain logic to the system, in that former rebels may be potentially very valuable assets in finding other rebels – hence the expression "it takes a thief to catch a thief."[80] Having former rebels join the Kadyrovtsy also means, from Kadyrov's point of view,

[77] Mikhail Duguzhev, "Karachyevo-Cherkesiya: Prezident pod davleniyem," *IWPR* [Institute for War & Peace Reporting], No. 373, January 15, 2007; Andrei Smirnov, "Kremlin Appoints New Government in Karachaevo-Cherkessia," *EDM*, February 16, 2005. See also: Fatima Tlisova, "Karachaevo-Cherkessia: An Inside Look," Paper presented at the North Caucasus Conference, Jamestown Foundation, September 14, 2006, p. 3.
[78] Khrabryy 2004; Rechkalov, "Armiya Basayeva."
[79] Musa Muradov, "Informatora Shamilya Basayeva likvidirovali dvazhdi," *K-D*, August 24, 2005; Vadim Rechkalov, Marshruty Basayeva," *Izvestiya*, December 9, 2004.
[80] On the effectiveness of this practice, see Lyall 2010.

that they won't join the forces of a different, pro-Moscow Chechen militia leader, such as former Grozny mayor Bislan Gantamirov. Kadyrov secures their exclusive loyalty, making them members of his "clan." More generally, providing employment for former fighters is a common feature of post-civil war settlements.[81] But since the civil war is not yet over, despite Russian claims, the risk of rebels-turned-cops sharing information with the insurgents seems high. Indeed, in April 2006, there were reports of an entire group of Kadyrov's security personnel, numbering 40–100 people, going back over to the side of the insurgents.[82]

Russian army troops in Chechnya see little difference between the Kadyrovtsy and the insurgents. One soldier remarked that the Kadyrovtsy are "a legalized bandit formation … no different from the rebels." During the 2008 dispute between Kadyrov and the Yamadayev brothers, the commander of the Vostok battalion, Sulim Yamadayev, made a similar accusation, stating that the Chechen police was composed mainly of amnestied rebels, prepared at any moment to "once again go into the mountains" to fight against Russian troops. Lieutenant-General Yuriy Netkachev, a former army commander in the North Caucasus, stated at the same time that the Ministry of Defense had made a mistake by creating "mono-ethnic units" in Chechnya. He blamed the dispute between the Kadyrovtsy and the Yamadayev brothers on the dominance of "clan relations" over "common sense." He observed that "service regulations should rule in the army, not ethno-cultural, kinship traditions and values."[83]

A related recruiting practice, although not strictly patrimonial, is the widespread enlisting of fighters as "agents" by the FSB or other power ministries. Of course, in itself this is a common intelligence practice. But it is striking how frequently these "agents" have been implicated in subsequent attacks. For example, a Dagestani fighter with close ties to Basayev, Rasul Makasharipov, was arrested in 2002, made a deal with the FSB and received amnesty, and was subsequently killed in a shootout with police in 2005, accused of leading a rebel group responsible for the murder of multiple police officers.[84] John Dunlop documented several cases of terrorists involved in either the 2002 *Nord-Ost* attack in Moscow or the 2004 Beslan raid having previously been

---

[81] For an introduction to the literature on "Disarmament, Demobilization, and Reintegration" after civil wars, see: Michael Brzoska, "Embedding DDR Programmes in Security Sector Reconstruction," in Alan Bryden and Heiner Hänggi, eds., *Security Governance in Post-Conflict Peacebuilding* (Munster: Lit Verlag, 2005), pp. 95–114.

[82] Bakhtiyar Akhmedkhanov, "Mulla, ty zachem uvel moikh lyudey?" *MN*, March 24, 2006; Arkady Ostrovsky, "Kadyrov's 'legalised bandits' bring lawlessness to Chechnya," *Financial Times*, January 4, 2006; Liz Fuller, "Who Is Out to Discredit the Chechen Police, and Why?," *RFE/RL*, February 1, 2007.

[83] Ostrovsky 2006; Vladimir Mukhin, "Spetsnaz spotknulsya na teypovykh protivorechiyakh," *Nez. Gaz.*, April 21, 2008.

[84] Khinshteyn 2006; Paul Tumelty, "Chechnya and the Insurgency in Dagestan," *CW*, May 11, 2005; Vyacheslav Izmaylov, "Spetsprikrytiye dlya terroristov," *Nov. Gaz.*, September 17, 2001.

released due to deals with the FSB or the police. It seems plausible that the state officials making these deals at least occasionally benefit financially from them, but at a minimum, an effective agency would have better control over its intelligence assets.[85]

To an important extent, Putin's relationship with the Kadyrovs, especially Ramzan, was patrimonial from the beginning. After his father's assassination in 2004, Ramzan Kadyrov met with Putin in the Kremlin – famously wearing a blue track suit – and received Putin's endorsement. Kadyrov always made clear that his loyalty to Putin was personal, not institutional. For example, in June 2007, while arguing that Putin should stay as president for a third term, Kadyrov stated:

Putin gave the Chechen nation its second life! Allah appointed him to his position.... I respect Putin not only as president, but also as a personality. I am not a FSB person or a GRU [military intelligence – B.T.] person, I am a Putin person. His policies, his word is the law for me. We are travelling along his road. Putin saved our people, he is a hero. He not only saved us, he saved Russia.... Putin is a gift from God, he gave us our freedom.[86]

Kadyrov's rule in Chechnya was also patrimonial in the classic sense that he treated the republic as his personal property. As Audit Chamber head Sergey Stepashin joked in 2009, "The whole republic belongs to Ramzan Kadyrov."[87]

The Russian state under Putin remained patrimonial in important respects. The development of rational-legal bureaucratic norms was particularly far away in the power ministries in the North Caucasus, where personalistic and familial modes of recruitment and advancement tended to predominate.

Monitoring

Police patrol monitoring relies on some parts of the state checking on the behavior of other parts, whereas fire alarm monitoring looks to outside actors, such as the media or civil society, to keep tabs on state officials. Putin exhibited a strong preference for police patrols over fire alarms during his presidency, and the ability of outside actors to help monitor the state was generally eroded.

In the North Caucasus, arguably there has been less monitoring of either type than in the rest of Russia. Although many brave journalists and NGO activists have sought to provide information on the state of affairs in the region, and because of their efforts it is generally available to interested

---

[85] Dunlop 2006. Dunlop concludes that these connections between the special services and the rebels suggest that the FSB is directly responsible for the *Nord-Ost* attack. But it seems at least as plausible that the rebels were manipulating their "sponsors" rather than the other way around.

[86] Musa Muradov, "'Putin – dar bozhiy'," *K-V*, June 18, 2007.

[87] *Ren TV* via *BBC Monitoring*, "Russian auditor praises defence minister; says Chechen leader owns republic," May 25, 2009 [JRL 2009-#99, May 28, 2009].

observers both inside and outside Russia, the state has limited the ability of these groups and individuals to publicize such facts and analysis on a broad scale in Russia. The situation seems closest to what Pablo Policzer calls "blind coercion," in which neither internal nor external monitors know much about law enforcement and security behavior at the local level. Policzer states that Argentina during the military dictatorship (1976–1982) had this form of monitoring state coercion.[88]

In the first Chechen War, critical media coverage of government policy and military performance helped turn the public against the war. In the period after the 1996 truce, it became increasingly dangerous for journalists to travel to the region because of the threat of kidnapping. During the second Chechen War, the government limited the ability of the media to cover the war, and the takeover of the NTV television station by pro-Kremlin forces effectively removed the main source of critical televised reporting about the war.[89] Tenacious reporters like Anna Politkovskaya continued to cover the war, publishing multiple articles in the independent *Novaya Gazeta* as well as several books. But Putin's statement shortly after her murder in October 2006 that she was not that well known in Russia beyond journalistic and human rights circles and that she did not influence popular opinion, although arguably in poor taste, was probably accurate.[90] NGOs like Memorial have also continued to produce valuable information on the situation in the region, but, again, it is likely their work is better known outside Russia than inside it.

More generally, the level of public accountability of state bodies is lower in the ethnic republics of the North Caucasus than elsewhere in Russia. One proxy for accountability is the regional index of democracy compiled by Nikolay Petrov and Aleksey Titkov of the Carnegie Moscow Center. They provide an annual assessment of the level of democracy in every region in Russia except Chechnya by combining ten different measures (on elections, the media, parties, civil society, etc.). The averages for the years 2003–2007 showed that Dagestan, Adygeya, Karachayevo-Cherkesiya, North Ossetia, Kabardino-Balkaria, and Ingushetia were all below the national average, with Dagestan the best-performing republic in the region (tied for sixty-fourth out of eighty-eight), and KBR finishing in absolute last place (eighty-eighth out of eighty-eight).[91]

---

[88] Pablo Policzer, *The Rise and Fall of Repression in Chile* (Notre Dame, IN: University of Notre Dame Press, 2009).

[89] Andrew Jack, *Inside Putin's Russia* (Oxford: Oxford University Press, 2004), pp. 116–117; Mark Kramer, "Guerrilla Warfare, Counterinsurgency and Terrorism in the North Caucasus: The Military Dimension of the Russian-Chechen Conflict," *Europe-Asia Studies*, 57, 2 (March 2005), pp. 257–258.

[90] Vladimir Putin, "Otvety na voprosy, zadannye vo vremya interv'yu telekanalu ARD (Germaniya)," October 10, 2006.

[91] N.V. Petrov and A.S. Titkov, "Indeks demokratichnosti," *Sotsial'nyy atlas rossiyskikh regionov*, multiple years. I thank Nikolay Petrov for providing me with the most recent data: personal communication, June 9, 2008.

The ability of Russian security and military personnel, and affiliated groups like the Kadyrovtsy, to engage in the predatory activities described in this chapter is further indication of the lack of meaningful oversight of their activities. John Russell noted that all of the various warring parties in Chechnya "can carry out the most arbitrary and brutal of crimes against civilians with impunity." The conviction of Colonel Yuriy Budanov of the 2000 kidnapping and murder of an eighteen-year-old Chechen woman he believed was collaborating with the rebels was widely perceived as an exception, desired by the Kremlin for public relations purposes, and not an indication of a greater desire to hold soldiers accountable for war crimes.[92] The spread of predatory tactics, such as torture and kidnapping, to Ingushetia has also been documented. State officials responsible for these tactics are rarely held accountable.[93]

Finally, it should be noted that the internal sense of mission that can motivate the behavior of state officials when there is no effective monitoring also seems to be absent in the power ministries in the North Caucasus. The one notable exception to this may be among the Kadyrovtsy. Kadyrov himself seems to not be motivated solely by material inducements, although these have been abundant and probably were his primary motivation for years. Anna Matveeva contended in 2007 that Kadyrov was refashioning himself as a "traditional Caucasian hero: merciless to his enemies, generous to his subordinates, respectful of tradition." He spoke of himself in the third person as someone with "authority, power, a leader that people respect," and as someone who carried out "a historically important step – when Kadyrov united the [Chechen] people."[94]

Although much of Kadyrov's public persona is clearly bluster, he does seem to understand the need to build some kind of legitimacy and move away from pure repression. He even met with Memorial activists in 2008 to discuss the human rights situation in Chechnya. After the meeting, chair of the Memorial board of directors, Oleg Orlov, stated that Memorial and Kadyrov had agreed on the need to observe human rights and punish those guilty of such violations. Orlov also expressed satisfaction with the sharp decline in cases of torture. Given Kadyrov's past crimes, the whole affair sounds morally repugnant, but it also brings to mind Tilly's observation that "war making and state making – quintessential protection rackets with the advantage of legitimacy – qualify as our largest examples of organized crime."[95] Overall, the enlistment of Chechens to play the lead role in violent state building seems

[92] Russell 2007, p. 104; Baker and Glasser 2007, pp. 99–120 (esp. pp. 117–118).
[93] Memorial, "Eskalatsiya konflikta ...," 2006; Memorial 2008.
[94] Matveeva 2007, pp. 7–8; Muradov 2007.
[95] "Kadyrov Meets with Memorial Activists," CW, 9, 8 (February 29, 2008); Charles Tilly, "War Making and State Making as Organized Crime," in Peter B. Evans, Dietrich Rueschemeyer, and Theda Skocpol, eds., *Bringing the State Back In* (Cambridge: Cambridge University Press, 1985), p. 169. The whole episode seems even more grotesque after the 2009 killing of Memorial activist Nataliya Estemirova, a killing that Orlov blamed on Kadyrov: see Chapter 8.

to have elevated a sense of mission among key cadres compared to the attitude of Russian troops earlier in the war.[96] It probably goes without saying that whatever sense of mission does exist among the Kadyrovtsy, it is not marked by either professional norms or a commitment to serving the public fairly, which I have argued are central to building state quality.

CONCLUSIONS AND PROSPECTS

Did Putin achieve his "historic mission?" The North Caucasus remained highly unstable at the end of his presidency, and the relative quiet of the last three years of his presidency was only a success compared to earlier in his tenure and to predictions of impending catastrophe. But it would also be a mistake to assume that nothing had changed. The level of political violence and terrorism in the region was generally lower in 2006–2007 than it was in 2004–2005. From Putin's point of view, a temporary improvement may have been sufficient. When he left office in May 2008, he could make a plausible claim to success at fulfilling his "historic mission." Tatyana Lokshina, chair of the human rights organization Demos, asserted in 2006 that Putin's key goal was keeping "the lid shut over the boiling pot" in Chechnya until 2008. Lokshina argued that this was an important factor explaining Putin's support for Ramzan Kadyrov.[97]

At the same time, the situation in the region remained potentially volatile and could be upset by a major successful terrorist attack, whether against a critical facility or even specific individuals, such as Kadyrov. Moreover, since Kadyrov's loyalty to Moscow, in patrimonial style, was more a personal connection with Putin than an impersonal commitment to the Russian state, his "Frankenstein" characteristics could indeed become evident in the next several years, particularly depending on Putin's future role in government and Kadyrov's relationship with Medvedev. Many observers and experts maintain that the violent instability in the region is due in part to the counterproductive behavior of coercive organs. Massive corruption and indiscriminate use of violence, these analysts contend, is simply making the problems of the region worse, actually creating the extremists and terrorists the government claims to be fighting. For example, Arkady Ostrovsky argued in 2008 that "Russia's colonial methods" were "the main cause of instability," brought about by "state-sponsored repression, corruption and lawlessness that alienates and radicalises the population and drives young men into the hands of Islamist militants."[98] Additionally, the

---

[96] On the cynicism and indifference of Russian troops during the First Chechen War, see: Lieven 1998, pp. 46–55, 212–218.

[97] Julie Corwin, "Chechnya: Activist Discusses Republic's Political Situation," *RFE/RL*, May 28, 2006.

[98] Arkady Ostrovsky, "The wild south," *The Economist: Enigma Variations* (Special report on Russia), November 29, 2008. Further possible citations here are legion. Examples include: Dunlop and Menon 2006; Khinshteyn 2006; Politkovskaya 2006; Naturov 2006; Memorial, "Eskalatsiya konflikta ..."; Anatoliy Tsyganok, "Neshtatnaya krovavaya trenirovka," *Polit.ru*, October 15, 2005.

archetypal example of a predatory state, Zaire under Mobutu Sese Seko, lasted only as long as Mobuto received massive subsidies from the United States and collapsed once external support was withdrawn.[99] The 2008–2009 economic downturn hindered Russia's ability to subsidize the region and arguably contributed to a subsequent upswing in violence.[100]

Studies of revolutions suggest that the type of state that post-communist Russia has had in the North Caucasus is the kind most likely to provoke revolution: simultaneously repressive, patrimonial, and organizationally weak.[101] There is little doubt that Russia's state apparatus in the region is both patrimonial and repressive and, despite its large physical presence and recent improvements in terms of public security, is still organizationally weak in the sense that its coercive structures perform poorly at some of their core tasks. For example, in September 2007, the last month of Kozak's stint as presidential envoy, he severely criticized the police in Ingushetia for their ineffectiveness in halting a wave of attacks and political murders. He called for a "purge" of the ranks to get rid of the "fellow travelers of the rebels, the corrupt, and the traitors."[102] Although revolution seems unlikely, the current nature of Russian state coercive organs in the North Caucasus gives little reason for confidence about long-term political order.

On the other hand, Tilly is clearly right that violent repression sometimes works. Some recent literature on counterinsurgency operations and imperial occupation suggests that harsh methods similar to those used by Russia and Kadyrov in Chechnya can lead to victory. And civil wars typically end not with a settlement, but one side achieving a dominant victory.[103] It is thus possible that the trend toward reduced violence and greater stability in the region that started in Putin's second term will continue. Will a short-term imposition of order lead to long-term state building? This is the puzzle that faces not only the North Caucasus, but Russia as a whole.

In thinking about this issue, it is worth considering more explicitly the relationship between state capacity and state quality, which for most of the book have been treated independently. We saw in the North Caucasus, for example, how power ministry corruption not only demonstrated the low quality of the Russian state in terms of its ability to serve the population in a fair manner,

[99] Peter B. Evans, "Predatory, Developmental, and Other Apparatuses: A Comparative Political Economy Perspective on the Third World State," *Sociological Forum*, 4, 4 (1989), pp. 561–587.

[100] Valery Dzutsev, "Moscow Reduces Aid to the North Caucasus: Jeopardizing the Precarious Security Environment ," EDM, 6, 169 (September 16, 2009).

[101] Jeff Goodwin, *No Other Way Out: States and Revolutionary Movements, 1945–1991* (Cambridge: Cambridge University Press, 2001). For a brief application of this logic to the North Caucasus, see: Georgi Derluguian, "The Coming Revolutions in the North Caucasus," *PONARS Policy Memo*, 378 (December 2005).

[102] Vladimirova and Trifonov 2007. For similar Kozak complaints about the ineffectiveness of law enforcement in Dagestan, see: International Crisis Group 2008, p. 16.

[103] Lyall 2009; Gil Merom, *How Democracies Lose Small Wars* (Cambridge: Cambridge University Press, 2003); James D. Fearon, "Iraq's Civil War," *Foreign Affairs*, 86, 2 (March/April 2007), p. 8.

but also had direct implications for the capacity of the state to prevent terrorist attacks. Furthermore, predatory officials who serve their own interests over those of either the powers that be or society as a whole are not likely to be effective in fighting crime, given that they are busy engaging in it themselves. In the final chapter, I ask whether a strong state can be built in Russia if state quality remains a low priority.

8

State Capacity and Quality Reconsidered

> I completely understand how much remains to be done to make the state genu-
> inely fair and attentive to its citizens.... I will give special attention to the fun-
> damental role of law, which is the basis for both our state and our civil society.
> We must achieve true respect for the law and overcome legal nihilism, which
> seriously hinders development today.
>
> Dmitriy Medvedev, May 2008[1]

Dmitriy Medvedev was inaugurated as Russian President in May 2008, bringing to a formal end the eight years of Vladimir Putin's presidency. However, it
was Putin more than the Russian citizenry who was responsible for Medvedev's
ascent to the presidency, and Medvedev immediately appointed Putin as his
Prime Minister. Together Putin and Medvedev established what came to be
known as a "tandemocracy" in which they share power. From the beginning,
Medvedev developed a reputation as more "liberal" than Putin, railing against
corruption and "legal nihilism." In the terminology of this book, Medvedev
marked improving "state quality" as one of his key priorities, something that
he noted at his inauguration was a weak point for the Russian state.

This chapter concludes with a look at the future of Russian state building. To address that issue, we need to evaluate the extent to which presidential agency can change the trajectory of the Russian state; perhaps Russia is
"doomed" to have a certain type of state due to its circumstances. Historically
the strength of the Russian state has varied over the centuries, but a disregard
for state quality has been fairly constant. Thus we also need to explore the
logical connections between state capacity and state quality.

This concluding chapter has five major sections. First, I briefly recap the key
arguments of the book so far. Second, I use cross-national quantitative data
to assess the extent to which structural features such as the level of economic
development, resource dependence, and post-Soviet legacies can account for

---

[1] Dmitriy Medvedev, "Vystupleniye na tseremonii vstupleniya v dolzhnost' Prezidenta Rossii,"
May 7, 2008.

the current level of Russian state capacity and quality. Although all three of these factors are associated with stateness, they alone cannot explain the weakness of the Russian state at the end of Putin's presidency. In the third section, I thus critically evaluate Putin's approach to state building, arguing that his state-building strategy did not address patrimonial practices in the power ministries, privileged internal "police patrols" over external "fire alarms" in terms of monitoring state agencies, and failed to instill a mission of protection of the population in law enforcement personnel, which led to the continued dominance of repressive and predatory practices. The fourth section returns to the social science literature on the state to probe the connection between state quality and state capacity. I argue that a constitutionalist approach to state building is preferable to an authoritarian one, not just in terms of building state quality, but state capacity as well. In the fifth and final section, I offer some concluding thoughts on the future of Russian state building.

STATE BUILDING AND RUSSIA'S POWER MINISTRIES: A RECAP

The Weberian approach to the state emphasizes controlling coercion. In a very practical sense, in established states this means the military, the police, and other affiliated agencies such as law enforcement and intelligence – what Russians call the "power ministries." Investigating the politics of the power ministries thereby provides a useful way to bring the abstract notion of state building into clearer focus.

The power ministries had played an important role in domestic politics under Boris Yeltsin, most obviously during the October 1993 events and the Chechen War, but they grew in particular prominence under Putin. Officials with power ministry backgrounds, known as *siloviki*, were seen as particularly influential and were often held responsible for Putin's authoritarian turn. This view has a lot to recommend it. These agencies received large and growing budgets, were headed by close Putin allies, and power ministry personnel were an important presence in national and regional politics.

Although the view of Putin's Russia as a siloviki-dominated police state possesses an important element of truth, it also can be misleading. A more complete picture of siloviki influence can be obtained by using three different lenses, what I call the cohort, clan, and corporate approaches. Thinking of the siloviki as a *cohort* captures their prominence throughout the state under Putin and points to commonalities in organizational culture among the power ministries, but overstates the cohesiveness of these officials. The *clan* approach to Russian politics focuses on competing groups of top elites who forge stable alliances based on past service together and common interests, alliances that can cross bureaucratic lines and indeed the state-business divide. This perspective points to the importance of patrimonial links in Russian politics and also opens up the possibility of splits within the siloviki cohort. Indeed, there seemed to be at least two powerful siloviki clans fighting for influence during the pivotal 2007–2008 years of the Putin-Medvedev succession. Finally,

bureaucratic politics remained important to understanding the power ministries, with *corporate* (organizational) interests often in conflict between the
different power ministries. Through this lens one could see that the key power
ministry was the FSB (Federal Security Service), the KGB successor, which
had the most domestic political clout and indeed somewhat colonized the two
other main power ministries, the Ministry of Defense and the Ministry of
Internal Affairs (MVD). In the long-running Russian battle between the military and the secret police, and the secret police and the regular police, under
Putin, the professional officers of the armed forces and the militia were much
weaker than the "Chekists" from the KGB/FSB.[2]

A detailed understanding of the power ministries and the siloviki, as well
as the politics of these agencies and officials, helps make sense of the direction and results of post-Soviet Russian state building. Both Yeltsin and Putin
highlighted state weakness as a key problem. Putin especially made building
state capacity the centerpiece of his presidency. Conceptually, state capacity
refers to whether a state is capable of taking decisions and ensuring that its
officials implement them, but this basic idea is complicated by two different types of decisions: routine and exceptional. In a strong state, bureaucrats
should carry out their jobs in compliance with laws and regulations, but what
about extralegal (exceptional) decisions by superiors? This also is a type of
capacity, but of a different sort than that exhibited by regular compliance with
routine decisions.

This ambiguity in the concept of state capacity stands out in an exploration of the role of the power ministries in Russian politics. Under Putin, the
biggest increase in power ministry capacity came in the rebuilding of what
Mark Beissinger, writing about the late-Soviet period, called a "regime of
repression" – the use of state coercive bodies, especially law enforcement, to
weaken or neutralize threats to the regime. The extraordinary nature of law
enforcement compliance with executive decisions was clear in the differen-
tial treatment of individuals and groups, such as political parties and candidates or powerful oligarchs, depending on their relationship with Putin and
his allies. In contrast, in the sphere of routine power ministry responsibilities,
such as fighting crime and terrorism and upholding private property rights,
the capacity of the Russian state increased only slightly or not at all compared
to the Yeltsin years. On the other hand, in the related area of fiscal capacity, the use of state coercive capacity arguably did lead to a greater ability to
extract taxes from society.

The power ministries and siloviki officials also played a pivotal role in one
of the major initiatives of Putin's first term: federal reform. Under Yeltsin,
considerable power had flowed to the regional level, including over the activity of notionally centralized law enforcement organs. Putin launched a series
of initiatives to recentralize state power, including the creation of seven federal districts (*okrugs*) between the center and the regions, and relied heavily

---

[2] "Chekists" from the original name of the KGB, the Cheka.

on control over coercion to carry out these reforms. The power ministries mattered not just because they were a natural base for Putin's reforms, but because other institutions used to manage the federal bargain in democratic federations, such as political parties and the courts, were too weak to play this role. The ability to control appointments and the main activities of regional law enforcement organs served to weaken the power of Russia's governors, whose status was reduced even further after the 2004 shift from elections to appointments for regional leaders. Arguably Putin's federal reforms amounted to an assault on federalism itself. This recentralization of power, however, did not amount to an appreciable increase in state capacity in terms of routine decisions, as the power ministries at the okrug and regional level were subject to manipulation by the center.

The weakening of the central government in post-Soviet Russia was most apparent in the North Caucasus. The ongoing war in Chechnya, which by 2010 had been raging off and on for more than fifteen years, suggested that in its southern republics, Russia was still in the first stage of state building: the formation of a state through acquisition of a monopoly over legitimate violence. Events such as the 2004 Beslan school terrorist attack demonstrated that not only was the Chechen problem not under control, but that it threatened to spread to the rest of the North Caucasus. However, in the last years of Putin's presidency, there was a substantial drop in violence in Chechnya. It appeared that an influx of resources and the delegation of a free hand to a powerful local "bandit," Chechen President Ramzan Kadyrov, had stanched the bleeding. On the other hand, the North Caucasus as a whole remained highly unstable and witnessed a renewed surge of violence in 2008–2009.

Overall, then, Putin's efforts to build state capacity yielded mixed results in the coercive realm. Fiscal capacity increased, as did the ability to repress regime opponents. Murder rates declined during his second term, although they remained quite high on a cross-national basis. In the last years of his presidency, 2006–2007, there did seem to be improvement in the North Caucasus and with the battle against terrorism more generally. But compared to the Yeltsin period, the levels of violent crime and terrorism were roughly equal, suggesting that there was less to Putin's project than many analysts, Russian and otherwise, have claimed. The insecure nature of property rights for businesses of all sizes also reflected the inability of law enforcement agencies to fulfill a key routine task as defined by law.

Thinking of state formation in terms of not just state capacity but also state quality leads to further doubts about the progress of Russian state building. State quality refers to the extent to which officials act in a fair and impartial manner that serves the public interest. Recent scholarship on the quality of government represents an important contribution to the state-building literature, as an examination of Russia demonstrates. Corruption and the weakness of the rule of law have been persistent problems in post-Soviet Russia, including in the very structures that are supposed to fight corruption and uphold the rule of law. Power ministry personnel are more oriented toward serving their own personal interests or those of the powers that be than those of society as a whole; predation and repression dominate over protection in terms of law enforcement behavior and norms.

Predatory behavior of power ministry personnel, and their relative lack of commitment to protecting the society they are supposed to serve, has generated a persistent lack of trust by Russian citizens in law enforcement structures. Civil society groups have tried to engage the police in order to change their predatory practices and norms in a more liberal and rational-legal direction, and they have had some success. But a campaign against human rights NGOs, especially those with foreign funding, in Putin's second term rendered uncertain future prospects for cooperative state-society partnerships in the power ministry realm. This was one of several ways in which efforts to improve state quality in the coercive sphere were undermined by Putin's state-building approach.

Why does the Russian state, particularly in the coercive realm, remain low in quality and uneven at best in terms of capacity? I highlighted three issues related to public administration and bureaucratic practices to explain the trajectory of Russian state building. First, Russia's power ministries, in terms of bureaucratic type, are patrimonial rather than rational-legal. The dominance of informal and personalistic practices impedes both state capacity and quality. Second, the state's strategy for monitoring officials relied primarily on empowering internal state oversight while emasculating the more effective external oversight mechanisms present in civil society. Monitoring weaknesses made it easier for bureaucrats to focus on their own interests rather than those of citizens, to "shirk" rather than "work." Third, in terms of organizational mission, there was a failure to instill a new set of values among power ministry personnel that would lead them to consistently work for more general interests. On this point, however, in Putin's second term, there was a more concerted effort to promote a traditional "Russia idea" in which potential threats from internal and external enemies were used to justify ideological commitment to the regime. Arguably, this project did contribute to an increase in state capacity in the coercive realm, although by its very nature this ideological message did not seek to promote higher state quality.

In summary, I have tried to show how the beliefs of those state officials who wear uniforms and carry guns, and the constraints under which they operate, affect their actions, and the consequences of these actions for Russian political development. I have been particularly motivated by a desire to make the study of state building as concrete and specific as possible, focusing in detail on a small number of coercive agencies in one state in a rather limited period of time in historical terms. At the same time, I have used a range of comparative data to help situate the Russian case in a broader context. In the next section, I move further toward a more explicitly comparative investigation by probing the extent to which the problems of the Russian state are caused by larger processes and forces less subject to the decisions and strategies of political leaders and state officials.

CAPACITY AND QUALITY IN COMPARATIVE PERSPECTIVE: IS RUSSIAN STATE WEAKNESS STRUCTURAL?

One difficulty in the study of state building is how to make valid comparisons across countries. Stateness has multiple dimensions. Once the "politics of sovereignty" are over and a state has been formed with some minimal degree of integrity, the process of making an existing state stronger (or weaker) continues. Scholars have, at the most basic level, distinguished between state capacity/infrastructural power – the ability of the state to make and implement decisions in its territory – and state autonomy/despotic power – the degree of independence of the state from society in making and implementing decisions. Within the category of state capacity, there are multiple further dimensions to consider; for example, William Tompson distinguishes between coercive, extractive, regulatory, rule-making, and administrative capacity.[3] I have argued that state quality should also be at the center of comparative studies of the state.[4]

A challenge as difficult as the conceptual issues, particularly in comparative work, is the methodological one of how to measure stateness. Qualitatively inclined comparativists have used the case study method to explain the diverging trajectories of weak and strong states, often comparing extreme cases of weakness (Sierra Leone, Nigeria) to equally clear cases of strength (Israel, South Korea).[5] Large-N cross-national comparisons tend to rely, in contrast, on standard measures, such as tax revenue as a percentage of GDP, for which there are data for the majority of countries in the world.[6] In this respect, the cross-national study of stateness received a big boost in the 1990s due to the World Bank Worldwide Governance Indicators (WGI) project, whose measures are widely used by scholars. A key virtue of this project, besides its comprehensiveness and aggregation of numerous data sources, is the attention to multiple dimensions of "governance." Throughout the book, I have used five of their six categories as rough indicators of state capacity and state quality.[7] I used political stability/absence of violence and government effectiveness as

---

[3] See Chapter 1 for a discussion of these issues. On the politics of sovereignty, see: Vadim Volkov, *Violent Entrepreneurs: The Use of Force in the Making of Russian Capitalism* (Ithaca, NY: Cornell University Press, 2002), p. 156. Tompson's categories are from: William Tompson, "Putting Yukos in Perspective," *Post-Soviet Affairs*, 21, 2 (2005), pp. 159–181.

[4] The first book-length study with detailed attention to state quality is: Verena Fritz, *State-Building: A Comparative Study of Ukraine, Lithuania, Belarus, and Russia* (Budapest: Central European University Press, 2007).

[5] These comparisons can be found in two exemplary studies: Joel Migdal, *Strong Societies and Weak States: State-Society Relations in the Third World* (Princeton, NJ: Princeton University Press, 1988); Atul Kohli, *State-Directed Development: Political Power and Industrialization in the Global Periphery* (Cambridge: Cambridge University Press, 2004).

[6] Some quantitatively inclined scholars simply throw up their hands at trying to measure state capacity, as Steve Fish does when he observes that "measuring the strength of the state is tricky and will not be attempted here." M. Steven Fish, *Democracy Derailed in Russia: The Failure of Open Politics* (Cambridge: Cambridge University Press, 2005), p. 213.

[7] The one left out is "regulatory quality," which is least connected to state coercion. See the discussion in Chapter 1 on the WGI.

proxies for state capacity, and voice and accountability, rule of law, and control of corruption as indicators of state quality.

It is particularly important to situate Russia comparatively because there is a major disagreement among specialists about whether or not Russia after Putin is a strong state. Although there was general agreement about the weakness of the Russian state under Boris Yeltsin, no such consensus exists about Russian stateness today. WGI measures, as the most commonly used cross-national measures, shed some light on this debate. Russia is a relative underperformer in all five of the WGI categories used in this book. With the exception of government effectiveness, in which Russia's scores place it around the fortieth percentile of states in the world, Russia's scores place it in the bottom quarter of world states.[8]

For the statistical analysis that follows in this section, I create state capacity and state quality indexes by averaging the separate components of WGI scores. Thus, the state capacity index is the average of a country's scores for political stability/no violence and government effectiveness, and the state quality index is the average of a country's score for rule of law, control of corruption, and voice and accountability. WGI scores range from a high of 2.5 to a low of −2.5, so state capacity and state quality scores are on the same scale.[9] WGI data for 2007 were used to construct state capacity and state quality indexes for 163 countries in the world. The state capacity index ranges from −1.97 (Democratic Republic of Congo) to 1.86 (Iceland), and the state quality index ranges from −1.53 (Turkmenistan) to 2.0 (Iceland again). Although the correspondence between WGI measures and the concepts of state capacity and state quality is necessarily imperfect, these indexes seem more likely to capture what I mean by these terms than a single measure, either from the WGI or something separate, like a measure of fiscal capacity.

The extent to which Russia lags behind other countries in terms of stateness is clear when we compare Russian state capacity and state quality indexes to the rest of the world. Figure 8.1 shows how Russia compared to other states in terms of state capacity at the end of Putin's presidency. The state capacity index was plotted relative to per capita Gross National Income (GNI) in U.S. dollars, using 2007 World Bank purchasing power parity (PPP) figures.[10] Not surprisingly, richer countries tend to have higher state capacity scores.[11] The trend line on the figure is log rather than linear, which takes into account the intuitive notion that an extra $1,000 in per capita GNI has a much bigger

---

[8] See Figures 3.1, 3.4, 5.1, 5.2, 6.6.

[9] The variance of the components in actuality is somewhat less than 5, but the actual variance is roughly similar for each of the components (ranging from 3.68 to 4.09), so no single component is driving the average score in the index.

[10] World Bank, *World Development Indicators* (WDI), 2007.

[11] R = .745. This link between economic development and state capacity is well established. Indeed, some scholars have gone so far as to use GDP per capita as a proxy for state capacity, although this seems a bit of a stretch: James Fearon and David Laitin, "Ethnicity, Insurgency, and Civil War," *American Political Science Review*, 97 (2003), pp. 75–90.

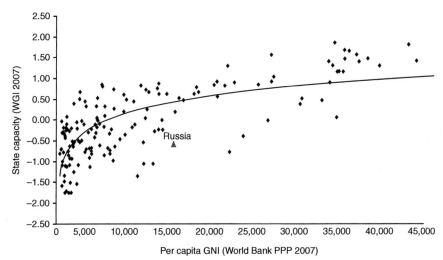

FIGURE 8.1. State capacity and per capita GNI.

effect for a country whose per capita GNI is $3,000 compared to one whose per capita GNI is $30,000. For our purposes, the most important point is that Russia has very low state capacity, even toward the end of Putin's tenure as president, relative to what one would expect given its wealth (GNI per capita PPP of $14,400 in 2007). There were fifty-three countries with a state capacity score below –.50 in 2007, but only six of those had a GNI per capita over $10,000: Lebanon, Iran, Venezuela, Equatorial Guinea, Belarus, and Russia. To put it differently, a low state capacity score is not in itself unusual; what *is* unusual, and what makes Russia such an outlier, is having such a low score while being relatively wealthy on a per capita basis.

A similar performance is evident when looking at state quality. Figure 8.2 follows the same format as Figure 8.1, but uses the state quality index – the average of WGI scores for control of corruption, rule of law, and voice and accountability – instead of the state capacity index. Once again, there is a strong correlation between wealth and state quality.[12] Once again, Russia is a serious underperformer in terms of state quality. Only four countries with GNI per capita of more than $10,000 score lower than Russia for state quality: Equatorial Guinea, Venezuela, Iran, and Belarus. Russia (score = –.96) outperformed Equatorial Guinea, which in 2007 had a state quality score of –1.47 despite having a GNI per capita of more than $20,000, but this is faint praise indeed.

Russian state capacity and state quality, according to these indicators, is more akin to states whose GNI per capita is less than $5,000 than its peers in the $12,000–$15,000 range, such as Chile, Croatia, Malaysia, and Mexico. In

[12] R = .769.

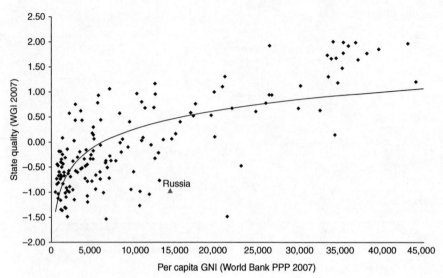

FIGURE 8.2. State quality and per capita GNI.

terms of wealth, Russia is in the top third of countries in the world, whereas in state capacity and state quality, it is in the bottom third. Although these data do not settle definitively the question of whether Russia after Putin should be thought of as a strong state, combined with other evidence they support the arguments of those who contend that the Russian state remains quite weak.

These results also bear on the famous (to Russianists, at least) "normal country" thesis of Andrei Shleifer and Daniel Treisman. Shleifer and Treisman argued in 2004 that Russia got a bad rap by many outside observers, partially because Westerners mistakenly thought of Russia as a "highly developed, if not wealthy, country." In contrast, they argued, Russia was best compared to other middle-income countries. Seen in this light, they concluded, the problems Russia faces with issues such as corruption, inequality, and restrictions on democracy were comparable to those of other states at similar levels of income.[13]

Shleifer and Treisman were undoubtedly correct that it would be not only unwise but unfair to expect Russia to look like the developed capitalist democracies of Western Europe, North America, and East Asia a mere decade or two after the Soviet collapse. In terms of stateness, however, Russia is not a "normal" middle-income country either.[14] Many of the states in the middle-income

---

[13] Andrei Shleifer and Daniel Treisman, "A Normal Country," *Foreign Affairs*, 83, 2 (March/April 2004), p. 37. A more detailed version of the argument is: Andrei Shleifer and Daniel Treisman, "A Normal Country: Russia after Communism," *Journal of Economic Perspectives*, 19, 1 (Winter, 2005), pp. 151–174.

[14] For a comparison of Russia to other middle-income countries using WGI data, with different methods but similar results to those shown here, see: William Zimmerman, "'Normal Democracies' and Improving How They Are Measured: The Case of Russia," *Post-Soviet Affairs*, 23, 1 (2007), pp. 11–13.

range, such as Uruguay, Botswana, Malaysia, and Chile, have made important strides toward the "civil state" category of high state capacity and high state quality. Although other middle-income countries remain "weak states," such as Iran, Belarus, and Mexico, these countries are outliers, not the norm.[15] As Steven Fish and William Zimmerman have separately pointed out, Russia is also an underperformer in democracy given its level of wealth.[16]

The level of economic development is one of the most important structural influences on state capacity and quality, and the data discussed here provide further evidence for this argument. Figures 8.1 and 8.2 show quite clearly that Russia is a serious underperformer in both categories of stateness given its wealth. The underlying data also serve to highlight another potentially important structural factor: resource dependence. As noted earlier, countries like Equatorial Guinea, Iran, and Venezuela are also relatively weak states given their level of economic development. These countries are united, of course, by a heavy reliance on natural resources, specifically oil and gas, for their wealth.[17]

A large literature on the "resource curse" connects natural resource dependence to a variety of political and economic ills. Most relevant for our purposes, resource dependence correlates globally with weak state capacity, poor governance, and corruption. Several causal mechanisms have been posited to explain this tendency, including disincentives to build a strong and effective bureaucracy because of the ease of raising nontax revenue, easy opportunities for rent seeking, and the use of rents both as a patronage mechanism and to fund strong coercive apparatuses. Resource dependence is also connected to authoritarianism for similar reasons.[18]

Another potential important influence on stateness that is arguably structural is the legacy of communist rule. Communist legacies can and have been conceptualized in many different ways – cultural, political, economic, and so

---

[15] These categorizations are based on whether these countries, all with annual per capita incomes between $10,000–$15,000 in 2007, had state capacity and state quality scores above or below zero in the 2007 WGI data. See Figure 1.1.

[16] Zimmerman 2007; Fish 2005, pp. 98–105. Another useful evaluation of the normal country thesis is: Peter T. Leeson and William N. Trumbull, "Comparing Apples: Normalcy, Russia, and the Remaining Post-Socialist World," *Post-Soviet Affairs*, 22, 3 (2006), pp. 225–248.

[17] Other oil- and gas-rich countries that seriously underperform in both state capacity and quality given their level of wealth are Libya, Turkmenistan, and Saudi Arabia.

[18] A good overview of many of these findings and arguments is: Erika Weinthal and Pauline Jones Luong, "Combating the Resource Curse: An Alternative Solution to Managing Mineral Wealth," *Perspectives on Politics*, 4, 1 (March 2006), esp. pp. 36–38. See also: Michael L. Ross, "The Political Economy of the Resource Curse," *World Politics*, 51, 2 (January 1999), esp. pp. 312–319. Quantitative evidence on the connection between resource-based economies and "the capacity and quality of government" is in: Jonathan Isham et al., "The Varieties of Resource Experience: How Natural Resource Export Structures Affect the Political Economy of Economic Growth," *World Bank Economic Review*, 19, 2 (October 2005), pp. 141–174 (quote p. 150). On oil and democracy, see: Michael L. Ross, "Does Oil Hinder Democracy?", *World Politics*, 53, 3 (April 2001), pp. 325–361. On the relevance of these arguments to Russia, see: Fish 2005, pp. 114–138.

on. For our purposes, we are most interested in the institutional legacies that could influence stateness in the post-communist period, such as particular types of bureaucratic or legal systems that affect whether the state can effi-ciently take and implement decisions or pursue the public interest in a disinter-ested way. The most well-known writing on Leninist legacies is by Ken Jowitt, who argued immediately after the revolutions of 1989 that in Eastern Europe, "the new institutional patterns will be shaped by the 'inheritance' and legacy of forty years of Leninist rule." He emphasized the sharp distinction, even "antagonism," between the public and private realms in Eastern European communist societies, and noted that, in Weberian terms, "what no Leninist regime ever did was create a *culture of impersonal measured action.*"[19]

Jowitt was aiming in particular at what he believed was an underly-ing Panglossian tendency in the "transitions to democracy" literature as imported to Eastern Europe. "Fragmentation" and "authoritarian oligarchy" seemed more likely to him than democracy. In hindsight, especially concern-ing Central and Eastern Europe, Jowitt was overly pessimistic, although he did conclude that if Western Europe "adopted" Eastern Europe, more civ-ic-minded forces could be strengthened in the region. The post-communist region has been marked by more diversity than the notion of "Leninist lega-cies" seems to imply, although some of his more pessimistic assumptions were met in much of the former Soviet Union and in the Balkans in the 1990s.[20] Further, there does seem to be consensus on the idea that post-communist "transitions" were particularly complicated by their multiple ("triple" or even "quadruple") components, involving not just political regime change, but also systemic economic reform, and, in many countries, nation and state building as well.[21]

Cross-national statistical analysis provides one way to examine more fully the influence of structural factors such as wealth, resources depen-dence, and Leninist institutional legacies on state building. Although this type of analysis cannot establish causality and underlying causal mecha-nisms, it can show whether certain variables are associated with each other and provides a technique for controlling for the influence of other variables. Here I use multivariate regression to establish whether there is a relationship

[19] Ken Jowitt, *New World Order: The Leninist Extinction* (Berkeley, CA: University of California Press, 1992), pp. 285, 287, 291 (empahsis in original).

[20] Books that in whole or in part evaluate the "Leninist legacies" idea include: Grzegorz Ekiert and Stephen E. Hanson, eds., *Capitalism and Democracy in Central and Eastern Europe: Assessing the Legacy of Communist Rule* (Cambridge: Cambridge University Press, 2003); Vladimir Tismaneanu, Marc Morjé Howard, and Rudra Sil, eds., *World Order after Leninism* (Seattle, WA: University of Washington Press, 2006), esp. the chapters by Marc Morjé Howard and Grigore Pop-Eleches.

[21] Claus Offe, "Capitalism by Democratic Design? Democratic Theory Facing the Triple Transition in East Central Europe," *Social Research*, 58, 4 (1991), pp. 865–881; Taras Kuzio, "Transition in Post-Communist States: Triple or Quadruple?," *Politics*, 21, 3 (2001), pp. 168–177.

between these structural variables and state capacity and state quality, using the indexes I created from the 2007 WGI data.[22] I report these results in Tables 8.1 and 8.2.

In Table 8.1 I model state capacity as a function of wealth, resource dependence, and post-communist and post-Soviet region. The measures for state capacity and wealth are the same as those used for Figures 8.1 and 8.2; state capacity is an index using 2007 WGI data and wealth is log GNI per capita PPP, from the 2007 *World Development Indicators* (WDI). The resource dependence variable also comes from the WDI, combining "fuel exports as percentage of merchandise exports" and "ores and metals exports as percentage of merchandise exports." Data are available for a total of 150 countries for this variable.[23] For region, a dummy variable was assigned to twenty-six post-communist countries in Model 1 and twelve post-Soviet countries (excluding the Baltic states) in Model 2.[24]

Both wealth and resource dependence are correlated with state capacity, with greater wealth associated with higher capacity and resource dependence correlated with lower capacity. These findings are not surprising and confirm those of other studies, although the measure of state capacity here is different than in other work.[25] Being a post-communist state is associated with somewhat lower state capacity scores, but the result is not statistically significant. The post-Soviet variable (Model 2), however, is statistically significant at the .10 level, which means that there is less than a 10 percent probability that this result is due to chance.[26]

In Table 8.2, I estimate state quality as a function of wealth, resource dependence, and belonging to the post-communist and post-Soviet region; the

---

[22] I thank Mark Beissinger for suggesting these tests and for providing an initial model of how to conduct the analysis, and Honggang Tan for conducting a revised form of the analyis. Richard Bodnar helped with data collection, and Jon Hanson provided advice on data sources for the resource dependence variable.

[23] One hundred sixty-three countries were in the dataset for Figures 8.1 and 8.2. To keep the number of countries as high as possible, for the resource dependence variable we used the most recent measure available from the period 2000–2006 for each country. This measure of resource dependence is not the only possible measure, but it is one of the most widely used ones, and WDI data cover a large number of countries. This is the measure used by Fish 2005, one of the best-known applications of the resource-curse literature to Russia.

[24] Post-communist are: Albania, Armenia, Azerbaijan, Belarus, Bulgaria, Croatia, Czech Republic, Estonia, Georgia, Hungary, Kazakhstan, Kyrgyzstan, Latvia, Lithuania, Macedonia, Moldova, Mongolia, Poland, Romania, Russia, Slovakia, Slovenia, Tajikistan, Turkmenistan, Ukraine, and Uzbekistan. Data were not available for Serbia, Montenegro, or Bosnia. Post-Soviet are: Armenia, Azerbaijan, Belarus, Georgia, Kazakhstan, Kyrgyzstan, Moldova, Russia, Tajikistan, Turkmenistan, Ukraine, and Uzbekistan.

[25] On resource dependence and state capacity, see note 18. The finding that richer countries tend to have stronger states is practically axiomatic, although obviously the effect can also run the other way: stronger states may produce higher rates of growth. See, for example: Adam Przeworski et al., *Democracy and Development: Political Institutions and Well-Being in the World, 1950–1990* (Cambridge: Cambridge University Press, 2000), pp. 162–166.

[26] $p = .06$.

TABLE 8.1. *State Capacity (Dependent Variable) and Structural Factors (Wealth, Resource Dependence, Region)*

	Model 1	Model 2
Ln per capita GNI (PPP)	.526***	.518***
	(.034)	(.034)
Natural resource	−.009***	−.008***
dependence	(.001)	(.001)
Post-communist	−.137	
	(.115)	
Post-Soviet (excl. Baltics)		−.307^
		(.164)
Constant	−4.337***	−4.281***
	(.301)	(.299)
N	150	150
R-Squared	.652	.657
Adj. R-Squared	.645	.650

Notes: Standard errors in parentheses. Significance Level: ^ $p < .10$; * $p < .05$; ** $p < .01$; *** $p < .001$.
Data Sources: World Bank: WGI; World Bank World Development Indicators.

TABLE 8.2. *State Quality (Dependent Variable) and Structural Factors (Wealth, Resource Dependence, Region)*

	Model 1	Model 2
Ln per capita GNI (PPP)	.551***	.530***
	(.034)	(.033)
Natural resource	−.01***	−.009***
dependence	(.001)	(.001)
Post-communist	−.428*** (.113)	
Post-Soviet (excl. Baltics)		−.690***
		(.162)
Constant	−4.467***	−4.318***
	(.298)	(.294)
N	150	150
R-Squared	.688	.696
Adj. R-Squared	.682	.689

Notes: Standard errors in parentheses. Significance Level: * $p < .05$; ** $p < .01$; *** $p < .001$.
Data Sources: Same as Table 8.1.

measures are the same as those already described. Once again, both the per capita income and resource dependence variables are statistically significant and in the expected direction (higher income increases state quality, greater resource dependence decreases state quality). Most interestingly, both the post-communist and post-Soviet variables are statistically significant at the .001 level. Indeed, the observed effects are quite large. The state quality variable is

TABLE 8.3. *Predicted Values for State Capacity and State Quality Compared to Actual Russian Scores*

State Capacity

Lower middle income ($4,516 per capita GNI) and high natural resource dependence (61.79%) country = −.41

Upper middle income ($10,986 per capita GNI) and high natural resource dependence (61.79%) country = .04

Lower middle income ($4,516 per capita GNI), high natural resource dependence (61.79%), post-Soviet (non-Baltic) country = −.72

Upper middle income ($10,986 per capita GNI), high natural resource dependence (61.79%), post-Soviet (non-Baltic) country [i.e., Russia]= −.27

Actual Russian score = −.58

State Quality

Lower income ($1,296 per capita GNI) and high natural resource dependence (61.79%) country = −1.07

Upper middle income ($10,986 per capita GNI) and high natural resource dependence (61.79%) country = .05

Lower middle income ($4,516 per capita GNI), high natural resource dependence (61.79%), post-Soviet (non-Baltic) country = −1.10

Upper middle income ($10,986 per capita GNI), high natural resource dependence (61.79%), post-Soviet (non-Baltic) country [i.e., Russia]= -.64

Actual Russian score = −.96

---

on a 5 point scale from −2.5 to +2.5, with actual scores ranging from −1.53 to 2.00. Being a post-communist country has the effect of dropping one's state quality score by .428 points on this scale, and being a post-Soviet country drops one's score by .690, an almost 14 percent decline on the notional scale and an almost 20 percent decline when compared to actual scores, even when controlling for wealth and resource dependence. This result suggests that post-communist and especially post-Soviet countries have much lower state quality – rule of law, control of corruption, and voice and accountability – than one would normally expect given other structural conditions. There does appear to be a Leninist legacy in state quality in particular, which implies that building state quality is a harder and lengthier process than building capacity.

We are especially interested in whether Russia's relatively weak state capacity and state quality can be explained in structural terms. To get at that issue, I calculated predicted values for state capacity and state quality, which are shown in Table 8.3. Countries were grouped into four income categories: lower income, lower middle income, upper middle income, and upper income. The four categories are of roughly equal size, with thirty-eight countries in the lower income and lower middle income groups and thirty-seven in the upper middle income and upper income groups. Then average incomes were calculated for each group: lower income = $1,296; lower middle income = $4,516; upper middle income = $10,986; upper income = $32,463. Three categories were created for resource dependence – low, middle, and high – with fifty countries in each group. Then the average percentage of natural resource exports was calculated for each group: low dependence = 2.25%; middle dependence = 11.95%; high dependence = 61.79%.

According to these categories, Russia is an upper middle income, high resource dependence, post-Soviet country. A "typical" upper middle income country with high resource dependence would be expected to have a state capacity score of .04. A country with these features from the Post-Soviet region, like Russia, has a predicted state capacity score of –.27. Russia's actual score, however, for state capacity in 2007 was –.58, considerably below the predicted value. Table 8.3 also shows predicted values for high resource dependence countries in the lower middle income category for both the Post-Soviet region and worldwide. Russia's actual score (–.58) was also lower than the predicted value for much poorer countries ($4,516 GNI per capita) with high natural resource dependence (–.41), although slightly higher once the effects of the Post-Soviet region are included (–.72).

We see a similar underperformance in terms of predicted values for state quality. A "typical" upper middle income country with high resource dependence would be expected to have a state quality score of .05. A country with these features from the post-Soviet region, like Russia, has a predicted state capacity score of –.64. Russia's actual score, however, for state quality was –.96, considerably below the predicted value. Indeed, Russia's state quality score is quite close to the predicted value of a lower income country ($1,296 per capita GNI) with high natural resource dependence (–1.07).

Overall, these results indicate that in terms of stateness, Russia by the end of Putin's presidency was still a serious underperformer in state capacity and especially state quality, even when controlling for key structural variables like wealth and resource dependence. Although Russia is a relatively poor country compared to Western Europe and North America, it is relatively rich when compared to much of the world. Although Russia's dependence on natural resources and its status as a post-communist/post-Soviet state probably contribute to its stateness problems, these problems exist in Russia to a greater extent than these features would lead us to expect. Russian state weakness cannot be explained solely in structural terms.

Throughout the book, I have stressed organizational factors more subject to manipulation – bureaucratic type, monitoring strategy, organizational mission – than structural variables for the capacity and quality of Russia's power ministries. This section has provided quantitative data to suggest that Russian state weakness overall may be driven in part by Leninist legacies and the political "resource curse," but that these structural factors cannot in themselves account for the state of the Russian state.

It is also worth noting that the organizational factors that I highlight provide, at least in part, plausible causal pathways between structural factors and stateness. To put it differently, we can reconceptualize my key explanatory variables as intervening ones between structural factors and the dependent variable of stateness. Logically there are possible causal connections between

Russia's Leninist history and hydrocarbon dependence and administrative issues like bureaucratic type, monitoring strategy, and organizational mission. I will briefly explore each of these issues.

Patrimonial administration was a persistent feature of Leninist regimes; indeed, Conor O'Dwyer refers to the "Leninist patrimonial state." Both the Imperial Russian and Soviet bureaucracy exhibited strong patrimonial tendencies, and patrimonialism has persisted in many former Leninist regimes in Eastern Europe and the former Soviet Union.[27] For this reason, the dominance of patrimonial administration over rational-legal bureaucracy in post-Soviet Russia is perhaps not a surprise. On the other hand, O'Dwyer and Anna Gryzmala-Busse both contend that some post-socialist states have made significant progress in building more Weberian bureaucracies, although they disagree on some specific cases.[28] Moreover, studies of post-communist policing show that Russia lags behind other countries in the region in creating more professional police.[29] Resource dependence also may contribute to patrimonialism in state administration. The opportunities for rent seeking provided by resource wealth create incentives to make appointments based on personal or family ties rather than professional qualifications; this is one component of the "rentier state" argument.[30]

Resource dependence and Leninist legacies may also influence the type of monitoring strategy pursued. In a country in which state finances come from resource rents rather than taxing citizens, and state elites and officials enrich themselves from these rents, it is less likely that strong external watchdogs will emerge to challenge the state. Citizens have fewer incentives to monitor the state (because they do not pay many taxes), and corrupt state officials will have good reasons to discourage a vibrant civil society in terms of NGOs and a free press.[31] Moreover, in communist systems, the Party, the secret police, and the procuracy provided internal monitoring over state officials; real external monitors in terms of a free press or independent civil society were absent. This legacy, along with the mutual alienation between the public and

[27] See the discussion in Chapters 1 and 5.

[28] Specifically, O'Dwyer sees the Czech Republic as a success of Weberian state building and Poland as a failure, whereas Gryzmala-Busse contends that Poland was a relative success and the Czech Republic a failure: Conor O'Dwyer, *Runaway State-Building: Patronage Politics and Democratic Development* (Baltimore: The Johns Hopkins University Press, 2006); Anna Gryzmala-Busse, *Rebuilding Leviathan: Party Competition and State Exploitation in Post-Communist Democracies* (Cambridge: Cambridge University Press, 2007).

[29] Marina Caparini and Otwin Marenin, eds., *Transforming Police in Central and Eastern Europe: Process and Progress* (Munster, Germany: Lit Verlag, 2004), esp. the summary tables in the appendix.

[30] See, for example: Weinthal and Jones Luong 2006, p. 38; Rolf Schwarz, "The Political Economy of State-Formation in the Arab Middle East: Rentier States, Economic Reform, and Democratization," *Review of International Political Economy*, 15, 4 (October 2008), p. 615.

[31] Discussions include Ross 1999, p. 312; Fish 2005, pp. 114–138; Weinthal and Jones Luong 2006, p. 38.

private spheres that Jowitt discussed, may continue to impede civil society development, as Marc Morje Howard has argued.[32]

Finally, in terms of organizational mission, Leninist legacies may also play a role in the inability to create a new goal that encourages public-interested behavior on the part of state officials.[33] Well before the Soviet collapse, Kenneth Jowitt identified the loss of a "combat task" among Party cadres as a key source of corruption and a potential threat to regime stability. In his Leninist legacies article, Jowitt returned to this issue and noted the absence of both "a culture of impersonal measured action" and a form of civic public spirit that would bolster open politics. Stephen Hanson has similarly emphasized how the Communist past has discredited the very idea of an overarching ideological project in Russia, and how the concomitant lack of loyalty on the part of state officials leads to state weakness.[34]

It should be emphasized that, although structural factors can influence organizational issues like bureaucratic type, monitoring strategies, and institutional mission, they are not a sufficient explanation for Russian state weakness. First, statistical regression establishes general tendencies and propensities, and in cross-national research there is usually plenty of real-world variation. For example, Botswana is heavily reliant on diamond exports and Chile is very dependent on copper exports, but both countries have high state capacity and quality scores. Similarly, the post-communist region exhibits substantial variation between the generally weak states of Central Asia and some of the stronger states of Central and Eastern Europe like Estonia, Slovenia, and the Czech Republic.

Second, although Russia's oil and gas dependency and communist past may contribute to state weakness, its relative wealth globally would lead us to expect a much stronger state than it currently has. Although relative wealth can explain partially why Russia lags behind wealthy countries such as South Korea or Spain, it cannot explain why it also ranks behind middle income countries such as Botswana or Brazil. As the predicted values in Table 8.3 show, even taking resource dependence and a communist past into account, the Russian state is still weaker than one would expect given its per capita gross national income.

Third, and most generally, any convincing explanation for stateness at the level pursued in this book, that of "the organizations and individuals who establish and administer public policies and laws," must deal with the choices made by state officials and elites.[35] As Richard Samuels has argued, political leaders

---

[32] Marc Morjé Howard, *The Weakness of Civil Society in Post-Communist Europe* (Cambridge: Cambridge University Press, 2003).

[33] Resource curse arguments seem less relevant for the organizational mission issue.

[34] See, for example: Stephen E. Hanson, "The Uncertain Future of Russia's Weak State Authoritarianism," *Eastern European Politics and Societies*, 21, 1 (February 2007), esp. pp. 72–74.

[35] Margaret Levi, "Why We Need a New Theory of Government," *Perspectives on Politics*, 4, 1 (March 2006), p. 6.

can "stretch constraints" imposed by structural forces.[36] Russian history over the last twenty-five years bears this point out; Mikhail Gorbachev, Boris Yeltsin, and Vladimir Putin all had an enormous influence on the path that Russia has taken. Leadership strategy, and not just structure, matter for state building.

THE ROLE OF AGENCY: PUTIN'S DISAPPOINTING STATE-BUILDING PROJECT

Thinking about the role of Gorbachev, Yeltsin, and Putin takes us from cross-national to temporal comparison. Russia is a relatively new state formed in the aftermath of the Soviet collapse. Continuing Russian state weakness, in this view, is best explained by this cataclysmic event. As Vladimir Putin noted in 2005 on the first anniversary of the Beslan tragedy, "after the collapse of the Soviet Union our country sustained enormous damage in every respect ... in the first half of the 1990s our armed forces and special services were in a state of 'knock-out,' a half-decayed condition."[37] To put it baldly, if anyone was to blame for the condition of the post-Soviet state, it was Mikhail Gorbachev and Boris Yeltsin, not Vladimir Putin.

We have already seen how being a post-Soviet state has a powerful and negative effect on state quality and a smaller but noticeable effect on state capacity. Certainly the consequences of the Soviet collapse partially account for the weakness of the Russian state; indeed, it is possible that simply state newness, and not any specific Leninist legacy, accounts for the low stateness of the entire region. State building is inherently a long-term process.[38] But if any post-Soviet state was not new, it was Russia, which has a centuries-long history and inherited the institutional apparatus of the Soviet state.

The part of the story about Russian state weakness that is harder to credit is that Putin was a powerful state builder. This perspective has been embraced by many, including Putin himself, top American Russia specialists such as Thomas Graham (senior director for Russia on the U.S. National Security Council staff in 2004–2007), influential scholars of comparative state building such as Charles Tilly, and, not least, a large majority of the Russian population, who blame Gorbachev and Yeltsin for the turmoil and destitution of the 1990s and laud Putin for the stability and economic growth of the 2000s. The journalist C.J. Chivers maintained, "Putin's signature legacy" was the building "of a more sophisticated and rational police state than the failed USSR."[39]

---

[36] Richard J. Samuels, *Machiavelli's Children: Leaders and Their Legacies in Italy and Japan* (Ithaca, NY: Cornell University Press, 2003).

[37] Vladimir Putin, "Nachalo vstrechi s zhitelyami Beslana, postradavshimi v rezul'tate terakta 1–3 sentyabrya 2004 goda," September 2, 2005.

[38] See the stimulating essays by Dietrich Rueschemeyer and Thomas Ertman in: Matthew Lange and Dietrich Rueschemeyer, *States and Development: Historical Antecedents of Stagnation and Advance* (New York: Palgrave Macmillan, 2005).

[39] Thomas Graham, "A Modernizing Czar," *Wall Street Journal Europe*, January 22, 2008; Charles Tilly, *Democracy* (Cambridge: Cambridge University Press, 2007), pp. 136–137;

The evidence presented in this book calls this view of the Putin presidency into question.[40] These arguments were summarized earlier and will not be repeated here. And it must be acknowledged that in Putin's last few years, there were improvements in some aspects of state capacity in the coercive realm, such as a declining murder rate and fewer major terrorist attacks. This change was particularly evident in Chechnya, although other parts of the North Caucasus, such as Ingushetia and Dagestan, were more unstable at the end of Putin's presidency than at the beginning. In terms of state quality, there is little evidence of improvement and some evidence of decline, both in general and in the power ministries. Corruption, predation, and the "unrule of law" remained pervasive. Overall, given the demonstrated causal link between wealth and state quality and capacity, the relative *absence* of change is disappointing in light of the substantial economic growth in Russia since 1999 (Russian GDP increased from $200 billion in 1999 to $1.3 trillion in 2008, a 7 percent average annual increase).[41]

One way of depicting this relative lack of change under Putin is by plotting Russia's state capacity and state quality scores from WGI over time. Figure 8.3 shows Russia's scores for these measures from 1996 (the middle of Yeltsin's presidency) to 2007 (the last year of Putin's presidency). Several points are evident. First, with the exception of 1996, when Russia had a particularly low state capacity score, Russia did not change much in terms of WGI scores over the decade of 1996–2007. Recall that the range of possible scores is −2.5 to 2.5. Between 1998 and 2007, Russia's scores for both state capacity (−.45 to −.68) and state quality (−.73 to −.96) stayed in a quite narrow range. Second, the figure shows a slight increase in state capacity and a decrease in state quality during Putin's presidency. Third, these data suggest that in the first years of Putin's presidency, a positive project of state building was underway, but that this project stalled and faltered in subsequent years (compare 2002–2003

C.J. Chivers, "Power. The Vladimir Putin Story," *Esquire*, October 1, 2008. See also: Vladimir Popov, "The State in the New Russia (1992–2004): From Collapse to Gradual Revival?" *PONARS Policy Memo*, 342 (November 2004); John P. Willerton, Mikhail Beznosov, and Martin Carrier, "Addressing the Challenges of Russia's 'Failing State': The Legacy of Gorbachev and the Promise of Putin," *Demokratizatsiya*, 13, 2 (Spring 2005), pp. 219–239; Andrei P. Tsygankov, "Modern at Last? Variety of Weak States in the Post-Soviet World," *Communist and Post-Communist Studies*, 40 (2007), pp. 423–439, esp. 433–434; Ottorino Cappelli, "Pre-Modern State-Building in Post-Soviet Russia," *Journal of Communist Studies and Transition Politics*, 24, 4 (2008), pp. 531–572; Gerald M. Easter, "The Russian State in the Time of Putin," *Post-Soviet Affairs*, 24, 3 (2008), pp. 199–230.

[40] Other skeptical accounts include: Fish 2005; S. Mohsin Hashim, "Putin's Etatization project and limits to democratic reforms in Russia," *Communist and Post-Communist Studies*, 38 (2005), pp. 25–48; Michael McFaul and Kathryn Stoner-Weiss, "The Myth of the Authoritarian Model," *Foreign Affairs*, 87, 1 (January/February 2008), esp. pp. 73–77. Note especially Fish's observation that "given the hyperpersonalization of power at the center, it is difficult to conclude that Putinism really strengthens overall state capacity. Building personal power and building institutions are not the same thing." Fish 2005, p. 270.

[41] World Bank, *World Development Indicators*.

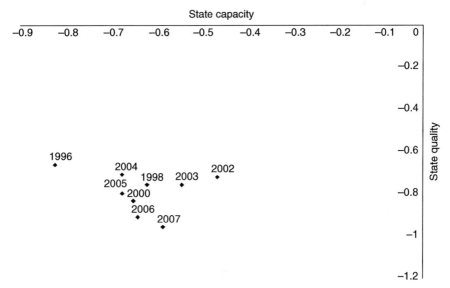

FIGURE 8.3. Russia: State capacity versus state quality (WGI).

to 2006–2007). Although these data are only illustrative and are not focused specifically on the power ministries, they are broadly consistent with the more detailed qualitative evidence provided throughout the book.

Focusing more specifically on the power ministries, we see some increases in state capacity under Putin, especially in the rebuilding of a "regime of repression" by which law enforcement personnel can be mobilized for extraordinary tasks. Indeed, to the extent that this regime of repression became institutionalized, attacks on regime opponents stopped being extraordinary tasks and became routine ones.[42] Despite rhetoric that emphasized both state capacity and state quality, the overall trajectory under Putin in the coercive realm was toward a slight increase in state capacity and slight decline in state quality. In terms of the three state types set out in Chapter 1, Russia remained a weak state but moved closer to being a police state and further away from being a civil state (see Figure 8.4).

This result is disappointing because the greater distance from the cataclysm of the Soviet collapse, plus significantly greater economic and political resources, should have made possible a noticeable increase in not only capacity but quality. However, a state-building strategy that did not address patrimonial practices in the power ministries, that privileged internal "police patrols" over external "fire alarms," and that failed to instill a mission of protection of the population in law enforcement personnel led to the continued dominance of repressive and predatory practices. The state's monopoly of force is not used to protect the interests of society as a whole.

[42] See the discussion in Chapter 3 on the 2008 creation of the MVD Department for Countering Extremism.

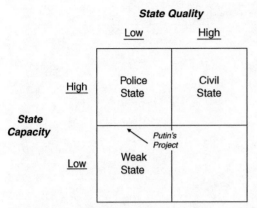

FIGURE 8.4. Weak state to police state? State building under Putin.

When Putin came to power, the first stage of state building – the formation of a state with a monopoly on legitimate violence – had been more or less
completed in Russia (Chechnya was an obvious exception). Vadim Volkov
demonstrated how over the course of the 1990s, the most important change in
controlling coercion was the weakening of the mafia groups that arose around
the time of the Soviet collapse. The decline of the mafia was accompanied both
by the rise of private security as a legitimate business and various forms of corruption and predation, such as "roofing," carried out by state law enforcement
agencies. As Volkov put it, "the first step in reconstructing the state has been
made: the bandit has gone; the state employee has taken his place. The second step – making him act as a state employee rather than a bandit – is still a
problem."[43]

Analytically, Volkov conceived of the Yeltsin era as a period in which the
dominant form of coercion, at least with respect to property rights, moved from
the private and illegal sphere (the mafia) in two different directions: toward
the private and legal and public and illegal spheres. What was not achieved
was the ideal state (what I call a civil state) in which property rights are protected by public bodies acting in their legal capacity (see Figure 8.5).[44]

In terms of the adapted version of Volkov's typology shown here, the central conclusion about the Putin era is consistent with that based on WGI
data: The process of state building largely stalled. A Weberian state was not
built, and not because too much control over coercion remained in private
hands, but because too much public coercion was exercised illegally and arbitrarily. The move into the public and legal cell in the coercion typology did not
take place. That is, predation dominated over protection in power ministry
behavior – state employees acted like bandits. Moreover, the selective use of

[43] Vadim Volkov, "The Selective Use of State Capacity in Russia's Economy: Property Disputes
and Enterprise Takeovers After 2000," *PONARS Policy Memo*, 273 (October 2002).
[44] Volkov, *Violent Entrepreneurs*, 2002, pp. 167–169.

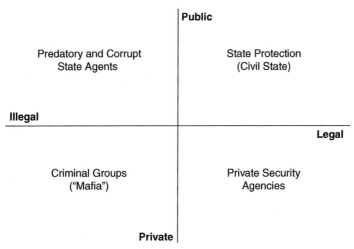

FIGURE 8.5. Control over coercion: A typology.

power ministry repression against state opponents undermined the creation of a civil state rooted in the rule of law.

The failure to build a civil state was recognized, at least rhetorically, by Putin's successor Dmitriy Medvedev. Indeed, if we compare Putin's first "State of the Union" speech to Medvedev's, there are significant commonalities. In July 2000, Putin spoke at length about the need to build a "strong," "effective," and "democratic" state, noted the "privatization" of state functions and institutions and the problem of corruption, and emphasized the need for state service "professionals" who act in compliance with the law. He also bemoaned the weakness of civil society, which in a democratic state should be a "partner of the state." Eight years later, in November 2008, Medvedev asserted that "the state bureaucracy is the same as it was 20 years ago," with too much power and inclined to restrict peoples' freedoms, cause "nightmares" for business, take control over the press, interfere in the electoral process, and pressure the courts. The state thus dominates all spheres of activity, "which is absolutely ineffective and creates only one thing – corruption. This system gives birth to widespread legal nihilism" and inhibits the development of the economy and democracy. Medvedev stressed that "a strong state and an all-powerful bureaucracy are not the same thing," and that the former needs a developed civil society whereas the latter is a threat to it.[45] This common ground between Putin's and Medvedev's first state of the nation speeches shows how little progress was made in reforming how state officials behave during Putin's presidency; Medvedev's speech was also an implicit indictment of his predecessor's performance as state builder.

---

[45] Vladimir Putin, "Vystupleniye pri predstavlenii yezhegodnogo Poslaniya Prezidenta Rossiyskoy Federatsii Federal'nomu Sobraniyu Rossiyskoy Federatsii," July 8, 2000; Dmitriy Medvedev, "Poslaniye Federal'nomu Sobraniyu Rossiyskoy Federatsii," November 5, 2008.

In Putin's first years, there was considerable hope, and some promising signals, that his state-building efforts would pave the way for an increase in both state capacity and state quality. First, as Alexei Barabashev and Jeffrey Straussman noted, "a renewed effort was made to jump-start" administrative reform after 2000, receiving the attention of top Kremlin officials like Dmitriy Kozak, as well as a group of academic specialists committed to a more modern, rational-legal civil service. Second, the federal reforms launched in 2000 had the potential to limit the worst excesses of regional leaders and law enforcement officials. A series of legal and economic reforms also raised hopes that the Russian state would become less corrupt and more compliant with the law.

In hindsight, these efforts did not lead to movement toward a civil state. Federal reform, rather than being a positive-sum affair that made all levels of government more effective, drastically shifted power toward the center in many respects without encouraging greater respect for the law or greater efforts to serve the population. Administrative reform also was both delayed and watered down, and then watered down further in the implementing decrees and regulations, not to mention actual practice; overall, there was a big gap between initial aspirations and actual reforms on the ground.[46]

More generally, toward the end of Putin's first term and moving into his second term, there seemed to be a shift toward a harder line in the Kremlin. Key milestones in this period were the Yukos affair in 2003, the Beslan terrorist incident in 2004, the "Rose" and Orange" "revolutions" in neighboring Georgia and Ukraine in 2003 and 2004, and the spontaneous social benefits protests in early 2005. A sense of being under siege seemed to grip Putin and his team. The response to Beslan and the "colored revolutions," with increased warnings about foreign and domestic enemies and the articulation of the ideology of "sovereign democracy," was the most obvious public manifestation of this harder line.

In terms of state building, the effects of this evident change were somewhat contradictory. A change for the worse came in the dominant type of monitoring. "Fire alarms" like a free press and a vigorous civil society, including those groups that targeted corruption and predation in the power ministries, found themselves under threat. On the other hand, arguably the new ideology appealed to power ministry personnel, who by inclination are *gosudarstvenniki* (statists) sympathetic to the traditional "Russian idea" of rallying the state to resist domestic and foreign enemies. This may have provided a stronger sense of institutional mission of service to the state, although not to society as a whole, which was reflected in some increase in state capacity but a decrease in state quality.[47]

The influence of the siloviki in general and Chekists in particular played an important role in the direction of Putin's state-building project. Initial

---

[46] On these points, see the discussions in Chapters 4 and 5.
[47] See the discussion in Chapter 3.

commentary about Putin contrasted his KGB past with his 1990s experience in "democratic St. Petersburg," wondering which was the "real" Vladimir Putin. An either/or answer here would be too simplistic, but the three different lenses for viewing the siloviki give us some insight.[48] As a cohort, the expanding presence of siloviki throughout government strengthened those whose statist views privileged order and stability over freedom and public accountability. As a clan, the victory of the Sechin-Ustinov-Patrushev siloviki group over the remnants of the Yeltsin "family" (particularly Chief of the presidential administration Aleksandr Voloshin and Prime Minister Mikhail Kasyanov) during the Yukos affair further cemented a harder approach to state building. As a corporate (bureaucratic groupings) issue, the domestic domination of the FSB fed into a campaign against foreign influence and the links of external actors with domestic reformers. The Chekist self-image, articulated in the writings of Viktor Cherkesov, which argued that they were the last and most reliable defense against Russian state collapse, justified certain choices about what kind of state to have and how to build it.

Arguably, Putin's approach to state building was based on a mistaken understanding about what stage of state building Russia confronted when he came to office in 2000. The first phase of state building – state formation in which a monopoly on legitimate violence is acquired – should be distinguished from a second phase that seeks to build the capacity of an already existing state. Clearly Putin was heavily influenced by the shock of the Soviet collapse, which in 2005 he termed "the greatest geopolitical catastrophe of the 20th century," and the Chechen War, which really was a crisis of state formation. Indeed, while still acting President in early 2000, he explicitly linked Chechnya to the Soviet collapse, arguing that the situation in the North Caucasus was "a continuation of the collapse of the USSR" and that "if we don't stop it now, immediately, Russia as a state in its current form will cease to exist."[49] This was an overreaction, as Matthew Evangelista has persuasively demonstrated, but there is little reason to doubt that this was how Putin and many other top officials felt at the time.[50] Both his professional background and the weight of responsibilities he faced after being elevated to the top rung of Russian politics so quickly played into this mindset.

Taking agency seriously ultimately implies that a different leader would have seen Russia's stateness problem differently, and could have chosen a different strategy, even in the face of the structural constraints he or she faced. What would an alternative strategy look like? And will Dmitriy Medvedev follow that route? These are the central questions of the final two sections.

[48] See the discussion in Chapter 2.

[49] N. Gevorkyan, A. Kolesnikov, and N. Timakova, *Ot pervogo litsa* (Moskva: Vagrius, 2000), p. 133.

[50] Matthew Evangelista, *The Chechen Wars* (Washington, DC: Brookings Institution Press, 2002).

CONNECTING STATE CAPACITY AND STATE QUALITY

Most studies of coercion and the state focus on the first stage of state building, when a monopoly over legitimate violence becomes more or less established – the "politics of sovereignty." This phase of state building is frequently
treated in the historical literature as a messy and violent affair, one in which,
as Charles Tilly famously argued, state building looks an awful lot like organized crime. Issues such as accountability and the rule of law are usually considered secondary, although Tilly did argue that in those regions in which
capital was more abundant, the state-building path was less coercive and more
dependent on bargains with wealthy interests.[51]

States in the contemporary world still trying to establish a monopoly on
legitimate violence do so in very different circumstances than those in early
modern Europe, as many scholars have noted.[52] Of the many differences, one
crucial one is that state formation has gone global, not only in the powerful influence of external coercion and capital, but also in the attention paid
to the process by a variety of watchdogs in the media, NGOs like Amnesty
International, and international organizations like the United Nations. These
external watchdogs highlight concerns related to state quality in a way that
state builders in other eras did not have to face.

This difference in context is important for thinking about the relationship between state capacity and state quality, including in the coercive realm.
Concern with the quality of state coercive organs is found most directly in the
largely policy-focused literature on "security sector reform." Security sector
reform (SSR) as a concept grew out of the work of international development
agencies and NGOs to transform the functioning of the military, police, and
intelligence services in democratizing or post-conflict countries.[53] Much of
this literature argues that there is no trade-off between capacity and quality
building. For example, Robin Luckham writes that "democratic accountability and the rule of law are not luxuries that can safely be postponed until
order and security are restored; they are inseparable from the latter."[54] Other

---

[51] Charles Tilly, "War Making and State Making as Organized Crime," in Evans, Rueschemeyer,
    and Skocpol 1985, pp. 169–191; Charles Tilly, *Coercion, Capital, and European States, AD
    990–1992* (Cambridge: Blackwell, 1992).
[52] My treatment of this literature is in: Brian D. Taylor and Roxana Botea, "Tilly Tally: War-
    Making and State-Making in the Contemporary Third World," *International Studies Review*,
    10, 1 (Spring 2008), pp. 27–57.
[53] Introductions include: Chris Smith, "Security-Sector Reform: Development Breakthrough
    or Institutional Engineering?" *Journal of Conflict, Security, & Development.* 1 (2001),
    pp. 5–19; Jane Chanaa, *Security Sector Reform: Issues, Challenges, and Prospects. Adelphi
    Paper 344.* London: Oxford University Press, 2002.
[54] Robin Luckham, "Democratic Strategies for Security in Transition and Conflict," in Gavin
    Cawthra and Robin Luckham, eds., *Governing Insecurity: Democratic Control of Military
    and Security Establishments in Transitional Democracies* (London: Zed Books, 2003), p. 21.
    See also: Nicole Ball, "Strengthening democratic governance of the security sector in conflict-
    affected countries," *Public Administration and Development*, 25, 1 (February 2005), pp. 25–38.

scholars, however, suggest that order and security can logically be separated from accountability and the rule of law when analyzing the first phase of state building, and the historical and comparative record would seem to be on their side.[55]

Of course, the difference between creating a state (stage 1) and building the capacity of an existing state (stage 2) may be clearer in theory than in practice. This is particularly true because "all state building is local," so it is possible that different areas of the same country will be at different stages.[56] But it is crucial to recognize this difference, because the relationship between state quality and state capacity varies across stages. Francis Fukuyama puts his finger on the crucial difference when he notes that what I call the first stage of state building involves "the concentration of the means of coercion," whereas enhancing what I call state quality requires "*limiting* the central state's authority to coerce."[57] In most cases, simultaneously trying to concentrate and limit state control over coercion will be impossible. But once concentration has taken place and a state has been created, it may actually enhance state capacity to limit the central state's power to arbitrarily coerce. State bureaucracies, including law enforcement ones, that serve the public in a fair and impartial manner often will have higher capacity than those who only serve state rulers' interests. Indeed, as Thomas Carothers argues convincingly, once the first stage of state formation is completed and a basic monopoly over legitimate violence has been more or less established, attempts to hinder liberalization as part of a "sequencing" strategy are unlikely to help the stated goal of creating "competent, impartial state institutions" and will likely delay progress on this front.[58]

Carothers' argument was part of a recent round of the perennial debate about the connection between state building and democratization. I have downplayed democratization as an issue in this book, which is focused on state building in the coercive realm. Although the concept of state quality is clearly related to democracy, they are not equivalents. It is possible to have state institutions that uphold the interests of the population in a fair manner without democracy, both in theory and in practice. Relatively clean government and the rule of law have existed without democracy, and democracy can

---

[55] Thomas Carothers, "The 'Sequencing' Fallacy," *Journal of Democracy*, 18, 1 (January 2007), p. 19; Roland Paris, *At War's End: Building Peace after Civil Conflict* (Cambridge: Cambridge University Press, 2004), esp. pp. 179–211.

[56] Diane E. Davis, "Contemporary Challenges and Historical Reflections on the Study of Militaries, States, and Politics," in Diane E. Davis and Anthony W. Pereira, eds., *Irregular Armed Forces and Their Role in Politics and State Formation* (Cambridge: Cambridge University Press, 2003), p. 29.

[57] Francis Fukuyama, "Liberalism versus State-Building," *Journal of Democracy*, 18, 3 (July 2007), p. 11. In Chapter 1, I argued, following Norbert Elias, that in the coercive realm, state quality is built when the state's monopoly of force is wielded not primarily for the interests of the ruler(s), but for society as a whole.

[58] Carothers January 2007; Thomas Carothers, "Misunderstanding Gradualism," *Journal of Democracy*, 18, 3 (July 2007), pp. 18–22 (quote p. 19).

exist without the rule of law and with high corruption.[59] In particular, you can have high state quality in an authoritarian state when state officials have high status and a public service ethic.[60] For the most part, however, democracy is likely to be conducive to building state quality in the contemporary world. As Carothers notes, "outside East Asia, autocratic governments in the developing world have a terrible record as builders of competent, impartial institutions."[61]

This is not surprising if we contrast Thomas Ertman's two alternative strategies for state building in established states: authoritarian (or monocratic) and constitutionalist (power-sharing). In a similar vein, Hanna Back and Axel Hadenius distinguish between "steering from above" and "steering from below." Although writing about very different periods, both approaches are interested in the influence of regime type on state building. Further, they all recognize that the authoritarian approach, or steering from above, can increase state capacity, and that neither approach is guaranteed of success. However, Ertman notes that the authoritarian approach "depends almost entirely on the degree of vigilance and the quality of supervision exercised by the executive, a condition subject to a high degree of contingency." In contrast, in the power-sharing solution, or steering from below, there are multiple possible checks dependent on a wider range of actors. To put it differently, fire alarms are a more robust monitoring mechanism than police patrols. Back and Hadenius contend, "the state's bureaucratic capacity can be *enhanced* if other actors in society are invited to take part in directing and reviewing the actions of the administrative apparatus."[62]

Why did Putin embrace a monocratic approach to state building, one which neglected state quality and ultimately failed to bring about a marked improvement in state capacity as well? There is no simple answer to this question. Indeed, there is a plausible argument to be made that Putin and his allies were not interested in rebuilding the Russian state at all, despite abundant rhetoric to the contrary. Rather, they were motivated first of all by the desire to extract

---

[59] Based on WGI and Freedom House data, for example, Singapore is a country with low democracy and high state quality, and Mongolia is a country with high democracy and low state quality.

[60] On the importance of high status and a shared ethic (or organizational culture) in building effective state bureacracies, see, for example: Dietrich Rueschemeyer and Peter B. Evans, "The State and Economic Transformation: Toward an Analysis of the Conditions Underlying Effective Intervention," in Peter B. Evans, Dietrich Rueschemeyer, and Theda Skocpol, eds., *Bringing the State Back In* (Cambridge: Cambridge University Press, 1985), p. 51; Dietrich Rueschemeyer, "Building States – Inherently a Long-Term Process? An Argument from Theory," in Lange and Rueschemeyer 2005, pp. 146–147.

[61] Carothers July 2007, p. 19. See also the contributions of Edward Mansfield and Jack Snyder, Francis Fukuyama, and Shari Berman to this debate in *Journal of Democracy*.

[62] Thomas Ertman, *Birth of the Leviathan: Building States and Regimes in Medieval and Early Modern Europe* (Cambridge: Cambridge University Press, 1997), pp. 323–324; Hanna Back and Axel Hadenius, "Democracy and State Capacity: Exploring a J-Shaped Relationship," *Governance*, 21, 1 (January 2008), p. 16.

rents from the oil and gas industry. In other words, they were more interested in looting the state than building it. This explanation is consistent with Douglass North's observation that "if the state has coercive force, then those who run the state will use that force in their own interest at the expense of the rest of society," as well as Venelin Ganev's argument that the weakness of post-communist states in general can be explained by an "elite predatory project" of "extraction from the state."[63] It has been articulated by both Russian and Western critics of Putin.[64]

Let us assume, however, that Putin's public commitment to state building was genuine. As argued earlier, it may be that Putin's "steering from above" strategy was based on both a flawed notion of sequencing and a misperception that Russia in 2000 was still in the first stage of state formation, which was true in Chechnya but not throughout the Russian Federation. Putin's inclination, supported by other siloviki, to treat the entire state as if it was so fragile that it was on the verge of collapse led Russia under Putin to adopt a state-building strategy designed, as Fukuyama put it, to "concentrate the means of coercion." Eschewing a power-sharing approach to state building, however, allowed the continuation of widespread predation by coercive bodies, which ultimately made the state less effective.

Putin voiced his preference for "steering from above" quite openly in an illuminating comment toward the end of his presidency. Putin argued that Russia needed another fifteen to twenty years of "manual steering." He stated:

We, emerging from a deep systemic crisis, were forced to do a lot in a so-called "manual regime." When will that time arrive when most things, or the basic things, can function in an automatic regime? After we create the necessary legal conditions and mechanisms, when all elements of a market economy work to the full extent.... This demands time.... When the legal, and economic, and social base has grown up and become stable, then we will not need manual steering.... I think that will be in 15–20 years.[65]

Of course, the standards set out by Putin are quite demanding, and it seems likely that even after fifteen-to-twenty years, the elements identified by Putin will not "work to the full extent." This is another flaw in the sequencing strategy – when do you know that state institutions are capable of functioning effectively without "manual steering?" Further, the political barriers to moving toward "steering from below" are likely to become higher as those who benefit from the existing political order get more deeply entrenched.

---

[63] Douglass C. North, *Institutions, Institutional Change and Economic Performance* (Cambridge: Cambridge University Press, 1990), pp. 59–60; Venelin I. Ganev, "Post-Communism as an Episode of State Building: A Reversed Tillyan Perspective," *Communist and Post-Communist Studies*, 38, 4 (2005), p. 432.

[64] Artemi Troitsky, "Alice-in-Wonderland Russia," *openDemocracy*, March 14, 2005 [www.opendemocracy.net]; Anders Aslund, "Unmasking President Putin's Grandiose Myth," *MT*, November 28, 2007.

[65] Vladimir Putin, "Otvety na voprosy zhurnalistov posle pryamogo tele- i radioefira ("Pryamaya liniya s Prezidentom Rossii")," October 18, 2007.

Western scholars who, contrary to my argument, conclude that Putin's contribution to state building was generally positive tend to adopt one of two possible lines of reasoning. The first is to argue that Russia in 2000 was still at the first stage of state building. For example, Ottorino Cappelli contends that Russia after Yeltsin was coming out of a "pre-modern" or "feudal" phase, and that it was necessary for Putin to use a combination of force and patronage to establish a rudimentary state analogous to early-modern West European absolutist monarchies. It was too early to think about building what I call a civil state.[66] As I have argued earlier, this position seriously overstates the weakness of the Russian state at the time Putin took power. To take one example: a state whose fiscal capacity allows it to extract more than 30 percent of GDP from society in the form of revenue, as it did under Yeltsin, is hardly comparable to European feudalism of 500 years ago. Most centrally, outside Chechnya, the state by 2000 had more or less successfully claimed a monopoly of legitimate violence, and thus completed the first stage of state building.

The second general approach that positively evaluates Putin's rule maintains that, for historical reasons, Russia can only be a strong state if it is a police state. This argument is best articulated by Gerald Easter, who refers to Russia under Putin as a "normal police state." It is normal in that, throughout history, Russia has only had a strong state when society is subordinate to the state and the control of wealth and power is centralized in the executive. To put it differently, only the monocratic or "steering from above" model works in Russia – the constitutionalist path or "steering from below," what Easter labels the "liberal state," is an illusion. Like Cappelli, Easter contends that the dominance of liberal norms among analysts leads to a failure to understand Russia not as we would like it to be, but as it really is.[67] I am somewhat sympathetic to Easter's "realist" reading of the Russian state, particularly his emphasis on the importance of coercion to Russian state building. On the other hand, Russian society has changed a great deal from the time of Ivan the Terrible, Peter the Great, or Joseph Stalin. The international context is also much different for Russia. In these changed conditions, the civil state ideal should be no more unattainable for Russia than it is for other middle-income developing states, including those in the post-communist world. Yet Russia seriously underperforms compared to its peers not just in terms of state quality, but also state capacity. This is perhaps my central disagreement with Easter's position, and it's an empirical one: Steering from above under Putin did not work.

In the Russian case, we can see how the monocratic strategy, which disregards state quality in a way that the constitutionalist state-building strategy would not, has negative consequences for state capacity as well. Corrupt

---

[66] Cappelli 2008.
[67] Easter 2008. Another stimulating essay with a similar line of argument is: Stefan Hedlund, "Vladimir the Great, Grand Prince of Muscovy: Resurrecting the Russian Service State," *Europe-Asia Studies*, 58, 5 (July 2006), pp. 775–801.

and predatory law enforcement agents not only neglect serving the population but also even neglect their actual jobs, like fighting corruption and terrorism. Possible examples of this problem are legion, but here is one that is illustrative. In the 2000s, during the time that Putin was president, there were multiple cases of wealthy businessmen or members of their family being kidnapped and held for ransom. Investigative journalists turned up evidence that several former power ministry personnel, including one gang's reputed leader, were involved in these kidnappings. This gang seemed to have powerful contacts inside law enforcement organs that protected it and shared information. Moreover, active law enforcement officers often showed little interest in investigating these kidnappings unless they were paid by relatives of the victim. Indeed, law enforcement officers would present themselves to family members with various schemes to help free their loved one – for a price, of course. Kidnappings were not heinous crimes to be solved, but simply another opportunity for corruption and predation.[68]

Russian observers early in the Medvedev presidency noted how the inattention to state quality under Putin, in terms of law enforcement personnel who served the public in a fair and impartial manner, weakened Putin's goal of strengthening the state. Yuliya Latynina used the kidnapping phenomenon discussed in the previous paragraph to evaluate the state of Putin's "power vertical" after his term had run out. Echoing Volkov, she noted that under Putin, just like in the early 1990s, businessmen were being kidnapped, but now instead of being done by "bandits," it was being done by "those who work in the secret services, or those who have a protector there." Pointing to other scandalous events, like the unsolved murders of multiple journalists and armed criminal raids on passenger planes at one of Moscow's major airports, Latynina maintained that state leaders were not interested in a well-functioning law enforcement system. Average law enforcement personnel were given to understand that they were free to make money by shaking down businesses as long as they would "protect the regime that allowed them to frighten businessmen." Such a system, she concluded, hardly qualified as a "power vertical." The Russian journalist and legal expert Leonid Nikitinskiy made a similar point, contending that Putin had not create a "power vertical" or a "dictatorship of the law," as he had promised in 2000. He had not created a "police state" either, because in a police state, "there is strict discipline," not a "fiction" of vertical power. Russia's system, Nikitinskiy stated, was more like a form of feudalism in which officers might serve their direct boss but hardly the administrative hierarchy as a whole.[69]

---

[68] Sergey Kanev, "Kto razreshil?," *Nov. Gaz.*, June 1, 2009; Vladislav Trifonov and Oleg Rubnikovich, "Militsioner sluzhil u urugvayskikh pokhititeley," *K-D*, June 2, 2009; Sergey Kanev, "'Kryshi' i podvaly," *Nov. Gaz.*, June 22, 2009.

[69] Yuliya Latynina, "O vertikali vlasti," *Yezhednev. Zh.*, June 2, 2009; Leonid Nikitinskiy, "Diktatura menta," *Nov. Gaz.*, April 27 and 29, 2009.

The widespread corruption and predation in Russian power ministries is not an inevitable consequence of a monocratic state-building strategy, but it is more likely than in the constitutionalist approach. One thing that can partially compensate for the shortcomings of the monocratic approach to state building is a strong sense of institutional mission on the part of officials, such as was seen in the early decades of communist rule in the Soviet Union and China. In Russia, this sense of mission has often come from a widely held belief among the political elite that the state was under serious external threat. Putin appealed to this idea, particularly in his second term, which seemed to rally power ministry officials behind his state-building project. At the same time, Putin's ideological project was in some respects incoherent, which can be seen in the very label "sovereign democracy." Russia moved in an authoritarian direction while simultaneously claiming to be strengthening its democracy, at least in part because of liberal democracy's hegemonic status as the most appealing form of government in the world.[70] This ideological incoherence did not provide a strong enough sense of mission to overcome the existing incentives for rent seeking in a patrimonial, weakly monitored system.

Overall, absent a strong ideological commitment to the legitimacy of authoritarian state building among officials themselves, the monocratic strategy tends toward major deficiencies in state quality (rule of law, accountability) that ultimately also undermine state capacity. In established states in the contemporary era, it has become increasingly difficult to raise capacity without attending to quality; for states in the second stage of state building, quality and capacity tend to go together. The exception are states that are (or aspire to be) police states, like those of East Asia (China and Singapore) or of the former Soviet Union (Turkmenistan, Kazakhstan, Belarus).[71] Belarus and Turkmenistan are hardly models for Russia, and indeed they are poor performers in both state capacity and state quality; they are better at maintaining order than serving the public in a fair and impartial manner, but they are not particularly good at taking and implementing policies in an efficient manner. Kazakhstan is a more successful state, but whether its version of resource-dependent patrimonial presidentialism can survive after Nursultan Nazarbayev leaves the scene remains an open question.

Ultimately the constitutionalist approach, or "steering from below," is more likely to create both state capacity and quality. Ertman notes that the constitutionalist path has the best chance of eliminating patrimonialism and building

---

[70] Francis Fukuyama, *The End of History and the Last Man* (New York: The Free Press, 1992).

[71] These countries were chosen as examples because there is a greater than .5 difference between their state capacity and state quality scores. There is also a subset of countries with state quality scores considerably higher (>.5) than their state capacity scores. Most of these are countries facing a serious secessionist or terrorist threat, such as India, Israel, and Spain. In these cases, the political stability/no violence scores pulls down the state capacity index.

a strong, rational-legal state if there are "strong, participatory localities."[72] Desmond King and Robert Lieberman, in a review of recent literature, similarly observe that "the new comparative politics of the state ... suggests that fragmentation by itself need not be debilitating to state development.... The relationship between alternative sites of power and the state is not always zero-sum. Federalism ... can also be a lever for advancing the reach and functionality of the national state."[73] In this respect, Putin's authoritarian state-building project, which weakened federalism and targeted civil society groups in opposition to the state, was particularly misguided. In the coercive realm, a more appropriate approach to developing both state capacity and state quality would have considered options for decentralizing parts of the police and ways to empower civil society monitoring of the power ministries.[74]

Although Putin's impulse toward centralization and "manual steering" may be understandable, given his background, his allies, and the situation he inherited, it is unlikely to create the conditions for the type of institutional development – strengthening civil society and the rule of law, reducing corruption – that he was rhetorically committed to as president. In established states in the contemporary era, the path to a strong state, paradoxically, involves sharing power.

THE FUTURE OF RUSSIAN STATE BUILDING

Medvedev's early rhetoric, first as a candidate and then as president, suggested he understood how an overly centralized, unaccountable state had created conditions for corruption and the "unrule of law" to flourish.[75] Indeed, the notion of "state quality" was embraced rhetorically by leading officials and elites. At the St. Petersburg International Economic Forum in June 2008, the theme featured in several prominent speeches. For example, First Deputy Prime Minister Igor Shuvalov argued that a key problem in Russian economic development was that for 300 years, Russia's elite had been motivated by a desire to "catch up and overtake the West." This approach to modernization led to a "one-sided" fixation on quantitative measures that neglected the issue of "becoming a country in which it is comfortable for people to live." Shuvalov stressed, "rather than pursuing certain [quantitative] indicators, we should set our sights on qualitative change in the economy and the quality of life." This would include maintaining the environment, improving the population's

---

[72] Ertman 1977, pp. 323–324.
[73] Desmond King and Robert C. Lieberman, "Ironies of State Building: A Comparative Perspective on the American State," *World Politics*, 61, 3 (2009), p. 574.
[74] See Chapters 4 and 6. Police-NGO relations were equally strained in Medvedev's first year as president: Pavel Chikov, "Krepit' zashchitu ot naroda," *Nov. Gaz.*, July 22, 2009.
[75] "Kandidat v prezidenty Dmitriy Medvedev oglasil svoi predvybornye tezisy," *Newsru.com*, January 22, 2008; Dmitriy Medvedev, "Vystupleniya na V Krasnyarskom ekonomicheskom forume," February 15, 2008 [http://www.medvedev2008.ru]; Medvedev, "Poslaniye Federal'nomu Sobraniyu Rossiyskoy Federatsii," November 5, 2008.

health, and "the growth of societal trust toward basic institutions, first of all toward judicial and law enforcement activity." Anatoliy Chubais, the controversial privatization tsar from the Yeltsin administration, echoed Shuvalov and drew the logical political implications, contending that "the state must be judged from the point of view of the quality of services that it provides for the country as a whole. In my understanding, it is impossible to evaluate the quality of this service without real give and take and a truly competitive political mechanism."[76]

Of course, rhetoric in itself does not translate into policy change. Putin had on multiple occasions made similar statements. For example, in his 2005 state of the nation speech, he maintained, "task number one for us remains raising the effectiveness of state administration, strict observance of the law by bureaucrats, the provision of quality public services to the population."[77] But Medvedev already had a reputation as a relative "liberal" in the Putin administration, a counterweight to the siloviki clan around Igor Sechin, and he continued to speak out on these issues after becoming president. For example, in July 2008, he denounced patrimonialism in state administration, observing that "decisions about filling positions" are sometimes made "on the basis of acquaintance, personal allegiance or, even worse, for money – that is, offices can be bought." He also attacked predation, demanding that "our law-enforcement and state institutions should stop terrifying business."[78] He launched a series of anticorruption and legal reforms, although most observers were skeptical that they would have much effect without larger changes in the political system.[79]

Medvedev's personal views and inclinations also may matter little for the future of Russian state building. Vladimir Putin, who became prime minister and the leader of the dominant United Russia party, showed little sign in Medvedev's first two years that he had any intention of relinquishing real power. Russian pundits labeled the political system a "tandemocracy," with Putin and Medvedev sharing power. The nature of the Putin-Medvedev relationship, and whether Medvedev was simply warming the presidential throne for Putin's inevitable return in 2012, was the biggest mystery, and the most hotly debated topic, of Medvedev's early presidency. The amending of the

---

[76] I.I. Shuvalov, "Vystupleniye Pervogo zamestitelya Predsedatelya Pravitel'stva Rossii I.I. Shuvalova na XII Peterburgskom Mezhdunarodnom ekonomicheskom forume v Sankt-Peterburge," www.government.ru, June 8, 2008; Alison Smale, "Money Talks at Russian Forum as Business Leaders See Past Hurdles to Investing," *NYT*, June 9, 2008. See also the editorial in Russia's leading business paper on the "quality deficit:" "Defitsit kachestva," *Vedomosti*, July 1, 2008.

[77] Vladimir Putin, "Poslaniye Federal'nomu Sobraniyu Rossiyskoy Federatsii," April 25, 2005.

[78] Nikolaus von Twickel, "Medvedev Admits Posts for Sale," *MT*, July 24, 2008; Brian Whitmore, "Beware The Russian Bear Market," *RFE/RL*, July 31, 2008.

[79] Brian Whitmore, "Russia's Judicial Counter-Reformation," *RFE/RL*, January 7, 2009; Roland Oliphant, "Tilting at the Windmills of Corruption," *RP*, May 28, 2009; Ira Iosebashvili, "European Watchdog Castigates Courts," *MT*, June 24, 2009.

Constitution in late 2008 to allow the president to serve two consecutive six year terms furthered speculation about Putin's long-term plans. Surveys conducted on the first and second anniversaries of Medvedev's presidency found that 66–68 percent of citizens believed that Medvedev is "under the control of Putin and [his] entourage," with only 19–22 percent contending that Medvedev "pursues an independent policy."[80]

Under Medvedev, most top government officials were holdovers from the Putin era. That said, there were some important personnel changes, especially among the siloviki. In May 2008, Nikolay Patrushev and Viktor Cherkesov lost their posts at the top of the FSB and FSKN (the narcotics control agency), and Igor Sechin and Viktor Ivanov were moved out of the Kremlin. All of them landed new jobs, including some influential ones – for example, Patrushev became Secretary of the Security Council, Sechin became a deputy prime minister, and Ivanov became head of the FSKN. This reshuffling had several likely motivations. Most centrally, with Medvedev in the presidency, the FSKN was no longer needed as a counterweight to the siloviki clan, with its powerful strongholds in the FSB and the Kremlin; as Latynina put it, Medvedev himself was now the main counterweight. The new FSB head, Aleksandr Bortnikov, was seen by most analysts as either a Medvedev ally or as a more apolitical technocrat. The May 2008 reshuffle seemed to mark the end of the 2007–2008 siloviki clan wars, or at least a temporary cease-fire. The tandemocracy of Medvedev and Putin could agree on the need for this cease-fire while allowing leading siloviki officials to maintain some political and, equally important, economic influence.[81]

Medvedev's timing in assuming the presidency seemed as unlucky as Putin's timing had been lucky. Putin came to office a year after the 1998 economic crisis of devaluation and default, which, along with a more general postcommunist recovery and rising world oil prices, paved the way for the rapid economic growth of the Putin years. Medvedev took office on the eve of the world economic "Great Recession," which brought Russia's economic growth to an abrupt halt and also contributed to a substantial drop in world energy prices, although these prices remained much higher than they had been during Yeltsin's presidency.

Moreover, the situation in the North Caucasus remained highly unstable and in some respects seemed to worsen. In October 2008, Medvedev sacked the disgraced president of Ingushetia, Murat Zyazikov, after the opposition

[80] Fred Weir, "Who Is Really Running Russia?" *Christian Science Monitor*, July 19, 2009; "Russian Poll: Medvedev Still in Putin's Shadow," *RFE/RL*, May 11, 2010.

[81] On continuity among state elite, including siloviki, see: "Medvedev: Prezident ili po-prezhnomu naslednik?" *EM*, March 1, 2009; Andrey Ivochkin, "Ol'ga Kryshtanovskaya: 'Putin u nas vser'ez i nadolgo'," *Nov. Gaz.*, August 6, 2008. On the May 2008 reshuffle, see: Francesca Mereu and Max Delany, "A Lineup Aimed at Taming Siloviki," *MT*, May 15, 2008; Yuliya Latynina, "Sprashivayte u ofitsial'nikh dilerov," *Nov. Gaz.*, June 16, 2008. On Bortnikov, see: Roman Shleynov, "Donoschiki snaryadov," *Nov. Gaz.*, April 26, 2007; Andrey Soldatov, "Spetssluzhbam ukazali put' polkovnika Undervud," *Yezhednev. Zh.*, May 13, 2008.

journalist Magomed Yevloyev was shot while in police custody, but this did little to stop the violence in the region. Indeed, Zyazikov's successor, Yunus-Bek Yevkurov, a retired army colonel, was seriously injured in a car bomb attack in June 2009. Also in June 2009, the Dagestani Interior Minister, Adilgerei Magomedtagirov, was shot and killed. In July 2009, a leading Chechen human rights activist with the organization Memorial, Nataliya Estemirova, was abducted and murdered. The head of Memorial, Oleg Orlov, accused Chechen President Ramzan Kadyrov of being responsible for the murder, adding that "it apparently suits President Medvedev to have a murderer as head of one of the regions of the Russian Federation." Estemirova's murder was only one of a number of killings after Medvedev became president that appeared to be the responsibility of Kadyrov; prominent individuals who had crossed Kadyrov were killed in Grozny, Moscow, Vienna, and Dubai in 2008 or 2009. Attacks on law enforcement personnel and civilians remained a frequent occurrence in the North Caucasus, especially in Ingushetia and Dagestan. After Estemirova's murder, a group of thirty-nine leading Russian human rights activists issued an open letter condemning the "anti-constitutional" and "criminal" policies being pursued in the North Caucasus, which involve killings, kidnappings, and torture, "committed by the siloviki and groups close to them, acting as 'death squads'." Moscow's ability to keep the lid on events in the region seemed to be slipping, and the capacity to keep providing massive economic subsidies – a key feature of North Caucasus policy in Putin's second term – was threatened by the economic crisis.[82] Moreover, terrorism from the North Caucasus once again returned to central Russia, with the November 2009 attack on a Moscow-St. Petersburg train that killed twenty-eight people and a March 2010 attack on the Moscow subway that killed forty people.[83]

In the power ministry realm more generally, Medvedev faced a series of challenges. Most prominent, perhaps, was the "five day war" with Georgia in August 2008. Although the Russian military largely had its way with the outgunned Georgian army, multiple tactical and operational deficiencies gave renewed impetus to the military reform efforts of Defense Minister Anatoliy Serdyukov. The economic crisis, however, threatened these efforts, and there was stiff resistance from the uniformed military.[84]

---

[82] The quotes from Orlov and the open letter are from: "Natalya Estemirova Kidnapped in Grozny, Found Dead in Ingushetia," *EDM*, July 16, 2009; "Ubiystvo Natal'i Estemirovoy – prigovor gosudarstvennoy politike," *Yezhednev. Zh.*, July 17, 2009. Further information and analysis of the events in the North Caucasus in 2008–2009, beyond that referred to in Chapter 7, include: Mikhail Solodovnikov, "Byuro ispolneniya teraktov," *Russkiy reporter*, August 20, 2009; Aleksandr Cherkasov, "Ikh ubivayut pervymi," *Yezhednev. Zh.*, July 16, 2009; Claire Biggs, "A String of Silenced Voices on Chechnya," *RFE/RL*, July 16, 2009; Aleksey Malashenko, "Kavkazskiye gorki," *NV*, July 6, 2009; Amnesty International, *Russian Federation: Rule WithOut Law: Human Rights Violations in the North Caucasus*, June 30, 2009.

[83] Sergey Minenko, Anatoliy Karavayev, Viktor Paukov, "Iz-pod zemli," *VN*, March 30, 2010.

[84] V.V. Shlykov, "Tayny blitskriga Serdyukova," *Rossiya v Global'noy Politike*, 6 (November–December 2009); Dale R. Herspring and Roger N. McDermott, "Serdyukov Promotes Systemic Russian Military Reform," *Orbis*, 54, 2 (2010), pp. 284–301.

Most centrally for this book, a series of episodes in 2009 led to a heightened focus on corruption and predation in the police. The biggest spark was the so-called Yevsyukov affair. Major Denis Yevsyukov, head of a police district in southern Moscow, went on a drunken shooting spree in a Moscow super-market in April 2009, killing two people and wounding seven. Yevsyukov, it turned out, had a whole series of blemishes on his record but had been protected due to patrimonial links, most directly to his father, who had served under the head of the Moscow GUVD, Vladimir Pronin, in Kursk. Pronin was sacked after the Yevsyukov incident, but the affair led to an outpouring of stories on patrimonialism and corruption in the Moscow police, including the struggle in the Moscow police between the "Moscow" and "Kursk" clans, the selling of positions and ranks, the wholesale involvement of the police in "roofing" and other corrupt and predatory practices, and the low professional standards of the militia. The head of the Duma Security Committee, Vladimir Vasilev, remarked that the cadres' problem in the law enforcement organs was so bad that many of those serving now "in different circumstances might be sitting in prison."[85]

The Yevsyukov affair turned out to be such a loud and resonant "fire alarm" that the pathologies of Russian law enforcement structures, especially the police, became one of the biggest stories of 2009. The press, including state-controlled media, reported on murders, rapes, and other crimes com-mitted by police officers. Polling data showed that public distrust of the police remained as high as it was under Yeltsin and Putin.[86] Even more remarkably, perhaps, was that police officers themselves began to come forward to pub-licly complain about corruption in the police, the "quota system" for evaluat-ing police effectiveness that led them to cook the books through a variety of standard unethical schemes, and their own poor living conditions. As befits our age, YouTube was the most popular venue for these passionate outbursts. The business daily *Vedomosti* noted at the end of 2009 that the evident cri-sis in Russian law enforcement showed how little had come of the ten-year campaign to strengthen the state, and that such vital public goods as domes-tic security were not adequately provided. The Russian militia, *Vedomosti* observed, worked not to defend the security and rights of citizens, but for "the interests of the powers that be" or for their own financial gain.[87]

[85] Leonid Nikitinskiy, "Vladimir Vasil'ev: V militsiyu popadayut lyudi, kotoriye mogli by sidet' v tyur'me," *Nov. Gaz.*, July 10, 2009. Noteworthy articles on the Yevsyukov affair and problems in the police include: Georgiy Satarov, "Na kholodnuyu golovu," *Yezhednev. Zh.*, May 6, 2009; Vladimir Perekrest, "Podlog, vzyatka, vorovstvo," *Izvestiya*, May 8, 2009; Il'ya Barabanov, "Dokhodnoye mesto," *NV*, May 18, 2009; Vladimir Demchenko, "Lider profsoyuza mil-itsionerov Mikhail Pashkin: 'General'skaya dolzhnost' v Moskve stoit million dollarov," *Izvestiya*, May 21, 2009; Sergey Kanev, "Klanoviye meropriyatiya," *Nov. Gaz.*, May 25, 2009; Kevin O'Flynn, "Police Crime Wave Sparks Talk of Reform in Russia," *NYT*, June 28, 2009.

[86] "Rossiyane ne doveryayut pravookhranitel'nym organam," *Levada Tsentr*, February 16, 2010 [http://www.levada.ru/press/2010021605.html]. For data from the Yeltsin and Putin years, see Chapter 6.

[87] "Ot redaktsii: Krizis obshchego blaga," *Vedomosti*, December 30, 2009. A good overview of what it dubbed the "year of the cop" was: Yaroslav Zagorets, "God menta," *Lenta.ru*,

Medvedev was forced to respond to the crisis in Russian law enforcement. He issued several decrees on police reform in late 2009 and early 2010. He vowed to trim the size of the police by 20 percent by 2012 while raising salaries for those who remained. Several secondary functions were stripped from the MVD, and a new "Law on the Militia" was drafted. The police once again vowed to reform the method for evaluating police performance and to move away from quotas in their performance statistics. More radical proposals were debated, including separating the federal criminal police from the local public-order police (see the discussion in Chapter 4), or even dismantling the MVD entirely and starting over. At the time this book went to press, it was too early to say what the results of this reform activity would be.[88]

Regardless of the ultimate outcome of this latest round of police reform, the Yevsyukov affair was a fitting symbol of the state of Russia's coercive organs nearly two decades after the Soviet collapse. Both the capacity and quality of Russian law enforcement was judged as highly deficient, from the president down to ordinary citizens. It did not have to turn out this way. Other postcommunist states had managed to significantly reform their law enforcement structures.[89] This was obviously most true in countries that aspired to and were able to join the European Union, which gave those countries significant material and moral inducements to reform their bureaucracies. But even tiny and poor Georgia was able to radically reform its police after the 2003 Rose Revolution. The size of the force was radically cut, with many officers dismissed. More stringent and professional procedures for recruiting, training, and retaining officers were put in place. Those who made the grade were rewarded with significantly higher salaries – from $30 per month in 2003 to $500 per month in 2008 – and more stable career prospects, as well as higher pensions. New oversight bodies were also created. Although there were still problems with the police, including questions about their use against opposition protestors and the extent to which the personnel reforms were followed in practice, by most accounts, police corruption dropped significantly, and public trust in the police increased enormously.[90]

December 30, 2009. Note that the Russian word used here, "*ment*," carries a negative connotation, so "year of the pig" would be another possible translation of the phrase.

[88] Irina Granik and Aleksandr Igorev, "Bez vytrezviteley, no s prezhnim ministrom," *K-D*, February 19, 2010; Afanasiy Sborov, "Instruktsiya dlya 'oborotney'," *K-V*, February 1, 2010; Viktor Paukov, "MVD: modernizatsiya vnutrennikh del," *VN*, December 25, 2009.

[89] Caparini and Marenin 2004.

[90] Author's interview with Natia Gvazava (head of international department) and Dato Korakhashvili (head of legal department), Georgian Ministry of Internal Affairs, June 2008; Alexander Kupatadze, Giorgi Siradze, and Giorgi Mitagvaria, "Policing and Police Reform in Georgia," in Louise Shelley, Erik R. Scott, and Anthony Latta, eds., *Organized Crime and Corruption in Georgia* (New York: Routledge, 2007), pp. 93–110; Jozsef Boda and Kornely Kakachia, "The Current Status of Police Reform in Georgia," in Philipp H. Fluri and Eden Cole, eds., *From Revolution to Reform: Georgia's Struggle with Democratic Institution Building and Security Sector Reform* (Vienna: Lavak, 2005): accessed at http://www.dcaf. ch/; Yekaterina Savina, "Lechit' ili udalyat'?," *NV*, May 18, 2009.

State building takes time, and improving state quality and state capacity in the coercive sector will be a major challenge in a country as large and diverse as Russia. Law enforcement is one of the most difficult sectors to reform. But Russia does *have* a state, and considerable economic resources; both capacity and quality could be built. A reform effort would need to tackle the bureaucratic type, monitoring approach, and organizational mission of the power ministries.

Perhaps most important is whether Medvedev, Putin, or any other future leader can articulate a clear and appealing ideological project for the Russian state that will be embraced by officials. There are two major alternative ideological projects. First, Russia's leaders could set the goal of building a civil state with both high capacity and high quality. This was seemingly Boris Yeltsin's goal, but the effort failed. Although Putin often spoke in this language as president, it was not a high priority. Medvedev seems to be trying to revive this project with his program of liberal modernization, which he dubbed "Forward, Russia!"[91] Such an ideological project would require greater liberalism and democracy, a completely different direction than the one Putin pursued. This civil state option remains a minority tradition in Russia, but it is far from dead.

The second possible ideological project is to revive the "Russian idea" that justifies a traditional service state, moving Russia toward the police state category. If implemented, this state-building approach would increase capacity but not quality. This type of state was seemingly Putin's goal, and it has substantial support among the elite in general and the siloviki in particular, but by 2008, it had not been achieved, although some signs of progress toward building this type of state were evident in his second term.

Weak state capacity and quality are likely to persist in the power ministries unless one of these two visions is institutionalized ("infused with value") throughout the state bureaucracy.[92] Although in the first years of Medvedev's presidency, there were some signals that he would pursue the goal of a democratic civil state, it seemed that he lacked the power to pursue such a vision. If Vladimir Putin returns as president in 2012, we may find out if his authoritarian state-building project has staying power. The evidence from this book suggests that, in the coercive realm, it is likely to fail.

---

[91] Dmitriy Medvedev, "Rossiya, vpered!," *Gazeta.ru*, September 10, 2009; Dmitriy Medvedev, "Poslaniye Federal'nomu Sobraniyu Rossiyskoy Federatsii," November 12, 2009.

[92] Philip Selznick, *Leadership in Administration: A Sociological Interpretation* (Berkeley, CA: University of California Press, 1957), p. 17.

Appendix A

Publication Abbreviations

AiF	*Argumenty i Fakty*
CW	*Chechnya Weekly*
EDM	*Eurasia Daily Monitor*
EM	*Ekho Moskvy*
JIR	*Jane's Intelligence Review*
JRL	Johnson's Russia List
K-D	*Kommersant"-Daily*
K-V	*Kommersant"-Vlast'*
KP	*Komsomol'skaya Pravda*
KZ	*Krasnaya Zvezda*
MK	*Moskovskiy Komsomolets*
MN	*Moskovskiye Novosti*
MT	*Moscow Times*
Nez. Gaz.	*Nezavisimaya Gazeta*
NI	*Novye Izvestiya*
Nov. Gaz.	*Novaya Gazeta*
NV	*Novoye Vremya*
NVO	*Nezavisimoye voyennoye obozreniye*
NYT	*New York Times*
PG	*Parlamentskaya Gazeta*
RAD	*Russian Analytical Digest*
RFE/RL	*Radio Free Europe/Radio Liberty*
RG	*Rossiyskaya Gazeta*
RN	*Russkiy Newsweek*
RP	*Russia Profile*
RRB	*Rossiyskiy Regional'nyy Byulleten'*
RRR	*Russian Regional Report*
VN	*Vremya Novostey*
WP	*Washington Post*
Yezhednev. Zh.	*Yezhednevnyy Zhurnal*
Yezhenedel. Zh.	*Yezhenedel'nyy Zhurnal*

Appendix B

Interview Index

Note: All titles are at time of interview and are for identification purposes only. Respondents who requested anonymity are listed at the end of each section.

Moscow

M-1: V. Abramkin, Director, Moscow Center for Prison Reform (March 2003)

M-2: Ye. Albats, Professor and journalist, expert on FSB (December 2004)

M-3: L. Alpern', Deputy Director, Moscow Center for Prison Reform (July 2008)

M-4: D. Babich, Russian journalist (September 1999, May & June 2000, May 2001)

M-5: V. Bakatin, former Minister of Interior and Director of KGB, Soviet Union (April 2003)

M-6: A. Barabashev, Associate Dean, Public Administration, Moscow State University (December 2004)

M-7: A. Belkin, Council on Foreign and Defense Policy (September 1999, June 2000, May 2001, March 2003)

M-8: A. Bogaturov, Institute of USA and Canada (September 1999)

M-9: B. Dubin, Head of Department of Social-Political Research, Levada Center (July 2008)

M-10: B. Gavrilov, Investigative Co., MVD (March 2003)

M-11: K. Golovshchinskiy, Institute of Public Administration and Municipal Management, Higher School of Economics (July 2008)

M-12: A. Gol'ts, Defense Correspondent, *Itogi* (September 1999, May 2001)

M-13: K. Goryainov, MVD institute and Center for Justice Assistance Policing Program (March 2003)

M-14: P. Isayev, State Duma staff member (June 2002)

M-15: G. Khromov, Military Industrial Commission, Soviet Union (June 2000)

M-16: N. Klishch, Institute of Public Administration and Municipal Management, Higher School of Economics (July 2008)

M-17: I. Komaritsky, Center for Justice Assistance (INDEM) (December 2004)

M-18: A. Kortunov, Moscow Public Science Foundation (September 1999, June 2000)

M-19: M. Krasnov, former legal adviser to Boris Yeltsin, INDEM Foundation (April 2003)

M-20: V. Luneyev, Institute of State and Law (December 2002)

M-21: A. Novikova and O. Shepeleva, "Demos" Center (June 2008)

M-22: A. Obolonskiy, Deputy Chair of Department of Public and Municipal Administration, Higher School of Economics (June 2008)

M-23: N. Petrov, Carnegie Moscow Center (December 2002, December 2004)

M-24: M. Peyser, Center for Justice Assistance (December 2002)

M-25: A. Pikayaev, Carnegie Moscow Center (September 1999, June 2000)

M-26: M. Pogorely, Col. (retired) and Editor, *Nuclear Security and Safety* (June 2000)

M-27: V. Pristavko, State Duma staff member (June 2000)

M-28: P. Romashkin, Col. (retired), State Duma staff member (June 2000)

M-29: A. Salmin, President, Russian Social-Political Center (June 2000)

M-30: G. Satarov, former political adviser to Boris Yeltsin, President of INDEM (September 1999, December 2004, July 2008)

M-31: R. Simonyan, Deputy Chief of Staff, Human Rights Commissioner of Russian Federation (December 2004)

M-32: V. Slipchenko, Gen.-Maj. (retired), Academy of Military Science (May 2000)

M-33: L. Smirnyagin, former adviser to Boris Yeltsin on regional politics (May 2001)

M-34: V. Solovyev, Managing Editor, *Independent Military Review* (June 2000)

M-35: I. Sutyagin, Institute for USA and Canada (September 1999)

M-36: D. Trenin, Carnegie Moscow Center (September & October 1999, June 2000)

M-37: V. Tsygichko, Col. (retired), Soviet General Staff, Professor, Russian Academy of Science (June 2000)

M-38: S. Tyushkevich, Maj.-Gen. (retired), Professor (June 2000)

M-39: S. Vitsin, Deputy Chair, Presidential Council on Judicial Reform (April 2003)

M-40: A. Vladimirov, Gen. (retired), Army (September 1999)

M-41: V. Yarynich, Col. (retired), Soviet General Staff (June 2000)

M-42: S. Yushenkov, member of Duma Defense Co.,Col. (retired) (September 1999)

M-43: Ye. Zapodinskaya, Crime and Justice correspondent, *Kommersant Daily* (June 2002)

M-44: A. Zhilin, military journalist, Russian television (June 2000)

M-45: Anonymous, Department of Justice, US Embassy (March 2003, July 2008)

M-46: Anonymous, MVD Colonel, Professor, Moscow State Legal Academy (April 2003)

M-47: Anonymous, former MVD and Russian Interpol official (March 2003)

M-48: Anonymous, US Army Attache, US Embassy (September 1999, June 2000)

M-49: Anonymous, Western foundation staffer (December 2004)

M-50: Anonymous, law enforcement official, US Embassy (June 2008)

Nizhniy Novgorod

NN-1: R. Bikmetov, Nizhniy Novgorod State Technological Institute (April 2003)

NN-2: V. Kozyreva, Center for Justice Assistance (April 2003)

NN-3: A. Makarychev, Nizhniy Novgorod Linguistic University (April 2003)

NN-4: A. Marchenko, Center for Justice Assistance (April 2003)

NN-5: V. Sarychev, Public relations manager for Gorky Automobile Factory (GAZ) (April 2003)

NN-6: V. Yegorov, Nizhniy Novgorod Obkom Secretary, Communist Party (April 2003)

NN-7: Anonymous, Col., MVD Institute, Nizhniy Novgorod (April 2003)

NN-8: Anonymous, law enforcement oversight, Nizhniy Novgorod city administration (April 2003)

Novosibirsk

N-1: S. Araslanov, Yabloko party (June 2003)

N-2: T. Babanova, I. Baradachev, and S. Lindemann-Komarova, Siberian Initiative (June 2003)

N-3: S. Kurbatov, crime correspondent, TV NTN-4 (June 2003)

N-4: N. Latygina, Novosibirsk Women's Crisis Center (June 2003)

N-5: V. Lavskii, editor, *Kommersant Daily*, Novosibirsk (June 2003)

N-6: A. Nikolayev, Novosibirsk Oblast Council of Deputies (June 2003)

N-7: A. Soinov, Gen., Director, Novosibirsk MVD (June 2003)

N-8: D. Trostnikov, journalist, TV NTN-4 (June 2003)

N-9: D. Vinogradov, journalist, Novosibirsk Press Club, (June 2003)

N-10: A. Zhirnov, editor, TV NTN-4 (June 2003)

N-11: Anonymous, Colonel Main Directorate, Siberian Federal District, MVD (June 2003)

N-12: Anonymous, Novosibirsk Pardons Commission (June 2003)

N-13: Anonymous, junior Procuracy official (June 2003)

Saint Petersburg

P-1: N. Cherkesova, *Rosbalt* Press Agency, wife of V. Cherkesov, Presidential Representative, Northwest Federal District (December 2002)

P-2: A. Konstantinov, Center for Journalistic Investigations, author of *Bandit St. Petersburg* (December 2002, December 2004)

P-3: O. Korshunova, Saint Petersburg Law Institute of the General Procuracy, Russian Federation (December 2002)

P-4: O. Leikind, Open Society Institute (December 2002)

P-5: A. Markova, Vice Governor of St. Petersburg (December 2002)

P-6: B. Mikhailichenko, *Moscow News* (June 2000, December 2002)

P-7: G. Ovchinnikova, Saint Petersburg Law Institute of the General Procuracy, Russian Federation (December 2002)

P-8: B. Pustyntsev, Citizen's Watch NGO (December 2002, December 2004, July 2008)

P-9: M. Rodionov, Col. (retired), Professor, Saint Petersburg MVD University (December 2002)

P-10: A. Sangurov, President, "Strategy" Center (December 2004, July 2008)

P-11: N. Vinnichenko, Main Federal Inspector (December 2002)

P-12: Ye. Vyshenkov, retired police officer, Center for Journalistic Investigations (December 2002)

P-13: Anonymous, Col., Main Directorate, Northwest Federal District, MVD (December 2002)

P-14: Anonymous, Main Directorate, Northwest Federal District, MVD (December 2002)

Yekaterinburg

Ye-1: A. Aleksandrov, Sverdlovsk Oblast administration (June 2003)

Ye-2: V. Amirov, Colonel, *Urals Military News* (June 2003)

Ye-3: S. Belyayev, President, human rights organization "Sutyazhnik" (June 2003)

Ye-4: M. Kazantsev, Institute of Philosphy and Law (June 2003)

Ye-5: K. Kiselev, Deputy Director, Institute of Philosphy and Law (June 2003)

Ye-6: Ye. Makei, Lawyer, Ekaterina Crisis Center (June 2003)

Ye-7: T. Merzlyakova, Ombudsman, Sverdlovsk Oblast (June 2003)

Ye-8: S. Plotnikov, Center for Journalism in Extreme Situations, crime reporter (June 2003)

Ye-9: V. Rudenko, Director, Institute of Philosphy and Law (May 2001, June 2003)

Ye-10: S. Tushin, Yekaterinburg city administration (June 2003)

Ye-11: Yu. Voronin, Organized Crime Study Center, Urals State Law Academy (June 2003)

Ye-12: V. Zhitenev, Urals Academy of State Service (June 2003)

Ye-13: Anonymous, Col., MVD (June 2003)

Ye-14: Anonymous, Main Directorate, Urals Federal District, MVD (June 2003)

References

Note: This list of works cited includes only secondary literature such as books, book chapters, and journal articles. It does not include sources such as government documents, reports by international organizations and non-governmental organizations, newspaper and magazine articles, and so on.

Adsera, Alicia, Carlos Boix, and Mark Payne. "Are You Being Served? Political Accountability and Quality of Government." *Journal of Law, Economics, & Organization* 19, no. 2 (2003): 445–490.

Albats, Yevgenia. *The State within a State: The KGB and Its Hold on Russia – Past, Present, and Future.* New York: Farrar, Strauss, and Giroux, 1994.

Aleksandrov, Yuriy. "Besovstvo," *Otechestvennye zapiski* 2, no. 41 (2008). http://www.strana-oz.ru/

Alexseev, Mikhail A., ed. *Center-Periphery Conflict in Post-Soviet Russia: A Federation Imperiled.* New York: St. Martin's, 1999.

"Security Sell-Out in the North Caucasus, 2004: How Government Centralization Backfires." *PONARS Policy Memo* no. 344 (November 2004).

Allison, Graham T. *Essence of Decision: Explaining the Cuban Missile Crisis.* Boston: Little, Brown, and Company, 1971.

Andriyenko, Yu. V. "V poiskakh ob"yacneniya rosta prestupnosti v Rossii v perekhodnyy period: kriminometricheskiy podkhod." *Ekonomicheskiy zhurnal VShE* 5, no. 2 (2001): 194–220.

Arbatov, Alexei, et al., eds. *Managing Conflict in the Former Soviet Union: Russian and American Perspectives.* Cambridge, MA: MIT Press, 1997.

Aslund, Anders. "Russia's Success Story." *Foreign Affairs* 73, no. 5 (September/October 1994): 58–71.

Ayoob, Mohammed. *The Third World Security Predicament: State Making, Regional Conflict, and the International System.* Boulder, CO: Lynne Rienner, 1995.

Back, Hanna, and Axel Hadenius. "Democracy and State Capacity: Exploring a J-Shaped Relationship." *Governance* 21, no. 1 (January 2008): 1–24.

Baev, Pavel. "The Evolution of Putin's Regime: Inner Circles and Outer Walls." *Problems of Post-Communism* 51, no. 6 (November–December 2004): 3–13.

"Has Russia Achieved a Victory in Its War Against Terror?" *PONARS Policy Memo* no. 415 (December 2006).

"Putin's 'Crushing Blow' on Terrorism: Is Chechnya Really Pacified and Is Stability Restored in the North Caucasus?" Unpublished paper, June 2008.

"The Russian Armed Forces." *The Journal of Communist Studies and Transition Politics* 17, no. 1 (March 2001): 23–42.

"The Russian Military Campaign in the North Caucasus: Is a Victory in Sight?" Paper presented at the North Caucasus Conference, Jamestown Foundation, September 14, 2006.

"The Targets of Terrorism and the Aims of Counter-Terrorism in Moscow, Chechnya, and the North Caucasus." Paper for the annual meeting of the International Studies Association, Chicago, IL, March 2007.

Bahry, Donna. "The New Federalism and the Paradoxes of Regional Sovereignty in Russia." *Comparative Politics* 37, no. 2 (January 2005): 127–146.

Bakatin, Vadim. *Doroga v proshedshem vremeni.* Moscow: Dom, 1999.

Baker, Peter, and Susan Glasser. *Kremlin Rising.* Updated ed. Dulles, VA: Potomac Books, 2007.

Ball, Nicole. "Good Practices in Security Sector Reform." *Security Sector Reform: Brief 15.* Bonn: International Center for Conversion, 2000.

"Strengthening democratic governance of the security sector in conflict-affected countries." *Public Administration and Development* 25, no. 1 (February 2005): 25–38.

Banks, William C., Mitchel B. Wallerstein, and Renée de Nevers. *Combating Terrorism: Strategies and Approaches.* Washington, DC: CQ Press, 2008.

Barabashev, Alexei, and Jeffrey D. Straussman. "Public Service Reform in Russia, 1991–2006." *Public Administration Review* 67, no. 3 (May–June 2007): 373–382.

Barany, Zoltan. *Democratic Breakdown and the Decline of the Russian Military.* Princeton, NJ: Princeton University Press, 2007.

Barkey, Karen. *Bandits and Bureaucrats: The Ottoman Route to State Centralization.* Ithaca, NY: Cornell University Press, 1994.

Barnard, Chester I. *The Functions of the Executive.* Cambridge, MA: Harvard University Press, 1938/1966.

Barnes, Andrew. *Owning Russia.* Ithaca, NY: Cornell University Press, 2006.

Barnett, Michael N. "Building a Republican Peace: Stabilizing States after War." *International Security* 30, no. 4 (Spring 2006): 87–112.

Baron, Samuel H. *Bloody Saturday in the Soviet Union: Novocherkassk, 1962.* Stanford, CA: Stanford University Press, 2001.

Barylski, Robert V. *The Soldier in Russian Politics: Duty, Dictatorship, and Democracy under Gorbachev and Yeltsin.* New Brunswick, NJ: Transaction Publishers, 1998.

Bates, Robert H. *When Things Fell Apart: State Failure in Late-Century Africa.* Cambridge: Cambridge University Press, 2008.

Baturin, Yuriy, et al. *Epokha Yel'tsina: Ocherki politicheskoy istorii.* Moscow: Vagrius, 2000.

Bayley, David H. *Changing the Guard: Developing Democratic Police Abroad.* Oxford: Oxford University Press, 2006.

Patterns of Policing. New Brunswick, NJ: Rutgers University Press, 1985.

"The Police and Political Development in Europe." In Tilly, *The Formation of National States in Western Europe,* 328–379.

Bayley, David H., and Clifford D. Shearing. "The Future of Policing." In Newburn, *Policing,* 715–732.

Beck, Adrian, and Annette Robertson. "Policing in Post-Soviet Russia." In Pridemore, *Ruling Russia*, 247–260.

Public Attitudes to Crime and Policing in Russia. Leicester, United Kingdom: Scarman Centre, University of Leicester, 2002.

Bednar, Jenna, William N. Eskridge Jr., and John Ferejohn. "A Political Theory of Federalism," In *Constitutional Culture and Democratic Rule,* ed. John Ferejohn, Jack N. Rakove, and Jonathan Riley, 223–267. Cambridge: Cambridge University Press, 2001.

Beissinger, Mark R. *Nationalist Mobilization and the Collapse of the Soviet State.* Cambridge: Cambridge University Press, 2002.

Scientific Management, Socialist Discipline, and Soviet Power. Cambridge, MA: Harvard University Press, 1988.

"Structure and Example in Modular Political Phenomena: The Diffusion of Bulldozer/Rose/Orange/Tulip Revolutions." *Perspectives on Politics* 5, no. 2 (June 2007): 259–276.

Beissinger, Mark R., and Crawford Young, eds. *Beyond State Crisis? Postcolonial Africa and Post-Soviet Eurasia in Comparative Perspective.* Washington, DC: Woodrow Wilson Center Press, 2002.

Bennett, Gordon. *The Ministry of Internal Affairs of the Russian Federation.* UK: Conflict Studies Research Centre, 2000.

Beramendi, Pablo. "Federalism." In *Oxford Handbook of Comparative Politics,* ed. Carlos Boix and Susan Stokes, 752–781. Oxford: Oxford University Press, 2007.

Berman, Sheri. "Civil Society and the Collapse of the Weimar Republic." *World Politics* 49, no. 3 (April 1997): 401–429.

Bermeo, Nancy. "The Import of Institutions." *Journal of Democracy* 13, no. 2 (April 2002): 96–110.

Betz, David. "No Place for a Civilian?: Russian Defense Management from Yeltsin to Putin." *Armed Forces and Society* 28, no. 3 (Spring 2002): 481–504.

Blum, Douglas W., ed. *Russia's Future: Consolidation or Disintegration?* Boulder, CO: Westview Press, 1994.

Boda, Jozsef, and Kornely Kakachia. "The Current Status of Police Reform in Georgia." In *From Revolution to Reform: Georgia's Struggle with Democratic Institution Building and Security Sector Reform,* ed. Philipp H. Fluri and Eden Cole. Vienna: Lavak, 2005. http://www.dcaf.ch/

Boone, Catherine. *Political Topographies of the African State: Territorial Authority and Institutional Choice.* Cambridge: Cambridge University Press, 2003.

Braguinsky, Serguey. "Post-Communist Oligarchs in Russia: Quantitative Analysis." *Journal of Law and Economics* 52 (May 2009): 307–349.

Bremmer, Ian, and Samuel Charap. "The *Siloviki* in Putin's Russia: Who They Are and What They Want." *The Washington Quarterly* 30, no. 1 (2007): 83–92.

Brym, Robert J., and Vladimir Gimpelson. "The Size, Composition, and Dynamics of the Russian State Bureaucracy in the 1990s." *Slavic Review* 63, no. 1 (Spring 2004): 90–112.

Brzoska, Michael. "Embedding DDR Programmes in Security Sector Reconstruction." In *Security Governance in Post-Conflict Peacebuilding,* ed. Alan Bryden and Heiner Hänggi, 95–114. Munster: Lit Verlag, 2005.

Bukkvoll, Tor. "Their Hands in the Till: Scale and Causes of Russian Military Corruption." *Armed Forces & Society* 34, no. 2 (January 2008): 259–275.

"Waiting for the Next Beslan – Russia's Handling of Major Hostage-Takings." Norwegian Defence Research Establishment (FFI) Report No. 2007/01888, August 8, 2007.

Bunce, Valerie. "Comparative Democratization: Big and Bounded Generalizations." *Comparative Political Studies* 33, no. 6–7 (2000): 703–734.

Subversive Institutions. Cambridge: Cambridge University Press, 1999.

Burger, Ethan S., and Mary Holland. "Law as Politics: The Russian Procuracy and Its Investigative Committee." *Columbia Journal of East European Law* 2, no. 2 (2008): 143–194.

Burk, James. "The Military's Presence in American Society, 1950–2000." In *Soldiers and Civilians,* ed. Peter Feaver and Richard Kohn, 247–274. Cambridge, MA: MIT Press, 2001.

Burnham, William, and Thomas A. Firestone. "Investigation of Criminal Cases under the Russian Criminal Procedure Code." Unpublished paper, October 2007.

Cameron, Maxwell A., and Tulia G. Faletti. "Federalism and the Subnational Separation of Powers." *Publius* 35, no. 2 (Spring 2005): 245–271.

Caparini, Marina, and Otwin Marenin, eds. *Transforming Police in Central and Eastern Europe: Process and Progress.* Munster, Germany: Lit Verlag, 2004.

Cappelli, Ottorino. "Pre-Modern State-Building in Post-Soviet Russia." *Journal of Communist Studies and Transition Politics* 24, 4 (2008): 531–572.

Carothers, Thomas. *Aiding Democracy Abroad: The Learning Curve.* Washington, DC: Carnegie Endowment for Peace, 1999.

"Misunderstanding Gradualism." *Journal of Democracy* 18, no. 3 (July 2007): 18–22.

ed. *Promoting the Rule of Law Abroad: In Search of Knowledge.* Washington, DC: Carnegie Endowment for International Peace, 2006.

"The Backlash against Democracy Promotion." *Foreign Affairs* 85, no. 2 (March/ April 2006): 55–68.

"The End of the Transition Paradigm." *Journal of Democracy* 13, no. 1 (January 2002): 5–21.

"The Rule-of-Law Revival." In Carothers, *Promoting the Rule of Law Abroad,* 3–13.

"The 'Sequencing' Fallacy." *Journal of Democracy* 18, no. 1 (January 2007): 12–27.

Centeno, Miguel Angel. *Blood and Debt: War and the Nation-State in Latin America.* University Park, PA: The Pennsylvania State University Press, 2002.

Chanaa, Jane. *Security Sector Reform: Issues, Challenges, and Prospects.* Adelphi Paper 344. London: Oxford University Press, 2002.

Chebankova, Elena A. "The Limitations of Central Authority in the Regions and the Implications for the Evolution of Russia's Federal System." *Europe-Asia Studies* 57, no. 7 (November 2005): 933–949.

Cirtautus, Arista Maria. "The Post-Leninist State: A Conceptual and Empirical Examination," *Communist and Post-Communist Studies* 28, no. 4 (December 1995): 379–392.

Clapham, Christopher. *Africa and the International System: The Politics of State Survival.* Cambridge: Cambridge University Press, 1996.

Cleary, Matthew R., and Susan C. Stokes. *Democracy and the Culture of Skepticism: Political Trust in Argentina and Mexico.* New York: Russell Sage Foundation, 2006.

"Trust and Democracy in Comparative Perspective." In *Whom Can We Trust? How Groups, Networks, and Institutions Make Trust Possible*, ed. Karen Cook,Russell Hardin, and Margaret Levi, 308–338. New York: Russell Sage Foundation, 2009.

Cohen, Stephen F. *Failed Crusade: America and the Tragedy of Post-Communist Russia*. New York: W.W. Norton, 2000.

Collier, David, ed. *The New Authoritarianism in Latin America*. Princeton, NJ: Princeton University Press, 1979.

Colton, Timothy J., "Introduction: Governance and Postcommunist Politics." In Colton and Holmes, *The State after Communism*, 1–20.

"Perspectives on Civil-Military Relations in the Soviet Union." In *Soldiers and the Soviet State*, ed. Timothy J. Colton and Thane Gustafson, 3–43. Princeton, NJ: Princeton University Press, 1990.

"Putin and the Attenuation of Russian Democracy." In Herspring, *Putin's Russia*, 37–52.

Colton, Timothy J., and Stephen Holmes, eds. *The State after Communism: Governance in the New Russia*. Lanham, MD: Rowman & Littlefield, 2006.

Cottey, Andrew, Timothy Edmunds, and Anthony Forster. "The Second Generation Problematic: Rethinking Democracy and Civil-Military Relations." *Armed Forces & Society* 29, no. 1 (Fall 2002): 31–56.

Darden, Keith. "The Integrity of Corrupt States: Graft as an Informal State Institution." *Politics & Society* 36, no. 1 (March 2008): 35–60.

Das, Dilip K. "Challenges of Policing Democracies: A World Perspective." In Das and Marenin, *Challenges of Policing Democracies*, 3–22.

Das, Dilip K., and Otwin Marenin, eds. *Challenges of Policing Democracies: A World Perspective*. Amsterdam: Gordon and Breach, 2000.

Davis, Diane E. "Contemporary Challenges and Historical Reflections on the Study of Militaries, States, and Politics." In Davis and Pereira, *Irregular Armed Forces and Their Role in Politics and State Formation*, 3–34.

"Undermining the Rule of Law: Democratization and the Dark Side of Police Reform in Mexico." *Latin American Politics and Society* 48, no. 1 (2006): 55–86.

Davis, Diane E., and Anthony W. Pereira, eds. *Irregular Armed Forces and Their Role in Politics and State Formation*. Cambridge: Cambridge University Press, 2003.

de Figueiredo, Rui J.P, Jr., and Barry R. Weingast. "Self-Enforcing Federalism." *Journal of Law, Economics, & Organization* 21, no. 1 (April 2005): 103–135.

Demos. *Reforma pravookhranitel'nikh organov: preodoleniye proizvola*. Moscow: Demos, 2005.

Militsiya mezhdu Rossiey i Chechney: Veterany konflikta v rossiyskom obshchestve. Moskva: Demos, 2007.

den Boer, M.G.W. "Internationalization." In Mawby, *Policing Across the World*, 59–74.

Derluguian, Georgi. *Bourdieu's Secret Admirer in the Caucasus*. Chicago: University of Chicago Press, 2005.

"Recasting Russia." *New Left Review* 12 (November–December 2001): 5–31.

"The Coming Revolutions in the North Caucasus." *PONARS Policy Memo* no. 378 (December 2005).

Deryugin, Aleksandr. "Osobennosti rossiyskogo federalizma." *Neprikosnovennyy Zapas* no. 38 (June 2004). http://www.nlobooks.ru/rus/nz-online/

Desmond, Dennis. "The Structure and Organization of the Ministry of Internal Affairs under Mikhail Gorbachev." *Low Intensity Conflict & Law Enforcement* 3, no. 2 (Autumn 1994): 217–258.

de Waal, Tom. "Chechnya: The Breaking Point." In Sakwa, *Chechnya*, 181–197.

Diamond, Larry. *Developing Democracy: Toward Consolidation*. Baltimore: Johns Hopkins University Press, 1999.

"Thinking About Hybrid Regimes." *Journal of Democracy* 13, no. 2 (April 2002): 21–35.

Diamond, Larry, and Leonardo Morlino, eds. *Assessing the Quality of Democracy*. Baltimore: The Johns Hopkins University Press, 2005.

Dininio, Phyllis, and Robert Orttung. "Explaining Patterns of Corruption in the Russian Regions." *World Politics* 57, no. 4 (July 2005): 500–529.

Dodonov, V.N., and V.E. Krutskikh. *Prokuratura v Rossii i za rubezhom*. Moscow: Norma, 2001.

Domrin, Alexander N. "Ten Years Later: Society, 'Civil Society,' and the Russian State." *The Russian Review* 62, no. 2 (April 2003): 193–211.

Downing, Brian M. *The Military Revolution and Political Change: Origins of Democracy and Autocracy in Early Modern Europe*. Princeton, NJ: Princeton University Press, 1992.

Downs, Anthony. *Inside Bureaucracy*. Boston: Little, Brown and Company, 1967.

Dunlop, John B. *The 2002 Dubrovka and 2004 Beslan Hostage Crises: A Critique of Russian Counter-Terrorism*. Stuttgart: ibidem-Verlag, 2006.

"The August 1991 Coup and Its Impact on Soviet Politics." *Journal of Cold War Studies* 5, no. 1 (Winter 2003): 94–127.

"Putin, Kozak, and Russian Policy toward the North Caucasus." Paper presented at the North Caucasus Conference, Jamestown Foundation, September 14, 2006.

Dunlop, John B., and Rajan Menon. "Chaos in the North Caucasus and Russia's Future." *Survival* 48, no. 2 (June 2006): 97–114.

Dutkiewicz, Piotr, and Sergei Plekhanov. "The Politics of 'Mimicry': The Case of Eastern Europe." In *The Soldier and the State in the Post Cold War Era*, ed. Albert Legault and Joel Sokolsky, special issue, *Queen's Quarterly* 109 (December 2002): 113–142.

Easter, Gerald M. "Building Fiscal Capacity." In Colton and Holmes, *The State after Communism*, 21–52.

Reconstructing the State: Personal Networks and Elite Identity in Soviet Russia. Cambridge: Cambridge University Press, 2000.

"The Russian State in the Time of Putin." *Post-Soviet Affairs*, 24, no. 3 (2008): 199–230.

"The Russian Tax Police." *Post-Soviet Affairs* 18, no. 4 (2002): 332–362.

Eaton, Kent. *Politics beyond the Capital: The Design of Subnational Institutions in South America*. Stanford, CA: Stanford University Press, 2004.

Edmonds, Martin. *Armed Services and Society*. Boulder, CO: Westview Press, 1990.

Egnell, Robert, and Peter Halden. "Laudable, Ahistorical, and Overambitious: Security Sector Reform Meets State Formation Theory." *Conflict, Security & Development* 9, no. 1 (April 2009): 27–54.

Ekiert, Grzegorz, and Stephen E. Hanson, eds. *Capitalism and Democracy in Central and Eastern Europe: Assessing the Legacy of Communist Rule*. Cambridge: Cambridge University Press, 2003.

Elazar, Daniel. *Exploring Federalism.* Tuscaloosa, AL: University of Alabama Press, 1987.

ed. *Federal Systems of the World,* 2nd ed. Harlow, Essex: Longman Group, 1994.

Elias, Norbert. "Violence and Civilization: The State Monopoly of Physical Violence and Its Infringement." In *Civil Society and the State: New European Perspectives,* ed. John Keane, 177–198. London: Verso, 1988.

Elster, Jon. *The Cement of Society: A Study of Social Order.* Cambridge: Cambridge University Press, 1989.

Encarnacion, Omar G. "Civil Society Reconsidered (Review Article)." *Comparative Politics* 38, no. 3 (April 2006): 357–376.

Epstein, Rachel A. "When Legacies Meet Policies: NATO and the Refashioning of Polish Military Tradition." *East European Politics and Societies* 20, no. 2 (2006): 254–285.

Ertman, Thomas. *Birth of the Leviathan: Building States and Regimes in Medieval and Early Modern Europe.* Cambridge: Cambridge University Press, 1997.

"Building States – Inherently a Long Term Process? An Argument from Comparative History." In Lange and Rueschemeyer, *States and Development,* 165–183.

Evangelista, Matthew. *The Chechen Wars: Will Russia Go the Way of the Soviet Union?* Washington, DC: Brookings Institution Press, 2002.

"Ingushetia as a Microcosm of Putin's Reforms." *PONARS Policy Memo* no. 346 (November 2004).

Evans, Alfred B. Jr. "Civil Society in the Soviet Union?" In Evans, Henry, and Sundstrom, *Russian Civil Society,* 28–54.

"Putin's Legacy and Russian Identity." *Europe-Asia Studies* 60, no. 6 (August 2008): 899–912.

"Vladimir Putin's Design for Civil Society." In Evans, Henry, and Sundstrom *Russian Civil Society,* 147–158.

Evans, Alfred B. Jr., Laura A. Henry, and Lisa McIntosh Sundstrom, eds. *Russian Civil Society: A Critical Assessment.* Armonk, NY: M.E. Sharpe, 2006.

Evans, Peter. "Government Action, Social Capital, and Development: Reviewing the Evidence on Synergy." In *State-Society Synergy: Government and Social Capital in Development,* ed. Peter Evans, 178–209. Berkeley, CA: International and Area Studies, University of California, 1997.

"Predatory, Developmental, and Other Apparatuses: A Comparative Political Economy Perspective on the Third World State." *Sociological Forum* 4, no. 4 (December 1989): 561–587.

Evans, Peter, and James E. Rauch. "Bureaucracy and Growth: A Cross-National Analysis of the Effects of 'Weberian' State Structures on Economic Growth." *American Sociological Review* 64, no. 5 (October 1999): 748–765.

Evans, Peter B., Dietrich Rueschemeyer, and Theda Skocpol, eds. *Bringing the State Back In.* Cambridge: Cambridge University Press, 1985.

Favarel-Garrigues, Gilles. "Sovetskaya militsiya i eye bor'ba s rostom ekonimicheskikh prestupleniy v epokhu 'zastoya'." *Neprikosnovennyy Zapas* no. 42 (July 2005). http://www.nlobooks.ru/rus/nz-online/

Fearon, James D. "Iraq's Civil War." *Foreign Affairs* 86, no. 2 (March/April 2007): 2–15.

Fearon, James, and David Laitin. "Ethnicity, Insurgency, and Civil War." *American Political Science Review* 97, no. 1 (February 2003): 75–90.

Feaver, Peter D. *Armed Servants: Agency, Oversight, and Civil-Military Relations.* Cambridge, MA: Harvard University Press, 2003.

"Civil-Military Relations." *Annual Review of Political Science* 2 (1999): 211–241.

Filippov, Mikhail, Peter C. Ordeshook, and Olga Shvetsova. *Designing Federalism: A Theory of Self-Sustainable Federal Institutions.* Cambridge: Cambridge University Press, 2004.

Filippov, Victor V. "The New Russian Code of Criminal Procedure: The Next Step on the Path of Russia's Democratization." *Demokratizatsiya* 11, no. 3 (Summer 2003): 397–401.

Firestone, Thomas. "Criminal Corporate Raiding in Russia." *International Lawyer* 42 (2008): 1207–1229.

"The Russian Connection: Sex Trafficking into the United States and What the United States and Russia Are Doing about It." *International Organized Crime* 51, no. 5 (2003): 39–42.

Fish, M. Steven. *Democracy Derailed in Russia: The Failure of Open Politics.* Cambridge: Cambridge University Press, 2005.

Fogelson, Robert M. *Big-City Police.* Cambridge, MA: Harvard University Press, 1977.

Foley, Michael W., and Bob Edwards. "The Paradox of Civil Society." *Journal of Democracy* 7, no. 3 (July 1996): 38–52.

Forrest, Joshua B. "The Quest for State 'Hardness' in Africa." *Comparative Politics* 20, no. 4 (July 1988): 423–442.

Fortescue, Stephen. *Russia's Oil Barons and Metal Magnates: Oligarchs and the State in Transition.* New York: Palgrave Macmillan, 2006.

Fritz, Verena. *State-Building: A Comparative Study of Ukraine, Lithuania, Belarus, and Russia.* Budapest: Central European University Press, 2007.

Fukuyama, Francis. *The End of History and the Last Man.* New York: The Free Press, 1992.

"Liberalism versus State-Building." *Journal of Democracy* 18, no. 3 (July 2007): 10–13.

State-Building: Governance and World Order in the 21st Century. Ithaca, NY: Cornell University Press, 2004.

Fuller, William C., Jr. *The Internal Troops of the MVD SSSR.* College Station Papers No. 6. College Station, TX: Center for Strategic Technology, Texas A & M University, 1983.

Fung, Archon. *Empowered Participation: Reinventing Urban Democracy.* Princeton, NJ: Princeton University Press, 2004.

Gaffney, Henry, Ken Gause, and Dmitry Gorenburg. *Russian Leadership Decision-Making under Vladimir Putin: The Issues of Energy, Technology Transfer, and Non-Proliferation.* Alexandria, VA: CNA Corporation, 2007.

Gaidar, Yegor. *Dni porazhenii i pobed.* Moscow: Vagrius, 1997.

Gakaev, Dzabrail. "Chechnya in Russia and Russia in Chechnya." In Sakwa, *Chechnya*, 21–42.

Galeotti, Mark. "Organised Crime and Russian Security Forces: Mafiya, Militia, and Military." *Conflict, Security & Development* 1, no. 2 (April 2001): 103–111.

Ganev, Venelin I. "Post-Communism as an Episode of State Building: A Reversed Tillyan Perspective." *Communist and Post-Communist Studies* 38, no. 4 (September 2005): 425–445.

Gans-Morse, Jordan. "Searching for Transitologists: Contemporary Theories of Post-Communist Transitions and the Myth of a Dominant Paradigm." *Post-Soviet Affairs* 20, no. 4 (2004): 320–349.

Gavrilov, Boris. "Sledstevennyy apparat organov vnutrennykh del." *Otechestvennye zapiski*, no. 2 (2003). http://www.strana-oz.ru/

Sovremennaya ugolovnaya politika Rossii: tsifry i fakty. Moscow: Prospekt, 2008.

Gavrilova, Natalia S., et al. "Patterns of Violent Crime in Russia." In Pridemore, *Ruling Russia*, 117–145.

Gazukin, Pavel. "Vooruzhennye sily Rossii v postsovetskiy period." *Otechestvennye zapiski* no. 8 (2002): 125–147.

Geertz, Clifford. *The Interpretation of Cultures.* New York: Basic Books, 1973.

Gel'man, Vladimir. "The Unrule of Law in the Making: The Politics of Informal Institution Building in Russia." *Europe-Asia Studies* 56, no. 7 (November 2004): 1021–1040.

Gerber, Theodore P., and Sarah E. Mendelson. "Cauldron of Terrorism or Bowl of Kasha? What Survey Data Say About the North Caucasus." Center for Strategic and International Studies, unpublished manuscript, July 2006.

"Public Experiences of Police Violence and Corruption in Contemporary Russia: A Case of Predatory Policing?" *Law and Society Review* 421, no. 1 (March 2008): 1–44.

"Security through Sociology: The North Caucasus and the Global Counterinsurgency Paradigm." *Studies in Conflict & Terrorism* 32, no. 9 (September 2009): 831–851.

Gervasoni, Carlos. "Data Set Review: The World Bank's Governance Indicators (1996–2004)." *APSA-CP* 17, no. 1 (Winter 2006): 17–20.

Gevorkyan, Natal'ya A., Natal'ya Timakova, and Andrei Kolesnikov, eds. *Ot pervogo litsa: Razgovory s Vladimirom Putinym.* Moscow: Vagrius, 2000.

Gibson, James L. "Social Networks, Civil Society, and the Prospects for Consolidating Russia's Democratic Transition." *American Journal of Political Science* 45, no. 1 (2001): 51–68.

Gilinskiy, Yakov. "Challenges of Policing Democracies: The Russian Experience." In Das and Marenin, *Challenges of Policing Democracies*, 173–194.

Gissiner, Mark A. "The Role of NGOs in Civilian Oversight of the Police." In Kadar, *Police in Transition*, 187–195.

Glikin, Maksim. *Militsiya i bespredel: Kto oni – oborotni v pogonakh ili nashi zashchitniki?* Moscow: Tstenrpoligraf, 1998.

Goffman, Erving. *Asylums: Essays on the Social Situations of Mental Patients and Other Inmates.* Garden City, NY: Anchor Books, 1961.

Goldsmith, A., and C. Lewis, eds. *Civilian Oversight of Policing: Governance, Democracy and Human Rights.* Oxford: Hart Publishers, 2000.

Gomart, Thomas. *Russian Civil-Military Relations: Putin's Legacy.* Washington, DC: Carnegie Endowment for International Peace, 2008.

Goode, Paul. "The Puzzle of Putin's Gubernatorial Appointments" *Europe-Asia Studies* 59, no. 3 (May 2007): 365–399.

Goodwin, Jeff. *No Other Way Out: States and Revolutionary Movements, 1945–1991.* Cambridge: Cambridge University Press, 2001.

Goryainov, K.K., V.S. Ovchinskiy and L.V. Kondratyuk. *Uluchsheniye vzaimootnosheniy grazhdan i militsii: Dostup k pravosudiyu i sistema vyyavleniya, registratsii i ucheta prestupleniy.* Moscow: INFRA-M, 2001.

Graham, Thomas E., Jr. "The Fate of the Russian State." *Demokratizatsiya* 8, no. 3 (Summer 2000): 354–375.

Gregory, Frank, and Gerald Brooke. "Policing Economic Transition and Increasing Revenue: A Case Study of the Federal Tax Police Service of the Russian Federation, 1992–1998." *Europe-Asia Studies* 52, no. 3 (May 2000): 433–455.

Grindle, Merilee S., ed. *Getting Good Government: Capacity Building in the Public Sectors of Developing Countries.* Cambridge, MA: Harvard Institute for International Development, 1997.

Grzymala-Busse, Anna. *Rebuilding Leviathan: Party Competition and State exploitation in Post-Communist Democracies.* Cambridge: Cambridge University Press, 2007.

Gryzmala-Busse, Anna, and Pauline Jones Luong. "Reconceptualizing the State: Lessons from Post-Communism." *Politics & Society* 30, no. 4 (December 2002): 529–545.

Gudkov, Lev. "The Army as an Institutional Model." In *Military and Society in Post-Soviet Russia,* ed. Stephen L. Webber and Jennifer G. Mathers, 39–60. Manchester: Manchester University Press, 2006.

Gudkov, Lev, and Boris Dubin. "Privatizatsiya politsii." *Vestnik obshchestvennogo mneniya,* no. 1 (January–February 2006): 58–71.

Gudkov, Lev, Boris Dubin, and Anastasiya Leonova. "Militseyskoye nasiliye i problema 'politseyskogo gosudarsta'." *Vestnik obshchestvennogo mneniya,* no. 4 (July–August 2004): 31–47.

Hahn, Gordon M. "The Impact of Putin's Federative Reforms on Democratization in Russia." *Post-Soviet Affairs* 19, no. 2 (April–June 2003): 114–153.

"The *Jihadi* Insurgency and the Russian Counterinsurgency in the North Caucasus." *Post-Soviet Affairs* 24, no. 1 (2008): 1–39.

"Managed Democracy? Building Stealth Authoritarianism in St. Petersburg." *Demokratizatsiya* 12, no. 2 (Spring 2004): 195–231.

Hale, Henry E. "Civil Society from Above? Statist and Liberal Models of State-Building in Russia." *Demokratizatsiya* 10, no. 3 (June 2002): 306–321.

"Democracy or Autocracy on the March? The Colored Revolutions as Normal Dynamics of Patronal Presidentialism." *Communist and Post-Communist Studies* 39, 3 (2006) 305–329.

"The Makeup and Breakup of Ethnofederal States: Why Russia Survives Where the USSR Fell." *Perspectives on Politics* 3, no. 1 (March 2005): 55–70.

"Party Development in a Federal System." In Reddaway and Orttung, *The Dynamics of Russian Politics,* vol. 2, 179–211.

Why Not Parties in Russia? Democracy, Federalism, and the State. Cambridge: Cambridge University Press, 2006.

Hale, Henry E., and Rein Taagepera. "Russia: Consolidation or Collapse?" *Europe-Asia Studies* 54, no. 7 (November 2002): 1101–1125.

Hall, Peter A., and Rosemary C.R. Taylor. "Political Science and the Three New Institutionalisms." *Political Studies* 44, no. 5 (1996): 936–957.

Hanson, Philip. "The Russian economic puzzle: going forwards, backwards, or sideways?" *International Affairs* 83, no. 5 (September 2005): 869–889.

Hanson, Stephen E. "Defining Democratic Consolidation." In *Postcommunism and the Theory of Democracy,* Richard D. Anderson, Jr., M. Steven Fish, Stephen E. Hanson, and Philip G. Roeder, 126–151. Princeton, NJ: Princeton University Press, 2001.

"Instrumental Democracy: The End of Ideology and the Decline of Russian Political Parties." In *The 1999–2000 Elections in Russia: Their Impact and Legacy,* ed.

Vicki L. Hesli and William M. Reisinger, 163–185. Cambridge: Cambridge University Press, 2003.

"The Uncertain Future of Russia's Weak State Authoritarianism." *East European Politics and Societies* 21, no. 1 (February 2007): 67–81.

Harasymiw, Bohdan. "Policing, Democratization, and Political Leadership in Postcommunist Ukraine." *Canadian Journal of Political Science* 36, no. 2 (June 2003): 319–340.

Hashim, S. Mohsin. "Putin's Etatization project and limits to democratic reforms in Russia." *Communist and Post-Communist Studies* 38, no. 1 (March 2005): 25–48.

Hedlund, Stefan. "Vladimir the Great, Grand Prince of Muscovy: Resurrecting the Russian Service State." *Europe-Asia Studies* 58, no. 5 (July 2006): 775–801.

Helliwell, John F., and Jaifang Huang. "How's Your Government? International Evidence Linking Good Government and Well-Being." NBER Working Papers No. 11988, Cambridge: NBER, 2006.

Helmke, Gretchen, and Steven Levitsky. "Informal Institutions and Comparative Politics: A Research Agenda." *Perspectives on Politics* 2, no. 4 (December 2004): 725–740.

Hemment, Julie. "The Riddle of the Third Sector: Civil Society, International Aid, and NGOs in Russia." *Anthropological Quarterly* 77, no. 2 (Spring 2004): 215–241.

Henderson, Sarah L. *Building Democracy in Contemporary Russia: Western Support for Grassroots Organizations*. Ithaca, NY: Cornell University Press, 2003.

Hendley, Kathryn. "Putin and the Law." In Herspring, *Putin's Russia*, 99–126.

Herbst, Jeffrey. *States and Power in Africa: Comparative Lessons in Authority and Control*. Princeton, NJ: Princeton University Press, 2000.

Herd, Graeme P. "Russia: Systemic Transformation or Federal Collapse?" *Journal of Peace Research* 36, no. 3 (May 1999): 259–269.

Herspring, Dale R. *The Kremlin and the High Command: Presidential Impact on the Russian Military from Gorbachev to Putin*. Lawrence, KS: University Press of Kansas, 2006.

"Putin and the Re-emergence of the Russian Military." *Problems of Post-Communism* 54, no. 1 (January 2007): 17–27.

ed. *Putin's Russia: Past Imperfect, Future Uncertain*. 3rd ed. Lanham, MD: Rowman & Littlefield, 2007.

Herspring, Dale R., and Roger N. McDermott. "Serdyukov Promotes Systemic Russian Military Reform." *Orbis* 54, no. 2 (2010): 284–301.

Hintze, Otto. "Military Organization and the Organization of the State." In *The Historical Essays of Otto Hintze*, ed. Felix Gilbert, 178–215. New York: Oxford University Press, 1975.

Hislope, Robert. "Corrupt Exchange in Divided Societies: The Invisible Politics of Stability in Macedonia." In *Transnational Actors in Central and East European Transitions*, ed. Mitchell A. Orenstein, Stephen Bloom, and Nicole Lindstrom, 142–161. Pittsburgh, PA: University of Pittsburgh Press, 2008.

Hobbes, Thomas. *A Dialogue Between a Philosopher and a Student of The Common Laws of England*. Chicago: University of Chicago Press, 1971.

Hoffman, David E. *The Oligarchs: Wealth and Power in the New Russia*. New York: Public Affairs, 2002.

Holmes, Stephen. "Lineages of the Rule of Law." In *Democracy and the Rule of Law*, ed. Jose Maria Maravall and Adam Przeworski, 19–61. Cambridge: Cambridge University Press, 2003.

"The Procuracy and Its Problems: Introduction." *East European Constitutional Review* 8, no. 1–2 (Winter/Spring 1999). http://www1.law.nyu.edu/eecr/

Horowitz, Donald L. *Ethnic Groups in Conflict*. Berkeley, CA: University of California Press, 1985.

Hosking, Geoffrey. *Russia: People and Empire 1552–1917*. Cambridge, MA: Harvard University Press, 1997.

Hough, Jerry F. *The Soviet Union and Social Science Theory*. Cambridge, MA: Harvard University Press, 1977.

Howard, Marc Morjé. *The Weakness of Civil Society in Post-Communist Europe*. Cambridge: Cambridge University Press, 2003.

Hughes, James. *Chechnya: From Nationalism to Jihad*. Philadelphia, PA: University of Pennsylvania Press, 2007.

Hui, Victoria Tin-Bor. *War and State Formation in Ancient China and Early Modern Europe*. Cambridge: Cambridge University Press, 2005.

Huntington, Samuel P. *Political Order in Changing Societies*. New Haven, CT: Yale University Press, 1968.

The Soldier and the State: The Theory and Politics of Civil-Military Relations. Cambridge, MA: Belknap Press/Harvard University Press, 1957.

Huskey, Eugene. "Nomenklatura Lite? The Cadres Reserve in Russian Public Administration." *Problems of Post-Communism* 51, no. 2 (March–April 2004): 30–39.

"Putin as Patron: Cadres Policy in the Russian Transition." In *Leading Russia: Putin in Perspective*, ed. Alex Pravda, 161–178. Oxford: Oxford University Press, 2005.

Huskey, Eugene, and Alexander Obolonsky. "The Struggle to Reform Russia's Bureaucracy." *Problems of Post-Communism* 50, no. 4 (July–August 2003): 22–33.

Hutcheson, Derek S., and Elena A. Korosteleva, eds. *The Quality of Democracy in Post-Communist Europe*. London: Routledge, 2006.

Hyde, Matthew. "Putin's Federal Reforms and Their Implications for Presidential Power in Russia." *Europe-Asia Studies* 53, no. 5 (July 2001): 719–743.

Inglehart, Ronald, and Christian Welzel. *Modernization, Cultural Change, and Democracy: The Human Development Sequence*. Cambridge: Cambridge University Press, 2005.

Institute of Sociology (Russian Academy of Sciences). *Byurokratiya i vlast' v novoy Rossii: pozitsii naseleniya i otsenki ekspertov*. Moscow: Institute of Sociology, 2005.

"Interview with the Main Federal Inspector for the Perm Region." In Reddaway and Orttung, *The Dynamics of Russian Politics*, vol. 2, 485–491.

Isham, Jonathan, et al. "The Varieties of Resource Experience: How Natural Resource Export Structures Affect the Political Economy of Economic Growth." *World Bank Economic Review* 19, no. 2 (October 2005): 141–174.

Ivanov, Vitaliy. *Putin i regiony: Tsentralizatsiya Rossii*. Moscow: "Evropa," 2006.

Jack, Andrew. *Inside Putin's Russia*. Oxford: Oxford University Press, 2004.

Jackman, Robert W. *Power without Force: The Political Capacity of Nation-States*. Ann Arbor, MI: University of Michigan Press, 1993.

Jackson, Robert H., and Carl G. Rosberg. "Why Africa's Weak States Persist: The Empirical and Juridical in Statehood." *World Politics* 35, no. 1 (October 1982): 1–24.

Jacoby, Wade. *Imitation and Politics: Redesigning Modern Germany.* Ithaca, NY: Cornell University Press, 2000.

"Inspiration, Coalition, and Substitution: External Influences on Postcommunist Transformations (Review Article)." *World Politics* 58, no. 2 (July 2006): 623–651.

Javeline, Debra, and Sarah Lindemann-Komarova. "How We Assess Civil Society Developments: The Russia Example." *PONARS Eurasia Policy Memo* 34 (2008).

Johnson, Janet Elise. "Public-Private Permutations: Domestic Violence Crisis Centers in Barnaul." In Evans, Henry, and Sundstrom, *Russian Civil Society,* 266–283.

Jones Luong, Pauline, and Erika Weinthal. "Contra Coercion: Russian Tax Reform, Exogenous Shocks and Negotiated Institutional Change." *American Political Science Review* 98, no. 1 (2004):139–152.

Jordan, Pamela A. "Russia's Accession to the Council of Europe and Compliance with European Human Rights Norms." *Demokratizatsiya* 11, no. 2 (Spring 2003): 281–296.

Joseph, Richard A. *Democracy and Prebendal Politics in Nigeria: The Rise and Fall of the Second Republic.* Cambridge: Cambridge University Press, 1987.

Jowitt, Ken. *New World Order: The Leninist Extinction.* Berkeley, CA: University of California Press, 1992.

"Soviet Neotraditionalism: The Political Corruption of a Leninist Regime." *Soviet Studies* 35, no. 3 (July 1983): 275–297.

Jurix. *Etnicheski izbiratel'nyy podkhod v deystviyakh militsii v Moskovskom metro.* Moscow: Novaya Yustitsiya, 2006.

Kadar, András. *Police in Transition: Essays on the Police Forces in Transition Countries.* Budapest: Central European University Press, 2001.

Kahn, Jeffrey. *Federalism, Democratization, and the Rule of Law in Russia.* Oxford: Oxford University Press, 2002.

Kahn, Jeffrey, Alexei Trochev, and Nikolay Balayan. "The Unification of Law in the Russian Federation." *Post-Soviet Affairs* 25, no. 4 (2009): 310–346.

Kahn, Peter L. "The Russian Bailiffs Service and the Enforcement of Civil Judgments." *Post-Soviet Affairs* 18, no. 2 (April–June 2002): 148–181.

Kalmanowieci, Laura. "Policing the People, Building the State: The Police-Military Nexus in Argentina, 1880–1945." In Davis and Periera, *Irregular Armed Forces and Their Role in Politics and State Formation,* 209–232.

Karklins, Rasma. *The System Made Me Do It: Corruption in Post-Communist Societies.* Armonk, NY: M.E. Sharpe, 2005.

Katzenstein, Peter J. *Cultural Norms and National Security: Police and Military in Postwar Japan.* Ithaca, NY: Cornell University Press, 1996.

Katznelson, Ira, and Helen V. Milner. *Political Science: The State of the Discipline.* Cent. ed. New York: W.W. Norton & Co., 2002.

Kaufmann, Daniel, Aart Kraay, and Massimo Mastruzzi. "Growth and Governance: A Reply" and "Growth and Governance: A Rejoinder." *Journal of Politics* 69, no. 2 (May 2007): 555–562, 570–572.

"The Worldwide Governance Indicators Project: Answering the Critics." World Bank Policy Research Working Paper 4149, Washington, DC: The World Bank, March 2007.

Keck, Margaret E., and Kathryn Sikkink. *Activists beyond Borders: Advocacy Networks in International Politics.* Ithaca, NY: Cornell University Press, 1998.

Keenan, Edward L. "Muscovite Political Folkways." *Russian Review* 45, no. 2 (April 1986): 115–181.

Kenney, Charles D. "Horizontal Accountability: Concepts and Conflicts." In *Democratic Accountability in Latin America,* ed. Scott Mainwaring and Chris Welna, 55–76. Oxford: Oxford University Press, 2003.

Khramchikhin, Aleksandr. "Shestnadtsat' armiy i ni odnoy parallel'noy." *Otechestvennye zapiski,* no. 8 (2002): 183–191.

Kier, Elizabeth. *Imagining War: French and British Military Doctrine between the Wars.* Princeton, NJ: Princeton University Press, 1997.

King, Desmond, and Robert C. Lieberman. "Ironies of State Building: A Comparative Perspective on the American State." *World Politics* 61, no. 3 (July 2009): 547–588.

Klebnikov, Paul. *Godfather of the Kremlin: Boris Berezovsky and the Looting of Russia.* New York: Harcourt, 2000.

Kleinfeld, Rachel. "Competing Definitions of the Rule of Law." In Carothers, *Promoting the Rule of Law Abroad,* 31–73.

Kleinig, John. "Gratuities and corruption." In Newburn, *Policing,* 596–623.

Klimenko, Andrey, and Hugh Grant. "Russia Civil Service Modernisation: Pay Reform. Comparative Pay and Benefits Survey, Public and Private Sectors." Unpublished report, 2003.

Klyamkin, Igor', and Tat'yana Kutkovets. *Kremlevskaya shkola politologii: Kak nas uchat lyubit' Rodinu.* Moscow: "Liberal'naya missiya," 2006.

Knight, Amy W. "The Enduring Legacy of the KGB in Russian Politics." *Problems of Post-Communism* 47, no. 4 (July–August 2000): 3–15.

  "The KGB, Perestroika, and the Collapse of the Soviet Union." *Journal of Cold War Studies* 5, no. 1 (Winter 2003): 67–93.

  The KGB: Police and Politics in the Soviet Union. Boston: Unwin Hyman, 1990.

  Spies without Cloaks: The KGB's Successors. Princeton, NJ: Princeton University Press, 1996.

Kohli, Atul. "State, Society, and Development." In Katznelson and Milner, *Political Science,* 84–117.

  State-Directed Development: Political Power and Industrialization in the Global Periphery. Cambridge: Cambridge University Press, 2004.

Kolemasov, V.N., et al. *Kommentariy k Zakonu Rossiyskoy Federatsii "O militsii": Postateynyy.* Moscow: Os'-89, 2007.

Kolesnikova, O., L. Kosals, R. Ryvkina, and Yu. Simagin. *Ekonomicheskaya aktivnost' rabotnikov pravookhranitel'nykh organov postsovetskoi Rossii: Vidy, masshtaby i vliyaniye na obshchestvo.* Moscow: 2002.

Kondrat'ev, Sergei. "Urals Federal Okrug." In Reddaway and Orttung, *The Dynamics of Russian Politics,* vol. 1, 187–209.

Konitzer, Andrew. *Voting for Russia's Governors: Regional Elections and Accountability under Yeltsin and Putin.* Baltimore: Johns Hopkins University Press, 2005.

Konitzer, Andrew, and Stephen K. Wegren. "Federalism and Political Recentralization in the Russian Federation." *Publius* 36, no. 4 (Fall 2006): 503–522.

Korenev, A.P. ed. *Administrativnaya deyatel'nost' organov vnutrennikh del.* 3rd ed. Moscow: Moskovkaya Akademiya MVD, 2001.

Korzhakov, Aleksandr. *Boris Yel'tsin: Ot rassveta do zakata.* Moscow: Interbook, 1997.

Kotkin, Stephen. *Armageddon Averted: The Soviet Collapse 1970–2000.* Oxford: Oxford University Press, 2001.

Kotkin, Stephen, and Andras Sajo, eds. *Political Corruption in Transition: A Sceptic's Handbook.* Budapest: Central European University Press, 2002.

Kramer, Mark. "The Changing Context of Russian Federal Policy in the North Caucasus." *PONARS Policy Memo,* no. 416 (December 2006).

"Guerrilla Warfare, Counterinsurgency and Terrorism in the North Caucasus: The Military Dimension of the Russian-Chechen Conflict." *Europe-Asia Studies* 57, no. 2 (March 2005): 209–290.

"The Perils of Counterinsurgency: Russia's War in Chechnya." *International Security* 29, no. 3 (Winter 2004): 5–62.

Krasner, Stephen D. "Approaches to the State: Alternative Conceptions and Historical Dynamics (Review Article)." *Comparative Politics* 16, no. 2 (January 1984): 223–246.

Defending the National Interest: Raw Materials Investment and U.S. Foreign Policy. Princeton, NJ: Princeton University Press, 1978.

Kryshtanovskaya, Ol'ga. "Rezhim Putina: liberal'naya militoktratiya?" *Pro et Contra* 7, no. 4 (Fall 2002): 158–180.

Kryshtanovskaya, Ol'ga., and Stephen White. "Inside the Putin Court: A Research Note." *Europe-Asia Studies* 57, no. 7 (November 2005): 1065–1075.

"Putin's Militocracy." *Post-Soviet Affairs* 19, no. 4 (November–December 2003): 289–306.

Kugler, Jacek, and William Domke. "Comparing the Strength of Nations." *Comparative Political Studies* 19, no. 4 (July 1986): 39–69.

Kulikov, Anatoliy. *Tyazhelye zvezdy.* Moskva: Voyna i Mir, 2002.

Kupatadze, Alexander, Giorgi Siradze, and Giorgi Mitagvaria. "Policing and Police Reform in Georgia." In *Organized Crime and Corruption in Georgia,* ed. Louise Shelley, Erik R. Scott, and Anthony Latta, 93–110. New York: Routledge, 2007.

Kurtz, Marcus J., and Andrew Schrank. "Growth and Governance: Models, Measures, and Mechanisms" and "Growth and Governance: A Defense." *Journal of Politics* 69, no. 2 (May 2007): 538–554, 563–569.

Kuzio, Taras. "Transition in Post-Communist States: Triple or Quadruple?" *Politics* 21, no. 3 (September 2001): 168–177.

LaFree, Gary. "A Summary and Review of Cross-National Comparative Studies of Homicide." In *Homicide: A Sourcebook of Social Research,* ed. M. Dwayne Smith and Margaret A. Zahn, 125–145. Thousand Oaks, CA: Sage Publications, 1999.

Lange, Matthew, and Dietrich Rueschemeyer, eds. *States and Development: Historical Antecedents of Stagnation and Advance.* New York: Palgrave Macmillan, 2005.

Lapidus, Gail W. "Asymmetrical Federalism and State Breakdown in Russia." *Post-Soviet Affairs* 15, no. 1 (1999): 74–82.

La Porta, Rafael, et al. "The Quality of Government." *Journal of Law, Economics, & Organization* 15, no. 1 (March 1999): 222–279.

Lassman, Peter. "The Rule of Man over Man: Politics, Power, and Legitimation." In *The Cambridge Companion to Weber,* ed. Stephen Turner, 83–98. Cambridge: Cambridge University Press, 2000.

Leeson, Peter T., and William N. Trumbull. "Comparing Apples: Normalcy, Russia, and the Remaining Post-Socialist World." *Post-Soviet Affairs* 22, no. 3 (July 2006): 225–248.

Legan, Yusif. *KGB-FSB. Vzglyad iznutri.* vol. 2. Moscow: "Tsentrkniga," 2001.

Lenin, V.I. "The State and Revolution." In *Lenin: Selected Works*, 263–348. Moscow: Progress Publishers, 1968.

Letki, Natalia, and Geoffrey Evans. "Endogenizing Social Trust: Democratization in East-Central Europe." *British Journal of Political Science* 35, no. 3 (July 2005): 515–529.

Levi, Margaret. *Consent, Dissent, and Patriotism.* Cambridge: Cambridge University Press, 1997.

Of Rule and Revenue. Berkeley, CA: University of California Press, 1988.

"The State of the Study of the State." In Katznelson and Milner, *Political Science*, 33–55.

"Why We Need a New Theory of Government." *Perspectives on Politics* 4, no. 1 (March 2006): 5–19.

Levitsky, Steven, and Lucan A. Way. "The Rise of Competitive Authoritarianism." *Journal of Democracy* 13, no. 2 (April 2002): 51–65.

Levy, Jonah. *Tocqueville's Revenge: State, Society, and Economy in Contemporary France.* Cambridge, MA: Harvard University Press, 1999.

Lieven, Anatol. *Chechnya: Tombstone of Russian Power.* New Haven, CT: Yale University Press, 1998.

"Chechnya i zakony voyny." In Malashenko and Trenin, *Vremya yuga*, 230–248.

Lieven, Dominic. *Nicholas II: Twilight of the Empire.* New York: St. Martin's Press, 1993.

Lijphart, Arend. *Democracy in Plural Societies: A Comparative Exploration.* New Haven, CT: Yale University Press, 1977.

Patterns of Democracy. New Haven, CT: Yale University Press, 1999.

Linden, Carl A. *Khrushchev and the Soviet Leadership 1957–1964.* Baltimore: The Johns Hopkins Press, 1966.

Linz, Juan J., and Alfred Stepan. *Problems of Democratic Transition and Consolidation: Southern Europe, South America, and Post-Communist Europe.* Baltimore: Johns Hopkins University Press, 1996.

Lipman, Masha. "Constrained or Irrelevant: The Media in Putin's Russia." *Current History* 104, no. 684 (October 2005): 319–324.

Lipsky, Michael. *Street-Level Bureaucracy: Dilemmas of the Individual in Public Services.* New York: Russell Sage Foundation, 1980.

Littell, Jonathan. *The Security Organs of the Russian Federation: A Brief History 1991–2004.* Paris: PSAN Publishing House, 2006.

Luckham, Robin. "Democratic Strategies for Security in Transition and Conflict." In *Governing Insecurity: Democratic Control of Military and Security Establishments in Transitional Democracies,* ed. Gavin Cawthra and Robin Luckham, 3–28. London: Zed Books, 2003.

Luton, Larry. "The Relevance of U.S. Public Administration Theory for Russian Public Administration." *Administrative Theory and Praxis* 26, no. 2 (2004): 213–232.

Lyall, Jason. "Are Coethnics More Effective Counterinsurgents? Evidence from the Second Chechen War." *American Political Science Review* 104, no. 1 (February 2010): 1–20.

"Does Indiscriminate Violence Incite Insurgent Attacks?: Evidence from Chechnya." *Journal of Conflict Resolution* 53, no. 3 (June 2009): 331–362.

Lynch, Allen C. *How Russia Is Not Ruled: Reflections on Russian Political Development.* Cambridge: Cambridge University Press, 2005.

Malashenko, Aleksey, and Dmitriy Trenin. *Vremya yuga.* Moscow: Carnegie Moscow Center, 2002.

Mann, Michael. "The Autonomous Power of the State: Its Origins, Mechanisms, and Results." In *States in History,* ed. John A. Hall, 109–136. Oxford: Basil Blackwell, 1986.

The Sources of Social Power. 2 vols. Cambridge: Cambridge University Press, 1986–93.

Manor, James. "Making Federalism Work," *Journal of Democracy* 9, no. 3 (July 1998): 21–35.

March, James G., and Johan P. Olsen. *Rediscovering Institutions.* New York: Free Press, 1989.

Marenin, Otwin. "Democracy, Democratization, Democratic Policing." In Das and Marenin, *Challenges of Policing Democracies,* 311–331.

"Police Performance and State Rule: Control and Autonomy in the Exercise of Coercion (Review Article)." *Comparative Politics* 18, no. 1 (1985): 101–122.

ed. *Policing Change, Changing Police: International Perspectives.* New York: Garland Publishing, 1996.

Markedonov, Sergey. "Vernut'sya na Kavkaz." *Apologiya* 9 (December 2006). http://www.journal-apologia.ru/

Marx, Karl. "The Eighteenth Brumaire of Louis Bonaparte." In *The Marx-Engels Reader,* 2nd ed., ed. Robert C. Tucker, 594–617. New York: W.W. Norton, 1978.

Matveeva, Anna. "Chechnya: Dynamics of War and Peace." *Problems of Post-Communism* 54, no. 3 (May–June 2007): 3–17.

Mawby, R.I., ed. *Policing Across the World.* London: Routledge, 1999.

McAuley, Mary. "Prisons in Russia and the Rule of Law." In *Dictatorship or Reform?: The Rule of Law in Russia,* ed. Mary McAuley, Alena Ledeneva, and Hugh Barnes, 8–23. London: Foreign Policy Centre, 2006.

Russia's Politics of Uncertainty. Cambridge: Cambridge University Press, 1997.

McCubbins, Matthew D., and Thomas Schwartz. "Congressional Oversight Overlooked: Police Patrols versus Fire Alarms." *American Journal of Political Science* 28, no. 1 (February 1984): 165–179.

McFaul, Michael. "Russia's 'Privatized' State as an Impediment to Democratic Consolidation." *Security Dialogue* 29, no. 2 (June 1998): 191–199, 315–332.

Russia's Unfinished Revolution: Political Change from Gorbachev to Putin. Ithaca, NY: Cornell University Press, 2001.

"State Power, Institutional Change, and the Politics of Privatization in Russia." *World Politics* 47, no. 2 (January 1995): 210–243.

"Ukraine Imports Democracy: External Influences on the Orange Revolution." *International Security* 32, no. 2 (Fall 2007): 45–83.

McFaul, Michael, and Kathryn Stoner-Weiss. "The Myth of the Authoritarian Model." *Foreign Affairs* 87, no. 1 (January–February 2008): 73–77.

Medvedev, Sergei. "'Juicy Morsels': Putin's Beslan Address and the Construction of the New Russian Identity." *PONARS Policy Memo,* no. 334 (November 2004).

Mendeloff, David. "Commentary on North Ossetia and Ingushetia." In Arbatov et al., *Managing Conflict in the Former Soviet Union: Russian and American Perspectives,* 77–82.

Mendelson, Sarah E. "Anatomy of Ambivalence: The International Community and Human Rights Abuse in the North Caucasus." *Problems of Post-Communism* 53, no. 6 (November–December 2006): 3 – 15.

"Russian Rights' Imperiled: Has Anybody Noticed?" *International Security* 26, no. 4 (Spring 2002): 39–69.

Mendelson, Sarah E., and John K. Glenn, eds. *The Power and Limits of NGOs: A Critical Look at Building Democracy in Eastern Europe and Eurasia.* New York: Columbia University Press, 2002.

Merom, Gil. *How Democracies Lose Small Wars.* Cambridge: Cambridge University Press, 2003.

Mettler, Suzanne. *Soldiers to Citizens: The G.I. Bill And The Making Of The Greatest Generation.* Oxford: Oxford University Press, 2005.

Migdal, Joel. *State in Society: Studying How States and Societies Transform and Constitute One Another.* Cambridge: Cambridge University Press, 2001.

Strong Societies and Weak States: State-Society Relations in the Third World. Princeton, NJ: Princeton University Press, 1988.

"Studying the State." In *Comparative Politics: Rationality, Culture, and Structure,* ed. Mark Irving Lichbach and Alan S. Zuckerman, 208–236. Cambridge: Cambridge University Press, 1997.

Migdal, Joel S., Atul Kohli, and Vivienne Shue, eds. *State Power and Social Forces: Domination and Transformation in the Third World.* Cambridge: Cambridge University Press, 1994.

Mikhailovskaya, Inga. "The Procuracy and Its Problems: Russia." *East European Constitutional Review* 8, no. 1/2 (Winter–Spring 1999). http://www1.law.nyu.edu/eecr/

Miller, Steven E., and Dmitri Trenin, eds. *The Russian Military: Power and Policy.* Cambridge, MA: MIT University Press, 2004.

Moe, Terry M. "The New Economics of Organization." *American Journal of Political Science* 28, no. 4 (November 1984): 739–777.

Montinola, Gabriella, Yingyi Qian, and Barry R. Weingast. "Federalism, Chinese Style: The Political Basis for Economic Success." *World Politics* 48, no. 1 (1995): 50–81.

Moore, Mick. "Revenues, State Formation, and the Quality of Governance in Developing Countries." *International Political Science Review* 25, no. 3 (2004): 297–319.

Mukhin, A.A. *Kto est' mister Putin i kto s nim prishel?* Moscow: Gnom i D, 2002.

Munck, Gerardo L., and Richard Snyder. "Debating the Direction of Comparative Politics: An Analysis of Leading Journals." *Comparative Political Studies* 40, no. 1 (January 2007): 5–31.

Murawiec, Laurent, and Clifford C. Gaddy. "The Higher Police: Vladimir Putin and His Predecessors. *The National Interest* 67 (Spring 2002): 29–36.

Myagkov, Mikhail, Peter C. Ordeshook, and Dimitri Shakin. *The Forensics of Election Fraud: Russia and Ukraine.* Cambridge: Cambridge University Press, 2009.

Nekrasov, Vladimir F. *MVD v litsakh: Ministry ot V.V. Fedorchuka do A.S. Kulikova 1982–1998.* Moskva: Molodaya Gvardiya, 2000.

Trinadtsat' 'zheleznykh' narkomov. Moscow: Versty, 1995.

Nekrasov, V.F., et al. *Organy i voyska MVD Rossii: Kratkiy istoricheskiy ocherk.* Moskva: MVD Rossii, 1996.

Nettl, J.P. "The State as a Conceptual Variable." *World Politics* 20, no. 4 (July 1968): 559–592.

Newburn, Tim, ed. *Policing: Key Readings.* Cullompton, Devon, UK: Willan Publishing, 2005.

Nice, David C., and Patricia Fredericksen. *The Politics of Intergovernmental Relations.* 2nd ed. Chicago: Nelson-Hall Publishers, 1995.

Nikitinskiy, Leonid. *Tayna soveshchatel'noy komnaty.* Moscow: AST, 2008.

Nordlinger, Eric A. *On the Autonomy of the Democratic State.* Cambridge, MA: Harvard University Press, 1981.

Soldiers in Politics: Military Coups and Governments. Englewood Cliffs, NJ: Prentice-Hall, 1977.

North, Douglass C. *Institutions, Institutional Change and Economic Performance.* Cambridge: Cambridge University Press, 1990.

Structure and Change in Economic History. New York: Norton, 1981.

North, Douglass C., and Robert P. Thomas. *The Rise of the Western World: A New Economic History.* Cambridge: Cambridge University Press, 1973.

Nozick, Robert. *Anarchy, State, and Utopia.* New York: Basic Books, 1974.

Obolonsky, Alexander V. "The Modern Russian Administration in the Time of Transition: New Challenges versus Old Nomenclature Legacy." *International Review of Administrative Sciences* 65, (1999): 569–577.

Odom, William E. *The Collapse of the Soviet Military.* New Haven, CT: Yale University Press, 1998.

O'Donnell, Guillermo A. "Democracy, Law, and Comparative Politics." *Studies in Comparative International Development* 36, no. 1 (March 2001): 7–36.

"Horizontal Accountability in New Democracies." *Journal of Democracy* 9, no. 3 (July 1998): 112–126.

"On the State, Democratization, and Some Conceptual Problems: A Latin American View with Glances at Some Postcommunist Countries." *World Development* 21, no. 8 (August 1993): 1355–1369.

"Why the Rule of Law Matters." *Journal of Democracy* 15, no. 4 (October 2004): 32–46.

O'Donnell, Guillermo A., and Philippe C. Schmitter. *Transitions from Authoritarian Rule: Tentative Conclusions about Uncertain Democracies.* Baltimore: Johns Hopkins University Press, 1986.

O'Donnell, Guillermo, Jorge Vargas Cullell, and Osvaldo M. Iazzetta, eds. *The Quality of Democracy: Theory and Applications.* Notre Dame, IN: University of Notre Dame Press, 2004.

O'Dwyer, Conor. *Runaway State-Building: Patronage Politics and Democratic Development.* Baltimore: Johns Hopkins University Press, 2006.

Offe, Claus. "Capitalism by Democratic Design? Democratic Theory Facing the Triple Transition in East Central Europe." *Social Research* 58, no. 4 (Winter 1991): 865–892.

Olcott, Anthony. *Russian Pulp: The Detektiv and the Way of Russian Crime.* Lanham, MD: Rowman & Littlefield, 2001.

Orttung, Robert. "Key Issues in the Evolution of the Federal Okrugs and Center-Region Relations under Putin." In Reddaway and Orttung, *The Dynamics of Russian Politics*, vol. 1, 19–52.

"Russia." In Freedom House, *Nations in Transit 2007*, 333–357. Washington, DC: Freedom House, 2007.

Osipova, Olga. "North Ossetia and Ingushetia: The First Clash." In Arbatov et al., *Managing Conflict in the Former Soviet Union: Russian and American Perspectives*, 127–182.

Pakulski, Jan. "Bureaucracy and the Soviet System." *Studies in Comparative Communism* 19, no. 1 (Spring 1986): 3–24.

Pallin, Carolina Vendil. "The Russian Power Ministries: Tool and Insurance of Power." *Journal of Slavic Military Studies* 20, no. 1 (January–March 2007): 1–25.

Paris, Roland. *At War's End: Building Peace after Civil Conflict*. Cambridge: Cambridge University Press, 2004.

Pascal, Elizabeth. *Defining Russian Federalism*. Westport, CT: Praeger, 2003.

Payne, Rodger A. "Persuasion, Frames, and Norm Construction." *European Journal of International Relations* 7, no. 1 (March 2001): 37–61.

Pelfrey, William V. Jr., "Perceptions of Police Style by Russian Police Administrators." *The Journal of Slavic Military Studies* 18, no. 4 (December 2005): 587–598.

Pereira, Anthony W. "Armed Forces, Coercive Monopolies, and Changing Patterns of State Formation and Violence." In Davis and Pereira, *Irregular Armed Forces and Their Role in Politics and State Formation*, 387–407.

Perrow, Charles. *Complex Organizations: A Critical Essay*, 3rd ed. New York: McGraw-Hill, 1986.

Peters, B. Guy. *The Politics of Bureaucracy*, 5th ed. London: Routledge, 2001.

Petrov, Nikolai. "Federalizm po-rossiyski." *Pro et Contra* 5, no. 1 (Winter 2000): 7–33.

"Korporativizm vs regionalism." *Pro et Contra* 11, no. 4–5 (July–October 2007): 75–89.

"Naslediye imperii i regionalism." In *Naslediye imperiy i budushcheye Rossii*, ed. Aleksey Miller, 381–454. Moscow: Fond "Liberal'naya missiya," 2008.

"Naznacheniya gubernatorov: Itogi pervogo goda." *Brifing Moskovskogo Tsentra Karnegi* 3, no. 8 (April 2006).

"Regional Elections under Putin and Prospects for Russian Electoral Democracy." *PONARS Policy Memo* no. 287 (February 2003).

"The Security Dimension of the Federal Reform." In Reddaway and Orttung, *The Dynamics of Russian Politics*, vol. 2, 7–32.

"Seven Faces of Putin's Russia." *Security Dialogue* 33, no. 1 (March 2002): 73–91.

"*Siloviki* in Russian Regions: New Dogs, Old Tricks." *Journal of Power Institutions in Post-Soviet Societies*, no. 2 (2005). http://pipss.revues.org/

"Substituty institutov." *Otechestvennye zapiski*, no. 6 (2007). http://www.strana-oz.ru/

Petrov, Nikolai, and Darrell Slider. "Putin and the Regions." In Herspring, *Putin's Russia*, 75–97.

Pfeffer, Jeffrey. *Organizations and Organization Theory*. Boston: Pitman Publishing Inc., 1982.

Pipes, Richard. "Flight From Freedom: What Russians Think and Want." *Foreign Affairs* 83, no. 3 (May/June 2004): 9–15.

Poe, Marshall. *The Russian Moment in World History*. Princeton, NJ: Princeton University Press, 2003.

Policzer, Pablo. *The Rise and Fall of Repression in Chile*. Notre Dame, IN: University of Notre Dame Press, 2009.

Politkovskaya, Anna. *Putin's Russia: Life in a Failing Democracy.* New York: Metropolitan Books, 2004.

A Small Corner of Hell: Dispatches from Chechnya. Chicago: University of Chicago Press, 2003.

Vtoraya Chechenskaya. Moskva: Zakharov, 2002.

Ponomarev, Lev. "Revival of the Gulag? Putin's Penitentiary System." *Perspective* 16, no. 1 (November–December 2007). http://www.bu.edu/iscip/perspective.html

Popov, Vladimir. "The State in the New Russia (1992–2004): From Collapse to Gradual Revival?" *PONARS Policy Memo* no. 342 (November 2004).

Porter, Bruce D. *War and the Rise of the State: The Military Foundations of Modern Politics.* New York: The Free Press, 1994.

Posner, Daniel N. "Civil Society and the Reconstruction of Failed States." In Rotberg, *When States Fail*, 237–255.

Pratt, Travis C., and Christopher T. Lowenkamp. "Conflict Theory, Economic Conditions, and Homicide: A Time-Series Analysis." *Homicide Studies* 6, no. 1 (February 2002): 61–83.

Pribylovskiy, Vladimir. "Upravlyaemye vybory: Degradatsiya vyborov pri Putine." In *Rossiya Putina: Istoriya bolezni*, ed. Vladimir Pribylovskiy. Moskva: Tsentr Panorama, 2004.

Pridemore, William Alex. "Demographic, Temporal, and Spatial Patterns of Homicide Rates in Russia." *European Sociological Review* 19, no. 1 (2003): 41–59.

ed. *Ruling Russia: Law, Crime, and Justice in a Changing Society.* Lanham, MD: Rowman & Littlefield, 2005.

Primakov, Yevgeniy. *Vosem' mesyatsev plyus...* Moscow: Mysl', 2001.

Przeworski, Adam, et al. *Democracy and Development: Political Institutions and Well-Being in the World, 1950–1990.* Cambridge: Cambridge University Press, 2000.

Putnam, Robert D. *Bowling Alone: The Collapse and Revival of American Community.* New York: Simon & Schuster, 2000.

Making Democracy Work: Civic Traditions in Modern Italy. Princeton, NJ: Princeton University Press, 1993.

Quinlivan, James T. "Burden of Victory: The Painful Arithmetic of Stability Operations." *RAND Review* 27, no. 2 (Summer 2003): 28–29.

"Coup-proofing: Its Practice and Consequences in the Middle East." *International Security* 24, no. 2 (Fall 1999): 131–165.

Raghavan, R.K. "The Indian Police: Problems and Prospects." *Publius* 33, no. 4 (Fall 2003): 119–133.

Reddaway, Peter and Dmitri Glinski. *The Tragedy of Russia's Reforms: Market Bolshevism Against Democracy.* Washington, DC: United States Institute of Peace Press, 2001.

Reddaway, Peter and Robert W. Orttung, eds. *The Dynamics of Russian Politics.* Two Volumes. Lanham, MD: Rowman & Littlefield, 2004–2005.

Remington, Thomas F. "Putin, the Parliament, and the Party System." In Herspring, *Putin's Russia*, 53–73.

Remmer, Karen L. "Theoretical Decay and Theoretical Development: The Resurgence of Institutional Analysis." *World Politics* 50, no. 1 (October 1997): 34–61.

Remnick, David. *Resurrection: The Struggle for a New Russia.* New York: Vintage Books, 1998.

Reno, William. *Warlord Politics and African States.* Boulder, CO: Lynne Rienner, 1998.

Renz, Bettina. "Putin's Militocracy? An Alternative Interpretation of *Siloviki* in Contemporary Russian Politics." *Europe-Asia Studies* 58, no. 6 (September 2006): 903–924.

"Russia's 'Force Structures' and the Study of Civil-Military Relations." *Journal of Slavic Military Studies* 18, no. 4 (December 2005): 559–585.

Richardson, James F. *Urban Police in the United States.* Port Washington, NY: Kennikat Press, 1974.

Richter, James. "Civil Society in the New Authoritarianism." *PONARS Eurasia Policy Memo* no. 35 (2008).

"Integration from Below? The Disappointing Effort to Promote Civil Society in Russia." In *Russia and Globalization: Identity, Security, and Society in an Era of Change,* ed. Douglas W. Blum, 181–203. Baltimore: Johns Hopkins University Press, 2008.

"Putin and the Public Chamber." *Post-Soviet Affairs* 25, no. 1 (2009): 39–65.

Rieber, Alfred J. "Civil Wars in the Soviet Union." *Kritika* 4, no. 1 (Winter 2003): 129–162.

Riggs, Fred W. *Administration in Developing Countries: The Theory of Prismatic Society.* Boston: Houghton Mifflin, 1964.

Riker, William H. "Federalism." In *Handbook of Political Science,* vol. 5, ed. Fred I. Greenstein and Nelson W. Polsby, 93–172. Reading, MA: Addison-Wesley, 1975.

Federalism. Boston: Little, Brown and Company, 1964.

Rimskiy, V.L. "Predstavleniya intervyuiruyemykh o vozmozhnosti pridaniya rossiyskim pravookhranitel'nym organam sotsial'no oriyentirovannykh kachestv." In Demos, *Reforma pravookhranitel'nikh organov,* 393–410.

Rivera, Sharon Werning, and David W. Rivera. "The Russian Elite under Putin: Militocratic or Bourgeois?" *Post-Soviet Affairs* 22, no. 2 (April–June 2006): 125–144.

Roberts, Cynthia, and Thomas Sherlock. "Bringing the Russian State Back In: Explanations of the Derailed Transition to Market Democracy." *Comparative Politics* 31, no. 4 (July 1999): 477–498.

Rodden, Jonathan. *Hamilton's Paradox: The Promise and Peril of Fiscal Federalism.* New York: Cambridge University Press, 2006.

Roeder, Philip G. "Soviet Federalism and Ethnic Mobilization." *World Politics* 43, no. 2 (January 1991): 196–232.

Rose, Richard. "When Government Fails: Social Capital in an Antimodern Russia." In *Beyond Tocqueville: Civil Society and the Social Capital Debate in Comparative Perspective,* ed. Bob Edwards, Michael W. Foley, and Mario Diani, 56–69. Hanover, NH: University Press of New England, 2001.

Rose, Richard, and Doh Chull Shin. "Democratization Backwards: The Problem of Third-Wave Democracies." *British Journal of Political Science* 31, no. 2 (2001): 331–354.

Rose-Ackerman, Susan. *Corruption and Government: Causes, Consequences, and Reform.* Cambridge: Cambridge University Press, 1999.

Ross, Cameron. "Federalism and Electoral Authoritarianism under Putin." *Demokratizatsiya* 13, no. 3 (Summer 2005): 347–371.

"Municipal Reform in the Russian Federation and Putin's 'Electoral Vertical'." *Demokratizatsiya* 15, no. 2 (Spring 2007): 191–208.

Ross, Michael L. "Does Oil Hinder Democracy?" *World Politics* 53, no. 3 (April 2001): 325–361.

"The Political Economy of the Resource Curse." *World Politics* 51, no. 2 (January 1999): 297–322.

Rotberg, Robert I., ed. *When States Fail: Causes and Consequences.* Princeton, NJ: Princeton University Press, 2004.

Rothstein, Bo, and Jan Teorell. "What Is Quality of Government? A Theory of Impartial Government Institutions." *Governance* 21, no. 2 (April 2008): 165–190.

"Impartiality as a *Basic* Norm for the Quality of Government: A Reply to Francisco Longo and Graham Wilson." *Governance* 21, no. 2 (April 2008): 201–204.

Rudolph, Lloyd I., and Susanne Hoeber Rudolph. "Authority and Power in Bureaucratic and Patrimonial Administration: A Revisionist Interpretation of Weber on Bureaucracy." *World Politics* 31, no. 2 (January 1979): 195–227.

Rueschemeyer, Dietrich. "Building States – Inherently a Long-Term Process? An Argument from Theory." In Lange and Rueschemeyer, *States and Development,* 143–164.

Rueschemeyer, Dietrich, and Peter B. Evans. "The State and Economic Transformation: Toward an Analysis of the Conditions Underlying Effective Intervention." In Evans, Rueschemeyer, and Skocpol, *Bringing the State Back In,* 44–77.

Russell, John. *Chechnya – Russia's "War on Terror."* New York: Routledge, 2007.

Rustow, Dankwart. "Transitions to Democracy: Toward a Dynamic Model." *Comparative Politics* 2, no. 3 (April 1970): 337–363.

Rutland, Peter. "Putin's Economic Record: Is the Oil Boom Sustainable?" *Europe-Asia Studies* 60, no. 6 (August 2008): 1051–1072.

Ryavec, Karl W. *Russian Bureaucracy: Power and Pathology.* Lanham, MD: Rowman & Littlefield, 2003.

Sagramoso, Domitilla. "Violence and Conflict in the Russian North Caucasus." *International Affairs* 83, no. 4 (July 2007): 681–705.

Sakwa, Richard, ed. *Chechnya.* London: Anthem Press, 2005.

Salagaev, Alexander, Alexander Shashkin, and Alexey Konnov. "One Hand Washes Another: Informal Ties Between Organized Criminal Groups and Law-Enforcement Agencies in Russia." *The Journal of Power Institutions in Post-Soviet Societies,* 4/5 (2006). http://pipss.revues.org/

Samuels, Richard J. *Machiavelli's Children: Leaders and Their Legacies in Italy and Japan.* Ithaca, NY: Cornell University Press, 2003.

Satter, David. *Darkness at Dawn: The Rise of the Russian Criminal State.* New Haven, CT: Yale University Press, 2003.

Savyuk, L.K. *Pravokhranitel'nye organy.* Moskva: Yurist, 2001.

Schedler, Andreas, Larry Diamond, and Marc F. Plattner. *The Self-Restraining State: Power and Accountability in New Democracies.* Boulder, CO: Lynne Rienner, 1999.

Schwarz, Rolf. "The Political Economy of State-Formation in the Arab Middle East: Rentier States, Economic Reform, and Democratization." *Review of International Political Economy* 15, no. 4 (October 2008): 599–621.

Scott, Harriet Fast, and William F. Scott. *The Armed Forces of the USSR.* 3rd ed. Boulder, CO: Westview Press, 1984.

Scott, James C. *Seeing Like a State: How Certain Schemes to Improve the Human Condition Have Failed.* New Haven, CT: Yale University Press, 1998.

Selznick, Philip. *Leadership in Administration: A Sociological Interpretation.* Berkeley, CA: University of California Press, 1957.

Sharafutdinova, Gulnaz. "Why was democracy lost in Russia's regions? Lessons from Nizhnii Novgorod." *Communist and Post-Communist Studies* 40, 3 (September 2007): 363–382.

Sharafutdinova, Gul'naz, and Arbakhan Magomedov. "Volga Federal Okrug." In Reddaway and Orttung, *The Dynamics of Russian Politics*, vol. 1, 153–186.

Shattenberg, Suzanne. "Kul'tura korruptsii, ili k istorii rossiyskikh chinovnikov." *Neprikosnovennyy Zapas* 42 (2005). http://www.nlobooks.ru/rus/nz-online/

Shelley, Louise I. *Policing Soviet Society: The Evolution of State Control.* London: Routledge, 1996.

Shepeleva, Ol'ga. "Proizvol v rabote militsii: Tipichnye praktiki." In Demos, *Reforma pravookhranitel'nikh organov*, 29–50.

Shepeleva, Ol'ga, and Asmik Novikova. "Osnovnye problemy sovremennoy militsii." In Demos, *Reforma pravookhranitel'nikh organov*, 51–68.

Shlapentokh, Vladimir. "Trust in Public Institutions in Russia: The Lowest in the World." *Communist and Post-Communist Studies* 39, no. 2 (June 2006): 153–174.

Shleifer, Andrei, and Daniel Treisman. "A Normal Country." *Foreign Affairs* 83, no. 2 (March–April 2004): 20–38.

"A Normal Country: Russia after Communism." *Journal of Economic Perspectives* 19, no. 1 (Winter 2005): 151–174.

Shlykov, V.V. "Tayny blitskriga Serdyukova." *Rossiya v Global'noy Politike* 6 (November–December 2009). http://www.globalaffairs.ru/

Shumilov, A.Yu. *Novyy zakon o militsii: Uchebnoye posobiye*, 4th ed. Moscow: Shumilova I.I., 2002.

Sikkink, Kathryn. *Ideas and Institutions: Developmentalism in Brazil and Argentina.* Ithaca, NY: Cornell University Press, 1991.

Skocpol, Theda. "Bring the State Back In: Strategies of Analysis in Current Research." In Evans, Rueschemeyer, and Skocpol, *Bringing the State Back In*, 3–37.

States and Social Revolutions: A Comparative Analysis of France, Russia, and China. Cambridge: Cambridge University Press, 1979.

Skocpol, Theda, Marshall Ganz, and Ziad Munson. "A Nation of Organizers: The Institutional Origins of Civic Voluntarism in the United States." *American Political Science Review* 94, no. 3 (September 2000): 527–546.

Skuratov, Yuriy. *Variant Drakona.* Moscow: Detektiv-Press, 2000.

Slider, Darrell. "Putin's 'Southern Strategy': Dmitriy Kozak and the Dilemmas of Recentralization." *Post-Soviet Affairs* 24, no. 2 (April–June 2008): 177–197.

Smirnyagin, Leonid. "Federalizm po Putinu ili Putin po federalizmu (zheleznoy pyatoy)?" *Brifing Moskovskogo Tsentra Karnegi* 3, no. 3 (March 2001).

Smith, Chris. "Security-Sector Reform: Development Breakthrough or Institutional Engineering?" *Journal of Conflict, Security, & Development* 1, no. 1 (2001): 5–19.

Smith, Gordon B. *Reforming the Russian Legal System.* Cambridge: Cambridge University Press, 1996.

ed. *State-Building in Russia: The Yeltsin Legacy and the Challenge of the Future.* Armonk, NY: M.E. Sharpe, 1999.

"The Struggle over the Procuracy." In *Reforming Justice in Russia, 1864–1996: Reforming Justice in Russia 1864 – 1996: Power, Culture, and the Limits of Legal Order,* ed. Peter Solomon, 348–373. Armonk, NY: M.E. Sharpe, 1997.

Solnick, Steven L. "Federal Bargaining in Russia. *East European Constitutional Review* 4 (Fall 1995): 52–58.

"The Political Economy of Russian Federalism." *Problems of Post-Communism* 43, no. 6 (November/December 1996): 13–25.

Solomon, Jr., Peter H. "Administrative Styles in Soviet History: The Development of Patrimonial Rationality." In *What Is Soviet Now?: Identities, Legacies, Memories,* ed. Thomas Lahusen and Peter J. Solomon, Jr., 78–89. Berlin: Lit Verlag, 2008.

"Assessing the Courts in Russia: Parameters of Progress under Putin." *Demokratizatsiya* 16, no. 1 (Winter 2008): 63–73.

"The Criminal Procedure Code of 2001." In Pridemore, *Ruling Russia,* 77–98.

"The Reform of Policing in the Russian Federation." *The Australian and New Zealand Journal of Criminology* 38, no. 2 (2005): 230–240.

Solomon, Peter H., Jr. Todd S. Fogelsong. *Courts and Transition in Russia: The Challenge of Judicial Reform.* Boulder, CO: Westview Press, 2000.

Sperling, Valerie. "Introduction: The Domestic and International Obstacles to State-Building in Russia." In *Building the Russian State: Institutional Crisis and the Quest for Democratic Governance,* ed. Valerie Sperling, 1–23. Boulder, CO: Westview Press, 2000.

Organizing Women in Contemporary Russia: Engendering Transition. Cambridge: Cambridge University Press, 1999.

Starkey, Ken. "Durkheim and Organizational Analysis: Two Legacies." *Organization Studies* 13, no. 4 (1992): 627–642.

Stepan, Alfred. "Federalism and Democracy: Beyond the U.S. Model." *Journal of Democracy* 10, no. 4 (October 1999): 19–34.

The Military in Politics: Changing Patterns in Brazil. Princeton, NJ: Princeton University Press, 1971.

"Russian Federalism in Comparative Perspective." *Post-Soviet Affairs* 16, no. 2 (April–June 2000): 133–176.

"Toward a New Comparative Politics of Federalism, (Multi)Nationalism, and Democracy." In *Arguing Comparative Politics,* 315–361. Oxford: Oxford University Press, 2001.

Stepanova, E.A. *Voyenno-grazhdanskiye otnosheniya v operatsiyakh nevoyennogo tipa.* Moscow: Prava Cheloveka, 2001.

Stern, Jessica Eve. "Moscow Meltdown: Can Russia Survive?" *International Security* 18, no. 4 (Spring 1994): 40–65.

Stewart, Debra W., Norman A. Sprinthall, and Jackie D. Kem. "Moral Reasoning in the Context of Reform: A Study of Russian Officials." *Public Administration Review* 62, no. 3 (2002): 282–297.

Stinchcombe, Arthur L. "On the Virtues of the Old Institutionalism." *Annual Review of Sociology* 23 (1997): 1–18.

Stoker, Gerry. "Governance as Theory: Five Propositions." *International Social Science Journal* 50, no. 155 (March 1998): 17–28.

Stoner-Weiss, Kathryn. "Central Governing Incapacity and the Weakness of Political Parties." *Publius* 32, no. 2 (Spring 2002): 125–146.

Resisting the State: Reform and Retrenchment in Post-Soviet Russia. Cambridge: Cambridge University Press, 2006.

Surkov, Vladislav. "Russkaya politicheskaya kul'tura. Vzglyad iz utopii." In Russkaya politicheskaya kul'tura. Vzglyad iz utopii. Lektsiya Vladislava Surkova, ed. Konstantin Remchukov, 16–21. Moscow: Nezavisimaya Gazeta, 2007.

Tanner, Murray Scott. "Will the State Bring You Back In?: Policing and Democratization (Review Article)." Comparative Politics 33, no. 1 (October 2000): 101–124.

Taylor, Brian D. "Force and Federalism: Controlling Coercion in Federal Hybrid Regimes," Comparative Politics 39, no. 4 (July 2007): 421–440.

"Law Enforcement and Civil Society in Russia." Europe-Asia Studies 58, 2 (March 2006): 193–213.

"Law Enforcement and Russia's Federal Districts." In Reddaway and Orttung, The Dynamics of Russian Politics, vol. 2, 65–90.

Politics and the Russian Army: Civil-Military Relations, 1689–2000. Cambridge: Cambridge University Press, 2003.

"Putin's 'Historic Mission': State-Building and the Power Ministries in the North Caucasus." Problems of Post-Communism 54, no. 6 (November–December 2007): 3–16.

Russia's Power Ministries: Coercion and Commerce. Syracuse, NY: Institute for National Security and Counterterrorism, Syracuse University, 2007.

"The Soviet Military and the Disintegration of the USSR." Journal of Cold War Studies 5, no. 1 (Winter 2003): 17–66.

"Strong Men, Weak State: Power Ministry Officials and the Federal Districts." PONARS Policy Memo no. 284 (2002).

Taylor, Brian D., and Roxana Botea. "Tilly Tally: War-Making and State-Making in the Contemporary Third World." International Studies Review 10, no. 1 (Spring 2008): 27–57.

Tendler, Judith. Good Government in the Tropics. Baltimore: The Johns Hopkins University Press, 1997.

Theobald, Robin. "Patrimonialism." World Politics 34, no. 4 (1982): 548–559.

Thies, Cameron G. "State Building, Interstate and Intrastate Rivalry: A Study of Post-Colonial Developing Country Extractive Efforts, 1975–2000." International Studies Quarterly 48, no. 1 (2004): 53–72.

Thomson, Janice. Mercenaries, Pirates, and Sovereigns: State-Building and Extraterritorial Violence in Early Modern Europe. Princeton, NJ: Princeton University Press, 1994.

Tilly, Charles. Coercion, Capital, and European States, AD 990–1992. Cambridge: Blackwell, 1992.

Democracy. Cambridge: Cambridge University Press, 2007.

ed. The Formation of National States in Western Europe. Princeton, NJ: Princeton University Press, 1975.

"War Making and State Making as Organized Crime." In Evans, Rueschemeyer, and Skocpol, Bringing the State Back In, 169–191.

"Western State-Making and Theories of Political Transformation." In Tilly, The Formation of National States in Western Europe, 601–638.

Tismaneanu, Vladimir, Marc Morjé Howard, and Rudra Sil, eds. World Order after Leninism. Seattle, WA: University of Washington Press, 2006.

Titkov, Aleksey. "Krizis naznacheniy." Pro et Contra 11, no. 4–5 (July–October 2007): 90–103.

Tlisova, Fatima. "Karachaevo-Cherkessia: An Inside Look." Paper presented at the North Caucasus Conference, Jamestown Foundation, September 14, 2006.

Tompson, William. "Putting Yukos in Perspective." *Post-Soviet Affairs* 21, no. 2 (April–June 2005): 159–181.

Treisman, Daniel S. *After the Deluge.* Ann Arbor, MI: University of Michigan Press, 1999.

    The Architecture of Government: Rethinking Political Decentralization. Cambridge: Cambridge University Press, 2007.

    "Putin's *Silovarchs.*" *Orbis* 51, no. 1 (Winter 2007): 141–153.

Trochev, Alexei, and Peter H. Solomon, Jr. "Courts and Federalism in Putin's Russia." In Reddaway and Orttung, *The Dynamics of Russian Politics,* vol. 2, 91–122.

Troshev, Gennadiy. *Moya Voyna: Chechenskiy dnevnik okopnogo generala.* Moskva: Vagrius, 2002.

Tsygankov, Andrei P. "Modern at Last? Variety of Weak States in the Post-Soviet World." *Communist and Post-Communist Studies* 40, no. 4 (December 2007): 423–439.

    "Understanding Russian Regionalism." *Problems of Post-Communism* 54, no. 2 (March–April 2007): 72–74.

Ungar, Mark. *Elusive Reform: Democracy and the Rule of Law in Latin America.* Boulder, CO: Lynne Rienner, 2002.

Vachagaev, Mairbek. "The Chechen Resistance: Yesterday, Today and Tomorrow." Paper presented at the North Caucasus Conference, Jamestown Foundation, September 14, 2006.

van de Walle, Nicolas. "The Economic Correlates of State Failure." In Rotberg, *When States Fail,* 94–115. Princeton, NJ: Princeton University Press, 2004.

    "Meet the New Boss, Same as the Old Boss? The Evolution of Political Clientelism in Africa." In *Patrons, Clients, and Policies: Patterns of Democratic Accountability and Political Competition,* ed. Herbert Kitschelt and Steven I. Wilkinson, 50–67. Cambridge: Cambridge University Press, 2007.

Van Dijk, Jan. *The World of Crime: Breaking the Silence on Problems of Security, Justice, and Development Across the World.* Los Angeles: Sage Publications, 2008.

Van Evera, Stephen. *Guide to Methods for Students of Political Science.* Ithaca, NY: Cornell University Press, 1997.

Vidaver-Cohen, Deborah. "Ethics and Crime in Business Firms: Organizational Culture and the Impact of Anomie." In *The Legacy of Anomie Theory,* ed. Freda Adler and William S. Laufer, 183–206. New Brunswick, NJ: Transaction Publishers, 1995.

Volkov, Vadim. "'Delo Standard Oil' i 'delo Yukosa'." *Pro et Contra* 9, no. 2 (September–October 2005): 66–91.

    "Hostile Enterprise Takeovers: Russia's Economy in 1998–2002." *Review of Central and East European Law* 29, no. 4 (2004): 527–548.

    "Patrimonialism versus Rational Bureaucracy: On the Historical Relativity of Corruption." In *Bribery and* Blat *in Russia: Negotiating Reciprocity from the Middle Ages to the 1990s,* ed. Stephen Lovell, Alena Ledeneva, andAndrei Rogachevskii, 35–47. New York: St. Martin's Press, 2000.

    "Po tu storonu sudebnoy sistemy, ili pochemu zakony rabotayut ne tak, kak dolzhni." *Neprikosnovennyy Zapas,* no. 42 (July 2005). http://www.nlobooks.ru/rus/nz-online/

"The Selective Use of State Capacity in Russia's Economy: Property Disputes and Enterprise Takeovers After 2000." *PONARS Policy Memo* no. 273 (October 2002).

Violent Entrepreneurs: The Use of Force in the Making of Russian Capitalism. Ithaca, NY: Cornell University Press, 2002.

Waddington, P.A.J. *Policing Citizens: Authority and Rights.* London: UCL Press, 1999.

Waldner, David. *State Building and Late Development.* Ithaca, NY: Cornell University Press, 1999.

Walker, Edward W. *Dissolution: Sovereignty and the Breakup of the Soviet Union.* Lanham, MD: Rowman and Littlefield, 2003.

Wallander, Celeste A. "The Domestic Sources of a Less-than-Grand Strategy." In *Strategic Asia 2007–2008: Domestic Political Change and Grand Strategy*, ed. Ashley J. Tellis, and Michael Wills, 138–175. Seattle, WA: National Bureau of Asian Research, 2007.

Waller, J. Michael. *Secret Empire: The KGB in Russia Today.* Boulder, CO: Westview Press, 1994.

Ware, Robert Bruce. "Revisiting Russia's Apartment Block Blasts." *Journal of Slavic Military Studies* 18, no. 4 (December 2005): 599–606.

Watts, Ronald L. *Comparing Federal Systems in the 1990s.* Kingston, Canada: Institute of Intergovernmental Relations, Queens University, 1996.

Way, Lucan A., and Steven Levitsky. "The Dynamics of Autocratic Coercion after the Cold War." *Communist and Post-Communist Studies* 39, no. 3 (2006): 387–410.

Weber, Max. *Economy and Society*, ed. Guenther Roth and Claus Wittich. Berkeley, CA: University of California Press, 1978.

"Politics as a Vocation." In *Max Weber: Essays in Sociology*, ed. H.H. Gerth and C. Wright Mills, 77–128. New York: Oxford University Press, 1946.

Weber, Renate. "Police Organization and Accountability: A Comparative Study." In Kadar, *Police in Transition*, 39–70.

Weigle, Marcia A. "On the Road to the Civic Forum: State and Civil Society from Yeltsin to Putin." *Demokratizatsiya* 10, no. 2 (Spring 2002): 117–146.

Weiler, Jonathan. *Human Rights in Russia: A Darker Side of Reform.* Boulder, CO: Lynne Rienner, 2004.

Weinthal, Erika, and Pauline Jones Luong. "Combating the Resource Curse: An Alternative Solution to Managing Mineral Wealth." *Perspectives on Politics* 4, no. 1 (Mar. 2006): 35–53.

Weitzer, Ronald. *Policing under Fire: Ethnic Conflict and Police-Community Relations in Northern Ireland.* Albany, NY: State University of New York Press, 1995.

Wibbels, Erik. *Federalism and the Market: Intergovernmental Conflict and Economic Reform in the Developing World.* New York: Cambridge University Press, 2005.

"Madison in Baghdad?: Decentralization and Federalism in Comparative Politics." *Annual Review of Political Science* 9 (2006): 165–188.

Widner, Jennifer A. "Building Effective Trust in the Aftermath of Severe Conflict." In Rotberg, *When States Fail*, 222–237.

Wilhelmsen, Julie. "Between a Rock and a Hard Place: The Islamisation of the Chechen Separatist Movement." *Europe-Asia Studies* 57, no. 1 (January 2005): 35–59.

Willerton, John P., Mikhail Beznosov, and Martin Carrier. "Addressing the Challenges of Russia's 'Failing State': The Legacy of Gorbachev and the Promise of Putin." *Demokratizatsiya* 13, no. 2 (Spring 2005): 219–239.

Wilson, Graham. "The Quality of Government." *Governance* 21, no. 2 (April 2008): 197–200.

Wilson, James Q. *Bureaucracy: What Government Agencies Do and Why They Do It.* New York: Basic Books, 1989.

Woodruff, David. *Money Unmade: Barter and the Fate of Russian Capitalism.* Ithaca, NY: Cornell University Press, 1999.

Wright, Deil. *Understanding Intergovernmental Relations,* 2nd ed. Monterey, CA: Brooks/Cole, 1982.

Yel'tsin, Boris. *Prezidentskiy marafon: Razmyshleniya, vospominaniya, vpetchatleniya...* Moscow: AST, 2000.

Young, John F., and Gary N. Wilson. "The View from Below: Local Government and Putin's Reforms." *Europe-Asia Studies* 59, no. 7 (November 2007): 1071–1088.

Zack, Lizabeth. "The *Police Municipale* and the Formation of the French State." In Davis and Periera, *Irregular Armed Forces and Their Role in Politics and State Formation,* 281–302.

Zaslavsky, Viktor. "Nationalism and Democratic Transition in Postcommunist Societies." *Daedalus* 121, no. 2 (Spring 1992): 97–122.

Zimmerman, Ekkart. *Political Violence, Crises, and Revolutions: Theories and Research.* Cambridge, MA: Schenkman Publishing, 1983.

Zimmerman, William. "'Normal Democracies' and Improving How They Are Measured: The Case of Russia." *Post-Soviet Affairs* 23, no. 1 (Summer 2007): 1–17.

Zubarevich, Natalia. "Southern Federal Okrug." In Reddaway and Orttung, *The Dynamics of Russian Politics,* vol. 1, 111–152.

Index

accountability, 234–47
administrative resources, 95–6
Adygeya, 279
Aeroflot, 105
Afghanistan, 29, 87
Africa, 15, 108–9, 115
agency theory, 29, 30, 177
Akunin, Boris, 184
Albania, 94
Albats, Yevgenia, 62, 165
Alekseyeva, Lyudmila, 238
Alpern, Lyudmila, 230, 232
Alpha unit, 44, 81
Altus Global Alliance, 227
Amnesty International, 308
Andriyenko, Yuriy, 93
Andropov, Yuriy, 43
anomie, 31, 202
Antonov, A.A., 137
Argentina, 24, 115, 279
armed forces. *See* military
Arshavin, Andrey, 242
Arutyunov, Sergey, 273
August 1991 coup attempt, 79–80,
      119, 251
Avtovaz, 105

Babich, Dmitry, 42
Babushkin, Andrey, 241
Back, Hanna, 310
Baev, Pavel, 270
Bailiffs Service, 50
Bakatin, Vadim, 117–18, 152, 198, 201
Barabashev, Alexei, 201, 306
Basayev, Shamil, 88, 254, 255, 258, 261–2,
      274, 276
Bashkortostan, 120, 122, 137, 140, 145, 251

Basic Element, 165
Bastrykin, Aleksandr, 51, 60, 66,
      69, 199
Bayley, David, 28, 30, 33, 149, 215, 216,
      232, 243
Beck, Adrian, 201, 249
Bednar, Jenna, 114
Beissinger, Mark, 94, 286
Belarus, 18, 21, 116, 291, 293, 314
Belozerov, A.M., 137
Belyaninov, Andrey, 50, 60, 69
Belyayev, Sergey, 145
Berezovsky, Boris, 103, 104, 234
Beslan school siege, 25, 79, 82, 88, 109,
      148, 189, 209, 239, 245, 254, 256–7,
      277, 287, 306
Bobkov, Filipp, 103
bombings. *See* terrorism
Bordyuzha, Nikolay, 59
Bortnikov, Aleksandr, 317
Botswana, 293, 300
Brazil, 33, 92, 106, 115, 127
Brezhnev, Leonid, 55, 117,
      152, 208
British Petroleum, 106–7
Brother (Brat), 193
Browder, William, 106–7
Brym, Robert, 186
Budennovsk, 82
Bukkvoll, Tor, 88
Buksman, Aleksandr, 187
Bulbov, Aleksandr, 65,
      174–5
bureaucracy, types of, 26, 27–8
Burk, James, 32, 178, 272
Burma, 178
Business Week, 170

cadres, 185–200
  conditions of employment, 194–5
  professionalism, 197–200
  recruitment and retention, 188–94
Cameroon, 162
Canada, 114
Cappelli, Ottorino, 312
Carnegie Moscow Center, 279
Carothers, Thomas, 158, 215, 309–10
Center for Justice Assistance (CJA), 220,
  224–7, 231
Chayka, Yuriy, 60, 61, 65, 66, 174, 193
Chechnya, 251, 255, 287. *See also* North
  Caucasus
  and challenges to Russian central
    authority, 73, 120
  "Chechenization", 267, 270
  first Chechen war (1994), 250, 254–6, 266,
    279
  and radicalization of Chechen fighters, 254
  role of MChS, 42
  and Russian internal security budget, 55
  and the Russian military, 41, 168
  and Russian police, 183, 221–2
  second Chechen war (1999), 250, 255,
    260–1, 266, 268n54, 279
  and terrorist violence, 4, 82, 85–6, 209,
    256, 259, 260, 287
Chekist manifesto, 63, 65
Chekists, 43, 62, 63, 65, 204, 248, 286,
  306–7
Chemezov, Sergey, 60
Cherkesov, Viktor, 36, 49, 60, 63, 66, 112,
  131, 143, 174, 204, 307, 317
Chernogorov, Aleksandr, 143
Chernomyrdin, Viktor, 64, 188
Chile, 291, 293, 300
China, 314
Chivers, C.J., 258, 301
Chkhartishvili, Grigoriy, 184
Chubais, Anatoliy, 64, 316
Chuvash Republic, 227, 253n6
Cirtautus, Arista Maria, 74
Citizen's Watch, 220–4, 232, 237
citizenship, low intensity, 22
civil service, Russian, 187–8
civil society
  and building state quality, 213–7
  and the decline of accountability, 234–47
  different perspectives on, 214–6
  lack of trust in government, 205–12, 247
  law enforcement and, 217–34
  under Putin, 238
  "watchdog" model, 215–6

weakening of, 204–5
civil states, 19–20, 293, 304
civil-military relations, 40
clans, *siloviki*, 3, 37, 64–6, 174, 285, 307
Cleary, Matthew, 213
coercion
  and bureaucratic type, 27–8
  and economics, 99–107
  and institutionalizing new mission, 31–3
  at the local level, 22–4
  in the North Caucasus, 250–83
  and organizational monitoring strategy,
    29–30
  and state building, 33–5
  and state capacity, 16–24, 76–7
  state monopoly over, 14–15, 304–5
coercive agencies, state. *See* Federal Security
  Service (FSB); law enforcement; Ministry
  of Internal Affairs (MVD); police;
  specific agencies
cohorts, *siloviki*, 3, 37, 57–64, 132, 285, 307
Cold War, end of, 15
Colton, Timothy, 75, 76
commissioned cases, 165–7
Committee on State Security (KGB), 37, 38,
  43, 116
  break-up of, 43
  Ninth Directorate, 44
  organizational culture of, 62–3
  size of, 43
  successors to, 43–8
communism
  collapse of, 15
  legacy of, 293–4, 298–300
Communist Party, 58, 61, 79, 114, 116, 117,
  118
Communist Youth League (Komsomol), 58
Comoros, 115
Comparative Political Studies, 10
Comparative Politics, 10
Congress of People's Deputies (CPD), 80
Constitution, Russian, 52, 80, 119, 121–2,
  148, 230
Constitutional Court, 146
corporate actors, *siloviki*, 3, 37, 66–70,
  285–6, 307
corruption
  bribes, 164n23, 166, 167, 170–2, 269
  defined, 159
  forced takeovers, 165–6
  forms of, 162–9
  in the North Caucasus, 269–72
  organized crime, 76, 168–9, 211
  racial profiling, 163

roofing, 164–5, 170, 176
selling assets, 167–8
shakedowns, 162–4
and state quality, 18, 159–61, 287
as a system, 169–72
Three Whales Case, 50, 172–5
and Transparency International
Corruption Perceptions Index, 22,
160, 162, 271
Cottrell, Robert, 106
Council of Europe, 232
coups
August 1991, 79–80
October 1993 crisis, 80–1
and state capacity, 10, 77
Criminal Procedure Code (2002), 166
Croatia, 291
Cuba, 21
Czech Republic, 300
Czechoslovakia, 15

Dagestan
democracy in, 279
and the *Kadyrovtsy*, 268
killing of Interior Minister, 318
patrimonialism in, 275
political violence in, 4, 82, 84, 251, 255,
258, 260, 265, 318
and power ministry corruption, 271
stateness in, 266
Darden, Keith, 21–2
Davis, Diane, 23, 175
de Figueiredo, Rui, 114
de Waal, Thomas, 265
decisions, routine versus exceptional, 16–7,
108, 286
democracy
in Russia's regions, 279
and state quality, 18–19, 309–10
Democratic Republic of Congo, 290
democratization, 10–11, 64, 149, 214, 294,
309–10
demonstrations, policing of, 95
Demos, 281
Department for Combating Organized Crime
and Terrorism, 46
Department for Countering Extremism, 46,
99n73
Deripaska, Oleg, 165
Derluguian, Georgi, 275
Diamond, Larry, 115n16
Dininio, Phyllis, 271
Directorate of Internal Affairs (UVD), 125,
135

Divayev, Rafail, 137
Dorenko, Sergey, 110
Drachevskiy, Leonid, 131, 141
Dubai, 318
Dubin, Boris, 208
Dudayev, Dzhokar, 153, 251
Duma, 45, 46, 58, 97–8, 109, 173, 243, 244,
275, 319
Dunlop, John, 277

Easter, Gerald, 90, 102, 312
economic depression of 1990s, 52, 71, 93,
264
economics, coercion of, 99–107
property rights, 102–7
Economist, The, 105
Edwards, Bob, 214
elections, power ministries and, 95–8
Elias, Norbert, 22
EMERCOM. *See* Ministry of Civil Defense
and Emergency Situations (MChS)
enforcement partnership, 76
Equatorial Guinea, 291, 293
Ermoshkina, Inna, 187
Ertman, Thomas, 310, 314–5
Eskridge, William, 114
Estemirova, Nataliya, 318
Estonia, 300
Ethiopia, 115
European Code of Police Ethics, The, 221
European Union, 320
Evangelista, Matthew, 71, 307
Evans, Peter, 32, 178, 201

Fadeyev, Nikolay, 132
Family, the (Yeltsin), 56, 64, 66, 103–4, 307
Far Eastern District, 132
Federal Agency for Government
Communication and Information
(FAPSI), 44
Federal Border Service (FPS), 44, 67
Federal Customs Service (FTS), 50, 69, 133,
168, 172–5
federal districts, 3, 128–30, 286,
See also okrug; *specific districts*
and harmonization of laws, 139–41
and manipulation of law enforcement,
141–4
Federal Financial Monitoring Service, 133
Federal Guards Service (FSO), 44, 52, 167
Federal Penitentiary Service, 235, 243n109.
See also Federal Service for the
Administration of Sentences (FSIN),
prisons

Federal Registration Service (FRS), 223, 237
Federal Road Construction Administration, 41
Federal Security Service (FSB), 3, 44, 52, 56, 126, 286. *See also* Chekists; Committee on State Security (KGB)
   and apartment bombings, 83–5
   centralization of budget, 123
   and elections, 96–7
   lack of trust in, 208
   under Medvedev, 317
   and the MVD, 67
   under Putin, 65, 68–9
   at the regional level, 149
   and roofing, 164–5
   and terrorism, 87–8
   and Three Whales Case, 172–5
Federal Service for the Administration of Sentences (FSIN), 49–50, 229–30. *See also* Federal Penitentiary Service, prisons
Federal Service for the Control of the Narcotics Trade (FSKN), 49, 65, 204
   under Medvedev, 317
   and Three Whales Case, 172–5
Federal Service of Special Construction, 41
Federal Tax Police Service (FSNP), 49, 100, 104–5, 123, 132–3
federalism, 112–54
   and 1993 Constitution, 121–2
   and coercion, 115
   creation of federal districts, 128–30
   and decentralization of police, 150–4
   and economic factors, 147
   and harmonization of laws, 139–41
   nature of post-Soviet federation, 119–20
   political theory of, 114
   under Putin, 3, 287
   Russian units of, 120n36
   under Soviets, 119
   stages of, 116
   and state capacity, 154–5
Federation Council, 58, 104, 146
Federation Treaty, 120
feeding (*kormleniye*), 185–6
Ferejohn, John, 114
Filatov, Nikita, 193–4
Finland, 162
"fire alarms", 29–30, 245–6, 249, 278, 303, 306, 319
First Contact project, 225–6
Fish, Steven, 108, 289n6, 302n40
Foley, Michael, 214
Foreign Intelligence Service (SVR), 43, 52

Forrest, Joshua, 16
Fradkov, Mikhail, 61n70
France, 24, 47, 207, 222
Fritz, Verena, 18
Fukuyama, Francis, 19, 31, 34, 309, 311

Gaidar, Yegor, 81
Gambia, 160
Ganev, Venelin, 311
Ganeyev, Valentin, 172
Gantamirov, Bislan, 277
Gavrilov, Boris, 191, 226
Gazprom, 105, 106
Geertz, Clifford, 6
Georgia, 98, 236, 318, 320
Gerber, Theodore, 178, 180, 247, 271
Gergiyev, Valeriy, 242
Germany, 47, 151, 207, 222
Ghana, 162
Gimpelson, Vladimir, 186
Glazev, Sergey, 97, 147
Golovshchinskiy, Konstantin, 226
Goodwin, Jeff, 23
Gorbachev, Mikhail
   1991 attempted overthrow of, 43, 44, 79–80
   and decentralization, 117, 118–9, 152
   leadership strategy of, 301
   and militia, 189
   and the North Caucasus, 251
   and regime of repression, 94
Gorfinkel, Ilya, 145
Goryainov, K.K., 211
governance, 17, 289. *See also* state quality
governors (regional), 124–5, 126, 133, 149
Grachev, Pavel, 81
Graham, Thomas, 64, 127–8, 301
Great Britain, 207, 222
Gref, German, 65
Grozny, 256, 277, 318
Gryzlov, Boris, 46, 60, 65, 135, 226, 243
Gryzmala-Busse, Anna, 299
Guatemala, 94
Gudkov, Gennadiy, 165, 243
Gusinsky, Vladimir, 103, 104, 105, 110, 234
Gutseriyev, Khamzat, 96

Hadenius, Axel, 310
Hahn, Gordon, 97
Haiti, 94
Hamilton, Alexander, 123
Hanson, Philip, 105
Hanson, Stephen, 32, 201, 300
Harasymiw, Bohdan, 175

harmonization of laws, 139–41
Hedlund, Stefan, 110
Hermitage Capital, 106
Hobbes, Thomas, 115
Holmes, Stephen, 75, 76, 125–6
homicide rates
  in Chechnya, 260
  decline in, 211
  in Russia, 90–4, 287
  and state capacity, 72
Howard, Marc, 214, 300
Hughes, James, 254, 266–7
human rights organizations, 182–3, 212,
    227, 230, 271, 288
  Citizen's Watch, 220–4
  Demos, 281
  Human Rights Watch, 237
  Institute of Human Rights, 239
  Man and Law, 241
  Memorial, 260, 273, 279, 280, 318
humanitarian agencies, 42
Huntington, Samuel, 10, 13, 19, 28, 77
Huskey, Eugene, 75, 187
hybrid regimes, 3, 114–5, 147, 150

Iceland, 178, 290
ideology of statism, 72–3, 201, 288, 303,
    314, 321
INDEM. *See* Information for Democracy
    (INDEM) Foundation
India, 21, 87, 115, 127, 151–2
Indonesia, 160
Information for Democracy (INDEM)
    Foundation, 160n11, 208, 224–8, 231,
    271
infrastructural power, 12, 89
Inglehart, Ronald, 213
Ingush-Ossetian conflict, 251–4
Ingushetia
  democracy in, 279
  and the *Kadyrovtsy*, 268
  Medvedev's actions in, 317–8
  patrimonialism in, 276
  political violence in, 4, 251, 255, 256,
    258, 260, 282, 318
  presidential election in (2002),
    96–7, 263
  and stateness, 266
Institute of Human Rights, 239
Institute of Situational Analysis and New
    Technology (ISANT), 149
Institutional Revolutionary Party (Mexico),
    114
institutionalism, old, 31–2

intelligence agencies. *See* Committee on
    State Security (KGB); Federal Security
    Service (FSB); Foreign Intelligence
    Service (SVR)
Internal Troops, 46, 67, 99, 117, 123, 130,
    180. *See also* Ministry of Internal Affairs
    (MVD)
Investigative Committee of the Procuracy, 51,
    66, 69, 199
Iran, 291, 293
Iraq, 87
Iskhakov, Kamil, 132
Israel, 21, 87, 289
Italy, 207
Itogi, 128
Ivanov, Sergey, 40, 56, 59, 60, 65, 66, 68,
    130, 255, 317
Ivanov, Viktor, 60, 65
Izmaylov, Vyacheslav, 267
Izvestiya, 128

Jack, Andrew, 61
Jacoby, Wade, 219, 232
Japan, 14, 28, 217
Jowitt, Kenneth, 32, 74, 294, 300

Kabardino-Balkaria, 251, 256–7, 258, 260,
    265, 271, 273, 279
Kadyrov, Akhmad, 256, 266
Kadyrov, Ramzan, 251, 256, 262, 266,
    276–8, 280, 281, 287, 318
Kadyrovtsy, 267, 268, 274, 276, 280
Kahn, Jeffrey, 146
Kahn, Peter, 50
Kalinina, Yuliya, 257
Kampfner, John, 257
Kanakov, Arsen, 263
Karachayevo-Cherkesiya, 256, 276, 279
Kasyanov, Mikhail, 61n70, 65, 307
Katzenstein, Peter, 14, 217
Kazakhstan, 21, 314
Kazan, Tatarstan, 132, 169
Kazantsev, Viktor, 96
Kenney, Charles, 244
KGB. *See* Committee on State
    Security (KGB)
Khadzhikurbanov, Sergey, 169
Khalikov, Rappani, 261
Khamkhoyev, Beslan, 270
Khasbulatov, Ruslan, 80
Khimanych, Vladimir, 239
Khinshteyn, Aleksandr, 175, 189, 275
Khodorkovsky, Mikhail, 65, 76, 105
Khrushchev, Nikita, 43, 55, 79, 117, 152

kidnappings, 313
King, Desmond, 315
Kiriyenko, Sergey, 140, 142–3, 145
Kiselev, Konstantin, 141
Kislitsyn, Vyacheslav, 142
Klebanov, Ilya, 131
Kleinfeld, Rachel, 22, 158
Klimentev, Andrey, 145
Knight, Amy, 62
Komaritskiy, Ivan, 224, 225
Kommersant, 65
Komsomolskaya pravda, 163, 170
Konstantinov, Andrey, 190, 194, 235
kormleniye (feeding), 185, 194, 196
Kortunov, Andrey, 139
Korzhakov, Aleksandr, 45, 64, 68, 81, 103
Kostina, Olga, 239
Kotenkov, Aleksandr, 146
Kotkin, Stephen, 24
Kovalev, Nikolay, 68
Kovalskaya, Galina, 128
Kozak, Dmitriy, 65, 184, 262–5, 275, 282, 306
Kramer, Mark, 265
Krasnodar, 264, 271
Krasnov, Mikhail, 108, 152, 157
Kryshtanovskaya, Olga, 36–7, 57–8, 59, 62, 63
Kudrin, Aleksey, 61, 65
Kuksenkova, Irina, 269
Kulikov, Anatoliy, 95, 142
Kuzio, Taras, 73
Kvashnin, Anatoliy, 131–2
Kyrgyzstan, 236

Latygina, N.A., 228
Latynina, Yulia, 143, 176, 257, 272, 313
Latyshev, Petr, 130, 140, 142, 144–5
law enforcement. *See also* police, *specific agencies*
  central versus regional control, 122–8
  and civil society, 217–34
  corruption in, 161–76
  and government effectiveness, 89–91
  lack of trust in, 288
  loss of personnel, 189–94
  manipulation of in federal districts, 141–4
  and predation, 176–85, 211
  professionalism in, 197–200
  and regime of repression, 94–9
  and roofing, 164–5, 170, 176, 319
  routine versus exceptional tasks, 3, 16–17, 108, 286
  and state capacity, 88–99
  and state quality, 175–6
  types of, 181
Law on Civilian State Service (2004), 188
Law on Militia, 134–5, 145, 320
Law on State Civil Service (2007), 222
laws, harmonization of, 139–41
Lebanon, 291
Lebed, Aleksandr, 254
legacies, Communist, 293–4, 298–300
Legan, Yesif, 62–3
legitimacy, 19
Lenin, Vladimir, 43
Leningrad Oblast, 221, 242
Leonov, Nikolay, 63
Lepikhin, Nikolay, 142
Levada Center, 179, 180, 181–2, 207, 208, 209, 271
Levi, Margaret, 9, 10, 102
Levinson, Lev, 239
Levitsky, Steven, 95, 99
Libya, 21
Lieberman, Robert, 315
Linz, Juan, 19, 214
Lipman, Masha, 201
Lithuania, 18, 94
Lokshina, Tatyana, 281
Luckham, Robin, 308
Lukin, Vladimir, 182–3, 212, 227, 230
Luneyev, Viktor, 211
Luzhkov, Yuri, 64, 104, 137, 140, 148
Lysovsky Beer Factory, 166

mafia, 76, 102, 164, 166, 168–9.
  See also organized crime
Maggs, Peter, 51
Magomedtagirov, Adilgerei, 318
Main Administration of the Ministry of Internal Affairs (GU MVD), 133, 137, 212
Main Directorate for Special Programs (GUSP), 45
Main Directorate of Internal Affairs (GUVD), 137, 145, 221, 223, 242, 319
Main Guards Directorate (GUO), 45, 81
Main Intelligence Unit (GRU), 83
Mainville, Michael, 184
Makasharipov, Rasul, 277
Makashov, Albert, 61
Malaysia, 115, 291, 293
Man and Law, 241
Mann, Michael, 12, 16, 32, 74, 89
March of the Dissidents, 98
Marenin, Otwin, 11, 33, 177
Markova, Anna, 96, 139–40

Marx, Karl, 26
Maskhadov, Aslan, 254, 258
Matveeva, Anna, 280
Matviyenko, Valentina, 96, 223
McAuley, Mary, 221
McCubbins, Matthew, 29–30
McFaul, Michael, 74
media as watchdogs, 4
Media-MOST, 103–4, 105, 107
Medvedev, Dmitriy, 61, 65, 66, 70, 211, 307
  actions in the North Caucasus, 264, 317–8
  compared to Putin, 305
  and crisis in Russian law enforcement, 320
  election to presidency, 5, 148, 284
  as First Deputy Prime Minister, 195
  and patrimonialism, 199, 316
  and rule of law, 158
  state building strategy, 35, 315–21
  and state quality, 284, 313
Memorial, 260, 273, 279, 280, 318
Mendelson, Sarah, 178, 180, 247, 271
Merzlyakova, Tatyana, 153
Mexico, 92, 114, 115, 153, 175, 291, 293
Migdal, Joel, 8–9, 16, 23–4, 134
military. *See also* Ministry of Defense (MO)
  civil-military relations, 40
  corruption in, 168
  effects of economic depression on, 52–3
  reform of, 40, 318
  regionalization of, 126–8
  Soviet, 39
  trust in, 207
  and war in Chechnya, 67
military jamaats, 254
militia. *See* police
militocracy, 36–7, 70. *See also* siloviki
Ministry of Atomic Energy, 41
Ministry of Civil Defense and Emergency
    Situations (MChS), 41–3, 67, 172
Ministry of Communications, 41, 58
Ministry of Defense (MO), 38, 39–43, 68,
    267, 286. *See also* military
Ministry of Economic Development, 58
Ministry of Internal Affairs (MVD), 38, 286.
    See also police
  building trust in, 217
  centralization of budget, 123
  description of, 45–8
  at the district level, 132–3
  and elections, 96, 97
  and the FSB, 67
  and homicide statistics, 91
  Internal Troops, 46, 67, 99, 117, 123,
    130, 180

loss of personnel, 191–2
Main Administration of the Ministry of
    Internal Affairs (GU MVD), 133
  OMON, 165
  and opposition to decentralization, 152–3
  and organized crime, 168–9
  Public Council, 239, 240–1
  under Putin, 65, 68
  at the regional level, 123–4, 149
  and roofing, 164–5
  salaries in, 194–6
  size of, 46–7
  under Soviets, 117
Ministry of Justice, 46, 49–50, 55, 237
Mironov, Oleg, 230
Mobutu Sese Seko, 282
monitoring
  internal versus external, 29–30
  of law enforcement, 249
Moscow
  police salaries in, 195
  terrorist attacks in, 79, 85–6, 88, 209, 256,
    270, 277, 318
Moscow Center for Prison Reform, 230, 232
Moscow Times, 166
Moskovskiy Komsomolets, 98, 257–8
Mozambique, 21
Munck, Gerardo, 10
Muratov, Dmitriy, 60, 169
murder rates. *See* homicide rates
Murov, Yevgeniy, 45
Muslim republics, 260–1. *See also* North
    Caucasus; *specific republics*

Nalchik, 256–7, 258, 260
narcotics agency. *See* Federal Service for
    Control of the Narcotics Trade (FSKN)
Nashi, 98
National Antiterrorism Committee (NAC),
    88
National Congress of the Chechen People,
    251
national guards, 120
Nazarbayev, Nursultan, 314
neo-statist movement, 13, 16
Netherlands, 106, 223
Netkachev, Yuriy, 277
Nezavisimaya Gazeta, 68
Nezvlin, Leonid, 239
Nigeria, 94, 115, 127, 289
Nikitinskiy, Leonid, 197, 313
Nizhny Novgorod, 140, 142–3, 145,
    154, 166–7, 190, 192, 193, 224,
    225, 242

non-governmental organizations (NGOs), 4,
198, 205, 208, 214, 217–34, 288, 299
2006 law, 223, 228
Amnesty International, 308
Center for Justice Assistance (CJA), 224–7,
232
Citizen's Watch, 220–4, 232, 237
Demos, 242
government-organized (GONGO), 240
Memorial, 260, 273, 279, 280
"roofs" for, 233
Soprotivleniye, 239–40
state attitude toward, 236–7
watchdog role, 234, 248
Yekaterina Crisis Center, 220, 228–9
Nord-Ost theatre incident, 79, 86, 88, 209,
256, 270, 277
North Caucasus. *See also specific republics*
Beslan school siege, 82, 109, 148, 189, 209,
239, 245, 254, 256–7, 277, 287, 306
clashes between army, MVD, and FSB, 67
corruption in, 269–72
death squads in, 274
economic depression of 1990s, 264
first Chechen war (1994), 250, 254–6, 266,
279
humanitarian agencies in, 42
improvement in state capacity, 262–5
Ingush-Ossetian conflict, 251–4
Islamic radicals in, 82, 83, 84, 88, 254,
263, 265, 272, 273
media coverage of government policy, 279
under Medvedev, 317–8
monitoring, 278–81
overview of crisis in, 251–6
patrimonialism in, 275–8, 276
predation in, 272–4
role of repression in, 3–4, 265–9
second Chechen war (1999), 250, 255,
260–1, 266, 268n54, 279
state building in, 6–7
terrorist violence in, 82–3, 256–62, 256–7
and weakening of central government, 287
North, Douglass, 31, 102, 311
North Ossetia, 251, 255, 256, 260, 265, 269,
271, 279
Northwest Federal District, 131, 133,
134, 143
notary publics, 187
Novaya Gazeta, 107, 169, 173, 279
Novikova, Asmik, 242
Novocherkassk, 116
Novosibirsk, 134, 228
NTV television, 103, 279

Nurgaliyev, Rashid, 46, 60, 65, 68, 190, 217,
226, 230, 241

Obolonskiy, Aleksandr, 75, 201
October 1993 crisis, 44, 68, 79–81, 95, 285
O'Donnell, Guillermo, 19, 22, 28, 244, 245,
250, 251
O'Dwyer, Conor, 299
Offe, Claus, 73
okrug, 117, 286. *See also* federal districts
oligarchs, 3, 25, 36, 102–4
ombudsman office, 182–3, 212, 227, 230
O'Neill, Thomas P., 23
Orange Revolution (Ukraine), 4, 175
organizational mission, sense of, 4–5, 26,
31–3
organizations, typologies of, 34
organized crime, 76, 211
cooperation with power ministries, 168–9
mafia, 76, 102, 164, 166, 168–9
RUBOP, 125, 133, 164, 169
Orlov, Oleg, 280, 318
Orttung, Robert, 271
Ostrovsky, Arkady, 281
Other Russia, 98
Ovchinnikov, N.A., 242
Ovchinskiy, Vladimir, 142
oversight, state, 4, 26, 29–30, 280, 288

Pakistan, 87, 115
Pakulski, Jan, 186
Palestine, 15
Pamfilova, Ella, 221
Paraguay, 94
pardons, 235–6
patrimonialism
and bureaucratic type, 26–8
favoritism to family members, 187
in law enforcement, 199
under Medvedev, 316
in the North Caucasus, 275–8
under Putin, 4, 56, 70
in Russian bureaucracy, 59, 157, 186, 288,
303
in Soviet bureaucracy, 299
and Three Whales Case, 175
Patrushev, Andrey, 65
Patrushev, Nikolay, 44, 55, 56, 60, 65, 66, 69,
83, 130, 173, 187, 222, 233, 236, 317
Pelfrey, William, 179n68
People's Commissariat of Internal Affairs
(NKVD), 45
Pereira, Anthony, 15
Perm Region, 132

Petrov, Nikolay, 137, 138, 243, 279
Pichugin, Aleksey, 239
Piotrovskiy, Mikhail, 242
Poland, 47
police. *See also* law enforcement; Ministry of
    Internal Affairs (MVD)
  bribes, 170–2
  and civil society, 219–20
  Code of Professional Ethics, 198, 227
  and commissioned cases, 165–6
  conditions of employment, 194–6
  connections to organized crime, 168–9,
      211
  and corruption, 161–76
  decentralization of, 150–4
  and domestic violence, 228–9
  ethnic minorities in, 222–3
  history of centralization, 117
  and issuing of passports, 269–70
  local control of, 47–8
  loss of personnel, 189–94
  monitoring in North Caucasus, 278–81
  patrimonialism in, 199
  predation, 176–85
  professionalism in, 197–200
  and public encounters with police violence,
      180–5
  public trust in, 207, 216–7, 288
  at the regional level, 134
  and roofing, 164–5, 170, 211, 319
  and rotation of cadres, 135–7
  salaries, 194–6
  and selling assets, 167–9, 211
  shakedowns, 162–4, 211
  size of, 47–8
  and treatment of ethnic minorities, 240
  use of torture, 182–3
police patrols, 29–30, 248, 303
police performance scores (Van Dijk), 94
police power versus police action, 34, 183
police state, 1, 21, 301, 303, 304
Police Station Visitors Week, 227
policing, forms of, 30, 176–85
Policzer, Pablo, 30, 279
political party system, 146
politics of sovereignty, 14, 308
Politkovskaya, Anna, 169, 267, 279
polpreds (*polpredy*), 128, 130–8, 154
Poltavchenko, Georgiy, 130
Ponomarev, V.P., 137
Posner, Daniel, 215
power ministries. *See also individual
    agencies; siloviki*
  budgets under Yeltsin and Putin, 52–5

  and corruption in law enforcement, 161–75
  and corruption in the North Caucasus,
      270–2
  definition, 36–7, 285
  and elections, 95–8
  and exceptional decisions, 107–8
  and the federal districts, 130–2
  Federal Security Service, 39–43
  leadership under Yeltsin and Putin, 55–7
  Ministry of Defense (MO), 39–43
  Ministry of Internal Affairs (MVD), 45–8
  organizational culture of, 61–3
  the Procuracy, 50–2
  replacement of officials at regional level,
      134–8
  size of, 39
  and state building, 37, 285–8
  and state capacity, 107–11
  and terrorism, 86–8, 258
  and Yukos affair, 105
power vertical, 112, 128, 144–8, 155, 156,
    220, 313
predation, 32, 176–85
  in the North Caucasus, 269, 272–4
  by the police, 198–9, 211, 288
Presidential Pardons Commission, 234
Presidential Security Service (SBP), 45, 64,
    65, 81, 103–4
Pribylovskiy, Vladimir, 95–6
Primakov, Yevgeniy, 43, 59, 104
principal-agent theory, 29
prisons, 46, 49–50. *See also* Federal
    Penitentiary Service, Federal Service for
    the Administration of Sentences (FSIN)
Pristavkin, Anatoliy, 234
Procuracy, the, 3, 50–2
  and the 1993 Constitution, 122
  and 1999 Skuratov affair, 103–4
  centralization of budget, 123
  and coercion, 116
  at the district level, 132–3
  and elections, 96
  and harmonization of laws, 140–1
  Investigative Committee, 51, 66, 69
  and MOST incident, 104–5
  power struggles within, 125–6
  Procurator General, 50, 55, 61, 65, 103–4,
      139, 173
  under Putin, 69
  at the regional level, 135, 149
  and Three Whales Case, 172–5
  and Yukos affair, 105, 106
Procurator General, 50, 55, 61, 65, 103–4,
    139, 173

Pronin, Vladimir, 319
property rights, 3, 26, 102–7, 156, 286
protection rackets, 76, 273. *See also* roofing
Public Chamber, 238–9, 243
public councils, regional, 241–3
Public Order Militia (MOB), 124, 135
Pulikovskiy, Konstantin, 132, 141
Pustyntsev, Boris, 221, 222, 223, 224, 237,
　241, 242
Putin, Vladimir
　centralization of state power, 112–3, 138,
　　144–8, 286
　and conflict in North Caucasus, 250
　goals of, 2, 286
　and KGB past, 59–60, 307
　and patrimonial nature of administration,
　　56, 70
　and personnel changes at the regional level,
　　134–5
　popularity of, 108, 205–6
　possibility of future presidency, 321
　power ministry-big business relations
　　under, 104–7
　and power ministry leadership, 55–7
　as prime minister, 85, 316
　and property rights, 104–7
　regime as "militocracy", 36–7
　relationship to Medvedev, 284, 316–7
　rise to power, 59–60
　siloviki network of, 57, 60
　state building strategy of, 24–6, 71, 301–7,
　　310–13
　and state quality, 34–5, 156–7
Putnam, Robert, 31, 214

Rabinovich, Igor, 142
Rakhimov, Murtaza, 137, 148
Rapota, Grigoriy, 264
rational-legal bureaucracy, 27, 28
regime of repression, 3, 25, 72, 89, 94–9, 156,
　211, 286, 303
regimes, hybrid, 3
Regional Anti-Organized Crime Director
　(RUBOP), 125, 133, 164, 169.
　See also Ministry of Internal Affairs
　(MVD)
Renz, Bettina, 61
Republic of Komi, 191, 193
Republic of Mariy El, 241
republics, 251–3
resource dependence, 293, 298, 299–300
revolutions, colored, 4, 98, 109, 175, 236–7,
　238, 306
Riker, William, 114, 119

Robertson, Annette, 201, 249
Rodionov, Mikhail, 222
Roofing (*kryshevanie*), 164–5, 170, 176, 211,
　319
Rose-Ackerman, Susan, 245
Rosneft, 65, 105–6, 167, 187
Ross, Michael, 108
Rossel, Eduard, 126, 144, 148
Rostov, 264, 271
Rostovskiy, Mikhail, 98
Rothstein, Bo, 17–8
routine versus exceptional decisions, 16–17,
　108, 286
Royal Dutch Shell, 106
Rudenko, Viktor, 141
rule of law, 22, 157–61, 246, 287
Rushaylo, Vladimir, 46
Russell, John, 280
Rutskoy, Aleksandr, 80
Ryaguzov, Pavel, 169
Ryazan incident, 83–5

Sadullayev, Abdul-Khalim, 258
Samuels, Richard, 300–1
Satarov, Georgiy, 153, 187–8, 207–8, 224,
　226, 228
Satter, David, 184
Schwartz, Thomas, 29–30
Sechin, Igor, 56, 60, 65, 66, 69, 106, 167,
　174, 187, 316, 317
secret police. *See* Chekists; Committee on
　State Security (KGB); Federal Security
　Service (FSB)
Security Council, 58–9
security sector reform (SSR), 22n67, 216, 308
Selznick, Philip, 31, 201
Serdyukov, Anatoliy, 40, 187, 318
shakedowns, 162–4, 211
Shaymiyev, Mintimer, 137, 145, 148
Shchekochikhin, Yuri, 172, 174
Shelley, Louise, 189, 197
Shepeleva, Olga, 200, 242
Shevtsova, Lilia, 110
Shklar, Judith, 158
Shlapentokh, Vladimir, 207, 213
Shleifer, Andrei, 292
Shleynov, Roman, 107, 175
Shogenov, Khachim, 263, 273
Shoygu, Sergey, 42, 81, 187
Shurygin, Vladislav, 257
Shuvalov, Igor, 315
Shvartsman, Oleg, 167
Siberian Federal District, 131–2, 133, 141
Sierra Leone, 289

silovarchs, 106
siloviki. See also power ministries
    approaches to, 3, 37, 57, 64–6, 285, 307
    definition, 2, 37, 285
    military officers, 41
    organizational culture of, 61–3, 177
    at the regional level, 130–8
    rise of under Putin, 57, 60
Simonyan, Robert, 211
Singapore, 314
Skocpol, Theda, 9, 13
Skuratov affair, 61, 103–4, 107
Skuratov, Yuriy, 55, 103–4, 139
Slipchenko, V.I., 110
Slovenia, 300
Smirnov, Andrei, 255
Smirnyagin, Leonid, 118, 154
Smith, Gordon, 75
Smolin, Oleg, 237
Snyder, Richard, 10
Sobchak, Anatoliy, 59, 126, 143
Soinov, Aleksandr, 97, 134, 169, 211
Soldatov, Andrey, 248
Somalia, 29
South Korea, 300
Southern Federal District, 143, 262–3, 264,
    273. *See also* North Caucasus
sovereign democracy, 109, 220, 306, 314
sovereign power issues
    March 1996 crisis, 81, 107
    October 1993 crisis, 79–81, 107
Soviet Union
    bureaucracy in, 186
    collapse of, 1–2, 15, 24–5, 43, 46, 189, 251,
        292, 307
    Committee on State Security (KGB), 37, 43
    and decline of power ministries, 37–8
    as federation, 114, 118–9
    homicide rates in, 91
    legacy of Communism, 293–4, 298–300
    Ministry of Defense (MO), 37, 39, 41
    Ministry of Internal Affairs (MVD), 37
    and patrimonialism, 299
    and property rights, 102
    and recruitment of cadres, 188–9
Sovmen, Khazret, 263
Spain, 207, 300
Special Designation Police Detachments
    (OMON/OMSN), 46, 123, 124
spending, national defense and security, 52–5
Sperling, Valerie, 74, 75
spy-rock case, 228, 236
St. Petersburg, 64–5, 190, 194, 212, 220–4,
    235, 242, 315, 318

St. Petersburg International Economic
    Forum, 315
St. Petersburg liberals, 64
Stalin, Josef, 55, 109
state. *See also* state building; state capacity;
    state formation; state quality; stateness;
    states
    definition, 8–10
state building
    constitutionalist approach, 285
    and democratization, 309–10
    elements of, 35
    future of Russian state building, 315–21
    and political competition, 247
    under Putin, 2, 301
    role of agency, 301–7
    and Russian power ministries, 285–8
    shortcomings in Russia, 26
    stages of, 14, 265–6, 307
state capacity, 2–4
    definition, 16, 286
    and federalism, 154–5
    and fiscal capacity, 100–2
    and government effectiveness, 89–91
    and Gross National Income (GNI), 290–1
    increase under Putin, 72–3
    influence of post-Communist legacy, 5,
        293–300
    influence of resource dependence, 5,
        293–300
    influence of wealth, 5, 290–8
    and law enforcement, 72–3, 88–99
    in the North Caucasus, 256–69
    and the power ministries, 107–11
    and property rights, 102–7
    regime of repression, 94–9
    Russian homicide rates, 90–4
    and state quality, 16–24, 308–15
    structural weaknesses of Russian state,
        289–301
State Construction Committee, 41
State Fire Service, 42
state formation, 2, 11–12, 15, 23, 308
state integrity, 250
state quality, 2, 4
    and civil society, 213–7
    and corruption, 159–61
    definition, 17
    and democracy, 18–19, 309–10
    and economic development, 293
    influence of post-Communist legacy, 5,
        293–300
    influence of resource dependence, 5,
        293–300

influence of wealth, 5, 290–8
and legitimacy, 19
in the North Caucasus, 269–81
and political stability, 21
in Russian coercive organs, 156–7
and state capacity, 16–24, 308–15
stateness, 5, 12, 19, 25, 100, 289
states
civil, 19–20, 293, 304
police, 1, 21, 301, 303
totalitarian, 20
weak, 12, 21, 107, 216, 293, 297, 303, 304, 321
statism, 201
Stavropol, 264
Stepan, Alfred, 119, 128, 149, 214
Stepanova, Ekaterina, 42
Stepashin, Sergey, 59, 176, 278
Stokes, Susan, 213
Stoner-Weiss, Kathryn, 75, 76, 154
Straussman, Jeffrey, 201, 306
Surkov, Vladislav, 109
Sutyagin, Igor, 234
Sverdlovsk Oblast, 125, 126, 145
Switzerland, 151
Sychev, Andrey, 65, 207

takeovers, forced, 165–6
"tandemocracy," 5, 284, 317
Tatarstan, 120, 122, 132, 137, 138, 140, 145, 251
tax system, Russian, 100–1, 147, 286
Tendler, Judith, 33
Teorell, Jan, 17–18
terrorism
airplane bombings (2004), 258
Beslan school siege, 79, 88, 148, 189, 209, 239, 245, 254, 256–7, 277, 287, 306
in Budennovsk, 254
Grozny stadium bombing, 256
Moscow attacks, 79, 85–6, 88, 209, 256, 270, 277, 318
in Nalchik, 256–7, 258
National Antiterrorism Committee (NAC), 88
in the North Caucasus, 259–62
public fears of, 209–10
under Putin, 287
Ryazan incident, 83–5
and state capacity, 72, 82–8
Three Whales Case, 50, 172–5
Tilly, Charles, 9, 11–12, 13, 154, 266, 268, 280, 282, 301, 308
Titkov, Aleksey, 279

Titov, Konstantin, 140
Togo, 160
Tokarev, Nikolay, 60
Tomchak, Yuriy, 263
Tompson, William, 90, 106, 289
torture, police use of, 182–3
transitions
to democracy, 15–16, 32, 294
post-Communist, 73, 75, 294
Transparency International Corruption Perceptions Index, 22, 160, 162, 271
Treisman, Daniel, 106, 292
trust
and civil society, 205–12, 247
institutional versus interpersonal, 213
lack of, 4, 288
Tsyganok, Anatoliy, 87
Turkmenistan, 290, 314
Tushin, Sergei, 153
Tuva, 120, 253n6

Udmurtia, 122
Ukraine, 4, 18, 94, 98, 109, 116, 175, 236, 306
Ungar, Mark, 23–4
Union of Right Forces, 61
United Nations, 308
United Russian party, 41, 46, 143, 146, 148, 316
United States
federalism in, 114, 151
homicide rate in, 92
internal use of armed forces, 150
police, 47, 151, 182, 207, 222
and racial profiling, 163
Unity Party, 42
Urals Federal District, 133, 140, 141, 142, 144–5
Uruguay, 293
USSR. *See* Soviet Union
Ustinov, Vladimir, 55, 60, 61, 65, 106, 173, 187, 264

Vachagaev, Mairbek, 255
van de Walle, Nicolas, 108
Van Dijk, Jan, 94
Vargas, Getulio, 106
Vasilev, Vladimir, 319
Vedomosti, 319
Venezuela, 94, 115, 291, 293
Vera Institute of Justice, 232
Vienna, 318
Vinnichenko, Nikolay, 134, 139, 154, 211
violence, political, 77–88. *See also* coups; terrorism

Vladimirov, Aleksandr, 127
Volga Federal District, 140, 141, 142
Volgodonsk, 82
Volgograd, 264, 271
Volkov, Vadim, 14, 76–7, 162, 166, 201, 304
Voloshin, Aleksandr, 65, 307
Vorobev, Eduard, 61
Voronov, G.I., 126
Vympel unit, 44, 81

Waddington, P.A.J., 11
Wahhabism, 254, 273
Way, Lucan, 95, 99
weak states, 12, 20–1, 107, 216, 293, 297,
    303, 304, 321
weapons, sale of, 270
Weber, Max, 1
    definition of state, 8–10
    on legitimate violence, 77
    on patrimonialism, 27–8, 113
    on rational-legal bureaucracy, 16–17,
        27–8, 185
    on state control of coercion, 14, 285
Weigle, Marcia, 216
Weingast, Barry, 114
Weitzer, Ronald, 177
Welzel, Christian, 213
Wilson, Graham, 17–18
Wilson, James Q., 31, 34
World Bank Worldwide Governance
    Indicators (WGI), 5, 289
    Control of Corruption indicator, 160
    Government Effectiveness indicator, 89–90
    Political Stability/No Violence indicator,
        20–1, 77–8, 259, 290
    and Russia's state capacity scores, 302–4
    Rule of Law indicator, 158–9
    Voice and Accountability indicator, 244–5,
        247, 291
    wealth and resource dependence variables,
        295–8
World Politics, 10

Yakovlev, Vladimir, 143
Yakunin, Vladimir, 60
Yamadayev, Ruslan, 268, 277
Yamadayev, Sulim, 268, 277
Yegorov, Vladislav, 154
Yekaterina Crisis Center, 220, 228–9
Yekaterinburg, 191, 198, 211
Yeltsin, Boris
    and decentralization, 156
    and the "Family", 58, 64, 66,
        103–4, 307
    and federalism, 119–28, 138–9
    and maintaining public order, 94–5
    and the North Caucasus, 251, 254
    October 1993 crisis, 68, 79–81, 95, 285
    and power ministries, 55–7, 103–4
    and privatization of property, 102–3
    resignation of, 36, 81
    and Soviet-style state, 2
    state building strategy, 24, 26, 321
    and weakness of Russian state, 290, 301
Yevkurov, Yunus-Bek, 318
Yevloyev, Magomed, 318
Yevsyukov, Denis, 319, 320
YouTube, 319
Yugoslavia, 13, 15, 255
Yukos affair, 65, 102, 105, 167,
    239, 306, 307
Yushenkov, Sergey, 127

Zaire, 282
Zaostrovtsev, Yevgeniy, 173
Zaostrovtsev, Yuri, 173
Zavtra, 257
Zhilin, Aleksandr, 110, 147
Zhitenev, Vyacheslav, 194
Zolotov, Viktor, 45, 60, 65, 66
Zubkov, Viktor, 61, 187
Zubrin, Vladimir, 143
Zuyev, Sergey, 172
Zvyagintsev, Aleksandr, 140
Zyazikov, Murat, 96–7, 263, 270, 317–8